TURNI
THE WORLD UPSIDE DOWN

CARLOS G. MARTIN

Pacific Press® Publishing Association
Nampa, Idaho
Oshawa, Ontario, Canada

Edited by David C. Jarnes
Cover design by Dennis Ferree
Cover art by Justinen Creative Group

Martin Carlos G., 1953-
Turning the world upside down : how to be a radical witness for Jesus / Carlos G. Martin.
p. cm.
Includes bibliographical references.
ISBN 0-8163-1760-7 (pbk.)
1. Witness bearing (Christianity) 2. Witness bearing (Christianity)—Biblical teaching. 3. Bible. N.T. Acts—Criticism, interpretation, etc. I. Title

BV4520 .M37 2000
248'.5'088267—dc21

99-047235

00 01 02 03 04 • 5 4 3 2 1

Contents

Introduction

It seems clear that when Luke wrote Acts, he wanted to show how the work of preaching the good news of salvation expanded through the faithful witness of Christ's followers. Acts illustrates, in different ways, how the same could happen today.

Seventh-day Adventist church members are not satisfied with being silent witnesses. Many would be willing to become active "if they were taught how to begin."[1] Those who become discouraged with the apparent lack of results yielded by their attempts at witnessing "need to be instructed and encouraged."[2] In the narratives of the book of Acts, readers will find the instructions and encouraging examples they need. The guidelines have been preserved so that "the followers of Christ in every age might be impelled to greater zeal and earnestness in the cause of the Saviour."[3]

The topical approach to Acts followed here gives readers a contemporary perspective of the book, providing at the same time workable ideas that will enable them to serve more effectively as witnesses in the service of the Lord. Ellen White counseled, "The whole of the book of Acts should receive careful study. It is full of precious instruction; it records experiences in evangelistic work, the teachings of which we need in our work today."[4]

This study does not pretend to cover all the witnessing events in the book nor to consider all the possible issues related to witnessing. However, the issues chosen should provide readers with a clear picture of what Jesus expects from His followers today. It also aims to motivate the church in these last days to finish the work that was begun at Pentecost.

1. Ellen G. White, *Christian Service*, 59.
2. Ibid.
3. White, *The Acts of the Apostles,* 593.
4. White, *SDA Bible Commentary*, 6:1051.

Chapter 1

All Christians Are Witnesses

It takes about three minutes to go from the Adventist International Institute of Advanced Studies (AIIAS, pronounced *eye ess*) seminary to downtown Silang, in the Philippines. The cheapest mode of travel is the jeepney, a typical Philippine form of public transportation. I happened to be on my way to the market in a jeepney when another passenger asked a student of mine who was also on the vehicle, "Are you from AIIAS? You have beautiful buildings!"

"Yes," the student replied. "But the most beautiful thing about AIIAS is something you cannot see."

I noticed that everybody in the jeepney was now listening to the dialogue. After a pause, the student added, "What I like about AIIAS is that Jesus lives there."

"How's that?"

"Well, Jesus lives in my heart, and this is why I am so happy. You should come and worship with us this coming Saturday morning!"

What the student had done was not preaching. It was not evangelism. It was not a Bible study. It was just creative witnessing.

What are *witnessing* and *evangelism* and *discipleship*? In this chapter, I'll define these terms, which are basic for the topic discussed in this book. If we want to turn "the world upside down" (Acts 17:6), we need to understand these terms and know how we can exercise the activities they represent as the Holy Spirit creates opportunities for us.

A Few Basic Definitions

The first term is "witness." We are called to serve as witnesses (Acts 1:8). On the day of his baptism, Saul was charged to be a witness (22:15, 16).

Witnesses are people who can give a firsthand account of something. A witness is "one who can testify to the facts bearing on any specific question, because he has observed directly; also the attestation of the fact or facts involved."[1] Witnesses have seen or experienced something and are willing to share it with others.

Christian witnessing, then, is sharing with others our personal experience with Jesus. "The apostles gave witness to the resurrection of the Lord Jesus" (Acts 4:33). Jesus asked His disciples to be His witnesses (1:8).

When Peter told the people to repent (Acts 2:38), he had himself previously repented of his own lying, denial of Christ, and profanity (Matt. 26:69-75). Peter witnessed both to the necessity of repentance, and to the power of God to transform the repentant one. He declared, " 'We are His witnesses to these things' " (Acts 5:32). Experience lies at the foundation of all true witnessing.

> No man has any right to recommend to others what he has not himself tasted and tested. Some people need something to tell more than they need power to tell it. Too often we preach of things in which we have no personal experience. I earnestly ask: What have you to tell that makes you so eager for God to give you power to tell it?[2]

Witnessing is a natural result of conversion. One reason for lack of real witnessing among some of us is that we know little of Jesus and His power in our own lives. We cannot witness if we have nothing about which to witness. "That which we have seen and heard we declare to you, that you also may have fellowship with us" (1 John 1:3). Here may be found the tools and goals of witnessing. The apostles had seen and heard events that were undeniable. Christians are powerful witnesses when they have the joy and the assurance of their own salvation. Their goal is to lead others to the same experience.

It is of significance that the Greek word for "witness" is *martus*, which is the root of the English term *martyr.* Stephen is known as the first martyr (Acts 22:20).

> A martyr is one who is convinced of truth, and manifests it in life and death. The fires of persecution do not make martyrs; they simply reveal them. The man who is not already a martyr never lays down his life for the truth. The martyrs died, not that they might become martyrs, but because they were martyrs.[3]

When Jesus called Saul on the road to Damascus, He gave him clear instructions: " 'Go into Damascus; and there you will be told all things which are appointed for you to do' " (Acts 22:10). God has given to each member of the church an individual responsibility: "Not more surely is the place prepared for us in the heavenly mansions than is the special place designated on earth where we are to work for God."[4] Serving as a witness for Jesus, as an ambassador for Christ, is more than a responsibility. It is a privilege!

From a Christian perspective, then, witnessing is more than what we say at certain inspired moments. Witnessing involves all that we are and do.[5] We cannot avoid witnessing. However, we may do it in such a way that the Holy Spirit may use it for His purposes, or we may do it so poorly that those who observe us get a distorted understanding of what Christianity is all about. So the right question is not Should we witness? It is How are we witnessing?

Three Levels of Evangelism

A related term is "evangelism." This word does not appear in the New Testament, and the word "evangelist" appears only once in the book of Acts (chapter 21:8). Nevertheless, Acts is saturated with evangelism. Essentially, evangelism is a more purposefully oriented form of witnessing. To evangelize is to share the good news of salvation in such a way as to persuade nonbelievers to accept Jesus as Savior.

LIFESTYLE EVANGELISM	
Method:	Meeting felt needs
Aim:	To gain access to the heart
CONVERSATIONAL EVANGELISM	
Method:	Giving a testimony
Aim:	To facilitate the knowledge of the gospel
PERSUASION EVANGELISM	
Method:	Studying doctrines
Aim:	To lead nonbelievers to a commitment to Christ and His Church

Figure 1: Three approaches to evangelism.

There are three basic approaches to evangelism. The first and most basic may be described as lifestyle evangelism[6] (see Figure 1). This form of witnessing involves the impact of the Christian way of life. The Christian witnesses by living the gospel before nonbelievers, giving a positive testimony in deeds, attitudes, and conversation. Lifestyle evangelism emphasizes testimony by demonstration. Its goal is to touch people at the point of their felt needs.

Many Christians prefer a passive approach to witnessing. They explain that when they share a smile they are serving as witnesses for the Lord. No doubt the lifestyle of the early Christians, described in Acts 2:44-47, was a major factor in the growth of the church in those days. However, there were some more aggressive forms of lifestyle evangelism. Think of Dorcas, that committed Christian who lived in Joppa. Acts 9:36 tells us that "this woman was full of good works and charitable deeds." Verse 39 says that when she died, many widows showed Peter "the tunics and garments which Dorcas had made while she was with them." Effective lifestyle evangelism requires one to go where people are. The desired outcome is that the recipients will become open to more advanced forms of evangelism.

Conversational evangelism is a more intensified form of witnessing (see Figure 1). Its venue is the common places of daily life where Christians encounter other people. These encounters are those that occur naturally; in other words, the Christian involved hasn't planned them as witnessing occasions but does intentionally take advantage of opportunities that arise.

Conversational evangelism may take the form of a personal testimony or a full presentation of the gospel. The intent is to make nonbelievers aware of the blessings of the gospel. (Think of Philip talking with the eunuch on his way to Ethiopia [Acts 8:27-31] or Paul talking to King Agrippa [26:1-28].) Christian witnesses, especially those in urban settings, may have only a few minutes to share a testimony, so effective conversational evangelism necessitates some training. This means of evangelism requires only a commitment to witnessing, not a special spiritual gift. Most Christians should be able to participate in this form of witnessing.

The most intensified form of witnessing is called persuasion evangelism (see Figure 1). Persuasion evangelism intends to lead a nonbeliever to a point of decision. In other words, those who use this approach to evangelism not only proclaim the gospel but also seek to persuade nonbelievers to respond. Witnessing at this specialized level is synonymous with traditional definitions of evangelism, which is the presentation of biblical doctrines in the power of the Holy Spirit in such a way that people will be persuaded to accept Jesus as Savior and to serve Him in the fellowship of the church. For example, think of Peter preaching on the Day of Pentecost and inviting the multitude to be baptized (Acts 2:38) or of Paul, who "reasoned in the synagogue every Sabbath, and persuaded both Jews and Greeks" (18:4; see also other examples in 19:26; 28:23).

This form of evangelism may be done through personal Bible studies, small groups, or diverse forms of public evangelism. Most Christians may help with these specialized forms of witnessing, but the key persons involved generally need special spiritual gifts or proper training.

Am I a Disciple?

The definition of evangelism stated above refers to "the fellowship of the church," implying baptism. However, we should not consider baptism an end in itself. The expression "responsible church membership" envisions discipleship. Notice that Paul and Barnabas left the city of Derbe only after "they had preached the gospel to that city and *made many disciples*" (Acts 14:21, emphasis added).

One of the best known passages of the Bible is the Great Commission, found in Matthew 28:19, 20. These two verses contain four verbs. Though not obvious in many translations, in the original language three of the verbs are participles and only one is a verb of command. The first participle, "go," could be translated "as you go" or "while going." "Baptizing" and "teaching" are also participles. They indicate the method by which disciples are to be made. You make disciples by teaching and by baptizing people who have believed and are willing to obey all things Jesus commanded us. The one imperative of Matthew 28:19, 20 is "make disciples." This is the goal of the Great Commission.[7]

A disciple is the "follower of a master." The word *disciple* is related to the word *discipline*. A disciple is someone who follows the discipline taught by a teacher. In the church, the term is equivalent to "Christian." The book of Acts identifies disciples of Jesus as those who confess Him as the Christ. Discipleship also suggests the idea of total attachment to someone.

Disciples are people who have made a commitment to make Jesus Christ the Lord of their lives. Until newly baptized members are incorporated into active service in the church, they are not full disciples of Christ. Many are members of the church but not necessarily disciples of Christ.

> A disciple is a person who has been born again, joined the church, identified his or her spiritual gifts, accepted a role in the church compatible with those gifts, and is committed to fulfilling that role *without continual external motivation.*[8]

Disciples are people who have been born again by the Spirit of God. They are new creatures. They may not be perfect, but they are part of the family of God. For instance, the biblical disciple Peter was not perfect after Pentecost, but he was committed to Jesus and willing to obey Him.

So, the work of evangelism should not stop when a person has accepted Jesus as Savior and has been baptized. Discipling implies a continuing work, guiding a new convert toward maturity—toward the stage in which the disciple brings others to a saving relationship with Jesus.

Divine Commands

Why witness?

Believers witness for a number of important reasons. First, many people are seeking salvation and may even be praying for someone to teach them. Think, for instance, of the Ethiopian whose story is found in Acts 8. Like him, "all over the world men and women are looking wistfully to heaven." Like him, "many are on the verge of the kingdom, waiting only to be gathered in."[9] As we set out in obedience to Christ's command, we will discover people who are dissatisfied with their present religious experience. We will find these honest, seeking souls if we search for them!

Second, God wants people to be saved (2 Pet. 3:9). He rejoices when sinners repent (Luke 15:10). So, through witnessing we have the privilege of bringing joy to the heart of God.

A most important reason for witnessing is that we have the love of Christ in our hearts (2 Cor. 5:14). The experience of salvation will virtually compel us to serve as witnesses for Him. I know Christians who have developed the habit of carrying witnessing materials to give away to people they meet on the bus, in the market, and on the street. They may not be eloquent speakers, but they've discovered that doing *something* for Christ gives them one of the greatest satisfactions in life. Again, a Christian who has experienced salvation will inevitably want others to experience God's love.

> The church of Christ is God's appointed agency for the salvation of men. Its mission is to carry the gospel to the world. And the obligation rests upon all Christians. Everyone, to the extent of his talent and

> opportunity, is to fulfill the Saviour's commission. The love of Christ, revealed to us, makes us debtors to all who know Him not.[10]

Fourth, we also witness in obedience to God. Angels transmitted to the disciples the command to witness (Acts 5:19, 20; 8:26). However,

> as His representatives among men, Christ does not choose angels who have never fallen, but human beings, men of like passions with those they seek to save. Christ took upon Himself humanity, that He might reach humanity. Divinity needed humanity; for it required both the divine and the human to bring salvation to the world. Divinity needed humanity, that humanity might afford a channel of communication between God and man.[11]

Angels cannot do the work of witnessing. Angels can cooperate with people, but people must do the witnessing.

Philip had conducted a successful evangelistic series in Samaria. He had seen many conversions (Acts 8:5, 6, 12). Then he was directed to a desert road that led south from Jerusalem (Acts 8:26). Did Philip question the divine strategy? Did he weigh the masses dwelling in Samaria against the few who traveled that road? "He rose and went" (verse 27). That is obedience. God implanted in Philip a conviction, and then he ran to obey God (Acts 8:29, 30).

When Philip was on the desert road he saw a chariot approaching. He did not wait for the chariot to reach him. He went to meet it. "The gospel commission is the great missionary charter of Christ's kingdom. The disciples were to work earnestly for souls, giving to all the invitation of mercy. They were not to wait for the people to come to them; they were to go to the people with their message."[12] Philip was obedient to the divine instructions, and he saw results.

According to Acts 5:32, the Holy Spirit is "given to those who obey." The apostles told the Sanhedrin that they must witness in obedience to God and that they would not stop doing it just because the Sanhedrin ordered them to (Acts 5:27-29). Witnessing is a command, and the church is under orders. "Someone must fulfill the commission of Christ; someone must carry on the work He began to do on earth; and the church has been given this privilege. For this purpose it has been organized."*

*"The church of Christ on earth was organized for missionary purposes" (White, *Testimonies*, 6:295).

Witnessing is not something we do because it is the program of the local organization. Witnessing is a matter of obedience to Christ. Christian experience cannot be complete without it.

Luther declared at the council of Worms: "My conscience is captive to the Word of God, I cannot and will not recant anything, for to go against conscience is neither right nor safe. God help me. Amen."[13] Those were brave words. May present-day Christian witnesses emulate that willingness to obey God.

---

1. *SDA Bible Dictionary*, s.v. "Witness."

2. LeRoy E. Froom, *The Coming of the Comforter* (Hagerstown, Md.: Review and Herald, 1956), 104, 105.

3. Ibid., 106, 107.

4. Ellen G. White, *Christian Service*, 99.

5. Paul E. Little, *How to Give Away Your Faith* (Downers Grove, Ill.: InterVarsity, 1966), 23.

6. These ideas are taken from Elmer Towns, "Evangelism: The Why and How," in *Church Growth: State of the Art*, ed. C. Peter Wagner (Wheaton, Ill.: Tyndale, 1986), 43-45. His terms, however, differ.

7. C. Peter Wagner, *Strategies for Church Growth* (Ventura, Calif.: Regal Books, 1987), 50.

8. James W. Zackrison, *Power to Witness* (Nampa, Idaho: Pacific Press, 1993), 23. Italics in original.

9. White, *The Acts of the Apostles*, 109.

10. White, *Steps to Christ*, 81.

11. White, *The Desire of Ages*, 296.

12. *The Acts of the Apostles*, 28.

13. Quoted in Roland H. Bainton, *The Reformation of the Sixteenth Century* (Boston: Beacon, 1952), 61.

Chapter 2

Witnesses, Ministers, and Missionaries

In one of the churches I served in Texas, we began several series of evangelistic Bible studies related to the book of Revelation in the homes of various members. A twelve-year-old boy volunteered to teach one set of these studies. Afraid he might do more harm than good, I reminded him that his mother had already committed their home to another teacher. But I promised the boy that if he found a neighbor willing to study, I would give him a set of Bibles and lessons.

That very afternoon a lady approached me and asked, "Sir, do you think that a twelve-year-old boy can lead me in a Bible study on the book of Revelation?" Not knowing how to respond, I asked, "Why?" Then she told me how she had been praying for someone to help her to understand the book of Revelation. As she was praying, someone knocked on her door. To her surprise, she found a boy who asked, "Ma'am, do you want to study the book of Revelation with me?" Eventually, I baptized this lady. The experience illustrates again that God works through every church member who will let Him do so.

This chapter will review the often-forgotten doctrine of the ministry of all believers, the role of the pastor in equipping the church for service, and the enabling role of the Holy Spirit. We are told that the work of God on this earth will be finished when believers commit themselves to witnessing and unite their efforts with those of pastors and church leaders.[1]

All Believers Are Ministers

On the road to Damascus the Lord appeared and spoke to Saul. Shortly thereafter, through Ananias, God called him to be "a minister and a witness" (Acts 26:16). The Greek word for "ministry" is *diakonia*, meaning "service."* (You'll find this word in Acts 12:25; 20:24; 21:19.) The call to serve as a minister, however, is not limited to a few apostles, elders, church leaders, or pastors.

Scripture teaches that all believers are ministers and priests. The distinction that has been made between laity and clergy is not biblical. The Protestant Reformers insisted on the "priesthood of all believers"†—though within the general ministry to which all believers are called we recognize the function of some who are called to "a definite line of service"[2] such as deacons, elders, pastors. Those called to these roles assume their responsibilities after receiving the laying on of hands. These ordained "ministers should not do the work which belongs to the church, thus wearying themselves, and preventing others from performing their duty. They should teach the members how to labor in the church and in the community."[3]

It is interesting to note that in the early church, the laying on of hands was not limited to the ordination of deacons or elders (Acts 6:2-6; 13:3; 1 Tim. 4:14). This spiritual ritual was also used in praying for the sick and in asking for the gift of the Holy Spirit (Acts 9:17; 19:6). It is also interesting to note that primitive Christianity followed no unified approach to the laying on of hands. The ritual was very often associated with baptism; sometimes preceding it (9:17-19) and sometimes following immediately after (8:12-17). In either case, early Christians regarded the laying on of hands at the time of baptism as an important practice—as the frequent references to it in the writings of the early Fathers of the church show.[4]

All those who join the church by baptism thereby enlist themselves as ministers of the gospel. "By their baptismal vows they are pledged to make earnest, self-denying efforts to promote, in the hardest parts of the field, the work of soulsaving."[5] Among other meanings, baptism means incorporation into the community of the committed and an ordination for full participation in Christ's ministry.

Church members will feel little motivation to share the gospel with others if they think that the "official ministry" bears the responsibility of witnessing and ministry. If, at the time of baptism, believers are informed that they have been ordained into the church ministry by the laying on of hands, that they have taken "sacred vows" and have committed themselves

---

*"Ministry means not only the study of books and preaching. It means service." Ellen G. White, *SDA Bible Commentary*, 4:1159.

†Martin Luther said: "All Christians are truly priests and there is no distinction amongst them except as to office." *Works of Martin Luther* (Philadelphia: A. J. Holman, 1925), 2:66.

to fulfill the Great Commission, it will be much easier to involve them in missionary activities. It is in this context that the assertion "Every true disciple is born into the kingdom of God as a missionary"[6] acquires meaning.

Hovering and Shepherding

Paul had a pastoral burden for the churches. "After some days Paul said to Barnabas, 'Let us now go back and visit our brethren in every city where we have preached the word of the Lord, and see how they are doing' " (Acts 15:36). After returning "he departed [again] and went over all the region of Galatia and Phrygia in order, strengthening all the disciples" (18:23). Note that apparently Paul did not stay for a long time in these established churches. "The churches are to be looked after and cared for, but they are not to demand continuous labor. . . . Do not educate our churches to expect constant ministerial help."[7]

In the early years of our denominational history, the primary work of Adventist pastors was public evangelism. Every preacher was to be an evangelist. At the turn of the century, Seventh-day Adventists began inclining toward the model of evangelism followed by American Protestants—that of using professional evangelists like D. L. Moody and Billy Sunday. The result was that eventually pastors were seen as shepherds while evangelism was left in the hands of professionals.[8] The formerly itinerant pastors now became stationary.* Very soon members learned to depend on pastors and their preaching. And pastors began to spend much time "hovering" over the congregations.

Ellen G. White countered with this advice:

> Instead of keeping the ministers at work for the churches that already know the truth, let the members of the churches say to these laborers: "Go work for souls that are perishing in darkness. We ourselves will carry forward the services of the church. We will keep up the meetings, and by abiding in Christ, will maintain spiritual life. We will work for souls that are about us."[9]
>
> The ministers are hovering over the churches which know the truth while thousands are perishing out of Christ. If the proper in-

*John W. Fowler affirms that "the only real distinction between the evangelist and the pastor . . . is that one is itinerant and the other is stationary." *Adventist Pastoral Ministry* (Nampa, Idaho: Pacific Press®, 1990), 109.

> struction were given, if the proper methods were followed, every church member would do his work as a member of the body. He would do Christian missionary work. But the churches are dying, and they want a minister to preach unto them. . . . They should be taught that unless they can stand alone, without a minister, they need to be converted anew, and baptized anew. They need to be born again.[10]

> This is no time for the messengers of God to stop to prop up those who know the truth, and who have every advantage.[11]

> God has not given His ministers the work of setting churches right. No sooner is this work done, apparently, than it has to be done over again. Church members that are thus looked after and labored for become religious weaklings.[12]

> The parable of the lost sheep should be a lesson to every soul who has been rescued from the snare of Satan. We are not to hover over the ninety and nine, but to go forth to save the lost.[13]

In some parts of the world, a pastor has only one church. In other parts, the average pastor has a district with fifteen or more churches. In these areas the head elders do the pastoring. Actually, there is no biblical distinction between an elder (*presbyteros*), an overseer (*episkopos*), and a shepherd (*poimen*)—all terms present in Acts 20:17, 28. "All three of these words refer to the same people Paul is teaching, so that at least to a significant extent, we can consider them synonyms for each other."[14]

Statistics show that in those areas where the ratio of members to pastors is higher (for instance, 1,000 members for each pastor in contrast to 50 members), the church tends to grow more rapidly.[15] This is not to suggest that churches should not have pastors. It is not to suggest that the number of pastors in the field should be reduced. It simply indicates that the more the members are involved in ministry and in witnessing, the more the church grows.[16]

Who Is a Missionary?

Among other purposes Luke had in writing Acts, one goal seems clear—that of showing how Christ's mission expanded through the faithful witness of His followers. Acts illustrates, in different ways, how mission expansion should happen today.

A dictionary definition says that *mission* is "a sending forth with a special message to bring or with a special task to perform." In a few words, *mission* means "sending." Note that the words *mission* and *missile* have the same root! "The church's sending out to proclaim the gospel, to tell others of the redemption wrought for them on the cross, and, when they are converted by the Holy Spirit, to incorporate them into the church"[17] is "mission."

Scripture repeatedly describes God as "the One who sent" and Christ as "the One who is sent."[18] The heart of the gospel is that God sent the Son into the world that the world may be saved through Him (John 3:16, 17). Jesus is the archetype of a missionary. He linked His own mission with the mission of His followers: " 'As the Father has sent Me, I also send you' " (John 20:21). A missionary is one sent "where Christ's name is unknown" (Rom. 15:20, 21, *The New Testament: An American Translation*).

A missionary is someone sent across significant barriers to serve as a witness. Sometimes those barriers include distance and culture. But the main boundary a person has to cross in order to be termed a missionary is the barrier that separates those who are "strangers and foreigners" to Christ from the "members of the household of God" (Eph. 2:19).[19]

All those who are willing to go in obedience to the divine commission are missionaries. So, both those who go "overseas" and those who simply step across the street are serving God as missionaries. "God expects personal service from everyone to whom He has entrusted a knowledge of the truth for this time. Not all can go as missionaries to foreign lands, but all can be home missionaries in their families and neighborhoods."[20] In this sense it is easy to understand Ellen G. White's comments that "every Christian is to be a missionary," that "every true disciple is born into the kingdom of God as a missionary."[21]

Only a few members have the gift of being an evangelist, but every Christian has the role of being a witness. In Ellen White's writings, the expression "missionary work" refers to witnessing. "Wherever a church is established, all the members should engage actively in missionary work. . . . If every church member had sought to enlighten others, thousands upon thousands would today stand with God's commandment-keeping people."[22]

Gifts and Talents

Spiritual gifts differ from talents. Talents are endowments from God given at birth. Spiritual gifts, on the other hand, are endowments the Holy Spirit bestows upon people at their spiritual birth to enable them to help the church fulfill its divine mission. Natural talents may be used for personal gain or as a means of livelihood. Spiritual talents are meant to be used for the advancement of the kingdom of God even when matched with natural talents. The Lord may convert natural talents into spiritual gifts, "but sometimes a person is assigned spiritual gifts that are entirely different from natural talents."[23]

The book of Acts mentions most of the spiritual gifts listed in the New Testament: leadership (6:1-4), apostleship (1:26), tongues (2:4), evangelism (21:8), miracles (2:43), healings (5:16), discernment (13:9), martyrdom (7:60), prophecy (11:27), wisdom (6:10), teaching (13:1), pastoring (20:28), hospitality (16:15), helps (9:25-27), faith (11:24), and mercy (9:36, 39). While the Spirit does not equip everyone in the same way, everyone is expected to serve as a witness (1:8).* "Every Christian is a witness, but because we have different spiritual gifts, we might not all witness in just the same way."[24] Some are most comfortable participating in a health ministry. Others prefer to work in a supportive ministry such as in the distribution of literature or serving as ushers in an evangelistic series. Still others are especially gifted to be evangelists. "All men do not receive the same gifts, but to every servant of the Master some gift of the Spirit is promised."[25]

Partnership With the Holy Spirit

The book of Acts contains many examples of cooperation between humanity and divinity. According to Acts 5:32, Peter said to the council, " 'We are His witnesses to these things, and so also is the Holy Spirit.' " In Iconium the disciples spoke "boldly in the Lord, who was bearing witness to the word of His grace, granting signs and wonders to be done by their hands" (14:3). Speaking of Lydia, Luke says, "The Lord opened her heart to heed the things spoken by Paul" (16:14).

> The arguments of the apostles alone, though clear and convincing, would not have removed the prejudice that had withstood so much evidence. But the Holy Spirit sent the arguments home to hearts with divine power. The words of the apostles were as sharp

---

*"Believers receive a diversity of gifts, an indication that each has an individualized ministry. Yet every believer should be able to witness about his faith, sharing beliefs and telling others what God has done in his life. The purpose for which God gives each gift, no matter what it may be, is to enable its possessor to witness." [Gerard P. Damsteegt], *Seventh-day Adventists Believe . . .* (Hagerstown, Md.: Review and Herald, 1988), 212.

arrows of the Almighty, convicting men of their terrible guilt in rejecting and crucifying the Lord of glory.[26]

Because we know that soul winning depends on God's Spirit, we have often made the big mistake of assuming that it depends *only* on God's Spirit. God expects us to be His agents in reaping (see 1 Cor. 3:6). And reaping demands preparation. "Much careful thought and fervent prayer are required to know how to approach men and women upon the great subject of truth."[27]

It may sound strange, but divinity needs humanity—"for it required both the divine and the human to bring salvation to the world. Divinity needed humanity, that humanity might afford a channel of communication between God and man."[28] "When divine power is combined with the human effort, the work will spread like fire in the stubble."[29] For confirmation, just think of Peter witnessing with much power because he was "filled with the Holy Spirit" (Acts 4:8-10).

Some may argue that planning, preparing budgets, and setting goals are denials of the power of the Holy Spirit. However, we are told that "the agency of the Spirit of God does not remove from us the necessity of exercising our faculties and talents."[30] Furthermore, God "works according to great principles . . . and it is our part to mature wise plans and set in operation the means whereby God shall bring about certain results."[31]

Training for Ministry

Acts 19:9 states that Paul "gave daily addresses in the lecture-hall of Tyrannus" (*The Twentieth Century New Testament*). It seems that Paul was providing a form of systematic ministerial training, which he offered for a two-year period. Apparently, he gave a great deal of emphasis to evangelism and witnessing because Acts reports that as a consequence, "all who dwelt in Asia heard the word of the Lord" (19:10).

Paul's work in Ephesus provides a pattern for our churches today. In order to equip believers for ministry, the Lord has designated that local churches should be training centers. "Many would be willing to work if they were taught how to begin. They need to be instructed and encouraged. Every church should be a training school for Christian workers."[32]

The "official minister" should be a "specialized minister" in the business of training "lay ministers" who are in the "general ministry."

> Christian ministers . . . have a broader work than many have recognized. They are not only to minister to the people, but to teach

> them to minister. They should not only give instruction in right principles, but educate their hearers to impart these principles. . . . Every church member should be engaged in some line of service for the Master.[33]

In two other places the book of Acts mentions Paul offering some form of training. In Acts 11:26 we read, "For a whole year they [Barnabas and Saul] assembled with the church and taught a great many people." Since they met "with the church," this teaching activity may have been a form of training for members. The other reference is Acts 20:16-18. It says that when Paul was on his way to Jerusalem he made a stopover in Miletus and "called for the elders of the church" at Ephesus. This could be the equivalent to a present-day "leadership district meeting" or to a "leadership training seminar." Ellen G. White says that pastors should train others to participate with them in ministry.

> The minister should not feel that it is his duty to do all the talking and all the laboring and all the praying; he should educate helpers in every church. Let different ones take turns in leading the meetings, and in giving Bible readings; in so doing they will be calling into use the talents which God has given them, and at the same time be receiving a training as workers.[34]

Administrators *and* Witnesses?

The apostles sent Peter and John to assist Philip in Samaria. Apparently, some Jews among the converts in Jerusalem became concerned when they heard that large numbers of Samaritans were being baptized in Jesus' name. But the apostles saw in that event a partial fulfillment of Acts 1:8, and two of them went to confirm what Philip had done.

When Peter and John finished their mission in Samaria, "they returned to Jerusalem, preaching the gospel in many villages of the Samaritans" (Acts 8:25). The fact that they were top leaders in the church organization did not prevent them from participating in the primary function of the church, which is evangelism. All church leaders should remember that "to win souls to the kingdom of God must be their first consideration."[35] "The heart of the true minister is filled with an intense longing to save souls. . . . With invitations and pleadings, mingled with the assurances of God's love, he seeks to win souls to Jesus."[36]

Sometimes the agendas of church boards and executive committees give top priority to the details of church business. The *Church Manual* warns that

> the church board should permit no other business to interfere with planning for evangelism. Should other business be too time-consuming, the board may appoint subcommittees to care for specific areas of church business such as finance or church building projects. . . . In this way the resources of the board are conserved for its primary task—evangelism.[37]

Along these lines, Ellen G. White wrote of evangelism, "Nothing is to be permitted to hinder this work. It is the all-important work for time; it is to be far-reaching as eternity."[38]

Acts 8 relates another instance of a church leader's outreach while returning to his home base. As Philip ended his personal encounter with the Ethiopian eunuch and traveled back to his home town, "he preached in all the cities till he came to Caesarea" (verse 40; see also Acts 21:8). This passage tells us something about looking for witnessing opportunities while traveling; it says that Philip's experience with the Lord motivated him to testify wherever he was.

Acts 9:26 says that when Saul escaped from Damascus he went to Jerusalem. When he wrote about this visit later, he said: "I went up to Jerusalem to see Peter, and remained with him fifteen days. But I saw none of the other apostles except James, the Lord's brother" (Gal. 1:18, 19). Why couldn't Saul see the other apostles? This is just a conjecture, but it is easy to imagine that the apostles were out on the road by then—multiplying churches, training leadership for them, and thus edifying the church. Verse 31 indicates that the churches throughout Judea, Galilee, and Samaria became well established and consolidated. It seems logical that the apostles were heavily involved in this work. Verse 32 says that "Peter went through all parts of the country." In all probability, each of the twelve apostles was doing similar things. Peter did not limit his ministry to administrative functions within the shelter of the temple courts; no doubt, this is a good model for administrators today.

1. Ellen G. White, *Gospel Workers*, 352.
2. White, *The Acts of the Apostles*, 162.
3. White, *Christian Service*, 69.

4. Carlos G. Martin, "La Imposición de Manos en Hebreos 6:2" ["The laying on of hands in Hebrews 6:2"], School of Graduate Studies of Andrews University at Montemorelos University, Mexico, August 1979.

5. White, *Evangelism*, 354, 355.

6. White, *The Desire of Ages*, 195.

7. White, *Review and Herald*, 9 February 1905, 9.

8. For historical details about this shift in evangelistic methodology, see Howard B. Weeks, *Adventist Evangelism in the Twentieth Century* (Hagerstown, Md.: Review and Herald, 1969).

9. *Christian Service*, 171.

10. *Evangelism*, 381.

11. White, *Testimonies to Ministers*, 232.

12. White, *Testimonies for the Church*, 7:18.

13. *Testimonies to Ministers*, 232.

14. C. Peter Wagner, *Blazing the Way*, The Acts of the Holy Spirit Series (Ventura, Calif.: Regal Books, 1995), 195.

15. Mark Finley, *Fulfilling the Gospel Commission: Participant Study Guide* (Riverside, Calif.: Hart Publications, 1989), 13.

16. *SDA Minister's Manual*, 119; *Evangelism*, 382.

17. Arthur F. Glasser and Donald A. McGavran, *Contemporary Theologies of Mission* (Grand Rapids: Baker, 1983), 184.

18. See Francis M. DuBose, *God Who Sends: A Fresh Quest for Biblical Mission* (Nashville: Broadman, 1983), 64-66.

19. Gottfried Oosterwal, *Mission: Possible* (Nashville: Southern Publishing Assn., 1972), 90.

20. *Christian Service*, 9.

21. Ibid., 22; *The Desire of Ages*, 195.

22. *Testimonies for the Church*, 6:296.

23. James W. Zackrison, "Spiritual Gifts: Keys to Ministry," *Adult Sabbath School Lesson*, Teacher's Edition, January-March 1997, 14.

24. General Conference of Seventh-day Adventists, *Witnessing for Christ* (Washington, D.C.: Review and Herald, 1981), 12.

25. White, *Christ's Object Lessons*, 327. A whole chapter of this book, entitled "Talents," has very helpful material on spiritual gifts.

26. *The Acts of the Apostles*, 45.

27. *Testimonies for the Church*, 4:67.

28. *The Desire of Ages*, 296.

29. *Selected Messages*, 1:118.

30. White, *Counsels to Teachers*, 361.

31. *Evangelism*, 652, 653.

32. *Christian Service*, 59.

33. White, *The Ministry of Healing*, 148, 149.

34. White, *Gospel Workers*, 197.

35. Ibid., 31.

36. *The Acts of the Apostles*, 371.

37. *SDA Church Manual*, 1995 ed., 81, 82.

38. *Testimonies for the Church*, 5:456.

Chapter 3

The Recipients of Witnessing

It was the opening night of an evangelistic series in Jakarta, the capital city of Indonesia. There are almost 200 million Muslims in that country, so I was wondering about how receptive the audience would be. However, the challenge posed by the site of the evangelistic series—the Jakarta World Trade Center—caused me even more apprehension. As I saw businessmen, professionals, diplomats, and artists participating in the free buffet offered in the hall, I almost panicked. How could I, a simple pastor, address that select audience?

I went to a private room to seek refuge in the Lord. While praying for serenity and composure, a question struck my mind. Why was I so anxious? This was not *my* work, but *His*. There were church members praying for me at that very moment. I knew that I should not be so apprehensive. After all, though they were members of the upper class, I was a member of a royal family! I was an ambassador for the King of the universe, and my audience was composed of sinners who needed to hear my message!

In commissioning His disciples, Jesus indicated that they were to reach *all* people. We may paraphrase Him as saying that His followers were to carry the gospel message to those who live in Judea, plus the Samaritans and the Gentiles who live all around the earth (Acts 1:8). In this chapter we will review how the apostles dealt with different groups of people.

Dealing With Jews

According to Acts 2:5, 22, the first Christian sermon was directed to Jews. It is interesting to note that Jesus chose as His disciples only Jews from a very limited geographical area. None of them were Hellenistic Jews—Jews influenced by the Greek culture whose first language was Greek, such as those mentioned in Acts 6:1. Jesus chose Hebrew Jews raised in Palestine. In fact, with one exception, He chose all His disciples from fellow Galileans. Those who witnessed Jesus' ascension were "men of Galilee" (Acts 1:11). On the Day of Pentecost, the multitude wondered in amazement, " 'Are not all these who speak Galileans?' " (2:7).

What is the point for us today? Before attempting to reach out to those living beyond Galilee, Jesus secured for Himself a nucleus of people from the same cultural background.[1] In order for us to accomplish Jesus' ultimate purpose of making disciples of all nations (Matt. 28:19, 20), we also must establish a solid foundation. Before we attempt to reach out to people in another neighborhood or from another culture, we must first work among those who live around us and are part of our own culture. We must do this not only because they are our first responsibility but because it is strategically important. When the center has been well secured, the concentric circles can encompass those living farther away and those from other cultures.

Notice also that instead of calling his hearers "Jews," Peter addressed them as "men of Israel" (Acts 2:22). We too need to develop culturally relevant strategies to take the gospel to the Jewish people—like using the terms *Messiah* for *Christ* and *Yeshua* for *Jesus* when addressing people with Jewish background. And yes, we ought to attempt to reach them. Ellen White wrote, "It has been a strange thing to me that there were so few who felt a burden to labor for the Jewish people, who are scattered throughout so many lands."[2]

Dealing With Samaritans

Don Richardson began a book chapter with these thought-provoking words:

> Hundreds of millions of Christians think that Luke's Acts of the Apostles records the twelve apostles' obedience to the Great Commission. Actually it records their reluctance to obey it.[3]

According to Jesus' instructions, His disciples began the proclamation of the gospel in Jerusalem (Acts 1:8). However, the proclamation "throughout the regions of Judea and Samaria" began as a result of "a great persecution" (8:1, 4, 5).

The Samaritans and the Jews (abbreviated from *Judeans*) had erected barriers against each other. The gospel narratives reveal the sharp contention between the two peoples (see John 4:8, 9; Luke 9:51-54). The Samaritans had preserved their own traditions and social customs. They worshiped in Shechem at Mt. Gerizim, while the Jews worshiped at Jerusalem. Samaritans valued only the five books of Moses as Holy Scripture. Religiously and culturally, they rejected the Jews; and the Jews rejected the Samaritans.

Luke wrote that Philip "preached Christ" to the Samaritans (Acts 8:5). The disciples could have ignored them as offering little evangelistic potential. But they were quite responsive. Acts says that "the multitudes with one accord heeded the things spoken by Philip" (8:5, 6).

Philip did more than merely lecture. The record states that the crowd not only heard what he said but also *saw* what he *did*. The healings and the good news of the Messiah stirred the city to joy (Acts 8:8). By mingling with the Samaritans and reaching them at the point of their need, Philip followed a pattern Jesus had exemplified. "First meet the temporal necessities of the needy and relieve their physical wants and sufferings, and you will then find an open avenue to the heart, where you may plant the good seed of virtue and religion."[4]

In response to Philip's preaching many Samaritans requested baptism (Acts 8:12). How did the Jerusalem church react? John, the "son of thunder," had wanted to call down fire from heaven to destroy the Samaritans when they rejected Jesus (Luke 9:52-54). Now he joined Peter in visiting Samaria and praying for the Samaritans (Acts 8:14, 15). Perhaps the breaching of the barrier between Jews and Samaritans really occurred when the apostles laid their hands on them following their prayer for them. Jews had touched Samaritans! "In Christ all race prejudices, all national distinctions, are laid aside, and we are all brethren, engaged in the work of advancing the Redeemer's kingdom."[5]

Dealing With Gentiles

Paul and Barnabas habitually attended synagogue services (Acts 13:14; 17:2), and the synagogue authorities frequently offered these visiting Jews who appeared to have something to say an opportunity to speak (13:15). According to Luke's record, on one occasion, after Paul preached to them about forgiveness of sin and justification by faith, Gentiles attending the synagogue "begged that these words might be preached to them the next Sabbath" (13:38-42).

These Gentiles were known as "God-fearers." This group comprised Gentiles who were strongly attracted to the monotheism and high moral and ethical standards of the Jewish faith. They worshiped Jehovah God and had agreed to adhere to the Jewish law to the best of their abilities but had not taken the more radical step of becoming Jewish proselytes through circumcision. (Proselytes were Gentiles, who, attracted to Judaism's monotheism, ethical standards, and messianic hopes, had adopted the complete range of Jewish beliefs and practices, including circumcision.)

On the next Sabbath a great crowd of Gentiles gathered for worship (Acts 13:44).* These Gentiles begged the apostles for more preaching and teaching. No doubt these Gentiles were hungry for spiritual food; they had already demonstrated interest by attending synagogue services. And Paul had a message of hope for them.

Dealing With Non-receptive People

The book of Acts records the apostles' testimony to the "hard to reach." Because Peter and John had caused some disturbances with their preaching, they were sent to jail (Acts 4:3). On the next day they were brought before "the council" (4:15)—a reference to the Sanhedrin, which consisted of seventy members, referred to here as "rulers, elders, and scribes" (4:5). It was the chief judicial body of the Jews at that time, so Peter and John had been taken right to the top.

The question, " 'By what power or by what name have you done this?' " gave Peter a chance to testify to them about the power of Jesus (Acts 4:7-12). Surely he remembered that Jesus had said, " 'You will be brought before kings and rulers for My name's sake. But it will turn out for you as an occasion for testimony' " (Luke 21:12, 13).

Paul, too, spoke before challenging groups. In visiting Athens, he, as always, witnessed among the Jews. But he also went daily to the marketplace seeking an opportunity to testify to those Gentiles who gathered there (Acts 17:17). Among those who talked with Paul were Epicurean and Stoic philosophers (verse 18), representatives of two popular philosophies of the time. These philosophers took Paul, this "proclaimer of foreign gods," to the Areopagus, or Mars Hill, to hear him out (17:18, 19).

Witnessing to these intellectuals was not an easy task. Greek philosophy assumed that humans could find truth in themselves, that no external revelation was necessary. Paul fitted his address to the audience. He used a rational approach to deal with these educated Greek philosophers. The Greek and Western mindset tends to organize everything in rational categories (the intellectual

---

*Here we find another evidence that the Sabbath was made for all humankind (Mark 2:27) and not only for Jews. We also see that God did not intend the Sabbath only for Old Testament times. The book of Acts refers to the Sabbath many times (13:14, 42, 44; 16:13; 17:2; 18:4). It is still a part of God's plan (Heb. 4:4-9). It will be observed in the earth made new (Isa. 66:22, 23), where worshipers of "every nation, tribe, tongue, and people" will meet before the Lord on His day. This is why the apostles led Gentiles in worship on Sabbath.

roots of systematic theology).*

To the Greeks Paul tried to transmit the content of the gospel in the Greek pattern of thought. Following a sound principle of witnessing, Paul began where the Athenians were (Acts 17:22, 23) and proceeded to preach to them in terms they could understand.

> Christ drew the hearts of His hearers to Him by the manifestation of His love, and then, little by little, as they were able to bear it, He unfolded to them the great truths of the kingdom. We also must learn to adapt our labors to the condition of the people—to meet men where they are.[6]

That Paul showed understanding of Stoic ideas (verse 28) is not to say that he accepted them. He tried to find common ground because he was laying the groundwork for a gospel appeal. We are instructed to do our best to find common ground before we move into deeper subjects.

> When you are laboring in a place where souls are just beginning to get scales from their eyes . . . be very careful not to present the truth in such a way as to arouse prejudice, and to close the door of the heart to the truth. Agree with the people on every point you can consistently do so. Let them see that you love their souls, and want to be in harmony with them so far as possible.[7]

The mission to Athens was less than a striking success. Sometimes the results of an evangelistic effort relate to the evangelist's approach. Paul later realized that eloquence and an intellectual presentation of the gospel was not the most effective approach (1 Cor. 2:1, 2). However, the real problems in Athens were not related to evangelistic strategies, but to the audience. "In their pride of intellect and human wisdom may be found the reason why the gospel message met with comparatively little success among the Athenians."[8]

The book of Acts mentions several conversions among the "hard to reach": "A great many of the priests" (6:7), "a eunuch of great authority under Candace

---

*"Many times, missionaries in our day have perpetuated the kind of ministry Paul used in Athens. We have tended to rationalize the gospel and present Christ to the lost in the weight of logical arguments." (Peter Wagner, *Blazing the Way*, The Acts of the Holy Spirit Series [Ventura, Calif.: Regal, 1995], 117. In many non-Western areas people approach truth through stories, parables, proverbs, or drama. That's one of the reasons why, when preachers follow Western patterns of thought, Christianity is perceived as a foreign religion.

the queen of the Ethiopians" (8:27), and "proconsul, Sergius Paulus, an intelligent man" (13:7). People in positions of authority and leadership in the world do need the gospel too. "It requires moral courage for them to take their position for Christ. Special efforts should be made for these souls, who are in so great danger, because of their responsibilities and associations."[9]

> The intelligent, the refined, are altogether too much passed by. The hook is not baited to catch this class, and ways and methods are not prayerfully devised to reach them with truth that is able to make them wise unto salvation. Most generally the fashionable, the wealthy, the proud, understand by experience that happiness is not to be secured by the amount of money that they possess, or by costly edifices, and ornamental furniture and pictures. They want something they have not. But this class are attracted toward each other, and it is hard to find access to them; and because of this many are perishing in their sins who long for something that will give them rest and peace and quietude of mind. They need Jesus, the light of righteousness.[10]

Notice that those in the upper classes "are attracted toward each other, and it is hard to find access to them." They may not be attracted to the gospel through traditional evangelistic strategies. One way to reach them is through believers belonging to the same social class.

> God calls for earnest, humble workers, who will carry the gospel to the higher class. There are miracles to be wrought in genuine conversions—miracles that are not now discerned. The greatest men of this earth are not beyond the power of a wonder-working God.[11]

Witnessing among secular urbanites has never been easy, and it may be very difficult, but it pays.

Dealing With Receptive People

Missiologists speak of "receptive people." They suggest "the strategy of concentrating the maximum number of workers among receptive segments of population while not bypassing the resistant."[12]

To break down the disciples' prejudice against the Gentiles, who were more receptive than the Jews, God directed Peter to Cornelius, a centurion in the Roman army. Cornelius was a God-fearer, and at that time God-fearers were the Gentiles by far the most receptive to the gospel. He was "a devout man and one who feared God with all his household, who gave alms generously to the people, and prayed to God always" (Acts 10:2). Cornelius was fasting and praying when an angel spoke to him (10:30, 31). The instruction he received concerned his own salvation and that of his household (11:14), so his prayer may have been related to these matters.

When Peter followed God's directions, he ended up in Cornelius's home, the house of a Gentile—something unthinkable for a Jew (Acts 10:28). "The love of God, sanctifying the soul, breaks down the wall of partition between the customs and practices of different individuals and nations. The great principles of Bible truth bring all into perfect harmony."[13] Peter's experience opened the early church to the needs of the world. And today, "all over the world men and women are looking wistfully to heaven. Prayers and tears and inquiries go up from souls longing for light, for grace, for the Holy Spirit. Many are on the verge of the kingdom, waiting only to be gathered in."[14]

Acts reveals that Paul also focused on the responsive. When the Jews to whom he preached rejected the gospel, he turned to responsive Gentiles (Acts 13:46; 18:6).

The "God-fearers" of Bible times were good prospects; they were interested persons. People like Cornelius should be in our prospect files. All churches should have prospect files. People who have already had some contact with the church and are ready for baptism are "Class A" prospects; "Class B" are those who are related to members, interests discovered by literature evangelists, and people who have already attended church services and evangelistic meetings. "Class C" prospects are people who may respond to your approaches, such as those with whom you have had conversational contact or newcomers to your neighborhood. According to the *Church Manual*, each church should have an "interest coordinator," and this person should be a member of the church board.[15]

In commenting about Cornelius, Ellen G. White wrote, "There are in our world many who are nearer the kingdom of God than we suppose."[16] Many nonbelievers are earnestly searching for truth and may even be praying for someone to teach them. "Many are waiting to be personally addressed."[17] We will find these sincere souls if we search for them!

---

1. C. Peter Wagner, *Spreading the Fire*, The Acts of the Holy Spirit Series (Ventura, Calif.: Regal Books, 1994), 52.

2. Ellen G. White, *Evangelism*, 578.

3. Don Richardson, "The Hidden Message of 'Acts,' " in *Perspectives on the World Christian Movement: A Reader* (Pasadena, Calif.: Carey, 1981), 89.

4. White, *Testimonies for the Church*, 4:226.
5. White, *Fundamentals of Christian Education*, 203.
6. *Evangelism*, 484, 485.
7. White, *Historical Sketches of the Foreign Missions*, 122.
8. White, *The Acts of the Apostles*, 240.
9. Ibid., 139, 140.
10. *Evangelism*, 556.
11. *The Acts of the Apostles*, 140.
12. C. Peter Wagner, Win Arn, and Elmer Towns, *Church Growth: State of the Art* (Wheaton, Ill.: Tyndale, 1986), 291.
13. White, *Review and Herald*, 3 November 1885, 673.
14. White, *Christian Service*, 57.
15. See the *SDA Church Manual*, 1995 ed., 61.
16. *The Acts of the Apostles*, 140.
17. *The Desire of Ages*, 141.

Chapter 4

Growing Witnessing

Throughout the book of Acts the reader finds repeated reports of church growth. The book "is intended to be a paradigm of how the kingdom of God would spread worldwide through the centuries until Jesus returns."[1] There is an evident progression in these reports:

1:15—An original nucleus of 120 disciples
2:41—Three thousand were baptized on Pentecost
2:47—There were daily additions to the church
4:4—The number increased to 5,000 men plus women
5:14—Multitudes were added to the Lord
6:1—Addition changed to multiplication
6:7—The number of the disciples multiplied
9:35—An entire town was committed to Christ
11:24—A great many people added to the Lord
16:5—Churches increased in number daily
19:10—All Asia heard the Word of the Lord
21:10—Myriads of Jews believed

This chapter will consider the concept of church growth and review selected principles that may help the church to fulfill its mission. When the latter happens, Jesus will come to claim His own.

Church Growth

The reports listed above provide descriptions of different forms of *numerical* growth. However, Acts also contains reports of *spiritual* growth—see, for example, chapter 9:31: "The churches throughout all

Judea, Galilee, and Samaria had peace and were edified. And walking in the fear of the Lord and in the comfort of the Holy Spirit, they were multiplied." Church growth, then, "is the balanced increase in quantity, quality, and organizational complexity of a local church."[2]

Missiologists describe four kinds of church growth.[3] The first may be described as "internal growth." It relates to the church's own progress. Churches need to be edified. The members' growth in grace and Christlikeness are prerequisites for other forms of church growth. Internal growth is not evangelism; it is designated E-0 (see Figure 2), indicating that the church is not yet "reaching out." However, *spiritual growth* is essential.

	Faith		Distance		Culture	
E-0	‖	E-1	‖	E-2	‖	E-3
Believers	‖	Nonbelievers	‖	Nonbelievers Distance	‖	Nonbelievers Distance Culture
Spiritual growth		Expansion growth		Extension growth		Bridging growth
Internal growth		Evangelism		Church planting		Missionaries

Figure 2. Four kinds of church growth.

A second form of growth takes place through what is commonly called "evangelism." This form of church growth sees people being added to the local church by conversion. It happens when the church reaches out and incorporates people from the surrounding community. In this case churches grow by "multiplying disciples." Because members cross only one invisible barrier, the barrier dividing believers from nonbelievers, this form of evangelism is called E-1 (see Figure 2). Because the church grows in size, this form of church growth is called *expansion growth*.

A third form of church growth is called "church planting." It happens when a "mother church" establishes new congregations. Multiplying churches is sometimes the best option for a church that is growing and wants to keep growing, because buildings have their limitations. Church planting crosses two barriers: it not only reaches out across the invisible barrier between believers and nonbelievers but also solves the obstacle of distance by planting new congregations in other neighborhoods. The church is branching across distance, so this growth is described as *extension growth* (designated E-2; see Figure 2).

The fourth form of church growth involves doing what Paul did and others are still doing: planting churches among people who are culturally different. It may require leaving the home country and learning another language. As missionaries reach out to nonbelievers and establish new congregations for people of a different culture, they are crossing a third barrier, culture. This form of evangelism that reaches other cultures is called E-3 (see Figure 2). Those who participate in this form of evangelism, in *bridging growth*, are traditionally called *missionaries*.

According to this understanding of evangelism and church growth, one need not go abroad to be an E-3 missionary, and not all those who do go abroad are missionaries. For instance, a Korean pastor nurturing members of a Korean-speaking church in South America is providing E-0 church growth. A Brazilian evangelist preaching to Portuguese-speaking nonbelievers in Angola, Africa, is doing E-1. A believer in the Philippines who offers regular Sabbath-morning services in his own house in order to plant a new church is doing E-2. An English-speaking Australian pastor planting a church among Italian-speaking nonbelievers in Sydney is doing E-3. And, of course, a Japanese woman living in a remote village in Bangladesh in order to plant a church is an E-3 missionary.

Growth and Decline

As we've already seen, the early church grew very rapidly. If there were 3,000 baptized believers by Pentecost and 5,000 three months later, the disciples were winning an average of about 20 new converts a day. Indeed, Acts 2:47 speaks of daily additions to the church.

The Adventist system provides three ways to add more members to a church: 1. By transfer of membership (when members move from one Adventist church to another). 2. By profession of faith (when persons already baptized by immersion request to join the church. 3. By baptism.

But people interested in church growth must account for losses as well as gains. The early church also experienced losses; the earliest recorded were Ananias and his wife Sapphira (Acts 5:3-5, 10). A local Adventist church may delete a name from its records for one of four reasons: 1. Transfer of membership (when a member moves away to another Adventist church and requests his or her membership). 2. Apostasy (when the church considers that a certain course of action requires disfellowship). 3. When a member is adjudged "missing" (usually when a member cannot be located for at least two years). 4. Death.

In a given year the average congregation will lose up to 2 percent of its membership due to death, 3 percent to transfer, and 6 percent to reversion or apostasy.[4] Suppose, then, that a congregation of 100 members baptizes eight persons a year (including children!) and receives three by transfer. That congregation will likely find that in the same year about five have apostatized, one has gone missing, three have transferred out, and two have died. This is not growth; it's just maintaining a congregation!

		Gains			**Losses**
	+ 8	baptisms		- 5	apostasy
	+ 3	transfer in		- 1	missing
Total	+ 11			- 3	transferred out
				- 2	died
			Total	- 11	

Researchers have estimated that for a church to grow, one of every two persons who join the church should be added by conversion growth.[5] Important as they are, biological and transfer growth do not provide an accurate measure of a church's effectiveness in reaching the lost. On the other hand, evangelism alone will not provide net growth either. You could bring in a large number of converts in a year and still show a loss if the "back door" stands wide open for apostasies.

Using Numbers

There is a significant difference between the words "addition" and "multiplication." (Three *plus* three equals 6, but three *times* three equals nine.) English translations of Acts use both words to describe the fast growth-rate of the early church. In Acts 5:14 Luke writes of addition, and in chapter 6:1 we find multiplication used to refer to the fast and constant increase of the church.

In two of his church-growth reports, Luke provided numbers, using the word *number* seven times in Acts. In one case he spoke of 3,000 baptisms (Acts 2:41), while in another he mentioned 5,000 men (4:4).

Counting is not contrary to God's nature. God told Moses, "Take a census of all the congregation of the children of Israel." (Num. 1:2. Notice the name of the book, "Numbers.") The problem arises when people abuse numbers. David counted Israel in order to evaluate his own military strength, and that displeased God (see 1 Chron. 21:1, 7).[6] "Using numbers is not intrinsically right or wrong. It depends on motives."[7] I don't think that Luke should be charged with "numerolatry" because he showed interest in numbers.

Some Christians argue that they are not interested in numbers nor in church growth. They say, "What God requires from me is not numbers but faithfulness." There is truth in that affirmation. 1 Corinthians 4:2 says that "it is required in stewards that one be found faithful." However, it may be dangerous to use this argument as an excuse for not doing evangelism or for explaining losses. The Lord spoke His "well done, good and faithful servant" to workers who demonstrated faithfulness in growth, in doubling their number of talents (see Matt. 15:21, 23). Church-growth expert Donald McGavran says, "The numerical approach is essential to understanding church growth. The church is made up of countable people and there is nothing particularly spiritual in not counting them."[8]

God's purpose is to save souls from ruin and sin. He established the church to serve as His agency to fulfill His mission on earth. God sent Saul to the Gentiles " 'to open their eyes and to turn them from darkness to light, and from the power of Satan to God, that they may receive forgiveness of sins and an inheritance among those who are sanctified by faith in Me' " (Acts 26:18). The more sinners are saved, the more pleased is God. Combining evangelism and nurturing will maximize the church's success. Incorporating converts and retaining them are of equal importance in the work of saving souls. At the end, numbers do count. Ellen G. White said, "The losses and gains in this business are of great importance; for the results do not end with this life, but reach over into eternity."[9]

Planning Witnessing and Growth

Planning is the process of setting goals, organizing resources, and designing approaches by which the goals may be achieved.[10] "The best help that ministers can give the members of our churches is not sermonizing, but planning work for them."[11] The following are some guidelines for planning found in the book of Acts.

First of all, planning requires setting goals and objectives. Some people suppose that Paul simply went from place to place, preaching the gospel without any master plan. However, his missionary strategy appears to have been much bolder. At times he bypassed certain areas and cities, even places where his work was needed. He wanted to preach in strategic centers like Philippi, Thessalonica, Berea, Athens, and Corinth. He felt he must visit the imperial city of Rome (Acts 19:21). "It is essential to labor with order, following an organized plan and a definite object."[12] Planning is so essential that working without a plan is sinful: "It is a sin to be heedless, purposeless and indifferent in any work in which we may engage, but especially in the work of God."[13] Success follows "order and harmonious action."[14]

Planning demands vision. Paul did not stay in Ephesus, but he left his friends Aquila and Priscilla there to prepare the way for his return (see Acts 18:19; 19:1). His apology that he was not able "to stay a longer time" with the brethren at Ephesus (18:20) indicates that he planned ahead and had a definite schedule. He had an itinerary, planning to be in Jerusalem for the coming feast and then to return again to Ephesus (18:21).

Ellen G. White offered the following good advice not only for Christian witnesses, Bible workers, literature evangelists, and pastors, but also for all others who want to make the best use of their time: "As far as possible, it is well to consider what is to be accomplished through the day. Make a memorandum of the different duties that await your attention, and set apart time for the doing of each duty."[15]

Planning requires the identification of priorities, and it demands flexibility. Paul worked patiently in the synagogue at Ephesus for three months. But when opposition developed, making it impossible for him to continue in the synagogue, he moved the Christian disciples to the school of Tyrannus (Acts 19:8, 9). The apostles' adaptation to circumstances also reveals their flexibility. When they did not find a synagogue in which to preach, they "went out of the city to the riverside" and "sat down and spoke to the women" (16:13). When they were thrown into prison, they used that opportunity to witness for the Lord by "praying and singing hymns" (16:25) in such a way that the prisoners listened. They made the best out of the worst circumstances.

Planning means organization. Paul's distribution of his missionary forces at his departure from Macedonia suggests a degree of organization. When he went to Athens, he left Silas and Timothy in Macedonia (see Acts 17:14). When Timothy visited Paul at Athens, Paul soon sent him back to Thessalonica (1 Thess. 3:1, 2). Later, Paul welcomed Silas and Timothy at Corinth (Acts 18:5).

Witnessing and the Finishing of the Work

The book of Acts describes many deeds that, according to the enemies of the early church, "turned the world upside down" (Acts 17:6). And Revelation tells how the message of the three angels, carried by the millions of Sabbath keepers that they represent, is taken to "every nation, tribe, tongue, and people" (Rev. 14:6). These faithful witnesses are not waiting for something extraordinary to take place some day in the future under the influence of the "latter rain." Many are already participating in the finishing of God's work by knocking on doors and giving Bible studies to their friends, neighbors, and relatives. Others are even leaving their families to spend the rest of their lives witnessing in one or another of the thousands of people groups in which Adventists have no presence.

Despite their efforts, however, there are many people to whom no Christians are witnessing. About one third of the world's population identify themselves as Christians (including denominations and cults, nominal Christians and those who are Christian in background only). Another third of the world's population are nonChristians who live in relatively close contact with Christians. But the other third of the world's population will die without hearing the gospel unless committed Christians volunteer to leave the conveniences of their culture to go and witness to them.

Research tells us that there are some 5,257 ethno-linguistic population groups of about one million people each on planet Earth. As of 1995 Adventists had at least one church in each of some 3,200 of these groups. At that time, Adventists were facing the challenge of reaching 1,700 unentered segments—representing about two billion people—with absolutely no Adventist presence.[16]

Acts 19:10 reports aggressive witnessing activities by believers in Ephesus as a result of two years of training "so that all who dwelt in *Asia* heard the word of the Lord" (emphasis supplied). Luke wasn't referring to the Asian continent but to a province of the Roman Empire now called Asia Minor. However, his use of the term reminds us of the greatest challenge for Christianity: the evangelization of the Asian continent.

Think about this: One-third of the people of the world have never heard of Jesus and are dying without a viable chance to become Christians. In the least evangelized area of the world, included mostly in what is known as the "10/40 Window," "live 86 percent of the world's people groups, of which less than 2 percent are Christians."[17] Most of these people live in Asia.

Most of these nonentered groups require cross-cultural missionaries.

These kind of missionaries must be willing to learn another language and to live in another culture until the church is planted.

Acts 16:9, 10 relates Paul's experience of hearing a European asking him, an Asian, to "come over . . . and help us!" He brought the gospel into Europe in answer to that call. Today God is

> calling for men who are willing to leave their farms, their business, if need be their families, to become missionaries for Him. And the call will be answered. In the past there have been men who, stirred by the love of Christ and the needs of the lost, have left the comforts of home and the society of friends, even that of wife and children, to go into foreign lands, among idolaters and savages, to proclaim the message of mercy.[18]

Today millions of voices from nonentered people groups are still asking, "Come and help us!"

How will God finish His work? Through committed members willing to give up the conveniences of their home, town, family, church, and country—willing even to sacrifice life itself—to go "where Christ was not known" (Rom. 15:20, NIV). How will "every nation, tribe, language, and people" (Rev. 14:6) have the opportunity to hear the eternal gospel? We can't rely on shortwave radios or the Internet. Eighty-five percent of the world's poorest countries lie within the unevangelized world. They may never be reached through sophisticated means of massive communication. Evangelizing them "must be largely accomplished by persevering, individual effort; by visiting the people in their homes."[19] "Servants of God . . . will hasten from place to place to proclaim the message from heaven. By thousands of voices, all over the earth, the warning will be given. . . . Thus the inhabitants of the earth will be brought to take their stand."[20]

---

1. C. Peter Wagner, *Spreading the Fire*, The Acts of the Holy Spirit Series (Ventura, Calif.: Regal Books, 1994), 17.

2. Ron Jenson and Jim Stevens, *Dynamics of Church Growth* (Grand Rapids, Mich.: Baker, 1981), 10.

3. Ralph Winter described different kinds of evangelism in "The New Macedonia: A Revolutionary New Era in Mission Begins," in *Perspectives on the World Christian Movement: A Reader* (Pasadena, Calif.: Carey, 1981), 295-301. What follows incorporates and adapts ideas from C. Peter Wagner, *Strategies for Church Growth* (Ventura, Calif.: Regal Books, 1987), 116, 117.

4. Gary McIntosh and Glen Martin, *Finding Them, Keeping Them* (Nashville, Tenn.: Broadman, 1992), 10.

5. See Win Arn, *The Church Growth Ratio Book* (Pasadena, Calif.: Church Growth, 1987), 55.

6. See Ellen G. White, *Patriarchs and Prophets*, 747.

7. Wagner, *Strategies for Church Growth*, 43.

8. Donald A. McGavran, *Understanding Church Growth* (Grand Rapids, Mich.: Eerdmans, 1990), 93.

9. White, *Testimonies for the Church*, 5:411.

10. See Bernard M. Lall and Geeta R. Lall, *Dynamic Leadership* (Nampa, Idaho: Pacific Press, 1979), 67-79.

11. White, *Christian Service*, 80.

12. White, *Evangelism*, 94.

13. White, *Review and Herald*, 18 March 1884.

14. White, *Patriarchs and Prophets*, 376.

15. White, *Child Guidance*, 124, 125.

16. See Charles R. Taylor, "Measuring a Dream," *Adventist Review* 172 (8 June 1995), 8.

17. Bryant L. Meyers, *The New Context of World Mission* (Monrovia, Calif.: MARC, 1996), 33.

18. White, *The Acts of the Apostles*, 370

19. White, *Historical Sketches of Foreign Missions*, 150.

20. White, *The Great Controversy*, 612.

Chapter 5

Models for Witnessing

Most of us admire people whom we consider heroes, models, and examples. I remember Grandpa Pedro. He was baptized about one hundred years ago. In those days, becoming a Protestant was not an easy task in his corner of the world. The area where he lived could have been classified as a "nonentered area"!

After his conversion, Grandpa Pedro went to the forests and to the cities, through swamps and mountains, in order to proclaim the three angels' messages. Before preaching his prophetic messages, he performed tooth extractions, massages, and water treatments. Grandpa Pedro suffered persecution, but he established new congregations and built church buildings. The stories of his youth that he told moved me to want to be like him!

Obviously, Jesus modeled witnessing for us. And so did champions like Paul. But what about deacons or anonymous witnesses or simple laity? The book of Acts presents us with dynamic models for witnessing in the third millennium. While the following review is far from exhaustive, it gives us a glimpse of what God can do with common people as well as apostles.

The Martyrs

The Greek word translated "witness" is also the root of the English word *martyr*. Stephen is known as "the first Christian martyr."[1] According to Acts 6:5, he was "a man full of faith and the Holy Spirit." Verse 8 adds that he was "full of faith and power." Such a filling impels a person filled to act. Acts 1:8 indicates that the inevitable result of being filled with the Holy Spirit is to serve as a witness.

For Stephen, being faithful to Jesus meant more than just accepting a responsibility in the church and doing good works in the community. Stephen and his fellow deacon, Philip, "were fully qualified to instruct others in the truth, and they engaged in the work with great earnestness and success."[2]

A dispute with Stephen led those who "were not able to resist the wisdom and the Spirit by which he spoke" to lie against him, to provoke further tensions, and finally to murder him (Acts 6:9-12; 7:58). Witnessing can be a risky business. Stephen surely proved to be a "martyr" in the full sense of the term.

In time, a more extended persecution conducted by the Roman authorities replaced the wave of persecution that the Jews initiated. But the early Christians regarded persecution as a challenge, an opportunity to witness. There are many "well-authenticated cases of conversion of pagans in the very moment of witnessing the condemnation and death of Christians," wrote Stephen Neil.[3] This fact supports the contention of a second-century apologist, Tertullian, that "the blood of Christians is [the]seed" of the church.[4] Martyrs were witnesses indeed. Paul never could forget the courage and the testimony of the dying Stephen (Acts 22:20). His death witnessed as effectively as did the words he spoke when alive. To martyrs like Stephen the Lord has promised " 'Be faithful until death, and I will give you the crown of life' " (Rev. 2:10).

The Scattered Ones

After Stephen's death, "a great persecution arose against the church which was at Jerusalem; and they were all scattered throughout the regions of Judea and Samaria" (Acts 8:1). It seemed that Satan had won a major victory. Very soon, however, it was evident that he had not because "those who were scattered went everywhere preaching the word" (8:4).

> When they were scattered by persecution they went forth filled with missionary zeal. They realized the responsibility of their mission. They knew that they held in their hands the bread of life for a famishing world; and they were constrained by the love of Christ to break this bread to all who were in need.[5]

"Now those who were scattered after the persecution that arose over Stephen traveled as far as Phoenicia, Cyprus, and Antioch" (Acts 11:19). Antioch was the third largest city of the empire, next to Rome and Alexandria in size. Its population is estimated at between 250,000 and 800,000.[6] In those days, according to Josephus, most of the Jews in the Diaspora lived in Antioch.*

It is likely that the first wave of Christian "refugees" from Jerusalem settled in the Jewish quarter and witnessed only to the Hebrew and Greek Jews (Acts 11:19).[7] There were some, however, "from Cyprus and Cyrene [North Africa], who, when they had come to Antioch" (11:20), witnessed to the Greek Gentiles.† The conversions of the Ethiopian eunuch (8:27) and of Cornelius (10:1) were prototypes of individual conversions among the Gentiles, but they were not examples of Gentile church planting. It is in Antioch that we find the first intentionally cross-cultural witnessing.[8]

There were many other "nameless ones" who also witnessed. Unnumbered disciples testified about Christ throughout and beyond the Roman Empire amid both persecution and anonymity. "Every Christian was a witness," Neill wrote, and "nothing is more notable than the anonymity of these early missionaries."[9] Although the chroniclers of mission history today search in vain for the surnames of these witnesses, they are not nameless to God.

Tertullian, who wrote about seventy-five years after the death of the apostle John, affirms that Christianity had spread to include

> the varied races of the Gaetulians, and manifold confines of the Moors, all the limits of the Spains, and the diverse nations of the Gauls, and the haunts of the Britons—inaccessible to the Romans, but subjugated to Christ. . . . In all which places the name of the Christ who is already come reigns.[10]

Deacon and Evangelist

Acts 8 describes Philip's ministry. He was not an apostle but was one of the seven deacons (Acts 1:13; 6:5).†† He was also one of the scattered ones (cp. 8:1 with 8:4, 5). The only stories about both Stephen and Philip told in Acts describe them working as evangelists. (Nothing is known about the other five deacons named in Acts 6:5.)

**War*, vii. 3. 3. Jews were so numerous and influential in Antioch that their rights and privileges were recorded on tables of brass. *War*, vii. 5. 2. Quoted in Alfred Edersheim, *The Life and Times of Jesus the Messiah* (Grand Rapids: Eerdmans, 1971), 1:74.

†The KJV renders "Grecians," while the RSV and the NIV prefer "Greek." NEB renders "pagans." Following another line of authorities, the NKJV uses the term "Hellenists."

††Luke never wrote of "seven deacons," nor did he call Philip a deacon.

Deacons should not be limited to the work of looking after the needs of the poor, smiling at the door of the church, and serving at the tables (Acts 6:2). Stephen "did great wonders and signs among the people," and Philip preached, did miracles, and baptized (see 6:8, 10; 7:2-56; 8:5, 6, 38). Although he was a deacon, Philip was even known in the early church as "Philip the evangelist" (21:8).

Many seem to believe that the responsibility for missionary work rests on those related to the department of Lay Activities or Personal Ministries. However, we are told that "wherever a church is established, *all the members* should engage actively in missionary work."[11] This "missionary work" is not necessarily cross-cultural ministry nor public evangelism. Ellen G. White used the term "missionary work" to refer to witnessing—a work in which deacons and administrators, carpenters and professors, are expected to participate. Commenting on the example of Philip, she wrote,

> Not upon the ordained minister only rests the responsibility of going forth to fulfill this commission. Everyone who has received Christ is called to work for the salvation of his fellow-men. "The Spirit and the bride say, Come. And let him that heareth say, Come." Revelation 22:17. The charge to give this invitation includes the entire church. Every one who has heard the invitation is to echo the message from hill and valley, saying "Come."
>
> It is a fatal mistake to suppose that the work of soul-saving depends alone upon the ministry. . . . Why is it that many more do not respond to the call? Is it because they think themselves excused in that they do not stand in the pulpit? Let them understand that there is a large work to be done outside the pulpit by thousands of consecrated lay members.[12]

An Enthusiastic Beginner

Paul first appears in Acts as "Saul" (chapter 7:58) (from the Hebrew *Sha'ul*, meaning "asked [of God]") and is referred to by that name through chapter 13:9. Possibly he had more than one name. As he began his work among the Gentiles, he preferred the use of his Grecized Roman name, *Paulos*, or *Paul*.

Paul's first contact with Christianity came when Stephen was martyred (Acts 7:58; 8:1). He was very active in the period of persecution that immediately followed (8:3; 26:11). He was converted during one of his persecuting excursions against Christians. Acts contains three accounts of his conversion (chapters 9:1-9; 22:4-11; 26:9-18).

Paul did not eat or drink during the three days between his encounter with Christ and his baptism (Acts 9:9, 18, 19). "Immediately he preached the Christ in the synagogues" (9:20). This is logical because "the very first impulse of the renewed heart is to bring others also to the Saviour."[13]

Luke does not say what Paul did during the "many days" (Acts 9:23) that followed his conversion. But when Paul told his own story in the book of Galatians, he said that three years passed between his conversion and the trip to Jerusalem that Luke mentions (Acts 9:26; Gal. 1:18). Paul spent some of that period in Damascus and some in Arabia (Galatians1:17). In Damascus the Jews plotted to kill him, but he escaped (2 Cor. 11:32, 33). That's when he went to Jerusalem.

While in Jerusalem, Paul "spoke boldly in the name of the Lord Jesus" (Acts 9:29). He was not yet "Paul, the evangelist" nor "Paul, the missionary" but he was "Saul, the witness." Many in Jerusalem recognized him not only because they had known him from his youth (26:4), when he sat at the feet of Gamaliel, the most renowned rabbi of his day (22:3), but because he became a member of the Sanhedrin,[14] the chief judicial body of the Jews.

Paul was exercising his abilities and using opportunities to testify for his Lord. However, we learn in part through trial and error. Paul made a mistake common among new converts: he got into an argument—he "disputed against the Hellenists" (Acts 9:29). These Hellenists were Greek-speaking Jews. Possibly, there were among them some whose coats Paul had held while they murdered Stephen (7:58; cp. 6:9-12). These people tried to kill Paul (9:23). So the believers decided to send him away, back to his home town (9:30). They did it primarily because they wanted to save his life, but it is probable they also thought he was stirring up too much trouble. Like many new Christians, Paul's enthusiasm may have been outweighing his wisdom. We are advised to avoid debates, although sometimes they are unavoidable:

> Often, as you seek to present the truth, opposition will be aroused; but if you seek to meet the opposition with argument you will only multiply it, and that you cannot afford to do. Hold to the affirmative. Angels of God are watching you, and they understand how to impress those whose opposition you refuse to meet with argument. Dwell not on the negative points of questions that arise, but gather to your minds affirmative truths, and fasten them there by much study and earnest prayer and heart consecration.[15]

It is normal and desirable that newly baptized members share the gospel with their relatives, neighbors, and friends. However, they need special guidance at this point. They need to understand that witnessing requires tact and wisdom.

Paul's Missionary Strategies

In his epistles, Paul speaks in no uncertain terms of his mission (1 Cor. 1:17; 9:16-18). He makes it clear that his supreme mission is evangelism. Paul expects that his own example will inspire others to follow in his train, just as he follows Christ (1 Cor. 11:1; 4:16; Phil. 3:17; 1 Thess. 1:6; 2 Thess. 3:6, 7). George W. Peters concludes, "To follow Paul meant to pursue the path of evangelism."[16]

Paul's *modus operandi* was under the guidance of and subject to the control of the Holy Spirit. Luke's record in the book of Acts enables us to see Paul's strategies.[17]

First, Paul maintained close contact with the home base (Acts 14:28; 18:23). At the end of his missionary journeys he returned to Antioch. On at least five occasions he visited Jerusalem, and each time he conferred with the leaders there.

Second, he confined his efforts to four provinces: two in Asia—Galatia and Asia; two in Europe—Macedonia and Achaia. A missionary cannot work the entire world. Witnessing regularly in a specific geographical area will prove more productive than occasional efforts scattered everywhere.

Third, he concentrated on large cities such as Antioch, Ephesus, Philippi, and Thessalonica. He was able to be more effective by staying in strategic centers (see Acts 19:8). From major urban centers the gospel spread to nearby cities.

Fourth, he made the synagogue the scene of his chief labor (Acts 13:14; 14:1; 17:1-3; 18:4). In the synagogue he found Jews, proselytes, and God-fearing Gentiles, all of whom already had a knowledge of the one true God, an acquaintance with the Old Testament, and an expectation of the coming Messiah. Visiting rabbis were customarily invited to give a "word of exhortation" (13:15), and he took full advantage of this opportunity.

Fifth, he preferred to preach to responsive people. When the Jews rejected Paul, he turned to the Gentiles (Acts 13:46; 18:6). Sometimes the process of institutionalization forces a number of Christians to stay in unproductive areas, while other areas ready for harvest are neglected.

Sixth, he baptized converts on their confession of their faith. For instance, he baptized the Philippian jailer the same night he was converted

(Acts 16:33). Paul himself was baptized immediately (9:18). However, while the Bible does not specify a period of time between conversion and baptism, it certainly does require a responsible decision, repentance, and willingness to follow the Word of God.

Seventh, he stayed in each place where he worked long enough to establish a church (Acts 18:11; 19:10; 20:3, 31). In every city, with the possible exception of Athens, he left behind a strong and growing church that could carry on after his departure.

Eighth, he made ample use of fellow workers such as Barnabas, John Mark, Silas, Timothy, Luke, and Epaphras. He was not a solitary evangelist, but rather the commanding officer of a large circle of missionaries.

Ninth, Paul aimed at transcultural witnessing. He was willing to carry the gospel "where Christ was not known" (Rom. 15:20, Beck). He went to Greece (Acts 17:15, 16) and was willing to go to Spain (Rom. 15:24). The finishing of our work demands that we penetrate nonentered areas of the world and of our own neighborhoods.

Tenth, he "taught publicly and from house to house" (Acts 20:20). He used different evangelistic strategies according to the circumstances. He was flexible as necessary to reach as many people as possible (1 Cor. 9:19-23).

A Dynamic Duet

Acts 18:1-3 gives us a good deal of information about Aquila and his wife, Priscilla. Aquila was a Jew born in the Roman province of Pontus, on the shore of the Black Sea. He and his wife had lived in Rome. It is possible that they were already Christians when Paul met them at Corinth. The second-century writer Suetonius relates that in Rome the Jews had disagreed violently over a person named "Chrestus"—very likely Christ—so that synagogue life was disrupted.* At about that time, A.D. 49, the Roman Emperor Claudius expelled the Jews from Rome. It was because of that expulsion that Aquila "had recently come from Italy with his wife Priscilla."

Paul arrived in Corinth alone, having left his partners Silas and Timothy at Thessalonica (Acts 17:14). Soon he discovered Aquila and Priscilla, who were working at tentmaking, the same trade as he (18:1-3). Notice that

*An inference is that the disorder resulted from the introduction of Christianity into one or more of the synagogues of the city. R. C. H. Lenski disagrees on the basis that in Acts 28:17-29 the leading Jews of Rome readily came to Paul, *The Acts of the Apostles* (Minneapolis: Augsburg, 1961), 745. Lenski, however, admits that Tacitus uses *Chrestianos* as a name for Christians.

Paul "went to them." He must have enjoyed working with this couple with whom he had not only the ties of nationality and faith but also of vocation. Eventually they became some of his closest friends. They are remembered because of their involvement with Paul and his mission and because of their commitment to God and His work.

Aquila and Priscilla opened their own home for church meetings (1 Cor. 16:19), which must have been as much a burden for them as it is for us today. When Paul returned to Palestine, probably in the fall of A.D. 52, the couple accompanied him as far as Ephesus (Acts 18:18, 19). There they met Apollos (18:24-26). By the time Paul wrote his letter to the Romans, Priscilla and Aquila were back in that city, where they again established a church in their house (Rom. 16:3-5). The greetings Paul sent to Timothy from Rome suggest that the couple had returned to Ephesus by the time of his imprisonment (2 Tim. 4:19). Their mobility suggests something about their personality and may have been a major blessing for the spread of the gospel.

Priscilla and Aquila functioned very well as a team. Evidently, they both shared their views of service and supported each other in ministry. Interestingly, the majority of the New Testament references to them list Priscilla first (Acts 18:18; Rom. 16:3; 2 Tim. 4:19), a mark of her influence as a Christian in her own right.

The fact that Paul mentioned the couple in several letters indicates that he considered them to be extremely valuable lay workers in the churches to which they belonged. Perhaps Paul noticed that they also had the missionary gift and so encouraged them to exercise it by planting churches and by accompanying him in pioneer missions (Acts 18:18, 19). Evidently, Paul did very well in inspiring these two lay people to become committed to missionary work.

Many members in our churches today don't know how to use their gifts, and some don't even know which gifts they have. Sometimes church members seem to believe that only pastors can carry forward God's work successfully.

> There is altogether too much unused force in our churches. There are a few who devise, plan, and work; but the great mass of our people do not lift their hands to do anything for fear of being repulsed, for fear that others will regard them as out of their place.[18]

Sometimes pastors seem to be reluctant to do what Paul did with Priscilla and Aquila. "The work of God is retarded by criminal unbelief in his power to use the common people to carry forward his work successfully."[19] Paul's success was due, among others things, to encouraging people like Aquila and Priscilla to use their gifts.

God's work today will be finished by witnessing Christians, anointed evangelists, people filled by the Holy Spirit. It will be finished when witnessing scholars and administrators, witnessing carpenters and secretaries, witnessing doctors and nurses, witnessing teachers and farmers, witnessing lawyers and shoemakers, witnessing men and women who comprise our church membership, "rally to the work, and unite their efforts" with those of Spirit-filled pastors and church officers.[20]

---

1. See, e.g., Ellen G. White, *The Acts of the Apostles*, 97.
2. Ibid., 90.
3. Stephen Neill, *A History of Christian Missions* (New York: Penguin, 1964), 39.
4. Tertullian, *Apology* 50.13. Loeb Classical Library, 227.
5. *The Acts of the Apostles*, 106.
6. *SDA Bible Dictionary*, rev. ed. (1970), s.v. "Antioch."
7. *The Acts of the Apostles*, 155.
8. C. Peter Wagner, *Lighting the World*, The Acts of the Holy Spirit Series (Ventura, Calif.: Regal Books, 1995), 102.
9. Neill, *History of Christian Missions*, 22.
10. Tertullian, *An Answer to the Jews*, ch. 7, found in *Ante-Nicene Fathers*, 3:158.
11. Ellen G. White, *Testimonies for the Church*, 6:296; emphasis added.
12. *The Acts of the Apostles*, 110, 111.
13. White, *The Great Controversy*, 70.
14. *The Acts of the Apostles*, 112.
15. *Testimonies*, 9:147, 148.
16. George W. Peters, *A Biblical Theology of Missions* (Chicago: Moody, 1972), 133.
17. Adapted from J. Herbert Kane, *Christian Missions in Biblical Perspective* (Grand Rapids: Baker, 1976), 73-84.
18. White, *Review and Herald*, 9 July 1895.
19. White, ibid., 16 July 1895.
20. Paraphrased from White, *Gospel Workers*, 352.

Chapter 6

The Tools for Personal Witnessing

"I am not interested in strategies—they're tools of the devil. I depend on the Holy Spirit alone!" Have you ever heard this argument? Some believers seem to believe that human tools and strategies are incompatible with the Holy Spirit. And they *are* poor substitutes. Nevertheless, some approaches to evangelism are productive and others are faulty.

During the years I served as a pastor, I conducted many evangelistic series. In time, I learned that people who have responded to an altar call have not necessarily made a firm decision for Christ yet. I discovered that when people who have made decisions in public meetings are not followed up by means of personal visitation, most of them won't complete their commitment. This chapter will focus on strategies for personal witnessing, for which we are told there is no substitute:

> By personal labor reach those around you. Become acquainted with them. Preaching will not do the work that needs to be done. Angels of God attend you to the dwellings of those you visit. This work cannot be done by proxy. Money lent or given will not accomplish it. Sermons will not do it. By visiting the people, talking, praying, sympathizing with them, you will win hearts.[1]

Three Approaches to Witnessing

Witnessing strategies may be divided into three categories (see Figure 3). The first comprises the primary forms of witnessing such as literature ministry, health ministry, language schools, and similar forms of ministry. They are not designed as strategies to present the whole truth and to persuade people to join the church. Rather, they serve as what some describe as "ground preparation." Since they touch people at the point of their needs, they are also described as "entering wedges."

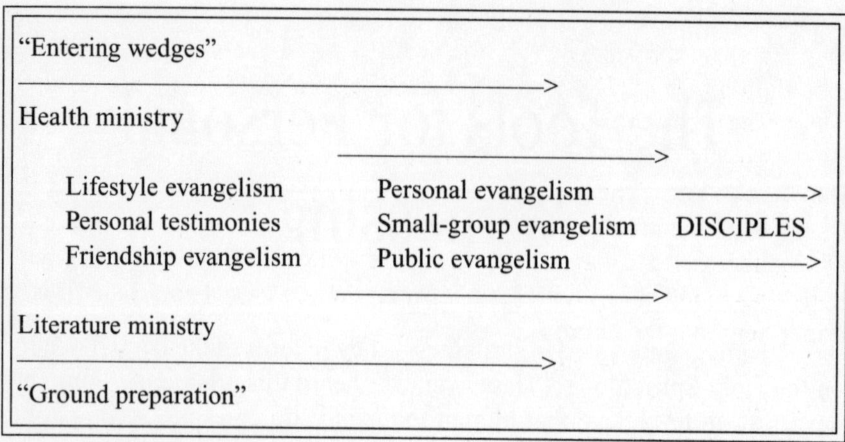

Figure 3: Three stages of witnessing

Like the first category, the second—which includes lifestyle evangelism, friendship evangelism, and personal testimonies—aims to gain access to the heart. However, the forms of witnessing in this category are more candid in their demonstration of Christianity. They serve as a bridge between the primary entering paths to the heart and the deeper levels of witnessing involving doctrinal presentations.

The immediate goal of the third set of witnessing activities is baptism. Personal evangelism, lay evangelism through small groups, and public evangelism aim to lead a person into the study of the Bible and Christian doctrines so that the receptor will make a responsible decision for church membership. These strategies seek to "teach them all things." An underlying assumption behind these approaches is that the gospel commission intends that our witnessing produce disciples.

Friendship Evangelism

"Friendship evangelism means that wherever you are, whatever you are doing, you consciously work at building relationships that will open doors to lead people to the gospel."[2] This approach to witnessing works effectively because of networks, which are groups of people "who relate informally through voluntary associations, professional contacts, family or racial ties, or other connections."[3]

Several stories in Acts demonstrate that the growth of the church took place mostly through networks of personal relationships. Lydia, the businesswoman from Philippi, was baptized with her household (Acts 16:14, 15). The Philippian jailer "believed in God with all his household," and they were baptized together on the night of his conversion (16:30-34). In preparation for Peter's arrival, Cornelius "had called together his relatives and close friends" (10:24).

Two facts underline the importance of what has been called "friendship evangelism." The question "How did you join the church?" elicits the first. Most church members (60 to 90 percent) would stress the influence of neighbors, friends, and relatives.[4] The second is that the closer the relationship a member has with nonbelievers, the less costly and easier it is to bring them into the church.[5]

Friendship, however, is more than an evangelistic tool. Friendship with other church members is the first step of a new believer's assimilation into the church. If new members don't have a minimum of seven friends in the church within the first six months, they will be on their way out the back door.[6]

Lifestyle Evangelism

Lifestyle evangelism refers to the process through which the everyday words and deeds of a maturing Christian draw others to Christ. It involves living a good testimony before the lost and thus developing opportunities to present the gospel. This method of attracting people to Christ and His church takes time, yet it is foundational.

> It is not only by preaching the truth, not only by distributing literature, that we are to witness for God. Let us remember that a Christlike life is the most powerful argument that can be advanced in favor of Christianity.[7]

Love in action is most effective when coupled with the verbal presentation of God's love. This was one of the keys for the rapid growth of the apostolic church. Think of the lifestyle of the first Christians. Many expressions in the first chapters of Acts suggest the idea of "togetherness." In Acts 1:14 we find that they "all continued with one accord in prayer and supplication." "When the Day of Pentecost had fully come, they were all with one accord in one place" (2:1).

> The "all" of the text included apostles, disciples, and the other followers assembled. The "in one place" was the transient phase, but the "of one accord" is the eternal condition. The place means nothing today, but the *accord*, or unity, means everything.[8]

After Pentecost "they continued steadfastly in the apostles' doctrine and fellowship, in the breaking of the bread and in prayers. . . . Now all who believed were together, and had all things in common" (Acts 2:42, 44). Perhaps the most significant expression here is the word "fellowship." It describes a mutual relationship, which should be the goal of every church fellowship. They kept together as one body and treated each other accordingly.

> The proclamation of the gospel was to be world-wide in its extent, and the messengers of the cross could not hope to fulfill their important mission unless they should remain united in the bonds of Christian unity, and thus reveal to the world that they were one with Christ in God.[9]

About thirteen years after Pentecost, "the disciples were first called Christians" (Acts 11:26). Before then they were called those "who were of the Way" (9:2), "believers" (5:14), or "disciples" (1:15). The title "Christian" may have arisen from local gossip: "Those people are always talking about Christ!" The followers of the Way in Antioch were so committed to Christ that almost inevitably they were called "Christians."

> Living, as they were, in the midst of a people who seemed to care but little for the things of eternal value, they sought to arrest the attention of the honest in heart, and to bear positive testimony concerning Him whom they loved and served. In their humble ministry they learned to depend upon the power of the Holy Spirit to make effective the word of life. And so, in the various walks of life, they daily bore testimony of their faith in Christ.[10]

In the last chapter of Acts there is another simple detail that illustrates the quality of life of these early Christians. A group of faithful disciples, knowing that a group of fellow Christians was on their way to Rome, came to meet them. They traveled "as far as Appii Forum and Three Inns" and accompanied Paul and his party from there back to Rome. Paul found that act of love very meaningful: "When Paul saw them, he thanked God and took courage" (Acts 28:15). Acts of love to fellow believers are not only a responsibility of the church but also a primary form of witnessing.

Personal Bible Studies

Apollos, born in the Egyptian city of Alexandria, was a Jewish convert to the message of John the Baptist. Luke described him as an "eloquent man" and "fervent in spirit" (Acts 18:24, 25). When Aquila and Priscilla heard him preach in the synagogue at Ephesus, they realized that he knew the plan of salvation only incompletely. So they "took him aside and explained to him the way of God more accurately" (18:26).

Sometimes the personal Bible studies that the book of Acts mentions took place in unusual circumstances and places. Philip offered a Bible study to an African man while traveling in his chariot (Acts 8:35-39). Paul and Silas studied the Bible with a jailer after midnight when an earthquake had opened the doors of the prison (16:25, 26). The disciples "spoke the word of the Lord to him and to all who were in his house" (16:32).

Personal Bible studies covering biblical doctrines are the most important tool of personal evangelism leading to baptismal decisions. They may be conducted on a one-on-one basis or with small groups. In the early days of Adventism question-and-answer Bible studies were called "Bible readings." They got this name because the preacher or teacher would ask a question and then direct the student to read the Scripture texts that answered that question.

"The plan of holding Bible readings was a heaven-born idea. There are many, both men and women, who can engage in this branch of missionary labor."[11] "Among the members of our churches there should be more house-to-house labor, in giving Bible readings."[12]

Here's a suggested approach to a Bible study:

a. Begin with a short (3-5 minute), pleasant, informal visit.

b. Pray, asking for God's guidance.

c. Begin the study. Let the student participate as much as possible by responding to your questions, looking up and reading texts, and asking questions of you. In most cases seven to ten Bible texts will be enough to show what the Bible says about a certain doctrine, though some people may require a deeper study. Ascertain whether the student understands the lesson by asking such questions as "Is this what you have believed?" and "Does this seem reasonable to you?"

d. Secure a decision at the end of each Bible study. You can do so by asking three questions: 1) "Do you understand this subject?" 2) "Do you have questions about this subject?" (Answer any questions they may have.) 3) "Are you willing to _______ (put into practice whatever the study has been about; e.g., accept Jesus' forgiveness for your sins, keep the Sabbath, etc.)?"

e. Close with a short prayer and invite the student to tell God through prayer about his or her willingness to live what he or she has learned. Generally, your Bible study should not take more than 30-40 minutes.

"All who can should do personal labor. As they go from house to house, explaining the Scriptures to the people in a clear, simple manner, God makes the truth powerful to save. The Saviour blesses those who do this work."[13]

Personal Testimony

Another witnessing method is the personal testimony. In a personal testimony a witness recounts what he or she has experienced of the power of Christ.[14]

> Our confession of His faithfulness is Heaven's chosen agency for revealing Christ to the world. . . . That which will be most effectual is the testimony of our own experience. . . . These precious acknowledgements . . . , when supported by a Christlike life, have an irresistible power that works for the salvation of souls.[15]

Personal witnessing in the form of spontaneous testimonies differs from a Bible study in that a testimony has as its primary purpose the demonstration of the transforming power of Jesus rather than the teaching of doctrines. Testimonies intend to create in the heart of the listener a desire for a similar experience. Your personal testimony is the account of "how blessed you have been since you gained an experience in His service," and of "the gladness and joy that there is in the Christian life."[16]

A personal testimony should not be an autobiography. A Christian witness should be able to give his or her testimony in three minutes or less. One may share it in a hurry, sometimes in unconventional places, such as on the street, on a bus, or while waiting in a line.

Paul's testimonies illustrate this form of witnessing. The book of Acts contains three accounts of Paul's conversion; one by Luke (9:1-19), and two by Paul himself (22:6-16; 26:12-18). Each testimony contains three essential elements: First, "my life before I became a Christian." (Acts 22:3-5 contains Paul's "before Christ" story.) This part of the testimony seeks to give the listener something to identify with. If the listeners see similarities between their own experience and that of the witness, they will be more likely to accept the solutions the believer has found. Avoid the common mistake of dwelling too much on this first part of the testimony.

Second, "how I became a Christian." (For Paul's example, see Acts 22:6-11.) All Christians should be able to testify of their commitment to Christ. Sometimes the witness can describe how God answered a prayer or how a particular victory made Jesus real to him or her.

Third, "what Jesus Christ now means in my life." (Paul testified that he was called to serve as a witness for Jesus; see Acts 22:13-21.) Christian witnesses may tell how their life has changed and something of the joy they experience in following Jesus. An emphasis on the warmth and friendliness the believer has found in the church usually strikes a responsive chord in the hearts of lonely people.

Witnessing through testimonies grows out of our commitment to Jesus; it does not require the gift of evangelism.

Witnessing in the Neighborhood

For a time Paul "reasoned in the synagogue [of Corinth] every Sabbath" (Acts 18:4). The day came when the Jews "opposed him and blasphemed," so Paul decided not to work among them anymore (18:6). However, he did not need to go far to continue his work. "He departed from there and entered the house of a certain man named Justus, . . . whose house was next door to the synagogue" (18:7).

Paul's preaching took on new power in Corinth after Silas and Timothy came from Macedonia (Acts 18:5). Some Jews were driven to blasphemy by their rejection of Jesus. Then, in a dramatic scene, Paul "shook his garments" (verse 6) and announced his turning to the Gentiles. Among the Gentiles there were many who were attracted to the Jewish faith. Justus was one of these "God-fearers."

Justus's case illustrates the importance of missionary work in the neighborhood. "Not all can go as missionaries to foreign lands, but all can be home missionaries in their families and neighborhoods."[17] "There are souls in your neighborhood who, if they were judiciously labored for, would be converted."[18]

Witnessing in the neighborhood includes much more than smiling or just saying "Good morning, how are you?" to your neighbors and talking about the weather. Witnessing aims to lead a person to serve Jesus in the fellowship of the church. However, friendship with your neighbors is virtually a prerequisite before you approach them on spiritual matters.

> Visit your neighbors in a friendly way, and become acquainted with them.[19]

> Go to your neighbors one by one, and come close to them till their hearts are warmed by your unselfish interest and love. Sympathize with them, pray for them, watch for opportunities to do them good.[20]

After cultivating such relationships for a while, Christian witnesses may invite their neighbors to a once-a-week neighborhood Bible class in the Christian's home or to personal Bible studies in their own home. Perhaps the neighbors would never go to church or to the Christian's home on their own initiative, but after proper cultivation the Christian can invite them to "come and see" (John 1:45, 46).

> Christ's method alone will give true success in reaching the people. The Saviour mingled with men as one who desired their good. He showed His sympathy for them, ministered to their needs, and won their confidence. Then He bade them, "Follow Me."[21]

Visitation

We might never have heard of Ananias had he not been involved in ministering to Saul of Tarsus. Luke describes him simply as "a certain disciple" (Acts 9:10). God needed Ananias for a specific task. He was to visit a certain house. But God made clear to Ananias that he was to seek out Saul of Tarsus. Everybody knew that Saul was too prejudiced, too antagonistic, to be interested in the Christian gospel. Consequently, Ananias was reluctant to go, and understandably so. But God let him know that He had prepared the way for his visit. So Ananias reconsidered his attitude and went.

Ananias's approach was simple, friendly, direct. He addressed his prospect as "brother Saul" (9:17), which was an act of faith. And his obedience was rewarded with the accession to the church of a notable convert.

Ananias's experience should encourage those who visit friends and acquaintances as messengers and ambassadors for Christ.

Ellen White found direct comparisons between Acts' portrayal of the circumstances leading to Saul's baptism and to that of Cornelius.[22] Both stories illustrate the importance of visiting people in their homes, which is the heart of successful evangelistic efforts. Ellen White also wrote, "It is not preaching that is the most important; it is house-to-house work, reasoning from the Word, explaining the Word. It is those workers who follow the methods that Christ followed who will win souls for their hire."[23]

Her counsel proves true in experience. For instance, evangelists know that people who respond to an altar call following a sermon on the topic "The True Church" are not necessarily saying that they are willing to join the church. Generally, people will confirm such a decision only in a private conversation. Public evangelism needs to be accompanied by the personal ministry of visitation.

> When both are combined, with the blessing of God, a more perfect and thorough work may be wrought; but if we can have but one part done, let it be the individual labor of opening the Scriptures in households, making personal appeals, and talking familiarly with the members of the family, not about things of little importance, but of the great themes of redemption.[24]

We cannot convert sinners; only the Holy Spirit can. He uses the "foolishness of preaching" through pastors and evangelists. But preaching produces the best results when combined with the personal work of consecrated Christians, even the humblest of people.

---

1. Ellen G. White, *Christian Service*, 117, 118.
2. James W. Zackrison, *Power to Witness* (Nampa, Idaho: Pacific Press, 1993), 48.
3. Ray Bakke and Jim Hart, *The Urban Christian* (Downers Grove, Ill.: InterVarsity, 1987), 14.
4. Donald G. McGavran, *Understanding Church Growth* (Grand Rapids, Mich.: Eerdmans, 1990), 225.
5. Win Arn and Charles Arn, *The Master's Plan for Making Disciples* (Pasadena, Calif.: Church Growth, 1982), 169.
6. Win Arn, *The Church Growth Ratio Book* (Pasadena, Calif.: Church Growth, 1987), 23.
7. *Christian Service*, 26.
8. LeRoy E. Froom, *The Coming of the Comforter* (Hagerstown, Md.: Review and

Herald, 1956), 109.

9. White, *The Acts of the Apostles*, 90.

10. Ibid., 158.

11. White, *Evangelism*, 456.

12. *Christian Service*, 142.

13. *Evangelism*, 442.

14. Many ideas in this section were taken from General Conference of Seventh-day Adventists, *Witnessing for Christ* (Hagerstown, Md.: Review and Herald, 1975), 43-50.

15. White, *The Desire of Ages*, 347.

16. *Evangelism*, 486.

17. *Christian Service*, 9.

18. *Evangelism*, 114.

19. White, *Welfare Ministry*, 78.

20. *Christian Service*, 116.

21. Ibid., 119.

22. White, *The Life and Epistles of the Apostle Paul*, 94.

23. White, *Gospel Workers*, 468.

24. *Christian Service*, 121.

Chapter 7

Approaches to Witnessing

A newly baptized member shared with his friends his new-found beliefs about the Sabbath, unclean meats, and the importance of paying tithe—all in one session! This was not Jesus' method. "Christ drew the hearts of His hearers to Him by the manifestation of His love, and then, little by little, as they were able to bear it, He unfolded to them the great truths of the kingdom."[1] Soul winning is a science.[2] This chapter will consider selected guidelines for effective witnessing.

> Mechanics, lawyers, merchants, men of all trades and professions, educate themselves that they may become masters of their business. Should the followers of Christ be less intelligent, and while professedly engaged in His service be ignorant of the ways and means to be employed? The enterprise of gaining everlasting life is above every earthly consideration. In order to lead souls to Jesus there must be a knowledge of human nature and a study of the human mind. Much careful thought and fervent prayer are required to know how to approach men and women upon the great subject of truth.[3]

The Whole Counsel of God

When Paul visited the city of Ephesus for the last time, he decided to meet in Miletus with all the leaders of the house churches of Ephesus (Acts 20:17, 25). Paul reminded them of the integrity of his own career and asked them to fulfill faithfully the responsibilities of their office. It was in this setting that Paul told them, "For I have not shunned to declare to you the whole counsel of God" (20:27).

The expression "the whole counsel of God" refers to "the entire will of God, every doctrine and every truth of God, omitting, altering, toning down nothing."[4] "The minister of Christ is not to present to the people only those truths that are the most pleasing, while he withholds others that might cause them pain."[5] However, a witness whose purpose is to lead a nonbeliever to the knowledge of Jesus and His truth "must not feel that the whole truth is to be spoken to unbelievers on any and every occasion. He should study carefully when to speak, what to say, and what to leave unsaid."[6]

"It is quite obvious that the subject sequence in a strongly Roman Catholic country would be entirely different from that followed in a strongly Protestant land."[7] That's true too when the target audience has a Hindu, Buddhist, or Muslim background. "The classes of people you will meet with decide for you the way in which the work should be handled."[8] Following are steps leading to "the whole counsel of God."

Preparatory activities are what evangelists call "groundwork." They may take several months, even years. One must secure the confidence of the community in order to gain a hearing. Approaches will vary according to several factors, such as culture, location, and circumstances. Approaches may include community services, English classes, personal testimonies, cooking classes, friendship evangelism, and farming projects.

Preparatory subjects are necessary for an evangelistic series that targets people with a secular or non-Christian background. Basically, this phase aims to attract them to meetings sponsored by Christians. The subjects should deal with the perceived needs of the targeted audience. They should establish confidence in Christianity and in the Bible. Some "entering wedges" are lectures on health, seminars on family life, and smoking-cessation and stress-control programs.

Introductory doctrines are necessary for non-Christians and for nominal Christians (those who have a Christian background but either do not have a commitment to Jesus or do not know the Bible). Only when this foundation has been established can the evangelist move to the next phase. Topics in the introductory phase include the Bible, God's character, the Trinity, and prayer. "Speak to them . . . upon points of doctrine on which you can agree. Dwell on the necessity of practical godliness. Give them evidence that you are a Christian, desiring peace, and that you love their souls."[9] This is what Stephen did (Acts 7:2-53). His address moved from what they agreed (patriarchs, Moses, Solomon) to the controversial issue of Jesus.

Foundational doctrines provide the starting point for an audience with a solid Christian background. These doctrines include sin, salvation, forgiveness, Second Coming, signs of the Second Coming, new earth, and judgment.

Distinctive Adventist doctrines should never be discussed in personal or public evangelism before the foundational doctrines have been properly understood and, ideally, accepted. These distinctive doctrines include the law, Sabbath, death, millennium, baptism, health, stewardship, sanctuary, true church, Spirit of prophecy, and Christian lifestyle.

The Contents of Witnessing

As we have already noted, there are major differences between witnessing and evangelizing. Evangelism has to do with biblical doctrines, while witnessing focuses on one's relationship with Christ. We may call evangelism an advanced form of witnessing. The content and purpose of witnessing do not demand that the witness have a specific spiritual gift. However, one must have the gift of evangelism to evangelize.

As an evangelist, Paul declared "the whole counsel of God"; in other words, all the "fundamental doctrines." Believers in Jerusalem had "filled Jerusalem" with their doctrine, or teachings (Acts 5:28). As evangelists, they preached "the word of God" (13:5; cf. 8:4, 25; 16:32; 19:10), "the gospel" (8:25; cp. 13:32), "the things concerning the kingdom of God" (8:12; 19:8; 28:23; 28:31).

As witnesses, the apostles testified of what Jesus did before dying on the cross (Acts 10:39) but especially of His resurrection (2:32, 3:15; 4:33; 5:32; 10:41; 13:31). They could not "but speak the things" which they had "seen and heard" (4:20). Saul was called to serve as a "witness to all men" (22:15)—both of the things which he had seen and of the things which would be revealed to him later (26:15, 16). All Christians are called to be witnesses of Christ's power (1:8).

The apostles' testimony centered on justification by faith. They taught "repentance toward God and faith toward our Lord Jesus Christ" in order to receive "forgiveness of sins" (Acts 20:21; 13:38). Jesus was the heart of their message, from the first sermon to the last verse (2:22-36; 28:31; see also 3:14; 4:2, 10, 33; 5:42; 8:5, 12, 35; 11:20; 17:3; 18:5, 28; 26:22). The Christian witness should give highest priority to leading people to Jesus Christ. Securing a decision for Jesus will facilitate the presentation of all the other biblical doctrines. "If those who today are teaching the word of God, would uplift the cross of Christ higher and still higher, their ministry would be far more successful."[10]

Leading to a Decision

The last chapter of Acts depicts the apostle Paul's attempt to persuade his listeners to accept Jesus (28:23). Persuasion means "to bring another person to a point of view." According to the divine principle of free will, we cannot use any form of coercion. But we can help people by providing all necessary information, by answering objections, by making the options very clear, by inviting them to side with the truth, and by affirming them as they make the right decisions. Paul assured the Philippian jailer, " 'Believe on the Lord Jesus Christ, and you will be saved, you and your household' " (16:31).

Ultimately, witnessing aims to lead a person to a decision to accept the gospel. Similarly, evangelism aims to persuade people (1) to accept Jesus and His truth, and (2) to serve Him in the fellowship of the church. These two objectives of evangelism are intimately related; you cannot get one without the other.

Evangelists can help a person make a positive decision concerning a point of doctrine by asking three leading questions: 1) "Is this subject clear to you?" (Generally, the person will say Yes.) 2) "Do you have any questions related to this subject?" (If there is a question, the evangelist should answer the question and then ask the first two leading questions again, continuing to repeat these steps until there are no more questions.) 3) "Do you really believe in this subject? Will you act upon it?" Ananias asked Saul, " 'Why are you waiting? Arise and be baptized, and wash away your sins, calling on the name of the Lord' " (Acts 22:16).

"The secret of our success and power as a people advocating advanced truth will be found in making direct, personal appeals to those who are interested, having unwavering reliance upon the Most High."[11] Those whose survival depends on selling, like literature evangelists and business people, know very well the importance of asking for a decision. You are not likely to get one if you do not ask for it.

Effective evangelism includes a carefully sequenced process that leads the nonbeliever through progressive decisions to the acceptance of the whole truth. Every Bible study and sermon should include an appeal. Doing so prepares the audience or the prospect for a future, major decision. The person who has responded positively every night will find it easier to respond positively when the evangelist makes the appeal for baptism. If, on the other hand, the evangelist makes no invitation during the series, the altar call or the appeal for baptism at the end of the series will take the hearers by surprise and many will not respond who might have otherwise. The principle of encouraging progressive decisions is valid for both personal and public evangelism.

Appeals are evangelistic tools whose purpose is to invite listeners to use their wills to make decisions based on what they already know about the gospel truth. The most important decision a sinner can make is to accept Jesus as Savior; all other decisions depend on this one. The first two recorded sermons in the book of Acts included powerful appeals to repent, be converted, and accept Jesus as Savior (Acts 2:38, 40; 3:19, 26).

> There are souls in every congregation who are hesitating, almost persuaded to be wholly for God. The decision is being made for time and for eternity; but it is too often the case that the minister has not the spirit and power of the message of truth in his own heart, hence no direct appeals are made to those souls that are trembling in the balance. The result is that impressions are not deepened upon the hearts of the convicted ones; and they leave the meeting feeling less inclined to accept the service of Christ than when they came. They decide to wait for a more favorable opportunity; but it never comes.[12]

In calling for progressive decisions: First, lead the people to decide for Christ before presenting testing truths. Soften their hearts by presenting the cross. "Christ and Him crucified" is "the foundation of the gospel."[13] John Fowler explains that every evangelistic message should end with an appeal to accept Jesus as Savior:

> When a person makes a decision of this nature it will generally indicate a willingness to accept all of the truths they have learned in the meeting. Specific calls to keep the Sabbath and to join the true church will not often be necessary. To accept Christ is to accept what Christ taught and what Christ is doing, which is the primary focus of all the prophetic teachings of Scriptures and all the doctrines found in the Bible.[14]

Second, do not present testing truths until you are reasonably sure that the person has been converted. "When they surrender heart and mind and will to God, they are then prepared candidly to weigh evidence in regard to these solemn, testing truths."[15]

Third, when the people understand the truth, they should be urged to decide to obey it. Paul confronted King Agrippa with a straight question, " 'Do you believe the prophets? I know that you do believe' " (Acts 26:27). "Bring the people to the point to decide. Show them the importance of the truth—it is life or death."[16]

The evangelist, the preacher, and the Christian witness are "ambassadors for Christ" and, as such, they should appeal for a decision as though God were pleading through them (see 2 Cor. 5:20). It is sobering to realize that the answer to their invitations has eternal consequences. "Many a precious soul balances for a time, and then takes his position on the side of error, because he does not have this personal effort at the right time."[17] Most evangelists know that very few people will make a decision unless they are asked to do so. This is why "in every discourse fervent appeals should be made to the people to forsake their sins and turn to Christ."[18]

> If words are not spoken at the right moment, calling for decision from the weight of evidence already presented, the convicted ones pass on without identifying themselves with Christ, the golden opportunity passes, and they have not yielded, and they go farther and farther away from the truth.[19]

Expressing a Commitment

According to Acts 8:36, the Ethiopian eunuch said, " 'See, here is water. What hinders me from being baptized?' "

Philip answered, " 'If you believe with all your heart, you may.' "

The eunuch confessed, " 'I believe that Jesus Christ is the Son of God' "(8:37).

A confession of faith is a statement of faith in Jesus. Even though an oral confession is not a prerequisite for baptism, a public testimony always affirms a private decision; so it is useful in evangelism.

Some of the ancient manuscripts of the Bible do not contain the eunuch's confession of faith (Acts 8:37), so many modern translations omit it. However, the New Testament records other confessions of faith (see, e.g., Matt. 14:33; John 6:69). Matthew 10:32, 33 indicates that Jesus said, " 'Whoever confesses Me before men, him I will also confess before My Father who is in heaven.' " And Paul wrote, "If you confess with your mouth the Lord Jesus and believe in your heart that God has raised Him from the dead, you will be saved" (Rom. 10:9). People can use this spiritual exercise as a powerful weapon for battling the devil and to affirm one's faith in Jesus (Rev. 12:11).

Here's a suggestion for preachers, Sabbath School teachers, Bible instructors, lay evangelists, pastors, and all others doing evangelism: After presenting salvation and forgiveness, ask the audience to express a short confession of faith. Ask them to make the name of Jesus part of this confession, for "whoever calls upon the name of the Lord shall be saved," "for there is no other name under heaven given among men by which we must be saved" (Rom. 10:13; Acts 4:12).

Those using this approach should illustrate to their hearers what they mean by a "short confession of faith." They might suggest such confessions as "Jesus is my Savior," "I accept Jesus as my personal Savior," "Jesus is the King of my heart," "I want to follow Jesus," "I give my heart to Jesus," and "I renew my commitment to Jesus." Of course, church members and visitors can participate together in this exercise. The evangelist should assure the audience that heaven rejoices when someone confesses Jesus, that those who believe in the name of the Lord have "the right to become children of God," and that those "who believe in the name of the Son of God . . . have eternal life" (John 1:12; 1 John 5:13).

Will You Be Baptized?

While confessing one's faith serves an important purpose, baptism is the prescribed ceremony for expressing publicly one's renunciation of the world. In the book of Acts we find three requirements for baptism. First, candidates should receive proper instruction (Acts 2:41; cf. 16:32). Second, they should believe on the Lord Jesus Christ (8:36, 37; cf. 16:31-33). And third, sinners should repent of their sins (2:28).

When Philip encountered the Ethiopian eunuch, that man knew something about the Jewish faith; he was reading Isaiah 53, though he didn't understand its meaning. So, "beginning at this Scripture," Philip "preached Jesus to him" (Acts 8:35). Evidently Philip talked about the cross, about the importance of confessing Jesus, and about baptism. As Philip preached Jesus to him, the eunuch requested baptism, and Philip baptized him on the spot (verse 39).

Even more dramatic is the story of the first Christian baptism in Europe. The Philippian jailer almost certainly came from a heathen background and, consequently, had not had much opportunity to know about the true God. Philippi contained too few Jews even to have a synagogue (Acts 16:13). Despite this, Paul baptized the jailer sometime between midnight and sunrise the very night of his conversion (16:25, 33, 35). Notice, however, that his "qualification" for baptism included not only his accepting the invitation to "believe on the Lord Jesus Christ" (verse 31) but also the apostles' speaking "the word of the Lord to him and to all who were in his house" (verse 32).

Ananias asked Saul a question that soul winners know very well: "Why are you waiting? Arise and be baptized, and wash away your sins, calling on the name of the Lord" (Acts 22:16). The man who later would be known as the apostle Paul did not eat or drink from the time he met Jesus until after he was baptized (9:18, 19).

The New Testament contains no evidence that the early church required a waiting period—long or short—between conversion and baptism. In fact, our *Church Manual* provides no guidelines concerning this issue. It simply states that candidates should be baptized only when they are "familiar with and committed to all fundamental beliefs and related practices of the church and are prepared to assume the responsibilities of church membership."[20] "When they give evidence that they fully understand their position, they are to be accepted."[21]

Soul winners, whether lay or professional, will bring more people into God's kingdom when they work empathetically, starting where people are spiritually and leading them step by step into a full profession of Christ and acceptance of the teachings of His Word.

---

1. Ellen G. White, *Evangelism*, 484.
2. White, *Ministry of Healing*, 398.
3. White, *Testimonies for the Church*, 4:67.
4. R. C. H. Lenski, *The Interpretation of The Acts of the Apostles* (Minneapolis, Minn.: Augsburg, 1961), 845, 846.
5. White, *The Acts of the Apostles*, 394.
6. White, *Gospel Workers*, 117.
7. Roy Allan Anderson, *The Shepherd-Evangelist* (Hagerstown, Md.: Review and Herald, 1950), 167. Other experienced evangelists had similar concerns.
8. White, Letter 97a, 1901.
9. *Gospel Workers*, 120.
10. *The Acts of the Apostles*, 209.
11. White, *Review and Herald*, 30 August 1892.
12. *Evangelism*, 279, 280.
13. *Gospel Workers*, 158.
14. John W. Fowler, *Evangelism 2000: Proclaiming Christ in the 21st Century* (Nampa, Idaho: Pacific Press, 1994), 55.
15. *Evangelism*, 485.
16. *Testimonies for the Church*, 1:152.
17. *Evangelism*, 425.
18. *Testimonies for the Church*, 4:396.
19. *Evangelism*, 283.
20. *Seventh-day Adventist Church Manual* (Silver Spring, Md.: General Conference of Seventh-day Adventists, 1995), 28.
21. White, *Testimonies to Ministers*, 128.

Chapter 8

An Environment for Witnessing

One Sabbath while my family and I were on vacation, we attended church services in a city we had not visited before. We wanted to be part of our Adventist family in that city, but no greeter was at the door to welcome visitors and members. Not having a hymnal, I approached a person who was singing alone and tried to read the words of the hymn he was using. Instead of sharing the hymnal with me, this person moved away and ignored me! The teacher of the Sabbath School class we joined didn't recognize us in any way. And throughout that morning, nobody approached us. If we had been nonbelievers attending church for the first time, we probably would never have returned to that church!

Some churches grow, but others are stagnant. Why? Researchers have found that both external and internal factors affect the way a church operates and how the members interact with the community.[1] Among the external factors are national contextual factors such as persecution, war, and economic conditions. Local contextual factors include urbanization, industrialization, and population growth. But it's the internal factors that are the most crucial for effective evangelism and witnessing.

Internal factors include denominational policies, institutions, and priorities. Other internal factors concern the local congregation—for instance, some churches are "cold" while others are "on fire." Visitors have a special sensitivity to a church's "climate"—in other words, "the combination of factors which determine how it feels to be part of the church."[2] They decide within the first five minutes whether or not they will return to that church. In a church with the right climate, visitors feel accepted and members are highly motivated to bring friends and acquaintances and to participate in witnessing activities.

A study of the book of Acts provides glimpses of other internal factors that motivated and maximized the early Christians' witnessing efforts. Applying them in our churches today would offer results similar to those they experienced.

Three Purposes, Four Functions

Acts 2:42-47 describes the church life of the early believers. The activities of these believers were based on three purposes and devoted to four functions essential to a vibrant Christian life. All church meetings should aim to fulfill these three purposes and four functions (see Figure 5).

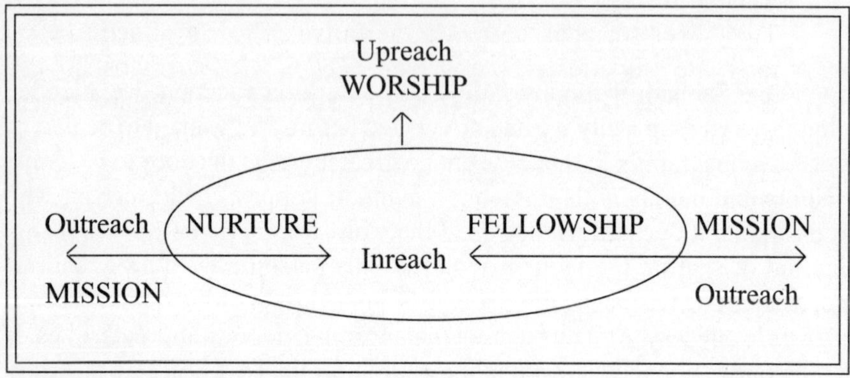

Figure 5: Ingredients of a vibrant church life

1) An* upward *purpose: to glorify God. According to Luke 24:53, the disciples "were continually in the temple, praising and blessing God." WORSHIP is the first of the four functions. Praise characterized the early Christians' worship (Acts 2:47). They also spent much time in prayer, another important aspect of worship (1:14; 2:42).

2) An* inward *purpose: to grow spiritually and to enjoy fellowship with the brethren. Two functions relate to this inward purpose. NURTURE is the second of the four functions. Notice that the early Christians were devoted to the apostles' doctrine (Acts 2:42). Through their devotion to the inspired words they received the spiritual food needed for healthy spiritual growth—growth into the likeness of Christ.

The third function, also a part of the inward purpose, is FELLOWSHIP. "All the believers were together, and had everything in common" (Acts 2:44, NIV; also 4:32). They even ate together (2:46). Christian fellowship is not merely a subjective feeling of belonging. It differs from membership in a tennis club or civic group. Christian community is more akin to the commitment of love and obligation we have toward members of our own family.

3) An **outward** ***purpose: to preach the gospel.*** This purpose encompasses the fourth important function of any church group, which is MISSION. The early church demonstrated a sense of mission as no other church in history had. Though a group of individuals shares together worship, nurture, and community, they will not be a legitimate church if they remain focused inward. The concept of mission includes such things as evangelism and soul winning. As a result of active outreach, the early disciples received new converts into church membership every day (Acts 2:47).

A Peculiar Lifestyle

The previous chapter discussed the early Christians' effectiveness in what today we call "lifestyle evangelism." *Fellowship* is perhaps the word that best describes their lifestyle. They expressed their fellowship in practical ways: "All who believed were together, and had all things in common, and sold their possessions and goods, and divided them among all, as anyone had need" (Acts 2:44, 45). They displayed Christian charity as a result of the inward communion they were committed to. A healthy congregation in our day will ensure that fellowship is an integral part of their church life.

The early Christians also expressed their faith in other practical ways. The book of Acts, for instance, contains many examples of commitment to the community expressed in the form of hospitality. Acts says that "breaking bread from house to house, they ate their food with gladness and simplicity of heart" (2:46). When the gospel first entered Europe, newly converted Lydia begged the itinerant evangelists to stay in her house (16:15).

Paul and his team visited the Phoenician port city of Tyre on his way back to Jerusalem at the end of his third missionary journey. Finding some believers, the missionaries stayed with them for a week. When Paul departed from Tyre, the believers, "with wives and children," accompanied the evangelists till they were out of the city (21:5).

Acts closes with Paul on his way to Rome. In Puteoli he found believers who urged the apostle to stay a week with them (28:14). Then a delegation of Christians in Rome traveled some forty miles to Appii Forum to meet the imprisoned apostle. "When Paul saw them, he thanked God and took courage" (28:15).

Dorcas, a woman of Joppa who was known as a great friend and helper of the poor (Acts 9:36-39), revealed another form of Christian charity. From the list of spiritual gifts mentioned in Romans 12:6-8, we infer that Dorcas had a cluster of gifts related to giving with liberality and showing mercy. Like

Dorcas, many members of the church "feel genuine empathy and compassion for individuals, both Christian and nonChristian, who suffer distressing physical, mental, or emotional problems."[3] This sense of compassion that leads a person to serve those in need—including those society considers outcasts—comes from God.

Referring to the work of Dorcas and other noble characters of the Bible, Ellen G. White says, "Such patient, prayerful, and persevering fidelity as was possessed by these saints of God is rare; yet the church cannot prosper without it."[4] In a very special way, these persons may cooperate with evangelistic activities: "First meet the temporal necessities of the needy and relieve their physical wants and sufferings, and you will then find an open avenue to the heart, where you may plant the good seeds of virtue and religion."[5]

By exercising this gift, believers may reflect Jesus' ministry. He "went about doing good and healing all who were oppressed by the devil" (Acts 10:38), modeling for us a life of service. Jesus' ministry encompassed an integral missionary program. He not only preached the gospel, He

> fed the hungry and healed the sick. By the good He accomplished, by His loving words and kindly deeds, He interpreted the gospel to men. . . .
>
> Christ's work in behalf of man is not finished. It continues today. In like manner His ambassadors are to preach the gospel and to reveal His pitying love for the lost and perishing souls. By an unselfish interest in those who need help they are to give a practical demonstration of the truth of the gospel.[6]

A Praying Church

From its very beginning, Acts also characterizes the early church as a praying church. In the days before Pentecost, believers "continued with one accord in prayer and supplication" for the promised blessing (Acts 1:14; Luke 24:49). "Under the influence of the Spirit, words of penitence and confession mingled with songs of praise for sins forgiven."[7] Sincere supplication and confession combined with praise and worship is still an unfailing formula for drawing near to God. Prayer became a distinctive characteristic of this small but growing church. The following examples reveal the prayer experience of the early Christians.

Possibly during the Passover of A.D. 44, Herod ordered the arrest of Peter in order to please his opponents (Acts 12:1-4). He planned to give

Peter to the people much as Pilate gave Jesus to the people. Peter was placed in maximum security, but "constant prayer was offered to God for him by the church" (12:5). Early Christians did not have churches like those we're familiar with today. For this occasion they met in the house of John Mark, the same person who later wrote one of the Gospels.

This pattern of prayer meetings in homes worked very well two thousand years ago, and it is still one of the keys to success used by today's fastest growing churches. Many churches offer prayer meetings in the neighborhood where members live, which harmonizes with inspired advice. "Why do not two or three meet together and plead with God for the salvation of some special one, and then for still another?" Ellen White asked, "If there is a large number in the church, let the members be formed into small companies, to work not only for the church members, but for unbelievers. . . . As they work and pray in Christ's name, their numbers will increase."[8]

Were those early believers praying for Peter's release? For a mercifully quick execution? For the will of the Lord to be done? How does one pray under such circumstances? The prayers of that group were answered even while they prayed. One can easily imagine what happened after Peter "departed and went to another place" (Acts 12:17). No doubt, that prayer meeting became saturated with praises!

The chapter "The Prayer and Missionary Meeting" of the book *Christian Service* offers the following suggestions for such meetings: First, there should be much participation. "Our prayer and social meetings should be seasons of special help and encouragement. Each one has a work to do to make these gatherings as interesting and profitable as possible."[9]

Second, they should be permeated with praise. "Far more than we do, we need to speak of the precious chapters in our experience." "To praise God in fullness and sincerity of heart is as much a duty as is prayer."[10]

Third, as the chapter name suggests, our prayer meetings should be integrated with missionary reports and training.

> Do not imagine that you can arouse the interest of the young by going to the missionary meeting and preaching a long sermon. Plan ways whereby a live interest may be aroused. From week to week the young should bring in their reports, telling what they have tried to do for the Saviour, and what success has been theirs. If the missionary meeting were made an occasion for bringing in such reports, it would not be dull, tedious, and uninteresting. It would be full of interest, and there would be no lack of attendance.[11]

> Let the missionary meeting be turned to account in teaching the people how to do missionary work.[12]

When the occasion required it, Jesus spent "all night in prayer with God" (Luke 6:12, 13). When the disciples considered it appropriate, they asked the apostle Paul to preach "until midnight" and "talked a long while, even till daybreak" (Acts 20:7, 11). In some parts of the world, Adventist believers gather together for special all-night prayer meetings. As we approach the end, perhaps we may see more of these intense seasons of prayer.

Commitment to the Kingdom

The leaders' attitude towards witnessing and evangelization also played a crucial role in the success of the early church. Paul and Barnabas began their first missionary journey together by visiting several urban centers: Antioch, Iconium, Listra, and Derbe. Antiochians "expelled them from their region" (Acts 13:50). In Iconium, both Jews and Gentiles tried to "abuse and stone them," so they fled that city (14:5, 6). Paul was stoned again at Lystra, under the instigation of Jews from Antioch and Iconium (14:19). From there he went to Derbe (14:20).

When they left Derbe, however, they did not continue forward but instead decided to retrace their steps and return to enemy territory, "to Lystra, Iconium, and Antioch" (14:21)! Why? They had "made many disciples" in those cities. They decided that even though they were risking their lives, they had to return to strengthen the new converts. The apostles warned the new converts that they also would suffer tribulations in their Christian experience (14:22).

The apostles returned because they were committed to extending God's kingdom. Extending God's kingdom definitely requires commitment.

> In his farewell to the Church Missionary Society before setting out for Uganda, Alexander MacKay said: "Within six months you will probably hear that one of us is dead. When the news comes, do not be cast down; but send someone else immediately to take the vacant place." How prophetic his words were! Within three months one of the party of eight was dead; within a year five had died; and at the end of two years MacKay himself was the sole survivor. In the face of overwhelming odds he struggled on for twelve years until he too was felled by the fever.[13]

The rulers, elders, and scribes of the Sanhedrin marveled when they saw that Peter and John witnessed without fear (Acts 4:5, 13). But the apostles prayed for more courage to proclaim God's Word (4:29). When the church leaders prayed for power in witnessing (4:29), the Lord immediately answered their prayers by filling them again with the Holy Spirit, so that "they spoke the word of God with boldness" (4:31). Paul manifested this boldness in witnessing immediately after his baptism and on many other occasions, such as when he and Barnabas were threatened in Iconium and as he preached in the synagogue in Ephesus (9:27, 29; 14:3; 19:8). When he went to Jerusalem for the last time, he boldly confessed that he was ready to die "for the name of the Lord Jesus" (21:13).

Our church today also needs to pray for the Holy Spirit.

> The Lord is more willing to give the Holy Spirit to those who serve Him than parents are to give good gifts to their children. For the daily baptism of the Spirit every worker should offer his petition to God. . . . The presence of the Spirit with God's workers will give the proclamation of truth a power that not all the honor or glory of the world could give.[14]

Witnessing That Converts

A study of the book of Acts reveals some recurrent themes in the witnessing it describes. In Acts 20:21 Paul recounts how he testified to both Jews and Gentiles about "repentance toward God and faith toward our Lord Jesus Christ." His message paralleled that of Peter on Pentecost, " 'Repent, and let everyone of you be baptized in the name of Jesus Christ' " (2:38).

Peter's invitation on Pentecost, in turn, was closely related to the consistent cry of John the Baptist (Matt. 3:2). The ancient prophets also called on Israel to turn or "return" to God (Isa. 31:6; Joel 2:12, 13). That invitation included everyone; all were to repent (Acts 3:19). The rite of baptism symbolizes repentance, and everyone is to be baptized.

> When Peter told the people to "repent" he had himself repented of his own lying, denial, and profanity at the time of his witnessing. So he witnessed both to the necessity of repentance, and to the power of God to transform the repentant one. He declared, "We are witnesses of these things." Acts 5:32. Are you and I? Verily, experience lies at the foundation of all true witnessing.[15]

Many members have felt frustrated at the lack of results from their witnessing about the Sabbath, tithe, or health reform. Even though these doctrines are important, the book of Acts reveals that the witnessing of those early Christians was Christ-centered. It characterizes Philip as an evangelist (Acts 21:8). He "went down to the city of Samaria and preached Christ to them" (8:5). Later in the same chapter we find him witnessing to an Ethiopian eunuch. "Philip opened his mouth, and beginning at this Scripture, preached Jesus to him" (8:35). And Philip saw "multitudes with one accord" responding to his approach to evangelism (8:6, 12).

Adventist evangelism has been characterized by the presentation of biblical doctrines, which is indispensable. However, many limit the content of their messages just to doctrines. We need to learn how to apply this fundamental concept of evangelism: no matter what doctrine we are preaching, we always have to invite our hearers to accept Jesus as Savior. "No discourse should ever be preached without presenting Christ and Him crucified as the foundation of the gospel."[16] The preacher "will not dismiss a congregation without presenting before them Jesus Christ, the sinner's only refuge, making earnest appeals that will reach their hearts."[17]

Study of the first chapters of Acts will show that Peter did not fail to present Jesus as the main subject of his sermons (Acts 2:22-36; 3:12-26; 4:8-12; 5:29-32). "The greatest work, the noblest effort, in which men can engage, is to point sinners to the Lamb of God."[18] Witnesses must remember that there is power in the name of Jesus, that "there is no other name under heaven given among men by which we must be saved" (4:12). These instructions apply not only to public evangelistic meetings but to personal evangelism and church services as well.

The witness who presents a personal testimony before a nonbeliever should not focus on doctrinal matters such as the Sabbath or stewardship. A personal testimony should transmit the joy found in accepting the salvation Jesus offers. Ellen G. White assures us that Christ-centered witnessing will "touch invisible cords, whose vibrations will ring to the ends of the earth, and make melody through eternal ages."[19]

First Things First

The witness who does evangelism should secure a decision to accept Jesus as Savior before moving to our distinctive doctrines. Once this is done, he should teach the whole truth. In Matt. 28:20 Jesus instructed his followers that they should make disciples by "teaching them to observe all things" He had commanded them. But even these doctrines have a logical sequence.

Those who want to serve as effective witnesses must understand that, for nonbelievers, many of our doctrines are not good news. The Second Coming is *the end of the world*! Keeping the Sabbath means refraining from work and forgoing the money they might have earned on that day. But we can transform all doctrines into good news. The doctrines of the law and of hell, for instance, become good news as we present them in the context of forgiveness and salvation. Before nonbelievers can understand the doctrine of victory over sin, they must first hear "the gospel of the grace of God" (Acts 20:24). John Fowler affirms that "this kind of preaching will consistently win people to Christ and His church."[20]

When our preaching ministries don't focus on Christ, "there is little incentive for our members to bring their nonAdventist friends to church. If they bring their neighbors and friends and we preached Christ and made calls to accept and follow Him, it would bring a new dynamic into our churches as it does our public meetings."[21]

When "Paul and his party" went to Antioch in Pisidia, they "went into the synagogue on the Sabbath day" (Acts 13:13, 14). There, in his first recorded sermon, Paul addressed two audiences simultaneously: Jews and Gentile God-fearers (Acts 13:16-41). In the introduction of his sermon, Paul established a point of contact with the Jews. He affirmed that they were God's chosen people. Then he identified himself with the Jewish audience by making reference to "our fathers," and after a brief review of Jewish history, identified Jesus as the long-awaited Messiah (see verses 17, 23).

Paul proceeded to affirm something unthinkable for his Jewish audience: that salvation was available not only to the "sons of the family of Abraham," but also to the God-fearers (Acts 13:26). The heart of Paul's sermon in Antioch is in verses 38, 39, which say that "forgiveness of sins" and justification are available to "everyone who believes."

Justification is the divine act of acquittal, of declaring a repentant sinner released from the guilt of sin and restored to divine favor. We are "justified freely by His grace through the redemption that is in Christ Jesus" (Rom. 3:24). "The moment we ask for forgiveness in contrition and sincerity, God forgives."[22] Such preaching stirred the interest of the receptive God-fearers, who "begged that these words might be preached to them the next Sabbath" (Acts 13:42). "The next Sabbath almost the whole city came together to hear the word of God" (13:44). Because the apostles' Christ-centered approach touched the hearts of the people, "the word of the Lord was being spread throughout all the region" (13:49).

> More people than we think are longing to find the way to Christ. Those who preach the last message of mercy should bear in mind that Christ is to be exalted as the sinner's refuge. Some ministers think that it is not necessary to preach repentance and faith; they take for granted that their hearers are acquainted with the gospel. . . . But many people are sadly ignorant in regard to the plan of salvation; they need more instruction upon this all-important subject than upon any other.[23]

Witnessing, outreach, is an important part of the makeup of healthy churches and healthy Christians. And more than anything else, witnessing means preaching Christ and His forgiving grace.

---

1. See Bob Waymire and C. Peter Wagner, *The Church Growth Survey Handbook* (Milpitas, Calif.: Global Church Growth, 1984), 23, 24.
2. Ron Jenson and Jim Stevens, *Dynamics of Church Growth* (Grand Rapids: Baker, 1981), 98.
3. C. Peter Wagner, *Your Spiritual Gifts Can Help Your Church Grow* (Ventura, Calif.: Regal Books, 1994), 223.
4. Ellen G. White, *Testimonies for the Church*, 5:304.
5. Ibid., 4:227.
6. White, *Welfare Ministry*, 56, 57.
7. White, *The Acts of the Apostles*, 38.
8. *Testimonies for the Church*, 7:21, 22.
9. White, *Christian Service*, 211.
10. Ibid., 212, 213.
11. Ibid., 212.
12. Ibid., 211.
13. J. Herbert Kane, *A Concise History of the Christian World Missions* (Grand Rapids: Baker, 1985), 97, 98.
14. *The Acts of the Apostles*, 50, 51.
15. LeRoy E. Froom, *The Coming of the Comforter* (Hagerstown, Md.: Review and Herald, 1956), 105.
16. *Gospel Workers*, 158.
17. *Testimonies for the Church*, 4:316.
18. *Gospel Workers*, 18.
19. Ellen G. White, *The Desire of Ages*, 823.
20. John W. Fowler, *Evangelism 2000: Proclaiming Christ in the 21st Century* (Nampa, Idaho: Pacific Press®, 1994), 41.
21. Ibid., 52.
22. White, *Signs of the Times*, 4 September 1893.
23. White, *Evangelism*, 185, 186.

Chapter 9

Structures for Witnessing

In one of the churches I served as a pastor, nobody wanted to be lay activities director. In time I learned the reason: somehow the members had developed the mistaken idea that the person who held this office was responsible for all outreach efforts! That church had not taken advantage of the structures for witnessing available in all Adventist churches.

Everything the church does should contribute to the goal of accomplishing God's mission. In the words of Ellen White, "The church of Christ on earth was organized for missionary purposes."[1] Within the formal organization of the world church, members cooperate in the fulfillment of the Great Commission and in the finishing of God's work. Members of a local congregation may get organized for witnessing by dividing their territory, organizing small groups, creating teams, and sending their own "missionaries" to "nonentered areas" in their territory. This chapter considers some of these possible approaches to witnessing.

Organizational Beginnings

The first chapters of the book of Acts contain evidences of a proto-organization. In addition to the foundational apostolic structure, there were networks among the subgroups of believers. The "Hellenists" mentioned in Acts 6:1 were Greek-speaking Jews influenced by Greek culture. They probably constituted the largest subgroup within the Jewish diaspora. Such ethnic groups as Mesopotamian Jews, Egyptian Jews, and Asian Jews were also represented (see Acts 2:9-11).

The "number of the disciples was multiplying" (Acts 6:1). R. C. H. Lenski says, "It has been conservatively estimated that at this time the total number of the disciples was between twenty and twenty-five thousand."[2] With so many members interacting, it was almost unavoidable that tensions would emerge. The Hellenists complained that the Hebrews were overlooking their widows in the daily dispensation of support. The accusation was not directed against the apostles, although they must be classed as Hebrews. Apparently, the apostles had used assistants from this class for dispensing the needed charity.

No doubt the twelve discussed the matter among themselves. But they did not make a decision on their own. They called the members and proposed that others do some of the tasks they were performing (Acts 6:2, 4). They suggested the number of helpers and named the qualifications these people should have but left the selection of personnel to the congregation (6:3).

When the first group of believers thought of the *church*, "the term did not mean an ecclesiastical organization in the sense which it later acquired. The emphasis was on community rather than organization."[3] However, as the number of the disciples multiplied, it became evident that the apostles needed help to oversee special lines of work. "The organization of the church at Jerusalem was to serve as a model for the organization of churches" in other parts of the world.[4] Later, "when in various parts of the world many groups of believers had been formed into churches, the organization of the church was further perfected."[5]

Without a plan and without proper delegation of responsibilities, no amount of dedication and zeal will result in total saturation of the community with the truth. The apostles couldn't do everything, and pastors should not attempt to do all the church's tasks. Pastors alone cannot and will not finish God's work. "The work of God in this earth can never be finished until the men and women comprising our church membership rally to the work, and unite their efforts with those of ministers and church officers."[6]

> Those who have the spiritual oversight of the church [pastors, elders, personal ministries leaders, Sabbath School leaders, etc.] should devise ways and means by which an opportunity may be given to every member of the church to act some part in God's work. . . . Plans have not been clearly laid and fully carried out, whereby the talents of all might be employed in active service. There are but few who realize how much has been lost because of this.[7]

Jesus Himself taught the apostles to delegate responsibilities. Soon after He called the twelve disciples, Jesus sent them out on a special mission limited to the sons and daughters of Israel (Matt. 10:5, 6). About a year later He sent forth seventy more followers (Luke 10:1-17). "These men He purposed to train and educate as the leaders of His church. They in turn were to educate others, and send them out with the gospel message."[8] When the leaders of the early church followed Jesus' example of delegation of responsibilities, the "word of God spread, and the number of the disciples multiplied greatly in Jerusalem" (Acts 6:7).

Many early Adventist believers regarded some kind of church government as imperative if order were to prevail and the movement were to grow and achieve its goals.* In 1860 a church name, "Seventh-day Adventists," was chosen and a legal body created to hold church property. In 1861, the grouping of organized churches in Michigan led believers to organize the first conference. And in 1863, Adventist members organized the General Conference to ensure that all the several conferences might work as one.[9]

Organizational Unity

The apostles were the natural leaders of the early church. Several cases illustrate how they provided cohesion. Philip's evangelistic work in Samaria resulted in many baptisms. "When the apostles who were at Jerusalem heard that Samaria had received the word of God, they sent Peter and John to them" (Acts 8:14). Similarly, when the news that many Greeks had "believed and turned to the Lord . . . came to the ears of the church in Jerusalem," they sent Barnabas to survey the situation (11:21, 22). For at least two decades the church in Jerusalem was regarded as the headquarters of the developing movement.[10]

Paul and Barnabas felt accountable to Antioch, so when they returned to that city "where they had been commended to the grace of God . . . and gathered the church together, they *reported* all that God had done with them" (14:26, 27; emphasis added). However, while Paul made Antioch his headquarters during the heyday of his missionary career, he also maintained contact with the church in Jerusalem. Barnabas and he "reported" to the Jerusalem council "all things that God had done with them" (15:4). And in his last visit to Jerusalem, Paul "told in detail those things which God had done among Gentiles through his ministry" (21:19). Accountability is an essential part of an efficient organization.

---

*On the other hand, during this early period many believers and leaders strongly opposed church organization.

From the beginning, the Lord instructed converts to join the organized church. "He did not give Paul an experience, in his conversion to truth [Acts 9:10-18], independent of His church recently organized upon the earth."[11] The organizational unity of the church was important in the book of Acts and is still important in the process of witnessing because "the Redeemer of the world does not sanction experience and exercise in religious matters independent of His organized and acknowledged church, where He has a church."[12]

When some disciples from Judea went to Antioch with teachings that created "dissension and dispute" among the brethren, "they determined that Paul and Barnabas and certain others of them should go up to Jerusalem, to the apostles and elders, about this question" (Acts 15:2).

> It is worthwhile pointing out that the church council set up in Jerusalem presented a Christian counterpart to the Jewish Sanhedrin. It had oversight of spiritual and material needs in Jerusalem and extended its authority over the churches in Judea. . . . The authority of the council was legislative, executive, judicial, and disciplinary, and was the ultimate authority in the church.[13]

The Jerusalem council, which preserved the unity of the early church, took place about eighteen years after Pentecost (Gal. 1:18; 2:1). In a similar way, "when the judgment of the General Conference, which is the highest authority that God has upon earth, is exercised, private independence and private judgment must not be maintained, but be surrendered."[14] However, "there are little companies continually rising who believe that God is only with the very few, the very scattered, and their influence is to tear down and scatter that which God's servants build up. . . . They stand separate from the people whom God is leading out and prospering, and through whom He is to do His great work."[15] In 1905 Ellen White stated: "We cannot step off the foundation that God has established. We cannot now enter into any new organization; for this would mean apostasy from the truth."[16]

First-century Christians expressed unity with the church organization by sending offerings. For instance, Paul took "alms and offerings" he had collected to Jerusalem (Acts 24:17). During the period of his ministry in Ephesus (Acts 18:18-20:38), Paul and his friends gathered funds for the poor in Jerusalem. Even though Luke does not discuss Paul's collection methodology, Paul's letters indicate he attached great significance to the offering (Rom. 15:26; 1 Cor. 16:1-4; 2 Cor. 9:1-8). He sensed that the ministry of essentially Gentile churches to the church at Jerusalem could bind the two segments of Christianity closer together. So he sought to involve as many Gentile churches as possible, taking offerings in the churches of Galatia (1 Cor. 16:1), Achaia (1 Cor. 16:2; 2 Cor. 8:10-15), and Macedonia (2 Cor. 8:1-5). These offerings were a joint effort, many churches working together in Christ's mission.

Ordination for Witnessing

In chapter 2, we saw that baptism is an ordination to the "ministry of all believers." The reception of the Holy Spirit enables believers to be "witnesses . . . to the ends of the earth" (Acts 1:8). Of Paul's ordination of those baptized in Ephesus (Acts 19:6), Ellen G. White wrote, "Thus they were qualified to labor as missionaries in Ephesus and its vicinity and also to go forth to proclaim the gospel in Asia Minor."[17] Paul ordained the membership of an entire church by the laying on of hands on the day of their baptism, enabling the members to go out and preach the gospel.

> All to whom the heavenly inspiration has come are put in trust with the gospel. All who receive the life of Christ are ordained to work for the salvation of their fellow men. For this work the church was established, and all who take upon themselves its sacred vows are thereby pledged to be coworkers with Christ.[18]

The practice of ordination by the laying on of hands for the commissioning of church officers has its roots in the church's very beginning. When the church chose seven deacons to serve in a special ministry of service, they were "set before the apostles; and when they had prayed, they laid hands on them" (Acts 6:6). The Holy Spirit instructed the prophets and teachers of Antioch to separate Barnabas and Paul for the work to which He had called them. "Then, having fasted and prayed, and laid hands on them, they sent them away" (13:3).

Ordination is an act of commission by the church that acknowledges God's call, publicly sets the individual apart, and appoints that person to serve the church in a special capacity. The following five points are an expansion of this definition gathered from the inspired records of the ordination of Paul and Barnabas.

1) *"An act of commission . . ."* "Before being sent forth as missionaries to the heathen world, these apostles were solemnly dedicated to God by fasting and prayer and the laying on of hands."[19]

2) *"By the church . . ."* "The circumstances connected with the separation of Paul and Barnabas by the Holy Spirit to a definite line of service show clearly that the Lord works through appointed agencies in His organized church."[20]

3) *"That acknowledges God's call. . . ."* "Their ordination was a public recognition of their divine appointment to bear to the Gentiles the glad tidings of the gospel."[21]

4) *"That publicly sets the individual apart. . . ."* God "instructed the church by revelation to set them apart publicly to the work of the ministry."[22]

5) *"To serve the church in a special capacity."* "Thus they were authorized by the church, not only to teach the truth, but to perform the rite of baptism and to organize churches, being invested with full ecclesiastical authority."[23]

When Paul and Barnabas returned to the churches they had established during their first missionary journey, they "appointed elders in every church" (Acts 14:23). Paul organized these churches soon after their members had become Christians, which shows that organization is essential for maintaining the spiritual life and growth of the church. The appointment of elders was part of the process. Even though Acts does not mention formal ordination here, doubtless it also took place, with prayer and fasting (see 1 Tim. 4:14; 5:22; 2 Tim. 1:6).

Organized Witnessing

One of the first instructions the resurrected Lord gave to the nascent church was to be His witnesses "in Jerusalem, and in all Judea and Samaria, and to the end of the earth" (Acts 1:8). The concept of territorial assignments is part of order and organization.[24] Jesus instructed His followers to expand their witnessing activities in concentric and expanding circles so that eventually the knowledge of the gospel would cover the whole earth.

God called Paul to serve Him as an apostle "to the Gentiles" (Acts 22:21; see also Rom. 11:13). In contrast, He called Peter to serve as an apostle to the circumcised (Gal. 2:7). The reader may wonder, *Where is my post of duty?* The answer is "Not all can go as missionaries to foreign lands, but all can be home missionaries in their families and neighborhoods."[25] The basic territory assigned to church members is their own families and neighborhoods. "Wherever a church is established, all the members should engage actively in missionary work. They should visit every family in the neighborhood, and know their spiritual condition."[26]

The *Church Manual* provides clear instructions in this respect:

> Since evangelism is the primary work of the church, the first item on the agenda of each church board meeting is to relate directly to the evangelization of the missionary territory of the church. . . . As far as possible, each family and member should be encouraged to accept an assignment of territory. Every home in the church territory will thus be assigned to a church member. The member will be encouraged to [make] . . . missionary contacts in every home of one section of that territory.[27]

In order to accomplish his work, Paul developed evangelistic teams; that is why Acts speaks of "Paul and his party" (Acts 13:13). He took Barnabas and John Mark as his companions on his first missionary journey. Then he chose Silas (15:40). In Lystra he asked Timothy to work with him (16:1, 3), and Acts and the Epistles mention many others of Paul's fellow workers.

Paul felt better when he was with his fellow workers (see 17:15; 1 Thess. 3:1; 2 Cor. 2:12, 13). But it was not solely his desire for companionship that dictated his preference for fellow workers. He did so because he wanted to increase the effectiveness of his ministry (see Mark 6:7; Luke 10:1). He believed in teamwork. And we are encouraged today to get organized in evangelistic teams for missionary service:

> Why do not believers feel a deeper, more earnest concern for those who are out of Christ? Why do not two or three meet together and plead with God for the salvation of some special one, and then for still another? In our churches let companies be formed for service. Let different ones unite in labor as fishers of men. Let them seek to gather souls from the corruption of the world into the saving purity of Christ's love. . . . Let them labor in Christlike love for those outside the fold, forgetting self in their endeavor to help others. As they work and pray in Christ's name, their numbers will increase.[28]

Witnessing Centers

One could describe the book of Acts as an account of how first-century Christians established local churches. But that doesn't include church buildings. During its first three hundred years, the Christian church used private houses as its primary places of worship.[29] The first Christian believers were Jews, and they continued worshiping God in the synagogues. When they met with other believers for fellowship, prayer, worship, or the Lord's Supper, they met in homes. The Greek word for "church," *ekklesia*, means simply "assembly," "gathering," "congregation." It does not mean "a church building."

From the beginning, homes appear to have been the location of the most important aspects of early church life. On the day of Pentecost, the Holy Spirit manifested His presence and power "as of a rushing mighty wind, and it filled all the *house* where they were sitting" (Acts 2:2, emphasis supplied). When Acts describes Paul's preconversion persecution of the church, it says he sought Christians not in the temple or in synagogues but in houses (8:3).

The New Testament speaks often of believers meeting in homes: in Priscilla and Aquila's house in Rome (Rom. 16:3-5) as well as in Corinth (1 Cor. 16:19), in Nymphas's house (Col. 4:15), and in Philemon's house (Phil. 1, 2). Acts indicates that homes were used for prayer meetings (12:12), for an evening of Christian fellowship (21:7), for "breaking bread" (2:46), for a whole night of prayer, worship, and instruction (20:7, 11), for impromptu evangelistic gatherings (16:32), for planned evangelistic meetings (10:22), and for instruction (5:42). Paul also worked out of home groups: in Thessalonica he used Jason's house as his base of operation (17:5-7), and in Corinth he "entered the house of a certain man named Justus" (18:7, 8).

Early Adventists followed a similar pattern. At first they "assembled for worship, and presented the truth to those who would come to hear, in private houses, in large kitchens, in barns, in groves, and in schoolhouses."[30] Early Adventist literature commonly designates evangelistic meetings conducted in homes as "cottage meetings." Ellen G. White pointed out that experience demonstrated that "the presentation of Christ in the family, by the fireside, and in small gatherings in private houses, is often more successful in winning souls to Jesus than are sermons delivered in the open air, to the moving throng, or even in halls or churches."[31] In some cases, these cottage meetings grew into organized churches.

According to Acts 9:31, when Christians walked "in the fear of the Lord and in the comfort of the Holy Spirit," churches multiplied in numbers. When we meet the same conditions today, we'll see the same results. "New churches must be established, new congregations organized. At this time there should be representatives of present truth in every city and in the remote parts of the earth."[32] Planting churches is the most effective strategy for church growth.*

Church planting means establishing new congregations in communities where the gospel witness is ineffective or inadequate. Church planting means proclaiming the gospel and gathering those who believe into fellowship groups in which they can worship, receive nurture, and work for others in the extension of the kingdom of God.

We should not limit our efforts at witnessing to smiling at our neighbors or sharing a testimony of our conversion with a nonbeliever or even sharing the gospel through a Bible study. If people who express their desire to follow Jesus are not subsequently folded into a local congregation, they will never become disciples of Jesus Christ. As the number of individuals who are evangelized increases, so also must the number of churches and the variety of churches increase. "Those who are the chosen of God are required to multiply churches wherever they may be successful in bringing souls to the knowledge of the truth."[33]

---

1. Ellen G. White, *Christian Service*, 72.
2. R. C. H. Lenski, *The Interpretation of The Acts of the Apostles* (Minneapolis: Augsburg, 1961), 239.
3. Donald Guthrie, *New Testament Theology* (Downers Grove, Ill.: InterVarsity, 1981), 732.
4. White, *The Acts of the Apostles*, 91.
5. Ibid., 91, 92.
6. White, *Gospel Workers*, 352.
7. *Christian Service*, 61.
8. *The Acts of the Apostles*, 17.
9. See details of organizational development of Seventh-day Adventists in Arthur Whitefield Spalding, *Origin and History of Seventh-day Adventists* (Hagerstown, Md.: Review and Herald, 1961), 1:291-311; also Andrew G. Mustard, *James White and SDA Organization: Historical Development, 1844-1881*, Doctoral Dissertation Series, vol. xii (Berrien Springs, Mich.: Andrews University Press, 1987), 163-92.
10. J. Herbert Kane, *Christian Missions in Biblical Perspective* (Grand Rapids: Baker, 1976), 74.
11. White, *Testimonies for the Church*, 3:430.
12. Ibid., 3:432, 433.
13. Walter R. Beach and Bert B. Beach, *Pattern for Progress* (Hagerstown, Md.:

---

*Experience has demonstrated that "the single most effective evangelistic methodology under heaven is planting new churches." C. Peter Wagner, *Church Planting for a Greater Harvest* (Ventura, Calif.: Regal, 1990), 11.

Review and Herald, 1985), 45.

14. *Testimonies for the Church*, 3:492.

15. Ibid., 1:417, 418.

16. White, *Selected Messages*, 2:390.

17. *The Acts of the Apostles*, 283.

18. White, *The Desire of Ages*, 822.

19. *The Acts of the Apostles*, 161.

20. Ibid., 162.

21. Ibid., 161.

22. Ibid.

23. Ibid.

24. See George E. Knowles, *How to Help Your Church Grow* (Hagerstown, Md.: Review and Herald, 1981), 68-80.

25. *Christian Service*, 9.

26. Ibid., 12.

27. *Seventh-day Adventist Church Manual* (Silver Spring, Md.: General Conference of Seventh-day Adventists, 1995), 80, 81.

28. *Testimonies for the Church*, 7:21, 22.

29. Metosalem Castillo, *The Church in Thy House* (Manila: OMF Literature, 1982), 56.

30. White, *Testimonies to Ministers*, 26.

31. *Gospel Workers*, 193.

32. *Testimonies for the Church*, 6:24.

33. *Testimonies to Ministers*, 199.

Chapter 10

Places for Witnessing

When I arrived at a small town in Central America for an evangelistic effort, the church members told me that the meetings would take place in the town square! Me, an educated Adventist minister preach in a town square? At first, I felt as if they had betrayed me or were abusing me. Since then, I have preached in public plazas several times, twice in the Philippines. I have to admit, however, that in the first meetings of a series in the open air I still feel quite awkward.

The book of Acts reveals a surprising variety of places where early Christians shared the gospel with others. The first, immediately after Pentecost, was "in the temple" (Acts 2:46; 3:1-9; 5:21). They also witnessed in the court (4:5-12), "in many villages" (8:25), on a chariot (8:28-31), in synagogues (13:5, 14; 14:1; 17:17; 18:4, 19; 19:8), by a river side (16:13), in a prison (16:23-25), "in the market" (17:17), "in the midst of the Areopagus" (17:22), in a school (19:9), on a ship (27:21-25), and in their lodgings (28:23).

What about the time? The records show that they witnessed during the week "at the hour of prayer" (Acts 3:1), "early in the morning" (5:21), "at midnight" (16:25), "daily" (5:42; 17:17; 19:9), and "from morning till evening" (28:23). Of course, they also shared the gospel on the Sabbath (13:42, 44; 16:13; 17:2; 18:4).

This chapter will consider some present-day approaches to witnessing inspired by the example of the early Christians. The selected cases of witnessing events that they participated in resemble those the modern Christian encounters.

Where the Sick Are

Take the case of a sick person. Very likely most readers of this book are not involved in full-time healing ministries. Neither was Paul. However, sooner or later most of us will have a relative or a friend, a fellow worker or a neighbor who suffers from some health problem. The sick person's first impulse may be to see a medical doctor. There is nothing wrong with physicians; Luke was one (Col. 4:14). Believers, however, may see in many of these cases an opportunity to talk about their confidence in God's power, to pray for the sick, and even to participate in the healing process.

Though we'd likely consider the apostle Paul an evangelist, he often carried out a healing ministry. On one occasion he met a leading citizen from the island of Malta whose father "lay sick of a fever and dysentery." Even though Luke, a physician, accompanied Paul, the evangelist "went in to him and prayed, and he laid his hands on him and healed him" (Acts 28:8).

Peter was a church administrator. However, the book of Acts says he also carried out itinerant ministry in the coastal plain area of Sharon (Acts 9:32). Lydda, today called Ludd, is a city located about eleven miles from Joppa. Peter found there—and through Jesus, healed—a man named Aeneas who had been bedridden for eight years (9:33, 34).

The use of the word "found" indicates Peter's interest in people. He sought them out. "We are not to wait for souls to come to us; we must seek them out where they are. . . . There are multitudes who will never be reached by the gospel unless it is carried to them."[1] Peter's outreach to Aeneas was not motivated by the desire for a larger membership nor a larger attendance nor even a larger budget. The compassion Jesus showed toward human suffering found expression also in Simon Peter. So must it be with us.

Aeneas's healing produced extraordinary results. "All who dwelt at Lydda and Sharon saw him and turned to the Lord" (Acts 9:35). Is this not the Lord's ultimate purpose? Evidently, Peter's ministry had larger goals than just to improve people's physical health. Peter preached repentance in such a way that people "turned to the Lord."

Just as was true of Peter's ministry, Adventist hospitals and sanitariums exist to do more than just to offer health services. After all, secular and nonChristian institutions may offer similar and even better services than Adventist hospitals do. "Medical missionary work is in no case to be divorced from the gospel ministry."[2] "Medical missionary work is to be a great entering wedge, whereby the diseased soul may be reached."[3]

Health evangelism is a tool that can prepare the beneficiaries to receive the "whole counsel of God." Think of Philip's ministry in Samaria.

Samaritans were not the most promising people group for evangelism. However, the Samaritan multitudes gave attention to "the things spoken by Philip, hearing and seeing the miracles which he did" (Acts 8:6, 7). In this case, as well as throughout the book of Acts, the healing ministry worked as an instrument that prepared people to listen to the full presentation of the gospel. The result was that many "men and women were baptized" (8:12).

Adventist health institutions exist as tools the church can use to fulfill the Great Commission. Medical missionary work functions as an "entering wedge" for the Seventh-day Adventist Church.[4] "There are ministerial duties devolving upon the head physicians of our sanitariums outside of the purely medical work. They must give heed to the urgent calls that come for soul-winning efforts."[5] On one occasion Ellen G. White reminded the leaders of an Adventist health establishment that "the great object of receiving unbelievers into the institution is to lead them to embrace the truth."[6]

Throughout her writings Ellen G. White consistently avoided using the term *medical work.* Adventist hospitals and sanitariums exist to actively proclaim the gospel. "*Medical missionary work* should be carried forward by the church in well organized efforts. It should be to the cause of God as the right hand is to the body. But the medical missionary work is not to take on undue importance. It should be done without neglecting other lines of work."[7]

The healing ministry is not relegated only to hospitals.

> Every church should be a training school for Christian workers. Its members should be taught how to give Bible readings, how to conduct and teach Sabbath-school classes, how best to help the poor and to care for the sick, how to work for the unconverted. There should be schools of health, cooking schools, and classes in various lines of Christian help work.[8]

Where the Family Is

Families have always played an important role in the extension of the gospel. The first person Paul baptized in continental Europe was a woman named Lydia, "a seller of purple from the city of Thyatira" (Acts 16:14). When God opened Lydia's heart to the gospel, she led her household to accept the good news so that "she and her household were baptized" (16:15). Paul and Silas were thrown into jail shortly after Lydia's conversion. When a providential earthquake freed them, "they spoke the word of the Lord to . . . [the jailer] and to all who were in his house. . . . Immediately he and all his family were baptized" (16:32, 33).

These cases do not justify infant baptism. Scripture offers no warrant for this practice. Lydia's household probably consisted of servants and employees. However, we may ask how young a child should be baptized. The following guidelines may help.

Those to be baptized must possess active faith (Acts 8:36-38). Since babies cannot exercise such faith, baptizing them makes no sense. However,

> children of eight, ten, or twelve years are old enough to be addressed on the subject of personal religion. . . . If properly instructed, very young children may have correct views of their state as sinners, and of the way of salvation through Christ.[9]

> When the happiest period of their life has come, and they in their hearts love Jesus and wish to be baptized, then deal faithfully with them. Before they receive the ordinance, ask them if it is to be their first purpose in life to work for God.[10]

> After faithful labor, if you are satisfied that your children understand the meaning of conversion and baptism, and are truly converted, let them be baptized. . . . If you consent to the baptism of your children and then leave them to do as they choose, feeling no special duty to keep their feet in the straight path, you yourselves are responsible if they lose faith and courage and interest in the truth.[11]

The first disciples had felt overwhelmed by the size of the task Jesus commissioned them to do. But they didn't begin by making plans to cover the whole world. They went "from house to house" (Acts 20:20), visiting people "in every house" (5:42), beginning in Jerusalem, then moving to all Judea and Samaria (1:8). It is our responsibility to reach the utmost corner of the earth. The work that began with so much witnessing will be finished in the same way. "How can the great work of the third angel's message be accomplished? It must be largely accomplished by persevering, individual effort, by visiting the people in their homes."[12]

Cornelius was a God-fearing Gentile. When he knew that Peter was coming to his house, he "called together his relatives and close friends" (Acts 10:24). When Peter arrived in Caesarea, he found a large group waiting for him. Modern Christian witnesses should also try to gain access to a person's inner circle.

> The lay members of our churches can accomplish a work which, as yet, they have scarcely begun. . . . They can distribute our publications, hold meetings in their homes, become acquainted with their neighbors, and invite them to come to these meetings.[13]

Where Believers Meet

As Paul, Silas, Timothy, and Luke arrived at Philippi, the first European city of their missionary journey, they learned that there was no synagogue there. So, they searched for a temporary place of worship outside the city. They found a prayer group of women by the stream Gangites, which ran into the river Strymon (Acts 16:13).*

We can infer two motives for Paul's party's Sabbath-day search for a place of worship. First, they naturally longed to fellowship with other Jews on the Sabbath, the appointed day for believers to gather and meet the Creator in worship (Ex. 20:8-11). God is with His children even though they be few (Matt. 18:20) and even if they gather by a riverside rather than in a synagogue or church (Acts 16:13).

Second, Paul and his fellow missionaries were looking for sincere people to whom they could impart their good news of salvation. That's why Paul regularly went to synagogues (Acts 13:14; 14:1; 17:1, 2; 18:4).

In Corinth, Paul "reasoned in the synagogue every Sabbath, and persuaded both Jews and Greeks" (Acts 18:4). The Sabbath School concept is relatively new, so suggesting that Paul's Corinthian Sabbath efforts were Sabbath School work may not be the most accurate interpretation. However, one can relate Paul's Bible studies at Sabbath services to the idea of using Sabbath School services as soul-winning tools. Sabbath School not only provides the opportunity to nurture existing members, but it also can be used to attract visitors, to prepare nonmembers for baptism, and to provide care and follow-up to newly baptized members.

"The Sabbath School should be one of the greatest instrumentalities, and the most effectual, in bringing souls to Christ."[14] Most people will have their first contact with the church through a Sabbath School. As visitors come to church for the first time, the warmth and the quality of the Sabbath

---

*At least ten men were required to organize a synagogue. R. C. H. Lenski, Interpretation of *The Acts of the Apostles* (Minneapolis: Augsburg, 1961), 655.

School program plays an important part in helping them to decide whether or not they will come back. How can these results be secured? Certainly not through a boring and repetitive Sabbath School program.

Visitors should be especially cared for. Instead of studying the regular Sabbath School Bible Study Guide, the visitors' class may systematically study biblical doctrines. "Many who listen frequently to sermons, even though the truth be presented in clear lines, learn but little. Often it would be more profitable if the Sabbath meetings were of the nature of a Bible class study."[15] The teacher of this special Sabbath School class should possess the gift of teaching and also the gift of evangelism.

When "Paul and his party" arrived in Pisidian Antioch, they "went into the synagogue on the Sabbath day" (Acts 13:13, 14). Paul used opportunities like this to preach the gospel. His messages helped many Jews, including proselytes, to accept Jesus as the Christ. But he also taught the gospel to the visiting Gentiles. On this occasion, Paul addressed the "men of Israel," or Jews, and the God-fearers, who were Gentiles (Acts 13:16). His message on justification by faith (13:38, 39) appealed to Gentiles in a special way. "The next Sabbath almost the whole city came together to hear the word of God" (13:44). Evidently, Paul knew how to combine worship with evangelism.

Worship evangelism is an attempt to make worship services an evangelistic tool. The preacher presents doctrinal subjects and in each sermon invites the worshipers to accept Jesus as Savior. Worship evangelism may be offered throughout the year, on a permanent basis, in the regular worship of a church.

In Corinth, "Paul was constrained by the Spirit, and testified to the Jews that Jesus is the Christ" (Acts 18:5). As a result, "many of the Corinthians, hearing, believed and were baptized" (18:8). Too often, however, "our ministers have merely sermonized, presenting subjects in an argumentative way, and scarcely mentioning the saving power of the Redeemer. Their testimony was destitute of the saving blood of Christ."[16]

Regardless of the distinctions between pastoral preaching and evangelistic preaching, Christ should be uplifted in every sermon and people given the opportunity to respond to Him. John Fowler goes as far as to say, "If our preaching fails to bring Christ to the people and the people to Christ, it is not Christian preaching."[17] Ellen White admonished, "No discourse should ever be preached without presenting Christ and Him crucified as the foundation of the gospel."[18] In other words, every sermon should move the audience closer to Jesus. "The science of salvation" should "be the burden of every sermon."[19]

If we would follow these guidelines, we would see many more conversions and renewals of commitment to Jesus in our church services.

Where the Multitudes Are

Acts 15-19 describes Paul working in five major urban centers: in Jerusalem, in Philippi, in Athens, in Corinth, and in Ephesus. As Paul visited the city of Athens, he experienced an intense indignation (Acts 17:16). "The glory he saw was utter shame. He was in no way humbled and abashed by the pride of this pagan flowering; he was only aroused to set the glory of God and of Christ where the glory of idolatry now spread itself."[20]

By contrast, it seems that in Corinth Paul was somehow discouraged by the opposition he had experienced (Acts 18:6). So the Lord appeared to him in the night and encouraged him. Of special significance to Paul—and to all those who have a burden for the multitudes in the cities—the Lord gave Paul the assurance that He had many sincere people in that city (18:10).

Our world today is fast becoming urbanized.* Industries, government, and education are generally concentrated in cities. And every day, masses of people continue to emigrate from the countryside to the urban centers. Urban poor, living in slum areas, comprise between a fourth and a half of the population of many of the largest cities in the world. For many reasons these urban poor are the most responsive group on earth today.[21]

When church members think of "missionaries," many immediately picture someone living in a forest or in the mountains. But with more than half of the world population living in urban areas today, we must develop new strategies and a new generation of missionaries who will work in urban centers.

I first experienced evangelism in a tent in Argentina. While today many Adventists dislike tent evangelism, experts say that "neutral places" are the best option for urbanites, who prefer "window-shopping the gospel" in "neutral territory."[22] I applied this advice in sophisticated Japan, and it worked!

Because cities are centers "where the enemy is served in every way, and where God is so often forgotten,"[23] believers have been encouraged to move

---

*In 1800, only 5 percent of the world's population lived in urban areas. By 1900, the figure had increased to 14 percent. In 1990, over half the world was urban. By 2050, approximately 79 percent of the world's population will live in cities. "Urban Growth Increases," *Reaching the Cities* 1 (Summer 1990): 1; Roger S. Greenway and Timothy M. Monsma, *Cities: Mission's New Frontier* (Grand Rapids: Baker, 1989), xiii.

out of the cities[24] as God opens the way. On the other hand, Ellen G. White urged "families that are well grounded in the truth" to "be scattered all over the country, in the towns, cities, and villages."[25] She insisted that "churches are to be built in the large cities"[26] and that believers should establish restaurants,[27] church schools,[28] clinics,[29] food stores, and treatment rooms[30] in the cities. All these urban institutions would be of little use if they were not established primarily with the purpose of actively working for the salvation of souls.

Where should we do evangelism? Wherever needy souls can be found.

---

1. Ellen G. White, *Christian Service*, 121.
2. White, *Testimonies for the Church*, 6:240.
3. White, *Evangelism*, 513.
4. Ibid., 513.
5. White, *Medical Ministry*, 190.
6. *Testimonies for the Church*, 1:560.
7. White, *Welfare Ministry*, 122; emphasis added.
8. White, *Ministry of Healing*, 149.
9. *Testimonies for the Church*, 1:400.
10. Ibid., 6:94.
11. Ibid., 6:94, 95.
12. *Welfare Ministry*, 97.
13. *Christian Service*, 178, 179.
14. White, *Counsels on Sabbath School Work*, 10.
15. *Evangelism*, 348.
16. White, *Gospel Workers*, 156.
17. John W. Fowler, *Evangelism 2000: Proclaiming Christ in the 21st Century* (Nampa, Idaho: Pacific Press, 1994), 40.
18. *Gospel Workers*, 158.
19. Ibid., 160.
20. Lenski, Interpretation of *Acts of the Apostles*, 708.
21. Viv Grigg, "Squatters: The Most Responsive Unreached Bloc," *Urban Mission* 6 (May 1989): 45.
22. Paul G. Hiebert, *Anthropological Reflections on Missiological Issues* (Grand Rapids: Baker, 1994), 177-185.
23. White, *Life Sketches*, 410.
24. White, *Country Living*, 24.
25. *Testimonies for the Church*, 8:244, 245.
26. Ibid., 5:382.
27. Ibid., 7:112.
28. White, *Child Guidance*, 306.
29. White, *Counsels on Health*, 547-556.
30. Ibid., 549.

Chapter 11

Errors and Setbacks in Witnessing

Trial and error is a tried-and-true method of learning. It is relatively easy to see the errors others make. We tend to believe, though, that the church the book of Acts describes was perfect. So some Christians find it difficult to think of Acts as a source of learning from the weaknesses and mistakes the first Christians made in their witnessing. But Acts reveals those errors for our instruction. In this chapter we will look at some of them.

"My Culture Is Better Than Yours"

When I arrived in Central America to serve as a pastor in a rural district, some of my churches were painted with bright colors. One in particular had colored papers hanging from the ceiling, as if a wedding service had just been held there. So I immediately set myself the task of cleaning up the mess and painting the interior all white, as a clean church should look. The members complied without saying much. However, some months later, one dared to mention to me that it seemed that their church was missing something—that it did not look like a happy church anymore. I had enforced my own cultural preferences on people who valued color.

Some early Christians demonstrated lack of cultural sensitivity and of theological understanding when they accused Peter after he had baptized Cornelius " 'You went in to uncircumcised men and ate with them!' " (Acts 11:3). Ethnocentrism is the practice of interpreting and evaluating behavior and objects by the standards of one's own culture rather than those of the culture to which they belong. It is judging other people's behavior by one's own values. Christian witnesses working among people of other cultures should remember that "all cultures are equally good—that no culture has the right to stand in judgment over the others."[1] Anthropologists call this "cultural relativism."[2] In the words of Ellen G. White, "The love of God, sanctifying the soul, breaks down the wall of partition between the customs and practices of different individuals and nations."[3]

We should not reject others, isolate ourselves, or force others to change their cultures because our culture differs from theirs. Some early Christians "traveled as far as Phoenicia, Cyprus, and Antioch, preaching the word to no one but the Jews only" (Acts 11:19). Some went as far as insisting to the Gentiles of Antioch that unless they were circumcised according to the custom of Moses, they could not be saved (15:1). In those days, Jews were forcing Gentiles to become Jews. Today it seems the opposite is true—Gentiles require Jews to become Gentiles in order to be accepted in the church, or Westerners force Asians to adopt Western patterns.

Faulty Contextualization

I spent a week on the beautiful island of Penang, Malaysia, and visited many Hindu shrines, Muslim mosques, and Buddhist temples. One can hardly find a common denominator among these faiths—except that in all of them worshipers remove their shoes when they enter sacred places. A Hindu asked me, "Do you remove your shoes in your house?"

I said, "Yes!" Most people living in Asia do remove their shoes in their homes.

"Well, if you remove your shoes when you enter into your house, why don't you remove your shoes when you enter God's house?"

His question started me thinking. Does the practice of removing one's shoes violate a biblical principle? No. I think Christians in Asia don't remove their shoes when they enter a church because missionaries didn't do it. Apparently, those early missionaries didn't handle the concept of contextualization well.

According to Acts 15:1, when some believers from Jerusalem went to Antioch, they "taught the brethren, 'unless you are circumcised according to the custom of Moses, you cannot be saved.' " C. Peter Wagner affirms that many missionaries have uncritically superimposed their own form of Christianity on converts in other cultures without realizing the damage they were doing. He says that the attitude of these men from Jerusalem "is the most blatant example of faulty contextualization recorded in the New Testament."[4]

Missiologists created terms such as *accommodation* and *contextualization* to describe the interaction between gospel and culture[5] (though groups having different philosophies of mission use the same terms, thus creating confusion).

Contextualization is the process of making the biblical text meaningful and applicable to a given society. Acceptable contextualization doesn't affect the content of the gospel but rather the forms in which it is presented. Any attempt to contextualize must preserve intact what we call the "twenty-seven fundamental beliefs."

Accommodation is the presentation of the gospel using local forms in order to produce the greatest impact on a given society. Ellen G. White advised,

> The people of every country have their own peculiar, distinctive characteristics, and it is necessary that men should be wise in order that they may know how to adapt themselves to the peculiar ideas of the people, and so introduce the truth that they may do them good. They must be able to understand and meet their wants.[6]

Successful witnessing "depends upon the simplicity of the message and its adaptation to the souls that are hungering for the bread of life."[7]

> Christ drew the hearts of His hearers to Him by the manifestation of His love, and then, little by little, as they were able to bear it, He unfolded to them the great truths of the kingdom. We also must learn to adapt our labors to the condition of the people—to meet men where they are.[8]

Sometimes accommodation and contextualization are called *indigenization*.* However, I prefer to see indigenization as the whole process by which the gospel is made relevant to a local culture. One major difference between accommodation and contextualization is that the former is done by outsiders while the latter is done by insiders. In this case, accommodation is indispensable as a first step, while contextualization is a further development.

---

*"If we, then, translate it into a native form without thought of preserving the meaning, we will end up in syncretism—the mixture of old meanings with the new so that the essential nature of each is lost. If we are careful to preserve the meaning of the Gospel, even as we express it in its native terms, we have indigenization." Paul G. Hiebert, "Culture and Cross-Cultural Differences," in *Perspectives on the World Christian Movement: A Reader*, eds. Ralph D. Winter and Steven C. Hawthorne (Pasadena, Calif.: Carey, 1981), 378.

In Acts 16:1-3 we find a good example of accommodation. "Paul wanted to have . . . [Timothy] go on with him. And he took him and circumcised him because of the Jews who were in that region." In the light of the council's decision (15:23-29), some may think Paul was compromising. However, "Paul was not violating any doctrinal principle, nor was he ashamed of the gospel. As a good missionary, he was wise enough and flexible enough to remove beforehand any possible social or cultural obstacle to the gospel of the Kingdom."[9] Paul's action harmonized with his declared philosophy: "To the Jews I became as a Jew, that I might win Jews; to those who are under the law, as under the law, that I might win those who are under the law" (1 Cor. 9:20). Even God Himself showed at Pentecost that He respects the cultures and languages of people. On that occasion the gospel was presented in cultural forms appropriate to each people group present (Acts 2:4-6).

Although the issue of Gentile circumcision is largely a thing of the past, other issues such as patterns of worship, styles of music, instruments used in worship, celebrations of transitions in life, and practices related to deceased ancestors continue to be discussed in some circles. It is apparent that much of these discussions grow out of ethnocentric ideas—the concept that a certain culture is superior to others.

Many differing cultural practices do not contradict the principles of the gospel. Those who want to draw others to Christ should respect these practices even though they differ from those of their own cultural practices. "Agree with the people on every point you can consistently do so. Let them see that you love their souls, and want to be in harmony with them so far as possible."[10] Local believers—rather than outsiders—should decide whether or not Christian men of that culture will wear pants and ties, whether or not Christians will remove their shoes when entering a church, cover their heads, play drums in church services, sit on the floor, or kiss each other.

Ethnic Divisions

Citizens of Thyatira identified Paul and Silas as Jews who troubled their city. Before the magistrates they accused the evangelists in terms of "us"—Romans—against "them"—Jews (Acts 16:20, 21). Too often ethnic hatred has plagued society. What may be surprising is that ethnic divisions also plagued the early Christians. "In those days . . . there arose a murmuring against the Hebrews by the Hellenists, because their widows were neglected in the daily distribution" (6:1).

Hellenists were non-native-born Jews whose first language was Greek rather than Hebrew. While the early church was bicultural, one of the groups, the Hebrews, provided the top leadership.

> Like many missionaries today, who have fallen into the error of assuming the leadership of churches in the new cultures to which they have been called, the apostles were probably talking behind the Hellenist believers' backs in Aramaic, a language the Hellenists could not understand. No wonder friction developed![11]

Luke described the neglect of the Hellenist widows as a class-discrimination offense. Neither Luke nor the apostles offer a defense for the partiality. The fault occurred because everyone was too busy. A group of poor women belonging to a particular cultural/language group happened not to receive "the daily distribution" and felt discriminated against.

"Then the twelve summoned the multitude of the disciples" (Acts 6:2). The fact that the apostles called a congregational meeting indicates they realized that the problem was serious. Later, a council of leaders resolved another conflict that arose (see Acts 15). In the Seventh-day Adventist Church we use both approaches. We believe that "in the multitude of counselors there is safety" (Prov. 11:14).

Moses' appointment of the seventy elders to care for his people (see Num. 11:10-16) may have offered the apostles a precedent. They advised the church to expand the leadership by involving other church members (Acts 6:3, 4). "They recognized that the Hellenists felt isolated from the power structure of the whole community."[12] So they chose seven men, whose Greek names indicate that they were Hellenists themselves.[13] These seven probably had already emerged as leaders among their own people group. The immediate result of this form of witnessing was that "the word of God spread, and the number of the disciples multiplied greatly in Jerusalem" (6:7).*

> The influence of the gospel is to unite God's people in one great brotherhood. . . . Worldly maxims and differences of nationalities are lost sight of in him. The love of God, sanctifying the soul, breaks down the wall of partition between the customs and

*Luke adds that many of the priests also became obedient to the faith (Acts 6:7). C. Peter Wagner suggests that "when the Hellenists became indigenized and moved out under their own leadership, the priests now could become a part of a more purely Hebrew Messianic community without compromising their own integrity" (*Spreading the Fire*, The Acts of the Holy Spirit Series [Ventura, Calif.: Regal Books, 1995], 189.)

practices of different individuals and nations. The great principles of Bible truth bring all into perfect harmony.[14]

Dissension Among Witnesses

In my first two years of denominational work, I served as Bible instructor for a series of evangelistic meetings. Several other workers participated as well. All of us, mostly young interns, wanted to lead as many people as possible to the baptismal waters. We were each assigned our territories, but in several cases circumstances led two or more workers to dispute over a soul. Arguments resulted: "This soul is mine!," "I saw him first!," "It's not fair!" On more than one occasion, these arguments perplexed and even discouraged the prospects.

Surprisingly, the first gospel workers also engaged in disputes. Paul and Barnabas, for instance, argued about John Mark, who, "departing from them, returned to Jerusalem" (Acts 13:13). Barnabas wanted to take John Mark with them on their next missionary trip. But "Paul insisted that they should not take with them the one who had departed from them in Pamphylia and had not gone with them to the work. Then the contention became so sharp that they parted from one another." (15:38, 39). The leaders of the church, however, understood that Paul and Barnabas were still doing God's work. They commended them "to the grace of God" (verse 40). It is possible to have unity of purpose even though opinions and strategies differ.

Shallow Conversions

Simon, a man who previously practiced sorcery, was baptized in a successful evangelistic effort that Philip conducted in Samaria (see Acts 8). Simon "was amazed, seeing the miracles and signs which were done" under Philip's ministry (verse 13). Simon's response to the Spirit's manifestations is disappointing but underscores the reliability of the Acts account: "When Simon saw that through the laying on of the apostles' hands the Holy Spirit was given, he offered them money" (8:18).* Peter's sharp rebuke, "You are poisoned by bitterness and bound by iniquity" (8:23), reveals the shallow nature of Simon's response. Mystified by the marvelous, he was not yet mastered by Jesus Christ! However, Peter offered him repentance, and Simon asked for intercessory prayer (8:22, 24).

Did Philip err in baptizing Simon? Sometimes evangelists make mis-

---

*Simon's attempt to purchase spiritual power (Acts 8:18, 19) gave the name "simony" to the medieval practice of selling and buying clerical positions.

takes in recommending people for baptism. But in Philip's defense, the Bible says, (8:13) "Simon himself . . . believed." Candidates for baptism should be properly instructed and "when they give evidence that they fully understand their position, they are to be accepted."[15] Jesus said, " 'The kingdom of heaven is like a dragnet that was cast into the sea and gathered some of every kind' " (Matt. 13:47, 48). This is a common situation in public evangelism. It was the case in Samaria.

Acts 18:24, 25 describes a somewhat similar situation. Apollos "had been instructed in the way of the Lord; and being fervent in spirit, he spoke and taught accurately the things of the Lord, though he knew only the baptism of John." In Ephesus, he led several to baptism. By the time Paul arrived at the city, there were about twelve converts (19:7). But Paul saw immediately that there was something lacking in their life and witness.

> The twelve men represented the product of their eloquent leader Apollos. If a preacher begins with mere eloquence, he usually ends with mere instruction. Too often the divine dynamic will be lacking; for a man can lift others only to the level on which he himself lives.[16]

Without preliminaries, Paul asked them a crucial question: " 'Did you receive the Holy Spirit when you believed?' "

They replied, " 'We have not so much as heard whether there is a Holy Spirit' " (Acts 19:2).

> The answers of the men so far had shown incomplete instruction, which fell short of what candidates for baptism ordinarily received, and also an incomplete spiritual experience, corresponding with their lack of knowledge.[17]

In Apollos's case, Aquila and Priscilla "took him aside and explained to him the way of God more accurately" (Acts 18:26). In the case of the Ephesian believers, "the apostle set before them the great truths that are the foundation of the Christian's hope."[18] These cases underline not only the importance of a thorough preparation before baptism but also the importance of a proper follow-up after converts are accepted into church membership.

Opposition and Persecution

In apostolic days, persecution rendered major setbacks. In many instances the enemies of the gospel used false charges to justify their persecution. They charged the apostles with agitation, if not insurrection (Acts 5:28). Still later, Christians were charged with divisiveness (14:4), with setting forth unlawful customs (16:20, 21), with turning the world upside down (17:6), with babbling about strange gods (17:18), with law-breaking (18:13), with diminishing business (19:26, 27), and even with bringing Gentiles into the temple (21:28). However, persecution has always motivated Christians to draw closer to and to commit themselves more fully to the Lord.

Space limitations will not allow a proper treatment of the different forms of persecution the book of Acts lists. Christian witnesses were put in prison (Acts 4:3; 5:18; 8:3; 16:23), beaten (5:40; 16:22, 23), suffered assassination attempts (9:23-25, 29; 14:5; 21:31; 23:12-15), endured opposition (13:45; 14:2; 17:13; 19:9, 23-41), were expelled from cities (13:50), and were stoned (14:19). Jesus never promised His disciples that they would not experience opposition; instead, He gave them words of hope and courage. "He knew that they would suffer persecution, that they would be cast out of the synagogues, and would be thrown into prison. He knew that for witnessing to Him as the Messiah, some of them would suffer death."[19]

"This history of truth has ever been the record of a struggle between right and wrong. The proclamation of the gospel has ever been carried forward in this world in the face of opposition, peril, loss and suffering."[20] Those who live in the end times should not expect better times ahead. The work that began with sacrifice will end with sacrifice.

There's a reason Acts records the mistakes and setbacks the first Christian witnesses knew: We're to learn from them. That way we can better represent our Lord and lead more people to trust Him for their salvation.

---

1. Paul G. Hiebert, *Anthropological Insights for Missionaries* (Grand Rapids: Baker, 1985), 101.

2. Merwin S. Garbarino, *Sociocultural Theory in Anthropology* (Prospect Heights, Ill.: Waveland, 1983), 101.

3. Ellen G. White, *Review and Herald*, 3 November 1885, 673.

4. C. Peter Wagner, *Lighting the World*, The Acts of the Holy Spirit Series (Ventura, Calif.: Regal Books, 1995), 227.

5. This chapter is based on ideas found in Carlos Martin's, "What Constitutes 'Acceptable Contextualization'?" *Asia Adventist Seminary Studies* 1 (1998): 19-25.

6. White, *Testimonies to Ministers*, 213.

7. White, *Christ's Object Lessons*, 231.

8. White, *Evangelism*, 484.

9. C. Peter Wagner, *Blazing the Way*, The Acts of the Holy Spirit Series, (Ventura, Calif.: Regal Books, 1995), 46.

10. White, *Historical Sketches*, 122.

11. C. Peter Wagner, *Spreading the Fire*, The Acts of the Holy Spirit Series (Ventura, Calif.: Regal Books, 1995), 175.

12. Thom Hopler, *A World of Difference* (Downers Grove, Ill.: InterVarsity, 1981), 86.

13. See Wagner, *Spreading the Fire*, 184-186.

14. White, *Review and Herald*, 3 November 1885, 673.

15. White, *Testimonies to Ministers*, 128.

16. LeRoy E. Froom, *The Coming of the Comforter* (Hagerstown, Md.: Review and Herald, 1956), 141.

17. "Unto What?" [Acts 19:3], *SDA Bible Commentary*, 6:372.

18. White, *The Acts of the Apostles*, 282.

19. Ibid., 21.

20. Ibid., 85.

Chapter 12

Power for Witnessing

The lay activities director of the church was very excited as he listened to the fiery Adventist preacher describing the latter rain during the sermon in the worship service. *Surely, now*, he thought, *many will come to participate in the witnessing activities this afternoon.* But only two members showed up at the announced time. What happened to the inspiration all the members received in the morning? No doubt many thought, *I'm too busy to do missionary work now. When I will receive the latter rain, I'll be a powerful witness for Christ.*

They're not alone in holding this idea. Ellen G. White wrote, "The impression concerning the Holy Spirit has been that this gift is not for the church now, but that at some time in the future it would be necessary for the church to receive it."[1]

The *SDA Bible Commentary* says, "The effect of the presence of the Holy Spirit is seen in enthusiastic witnessing for the faith."[2] Powerful witnessing comes from the combination of "both the divine and the human."[3] This chapter will examine the role of the supernatural in witnessing. We'll see that divine agencies are available now to enable Christian witnesses to participate with power in the finishing of God's work.

Boldness in Witnessing

Acts 4 mentions boldness in witnessing twice (verses 13, 31). Notice that in both cases a reference to the Holy Spirit precedes the mention: According to Acts 4:8, Peter was "filled with the Holy Spirit." And Acts 4:31 says that as "they were all filled with the Spirit, . . . they spoke the word of God with boldness." The disciples' courage manifested in witnessing was founded on the fact that "they had been with Jesus" (4:13).

The early Christians were so full of the Spirit of God, so persuaded of the relevance of their message, that people believed what they had to say. "They were not able to resist the wisdom and the Spirit by which he spoke" (Acts 6:10). The inspired conviction that they had the right message and that God was on their side enabled the disciples to turn the world of their time upside down (17:6). Under the power and influence of the baptism of the Holy Spirit, thousands were convicted and baptized.

The apostles' boldness and effectiveness in witnessing grew out of their reception of the Holy Spirit. Modern communicators of the Word need the same fullness of the Spirit in their lives. This experience is not a spiritual luxury; it is an essential condition for effective Christian service. "The human spirit fails unless the Holy Spirit fills."[4] The Laodicean condition in many of our churches, our indifference to urgent missionary appeals, and the lack of motivation to participate in soul-winning efforts signal that we're missing something in our lives. "If we were only vitalized by the Holy Spirit, there would be a hundred missionaries where there is now one."[5]

> If the fulfillment of the promise is not seen as it might be, it is because the promise is not appreciated as it should be. If all were willing, all would be filled with the Spirit. Wherever the need of the Holy Spirit is a matter little thought of, there is seen spiritual drought, spiritual darkness, spiritual declension and death. Whenever minor matters occupy the attention, the divine power which is necessary for the growth and prosperity of the church, and which would bring all other blessings in its train, is lacking, though offered in infinite plenitude.[6]

> As consecrated believers share with others the light they have received,they receive more and still more of the Spirit's power. . . . On the other hand, there are some who, instead of wisely improving present opportunities, are idly waiting for some special season of spiritual refreshing by which their ability to enlighten others will be greatly increased.[7]

Filled With the Spirit

No doubt Peter was filled with the Holy Spirit when he preached on Pentecost. But we shouldn't credit the powerful defense Acts 4 records to his keen powers and great courage. That defense came as a fulfillment of the Lord's promise: " 'Do not worry about how or what you should speak. . . . It is not you who speak, but the Spirit of your Father who speaks in you' " (Matt. 10:19, 20).

Someone has said that Acts of the Apostles could also have been named "Acts of the Holy Spirit." It was not only the apostles who were filled with the Spirit: Stephen, the first Christian martyr, was characterized as "a man full of faith and the Holy Spirit" (Acts 6:5; see also 7:55). Acts describes Barnabas similarly (11:24). As a result of his witness, "many people were added to the Lord." The same verse that says that Saul became Paul also says that this new convert ministered "filled with the Holy Spirit" (13:9). And Ephesians 5:18 commands all Christians to "be filled with the Spirit."

LeRoy E. Froom commented, "All the children of God are *born* of the Spirit; but it is another thing to be *filled* with the Spirit. It is one thing to *have* the Holy Spirit in a measure, or by measure; but quite different for *Him to have us fully*."[8] Those who are "filled with the Holy Spirit" receive a special empowering of the Spirit over and above the ordinary. For the lack of this, one's testimony is feeble and the spiritual life but partial. And whether or not one has received this baptism is a matter of life and death—the parable of the Ten Virgins clearly indicates this (Matt. 25:1-13).

Through the prophets, the Lord promised special outpourings of His Spirit (see Joel 2:23; Jer. 5:24). "The outpouring of the Spirit in the days of the apostles was 'the former rain,' and glorious was the result. But the latter rain will be more abundant."[9] Before we are ready for the latter rain, we must receive the former rain.

> We may have had a measure of the Spirit of God, but by prayer and faith we are continually to seek more of the Spirit. It will never do to cease our efforts. If we do not progress, if we do not place ourselves in an attitude to receive both the former and the latter rain, we shall lose our souls.[10]

Power Encounters

"A power encounter is a practical, visible demonstration that the power of God is greater than the power of the spirits worshiped or feared by the members of a given social group or by individuals."[11] A classical illustration from the Old Testament is Elijah's challenge to the priests of Baal (1 Kings 18:21). In the book of Acts, we find Paul meeting the Satanic power of a sorcerer whose name was Bar-Jesus (Acts 13:6). In Paphos, capital of Cyprus in those days, Paul met "the proconsul, Sergius Paulus, an intelligent man" (13:7). At the end of the story Luke "brings before his readers a dramatic power encounter, in which the Holy Spirit overthrew the evil one, the apostle confounded the sorcerer, and the gospel triumphed over the occult."[12]

These visible evidences of God's power over the powers of evil do not necessarily involve spectacular demonstrations of force. Jesus commanded us to go into Satan's territory to confront the power that holds people in spiritual blindness. Paul's call to turn Gentiles "from the darkness to light, and from the power of Satan to God" (Acts 26:18) indicates that witnessing and evangelism comprise one of the primary forms of power encounter. These encounters do not necessarily mean confrontations with magicians, diviners, mediums, spiritualists, and others like them. In fact, those who dialogue with such people "place themselves in communication with the powers of darkness and encourage evil angels about them."[13]

We should not intentionally precipitate a clash with demons. However, in the course of our witnessing we may find ourselves in the midst of situations where we face the challenge of Satan. Then we can claim deliverance in the name of Jesus. "Satan cannot endure to have his powerful rival appealed to, for he fears and trembles before His strength and majesty."[14]

According to Acts 3:6, Peter commanded a lame man " 'in the name of Jesus Christ of Nazareth, rise up and walk.' " In many instances the book of Acts sets forth Jesus' name as the means by which miracles are worked (3:6; 4:10; 16:18) and salvation is attained (2:21; 2:38; 4:12; 22:16). The full trust with which Peter uttered that name reveals his faith in his Master's promise (Mark 16:17, 18). "The name of the Lord became a symbol to the disciples of the glorious character and unlimited power" of Jesus.[15]

However, we cannot use Jesus' name as a magical incantation. The sons of Sceva tried that, but the evil spirit they were trying to master didn't respond to their command. "The man in whom the evil spirit was leaped on them, overpowered them, and prevailed against them" (Acts 19:14-16). Their experience warns us that no one who does not belong to Jesus should challenge Satan.

Adventists have clear instructions about "deliverance ministries":

> The work of declaring persons possessed of the devil, and then praying with them and pretending to cast out the evil spirits, is fanaticism which will bring into disrepute any church which sanctions such work.
>
> I was shown that we must give no encouragement to these

> demonstrations, but must guard the people with a decided testimony against that which would bring a stain upon the name of Seventh-day Adventists.[16]

Miracles Among Us?

Acts contains numerous references to miracles (3:1-9; 9:32-35, 38-43; 19:11, 12; 28:3-6, 8, 9), and specifically "signs and wonders" (2:22, 43; 4:30; 5:12; 6:8; 8:13; 14:3; 15:12). Indications of church growth follow at least three of the references to "signs and wonders" (2:43, 47; 5:12, 14; 8:6-13). "These evidences of divine approval had a powerful influence on those whose minds were open to conviction, and converts to the gospel multiplied."[17]

Miracles and supernatural manifestations were also common among early Adventists. Even though Ellen White never claimed to work miracles, many times she was called upon to pray for the sick, and miracles happened. Then she would say, "Christ is the great miracle worker. To Him be all the glory."[18] She recorded in volume two of *Spiritual Gifts* many miracles that occurred in answer to prayer in early Adventist history.*

Ellen White wrote that the miraculous scenes of Pentecost "are to be repeated" under the latter rain, "and with greater power."[19] She described what will happen then:

> Servants of God, with their faces lighted up and shining with holy consecration, will hasten from place to place to proclaim the message from heaven. By thousands of voices, all over the earth, the warning will be given. Miracles will be wrought, the sick will be healed, and signs and wonders will follow the believers. Satan also works with lying wonders, even bringing down fire from heaven in the sight of men. Thus the inhabitants of the earth will be brought to take their stand.[20]

Acts reveals that miracles occurred during the time of the early church. Miracles also took place in the early Adventist church one hundred fifty years ago. And we are told that under the influence of the latter rain the scenes of Acts will be repeated. Seventh-day Adventists should not disregard miracles. However, Ellen White warned that we should not consider miracles the hallmark of our ministry, for "the man who makes the working

---

*For instance, see how God intervened in cases of rheumatic fever (*Spiritual Gifts*, 2:42, 43), fits (ibid., 71, 72), coughing spells (ibid., 97), bloody dysentery (ibid., 100), brain inflammation (ibid., 122), cholera (ibid., 138), heart pain (ibid., 186, 187), and cancer (ibid., 184-187).

of miracles the test of his faith will find that Satan can, through a species of deception, perform wonders that will appear to be genuine miracles."*

The Role of Angels in Witnessing

Angels, "ministering spirits" (Heb. 1:14) who are usually invisible to human eyes, interacted many times with believers in the events registered in the book of Acts. An angel instructed Philip to go to the desert to meet the Ethiopian eunuch (Acts 8:26, 27), an angel of God appeared to Cornelius instructing him to send for Peter (10:3-5), and an angel of the Lord delivered Peter from prison (12:5-9). These stories illustrate "the closeness of the connection between heaven and earth."[21] We may be tempted to think that the work would be rapidly finished if angels would do the preaching. However, "as His representatives among men, Christ does not choose angels who have never fallen, but human beings, men of like passions with those they seek to save."[22]

As believers go out in obedience to the gospel commission, they may have the full assurance that angels accompany them on their mission.

> We need to understand better than we do the mission of the angels. It would be well to remember that every true child of God has the cooperation of heavenly beings. Invisible armies of light and power attend the meek and lowly ones who believe and claim the promises of God.[23]

The continual presence of guardian angels is one of the Christian's sweetest assurances. Angels also accompany the believer in missionary endeavors. "As he visits from house to house, opening the Scriptures to those whose understanding is darkened, angels of God will be close beside him to impress the heart of the one who is athirst for the water of life."[24]

Conditions for the Enabling Baptism

John the Baptist announced, " 'I indeed baptized you with water, but . . . [Jesus] will baptize you with the Holy Spirit' " (Mark 1:8). After His resurrection Jesus confirmed, " 'For John truly baptized with water, but

---

*_Selected Messages_, 2:52. Jesus warned that in the latter days "false christs and false prophets will arise and show great signs and wonders, so as to deceive, if possible, even the elect" (Matt. 24:24). Some of these manifestations are related to the gift of tongues. The Spirit of prophecy warns against such manifestations among Adventists, see _Testimonies for the Church_, 1:414.

you shall be baptized with the Holy Spirit' " (Acts 1:5). "Christ has promised the gift of the Holy Spirit to His church, and the promise belongs to us as much as to the first disciples. But like every other promise, it is given on conditions."[25] In this section we'll review some of those conditions.

The first condition is *surrender*. "As the disciples waited for the fulfillment of the promise, they humbled their hearts in true repentance and confessed their unbelief."[26] No doubt, it was not an easy thing to do, but they gave up ambitions, suspicion, murmuring, and criticism.

> There are many who believe and profess to claim the Lord's promise; they talk *about* Christ and *about* the Holy Spirit, yet receive no benefit. They do not surrender the soul to be guided and controlled by the divine agencies. . . . They want to manage themselves. This is why they do not receive the heavenly gift.[27]

As a young adult, Martha* did not have moral restraints. When a member of the church invited her to a Revelation Seminar, she was using drugs and living a promiscuous life. The gospel gave her new perspectives, but she found it difficult to abandon her past. One day she told me that she would fast until she knew she had surrendered all the corners of her life to Jesus. I promised her that I would fast with her for two days. A few days later, she called me from a police station. She had been arrested for preaching in the street! Martha had surrendered her life to Jesus.

A second condition is *a life consecrated to God*. "There is no limit to the usefulness of the one who, putting self aside, makes room for the working of the Holy Spirit upon his heart, and lives a life wholly consecrated to God."[28] The resulting lifestyle (see Acts 2:44-47; 4:32-35) will be more effective than many sermons.

A third condition is *a willingness to serve as a witness for Jesus*. "The Holy Spirit will come to all who are begging for the bread of life to give to their neighbors."[29] The early disciples understood that witnessing was a matter of simple obedience (Acts 5:29). And Acts 5:32 points to the great condition: The Holy Spirit is "given to those who obey." When "we have an enlightened people, that know by experience what it means to be laborers together with God," when "the largest portion of the church [become] laborers together with God," "when we have entire, wholehearted consecra-

---

*Not her real name.

tion to the service of Christ, God will recognize the fact by an outpouring of His Spirit without measure."[30]

A fourth condition is *prayer*. The disciples were continuing "with one accord in prayer and supplication" for the Holy Spirit (Acts 1:14). The Father gives the Holy Spirit to those who ask Him (Luke 11:13). "It is our work, by confession, humiliation, repentance, and earnest prayer, to fulfill the conditions upon which God has promised to grant us His blessing. A revival need be expected only in answer to prayer."[31]

In Acts 1:14 we read that the disciples prayed "with one accord." This adverbial phrase, which occurs ten times in Acts, is used to express oneness of heart and mind—they prayed together for the same purpose.

> The disciples prayed with intense earnestness for a fitness to meet men and in their daily intercourse to speak words that would lead sinners to Christ. Putting away all differences, all desire for the supremacy, they came close together in Christian fellowship.[32]

More than five hundred believers saw the Lord after His resurrection and before Pentecost (1 Cor. 15:6). However, only the apostles, certain women, and some of the other believers—one hundred twenty in all—"continued with one accord in prayer and supplication" (Acts 1:13-15). So only about one in four tarried as directed. "There may be some encouragement for us in that, in the light of conditions and tendencies of today. If we are looking for the whole church to receive the latter rain, that day will never come."[33]

We can receive a new baptism of the Holy Spirit every day. Doing so will enable us to live in holiness and witness for Jesus effectively.

> Morning by morning, as the heralds of the gospel kneel before the Lord and renew their vows of consecration to Him, He will grant them the presence of His Spirit, with its reviving, sanctifying power. As they go forth to the day's duties, they have the assurance that the unseen agency of the Holy Spirit enables them to be "laborers together with God."[34]

---

1. Ellen G. White, *Testimonies to Ministers*, 174.
2. "With the Spirit" [Eph. 6:18], *SDA Bible Commentary*, 6:1034.
3. White, *Christian Service*, 8.

4. John T. Seamands, *Tell It Well* (Kansas City, Mo.: Beacon Hill, 1981), 120.

5. White, *Counsels on Health*, 507.

6. White, *The Acts of the Apostles*, 50.

7. Ibid., 54.

8. LeRoy E. Froom, *The Coming of the Comforter* (Hagerstown, Md.: Review and Herald, 1956), 150. Italics in the original.

9. White, *Testimonies for the Church*, 8:21.

10. *Testimonies to Ministers*, 508.

11. C. Peter Wagner, *Lighting the World*, The Acts of the Holy Spirit Series (Ventura, Calif.: Regal Books, 1995), 154.

12. John R. W. Stott, *The Message of Acts* (Downers Grove, Ill.: InterVarsity, 1994), 220.

13. *Testimonies for the Church*, 3:485.

14. Ibid.,1:346

15. "Call" [Acts 2:21], *SDA Bible Commentary*, 6:144.

16. White, *Selected Messages*, 2:46.

17. *The Acts of the Apostles*, 177.

18. *Selected Messages*, 2:54.

19. White, *Christ's Object Lessons*, 121.

20. White, *The Great Controversy*, 611, 612.

21. *The Acts of the Apostles*, 152.

22. White, *The Desire of Ages*, 296.

23. *The Acts of the Apostles*, 154.

24. *Evangelism*, 489.

25. *The Desire of Ages*, 672.

26. *The Acts of the Apostles*, 36.

27. *The Desire of Ages*, 672, italics original

28. *Christian Service*, 254.

29. Ibid., 252.

30. Adapted from ibid., 253.

31. *Selected Messages*, 1:121.

32. *The Acts of the Apostles*, 37.

33. Froom, 108.

34. *The Acts of the Apostles*, 56.

Chapter 13

Post-Witnessing Activities

Have you heard the expression "Close the back door!" used in reference to the church? Evangelism brings people into the church through the "front door." We must do all we can to prevent those baptized from slipping out the "back door."[1]

I remember discouraging reports after one series of evangelistic meetings I conducted. It seems that most of the newly baptized had reverted to their old ways. Of course, my team and I were held at fault—the word was that we had baptized them prematurely or hadn't prepared them well enough. Soon thereafter in another series we baptized hundreds more. Though we followed the same approach as in the previous effort, report after report indicated that there were virtually no "backdoor" losses. What made the difference? The pastor of the district where I held the second effort—who was responsible for twelve congregations—had instituted a well-designed follow-up program.

Early Christians demonstrated much care for the newly baptized believers and for the congregations they planted. In this chapter we'll review their practices as found in the book of Acts and consider how we can "close the back door" today.

Follow Up for Young Churches

During Paul's first missionary journey, he and Barnabas visited several urban centers: Antioch, Iconium, Lystra, and Derbe. They suffered a lot of opposition there. The Antiochians "expelled them from their region" (Acts 13:50). In Iconium, both Jews and Gentiles tried to "abuse and stone them," and they had to flee (14:5, 6). Paul actually was stoned at Lystra, at the instigation of Jews from Antioch and Iconium (14:19). From Lystra, they went to Derbe (14:20). If they had continued onward, in a week or so they could have made it to Tarsus, Paul's hometown. Instead, "they returned to Lystra, Iconium, and Antioch" (14:21).

Why did Paul and Barnabas return to enemy territory at the risk of their lives? In Antioch, "almost the whole city" had attended Sabbath services (Acts 13:44). In Iconium, "a great multitude both of the Jews and also of the Greeks believed" (14:1). In Derbe, they had "made many disciples" (14:21). Acts says they decided to return to strengthen "the souls of the disciples" and to appoint elders in every church. The apostles knew the importance of what we today call follow-up. That's why they decided to risk retracing their steps.

Acts 13:43 says that after Paul and Barnabas preached justification by faith in Pisidian Antioch, "many of the Jews and devout proselytes followed Paul and Barnabas, who, speaking to them, *persuaded them to continue in the grace of God*" (emphasis added). We find Paul spending extended periods in many places, such as in Iconium ("a long time," Acts 14:3), in Corinth ("a year and six months," 18:11), in the province of Asia Minor ("for a time," 19:22), and in Greece ("three months," 20:2, 3). His ministry combined nurture with evangelism.

Acts pictures some of the elements of evangelistic follow-up. Acts 8:12 says that many Samaritans believed the good news "concerning the kingdom of God and the name of Jesus" that Philip preached there. They sealed their commitment through public baptism, and thus the church was firmly planted among them. Incorporation in the church through baptism is an indispensable ingredient of true evangelism.

However, "when the apostles who were at Jerusalem heard that Samaria had received the word of God, they sent Peter and John to them, who, when they had come down, prayed for them that they might receive the Holy Spirit" (Acts 8:14, 15). The work of the gospel does not end with baptism. The presence and ministry of the apostles in Samaria served, among other purposes, to let the Samaritans know that they were welcome in the fellowship of Christian believers, and they also helped nurture them after baptism.

The most concrete, lasting form of ministry Acts describes is church planting. To plant a church, one must do more than merely establish a meeting place or even baptize a group of believers. Only when leaders are functioning properly, members are actively participating in outreach, and the church is multiplying itself has a church really been planted.

Good follow up includes also the training of local leaders. When Paul was stoned in Lystra, the multitudes dragged him out of the city, supposing him to be dead (Acts 14:19). However, the Lord intervened, and suddenly Paul lifted up his head and rose to his feet (14:20). "Among those who had been converted at Lystra, and who were eyewitnesses of the sufferings of Paul, was one who was afterward to become a prominent worker for Christ. . . . This was a young man named Timothy."[2]

> When men of promise and ability were converted, as in the case of Timothy, Paul and Barnabas sought earnestly to show them the necessity of laboring in the vineyard. And when the apostles left for another place, the faith of these men did not fail, but rather increased. They had been faithfully instructed in the way of the Lord, and had been taught how to labor unselfishly, earnestly, perseveringly, for the salvation of their fellow men. This careful training of new converts was an important factor in the remarkable success that attended Paul and Barnabas as they preached the gospel in heathen lands.[3]

Acts says the disciples in Antioch sent a love offering "to the brethren dwelling in Judea" (Acts 11:29). It is significant that the ones who received the offering were not the apostles in Jerusalem but the elders of Judea (11:30). Apparently, the apostles had trained elders to take over the leadership of the local congregations in Judea. This was not a new idea; the apostles had previously requested assistance in order to have more time for other ministries (6:3, 4).

The picture in Acts of the organization of church life in Ephesus shows it to have been relatively simple. Before Paul departed after the riot described in Acts 19, he encouraged the "disciples" (20:1). From Miletus he sent for the Ephesian "elders" (20:17) [Greek: *presbyteros*]. Most likely, each of them led a relatively small congregation that met in someone's home. Acts records many evangelistic sermons, but the address recorded in chapter 20:18-35 is its only example of Paul's teaching of church leaders. His charge to the elders identifies them as "overseers [Greek: *episkopos*]" (verse 28), also translated as "bishops" or "guardians."

> The minister should not feel that it is his duty to do all the talking and all the laboring and all the praying; he should educate helpers in every church. Let different ones take turns in leading the meetings, and in giving Bible-readings; in so doing they will be calling into use the talents which God has given to them, and at the same time be receiving a training as workers.[4]

Discipleship and Training

Acts says that when the gospel was preached in Antioch in the first recorded attempt to reach Gentiles, "a great number believed and turned to the Lord" (Acts 11:19-21). Barnabas secured Paul's help, and for a whole year they "assembled with the church and taught a great many people" (11:26). Some translations render the phrase "in the church," perhaps implying that these meetings were for nonChristians. Most translations, however, say that "they assembled *with* the church," suggesting the idea that these meetings were for the purpose of training Christians.

Paul and Barnabas "taught a great many people." As a result of these training sessions the members of this newly established church became so active in identifying with Christ that soon they were known as "Christians." "The name was given because Christ was the main theme of their preaching, their teaching, and their conversation."[5]

What Paul and Barnabas did in Antioch to provide a proper follow-up for newly baptized members sets a pattern for a comprehensive approach to evangelism:

> Every church should be a training school for Christian workers. Its members should be taught how to give Bible readings [Bible studies], how to conduct and teach Sabbath-school classes, how best to help the poor and to care for the sick, how to work for the unconverted. There should be schools of health, cooking classes, and classes in various lines of Christian help work.[6]

While there is no question that new churches need nurture, we ought to remember that "the greatest help that can be given our people is to teach them to work for God, and to depend on Him, not on the ministers."[7]

> Ministers should not do the work which belongs to the church, thus wearying themselves, and preventing others from performing their duty. They should teach the members how to labor in the church and in the community.[8]

> Christian ministers . . . have a broader work than many have recognized. They are not only to minister to the people, but to teach them to minister.[9]

> The best medicine you can give the church is not preaching or sermonizing, but planning work for them.[10]

How can church leaders put new members to work? Doing so will require some planning. Here are some suggestions:

Invite new members to participate on the platform. They can announce an opening song, render a musical selection, or take a part in the Sabbath School program. A newly baptized member wrote his relatives: "I am a very important person in my church. . . . I am almost a preacher!" What had happened? The Sabbath after his baptism, I had invited this young man to announce the opening song of the worship service, which he did with much enthusiasm. As he returned to his chair, I said to him, "Congratulations! Only a little more training, and you would be a good preacher!" That experience encouraged him and gave him a sense of belonging to our church. "The elders and those who have leading places in the church . . . should arrange matters so that every member of the church shall have a part to act."[11]

Ask a new member to have Bible studies with a new interest. Ellen White said that the more a person seeks to impart light, the more light that person will receive.[12] She instructed us that each convert should receive an assignment to work for others immediately upon conversion "When souls are converted, set them to work at once."[13]

An ordained Roman Catholic deacon who had attended a Revelation Seminar volunteered to teach a series. I thought, *Why not?* After all, we are told that "everyone who is added to the ranks by conversion is to be assigned his post of duty."[14] Shortly thereafter I baptized not only this brother, Alfonso Garzon, but also some of those who had attended his Revelation Seminar!

Invite new members to accompany experienced members in visitation in order to learn how to do it. "Many would be willing to work if they were taught how to begin. They need to be instructed and encouraged."[15]

Encourage them to bring others to church. For about two years after their conversion, they will be the best soul winners of your church! Why? Most of their friends are not yet members of the church. They are in their "first love," and they want to see their friends in heaven. "The very first impulse of the renewed heart is to bring others also to the Saviour."[16] This is why the newly baptized Paul "preached the Christ in the synagogues" (Acts 9:20), and he did it boldly (9:27). "Every true disciple is born into the kingdom of God as a missionary. He who drinks of the living water becomes a fountain of life. The receiver becomes a giver."[17]

Paul started his second missionary tour in the area close to Antioch and then proceeded to Galatia, where he had established churches during his first missionary journey (Acts 13-14). As Paul and Silas "went through the cities, . . . the churches were strengthened in the faith, and increased in number daily" (Acts 16:4, 5).

However, the brevity of the record in Acts 15:40, 41 suggests that in his second missionary journey Paul had no intention of making a career of nurturing the new churches even though they would have liked him to stay around. Paul and Silas kept their visits short and moved on to the frontiers as quickly as possible. After training leadership they continued with their work of evangelization.

What was good church-planting practice in Paul's day is good church-planting practice in ours as well. Ellen G. White has counseled us regarding the relationship of ministers and well-established churches: "This is no time for the messengers of God to stop to prop up those who know the truth, and who have every advantage."[18] "The ministers who are hovering over the churches, preaching to those who know the truth, would better go into places still in darkness. Unless they do this, they themselves and their congregations will become dwarfed."[19] "The churches are to be looked after and cared for, but they are not to demand continuous labor. . . . Do not educate our churches to expect constant ministerial help."[20]

New churches, new church members, need nurture. But the very best nurture we can give them is to train them in soul winning and then to put them to work at it.

---

1. See Alan F. Hare, *Close the Back Door* (St. Louis, Missouri: Concordia, 1984); and Gary McIntosh and Glenn Martin, *Finding Them, Keeping Them* (Nashville: Broadman, 1992), 13.
2. Ellen G. White, *The Acts of the Apostles*, 184.
3. Ibid., 186, 187.
4. White, *Gospel Workers*, 197.
5. *The Acts of the Apostles*, 157.
6. White, *Ministry of Healing*, 149.
7. White, *Christian Service*, 58.
8. Ibid., 69.
9. *Ministry of Healing*, 148, 149.
10. White, *Evangelism*, 356.
11. *Christian Service*, 62.
12. See White, *Christ's Object Lessons*, 354.

13. *Evangelism*, 355.
14. White, *Testimonies for the Church*, 7:30; *Christian Service*, 74.
15. *Ministry of Healing*, 149.
16. White, *The Great Controversy*, 70.
17. White, *The Desire of Ages*, 195.
18. White, *Testimonies to Ministers*, 233.
19. White, *Review and Herald*, 9 February 1905, 9.
20. Ibid., 11 July 1899, 438.

How to Retain the Newly Baptized

The following suggestions were gleaned from the chapter "Establishing and Holding New Converts" in Ellen G. White's book Evangelism *(see pages 334ff).*

• **Visit them often, especially during the first year.** Paul demonstrated an intense desire to strengthen the churches he had established. Acts 15:36 tells us that "Paul said to Barnabas, 'Let us now go back and visit our brethren in every city where we have preached the word of the Lord, and see how they are doing.' " As the apostles returned to Antioch, Paul "departed and went over all the region of Galatia and Phrygia in order, strengthening all the disciples" (18:23). Ellen White counseled, "Like the apostle Paul, visit them often to see how they do" (p. 338). "As the shepherd of the flock he [the minister] should care for the sheep and the lambs. . . . He should visit every family" (pp. 346, 347).

• **Appoint spiritual guardians for them.** Many newly baptized persons do not feel a sense of belonging to the congregation where they are members. Friendship with other members is the first step toward their assimilation into the church. According to church-growth experts, each new member should have a minimum of seven friends in the church within the first six months; otherwise they will be on their way out the back door.* Ellen White wrote, "After individuals have been converted to the truth, they need to be looked after" (p. 351). The assigned person should be a loving friend, not a spy.

• **Begin a review of doctrines.** "After the first efforts have been made in a place by giving a course of lectures, there is really greater necessity for a second course than for the first" (p. 334). Use new members as helpers. They should invite their nonAdventist friends and relatives.

• **Keep them attending services.** Make your church services intensely interesting. "Do it just as perfectly as if the first effort had not been made" (p. 335).

• **Organize a Bible class on Sabbath morning.** "Many who listen frequently to sermons, even though the truth be presented in clear lines, learn but little. Often it would be more profitable if the Sabbath meetings were of the nature of a Bible class study" (p. 348).

• **Involve them in service to the community.** "They can be in many lines, according to their several abilities, useful in helping the church to come nearer to God and working in various ways to act upon the elements outside the church" (pp. 356, 357).

• **Teach them good devotional habits.** "Unite with the Spirit of the living God to present a bulwark around our people and around our youth" (p. 339). They need to learn how to study the Sabbath School lesson, how to hold family worship, and how to begin the Sabbath day.

• **Encourage them to read from the Spirit of Prophecy.** "*Patriarchs and Prophets* and *Great Controversy* are books that are especially adapted to those who have newly come to the faith, that they may be established in the truth" (p. 366).

• **Teach them our spiritual heritage.** They need to know the story of the Advent movement, Daniel and Revelation, the doctrines, the health message, true Christian stewardship, spiritual gifts, and the necessity of doing missionary work (pp. 343, 344, 363).

• **Encourage them to pray and work for the conversion of souls.** "Personal responsibility, personal activity in seeking the salvation of others, must be the education given to all newly come to the faith" (p. 354). "By their baptismal vows they are pledged to make earnest, self-denying efforts to promote, in the hardest parts of the field, the work of soulsaving" (pp.354, 355). Newly baptized believers are strengthened in the faith when they see others joining the church they love.

---

*Win Arn, *The Church Growth Ratio Book* (Pasadena, Calif.: Church Growth, 1987), 23.

Chapter 14

The Results of Witnessing

Ray and Dawn Spoon started pioneer work among the Palawano people on the Philippine island of Palawan in 1991. When occasionally they came down from their mountains, they would stop by our Philippine seminary, where they lectured several times in my Missionary Anthropology class. Their testimonies helped us to understand that sometimes we must wait longer than we want to see the results of our witnessing—their efforts didn't produce baptisms until 1997. Today there is a flourishing Adventist church among the Palawanos.

In 1996, my son Christian went as a student missionary to India to help John and Beth Baxter. In 1993, these missionaries were sent to a city of 300,000 in which there were less than one hundred Christians and no Seventh-day Adventists. They didn't see the first fruits of their witnessing until 1999.

There are times when Christian witnesses see immediate results. When the missionaries from Cyprus and Cyrene preached Jesus to the Hellenists, "a great number believed and turned to the Lord" (Acts 11:21). But the book of Acts also illustrates that there are times when results are slow in coming. Paul was persecuted by both Jews and Gentiles in Iconium (14:4-7). A setback, however, does not mean utter defeat. Paul returned to that city on the same journey (14:21), visited there again on his second missionary journey (16:2), and also possibly on his third (18:23).

Even though the message is sometimes rejected, the Christian witness still testifies in obedience to Christ. On Pentecost, some people said in derision that the disciples were simply drunk (Acts 2:13). Nobody likes to be the laughingstock of a multitude. But Peter stood up and provided a powerful explanation of what had happened, and later on that day "about three thousand souls were added to them" (2:41).

Think of Paul and Silas in Philippi. Their witnessing excursion in the first European city they penetrated ended in apparent failure: "The magistrates tore off their clothes and commanded them to be beaten with rods. And when they had laid many stripes on them, they threw them into prison, commanding the jailer to keep them securely. Having received such a charge, he put them into the inner prison and fastened their feet in the stocks" (Acts 16:22-24). From a human perspective, the day finished in a complete disaster.

However, the apostles were still witnessing! "At midnight Paul and Silas were praying and singing hymns to God, and the prisoners were listening to them" (16:25). The baptism of the jailer and his family on that same night testifies that what humans consider an apparent fiasco God regards as an opportunity to do something great. I want to see Paul and the Philippian jailer meet in heaven! Indeed, while we may or may not receive rewards for witnessing on this earth, they will certainly be evident in eternity.

Failure—or Success?

When Paul preached in Athens, the intellectual center of the world, the philosophers who had arranged for his talk did not accept his message. "When they heard of the resurrection of the dead, some mocked, while others said, 'We will hear you again on this matter.' So Paul departed from among them" (Acts 17:33). Many people consider his work there an example of a faulty evangelistic strategy. But the record indicates that "some men joined him and believed" (17:34). Paul didn't see a great number of people become Christians in Athens, but who said that success is measured only in terms of numbers? The fact that there were conversions in Athens tells me that God blessed Paul's work there, and that spells success. "If you fail ninety-nine times in a hundred, but succeed in saving the one soul from ruin, you have done a noble deed for the Master's cause."[1]

When I was a local pastor, I used to encourage every family in my district to offer their home as an evangelistic center. About twice a year twenty to thirty families began home seminars simultaneously, in preparation for a major evangelistic effort. When my family moved to a new neighborhood, Nolly, my wife, volunteered to offer a seminar in our home. She visited our neighbors and invited them to attend her seminar. On the opening night, however, only one lady showed up. My mother—a pastor's daughter—and my children participated in the Bible study. A few lessons later the lady was not able to attend anymore, and Nolly was quite disappointed and ready to quit. I asked our children—twelve and nine years old—what they thought about the seminar, and they said they liked answering the questions. So Nolly decided to consider the series as our family devotions. This somehow mollified her feeling that the home seminar had failed.

Some weeks later, our daughter, Melissa, challenged me: "Ask me any question about the church doctrines!" I questioned her for a few minutes just to let her know that I was paying attention to her. When I felt I had asked enough questions, she asked me a question in return: "Dad, don't you think that I'm ready for baptism?" So that was her point!

After I baptized our daughter, I asked Nolly: "Do you still feel that your seminar was a failure?" Of course not!

Remember: soul winning is God's work. Consequently, feelings of personal failure—or success—should not have a place in it. We are to cooperate with God in witnessing, but conversions are always God's work. "Workers for Christ are never to think, much less to speak, of failure in their work."[2] From the perspective of the Great Commission, failure is doing nothing. "When we give ourselves wholly to God, and in our work follow His directions, He makes Himself responsible for its accomplishment. He would not have us conjecture as to the success of our honest endeavors. Not once should we even think of failure. We are to cooperate with One who knows no failure."[3]

While we shouldn't regard the results of our soul-winning efforts as measures of our success or failure, that doesn't mean that we should consider those results meaningless. "The losses and gains in this business are of great importance, for the results do not end with this life, but reach over into eternity."[4] Soul winning requires divine as well as human efforts; conversion is always a miracle from God. But, in view of the eternal consequences, we should do our best to maximize the results.

The Finishing of the Work

The book of Acts describes many feats of Christians that, according to their enemies, "turned the world upside down" (Acts 17:6). And Revelation continues the story, telling how the message of the three angels, carried by the millions of Sabbath keepers whom they symbolize, will be taken to "every nation, tribe, tongue, and people" (Rev. 14:6). These faithful witnesses aren't waiting for something extraordinary to take place some day in the future under the influence of the latter rain. Many are already participating in the finishing of God's work by knocking on doors and giving Bible studies to their friends, neighbors and relatives. Others are leaving their families to spend the rest of their lives witnessing to thousands of people groups where there is no Adventist presence.

In the meanwhile, there are many people in the world with no witness. Think of this: Only about one fourth of the world's population is

Christian—this includes all Catholics and Protestants and all kinds of cults and sects. And while many of the world's nonChristians can learn about Christianity because they're in touch with Christians, many others have no such contact. In fact, about a third of the world's population living today will die without hearing about Jesus unless committed Christians volunteer to leave their cultures and go as missionaries.

How will God finish His work? Through committed members, willing to sacrifice the conveniences of their home, family, church, town, and country—willing even to risk life itself—to go "to places where the very name of Christ has not been heard" (Rom. 15:20, NEB). "Servants of God . . . will hasten from place to place to proclaim the message from heaven. By thousands of voices, all over the earth, the warning will be given."[5]

Paul arrived in Rome in depressing circumstances. "When the Christian churches first learned that Paul was to visit Rome, they looked forward to a signal triumph of the gospel in that city. . . . But their hopes were crushed by the tidings that Paul had gone to Rome as a prisoner."[6] There are many circumstances when doors seem to be closed: retirement, seclusion in a hospital, even the solitude of a jail. However, Paul's experience teaches us something. "Let not the follower of Christ think, when he is no longer able to labor openly and actively for God and His truth, that he has no service to render, no reward to secure."[7]

The book of the Acts of the Apostles concludes exuding a spirit of freedom: It describes Paul as "preaching the kingdom of God and teaching the things which concern the Lord Jesus Christ with all confidence, no one forbidding him" (Acts 28:31). To be sure, Paul was still a prisoner; but his bonds did not prevent him from proclaiming the gospel. In a sense, the reader forgets the bonds and celebrates the freedom of the good news.

Actually, Acts doesn't end with its final verses—for the work goes on through the ministry of many. All who are involved are important. Unless we all work together, the mission of reaching the world cannot be all that God intends. The same Jesus is standing at the right hand of God, absent from believers in the flesh yet present with them in the Spirit. Though the apostles have been replaced by modern witnesses, the same Spirit Who moved upon the church at Pentecost is acting today. The Acts of the Apostles is not a closed book so long as God's Spirit moves God's people into God's world to work together in Christ's mission.

What a Reward!

The rewards of witnessing are both present and future. In terms of immediate rewards, "those who give their lives to Christlike ministry know the meaning of true happiness. Their interests and their prayers reach far beyond self. They themselves are growing as they try to help others."[8] Seeing a former drug addict teaching a Sabbath School lesson, a former drunkard taking his friends to church, or a convicted criminal witnessing for Jesus to his fellow inmates may birth in us the feelings Paul expressed when he wrote, "You are our glory and joy" (1 Thess. 2:20).

There will also be an eternal reward: to see these souls in heaven!

> The redeemed will meet and recognize those whose attention they have directed to the uplifted Saviour. What blessed converse they will have with these souls! "I was a sinner," it will be said, "without God and without hope in the world; and you came to me, and drew my attention to the precious Saviour as my only hope. . . ." Others will say: "I was a heathen in heathen lands. You left your friends and comfortable home, and came to teach me how to find Jesus, and believe in Him as the only true God. I demolished my idols, and worshiped God, and now I see Him face to face. . . ."
>
> Others will express their gratitude to those who fed the hungry and clothed the naked. "When despair bound my soul in unbelief, the Lord sent you to me," they say, "to speak words of hope and comfort. You brought me food for my physical necessities, and you opened to me the Word of God, awakening me to my spiritual needs. . . . My heart was softened, subdued, broken, as I contemplated the sacrifice which Christ had made for me."[9]

What a joy it will be to see and to greet in heaven those to whom we have introduced Jesus and His salvation! What a joy it will be to hear the Lord say, "Well done!"

---

1. Ellen G. White, *Testimonies for the Church*, 4:132.
2. White, *Gospel Workers*, 19.
3. White, *Christian Service*, 261, 262.
4. *Testimonies for the Church*, 5:411.
5. White, *The Great Controversy*, 612.
6. White, *The Acts of the Apostles*, 463, 464.
7. Ibid., 465.
8. *Testimonies for the Church*, 9:42.
9. *Gospel Workers*, 518, 519.

Contents

CREDU IS A MULTI-MILLION POUND PROJECT CREATED BY...

IN PARTNERSHIP WITH...

THE WELSH EUROPEAN FUNDING OFFICE (WEFO) ACTS AS THE BODY RESPONSIBLE FOR THE IMPLEMENTATION OF THE STRUCTURAL FUNDS IN WALES ON BEHALF OF THE WELSH ASSEMBLY GOVERNMENT

CREDU Project

CREDU (which means "to believe" in Welsh) brings computer equipment, a portal of choice and skill learning opportunities to young people, enhancing the programmes and locations in which they are already working. The CREDU benefits are available to all young people in an environment in which they are already comfortable and therefore do not feel disadvantaged, daunted or discriminated against.

Launching this landmark project, Andrew Davies, Minister for Enterprise, Innovation & Networks said; "CREDU, and the Digilab network, will provide young people with the opportunity to learn essential ICT skills, which are vital to the continued transformation of Wales into a high-value, knowledge based economy. This is truly a landmark day for Wales, for the young people of Wales and for the future of Wales."

CREDU IN A NUTSHELL:

- 112 DIGILABS
- CREDU PORTAL

LOOK WHAT YOU CAN ACCESS IN **CREDU DIGILABS...**

* HIGH-SPEED INTERNET / BROADBAND LINKED COMPUTERS (WITH THE POTENTIAL FOR SPECIAL NEEDS ADAPTATION)
- DIGITAL CAMERAS
* VIDEO CAMERAS
- COLOUR PRINTERS
* SCANNERS
- VIDEO CONFERENCING EQUIPMENT
* MOBILE PENTABS
- LAPTOPS
(COMPLEMENTED BY THE LATEST SOFT-WARE)

CREDU PROJECT

CREATE CONTENT, PUBLISH CONTENT: LOOK WHAT YOU CAN DO IN CREDU DIGILABS...

FILM MAKING
MUSIC MAKING
MSN
CREATE A CV
ANIMATION
ACCESS QUALITY INFORMATION
DIGITAL STORYTELLING
DEVELOP SKILLS
LISTEN TO MUSIC
POSTERS
GRAPHIC DESIGN
BUDGETING TOOL
PROJECTS
MAKE FRIENDS
HAVE A GOOD TIME
PHOTOGRAPHY
WORD PROCESSING

...AND YOU CAN PUT ALL THIS ON THE CREDU PORTAL...

CREDU Portal

Zone 1: VIP

Register on the CREDU Portal and get all this fantastic stuff...your own VIP account with your own password-protected personal folder with personal e-mail address

Look what you get in VIP and what you can save in your scrapbook...

Manage your money
Calendar
Animation
CV
Video Clips
Songs
Images
Diary
Music

Plus you get to design your own avatar (like the zany picture in the box above) and compete in competitions to win CDs, DVDs etc.

www.credu.co.uk

CREDU PORTAL

ZONE 2: SPOTLIGHT

EVERY WEEK IN THE SPOTLIGHT ZONE, CHECK OUT THE THEME OF THE WEEK...

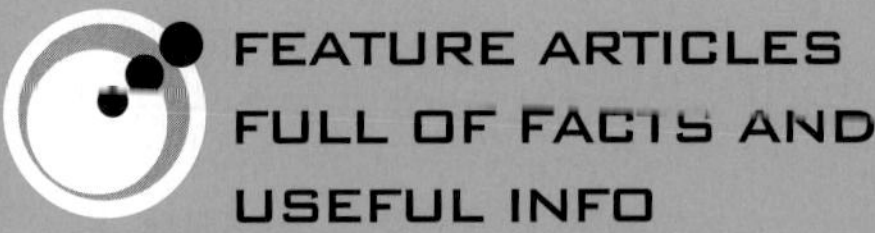

FEATURE ARTICLES FULL OF FACTS AND USEFUL INFO

WEEKLY & DAILY VOTES

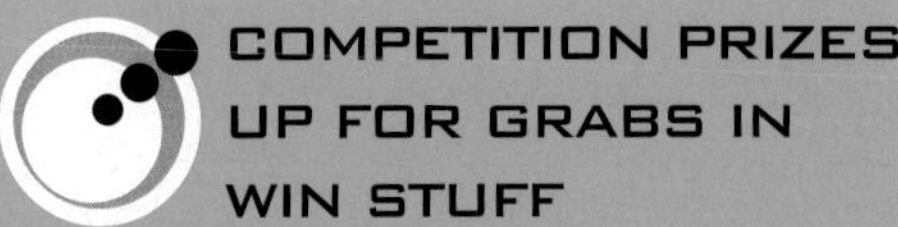

COMPETITION PRIZES UP FOR GRABS IN WIN STUFF

WWW.CREDU.CO.UK

ZONE 3: OURCREDU

OURCREDU IS THE COMMUNITY ZONE...

ABERCREDU IS AN ONLINE SOAP OPERA JUST 4 U! READ NEW EPISODES AND TAKE PART IN VOTES EVERY WEEK.

WANNA HAVE YOUR SAY ON LIFE, THE WORLD & EVERYTHING? CHECK OUT THE SHOUT FORUM

LIKE REAL LIFE STORIES?
CHECK OUT MY LIFE & STRIFE

LIKE DIGITAL STORIES?
CHECK OUT REALITY BITES

IF ANIMATION IS YOUR THING, CHECK OUT ANIMO AND IF YOU WANNA SEE SOME VIDEO CLIPS GO TO VIDEO. THERE IS SOMETHING FOR EVERYONE IN OURCREDU!

WWW.CREDU.CO.UK

CREDU PORTAL

ZONE 4: WANNA B

WANNA B IS ABOUT

JOBS, HOBBIES & AMBITIONS

WANNA B AN RSPCA OFFICER? WANNA KNOW HOW MUCH THEY GET PAID? WANNA KNOW HOW TO GET TO BE ONE? CHECK OUT PROFESSIONAL PROFILES FOR INFO ON LOTS OF DIFFERENT JOBS & ACTIVITIES

READ INTERVIEWS WITH PROFESSIONALS IN THE WORKPLACE AND DO YOUR CV ONLINE WITH OUR CV GENERATOR...ALL IN WANNA B

WWW.CREDU.CO.UK

CREDU PORTAL

ZONE 5: TRAIN UR BRAIN

HOW TO... WORKSHEETS WITH TIPS & ADVICE ON HOW TO DO THINGS OR MEET CHALLENGES ARISING FROM THE THEME OF THE WEEK...

FOR EXAMPLE, WHEN THE THEME WAS LIVE MUSIC, THE HOW 2 PACK WAS "HOW TO GET YOUR DEMO HEARD".

SOME OF THE TRAIN UR BRAIN PACKS ON THE CREDU PORTAL:
HOW 2...

- ANIMATE AN ACTION
- BE AN ETHICAL CONSUMER
- PLAN THE PERFECT HOUSE PARTY
- CHECK YOURSELF FOR CANCER
- START YOUR OWN BAND AND GET A GIG
- STAY STREET SAFE

WWW.CREDU.CO.UK

CREDU PORTAL

ZONE 6: CHILL

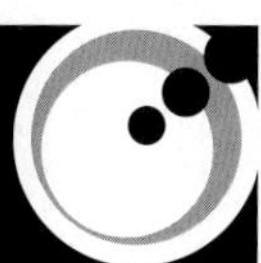

CHILL IS ABOUT FUN, FUN, FUN!!!

CHECK OUT EVENTS IN WOTZ UP WALES

CHECK OUT PICCIES AND IMAGES IN THE SNAPSHOW GALLERY

LISTEN TO MUSIC, SOUNDS & SONGS IN LOOPLOUNGE

TRY FOR THE HIGHEST SCORE IN THE GAMEZROOM - PIT YOUR WITS AGAINST THE BLOCKBOGGLER, THE SIZZLER AND THE BRAINTEASER

REMEMBER, IF YOU REGISTER ON THE PORTAL, YOU CAN UPLOAD YOUR OWN CONTENT INTO SNAPSHOW & LOOPLOUNGE

WWW.CREDU.CO.UK

CREDU PORTAL

ZONE 7: XPLOITS

XPLOITS IS ABOUT PROJECTS AND INITIATIVES

WANNA KNOW ABOUT OR PROMOTE YOUTH EXCHANGES, FUND-RAISING RALLIES, THEMED PROJECTS, COMMUNITY PROGRAMMES, LOCAL, NATIONAL AND INTERNATIONAL ACTIVITIES?

CHECK OUT XPLOITS!

WWW.CREDU.CO.UK

CREDU PORTAL

ZONE 8: IZONE

IZONE IS PACKED FULL OF

INFORMATION

- CLICK ON THE INFO INDEX FOR INFO ON THE CANLLAW ONLINE INFO INDEX TOPICS

- FIND YOUR NEAREST DIGILAB BY CLICKING ON DIGI

- FIND YOUR NEAREST INFO OUTLET BY CLICKING ON INFO

CHECK OUT HOT POTATOES FOR INFO ON CONTENTIOUS ISSUES OF THE MOMENT AND SEE NEWSBITES FOR NEWS ARTICLES FROM AROUND THE WORLD, EUROPE, UK & WALES

WWW.CREDU.CO.UK

CREDU Digilabs

Wanna do your CV online and send off for a job? wanna make a movie with your mates? wanna make music and record it? wanna learn animation and graphic design? wanna make a digital story? then check out your local digilab. Packed full of the latest in hardware & software and staffed by trained facilitators, digilabs are there for you! Learn new skills and become savvy in new technologies and digital media. CREDU - believe in your digital future...

CREDU DIGILABS

ANGLESEY

Canolfan Hyfforddiant Parys
Uned 2 * Stad Llwyn Onn * Amlwch * LL68 GBQ * http://parys.credu.co.uk

Labdigi Bodedern Digilab
Ysgol Uwchradd Bodedern * Bodedern * LL65 3SU * http://bodedern.credu.co.uk

Clwb Ieuenctid Llangefni
Plas Arthur * Ynys Môn * LL77 7EY
http://llangefni.credu.co.uk

Canolfan Jesse Hughes
Ffordd Kingsland * Hollyhead * LL65 2SP * http://jessehughes.credu.co.uk

Learning Skills Wales
The Old Stables * Tyddyn-y-waen
Llanfechell * Amlwch * LL68 0UF
http://learningskillswales.credu.co.uk

BLAENAU GWENT

Blaina Communities First Centre
108 High Street * Blaina * Brynmawr
NP13 3AF * http://blainacfc.credu.co.uk

Brynteg Digilab
Brynteg Youth Centre * Brynteg Terrace
Ebbw Vale * NP23 6NA
http://brynteg.credu.co.uk

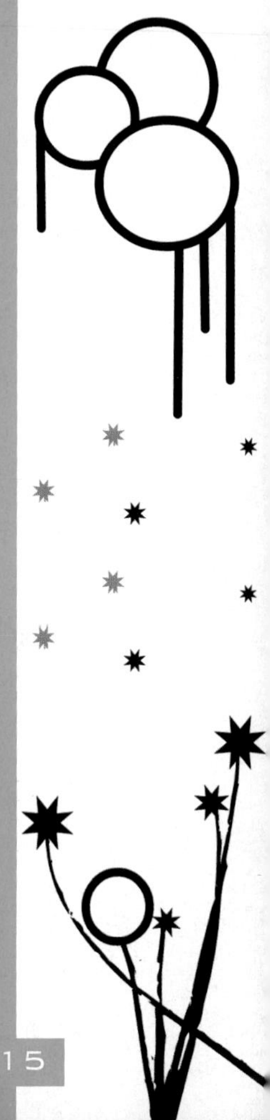

CREDU DIGILABS

BLAENAU GWENT CONT...

Ebenezer Babtist Church
Park Place * Abertillery * Blaenau Gwent
NP13 1HF * http://ebenezeryc.credu.co.uk

Abertillery Youth Centre
Station Hill * Abertillery * Blaenau Gwent
NP13 1UJ * http://abertilleryyc.credu.co.uk

Tredegar Youth Café
13 The Circle * Tredegar * NP22 3PS
http://tredegaryouthcafe.credu.co.uk

Another Planet Digilab
Shop 4 * Queensway * Garnlydan *
NP23 5EE * http://anotherplanet.credu.co.ul

Hill Top Log Cabin Digilab
69 Bethcar Street * Ebbw Vale
NP23 6HW * http://hilltop.credu.co.uk

BRIDGEND

Bridgend College Digilab
Cowbridge Road * Bridgend * CF31 3DF *
http://bridgendcollage.credu.co.uk

Pencoed College Digilab
Tregroes * Pencoed * CF35 5LG
http://pencoedcollege.credu.co.uk

Bridgend Info Shop Digilab
37 Caroline Street * Bridgend * CF31 1DW
http://bridgendinfoshop.credu.co.uk

CREDU DIGILABS

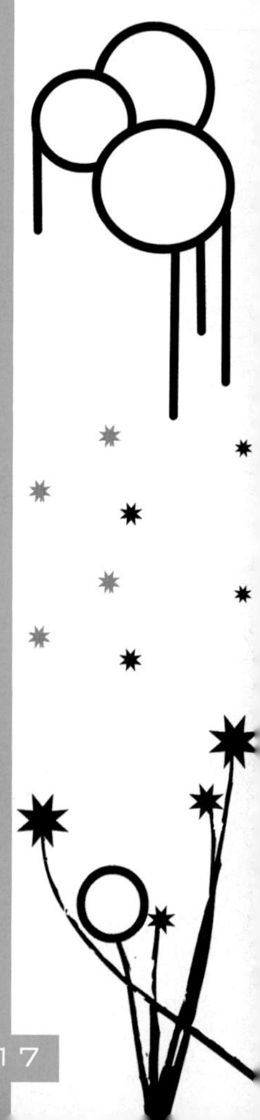

Ynysawdre Youth Centre Digilab
Ynysawdre Comp School * Heol yr Ysgol
Tondu * CF32 9EH
http://ynysawdreyc.credu.co.uk

KPC Youth Project Digilab
28 Heol Tegfryn * Pyle * CF33 6LL
http://kpcyouth.credu.co.uk

Creation - Blaengarw Workmans Hall
Blaengarw Workmans Hall * Blaengarw
CF32 8AW * http://blaengarw.credu.co.uk

Every Link Counts
Office 4, Llynfi Entersprise * Heol Ty Gwyn
Ind Est * Maesteg * CF34 0BQ
http://elc.credu.co.uk

Bethlehem Church Life Centre
Cefn Road * Cenf Cribur * CF32 0AA
http://bethlehemclc.credu.co.uk

CAERPHILLY

Canllaw Online Digilab
Van Road * Caerphilly * CF83 3ED *
http://www.credu.co.uk

Blackwood Stargate Digilab
Caerphilly Fast forward * Old Blackwood
Junior School * Pentwyn Road * NP12 1HN *
http://pefastforward.credu.co.uk

Aber Valley YMCA Digilab
Bryn Hafod Road * Abertridwr * CF83
4BH * http://abervalleyymca.credu.co.uk

CREDU DIGILABS

CAERPHILLY CONTINUED...

Young Wales Digilab
Unit 12 * Western Industrial Estate
Caerphilly * CF83 1BQ
http://youngwales.credu.co.uk

Learn About Wales Digilab
Unit 1, Former Magna Building
Pontygwyndy Ind Est * Caerphilly
CF83 2HU * http://learnabout.credu.co.uk

Phillipstown Community House
9 - 10 Penrhyn Terrace * Phillipstown
New Tredegar * NP24 6BG
http://phillipstownch.credu.co.uk

CARDIFF (OUTREACH)

Immtech Music and Multi Media Training
Unit C, Building 8 * Curran Road * Butetowr
CF10 5DF * http://Immtech.credu.co.uk

CARMARTHENSHIRE

Llandovery YMCA Digilab
Gerwin House * Market Square * Llandovery
SA20 0AB * http://llandoveryymca.credu.co.uk

Bwlch Youth Community Centre Digilab
Dafen Row * Morfa * Llanelli
SA15 2BJ * http://bwlchycc.credu.co.uk

CREDU DIGILABS

CARMARTHENSHIRE

Cwmaman Resource Centre Digilab
Station Road * Glanaman * Ammanford
SA18 1LQ * http://cwmamancentre.credu.co.uk

Streets Youth Project Digilab
Welfare Hall * Wind Street * Ammanford
SA18 3DN * http://streetsyp.credu.co.uk

Plant Dewi Digilab
21 King Street * Carmarthen * SA31 1BH
http://plantdewi.credu.co.uk

Carwe Digilab
Neuadd Carwe * Siloh Row * Carwe/Llanelli
SA17 4HP * http://carwe.credu.co.uk

Dr M'z Digilab
7 Queen Street * Carmarthen * SA31 1JR
http://drmz.credu.co.uk

Carmarthenshire Football Club Digilab
Richmond Park
http://carmsfootballclub.credu.co.uk

Newcastle Emlyn Youth Centre Digilab
Newcastle Emlyn Library * Church Lane
Newcastle Emlyn * SA38 9AB
http://newcastleemlynyc.credu.co.uk

Laugharne Youth Centre
Laugharne Community Centre * Laugharne
Carmarthen * SA33 4TE
http://laugharneyc.credu.co.uk

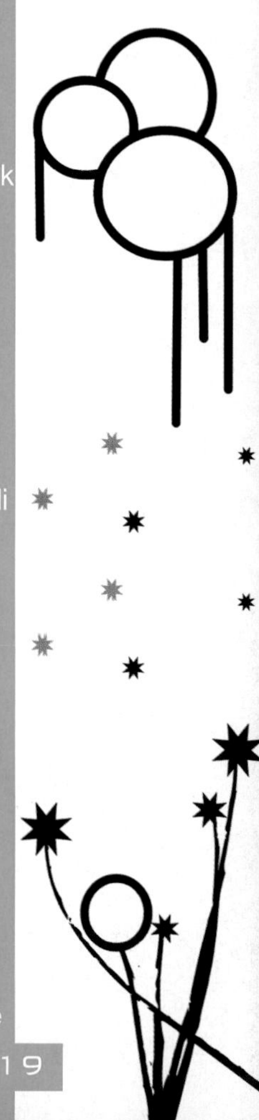

CREDU DIGILABS

CEREDIGION

YHA Borth Digilab
Morlais * Borth * Ceredigion
SY24 5JS * http://borthyha.credu.co.uk

CTC Aberaeron Digilab
Aberaeron Drop in Centre * Portland Place
Aberaeron * SA46 0IX * http://ctcaberaeron.credu.co.

Aberystwyth Arts Centre Digilab x 2
University of Wales Aberystwyth
Aberystwyth * SY23 3DE
http://aberystwythartscentre.credu.co.uk.

Gwersyll Llangrannog Digilab
Llangrannog * Llandysul * SA44 6AE *
http://urddllangrannog.credu.co.uk

CONWY

Conwy Youth Hostel Association Digilab
Lark Hill * Sychnant Pass Road
Conwy * LL32 8AJ
http://conwyyha.credu.co.uk

Llandudno Junction Youth Centre Digilab
Brickfield Terrace * Llandudno Junction
Conwy * LL31 9NG
http://llandudnojunction.credu.co.uk

Colwyn Bay Youth Centre Digilab
Douglas Road * Colwyn Bay * Conwy
LL29 7PE * http://colwynbay.credu.co.uk

CONWY CONTINUED...

Abergele Youth Action Café Digilab
Itaca, Hesketh House * Bridge Street
Abergele, Conwy * LL22 7HA
http://abergeleyc.credu.co.uk

Capel Curig Centre Digilab
c/o 2 Rhos Cottages * Capel Curig
LL24 0DY * http://capelcurig.credu.co.uk

DENBIGHSHIRE

Weston Spirit Rhyl Digilab
111 Stryd Fawr / High Street * Rhyl * LL18 1PR
http://westonspiritrhyl.credu.co.uk

Llangollen YHA Digilab
Tyndwr Hall * Tyndwr Road * Llangollen YHA *
LL20 8AR * http://llangollenyha.credu.co.uk

Rhyl Leisure Centre Digilab
Grange Town * Rhyl * Denbighshire
LL18 4BY
http://rhylyouthcentre.credu.co.uk

Prestatyn Youth Centre Digilab
Dawson Drive * Prestatyn * Denbighshire
LL19 8SU * http://prestatynyc.credu.co.uk

Llangollen Youth Centre Digilab
Willow Street * Llangollen * Denbighshire
LL20 8HH *
http://llangollenyc.credu.co.uk

CREDU DIGILABS

DENBIGHSHIRE CONTINUED..

West Rhyl Young People's Project Digilal
15 Bedford Street * Rhyl * Denbighshire
LL18 1SY * http://westrhylyp.credu.co.uk

Rhyl Youth Cafe Action Group Digilab
1 Elwy Street * Rhyl * LL18 1BS
http://ryag.credu.co.uk

ECTARC Digilab
Parade Street * Llangollen
LL20 8RB * http://ectarc.credu.co.uk

Ruthin Youth Centre Digilab
Denbigh Road * Ruthin
LL15 1NT * http://ruthinyc.credu.co.uk

GWYNEDD

Blaenau Ffestiniog Digilab
Heol Wyn Road * Canolfan Hamdden Blaer
Ffest * LL41 3UF
http://bffestiniogyc.credu.co.uk

Coleg Meirion-Dwyfor Dolgellau Digilab
Ffordd Ty'n y Coed * Dolgellau * Gwynedd
LL40 2SW
http://colegdolgellau.credu.co.uk

Canolfan Ieuenctid Caernarfon Digilab
Canolfan Ieuenctid Penyrallt
Penyrallt Isaf * Caernarfon
LL55 1NS * http://cicaernarfonyc.credu.co.u

CREDU DIGILABS

GWYNEDD CONTINUED...

Canolfan Cymunedol Bethesda
Canolfan Cefnfaes * Bethesda,Bangor
Gwynedd * LL57 3NG
http://cibethesdayc.credu.co.uk

Gwersyll yr Urdd Glan-llyn Digilab
Llanuwchllyn * Bala * Gwynedd
LL23 7ST * http://urddglanllyn.credu.co.uk

Coleg Meirion-Dwyfor Glynllifon Digilab
Ffordd Clynnog * Caernarfon * Gwynedd
LL54 5DU * http://colegglynllifor.credu.co.uk

Healthy Living Centre
Ty Cegin, Penrhyn Avenue * Maesgerchen
Bangor * LL57 1LR
http://tycegin.credu.co.uk

MERTHYR TYDFIL

Bedlinog Digilab
Bedlinog Resource Centre * Commercial
Street * Bedlinog * CF46 6RF
http://bedlinog.credu.co.uk

Treharris Boys and Girls Club Digilab
Forest Road * Treharris * CF46 5HG
http://treharrisbgc.credu.co.uk

The Dowlais Blast Engine House
High Street * Dowlais * CF48 3HA
http://pantdowlaisbgc.credu.co.uk

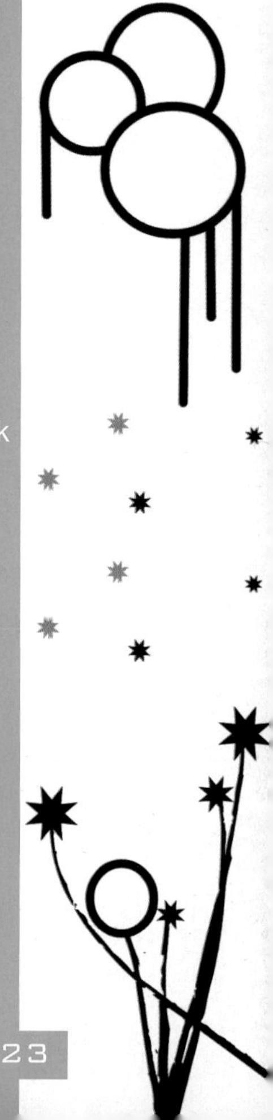

CREDU DIGILABS

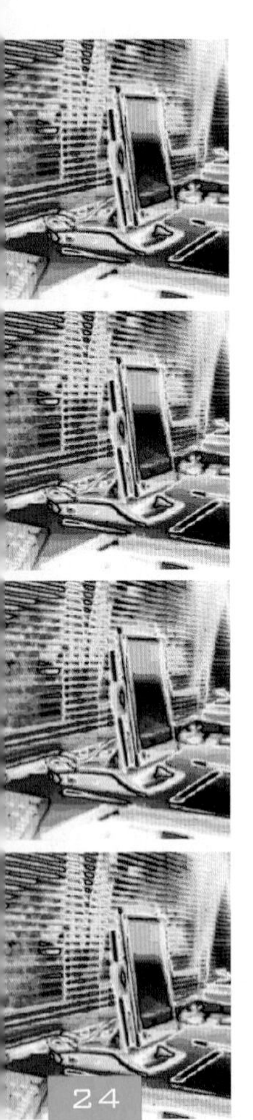

MERTHYR TYDFIL CONT...

Gellideg Digilab
Coed y Dderwen Community School
Gellideg Estate * Merthyr Tydfil
CF48 1LG * http://gellideg.credu.co.uk

Merthyr Tydfil Information Shop Digilab
Bus Station Building * Castle Street
Merthyr Tydfil * CF47 8BB
http://merthyrinfoshop.credu.co.uk

Afon Taf Community Education Digilab
Yew Street * Troedyrhiw * Merthyr Tydfil
CF48 4ED * http://afontafcec.credu.co.uk

Weston Spirit Merthyr Digilab
147a High Street * Merthyr tydfil
CF47 8DP * http://wessomerthyr.credu.co.uk

NEATH PORT TALBOT

Sandfields Community Education Day Cent
Seaway Parade * Sandfields * Port Talbot
SA12 7BL * http://sandfieldsyc.credu.co.uk

The Dulais Valley Partnership Youth Proj
The Youth Room * Seven Sisters Communit
Hall * Brynhyfryd Terrace, Neath * SA10 9B
http://dvp.credu.co.uk

St Joseph's Roman Catholic Comprehensive and Sixth form School
Newton Avenue * Port Talbot * SA12 6EY
http://stjosephs.credu.co.uk

CREDU DIGILABS

NEATH PORT TALBOT...

Croeserw Community Association
Sunny Crescent * Croeserw * Cymmer
SA13 3PG * http://croeserwcc.credu.co.uk

Glynneath Training Centre Digilab
Oddfellow Street * Glynneath * SA11 5DB
http://glynneath.credu.co.uk

YIP Cyber Café Digilab
New Sandfields * Bevin Avenue/Sandfields
Port Talbot * SA12 6JW
http://yipcybercafe.credu.co.uk

Ponty Project Digilab
The Stables * Herbert Street * Pontardawe
SA8 4EB * http://pontyproject.credu.co.uk

The Hideout Digilab
16 Forge Road * Port Talbot * SA13 1NU
http://hideout.credu.co.uk

Llandarcy Inclusive Learning Digilab
Llandarcy CC * Prettyman drive
Llandarcy * SA10 6HZ
http://llandarcyinst.credu.co.uk

PEMBROKESHIRE

The Tanyard Youth Project Digilab
Commons Road * Pembroke * SA71 4EA
http://tanyard.credu.co.uk

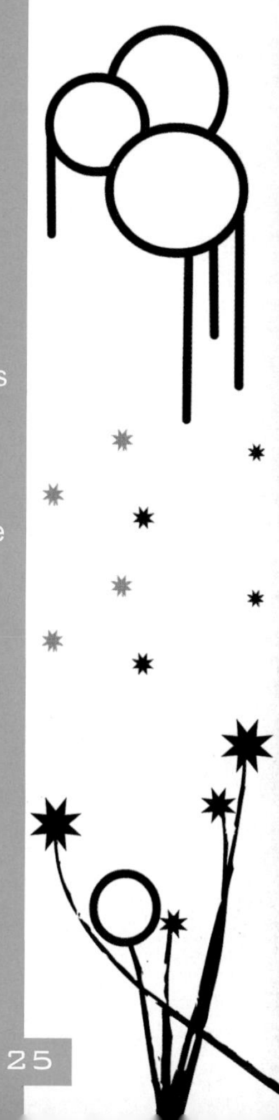

CREDU DIGILABS

PEMBROKESHIRE CONT...

Manobier YHA Digilab
Manobier * Near Tenby * Pembrokeshire
SA70 7TT * http://manobier.credu.co.uk

Neyland Youth Centre Digilab
Charles Street * Neyland * Pembrokeshire
SA73 1SA * http://neylandyc.credu.co.uk

Hubberston and Hakin Community Centre
Church Road * Hubberston * Milford Haven
SA73 3PL * http://hubberstonhakin.credu.co.uk

Tenby Youth Centre Digilab
Greenhill Avenue * Greenhill * Tenby
SA70 7LB * http://tenbyyc.credu.co.uk

Pembroke Dock Youth Centre
Bush Street * Pembroke Dock, Pembrokeshire
SA72 6HQ * http://pembrokedockyc.credu.co.uk

The Hive Digilab
Goshawk Road * Haverfordwest
SA61 2UB * http://hive.credu.co.uk

Point Digilab
Unity Hall * Rope Walk * Fishguard
SA65 9BT * http://point.credu.co.uk

Mitec - Milford Haven Digilab
The Docks * Milford Haven
SA73 3AA * http://milfordhaven.credu.co.uk

The Garage Youth Project
Dew St * Haverford West * SA61 1ST
http://garageyp.credu.co.uk

CREDU DIGILABS

PEMBROKESHIRE CONT...

Haverford West University Digilab
Merlins Bridge * Haverford West
SA61 1SZ * http://pembscoll.credu.co.uk

YHA Broad Haven
Broad Haven * Haverford West
SA62 3JH * http://broadhavenyha.credu.co.uk

RHONDDA CYNON TAFF

Tonypandy Community College Digilab
Room 14 * Llewellyn St * Penygraig/Tonypandy
CF40 1HQ * http://tonypandycc.credu.co.uk

Ferndale Community School Digilab
Rear of Excelsior Terrace * Maerdy * Ferndale *
CF43 4AL * http://ferndalecs.credu.co.uk

Continuing Education Centre Digilab
Crawshay Street * Ton Pentre * CF41 7EP *
http://crawshaystreet.credu.co.uk

Hawthorn High School Digilab
School Lane * Hawthorn
CF37 5AL * http://hawthornhigh.credu.co.uk

Beddau CEC Digilab
Bryncelynnog Comp School * Pencoedcae Rd
Beddau *CF38 2AE* http://beddaucec.credu.co.uk

Barnardos Open Door Project Digilab
21 Morgan Street * Pontypridd
CF37 2DS * http://barnardos.credu.co.uk

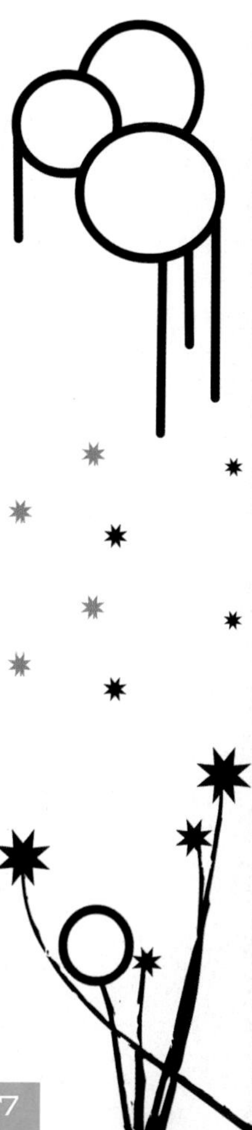

CREDU DIGILABS

R.C.T CONTINUED...

RCT People First Digilab
Old Bank Buildings * The Square, Porth
CF39 9NP * http://rctpeoplefirst.credu.co.uk

Miskin CEC Digilab
Clarence Street * Miskin * Mountain Ash
CF45 3BD * http://miskincec.credu.co.uk

E3 Project Porth Digilab
Porth County School * Cemetary Road
Porth * CF39 0BS * http://e3project.credu.co.uk

The Bridge Depot Digilab
Cowbridge Road * Pontyclun
CF72 9ED * http://thebridgedepot.credu.co.uk

Bryncynnon Strategy Digilab
Bryncynon Community Centre * Ynysboeth *
CF45 4BX * http://bryncynonstrategy.credu.co.uk

SWANSEA

Gendros Youth Support Centre Digilab
Gendros Avenue East * Gendros
SA5 8DE * http://gendrosysc.credu.co.uk

Gorseinon Youth Network Centre
Pontardulais Road * Gorseinon * SA4 2FE *
http://gorseinoncentre.credu.co.uk

Langland Bay Lifeguard Club Digilab
Langland Bay Road * Langland * SA3 4HQ *
http://langlandbaylc.credu.co.uk

CREDU DIGILABS

SWANSEA CONTINUED...

Swansea Foyer Digilab
Ty Tom Jones * 34 Alexandra Road
SA1 5DZ * http://swanseafoyer.credu.co.uk

Phoenix Centre Digilab
Powys Avenue * Townhill * SA1 6PH
http://phoenixcentre.credu.co.uk

Youth Offending Team Digilab
Llwyncelyn Campus * Cockett Rd * Cockett *
SA2 0FJ * http://swanseayot.credu.co.uk

Info Nation
47 Kingsway * Swansea * SA1 5HG
http://infonationswansea.credu.co.uk

TORFAEN

Wye Court Digilab
25 Wye Court * Thornhill * Cwmbran
NP44 5UL * http://wyecourt.credu.co.uk

Cwmbran Centre For Young People
Glyndwr Road * Town Centre * Cwmbran
NP44 1QS * http://ccyp.credu.co.uk

The Doorway Digilab
69 - 70 Broad Street * Blaenavon * Torfaen *
NP4 9HN * http://thedoorway.credu.co.uk

WREXHAM

There is also a pilot CREDU Digilab at
Victoria Youth Centre

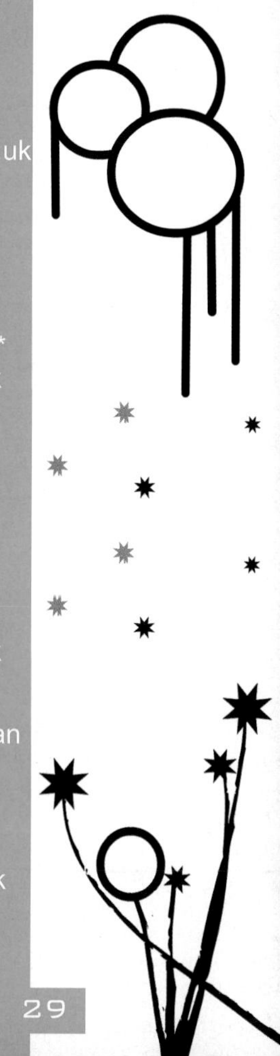

Check out articles by young writers on the CREDU Portal - www.credu.co.uk

(in My Life & Strife, Newsbites and Hot Potatoes)

Mental Health Matters

"All too often we look on being healthy as having a good diet, feeling physically fit and being free from physical illness or infection. Unknown to many, this is only a fragment of what being healthy means – many of us fail to recognise the need to examine our mental health and wellbeing also"

Basketball in Britain

"Michael Owen v Michael Jordan? No Contest. Basketball is one of the World's biggest sports, yet here in Britain, we resolutely refuse to accept it as part of our national culture"

Internet

"It was only recently (I've been in denial) that I realised just how dependant I am on the internet. It has become a big part of my life"

Sexuality

"I think that people are people and that you don't stop being who you are just because you're gay. You've got individual qualities and ideas that make you unique, same as everybody else, and your sexuality shouldn't come into it".

Dying to Diet?

"The pressure to be young, thin and tanned has never been as intense as it is in today's society"

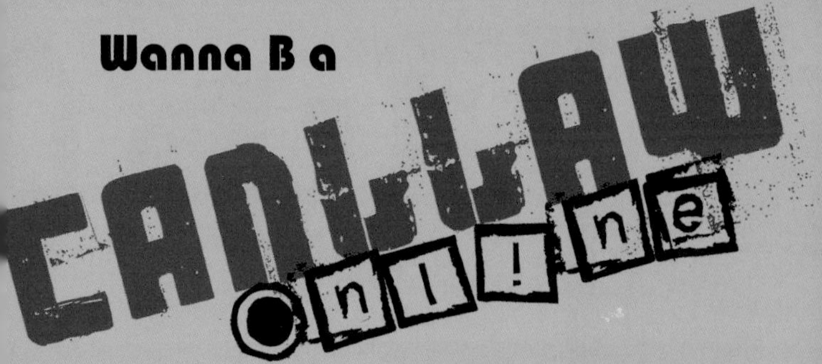

Young Writer?

Wanna see your words in print?

We're looking for young people to put pen to paper. You can write about anything you like: politics, the environment, anorexia, self-harm, recycling, tiddlywinks, space monkeys...it's up to you!!!

Join the Canllaw Online Young Writers' Initiative today and start writing tomorrow!

To join:

e-mail your name and postal address to ed@canllaw-online.com (title your e-mail "young writer") or **text** "young writer" and your name and address to 07800140769 or **send a postcard** to Ed at Canllaw Online, Suite 5, The Octagon, Caerphilly Business Park, Van Road, Caerphilly, CF83 3ED. Make sure you include your name and address.

INFO!

Fed up of not knowing what's happening for young people in your area, Wales, the UK? Find it difficult to find things to do? Bored, cheesed off and uninformed? Don't be frustrated, all that's about to change. No need to find out about things after they've happened... just step off the streets into a Canllaw Online INFO outlet. Get free leaflets, brochures and posters, advice, support and guidance, access to a range of other services, training and consultations and much more.

Look out for the signs on the streets and get in there! They're free, confidential, and friendly and give you the essential info you need on life, the world and everything.

 INFO Outlets – on the streets 4 you!

INFO
Siop I bobl ifanc yng Nghymru
Shop For young people in Wales

Info Shop – Expect to find friendly helpful staff who are trained to work with young people and will be able to answer your enquiries about any topic, ranging from training opportunities, travel advice and health, to news of local events, music venues, sports clubs and other exciting activities open to you. If they're unable to help you, they'll be able to put you in touch with someone who can, or may be able to arrange an appointment for you to see someone who specialises in your enquiry. Look out for them in your area, get in touch and pop in.

INFO Outlets – on the streets 4 you!

Info Zone – INFO Zones may be found in your local library, leisure centre, school, youth club, community centre, job centre or any building that young people visit. Here you'll be able to access quality information provided by trained staff who will be able to help you with your info needs in a relaxed and comfortable environment. Remember, every CREDU Digilab is also an INFO Zone (see pages 14-29)

INFO

Safe Point

I bobl ifanc yng Nghymru
For young people in Wales

Info Point – INFO Points can be found literally anywhere! Shopping centres, schools, burger bars, youth centres, careers offices, Jobcentres etc. Points are areas that have been designated as notice-boards, leaflet racks, wall-spaces and shelving areas containing info that you can look at and get the right contacts about services available. The points aren't always staffed by info-workers, but are a permanent display of opportunities, events, and services available for you.

Info Mobile – INFO mobiles can be seen travelling around local estates and town centres where they reach out to young people, like you, and communities that have limited access to suitable premises and services. The !NFO mobile carries loads of useful info and resources, and gives it out to young people in outlying communities who need to know what's available for them in other areas.

Find Your Nearest Info Outlet!

Anglesey

Jesse Hughes Youth Centre Info Zone
Jesse Hughes Youth Centre
Anglesey Youth Service, Holyhead,
LL77 7EY, 01248 752900

Blaenau Gwent

Catapult Youth Project Info Zone,
7-9 Commercial Street, Tredegar,
NP22 3DH, 01495 711499

Tredegar Youth Café Info Zone
13 The Circle, Tredegar, 01495 725579

Blaenau Gwent Info Zone @ Childrens
and Young Peoples Information
Service, Rachel Hicks/Scott Carey
Integrated Childrens Centre
Old Blaina School, High Street
Blaina, NP13 3BN, 08000 323339
Website: www.blaenau-gwent.gov.uk

Youth Forum Info Point, David Rees,
GAVO Offices, Festival Park, Victoria
Park, Ebbw Vale, 01495 306602

Sexual Health Info Point
Outreach Worker Nicola Marshall,
Arael Office, Aberbeeg Road,
Abertillery, NP13 2EG, 01495
212244 / 07968476297

Ebbw Vale Info Shop, 69 Bethcar
Street, Ebbw Vale, 01495 353100

Bridgend

Bridgend Info Shop, 37 Caroline
Street, Bridgend, CF31 1DW
01656 651585, Contact - Melonie Davies

Bridgend Mobile Info Service
Contact 07970 175812

Abercerdin Youth Centre Info Zone
Kenry Street, Evanstown
Gilfach Goch, Bridgend, 01443 674334

Archbishop McGrath Catholic School Info
Point, Archbishop Mcgrath Catholic
School, Bryn Road, Tondu, Bridgend,
CF32 9EH, call 01656 651585

Brackla Youth Centre Info Point, Brackla
Youth Centre, Brackla Community Hall,
Brackla, Bridgend, 01656 651585

Bridgend Drop In Info Point, Bridgend
Recreation Centre, Bridgend, 01656 651585

Brynteg Youth Centre Info Point
Brynteg Youth Centre, School
Premises, Ewenny Road, Bridgend
call 01656 651585 for details.

Bryntirion Youth Centre Info Zone
Bryntirion Youth Centre, School
Premises, Bryntirion Comprehensive
School, Merlin Crescent, Cefn Glas,
Bridgend, call 01656 651585

Garw Youth Centre Info Zone
Blaengarw Workmen's Hall
Blaengarw Road, Blaengarw
Bridgend, CF32 8HW, 01656 651585

Heol-y-Cyw Primary School Info
Point, Heol-y-Cyw Primary School,
High Street, Heol-y-Cyw, Bridgend,
CF35 6HY, 01656 651585

K.P.C Info Zone, K.P.C, 26 Heol
Tegfryn, Pyle, Bridgend, CF33 6LL
01656 749219

Llynderw Youth Centre Info Zone
Llynderw Youth Centre, Maesteg Lower Comprehensive School, Bridgend Rd, Maesteg, 01656 651585

Metro Centre Info Point
Metro Centre, 34A Penybont Road, Pencoed, Bridgend, 01656 651585

Nantymoel Youth Centre Info Point
Berwen Centre, Ogwy Street Nantymoel, Bridgend, 01656 651585

Noddfa Youth Centre Info Zone
Noddfa Youth Centre, Noddfa Chapel, Caerau Road, Caerau, Bridgend, 01656 730106

Ogmore Comprehensive School Info Point, Ogmore Comprehensive School, Spout Hill, Brynmenyn, Bridgend, CF32 9NA, 01656 651585

Ogmore Youth Centre Info Zone
Ogmore Youth Centre, St John Square, Ogmore Vale, 01656 842338

Pencoed School Info Point, Pencoed School, Coychurch Road, Pencoed, Bridgend, CF35 5LY, 01656 651585

Pencoed Youth Centre Info Point, Pencoed Youth Centre, Pencoed Comprehensive School, Coychurch Road, Pencoed, Bridgend, CF35 5LY, 01656 651585

Porthcawl Comprehensive Info Point
Porthcawl Comprehensive, 52 Park Avenue, Porthcawl, CF36 3ES call 01656 651585 for details.

Porthcawl Youth Centre Info Point
Porthcawl Youth Centre, School Premises, Porthcawl Comprehensive School, 52 Park Avenue, Porthcawl Bridgend, CF36 3ES, 01656 651585

Post 14 Project Info Zone, Post 14 Project, Riverside Offices, 20 Dunraven Place, Bridgend, CF31 1JD, 01656 651585

The Courthouse Info Point, The Courthouse, 4 Station Street, Maesteg, CF34 9AL, 01656 732613

Wildmill Drop In Info Point, 7 The Precinct, Wildmill, Bridgend, CF31 9SP, 01656 652539

Ynysawdre Comprehensive School Info Point, Ynysawdre Comprehensive School, Heol-yr-ysgol, Tondu, Bridgend, CF32 9EH, call 01656 651585 for details.

Ynysawdre Youth Centre Info Zone
Ynysawdre Youth Centre
Youth Wing, Ynysawdre School, Heol-yr-ysgol, Tondu, Bridgend, CF32 9EA, 01656 720230

Caerphilly

Gigabites e-café Info Point
Gigabites e-cafe, Shop 1 & 2
41 High Street, Bargoed
CF81 8RD, 01443 837792

Basement Youth Information Mobile, Crumlin 'Stute Hillside Road, Crumlin, Newport NP11 4QB, 01495 244064

Basement Youth Info Zone
Blackwood, 01495 233007

Info Zone @ Caerphilly Info Quest, St Ivors road, Pontllanfraith, 01495 230067

Cardiff

Butetown Youth Pavilion Info Zone Dumballs Road, Butetown, Cardiff, CF10 5FE, 029 2048 8666

Outreach Project Info Zone, c/o Cathays Youth and Community Centre, 36 Cathays Terrace, Cathays, 029 2037 3144

Cardiff Youth Project Info Point, CIC Office, Ysgol Gyfun Plasmawr, Heol Pentrebaen, Y Tyllgoed, Cardiff, CF5 3PZ, 029 2057 8245

Cathays Youth and Community Centre Info Zone, 36 Cathays Terrace, Cathays, Cardiff, 029 2037 3144

Dusty Forge Project Info Zone, Dusty Forge Project, 460 Cowbridge Road West, Ely, Cardiff, CF5 5B2, 029 2059 6849

Glantaf Youth Centre Info Point, Glantaf Youth Centre, Bridge Road, Llandaff North, Cardiff, CF14 2JL, 029 2056 1372

Grassroots Info Zone, Grassroots, City Centre Youth Project, Grassroots, 58 Charles Street, Cardiff, CF1 4EG 029 2023 1700

Heol Hir Youth Centre Info Zone Llanishen High School, Heol Hir Llanishen, Cardiff, CF14 5YL 029 2075 5663

North Ely Youth & Community Centre Info Zone, Pethybridge Road, Ely, Cardiff, CF5 3NN, 029 2059 2407

Powerhouse Youth Centre Info Shop Powerhouse Community Education Centre, Roundwood, Llanedeyrn Cardiff, CF23 9PN, 029 2054 9650

Radyr Youth Centre Info Zone Radyr Comprehensive, Heol Isaf Radyr, Cardiff, 029 2084 3177

SNAP Cardiff Info Zone, SNAP Cardiff, 10 Coopers Yard, Curran Road, Grangetown, CF10 5NB, 029 2038 4868

The Buzz Info Shop, "The Buzz" Info Project, Cardiff Youth Service, Penarth Road, Grangetown, 029 2066 6385

The Dome Youth Centre Info Zone Community Education Centre, Bryn Heulog, Pentwyn, CF2 7JF, 029 2054 9033

Trelai Youth Centre Info Point, Bishopston Road, Ely, CF5 5DY, 029 2056 6106

Ty Celyn Youth Centre Info Zone Cardiff High School, Llandennis Road Roath Park, CF23 6EG, 029 2076 3975

Waterhall Youth Centre Info Point Pentrebane Road, Fairwater Cardiff, 029 2056 4766

Whitchurch Youth Centre Info Zone Whitchurch High School (upper), Penlline Road, Cardiff, CF14 2XJ, 029 20 627363

Carmarthenshire

DR. Mz Youth Project Information Shop, 7 Queen Street, Carmarthen SA31 1JR, 01267 222786

Carmarthen Mobile Info Service Info Mobile, Moby - 01267 228273

Brynaman Youth Club Information Point, Church Hall, Church Lane Brynaman, SA18 1AD, 01269 822153

Glanamman Youth Club Information Point, Community Centre, High Street Glanamman, Ammanford, Carms SA18 1DX, 01269 823162

Youth Resource Centre Information Zone, Station Road, Glanamman, Ammanford, SA18 1LQ, 01269 822100

Streets Youth Project, Information Zone, The Welfare Hall, Wind Street Ammanford, SA18 3DN, 01269 596956

Carway Welfare Hall Information Point, Siloh Row, Carway, Kidwelly, SA17 4HP, 07748154280

Llandybie Youth Club Information Point, 129 Woodfield Road, Llandybie, Ammanford, SA18 3UT, 07769883827

Tycroes Youth Club Information Point, 27 Cwmferws Road, Tycroes, Ammanford, Carms, SA18 3TU, 07748154280

Trimsaran Welfare Hall Information Point, Llanelli Rd, Trimsaran, Kidwelly, Carms, SA17 4AA, 01554 810155

Tumble Youth Club Information Point Tumble Hall, Heol Y Neuadd, Tumble Cross Hands, SA14 6HR, 01269 841213

Bwlch Youth/Community Centre Information Zone, Dafen Row Morfa, Llanelli, SA15 2BJ 01554 749 782

Felinfoel Community Education Centre Information Zone, Tanyrodyn Felinfoel, Llanelli, SA15 4LN 01554 749882

Pembrey Community Education Centre Information Point, Mountain Road, Pembrey, Llanelli, SA16 0AJ, 01554 749782

Pwll Youth Club Information Point Pwll Community Education Centre Pwll, Llanelli, 01554 749782

Llwynhendy Youth Club Information Point, Llwynhendy Community Education Centre, Llwynhendy Carms, SA14 9DP, 01554 749 782

Llangennech Youth Club Information Point, The Pavilion, Llangennech, SA14 8UB

Carmarthen Community Information Point, Education Centre, Furnace Road Carmarthen, SA31 1EU, 01267 235413

Ferryside Youth Club Information Point, Griffiths Jones Centre, St Clears Carmarthenshire, SA33 4BT, 01267 231866

Kidwelly Youth Club Information Point Parc Stevens, Kidwelly, (01267) 253565

Llangain Youth Club Information Point Village Hall, Llangain,

Llanmiloe/Pendine Youth Club Information Point, 1 Cyscoed y Coed, Llanmiloe Carms, SA33 4TW

Llandeilo Youth Club Information Point Education Centre, Heol Rhosmaen Llandeilo, SA19 6LY

Laugharne Youth Club Information Point, Village Hall, Lagharne, Carms 01994 427266

Bancyfelin Youth Club Information Point, Bancyfelin Village Hall, Bancyfelin, Carms,

Llandovery Youth Club Information Point, YMCA Building, Llandover y, Carms, 01639 730481

Talley Youth Club Information Point Edwinsford Arms, Talley, Carms

Carmarthen library Information Zone Petre's Street, Carmarthen, SA31 1LN 01267 230873

Newcastle Emlyn Library Information Zone, Church Lane, Newcatle Emlyn 01239 711103

Llanelli Library Information Zone
Vaughan Street, Llanelli, SA15 3AS
01554 773538

Ammanford Library Information Zone
3 Wind Street, Ammanford
SA18 3DN, 01269 59 8150

Laugharne Library Information Zone
Laugharne Community Centre
Carmarthen, SA33 4TE, 01994 427874,
Any further Information on Info Outlets contact Rhys Morris on 07901 516292

Ceredigion

Aberaeron Youth Project Info Zone
Ground Floor, Youth Building, Portland Place, Aberaeron, Ceredigion
SA46 0AX, 01545 571572

CONWY - INFO ZONES

Colwyn Bay Youth Centre
Douglas Road, Colwyn Bay
Conwy, LL29 7PE, Tel: 01492 535961
Email :David.Price@conwy.gov.uk

Llandudno Junction Youth Centre
Brickfield Terrace, Llandudno Junction
Conwy, LL31 9NG, Tel: 01492 582365
Email:Paul.Hughes@conwy.gov.uk

CONWY INFO POINTS

Llandudno Youth Centre, Trinity Avenue
Llandudno, Conwy, LL30 2NQ
Tel: 01492 877326
Email:Howard.Thomas@conwy.gov.uk

Llysfaen Youth Centre, Ysgol-y-Cynfran
Llysfaen, Conwy, LL29 8SS
Tel:01492 518128
Email:Debbie.Owens@conwy.gov.uk

Towyn Youth Centre, Towyn Road
Towyn, LL29 9ER, Tel: 01745 337908
Email:Kristina.Kordiak@conwy.gov.uk

Penmaenmawr Youth Centre, Bangor Road, Penmaenmawr, Conwy
LL34 6LE, Tel: 01492 623634

Llanrwst Youth Centre, Watling Street
Llanrwst, Conwy, LL26 0LS

CONWY INFO MOBILE

The Bus Stop Project, Peulwys Community House, Peulwys, Old Colwyn,
LL29 9LG, Tel: 01492 512970
Email: Tomos.Jones@conwy.gov.uk

Denbighshire

Rhuddlan Info Shop for Young People
5 The High Street, Rhuddlan,
Denbighshire, 01745 591932

Llangollen Youth Hostel Info Zone
Tyndwr Hall, Tyndwr Road, Llangollen
Denbighshire, LL20 8AR, 0870 770 5932

Flintshire

Bagillt Youth & Community Centre Info Zone, Sunnyside, Holywell Road
Bagillt, Flintshire, 01352 710390

Buckley Clinic Info Point, The Health C
Padeswood Road, Buckley, Flintshire
CH7 2JL, 1244 545277

Chat Clinic Info Point, Deeside College
Kelsterton Road, Connah's Quay
Deeside, Flintshire, CH5 4BR
01352 710390

Connah's Quay Youth & Community Centre Info Zone, Golftyn Lane
Connah's Quay, 01352 710 390

Flint Clinic Info Point, Borough Grove
Flint, Flintshire, 01352 710390

Flint Youth & Community Centre Info Point, Borough Grove, Flint, 01352710390

Greenfield Youth & Community Centre Info Point, School Lane, Greenfield Flintshire, 01352 710390

Gronant Youth & Community Centre Info Point, Pentre Lane, Gronant, 01352710390

Holywell High School Info Point, The Strand, Holywell, CH8 7AW, 01352 710 390

Mold Alun High School Info Point, Wrexham Road, Mold, CH7 1EP, 01352 710390

Sealand Youth and Community Centre Info Point, Sandy Lane, Garden City, Sealand, Flintshire, CH5 2JH, 01352 710 390

Young People's Info Mobile, Bagillt Youth and Community Centre, Sunnyside, Holywell Road, Bagillt, Flintshire, 01352 710390

Children's Information Service Info Point Children's' Information Service, The Westwood Centre, Tabernacle Street Buckley, Flintshire, 01244 547017

FYI Flintshire Youth Information Shop Flintshire Youth Information, 79 High Street, Holywell, Flintshire, 01352 710390

Gwynedd

Llanberis Youth Hostel Info Point, Llwyn Celyn, Llanberis, Caernarfon, LL55 4SR, 0870 770 5928

Llywio'r Llwybr Info Shop for Young People in South Gwynedd, Tŷ Abermawddach 4 Stryd Fawr, Blaenau Ffestiniog LL41 3ES, 01766 832186

Merthyr Tydfil

Young Persons Information Shop, Bus Station Building, Castle Street CF47 8BB, 01685-727085

Outreach Project Mobile Info Bus Station Building, Castle Street CF47 8BB, 01685-725332

Pen-y-Dre CEC Info Point Gurnos, 01685-722104

Library Info Points
Central- 01685-723057
Dowlais- 01685-723051
Treharris- 01443-410517
library.services@merthyr.gov.uk

Gurnos Info-Shop - 01685-721992
Working Links Info Point Castle House, Glebeland Street Merthyr Tydfil, 01685-388105

Careers Centre Info Point 01685-358180

Job Centre Plus Info point, 1 Glebeland Street, CF47 8AU, 01685-302000

Gates Project Info Point, 01685-729941

Megabytes Info Point, 01443-692020

Gellideg Foundation Info Point 01685-383929

3 G's Info Point - 01685-359999

Monmouthshire

Abergavenny Library Info Point
Abergavenny Library, Usk CEC
18 Maryport Street, Usk
NP15 1AF, 01291 674605

Caldicot Library Info Point, Caldicot Library, Woodstock Way, Caldicot NP26 4DB, 01291 426425

Central Kaff Info Zone, Central Kaff Welsh Street, Chepstow, 01291 625396

The Attik Info Zone, The Attik 9 Monnow Street, NP25 3EG 01600 772033

Neath Port Talbot

Alltwen Youth Club Info Point, Cilybebyll Community Centre, Dyffryn Road, Alltwen, Pontardawe, SA8 3BX, 01639 861900

Blaengwynfi Youth Club Info Point Blaengwynfi Boys & Girls Club, 34-35 Jersey Road, Blaengwynfi, Port Talbot SA13 3TA, 01639 861900

Bryn Youth Club Info Point, Bryn Village Hall, Maesteg Road, Bryn, Port Talbot SA13 2RY, 01639 861900

Bryncoch Youth Club Info Point, Bryncoch Community Centre, Main Road, Bryncoch, Neath, SA10 7TT, 01639 861900

Cimla Youth Club Info Point, Cimla RFC Moorland Road, Cimla, Neath SA11 1JL, 01639 632562

Croeserw Digilab Info Zone, Croeserw Community Centre, Sunny Crescent Croeserw, SA13 3PG, 01639 861900

Crynant Youth Club Info Point, Crynant Community Centre, Woodland Road Crynant Neath, SA10 8RL, 01639 861900

Cwmllynfell Info Point, Cwmllynfell Welfare Hall, Gwliym Road, Cwmllynfell SA9 2GH, 01639 861900

Cwmteen Drop In Centre Info Point, Cwmafan YWCA, 23 Depot Road, Cwmafan, Port Talbot, SA12 9BA, 01639 861900

Cymmer Youth Club Info Point Cymmer Afan Comprehensive School School Road, Cymmer Port Talbot SA13 3EL, 01639 861900

Glyncorrwg Youth Club Info Point Glyncorrwg Community Centre Glyncorrwg, Port Talbot 01639 861900

Glynneath Youth Centre Info Point Glynneath Training Centre, Oddfellows Street, Glynneath, Neath Port Talbot SA11 5DB, 01639 861900

Hengwrt Youth Club Info Point Hengwrt Sports Hall, Llansawel Crescent, Briton Ferry, 01639 861900

Neath Port Talbot CBC Youth Service Info Point, Youth Service, Cymric House Bethany Square, Port Talbot SA13 1PQ, 01639 861900

Neath Port Talbot Council for Voluntary Service Info Point, Tŷ Margaret Thorne, 17-19 Alfred Street Neath, SA11 1EF, 01639 631246

Neath Port Talbot Youth Council Info Point, Youth Service, Cymric House Bethany Square, Port Talbot SA13 1PQ, 07855430966 01639 861900

Neath YMCA Info Point, Llety Nedd Pen-Dre, Neath, 01639 861900

Port Talbot YMCA Info Point, Talbot Road, Port Talbot, 01639 887034

Route 16 - Social Services Info Point Route 16, 11 High Street, Pontardawe SA8 4HU, 01792 832050

Sandfields Youth Club and Digilab Info Point and Zone, Sandfields Community Education Centre, Seaway Parade Port Talbot, SA12 7BL, 01639 861900

Seven Sisters Youth Club Info Point Seven Sisters Community Centre Brynhyfryd Terrace, Seven Sisters Neath, SA10 9DN, 01639 861900

SNAP Cymru Neath Info Zone, SNAP Cymru Neath, 43 Alfred Street Neath, SA11 1EH, 01639 632192

Taibach Youth Club Info Point, Taibach Community Centre, Margam Road Port Talbot, SA13 3BA, 01639 861900

Tonna Cyber Café Info Zone, Tonna Community School, School Road Tonna, Neath, SA11 3EJ, 01639 861900

Flexible Learning Programme Info Point Llandarcy Community Centre, Prettyman Drive, Llandarcy, 01639 861900

Youth Service – Duke of Edinburgh's Award Info Point, Llangatwg Comprehensive Schol, Cadoxton, Neath, SA10 8DB, 01639 861900

Youth Service Detached Team Info Point Taibach Library, Commercial Road Taibach, Port Talbot, 01639 790980

Newport

Newport Info Shop, 133 Commercial Street, NP20 1LY, 01633 784054

For further information regarding the following outreach provisions, please contact the Info Shop on 01633 784054.

Information Points
Graig Youth Centre * POD, YMCA Pillgwenlly * Gaer Community Office, Gaer * Maesglas Community Network Office, * Ringland Resource Centre, Ringland * Monnow Youth & Community Centre, Bettws * Streets Ahead Flat, Bettws

Information POINT Satellites
Hatherleigh Youth Club * Alway Café Youth Club * Ringland Youth Club
EDGE / Maindee Youth Club * Maesglas Youth Club * Gaer Youth Club * Duffryn Youth Club * Caerleon Youth Club
Underwood Youth Club

Information Zones – St Julians Info Zone

SNAP Cymru Gwent Info Point
SNAP Cymru Gwent, 17 Gold Tops
Newport, NP20 4PH, 012633 257128

PEMBROKESHIRE

Pembrokeshire Youth Information Co-Ordinator: Rose Davis, Tel: 01646 680863
Email: rose.davis@pembrokeshire.gov.uk

Pembrokeshire Youth Information Service
Email: youth.info@pembrokeshire.gov.uk
Text: 07770 568186
Website:
www.pembrokeshireyouthzone.co.uk

Pembrokeshire Youth Mobile Zone
Bringing information, advice and guidance to young people across Pembrokeshire. – 01646 680863

Youth Centres:
Information is available to young people at youth centres across Pembrokeshire:

Fishguard – The Bunkhouse Youth Centre Info Point, Rope Walk, Fishguard,
Tel: 01348 874713

Fishguard & Goodwick Young Persons Project Info Zone, The Point, Unity Hall, Ropewalk, Fishguard, Pembrokeshire, SA65 9BT, Contact: Dawn Nicholson
Tel: 01348 875467

Haverfordwest - The Garage Youth Centre Info Zone, Haverfordwest Community Learning Centre, Off Dew St, Haverfordwest, SA61 1ST
Tel: 01437 769523

Garth Youth and Community Project Info Zone, The Hive, Goshawk Road, Haverfordwest, Pembrokeshire, SA61 2UB, Contact: Anji Tinley
Tel: 01437 764655

Hubberston Youth Centre Info Zone
Hubberston Community Learning Centre, Church Rd, Hubberston, SA73 3PL
Tel: 01646 693216

Milford Haven - The Junction Youth Centre Info Point, Milford Haven Community Learning Centre, St Peters Road, Milford Haven, Tel: 01646 693727

Neyland Youth Centre - The Club-Info Zone Charles St, Neyland, Pembrokeshire, SA73 1SA, Tel: 01646 600614

Pembroke Dock Youth Centre Info Zone, Bush St, Pembroke Dock, SA73 6HQ, 01646 682823

Project Milford Info Point, 14 Fulke Street, Milford Haven, Pembrokeshire, SA71 4AE
Tel : 01646 693727

The Tanyard Youth Project Info Zone Commons Road, Pembroke, Pembrokeshire, SA71 4AE, Tel: 01646 680068

Tenby Youth Centre Info Zone, Tenby Community Learning Centre, Greenhill Avenue, Tenby, SA63 7HL, 01834 849182

Schools Info Points, School-based youth workers offer information points - visit the Youth Room at the following schools:

Milford Haven School Info Point, Steynton Road, Milford Haven, SA73 1AE

Pembroke School Info Point, Bush Pembroke, SA71 4RL

Sir Thomas Picton School Info Point Queensway, Haverfordwest, SA61 2NX

Tasker Milward School Info Point, Portfield Avenue, Haverfordwest, SA61 1EQ

The Greenhill School Info Point, Heywood Lane, Tenby, SA70 8BN

Ysgol Bro Gwaun Info Point, Heol Dyfed Fishguard, SA65 9DT

Ysgol Y Preseli Info Point Crymych, SA41 3QH

Powys

Radical Mobile Information for Young People Info Mobile (Powys South) Dolgerddon Hall, Dark Lane, Rhayader LD6 5DA, 01597 810 877
mail to radical@powys.gov.uk

Mayp Mobile Information Bus for Young People (Powys North)
For times in your area call - 01938 559130
mailto: mayp@ukonline.com

Rhondda Cynon Taff

R.C.T Youth Service Info Point
Beddau Community Education Centre
Pencoedcae Rd, Beddau, RCT
CF38 2AE, 01443 204551

Continuing Education Centre Info Zone
Crawshay Street, Ton Pentre
Tel - 01443 424400

SNAP Cymru Info Zone, 89 Talbot Road, Talbot Green, 01443 220150

Barnardo's Info Zone, 21 Morgan street Pontypridd, 01443 486645

Swansea

Info-Nation Info Shop, 47 The Kingsway Swansea, SA1 5HG, 01792 484010

Blaen-y-Maes Youth Support Centre Info Zone, Portmead Avenue, Blaen-y-Maes, Swansea, 01792 583469

Townhill Youth Support Centre Info-Zone Paradise park Info Zone, Powys Park, Townhill, Swansea, 01792 470270

Birchgrove Community Centre Info Point 72 Trewen Road, Birchgrove, 01792 324911

Bonymaen Community Centre Info Point Anne davies, Norwood House, Tydraw Road Bonymaen, Swansea, SA1 7BG, 01792 635418, Anne.davies2@swansea.gov.uk

Clase Community Centre Info Point 12 Second Avenue, Clase, SA6 7LM

Gorseinon Library Info Point 15 West Street, Gorseinon Swansea County Council SA4 4AA Carole.bonham@swansea.gov.uk

Llangyfelach Community Centre Info Point 8 Rockland Terrace, Waunwen, SA1 6FL

Penclawdd Community Centre Info Point 124 Pencaerfenni Park, Crofy, SA4 3SQ 01792 851717

Townhill, Gors & Mayhill Community Centres Info Point, Townhill Youth Support Centre, Paradise Park, Powys Park, Townhill Centre – 01792 470270

Waunarlwydd Community Centre, 63 Brithwen Road, Waunarlwydd, Swansea. SA5 4QT, 01792 635417

Youth Librarian Info Point, Library H.Q. County Hall, Oystermouth Road, Swansea. SA1 3SN, 01792 636319

Birchgrove Comprehensive Info Point, Birchgrove Road, Birchgrove, Swansea, SA7 9NB, 01792 535400

Daniel James Comprehensive School, 2 Heol Emrys, Primrose Court, Penlam, SA6 7AD

Bishop Gore School Info Point, Delabeche Road, Sketty, SA2 9AP, 01792 535400

Dylan Thomas Community School Info Point John Street, Cockett, Swansea SA2 0FR, 01792 610300

Morriston Comprehensive Info Point Heol Maes Eglwys, Morriston, Swansea SA6 6NH, 01792 797745

Penyrheol Comprehensive Info Point Pontarddulais Road, Gorseinon SA4 4FG, 01792 533066

Ysgol Gyfun Gwyr Info Point Talbot Street, Gowerton, Swansea SA4 3DB, 01792 872403

Pentrahafod School Info Point, Pentremawr Road, Hafod, SA1 2NN

Clydach Youth Club Info Point, Canoldra centre, Jockey Street, Swansea

SCVS Info Point, Voluntary Action centre 7 Walter Road, Swansea SA1 5NF

Dan-y-Coed Activity Centre Info Point Dan-y-Coed House, Huntington Close West Cross, Swansea, SA3 5AL

Borfa House Info Point, Port Eynon Swansea, SA3 1NN

Rhossili Activity Centre Info Point Middleton, Swansea, SA3 1RJ

Ty Gwaun Info Point, Llwyncelyn Campus,
Cockett Road, Cockett
Swansea County Council SA2 0FJ
01792 522851

Torfaen

Ashley House Youth Centre Info Point
Mount Pleasant Road, Pontnewydd
Cwmbran, Torfaen, 01633 869590

Blaenafon Information Shop Info Zone
The Doorway
69/70 Broad Street, Blaenafon
Torfaen, NP4 9NH, 01495 793109

Cwmbran Centre for Young People Info
Zone, Cwmbran Centre for Young People
Glyndwr Road, Cwmbran
Torfaen, 01633 875851

New Inn Info Shop Info Point
Zone 2, The Old Caretakers House
The Highway, New Inn, Pontypool
Torfaen, NP4 0PH
01495 762859

St Dials Info Point
Cocker Avenue
Cwmbran, Torfaen
01633 861190

Thornhill Youth Centre Info Point
Thornhill Community Centre
Leadon Court
Thornhill, Cwmbran, Torfaen

Tŷ Rosser Gwyn Info Point
Youth Activity Centre
Flats 1 & 2
Tŷ Rosser Gwyn Road
Varteg
Pontypool
Torfaen
NP4 7SQ
01495 774320

Coed Eva Youth Centre Info Point
Ton Road
Fairwater
Cwmbran
NP44 7LE
01633 862515

Vale of Glamorgan

Area 41 Info Zone
Area 41 & Vale Youth Forum
41 Holton Road
Barry, Vale of Glamorgan
CF63 4HB
01446 745670

Cowbridge Youth Centre Info Zone
Cowbridge Youth Centre
The Old Court
Westgate
Cowbridge
Vale of Glamorgan
CF71 7AH
01446 774460

Llantwit Major Youth Centre Info
Zone
Llantwit Major Youth Centre
Station Road
Llantwit Major
Vale of Glamorgan
CF61 1ST
01446 792141

Penarth Youth Project / Info Shop
Penarth Information Shop
1a Stanwell Road
Penarth
Vale of Glamorgan
CF64 2AB
029 2040 5305

WREXHAM

Wrexham Info Shop
2 North Arcade, Chester Street, Wrexham
(Entrance to the Peoples Market)
(01978) 358900
infoshop@wrexham.gov.uk

8 x INFO POINTS @

Yale College
Grove Road
Wrexham

Yale College
Bersham Road
Wrexham

Childrens Ward
Wrexham Maelor Hospital
Wrexham

Brynteg Community House
Brynteg
Wrexham

The Venue
Plas Madoc Estate
Wrexham

Centre for Creative Arts
Victoria Youth Centre
Wrexham

The Venture
Garner Road
Wrexham

Caia Park Partnership
Caia Park
Wrexham

Call the Info Shop on (01978) 358900 for times when these Info Points are open

WEBSITES

Young Newport Website
www.youngnewport.co.uk

Newport's Young Peoples Partnership has commissioned the www.youngnewport.co.uk website to give young people better information about the services, activities, and opportunities that are available for them in Newport & their 'entitlements'.

Sexual Health Info Shop Website
www.willynilly.org.uk

Note down your nearest Info Outlet:

What is Digital Storytelling?

Digital Stories are "mini-movies" created not by star Directors and major studios, but by anyone with a memory to share or a story to tell - using cameras, computers, scanners and their own photo albums. The Digital Storytelling movement is based on the belief that everyone has a story to tell and new technology means that people without big budgets behind them can create a short, personal "story film" that can be shown on a website or on DVD screen, even on terrestrial TV. The idea is to show the richness of life in our communities through stories made by the people of those communities.

The Digital Storytelling movement started in the early nineties in the USA, where the Center for Digital Storytelling in California has run many workshops teaching people how to do it. Thousands of people have taken part, creating stories based on their personal archives. In 2001, Photojournalist Daniel Meadows, inspired by this work in the USA, was seconded to BBC Wales to develop Capture Wales' Digital Storytelling Project.

Digital Storytelling

'I've thought of Digital Stories as "scrapbook television'. Short, personal, multimedia tales, told from the heart. They are rich on feeling, and - because, in theory, anyone can make them, and publish them on screens anywhere - they have the potential to be a very democratic kind of storytelling. The Wales of Capture Wales is not the media cliché post-industrial Wales of pit closures, redundant workers, quaint folk in pointy hats, Shirley Bassey, Tom Jones, Catherine Zeta Jones, and lovely mountains covered in sheep. No, it's the personal story of a country talking to itself".

Since then, encouraged by the pioneering work of the BBC, a number of Digital Storytelling projects have grown up across Wales, involving people from education, local government, information technology and the arts. A highly successful example is the Breaking Barriers project set up by Kate Strudwick, Senior Arts Development Officer for Caerphilly County Borough Council. "If you can give a voice to people whose voices are rarely heard, then you can encourage social inclusion. People of all ages can take part, learning new skills - all they need to have is a story to tell".

Everyone has a story to tell...

All over Wales, people are making Digital Stories about real-life experiences and each story is as individual as the person who made it. Digital Stories are two-minute personal films created by the storyteller, using their own photos, words and voice.

Capture Wales is the BBC's award-winning Digital Storytelling project which came out of a partnership formed in 2001 between BBC Wales and Cardiff University. At BBC Capture Wales workshops, people gather at venues like community centres, schools and village halls.

Regardless of previous computer experience, anyone can apply for a place on the workshop, because the BBC team shows people how to craft and record their stories, how to capture images and use video editing techniques to build their own Digital Story, using computers, digital cameras and scanners.

Everyone takes away not only a copy of their story but also a set of new skills learned during the workshop

Build your own Digital Story

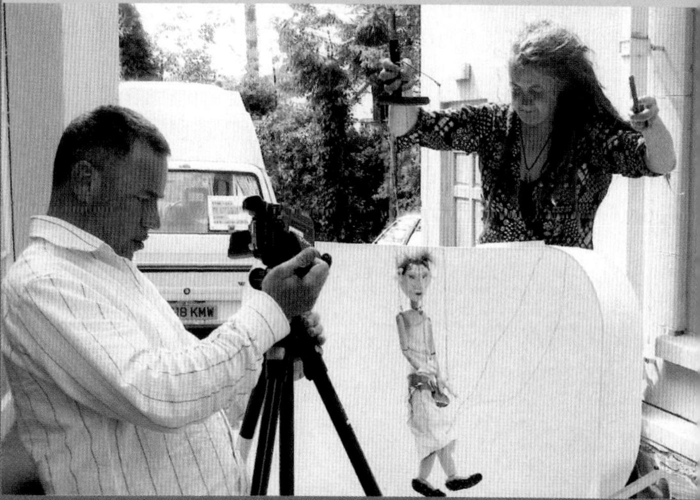

"I learned an awful lot, particularly about myself." - Tahir, Cardiff.

"Brilliant experience... we need more TV like this!" - Pete, Aberystwyth

Digital Stories appear on:

the web

bbc.co.uk/capturewales and **bbc.co.uk/cipolwgargymru**

the telly

BBC 2W - digital TV for Wales and on **'Your Stories'**, behind the red button on interactive, digital satellite services

the radio

Radio Cymru and **BBC Radio Wales**

You can find out more about Capture Wales by visiting the website.

'I made my first Digital Story in college when I was 14. It was like making a real movie'

Libby, Wrexham

www.yale-wrexham.co.uk/digitalstories

Yale College, Wrexham

BEING YOUNG AND ...

Being You

Everyone has a story to tell

Tell Yours

BEING YOUNG AND ...

Are you sick of being labelled? If you are, this project is for you

If you are young and...
a traveller, homeless,
a young parent...

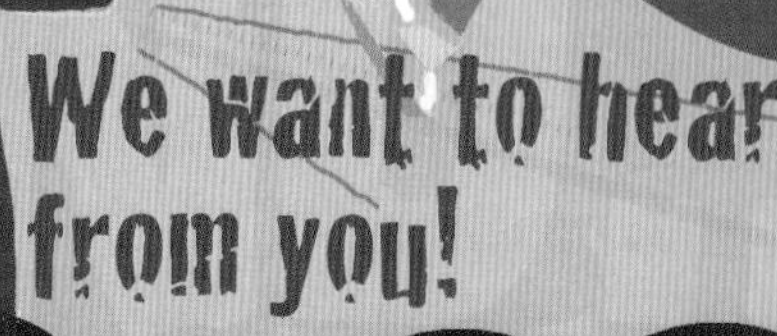

We want to hear from you!

BEING YOUNG AND ...

Canllaw Online is running a Digital Storytelling project called Being Young And... working with young people and CREDU Digilabs to stamp on stereotypes and turn labels on their heads, letting young people tell their own stories in their own unique ways. We are looking for stories about being young and... Being Me, Homeless, A Parent, Lesbian, Gay or Bisexual, Adopted, A Self Harmer, An Asylum Seeker, Bullied, Disabled, A Young Offender, Diagnosed With (Kidney Failure, Diabetes, Asthma, Eczema, an STI, ADHD, Dyslexia etc), Interested In (politics, volunteering, new media, music etc), Addicted To (gambling, games, smoking, alcohol, shopping, eating etc). But if you have a different story about your life as a young person, we want to know! We will share your story with other young people.

BEING YOUNG AND ...

Work with us to tell your tale!

Our staff will help you write a script, take and scan photographs, manipulate images, take video clips, record your voiceover and edit it all together to make your very own Digital Story.

We are running a seriese of workshops that you may want to take part in. Text your name, address and e-mail to 07800140769 (start your text with "Digistory") or e-mail ed@canllaw-online.com (texts will be charged at your normal rate, depending on your service provider. Remember to get permission from the bill-payer before texting).

Send in a story to snatch yourself a mobile phone!

Create your own Digital Story and send us the bits – we'll put it together for you and publish it on the CREDU Portal. All entries will go into a prize draw and the lucky person drawn as the winner will be able to pick out a pay-as-you-go mobile phone for themselves up to the value of £100!!! Are we good to you or what?

Simply write a small script (no more than 100 words) and put together up to 12 photos or drawings and send them in to Tell us a Story, Canllaw Online, Suite 5, The Octagon, Caerphilly Business Park, Van Road, Caerphilly, CF83 3ED. Closing date 31st March 2007. For competition rules, check out www.wise1520.info

under 26?

get money off stuff

get the Euro<26 Discount Card

to get your hands on a discount card, send proof of your age (copy of drivers license or passport) and your name, address and mobile number to euro26@canllaw-online.com or post to euro26, canllaw online, suite 5, the octagon, caerphilly business park, van road, caerphilly, cf83 3ed
(the card costs £7 or is free to 16-year-olds)

read on for discounts...

Culture & Going Out: Clubs & Venues

Megabowl Cardiff - 376 Newport Road, Cardiff, CF23 9AE, Tel 029 20 461666
Discount: Sunday to Thursday, buy one game and get one free

Culture & Going Out: Cultural Centres

Centre for Alternative Technology
Machynlleth, Powys, SY20 9AZ,
Tel 01654 70 59 52
Discount: £1.00 discount off admission

Centre for Alternative Technology

Glyn-Coch Craft Centre - Ffynnongain Lane, Pwll Trap, St Clears, Carmarthenshire, SA33 4AR
Discount: 10% off DIY Pottery & Ceramic Painting

Rhondda Heritage Park
Lewis Merthyr Colliery, Coed Cae Road, Trehafod, RCT, CF37 7NP
Discount: 20% off

Culture & Going Out: Museums and Galleries

Ceredigion Museum
Terrace Road, Aberystwyth, SY23 2AQ
Discount: 10% off items sold in the shop

Llangollen Motor Museum
Pentrefelin, Llangollen, LL20 8EE
Discount: 50p off admission price

Model House Craft & Design Centre
Bull Ring, Llantrisant, CF72 8EB
Discount: 10% on any goods purchased in the gallery or shop

Culture & Going Out: Miscellaneous

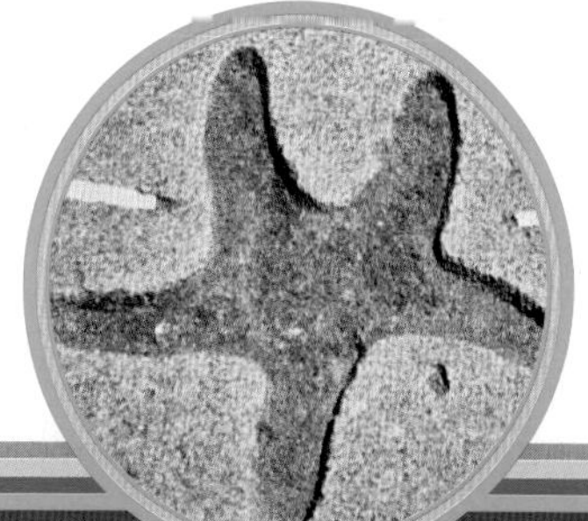

Anglesey Sea Zoo
Brynsiencyn, Anglesey
Discount: Group Rate

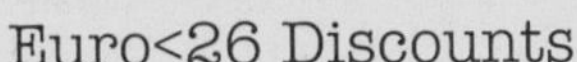

Education:

Driving Schools

Learn to drive with **Bob Lush School of Motoring**

Discount: £1 off every lesson

Bob Lush School of Motoring is an independent driving school run by a fully qualified DSA Approved Driving Instructor and member of the Motor Schools Association. We operate in the Cardiff, Penarth and Caerphilly areas. We provide all levels of driving instruction with lessons of one hour or two-hour duration and strive to provide a professional and friendly service at reasonable cost. Learning to drive is a serious business but it should also be enjoyable - the more you enjoy your lessons the quicker you will learn.

35 Hazel Tree Close, Radyr, Cardiff, CF15 8RS
Web site www.boblush-som.co.uk
email info@boblush-som.co.uk
Telephone 02920 843268
Mobile 07801 560343

Language Courses

Meirionydd Languages

Bodyfuddau, Trawsfynydd, Gwynedd, LL41 4UW

Discount: 10% off

Other Education

Computer@id

Training Centres across South Wales – phone 01792 610550 or e-mail training@computeraidwales.com or check out www.computeraidwales.com

Discount: 10% off standard 1 day ICT training courses

Health & Beauty: Hairdressers

Saks Hair & Beauty
11 St John Street, Cardiff, CF10 1GL
Tel: 029 20 382525 Cardiff@sakshairandbeauty.co.uk
Discount: 20% off services Monday to Thursday

Places to Eat: Fast Food

Discount: 15% off – collection only – at these Domino's Pizza: 254 Quarella Road, Bridgend 01656 668877 * Piccadilly Square, Caerphilly 029 20 882223 * 17 Holton Road, Barry 01446 420042 * Wain Bakery, Broadway, Pontypridd 01443 480680 * 356 Chepstow Road, Newport 01633 280011 * Malpas Road Retail Development, Malpas Road, Newport 01633 852222 * 3 Caradoc Road, Cwmbran 01633 833811 * High Street, Blackwood 01495 251133

Discount: 20% off all pizzas and starters at these Domino's Pizza: 206 Cowbridge Road East, Canton, Cardiff, CF5 1GX 029 20 232000 * 62 Crwys Road, Roath, Cardiff 029 20 229977 * Mermaid Quay, Cardiff Bay 029 20 451851

Places to Stay:

Guesthouses:

Anchor Guest House

Enville Road, Broad Haven, Haverfordwest, Pembrokeshire, SA62 3JN * www.anchorguesthouse.co.uk * 01437 781476

Discount: 10% off

Hotels

Tŷ Mawr Hotel - Llanbedr, Gwynedd, LL45 2NH * 01341 241 440

Tŷ Mawr HOTEL

Discount: April to October:

20% off Bed & Breakfast Monday – Thursday

10% off Bed & Breakfast Friday, Saturday and Sunday

Discount: November to March: 20% off Bed & Breakfast Monday – Sunday (Double room, per person per day, sharing, en-suite = £35 * Single room, per person per day, en-suite = £45)

Other Accommodation - **Hafod Elwy Hall**

Discount: Free midweek 3 night breaks offered in luxury 4 star historical home to young people, in return for 3 mornings (4 hours daily) worked on the land. Breakfast and dinner included. This is hard work so applicants must be willing and very fit. Breaks are in late June/early July 2007 with a possibility of Autumn dates if scheme goes well. Non-smoking establishment. For further information on property see www.hafodelwyhall.co.uk for further information on break telephone 01690 770345 or e-mail enquiries@hafodelwyhall.co.uk.

Hafod Elwy Hall . Bylchau . Denbigh . North Wales . LL16 5SP

YHA (Youth Hostel Association)

Independent travel at affordable prices! Whether you are planning on a short break to explore England and Wales or embarking on a year's odyssey around the world, you'll find a range of youth hostels in the locations you need. There are over 4,000 hostels in more than 80 countries and as you would expect, all of them provide you with a good night's sleep in friendly surroundings at an affordable price. YHA members always know what to expect, as all youth hostels must meet the International Youth Hostel Federation's safety and security standards.

If you are 14 or over you can stay in a hostel on your own or with friends, for a great way to experience your first holiday without your parents!

Discount: All Euro <26 card holders can take advantage of a special Under 26 membership offer of ONLY £5.00. To claim call 0870 770 8868 and quote reference Euro26-06 (Terms & Conditions apply). Students and Young People, not traveling as part of a group, can claim a concession of £3.00 from the Youth Hostels overnight charge on production of a valid Euro <26 card.

For more information or to make a booking visit www.yha.org.uk

Places to Stay: Hostels

YHA (Youth Hostel Association)

YHA Bangor (shown below)
Tan-y-Bryn, Bangor, Gwynedd, LL57 1PZ * 0870 770 5686
bangor@yha.org.uk

YHA Betws-y-Coed
Swallow Falls, Betws-y-Coed, Gwynedd, LL24 0DW
01690 710796
betwsycoed@yha.org.uk

YHA Borth
Morlais, Borth, Ceredigion, SY24 5JS * 0870 770 5708
borth@yha.org.uk

YHA Brecon
Groesffordd, Brecon, Powys, Wales, LD3 7SW * 0870 770 5718
brecon@yha.org.uk

YHA Broad Haven
Broad Haven, Haverfordwest, Pembrokeshire SA62 3JH
0870 770 5728
broadhaven@yha.org.uk

YHA Bryn Gwynant
Nantgwynant, Caernarfon, Gwynedd, LL55 4NP
0870 770 5732
bryngwynant@yha.org.uk

YHA Capel Curig
Plas Curig, Capel Curig, Betws-y-Coed, LL24 0EL
0870 770 5746
capelcurig@yha.org.uk

YHA Capel-y-Ffin
Capel-y-Ffin, Llanthony, nr Abergavenny, Monmouthshire NP7 7NP
0870 770 5748
capelyffin@yha.org.uk

YHA Cardiff
2 Wedal Road, Roath Park, Cardiff CF14 3QX
0870 770 5750
cardiff@yha.org.uk

Places to Stay: Hostels

YHA (Youth Hostel Association)

YHA Conwy
Larkhill, Sychnant Pass Road,
Conwy, LL32 8AJ
0870 770 5774
conwy@yha.org.uk

YHA Danywenallt (shown here)
Talybont-on-Usk, Brecon Powys,
LD3 7YS * 0870 770 6136
danywenallt@yha.org.uk

YHA Idwal Cottage
Nant Ffrancon, Bethesda, Bangor,
Gwynedd, LL57 3LZ
0870 770 5874
idwal@yha.org.uk

YHA Lawrenny
Lawrenny, Pembrokeshire,
SA68 0PN * 0870 770 5914

YHA Kings
Kings, Penmaenpool, Dolgellau,
Gwynedd, LL40 1TB
0870 770 5900
kings@yha.org.uk

YHA Llanberis
Llwyn Celyn, Llanberis,
Caernarfon, Gwynedd,
LL55 4SR
0870 770 5928
llanberis@yha.org.uk

YHA Llanddeusant
The Old Red Lion, Llanddeusant,
Carmarthenshire, SA19 9UL
0870 770 5930
llanddeusant@yha.org.uk

YHA Llwyn-y-Celyn
Libanus, Brecon, Powys, LD3
8NH
0870 770 5936
llwynycelyn@yha.org.uk

YHA Manorbier
Manorbier, nr Tenby,
Pembrokeshire, SA70 7TT
0870 770 5954
manorbier@yha.org.uk

Places to Stay: Hostels

YHA (Youth Hostel Association)

YHA Llangollen (middle)
Tyndwr Road, Llangollen,
Denbighshire, LL20 8AR
0870 770 5932
llangollen@yha.org.uk

YHA Marloes Sands
Runwayskiln, Marloes,
Haverfordwest, Pembs, SA62 3BH * 01646 636667 (01629) 592708 for bookings more than 7 days in advance)
reservations@yha.org.uk

YHA Penycwm
Whitehouse, Penycwm,
Haverfordwest,
Pembrokeshire, SA62 6LA
0870 770 5988
penycwm@yha.org.uk

YHA Pwll Deri
Castell Mawr, Trefasser,
Goodwick, Pembrokeshire,
SA64 0LR * 0870 770 6004
pwllderi@yha.org.uk

YHA Pen-y-Pass (shown here)
Pen-y-Pass, Nantgwynant,
Caernarfon, Gwynedd,
LL55 4NY
0870 770 5990
penypass@yha.org.uk

YHA Poppit Sands
Sea View, Poppit, Cardigan,
Pembrokeshire, SA43 3LP
0870 770 5996
poppit@yha.org.uk

YHA Rowen
Rhiw Farm, Rowen, Conwy,
LL32 8YW
0870 770 6012 (Bookings more than 7 days ahead: 0870 770 6113)

YHA Port Eynon (shown here)
Old Lifeboat House, Port Eynon,
Swansea, SA3 1NN
0870 770 5998
porteynon@yha.org.uk

Places to Stay: Hostels

YHA (Youth Hostel Association)

YHA Snowdon Ranger (shown below)
Rhyd Ddu, Caernarfon, Gwynedd, LL54 7YS
0870 770 6038
snowdon@yha.org.uk

YHA St Davids
Llaethdy, Whitesands, St David's, Pembrokeshire, SA62 6PR
0870 770 6042
StDavids@yha.org.uk

YHA Trefdraeth
Lower St Mary Street, Newport, Pembrokeshire, SA42 0TS
0870 770 6072
(+44) 1629 592708 for bookings more than 7 days in advance
reservations@yha.org.uk

Bunkhouses

YHA Blaencaron
Blaencaron, Tregaron, Ceredigion, SY25 6HL
0870 770 5700
reservations@yha.org.uk

YHA Dolgoch
Dolgoch, Tregaron, Ceredigion, SY25 6NR
0870 770 5976 (0870 770 8868 for bookings more than 7 days in advance)
dolgoch@yha.org.uk

YHA Tyncornel
Llanddewi-Brefi, Tregaron, Ceredigion, SY25 6PH
Reservation Department
0870 770 6113
tyncornel@yha.org.uk

Shopping: Body Care

Beauty Counter Direct
www.beautycounterdirect.co.uk

Discount:
Looking Good for Less! Discount Designer Beauty Brands.

Beauty Counter Direct is the fabulous online beauty retailer where you'll find top brands like D&G, Calvin Klein, Gucci, Clarins, Dior and many more, at up to 70% off high street prices.
Plus Euro <26 members can claim an extra 10% discount when you quote **Promotion Code: E26**
So now you can enjoy treating yourself to the latest celebrity must-have, or pamper family and friends with great gifts that won't break the bank.

To see the full range of beauty offers logon to
www.beautycounterdirect.co.uk
or telephone 0870 850 3196 to request a product list.

Shopping: Books

Siop Lyfrau'r Hen Bost
45 Stryd Fawr,
Blaenau Ffestiniog
Discount: 10% off

Shopping: Electrical

Ace TV & Video
158 Penarth Road, Grangetown, Cardiff, CF11 6NJ
Discount: 10% off

Beach Buoys
2 Marine Road, Broad Haven, Haverfordwest, Pembrokeshire, SA62 3JR
01437 781504
Discount: 15% off

Shopping: Body Care

Chevron Clothing Ltd
4 Henblas Street, Wrexham, LL13 8AD
Discount: 10% off

Oyster Clothing Ltd
28 Castle Arcade, Cardiff, CF10 1BW
Discount: 10% off

Weird Fish Retail Ltd
31 Royal Arcade, Cardiff, CF10 1AE
Discount: 10% off regular price merchandise (This does not include merchandise already reduced or offers in store. Not available online)

Shopping: Jewellery

North Wales Coins Ltd Jewellers
1B Penrhyn Road, Colwyn Bay, LL29 8LG
Discount: 10% off

Shopping: Music, CDs, etc.

Cardiff Violins
15-23 The Balcony,
Castle Arcade, Cardiff, CF10 1BY
Discount: 10% off (not to be used in conjunction with other offers or schemes)

Shopping: Sportswear, Sports Equipment

7twenty
15 Clwyd Street, Ruthin, Denbighshire, North Wales, LL15 1HF
Discount: 10% off

Tom Davies Cycles
312a Cowbridge Road East, Canton, Cardiff, CF5 1HW , 029 20 382999
Discount: 10% off

Top Sportswear & Equipment Ltd
14 Station Road, Ystradgynlais, Swansea, SA9 1NT
Discount: 10% off (including sales items but excluding school uniforms)

Sport & Leisure: Sport / Fitness

Gôl Football Centres
Lawrenny Avenue,
Canton, Cardiff
CF11 8BR.

Check out www.golcentres.co.uk

Discount: 20% off prices before 6pm Monday to Thursday and all day on Friday, Saturday and Sunday.

Simone's Health Clubs
15 Church Street, Monmouth, NP25 3BX
01600 772223
Discount: Student Membership prices: £28.00 per month & £25 joining fee

Sport & Leisure: Theme Parks

Greenwood Forest Park
Y Felinheli, Gwynedd, LL56 4QN
Discount: 10% off

Community Legal Service

FIND THE RED WORDS (OVER LEAF)….

Gwasanaeth Cyfreithiol Cymunedol

S	C	L	S	D	I	R	E	C	T
H	O	U	S	I	N	G	D	Z	Y
E	A	G	L	E	G	A	L	F	B
L	D	S	I	K	Q	D	J	H	E
P	V	C	B	C	G	E	R	I	N
U	I	A	H	I	I	B	A	E	E
B	C	X	F	V	Y	T	P	M	F
D	E	N	V	I	O	W	O	I	I
F	A	M	I	L	Y	B	T	R	T
L	E	G	A	L	A	I	D	C	S

legal services COMMISSION

COMISIWN gwasanaethau cyfreithiol

.... TO GET ADVICE

The LSC stands for the Legal Services Commission and is responsible for administering the budget for Legal Aid in England and Wales. This means that if you need Help with Advice and/or representation and cannot afford to pay for it yourself you could be eligible for Legal Aid via a specialist Solicitor, CAB (Citizen Advice Bureau) or other advice provider. Some examples of civil advice might be - a problem with Debt, Benefits, Housing or a Family matter. Alternatively you may need advice if you are accused of a crime and taken to a police station or if you have to appear in court about a criminal matter.

CLS Direct stands for Community Legal Services Direct. See over leaf for more ...

COMMUNITY LEGAL SERVICE DIRECT

If you want free high-quality legal information to help you deal with your legal problems, Community Legal Service Direct (CLS Direct) can help.

You can:

- read free legal information leaflets or legal help fact sheets
- search for a high-quality local legal adviser or solicitor
- search for legal information from a selection of the best advice websites in the UK
- find out if you qualify for legal aid
- if you qualify for legal aid call our national helpline 0845 345 4 345 for free advice about benefits, tax credits, housing, employment, education or debt problems.

  We are also on the web at:

www.clsdirect.org.uk

legal services COMMISSION

COMMUNITY LEGAL SERVICE AND THE ROLE OF THE LSC

The Community Legal Service (CLS) plays a vital role in helping to ensure that everyone has access to justice, in protecting your rights and in helping people to make improvements in their lives. It does this through providing independent high quality legal advice, representation, education and information.

As part of the CLS, The Legal Services Commission (LSC) directly funds legal services for eligible clients. Young people often need all sorts of advice and so if you need advice, you could be eligible for Legal Aid. Read on to find out more information ...

COMISIWN
gwasanaethau cyfreithiol

The Welsh Assembly Government wants every young person in Wales aged 11-25 to have the same rights or entitlements, things you are allowed/should have/have a right to. Rights come with responsibilities - for adults and for you as a young person. The things the Assembly thinks you should be entitled to are opportunities and choice:

1. Your Rights

a. To learn what your rights are and understand them - *Do you know what your rights are? There are lots of places where you can find out. Why not start by going to the Credu portal and accessing the Law and Rights section: http://www.credu.co.uk/izone/infoindex/law/*

b. Make sure you are able to claim them and to understand and accept the responsibilities arising from them - *Once you have found out your rights you may not fully understand them. There are plenty of people who can help you make sense of them like youth workers, teachers and information workers; why not ask at your local Info point or digilab about your rights and maybe look at doing a project to help you and your friends understand and make sense of your rights.*

2. Being Heard

It is your right to have the opportunity to be involved in making decisions, planning and reviewing an action that might affect you. Having a voice, having a choice, even if you don't make the decision yourself. Your voice, your choice.

Participation in decision making is very important for young people and in Wales there is a genuine commitment to ensuring young people have their say. There are lots of ways of getting involved in decision making. Every school in Wales should have a school council. Why not start by getting involved in this- you may wish to stand for election or at the very least you should ensure that your representative knows what your thoughts are. There are other organisations locally and nationally that you can get involved with too like the local youth forum or Funky Dragon http://www.funkydragon.org . You can also have your say in a number of ways through the Credu project – why don't you tell us what you think at the forum (http://forums.credu.co.uk/index.php; there are always lots of discussions taking place and you can tell us what you think about things, you can tell us what you like and what you really hate. You can also see what others think. You can also have you say by casting votes in our various votes in the Spotlight area of the Credu portal: http://www.credu.co.uk/spotlight/

3. Feeling good

To feel confident and feel good about yourself

There's lots to feeling good about yourself. It got a lot to do with your self esteem and confidence; find out more about this at http://www.canllaw-online.com/fe/family.asp?nodeidl2=240&level=3&nodeidl3=243. There are other things too that can help you feel good such as having a healthy diet and taking lots of exercise; why not check out the health section on the portal: http://www.credu.co.uk/izone/infoindex/health/.

You can also feel god by getting on well with others why not check out Family and Relationships section in the I section of the Credu portal: http://www.credu.co.uk/izone/infoindex/family/

a. To be able to learn about things that interest and affect you. *Getting the right education is one of the most important things you can do and in Wales there is a great opportunity to pick up learning at any stage and any age. It doesn't matter if you were good or bad at school you can always take up a new learning opportunity and find something that you enjoy and something that will contribute to your future. There are plenty of places that offer formal , informal and non formal learning opportunities, including a whole host of elearning and distance learning courses, so why not check out the Education section of the Credu portal: http://www.credu.co.uk/izone/infoindex/education/*

b. To enjoy the job that you do - *Work takes up a lot of time so it's really important to find a job that you like and can be good at. There are lots of ways in which you can get the right job for you; you can make sure you have the right skills and attitude that employers are looking for and that will help you get on. There are ways that you can present yourself to your best potential in your cv,in the way you look and how you communicate with others. Just remember your future employer needs someone like you as much as you need them so make sure that you understand each other and show that you can excel at a job given the right support and training.Why not look at the Employment and Training section of the Credu portal http://www.credu.co.uk/izone/infoindex/employment/ and find out what support Careers Wales can offer you in getting that perfect job - www.careerswales.com and www.cliconline.co.uk*

c. To get involved in the activities that you enjoy including leisure, music, sport and exercise, art, hobbies and cultural activities *Educative activities can be very interesting, enjoyable and relaxing and can extend beyond formal curricula. You have a right to take part in such activities and there are plenty of opportunities provided for you such as what your local Youth Service has on offer ; your local authority will offer a range of activities and national and local voluntary organisations will also have an exciting range of opportunities so why not check out the local info pages (505-527) and national and local voluntary organisation pages (528-529). Remember that the Credu project offers a whole range of such activities too through the portal and of course the 112 digilabs across Wales; find out where your nearest digilab is at http://www.credu.co.uk/izone/digilabs/*

5. Taking part / Getting Involved

To be involved in volunteering and to be active in your community - *There are loads of ways young people can volunteer and get involved in community activites gaining skills, making friends and enjoying the experience. There are loads of organisations that can help you – check out the national and local voluntary youth organisation pages (528-529). Why not ask at your local digilab about community and voluntary projects you can get involved with. Check out the Credu portal for information on Volunteering: http://www.credu.co.uk/spotlight/feature/?id=1695*

6. Being Individual

a. To be treated with respect and as an equal by everyone
b. To be recognised for what you have to contribute and of your achievments * c. To celebrate what you achieve
It is really important for young people to be themselves; to find out what they are all about, what they believe in and what makes them tick. You can find out lots of things about this area in the Family and Relationships bit on the Credu portal: http://www.credu.co.uk/izone/infoindex/family/. Why don't you put together a file/scrap – a kind of portfolio – with photos and descriptions of all the things you take part in from sport to drama and everything in between. You'll be surprised at how much you do when you think about it. Take a minute to be proud of your achievements!

7. Easy Access

Easy access in getting the best services that you should have, locally and nationally, and to have someone available to help you find them. *There are loads of services just for young people in Wales and you can find out more about these through you local digilabs and Info outlets http://www.credu.co.uk/izone/digilabs/ and in the local section and national and local voluntary youth organisation pages in this book (528-529). Don't forget all the many things the Credu project offers too as it's just for young people like you in Wales and is all about helping you reach your potential!*

8. Health & wellbeing

To lead a healthy life, both physically and emotionally
To be happy in life it helps to be healthy and there are loads and loads of things you can do to improve your health from eating a healthy balanced diet and taking lots of exercise through to relaxing and taking time out to chill when you're stressed. Find out more on the Credu portal at: http://www.credu.co.uk/izone/infoindex/health/

9. Access to information & guidance

To be able to get information, advice and support on a wide range of issues that affect your life, as and when you need it

In an increasingly complex society it is vitally important that young people can access quality information and have appropriate support to deal with such information.There are lots of information providers about and young people have a choice of services. Canllaw Online and the Credu project are all about information for young people and 2006 is the 21st year of the Canllaw Online initiative in Wales.A lot has happen since 1985 when young people and youth workers came together for the first time to look at a way to provide young people with the information they need;now there are Info Outlets across Wales where young people can access support and information relevant to their needs (http://www.credu.co.uk/izone/infooutlets/) and a variety of generic or special interest websites We use the Canllaw Info Index, a 10 heading classification system, to collate and sort information and offer a wide range of information under these headings (see next page)...

*Education * Employment and Training * Environment * World, Europe, Uk and Wales * Family and Relationships * Health * Housing * Law and Rights * Money * Sport and Leisure*

The Credu project has been developed to ensure that young people in Wales benefit from the latest technologies within the New Information Society and that young people can easily access quality information (via the Credu portal www.credu.co.uk)) and become the generators of digital content themselves by using all of the equipment on offer at digilabs.

Remember "Better information leads to better life choices"

10. safety & security

To live in a safe, secure home and community

It's important to have a safe place to live, a home that feels secure and a community that is the same. In other parts of the world this is not always the case – in Wales it is your entitlement as a young person.There are lots of ways in which we can all help to make our environments safer and more secure. We can learn to get on with our families , friends, neighbours and even enemies. We can stick to our own points of view but respect the fact that others are entitled to theirs even if we do not agree with them- check out the Family and Relationships section of the Credu portal (http://www.credu.co.uk/izone/infoindex/family/). We can help to ensure that people are law abiding by reporting crimes when we see them happening- check out the Law and rights section on the Credu portal (http://www.credu.co.uk/izone/infoindex/law/). We can help in local community activities and take pride in where we live, learning about our history and heritage.

Text in white and headings taken from Welsh Assembly Government (WAG) document on Extending Entitlement

The Electoral Commission

Make your vote count: Get involved in Politics

Radio 1 DJ Bethan Elfyn launches Democracy Disk

The Electoral Commission has produced a new interactive resource aimed at getting young people voting in next year's elections.

Democracy Disk is a CD-ROM that can be played on either your computer or CD player and features all the information you could want to know about Wales' politicians and democratic institutions.

From MEPs to local Councillors and MPs to AMs, Democracy Disk features interactive quizzes and games to help you learn who represents you on each level of government. But it isn't just an encyclopaedia of Welsh politics, Democracy Disk provides you with all the information you need to go out and get involved.

Presiding Officer Lord Dafydd Elis-Thomas AM encourages young people to vote in the 2007 National Assembly for Wales elections.

There are easy guides to registering to vote and how to vote, and tips on how you can get involved in politics like starting a local campaign, joining a youth council, or contacting your local representative.

The Electoral Commission

Make your vote count: Get involved in Politics

Exclusive to Wales, Democracy Disk features nine music tracks from Wales' most promising, up and coming artists.

Listen to the songs and help select the winning artist, who will play a part in the 2007 National Assembly for Wales elections, by voting for your favourite musician online.

Turnout among 18 - 24 year olds was only 16% at the 2003 National Assembly for Wales elections, and The Electoral Commission want to see a lot more young people voting in the 2007 Assembly elections.

We know that you feel strongly on the issues that affect you such as the environment, education, housing and the cost of your night out. So make your vote count, get Democracy Disk now and get involved!

To request your free copy of Democracy Disk contact the Electoral Commission on 02920 346800 or email infowales@electoralcommission.org.uk.

Canllaw Online Info Index

1 - Education

2 - Employment & Training

3 - Environment

4 - World, Europe, UK & Wales

5 - Family & Relationships

6 - Health

7 - Housing

8 - Law & Rights

9 - Money

10 - Sport & Leisure

1.1 Basic Skills
Basic Skills Essentials

1.2 School
A & AS Levels
Choices @ 16
Disability Education & Courses
Exams & Revision
GCSEs
Personal Development
Qualifications Essentials
School Essentials
SEN Special Education Needs
Welsh Baccalaureate

1.3 Social Issues at School
Bullying at School
Bunking off
Exclusion
Harassment
Teachers

1.4 College or Uni
College Essentials
Courses & Subjects
Degrees & Diplomas
Gap Years
Grants & Loans
Student Life
University Essentials

1.5 Home Learning
Community Education
Distance & E-learning
Education at Home

2.1 Training Schemes
Modern Apprenticeships
Skill Building
Training Essentials

2.2 Vocational Qualifications
City & Guilds
HNC & HND
NVQs & GNVQ

2.3 Unemployed?
Initiative
Jobcentre Plus
Retraining / New Trade
Princes Trust
Unemployed Essentials

2.4 Types of Work
Careers Essentials
Self Employment
Work Experience
Work from Home
Working UK
Working Abroad
Working Europe
Working Seasonal

2.5 Get that Job!
Applying for a Job
CVs & Application Forms
Interviews & Assessments
Recruitment Agencies

2.6 Grievances
Bullying in the Workplace
Employment Rights
Paid Leave & Maternity Leave
References
Sexual Harassment
Unfair Dismissal

2.7 New Job New Life
Contracts
Time off Work
Wages
Working Hours

2.8 Volunteering
Volunteering Abroad
Volunteering UK

3.1 The Animal Kingdom

Animal Rights
Animal Testing
Hunting
Pets
Wildlife, Zoos & Safari Parks

3.2 Environmental Issues

Biodiversity
Climate Change
Cloning & Genetics
Consumer Labelling
Earth
Famine & Drought
Farming & Agriculture
Flooding
Forest Fires
Logging
Over Population
Pollution
Renewable Energy
Sustainable Development

3.3 Get Active

Bin it!
Conservation
Countryside
Going Green
Recycling

Y Byd, Ewrop, DU, & Gymru
World, Europe, UK & Wales

5.1 Family & Relationship Issues

Abortion
Abuse
Adoption
Arguments
Attitudes & Stereotypes
Babies
Care
Children
Divorce
Family
Fostering
Friends
Marriage
Miscarriage
Parenthood
Peer Pressure
Young Carers

5.2 Love & Sex

Boyfriends & Girlfriends
Celibacy
Contraception
Dating
Falling in Love
Fertility
Kissing
Living Together
Making Love
Oral Sex
Orgasms
Sex Essentials
Sexuality
Splitting Up

5.3 Close to the Heart

Losing a Loved One
Problems & Emotions
Self Esteem
You

6.1 First Aid
First Aid Essentials

6.2 Substance Misuse
Alcohol
Drugs
Smoking

6.3 Mental Health
Anxiety
Compulsions
Depression
Panic Attacks
Phobias
Schizophrenia
Self Harm
Stress
Suicide

6.4 Relaxation & Coping
Counselling
Meditation
Relaxation
Sleeping & Dreaming

6.5 Diet & Exercise
Eating Disorders
Exercise & Keep Fit
Healthy Eating
Vegetarianism & Veganism

6.6 Medical Conditions
Acne
Allergies
Anaemia
Arthritis
Asthma
Autism
Burns
Cancer
Diabetes
Eczema
Epilepsy & Fits
Food Poisoning
Hay Fever
Headaches
Incontinence
M.E.
Meningitis
Stammering
Stings & Bites

6.7 Women's Health
Breasts
Cystitis
Genitals
Periods & PMS
Pregnancy
Thrush

6.8 Men's Health
Athletes Foot &
Jock Itch
Impotence
Penis
Prostate Cancer
Testicles

6.9 Looking Good?
Balding
Body Hair (shaving)
Body Odours
Cellulite & Stretch Marks
Dermatology
Flushing & Blushing
Hair & Scalp
Looking Your Best
Piercings
Plastic & Cosmetic Surgery
Sunbathing
Tattoos

6.10 Sexual Health
HIV & Aids
Safe Sex
STIs

6.11 Health Services
Alternative Medicine
Doctors
Donor Services
Emergencies
Eyes
Health Service
Injections & Immunisations
Patients' Rights
Teeth

Health
Iechyd
Health
Iechyd
Health
Iechyd
Health
Iechyd

Housing
Tai
Housing
Tai
Housing
Tai
Housing

8.1 Law & Police
Laws
Police

8.2 Your Legal Rights
Arrested?
Bail
Consumer Rights
Human Rights
Rights Essentials
Stop & Search

8.3 Crime
Abduction
Anti Social Behaviour
Crime Prevention & Personal Safety
Domestic Violence
Driving Offences
Drug Crime
Fraud
Murder & Manslaughter
Rape
Sex Trade
Sexual Harassment
Shoplifting
Smuggling
Stalking
Street Crime & Violence
Theft
Vandalism & Graffiti
Victims
Weapons & Firearms
Witnesses
Youth Crime

8.4 Punishment & Sentences
Criminal Records
Prison
Rehabilitation Centres
Remand
Young Offenders

8.5 Court Procedures
Courts
Jury Service
Trials

8.6 Discrimination
Discrimination Essentials
Equal Opportunities
Racism

8.7 Solicitors & Legal Services
Death & Wills
Legal Advice

Canllaw Online Info Index

9.1 Budgeting

Budgeting Essentials
Discount Cards

9.2 Financial Planning

Insurance
Interest Rates & Inflation
Investing
Pensions
Savings (ISAs, etc)
Stocks & Shares

9.3 Bank Accounts

Banks & Building Societies
Online Banking

9.4 Debt

Credit Cards
Debt Essentials
Gambling
Gambling
Hire Purchase (HP)
Loans
Overdrafts
Store Cards
Student Loan

9.5 Benefits

Benefits Essentials

9.6 Tax & NI

Income Tax
National Insurance
Value Added Tax (VAT)

1.1 Basic Skills

We use basic skills every day: when we talk to friends, read a newspaper, write a note, work out our change after buying a packet of crisps etc. Having good basic skills can help you achieve in the workplace, in education, at home and socially. At one time or another, we all struggle with basic skills. Many people hide their lack of basic skills from others rather than try to improve them. There is nothing to be ashamed of. In fact, it is thought that around one in seven people in the UK have serious problems with basic skills. For those who do have problems, there is help available. Many colleges and community projects offer courses in basic skills. It is also possible to study basic skills through home learning using books, tapes, videos or the Internet.

Dyslexia is a condition that inhibits the ability to read and write. Sufferers may not recognise letters or numbers well or may have trouble with writing. Around one in twenty people in the UK are dyslexic. If you have problems with reading and writing and think you might have dyslexia, there is help available for you. Inside school you may be entitled to specialised teaching, a tutor and oral help in examinations. Similar help plus support groups and guidance exists outside of school also.

The National Basic Skills Strategy for Wales
0845 602 1654
www.basic-skills-wales.org

Dyslexia Wales
01558 685 644
www.dyslexiawales.com

Basic Skills Agency
0207 405 4017
www.basic-skills.co.uk

Department for Education and Skills
0207 332 9535
www.dfes.gov.uk

Also check out:
> Distance & E-Learning
> Education At Home
> Qualifications Essentials
> Training Essentials
> Vocational Qualifications
> Careers Essentials

Following GCSEs (General Certificate of Secondary Education), A (Advanced) Levels are one of the next sets of qualifications available, taking two years of full-time study to complete in any of over 70 subjects. Although entry requirements vary to take most A Level subjects, it is usually necessary to gain a grade C or above in the same subject at GCSE level. In most subjects, students are assessed by exams taken at the end of each year, which account for between 70% and 80% of the mark. The rest of the grade is made up from coursework. Each grade has it's own number of UCAS points: an A grade is worth 120 points, B 100, C 80, D 60 and E 40 points.

An AS (Advanced Subsidiary) Level is the first year of A Level study. If a student completes only their first year, the results they achieve in their first year exams will be their AS Level grade. The number of UCAS points awarded to AS Levels is half of those given to A Levels.

AVCEs (Advanced Vocational Certificate of Education) are equivalent to A Levels but, featuring more coursework, place an emphasis on the application of theory. A full AVCE is worth two A Levels and a single AVCE is worth one. All A Level exams can be re-sat if your grades aren't adequate.

Welsh Joint Education Committee
02920 265 000
www.wjec.co.uk

BBCs AS Guru
www.bbc.co.uk/education/asguru

Project A Level
www.s-cool.co.uk

Careers Wales
0800 100 900
www.careerswales.com

Qualifications and Curriculum Authority
0207 509 5555
www.qca.org.uk

Also check out:

> Personal Development
> Exams & Revision
> Basic Skills Essentials
> Qualifications Essentials

Once you hit 16 and school is over, the world opens up to you. You can do whatever you want to take your life in the direction that you desire. Here are some of your options:

6th Form – You'll be able to study the subjects that you like in more depth and will gain vital education to take you forward in life.

College –College is a great chance for you to study subjects of your choice if those offered by your school are not suitable. You'll also get the chance to meet new people and enjoy the different atmosphere and educational style of college.

Employment – The world of work can offer so much. You can learn new skills, get responsibilities, improve your social life, have fun and best of all you get paid for it.

Employment with training – An apprenticeship can give you all of the above plus all of the new skills you'll be learning will count towards gaining a qualification.

Gap Year – Take a year out. You can spend time travelling or could volunteer for a charity. Both will be great fun and will open your mind to tons of new experiences.

You could also work from home, start your own business or re-take GCSEs if your results were not good enough for you.

Careers Wales
0800 100 900
www.careerswales.com

BBC - Education
www.bbc.co.uk/onelife/education

Hot Courses
0208 600 5300
www.hotcourses.com

Guide to Gap Years
www.gapyears.com

Also check out:
> College Essentials
> Training Essentials
> Careers Essentials
> Volunteering UK
> Volunteering Abroad
> Gap Years

Since the introduction of the Disability Discrimination Act, all educational institutions have had to provide the same level of education to everyone, regardless of disability where possible. This means that there is a world of educational opportunity open to you. However, it is necessary to think about the special needs that you have whether that be wheelchair access, specialist equipment or a support teacher and whether or not these needs will be met. It may be that the number of courses open to you at your local college is limited if they do not have adequate provisions for disabled people. However, there are specialist colleges that are specifically designed for disabled people. These are often residential colleges. So, choosing your own educational path is really just a matter of deciding what you want to do and where you want to go. If you have a disability, contact your local school or college, tell them what areas you are interested in and what your special requirements are.

Skill (National Bureau for Students with Disabilities)
www.skill.org.uk/wales/

MENCAP
www.mencap.org.uk/

Essential Aids (living aids for the disabled)
www.essentialaids.com

Disability Wales
www.disabilitywales.org

Choices and challenges for young disabled people
www.after16.org.uk

Special Needs Advisory Project for Wales
www.snapcymru.org

Also check out:

> Discrimination Essentials
> Equal Opportunities
> Disability Travel
> Disability Sport

There's no point in spending all of those hours, weeks, months and years studying if you don't put the effort into preparing for and taking exams. Just as important as the exam itself is the preparation. Before beginning your revision, draw up a schedule, allocating an adequate amount of time to each subject and taking into account other responsibilities like housework, a part-time job and socialising. You need to organise your revision materials (notes, books etc.) into a decent order – you don't want to spend your hour of revision searching through piles of paper to find your notes. If you think you've missed some important classes, ask your teacher to recommend a good study guide. Concentration during revision can be difficult so take regular short breaks, roughly five minutes every half an hour will keep your brain fresh. As far as the actual exam is concerned, you need to be 110% certain of where and when the exam is and you need to make sure that you leave in time to arrive at least 15 minutes before the start. It's also vital that you check that you have everything you need – pens, back-up pens, calculators etc. During the exam try not to be too nervous, take your time, read the question properly and remember that, whilst important, exams are not the end of the world!

BBC Revision Guide
www.bbc.co.k/schools/revision

Revision Advice and Help
01793 615 439
www.studysuccess.co.uk

Department for Education and Skills
0870 000 2288
www.dfes.gov.uk

Also check out:
> Stress
> Relaxation
> Qualifications Essentials
> Choices @ 16

The GCSE is the General Certificate of Secondary Education that's awarded to students who have completed the necessary assessment. There are over 45 GCSE subjects that can be studied. Subjects can be assessed in several ways; some are 100% course-work, some, 100% examination and others, a combination of both. Subjects either have a single GCSE award (the majority) but some bigger subjects have a dual award (two GCSEs) and other smaller ones are assessed with a GCSE Short Course (half a GCSE).

GCSEs are normally taken between the ages of 15 and 18. All students in Wales have to study and most take a GCSE in Maths, English, Science and Welsh. You also have to study RE and PE but taking a GCSE in these subjects is optional. In addition to these core subjects, pupils can take optional subjects in things like Art and Geography. Some subjects have tiered exam papers meaning that there are two different papers aimed at differing abilities. One paper is aimed at those expecting to achieve grades A-D, the other at C-G. Grades go from A*, which is the highest, to G. If you don't do as well as you had expected to in an exam, you can re-sit a paper and take the better mark out of the two results.

Welsh Joint Education Committee
02920 265 000
www.wjec.co.uk

BBC Revision Guide
www.bbc.co.uk/schools/gcsebitesize/

Official GCSE Guide
www.qca.org.uk/downloads/12815_student_gcse_guide_2005.pdf

Also check out:

> School Essentials
> Exams and Revision
> Basic Skills Essentials
> Choices @ 16
> Qualifications Essentials

Despite what some people would have you believe, being young isn't just about education. It is important though; after all, the skills and knowledge that you learn when you're young enable you to do the things that you enjoy when you're older. However, as well as gaining a decent educational grounding, being young is about finding yourself. As you grow older, you begin to realise what kind of person you are naturally. You'll find out exactly what type of people you like to hang out with, what gets you excited, what makes you mad and you'll discover the things you really enjoy and the things you really don't. Obviously, education does play a part in doing this for you (you may find that you really don't like maths for example!) but it's what you do in your spare time that can shape you as a person.

The world is a fascinating place, so get out there and get active. Try different things. If you find you don't like something, don't do it! Here are some of the things you could try: learn a new sport, take up a hobby like amateur dramatics or photography, do a course in something practical like flower arranging, learn a musical instrument, join a writing group.

The Duke of Edinburgh's Award
01753 727 400
www.theaward.org

BBC page on getting involved in film, music, writing, art and dance
www.bbc.co.uk/blast/

Careers Wales
0800 100 900
www.careerswales.com

Also check out:
- Choices at 16
- Basic Skills Essentials
- Attitudes @ Stereotypes
- Qualifications Essentials

Once you've negotiated the hurdles of your GCSEs, a whole world of qualifications opens up to you. It is up to you which subjects you choose to study and how you mix and match qualifications. Here is some basic information on the most popular qualifications:

National Vocational Qualification (NVQ)
NVQs are qualifications that are normally completed whilst at work. They show that a person can actually do a job rather than just do it in theory.

Advanced Extension Awards (AEA)
AEAs are aimed at the higher achieving students. Typically, the UK's top 10% of students in each subject may enter for the awards, which are usually taken at the same time as A Levels.

General National Vocational Qualification (GNVQ)
GNVQs are one or two year courses that are of a similar status as A Levels. They are currently being phased out and will no longer exist by 2007.

Key Skills
These are qualifications that deal with skills appropriate to many walks of life, including further education and the workplace. Subjects include Communication and Application of Number.

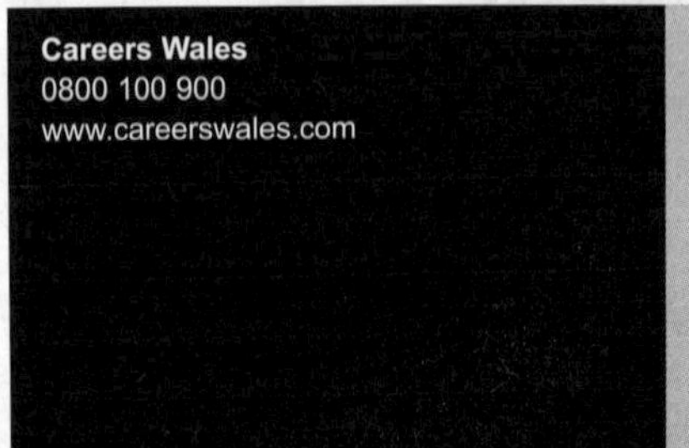

Also check out:
- College Essentials
- University Essentials
- Choices @ 16
- Courses and Subjects

"Don't do this!", "Stop that!", "...and what d'you think you're doing?"...School is chock full of rules. But every pupil has rights too. Schools have a code of conduct that spells out the school rules. Here are some of the main rules and rights you can expect:

Uniform – Most schools have a standard uniform that a pupil must wear. Religious variations depend on the school.
Attendance – Pupils must attend school regularly by law. Failure to do so may result in prosecution for the pupil's parents.
Detention – After-school detention is allowed, but both the pupil and their parents must be notified in advance. Detention cannot take place at a time that makes it unsafe for a pupil to walk home.
Vandalism – Obviously, vandalism will not be tolerated. A school can charge the pupil (or their parents) responsible for the cost of any damage.
Assemblies/Worship – Pupils must attend assemblies or worship as and when required unless their parents have withdrawn them on religious grounds.
Exclusion – Decisions on exclusion can only be made by head-teachers or acting head-teachers. Even if excluded from a school, pupils still have the right to free education.
Food – All schools must provide food and an eating area. Pupils whose parents are on income support are entitled to free meals.

Youth Information
www.youthinformation.com

Citizens Advice Bureau page on education on Wales
www.adviceguide.org.uk

Schoolsnet
www.schoolsnet.com

Also check out:
> Bullying at School
> Education at Home
> Bunking Off
> Exclusion
> Qualifications Essentials

1.EDUCATION

Special Educational Needs (SEN) 1.2 School

Those with Special Educational Needs (SEN) have difficulties or a disability that can make it harder for them to progress with their education than others of the same age. For example, they may have difficulty with speech, understanding or behaviour. The special educational needs of a student may be identified by a teacher, parents or by the student themselves. Once a need has been spotted, the school or college will find a way to help, such as a different style of teaching, extra equipment or help from an outside source, like an educational psychologist. No help will be forced onto a student. Instead, the student, the parents and the teachers will come to a mutual agreement about what help is required. Most educational institutions have provisions to help students with SEN.

Citizens Advice Bureau information on SEN
www.adviceguide.org.uk/em/index/family_parent/education/special_educational_needs/index/family_parent/education/special_educational_needs.htm

Snap Cymru
www.snapcymru.org

National Bureau for Students with Disabilities
0800 328 5050
/www.skill.org.uk

Careers Wales
0800 100 900
www.careerswales.com

Also check out:
> Disability Education and Courses
> School Essentials
> Choices @ 16

The Welsh Baccalaureate is an over-arching qualification that is taken in school or college by those aged 16+. At the moment, there are 24 schools and colleges that offer the Welsh Bac, but more and more are taking it up each year. It is comprised of two sections – Core Studies and Optional Studies. The bulk of the Baccalaureate, taking up 18-20 hours per week, is the Optional Studies section. This part of the qualification is the same as the everyday qualifications that are offered by most schools and colleges, so you can choose your own mix of GCSE's, A Level's, NVQ's etc. The Core Studies part of the Baccalaureate includes subjects such as Key Skills, Wales, Europe and the World and Personal and Social Education. This requires around four to five hours per week. There are two types of Baccalaureate – an Intermediate and an Advanced diploma. To achieve the Advanced diploma requires higher and better qualifications than the Intermediate diploma. By including Core Studies, The Welsh Bac is intended to give students a more rounded and fulfilling education than traditional qualifications. Recognising this, the number of UCAS points awarded to Core Studies (120) is the equivalent to achieving an A grade A Level.

Welsh Baccalaureate Qualification
02920 265 010
www.wbq.org.uk

Welsh Joint Education Committee
02920 265 000
www.wjec.co.uk

Careers Wales
0800 100 900
www.careerswales.com

Also check out:
> Personal Development
> Exams and Revision
> Choices @ 16
> Qualifications Essentials
> Careers Essentials
> School Essentials

Unfortunately, some form of bullying takes place in almost every school. It can be physical – kicking, pushing, punching, slapping etc. and/or it can be verbal – intimidation, name-calling, threats, humiliation etc. Both forms of abuse can be very damaging to victims of bullying. Emotional pain can be just as severe as physical pain and a combination of both can be terrifying. Groups or individuals can carry out bullying. Bullying occurs for a number of reasons, usually because those who bully need to make someone else feel bad or small in order to make themselves feel better. Whilst a victim of bullying may feel embarrassed, it is actually the bully who is weak, picking on one person to hide his or her own weakness. It is important that victims of bullying do not suffer in silence. If you are being bullied, keep a note of what happens and tell a friend, parent or teacher. All schools have an anti-bullying policy and methods of dealing with bullying so they should be able to help bullies come to terms with and change their unacceptable behaviour. If you're at school and see bullying occurring, do not ignore it or take the side of the bully to avoid trouble, be brave and tell a teacher or member of staff.

Bullying Online
www.bullying.co.uk

Childline
0800 11 11
www.childline.org.uk

Also check out:
> Attitudes & Stereotypes
> Harassment
> School Essentials
> Discrimination Essentials
> Personal Development

Skiving, wagging, skipping, bunking, call it what you want, truancy occurs and it probably always will. But, if you think it's harmless then think again. Students bunk off school for a number of reasons. Victims of bullying may be too scared to go to school; other students may find that their educational needs are not being met. Bunking off school will not help either of these problems. In both cases, it is vital that help is requested. With the right help from teachers and parents, bullying can be stopped and teachers can approach individual needs in a fresh way. Perhaps the main reasons for truancy are that students are bored and looking for excitement elsewhere or their parents think that it is more important for them to be doing something else, like Christmas shopping. Both of these reasons are unacceptable. It has been proven that those who have played truant at school have gone on to achieve less later on in life. Think about it – missed lessons = falling behind at school = lower GCSE results = less employment opportunities. In some cases, parents can be prosecuted for their children not attending school. It is also possible for a school to exclude an absent student.

Advisory Centre for Education (ACE)
0808 800 5793
www.ace-ed.org.uk

Childline
0800 11 11
www.childline.org.uk

Department for Education and Skills
0207 925 5466
www.dfes.gov.uk/schoolattendance

Also check out:
- School Essentials
- Bullying at School
- Choices @ 16
- Personal Development
- Unemployed Essentials

Excluding a pupil from school is a last resort. They will only do so if a pupil has broken the school's code of conduct. If a student has behavioural problems, the school will firstly work alongside the student and their parents to try and find a solution to them. If problems persist, it is only then that exclusion will be considered. The only person who can exclude a pupil is the school's head or acting head teacher. There are two types of exclusion that a school can use:

A fixed-period exclusion – Used when a student has breached discipline in a minor way. Exclusions usually last for between one and three days and rarely last for more than 15 days. In a school year, a pupil can only receive a maximum of 45 days of exclusion in total.

Permanent Exclusion – More likely to be used when a pupil commits a serious breach of school discipline. Even if a student has no previous record of bad behaviour or has not been excluded temporarily before, they may still be excluded permanently. In cases where an investigation is needed to decide whether a student is deserving of permanent exclusion, they may be excluded temporarily whilst a decision is made.

Citizens Advice Bureau guide to exclusion from school
www.adviceguide.org.uk/index/family_parent/education/problems_at_school.htm#Exclusion_from_school

Childline
0800 11 11
www.childline.org.uk

Bullying Online
www.bullying.co.uk

Also check out:
- School Essentials
- Home Learning
- Personal Development
- Choices @ 16
- Careers Essentials
- Stress

Harassment is similar in many ways to bullying. But, whereas bullying is about intimidating and belittling others, harassment refers mainly to inappropriate behaviour. It may involve improper touching or physical abuse, name-calling or discrimination due to your appearance, race, gender, sexuality or disability. Anyone can be a victim of harassment, just as anyone can be the perpetrator of harassment. So, it may come from boys to girls or vice versa and a pupil may harass a teacher or vice versa.

Most schools have anti-harassment policies and procedures to deal with any cases of it. If you feel that you are being harassed, either by another pupil or by a teacher, tell somebody. Suffering in silence will not help anyone. The harassment is likely to continue and those responsible will get away with it and consider their behaviour acceptable. Once a third party is aware of the situation, they can begin procedures to resolve the problem. This may mean getting all the involved parties together to talk about the problem and attempt to resolve it. If the harassment continues, pupils are protected by Government legislation, which can lead to exclusion for guilty pupils or dismissal for teachers.

Youth Information page on harassment
0116 242 7350
http://www.youthinformation.com/infopage.asp?snID=761

Bullying Online
www.bullying.co.uk

ACAS (making working life better)
0845 47 47 47
www.acas.org.uk

Also check out:
- School Essentials
- Bullying at School
- Bunking Off and Exclusion
- Racism
- School Essentials

Try to imagine standing up and talking in front of 30 people everyday. Then think about how difficult it must be to keep everybody interested. And what about making sure that nobody misbehaves? Now try and imagine how hard it must be to keep your sanity, let alone keep smiling. Being a teacher isn't easy. But they do it for the love of the job. Strangely enough, they do get satisfaction from seeing their pupils succeed and achieve! Whether that means a pupil getting an A grade or an E grade makes no difference. All that a teacher wants is for each pupil to realise what he or she is capable of. The relationship that you have with your teacher is the same as any – if you treat them with respect, you will earn similar respect in return. However, always remember that a teacher is in a position of power and they have a responsibility to make sure the whole class has a good education, meaning that they may need to discipline disruptive elements! They are there to help you and they will so long as they are treated in the right way.

Training and Development Agency for Schools
0870 4960 123
www.tda.gov.uk

National Union of Teachers in Wales
www.teachers.org.uk

Also check out:

> School Essentials
> Bunking Off and Exclusion
> Bullying at School
> Qualifications Essentials

One of the most popular options for pupils when they have completed their GCSEs is college. Some schools have a sixth form college, which will be much similar to school, although the dress code may differ. Students normally take A-Levels (usually three) at sixth form colleges. For pupils at a school without a sixth form college, there are other colleges that may teach a range of subjects and qualifications. Colleges differ from schools in many ways. Students are treated much more like adults than they are at school. There is usually no uniform and pupils are expected to take care of their own time keeping and attendance. Rather than constant discipline to keep students in check, lecturers and course tutors will monitor overall performance and attendance and may take action if they are falling behind. At college, students can pick and choose which subjects and qualifications they study. They may offer GCSEs, A-Levels and GNVQs in subjects as diverse as performing arts, metaphysics and cycle maintenance, as well as offering the more traditional subjects. Entry to college is usually gained by achieving the required GCSE grades, an application form and/or an interview. Obtain a prospectus or visit a college on their open day for more information.

Qualifications and Curriculum Authority
0207 509 5555
www.qca.org.uk

BBC Learning page
www.bbc.co.uk/learning

The National Union of Students
0871 221 8221
www.nusonline.co.uk

Universities and Colleges Admissions Services 0870 1122211
www.ucas.com

Guide to being a student
0207 189 8339
www.studentuk.com

Also check out:
> Qualifications and Subjects
> Community Education
> University Essentials
> Grants and Loans
> Student Life

Once you've completed your GCSEs, the world of education opens up to you. Colleges and universities offer a wide range of qualifications and subjects. You can take A-Levels, further GCSEs, GNVQs or A-Levels at college level and you can study for a Bachelors degree or an HND post-college. The range of subjects that are available once you leave school also increases dramatically. From the traditional subjects like English and Maths to practical courses such as Horticulture and less traditional ones like Travel and Tourism. When you are deciding which qualifications and subjects you are to study you should consider a number of factors. Think about what subjects you enjoy, what you are good at, what career path you wish to take and what style of learning and assessment suits you best. Some courses may be entirely theoretical, some may be completely based on practical work and others might feature a mixture of both. Courses can be assessed using exams, coursework, modules or a combination of all three. As you may be able to combine courses and qualifications, it's also worth considering which courses can be studied together. Some courses also include work experience or may offer a year abroad, so if that interests you then go for it!

Qualifications and Curriculum Authority
0207 509 5555
www.qca.org.uk

Learn Direct
0800 100 900
www.learndirect.co.uk

National Union of Students
0871 221 8221
www.nusonline.co.uk

Universities and Colleges Administration Service 0870 1122211
www.ucas.com

Worktrain (national jobs and learning website) 0845 6060 234
www.worktrain.gov.uk

Also check out:
- College Essentials
- University Essentials
- Qualification Essentials
- Degrees and Diplomas
- Student Life
- Gap Years

Anyone can study a degree or a diploma. It may be necessary to have certain qualifications to be accepted onto a course, but experience or proven ability may get you a place. Most degree courses take three years to complete but some take longer. Many courses also have an extra, 'sandwich', year, which is a year spent working in the industry or abroad, if studying a language. Each degree is classified, so a BA is a Bachelor of Arts and a BSc is a Bachelor of Science. Degrees are graded so that a 1st is the highest mark, then a 2:1, then a 2:2 and finally a 3rd. Whilst completing a degree, a student is known as an undergraduate and once they have graduated, they become known as a postgraduate.

There are several types of diploma. The BTEC National Diploma is a two-year course, which is often taken instead of A Levels; Higher National Certificates (HNC) take two years of part-time study to complete and Higher National Diplomas (HND) take two years of full-time study; and Foundation Degrees are employment-related qualifications that take one or two years to complete. All diplomas can be used as a stepping-stone to study a degree. Obtain a copy of a University prospectus for complete details of courses and the university.

Universities and Colleges Admissions Services
0870 1122211
www.ucas.ac.uk

The National Union of Students
0871 221 8221
www.nusonline.co.uk

Also check out:
> University Essentials
> Student Life
> College Essentials
> Qualifications Essentials
> Careers Essentials

After twelve or fourteen years of education at school, you'd be forgiven if you wanted to take a break from it all. Many people take a gap year for this reason. They may also take one because they don't know for sure what they want to do and need time to decide. Whatever your reasons, if you do take a gap year, make sure you use it well. Rather than take a break from education with no specific plan in mind, pre-arrange what you intend to do with your time. You might want to get a job so that you have some money for university, you could travel the world, volunteer for a charity or you may want to get some work experience so that you can get a taste for the sort of job that you may be considering as a career. But if you don't plan ahead, it can be all too easy to drift into a life of lazing around doing nothing, which one day you'll regret for sure! If you do plan on returning to university after your gap year, apply at the same time as the rest of your class.

The complete guide to gap years
www.gapyear.com

Plan your gap year
www.gap-year.com/browse.asp?catID=1155

Travel Tree (volunteering abroad and working holidays)
0870 350 3033
www.traveltree.co.uk

Gap Activity Projects (volunteering for young people)
0118 959 4914
www.gap.org.uk

Also check out:

> Travel Essentials
> Careers Essentials
> Flying Essentials
> Exchanges for Young People
> Volunteering Abroad
> Volunteering UK

Students starting university in Wales in 2006 will pay £1,200 for their first year of study. From 2007, each university will decide whether to charge between £0 and £3,000 per year of study with students that normally live in Wales and study at a Welsh higher education institution entitled to a non-repayable fee grant of £1,800. If studying outside of Wales, you'll have to pay fees of up to £3,000 per year. Loans of up to a maximum of £4,405 (£6170 if studying in London) and grants are available to help pay for fees and the cost of living. They are means-tested, meaning that the amount of money you're awarded depends on your family income. Students whose families are on lower incomes are likely to receive more money. Of course, loans need to be paid back at some point. In the present system, a graduate isn't required to begin repayment (with a low interest rate of around 3.2%) until they're earning a salary of £15,000 upwards. Once you're earning that much, your loan repayment will be automatically deducted from your pay as a percentage until it has been paid off. Grants are usually awarded for the students that need financial assistance the most. They do not need to be paid back. In Wales, there is an additional grant (the Assembly Learning Grant) that can be applied for.

Student Loans Company
0800 40 50 10
www.slc.co.uk/

Student Finance Wales
0845 602 8845
www.studentfinancewales.co.uk

National Union of Students
0871 221 8221
www.nusonline.co.uk

Welsh Assembly
02920 825 111
www.wales.gov.uk

Also check out:

> Budgetting Essentials
> Debt Essentials
> Student Life
> Loans
> Overdrafts

People often say that university is the best time of their lives. As well as the benefit of an education that can be much wider and more specialised than school education, university is a chance to learn more about yourself and life in general. At university, students are treated much more like adults than whilst at school or college. If you don't do the work or attend lectures, you won't be put in detention or shouted at. It will be left up to you to make sure you get the work done in whichever way you choose. The majority of students live away from home in either student halls or rented flats and houses. So, get used to cooking, cleaning, shopping and paying for bills. The social side of university is also very important. You'll meet a wide range of people and will find that your social options will become very wide indeed. Your first week at Uni is known as Fresher's Week and is a chance to make new friends, find your way around and join clubs and societies. All students must have a NUS card, which can give many discounts at local and high street shops. Students can also get an ISIC card, which can be used worldwide.

National Union of Students
0871 221 8221
www.nusonline.co.uk

Student UK
0207 189 8339
www.studentuk.com

International Student Identity Card
http://www.isic.org

BBC One Life
http://www.bbc.co.uk/radio1/onelife/

Also check out:
> Renting Essentials
> Courses and Subjects
> Grants and Loans
> Degrees and Diplomas

University application is done through a company called UCAS (Universities and Colleges Admissions Service). Applicants must complete a UCAS form, either on paper or online, which is then processed by UCAS. Each applicant can choose either six courses (costing £15 to apply) or just one (costing £5). Once your application is complete, you'll (hopefully!) receive an unconditional offer from your preferred option, meaning that you have already been accepted on to the course. If not, you may receive a conditional offer, which means that you will be accepted on to the course as long as you achieve certain grades or pass an interview. If you don't receive any offers, fear not. British universities have a system known as 'clearing'. This caters for anyone without a firm university offer. It involves getting directly in contact with universities to get spare university places. The deadline for applying to most courses is usually around mid-January, although applications for Oxford and Cambridge must be received by mid-October. There are also certain art and design courses that can be applied for in slightly different ways through UCAS (see their website for more details).

UCAS
0870 112 211
www.ucas.com

BBC (Welsh University Listings)
www.bbc.co.uk/radio1/onelife/education/uni_listings/wales.shtml

Student UK
0207 189 8339
www.studentuk.com

Higher Education and Research Opportunities in the UK 0191 227 3549
www.hero.ac.uk

Student Loans Company
0800 40 50 10
www.slc.co.uk

Also check out:
> Degrees and Diplomas
> Grants and Loans
> College Essentials
> Student Life
> Gap Years
> Courses and Subjects

Community education encompasses all kinds of courses that can be studied in your spare time at a local institution. That can mean evening or daytime courses that can be studied at local colleges, universities, community centres or councils. There are a wide range of subjects that can be studied in a variety of different learning styles. They are a great way to learn new skills and ideas and can help you meet new people with similar interests. You could study something that might help your career or your education such as English or Website Design or you could study something to improve your spare time such as Photography or Music. Courses usually run in conjunction with university term time, lasting for the equivalent of one term or an academic year or more. Community education courses are often charged for with the fee relating to the type of course. For example, a photography course (requiring the use of a large space and expensive technical equipment) will cost more than a theoretical course (requiring only a classroom and a lecturer). Some courses are subsidised for those less able to pay full fees and your work could pay for you to learn (if it's useful for them also). For details of community education courses, see your local careers adviser, council website, community centre or local education institutions.

The National Institute of Adult Continuing Education 0116 204 4200
www.niace.org.uk

Learn Direct
0800 100 900
www.learndirect-advice.co.uk

BBC Learning
www.bbc.co.uk/learning

Also check out:
- Training Essentials
- Careers Essentials
- Distance & E-Learning
- Education at Home

If turning up in a certain place at a certain time to get your education isn't your bag then distance and e-learning is the thing for you. Also known as correspondence courses, home learning or open learning, you can get your education through your home computer or through material sent to you in the post. This means that you can study when and where you want with no regard for timetables or rules – you can do it when the mood suits you. The types of courses that are available are wide and varied. You could study for a specific qualification or just take a course that could help a new or existing hobby. You might learn a new language, computer skills, creative writing or subjects like maths and humanities. You will be given a personal tutor who will be available for help and advice and some courses will offer the chance to communicate with other students to exchange ideas and discuss your learning. Most of these types of courses are charged for and will vary depending on the type and length of course. Discounted rates may be offered to the unemployed or those on a low income.

Hobson's Distance Learning
www.distancelearning.hobsons.com

Hot Courses
0208 600 5300
www.hotcourses.com

Open University
01908 274066
www.open.ac.uk

Linguaphone (learn a new language)
0800 136 973
www.linguaphone.co.uk

International Centre for Distance Learning
www-icdl.open.ac.uk

Learn Direct
0800 100 900
www.learndirect.co.uk

Also check out:

- University Essentials
- Careers Essentials
- Community Education
- Education at Home
- College Essentials
- Student Life

By law, all children are required to receive education. However, there is no law that states exactly where that education should come from so, whilst the majority of children are taught in schools, it is legal for family members to remove their child (or children) from school and teach them from home. All the parents have to do is prove to the local education authority that education is taking place. There are many reasons why a child may be taught from home. It could be that their parents believe that the National Curriculum does not offer what they want their child to receive. It could also be that their child has had a problem at school so would be better suited to home schooling. At home, a child can get more attention and will be able to learn at their own pace and ability. Your parents do not have to follow the National Curriculum or enter you for any examinations but they are able to do so if they wish. There are many aids to help parents teach their children at home including learning packs, CD ROMs etc. At the moment, the number of children taught at home is increasing.

Hobson's Distance Learning
www.distancelearning.hobsons.com

Hot Courses
0208 600 5300
www.hotcourses.com

Open University
01908 274066
www.open.ac.uk

Linguaphone (learn a new language)
0800 136 973
www.linguaphone.co.uk

International Centre for Distance Learning
www-icdl.open.ac.uk

Learn Direct
0800 100 900
www.learndirect.co.uk

Also check out:

> Exams and Revision
> GCSEs
> Basic Skills Essentials
> Distance and E-Learning
> Community Education
> Qualifications Essentials

Want to earn money whilst you learn? If so, a modern apprenticeship is the thing for you. Many employers offer modern apprenticeships so that whilst you are working and learning skills, you can also train for a qualification. You can learn new skills and key skills that can lead to an internationally recognised qualification. Usually, the qualification that you gain will be an NVQ, which will take between one and four years to complete. There is a huge choice of subject areas in which you can become an apprentice. From hands-on, practical industries such as the motor mechanic industry or agriculture to office-based areas such as administration, there will be an apprenticeship for you. The training is designed by employers so is specifically designed to train you for the workplace. Competition to be an apprentice is tough; you'll usually need around four GCSEs grade A-C and may have to pass an aptitude test to get onto the scheme. Most employers will also be looking out to check that you have the commitment and the drive to last the length of the course. A foundation modern apprenticeship is an entry level apprenticeship that will leave you with a Level 2 NVQ and can lead to studying for a modern apprenticeship.

Careers Wales
0800 100 900
www.careerswales.com

Connexions (Information and advice for young people on work and training)
08080 013 219
www.connexions-direct.com

Also check out:

> Basic Skills Essentials
> Training Essentials
> Qualifications Essentials
> Vocational Qualifications
> Careers Essentials
> Working UK

Making the most of your career is all about skills. To carry out a job successfully, you need not just to have the education but also the skills to back you up. There are many ways to gain the kinds of skills that you need to make your career a success. Traditional education is great for giving you the skills to learn, it can teach you many interesting and useful theories and skills. However, do not feel that you are limited to traditional education to learn what you need to know to get a job. Think about all of the other qualifications that exist. From NVQs to HNDs and City and Guilds, there are many other educational routes each offering a different method of learning what you want. Work experience is a great to get a real feel for what jobs are like. In a way, work experience is like a try-before-you-buy. In short, it's perfect for finding out if you do or don't like a particular job. You could also try other training schemes such as The Princes Trust, volunteering or daytime or evening learning to help you find your way. Think about the way that you prefer to learn and what it is that you want to learn and pick a training route that matches.

BBC Learning
www.bbc.co.uk/learning/

Basic Skills Wales
0845 602 1654
www.basic-skills-wales.org

Also check out:

> Training Essentials
> Vocational Qualifications Essentials
> Careers Essentials
> Qualifications Essentials
> Courses and Subjects
> Working UK

To continually improve, learn and work your way up the career ladder, training is an absolute necessity. Most companies offer training courses to their employees in any area that they think may be of use to them. As an employee, keep an eye out for training that may improve your skills in the workplace and don't be afraid to ask your employer to send you on the course. As well as improve your existing skills, training can teach you new skills or you can learn skills in a completely new area. As a young person, the opportunities for training are at their greatest. Training their staff young means that your employer will also benefit from you. The Time Off for Study or Training Law means that all 16 or 17 year olds who are not in full time education and are not qualified to Level 2 (roughly equivalent to 5 GCSEs) are entitled to paid time off work to receive training. Employers may also offer day release (where you are allowed to attend college one day per week). There are also countless other schemes such as Apprenticeships and Entry to Employment (e2e) that can provide training for young people.

Time Off For Study or Training Law
www.dfes.gov.uk

Work and learn at the same time
08080 013 219
www.connexions-direct.com

Also check out:
> Basic Skills Essentials
> Unemployed Essentials
> Time Off Work
> Vocational Qualifications
> Community Education
> Distance and E-Learning

With over 500 City and Guilds qualifications to choose from, they are an excellent way of improving your employability or introducing you to a new career. The courses that they run are usually more practical than traditional education, preferring to focus on teaching skills that are actually used within the workplace. City and Guilds qualifications are run from approved centres around the country and anyone can apply for them, no matter whether you are at school, college or in the workplace. They offer a range of qualifications including NVQs, Apprenticeships and Basic Skills, amongst many others. Each qualification is different, with every type of learner catered for. There are also seven different levels of entry for each qualification going from the most basic of knowledge up to professional level. City and Guilds qualifications are not free to complete. Each training centre individually chooses how much to charge for each course. To find out the City and Guilds courses that are available, contact City and Guilds and ask for a prospectus.

City and Guilds
0207 294 2800
www.city-and-guilds.co.uk

NVQs
www.dfes.gov.uk/nvq/

Qualifications and Curriculum Authority
0207 509 5555
www.qca.org.uk/

Also check out:

> Choices @ 16
> Qualifications Essentials
> Basic Skills Essentials
> Vocational Qualifications
> Exams and Revision
> Distance & E-Learning

Higher National Certificates (HNCs) and Higher National Diplomas (HNDs) are qualifications that are internationally recognised by both employers and educational establishments. Both of the Higher National qualifications can be gained through courses that are more practical than traditional education. Learning is more hands-on than theory-based learning. They can be used either to help you get a job or to get a place at university. A HNC usually takes one year of full-time study to complete (although it can be studied part-time) and is comprised of 12 modules. It can be used if you are unsure of committing to a subject for three years, to give you a feel for your chosen subject or to get you onto the second year of a similar degree course. HNDs take two years to complete and are comprised of 30 modules. They can be used to help you get into your chosen career or to gain entry onto the third year of a relevant degree course. The entry requirements for HNCs and HNDs vary but are normally lower than those required to get onto a degree course. Usually, one A Level at Grade E or above will be enough.

Aim Higher
www.aimhigher.ac.uk/student_info/hnc.cfm

Edexcel information on Higher National qualifications
0870 240 9800
www.edexcel.org.uk

Careers Wales
0800 100 900
www.careerswales.com

Also check out:
> Qualifications Essentials
> College Essentials
> University Essentials
> Vocational Qualifications
> Training Essentials
> Careers Essentials

NVQs & GNVQ

2.2 Vocational Qualifications

National Vocational Qualifications (NVQs) are based on the National Occupational Standards (NOS). The NOS describes what standard of competence people who work in certain professions are expected to achieve in order to carry out their jobs effectively. They come in five levels (1-5), with one being the most basic and five being the most complex level of certification. By achieving an NVQ it shows that you have the ability to do a job in practice rather than in theory. All learning is completed whilst at work; although some written work may be required to be done during your own time.

GNVQs (the 'G' stands for General) are qualifications that are studied for in college on a full-time basis for between one and two years. They are considered to be a more vocational alternative to studying GCSEs or A and AS Levels, depending on the level (Intermediate or Foundation) that you take. GNVQs are currently being phased out and will no longer be available from 2007, although any qualifications that have already been gained will still hold the same value. Advanced GNVQs have been replaced by Vocational A Levels and Foundation and Intermediate GNVQs have been replaced by vocational GCSEs.

Search for a qualification
www.dfes.gov.uk/section96/search/search.cfm

Qualifications and Curriculum Authority
0207 509 5555
www.qca.org.uk

BBC Learning
www.bbc.co.uk/learning

Also check out:

- Basic Skills Essentials
- Choices @ 16
- Qualifications Essentials
- College Essentials
- Training Essentials
- Careers Essentials

Initiative
2.3 Unemployed?

When employers look for new staff, there are a number of qualities that they look for beyond the obvious qualifications and work experience. One of these is initiative. Prospective employees who can show that they've used their initiative to improve themselves, to find work or to help others demonstrate that they'll be able to use that initiative in their new job. If you're unemployed and are having trouble finding work, there are a number of ways to use your initiative to make yourself more employable. Think about the type of work that you might like to do, look up all of the local companies that provide that kind of work, contact them and ask for work experience. You may want to think about setting up your own business. You could volunteer for charity organisations. There are heaps of courses out there that can teach you new skills and give you invaluable knowledge. Basically, you need to prove that you are going the extra mile to get to where you want to. If you can show that you're that well motivated when you're unemployed, employers will have no doubt how good an employee you'd make.

Business Eye
08457 96 97 98
www.businesseye.org.uk

Volunteering Wales
www.volunteering-wales.net

The National Council for Work Experience
0845 601 5510
www.work-experience.org

Jobcentre Plus
0845 6060 234
www.jobcentreplus.gov.uk

CWVYS Council for Wales for Volunary Youth Services
www.cwvys.org.uk

WCVA Wales Council for Voluntary Action
www.wcva.org.uk

Also check out:
> Volunteering
> Training Essentials
> Basic Skills Essentials
> Unemployed Essentials
> Personal Development

There are job centres all over the country, with most people in Wales having a convenient local office. They offer a dual service, providing benefits for the unemployed and helping jobseekers find suitable positions. If you are unemployed you need to get down to your local jobcentre and get registered immediately. You'll have to fill in a form and have an interview with someone at the centre. If you're aged 18 or over, you should be entitled to claim jobseeker's allowance. If aged between 16 and 18 and you're unemployed, you may be entitled to jobseeker's allowance – go to the Citizens Advice Bureau for advice. In some cases it may be possible to get jobseeker's allowance backdated if you can prove a good reason for your late claim. You must also prove that you are actively seeking and are available for work. When you register with the jobcentre, they will find out what sort of job you'd like to do and will try and find suitable roles, which they will recommend to you. They'll also give you advice on how to find and apply for jobs. You will also have to show that you have been putting the effort in to try and find a job.

Citizens Advice Bureau
www.citizensadvice.org.uk

Jobcentre Plus
www.jobcentreplus.gov.uk

Also check out:

> Benefits Essentials
> Unemployed Essentials
> Basic Skills Essentials
> Applying for a Job
> CVs & Application Forms

It is unrealistic to believe that everyone knows exactly what they want to do from an early age and ends up doing just that and enjoying it. Most people change their minds about what they want to do all the time. Before you leave school, that's not too much of a problem but once you start getting into University or employment, it can seem more difficult if you change your career aspirations. Once you're in a job, you'll usually have commitments (bills to pay etc.) so changing career paths might seem impossible. However, there is no reason to feel trapped in a job or career. Think and be sure about exactly what you want to do. Then work out exactly what training or experience you'll need to get there. You may have skills from your current job that can be transferred. Speak to a careers advisor to get advice on the best way to move on. You may be able to start a distance-learning course, study part-time, start a full-time course or take evening classes. You may be able to get work experience or a part-time job in the area of your choice. Remember there are always other options if you look hard enough for them.

Tips on building your career
www.coaching-life.co.uk

Channel 4's page on retraining
www.channel4.com/life/microsites/G/going_to_extremes/career.html

Careers Wales
www.careerswales.com

Volunteering Wales
www.volunteering-wales.net

Also check out:

> Qualifications Essentials
> Training Essentials
> Vocational Qualifications
> Careers Essentials
> Working UK
> Basic Skills Essentials
> Volunteering

The Princes Trust is a UK charity that aims to help people aged between 14 and 30 get their lives on track. They specialise in helping those who struggled at school, have been in care, the long-term unemployed or those who have been in trouble with the law. They do this in a number of ways:

- 12-week community projects that aim to improve communica tion, confidence, basic skills and could even have you working with a premiership football team.
- Providing support (including advice and low-interest loans and grants) for those looking to start their own businesses.
- Providing grants to help you get into work, training or educa tion and to help with group community projects.
- Running a course called Sound Live, which is aimed at people with musical talent who wish to develop their skills.
- Running projects working in Europe.
- Providing advice and support courses to those who have just left care.
- Run xl clubs for those in the last two years of school. xl clubs offer the chance for pupils to become involved in non-school projects.
- Provide support, advice, loans and grants to ex-offenders look ing to gain skills, training and employment.

The Prince's Trust
0800 842 842
www.princes-trust.org.uk

The National Association for the Care and Resettlement of Offenders
0207 582 6500
www.nacro.org.uk

Jobcentre Plus
0845 6060 234
www.jobcentreplus.gov.uk

Carelaw (information for young people and children in care)
http://nchacti01.uuhost.uk.uu.net/carelaw/

Also check out:
> Basic Skills Essentials
> Training Essentials
> Care
> Choices @ 16
> Unemployed Essentials
> Arrested?

2.3 Unemployed?

Being unemployed isn't much fun. It can be boring, repetitive and it can become easy to get stuck in a rut from which escape seems impossible. There are plenty of resources to help you out when you are unemployed though. Job Seekers Allowance is a twice-monthly payment made by the Government to the unemployed who are actively seeking a job. This payment enables the unemployed to live and to search for employment. As well as meeting certain criteria (explained on the Job Centre website), to get the payment, you need to prove that you are actively seeking employment. The amount of money available depends on your personal situation. Another service available to the unemployed is New Deal. This is another Government service that works one-to-one with those looking for work. They provide information, support and advice on looking for work, training and job preparation. Careers services are another stop-off point for those looking for work. In Wales, Careers Wales can offer help and advice on how to improve your career prospects.

New Deal
0845 606 2626
www.newdeal.gov.uk

Careers Wales
0800 100 900
www.careerswales.com

Jobcentre Plus
0845 60 60 234
www.jobcentreplus.gov.uk

Also check out:
> Training Essentials
> Careers Essentials
> Basic Skills Essentials
> Qualifications Essentials
> Applying for a Job

2.EMPLOYMENT & TRAINING

Most people spend 40 years or so in employment so it's worth making sure you choose a career that you enjoy. Some people know exactly what they want to do from a very young age. They're the lucky ones! The majority of people are either unsure of what career they want or they fall into a career by accident. You can help yourself by looking into what career would be right for you and what it takes to get into it. Think about the sort of things that you like doing. Do you like practical, hands-on work? Are you creative? Maybe you enjoy working with figures? Think about what sort of environment you'd like to work in. Do you mind getting your hands dirty? Would you enjoy working in an office? Perhaps you'd like to work outdoors? And think about what you're good at. Maybe you have a good scientific brain? Perhaps you're good with people or are a dab hand in the kitchen? Then find out what sort of jobs are suitable for you and what training is required to get into that job. The best places to go to find out this information are careers services. Most educational institutions have a careers department; Careers Wales also provides Wales-wide careers information.

Careers Wales
0800 100 900
www.careerswales.com

BBC's guide to careers
www.bbc.co.uk/radio1/onelife/work/

Also check out:
- Training Essentials
- Basic Skills Essentials
- Vocational Qualifications
- Personal Development

Making the decision to go self-employed usually carries more risk than ordinary employment, but if things work out well, the rewards can be many. There are two main ways that you can be self-employed. You can work on a freelance basis, meaning that you work for different companies either for a set period of time (also known as 'contract work') or to do a specific, one-off job. Otherwise, you can start your own business. For freelancers, the main risk is that work may not be constant so you might have to find other ways of generating money when there is none. Additionally, freelance workers don't receive the same benefits such as pension schemes, paid holiday and sick leave that employees do. However, freelance work has its benefits. It can be possible to make a good wage from it, you can choose when, where and who to work for and the work can be as varied as you want it to be. Business owners can enjoy the freedom to be their own boss and to be in control of their own destiny. The risk is obvious but the challenge to succeed is an exciting one, you'll get to work in your own chosen field and you'll get to make all of the important decisions.

Young Enterprise
01865 776845
www.young-enterprise.org.uk

Because You Can (Guide to starting your own business) 08457 96 97 98
www.becauseyoucan.com

Citizen's Advice Bureau self-employment checklist
www.adviceguide.org.uk/em/index/life/employment/self-employment_checklist.htm

New Deal
0845 606 2626
www.newdeal.gov.uk

Also check out.
> Work from Home
> Employment Rights
> Training Essentials
> National Insurance
> Tax
> Working UK

Work experience can be vital for your career. Most companies and organisations take in people on work experience. For the company, it gives them the chance to have someone help out for a while and may result in them finding someone that they want to employ. Work experience can help those who know exactly what they want from a career and those who have no clear idea of it. For those who know what job they want to do, work experience can be a way of making contacts, learning real job skills and actually getting a genuine feel for what the job and the industry are like. If you're unsure of your career, you can try work experience in differing roles that you think you may like. Eventually, you're bound to find one you like! Think about what sort of work you want to do and contact all relevant companies asking for work experience. Don't be afraid to explain exactly what you're looking for. Some companies may only ask you to complete some fairly menial tasks. This really is not what work experience is for so be sure that you will get to experience the job properly at some point. You're unlikely to be paid for your efforts but work experience can still make a huge difference to your CV and hence, your career.

The National Council for Work Experience
0845 6015510
www.work-experience.org

Careers Wales
0800 100 900
www.careerswales.com

European Work Experience Programme
0208 572 1114
www.ewep.com

Also check out:
- Careers Essentials
- Unemployed Essentials
- New Job New Life
- Training Essentials
- Basic Skills Essentials
- CVs and Application Forms

Working from home is currently gaining in popularity. There are different ways in which you might work from home. You may start your own business that can be run at home, work for a company that allows you to spend some working hours at home or you may work for a specialist home working organisation. There are pros and cons to working from home. You may find it easier to get on with your work and you won't have to worry about catching the bus in time either! In fact, you could do your work whilst wearing your pyjamas if you really wanted to! However, it may be difficult to separate home life from work life. If you are working from home, try sticking to office hours so that you can balance your work and home life and try and build a working area that is enclosed and can be shut off once you stop working. Many homeworkers work for home working organisations, which usually advertise on lampposts or by word of mouth. These jobs are usually what are known as piecework, involving sewing, packing envelopes or similar work. They are usually paid per item that you pack or sew etc. Be careful with these types of roles, as there are disreputable companies out there who operate illegally and often pay unreasonably. Research the company thoroughly before you commit to anything.

The Home Business Alliance
0871 474 1015
www.homebusiness.org.uk

eGrindstone (connecting homeworkers)
www.egrindstone.co.uk

The Teleworker Association
www.tca.org.uk

The National Group on Homeworking
0800 174 095
www.homeworking.gn.apc.org

Also check out:

> Applying for a Job
> Employment Rights
> Self Employment
> Careers Essentials
> Contracts
> Working UK

Your job may last for two weeks or twenty years. Either way, you should make the most of it. After all, roughly eight hours of work a day means that you'll spend a great deal of your life there. Working life is a melting pot of people of all ages, experiences and backgrounds. Some you'll like, some you won't. Your career will be made much brighter if you try your best to get along with everyone (especially your bosses!). Show willing to try out new things at work – your bosses will appreciate the effort even if you don't continue with it and if you do, they'll be impressed too, so you can't lose. Show initiative and be willing to work outside of your job description if needed. Don't let people push you around or make unreasonable demands, if you have a problem, tell someone. Do not accept discrimination of any kind. It shouldn't be tolerated and there are laws that should prevent it. Again, tell someone. When you learn new skills or do something particularly impressive, make a note of it on your CV, so that when you come to get a new job, you won't have to rack your brains to update your CV.

Equal Opportunities Commission
0845 601 5901
www.eoc.org.uk

Citizen's Advice Bureau (Basic Rights at Work)
www.adviceguide.org.uk/em/index/life/employment/basic_rights_at_work.htm

BBC Wales tips on writing CVs
www.bbc.co.uk/wales/raiseyourgame/trainingcoach/communication/cv_writing.shtml

Careers Wales
0800 100 900
www.careerswales.com

Also check out:
- Employment Rights
- Contracts
- Careers Essentials
- Applying for a Job
- CVs and Application Forms
- Interviews and Assesment

2.4 Types of Work

Many people choose to work abroad in different ways and for different reasons. You can volunteer, work whilst travelling, take seasonal or temporary jobs or work and live abroad permanently. Whilst working abroad you'll experience a different social and working culture, as well as picking up additional skills and experience. It can be great fun but remember that work is work wherever you are and serving drinks by the pool may not be much better than in the pub. Planning and preparation is key for those who are going to work abroad and there are plenty of organisations out there ready to help. The Department of Trade and Industry and Business Eye can provide useful information on regulations for working abroad (regulations on foreign workers differs between countries). The Chamber of Commerce can find useful organisations in your destination country. Travel agents can help with arranging seasonal work. Your local Job Centre has information on working abroad and can provide lists of vacancies too. Applications and CVs may be different abroad so speak to Careers Europe (through Careers Wales) for advice. The National Academic Recognition Information Centre can tell you if your qualification is internationally recognised. See links below for details of the above organisations.

The Department of Trade and Industry
0207 215 5000 www.dti.gov.uk

Business Eye 08457 96 97 98
www.businesseye.org.uk

The Chamber of Commerce 0207 654 5800
www.chamberonline.co.uk

Careers Europe 01274 829600
www.careerseurope.co.uk

National Academic Recognition Information Centre 0870 990 4088
www.naric.org.uk

Jobcentre Plus
www.jobcentreplus.gov.uk

Careers Wales
www.careerswales.com

Also check out:

- Careers Essentials
- Volunteering Abroad
- Travel Essentials
- Working Europe
- Working Seasonal
- Cultures

Working abroad in Europe is a great way to experience a new culture and a new working environment whilst gaining new skills and experience and, hopefully, having a lot of fun. You don't need a work permit to work in any EU state if you own an EU or British passport but, after three months you will need to obtain a residency permit from the local police. Some of the new EU states have varying working restrictions for foreign workers, so find out what they are first. For non-EU countries, you will need to have a work permit before taking up employment. When working abroad in Europe you will be subject to exactly the same sets of rules, regulations and rights as everybody else. Your first port of call if you're thinking about working abroad in Europe should be the Job Centre. They are part of the European Employment Services, which means that they have Europe-wide job vacancies and information on living and working conditions abroad in Europe. It's important to plan well before leaving to work abroad in Europe. Try and find out as much about the social and the working cultures in your chosen countries. There may be differences in language, dress codes and employment law as well as cultural differences such as body language.

Jobcentre Plus
0845 60 60 234
www.jobcentreplus.gov.uk

Careers Europe
01274 829 600
www.careerseurope.co.uk

Careers Wales
0800 100 900
www.careerswales.com

Also check out:

> Working Abroad
> Working Seasonal
> Careers Essentials
> Passports and Visas
> Travel Essentials
> Applying for a Job

Seasonal work can take place during any season but usually only lasts for anything up to six months so employment is on a casual basis. This means that jobs are often advertised in less formal ways than normal employment such as by word of mouth, in shop windows and that hours, pay etc. may also be less strictly regulated. In particular, keep an eye out from October, when employers start to look for additional staff to cover the Christmas period. Seasonal work can come in many forms. Typical work can be fruit picking, summer camp work, holiday work (bar work, entertainment, holiday rep etc.), child-care, sports instruction and shop work. Pay may be quite low for seasonal work but some positions may also include accommodation and/or food as well. Seasonal working can be a lot harder than it looks but it can be a lot of fun too. You'll make a whole host of new friends and may experience a new culture and lifestyle. Holiday companies are a good starting point to organise seasonal work but you may need to book ahead. If you go abroad without pre-arranged employment, make sure you have enough cash to keep you going, should work fail to materialise.

Any Work Any Where (Information on working across the globe)
www.anyworkanywhere.com

Pay Away
www.payaway.co.uk

Lonely Planet
0207 841 9000
www.lonelyplanet.com

Careers Europe
01274 829600
www.careerseurope.co.uk

Also check out:
> School Essentials
> Volunteering Abroad
> Travel Essentials
> Working Abroad
> Working Europe
> Money Abroad

2.5 Get that Job!

Getting the perfect job doesn't come easily for most people so don't expect that highly paid chocolate tasting job to waltz into your lap! Finding the right job to apply for can be tricky but with a bit of research, it becomes much easier. Look on the Internet, in local and national newspapers and in industry magazines. You might even find your ideal job advertised in a shop window, on a notice board or just from asking around in the right places. As long as you get out there and put some time into looking you'll eventually find what you're looking for. Then comes the time to apply for the job. This is the really difficult bit. Most jobs require you to fill in an application form or to send a CV and a covering letter. Do some research into the company and the industry to show that you've put the effort in and are interested in the role. Be careful to address every point made in the job and person specification. There is plenty of help available from websites and careers services that can give you advice on how to fill in application forms, write covering letters and CVs that will impress your prospective employers.

Careers Wales
0800 100 900
www.careerswales.com

UK Employment Services
0800 093 5412
www.getthatjob.net

Government advice on job application
www.direct.gov.uk

Prospects job application advice for graduates
www.prospects.ac.uk

Also check out:
- CVs and Application Forms
- Job Hunting
- Careers Essentials
- Interviews and Assesments
- Working UK

2.5 Get that Job!

If you want to get a job, the chances are you'll need to know how to fill in a job application form properly and/or have a well-produced, professional Curriculum Vitae (CV). A CV shows all your skills and experiences and is another way to sell yourself to prospective employers. These days, more and more jobs ask you to complete an application form rather than send in a copy of your CV but the information on both tends to end up the same anyway. You'll need to provide personal information, work and education experience, skills, training and other information like your hobbies and that sort of thing. Most application forms ask a general question like 'Why would you be the best person for this role?' This part of the form will make or break you! Always look at the job description and person specification and make sure that you cover all points made in them, detailing as best you can how you fit the criteria. Before writing on the actual form itself, try writing rough drafts so you don't make mistakes. It's always sensible to send a short covering letter with any CVs or application forms as well, to give your application that professional touch. Good luck!

Careers Wales
0800 100 900
www.careerswales.com

BBC guide to writing a CV
www.bbc.co.uk/radio1/onelife/work/cvs/cvs_intro.shtml

Job Centre
0845 60 60 234
www.jobcentreplus.gov.uk

Prospects guide to writing a CV
www.prospects.ac.uk/cms/ShowPage/Home_page/Applications_and_interviews/Applications/Compiling_a_CV/p!eXfdpk

Also check out:
> Applying for a Job
> Interviews and Assessments
> Working UK
> Careers Essentials
> Basic Skills Essentials

The majority of us dread interviews and assessments. It's a fact that some people are naturals when it comes to keeping calm under pressure and some of us aren't. However, most interviewers will be able to see beyond pure confidence. Saying the right thing at the right time is more important than how confident you appear. There are steps that everyone can take to improve interview technique. The first is to not worry too much about them. They aren't the most important things in the world; so don't get in a panic about them. Relax and try to be yourself as much as you can. Get a good night's sleep beforehand as yawning during an interview won't impress anyone. Dress smartly (men should always were suits if possible) unless you've been told otherwise. Concentrate on what is being said. This is harder than it looks, as most people's thoughts get pretty crowded when they're nervous. If you don't hear correctly or understand, just ask for the question or point to be repeated. Believe me, your honesty will be much more appreciated than a meaningless response. Additionally, prepare yourself by thinking up answers to some likely questions and some questions to throw back at the interviewers. Be interested, be enthusiastic and - one last thing - smile!

Careers Wales
0800 100 900
www.careerswales.com

The Student Zone's interview advice
01271 344 738
www.thestudentzone.com/articles/interviewadvice.html

Prospects interview and application advice page
www.prospects.ac.uk/cms/ShowPage/Home_page/Applications_and_interviews/p!eefmd

Also check out:
> Applying for a Job
> CVs & Application Forms
> Working UK
> Careers Essentials
> Relaxing

Recruitment agencies act like a middleman between those looking for jobs and employers looking for new recruits. They don't actually take money from those looking for work. Instead, if they match an employer with a vacancy, they charge the employer, not the employee. If you're looking for work, you can approach them to help you find exactly what you're looking for. They'll need to know specifically what sort of work you do and don't want to do, if you want permanent or temporary work, what sort of hours you can do and what sort of pay you're looking for. You'll also need to provide them with a current CV. They may give you advice on improving your CV, change it for you and interview you. Some agencies may also ask you to complete some simple tests such as typing and IT tests. Employers approach recruitment agencies with a list of vacancies and an idea of the type of people that they are looking for. It is then up to the agency to match the jobseeker up with the vacancy. They'll arrange the interview between the employer and you and will be responsible for letting you know if you got the job or not. They'll also be able to get feedback from employers if you don't get the job. Once you accept the job, you can contact the employer and the recruitment agency's job is done.

Careers Wales
0800 100 900
www.careerswales.com

BBC Guide to Work
www.bbc.co.uk/radio1/onelife/work/index.shtml

Also check out:
> Applying for a Job
> CVs and Application Forms
> Interviews & Assessments
> Careers Essentials
> Working UK

Bullying doesn't just take place at school, it can happen at work as well. It is equally unacceptable and you shouldn't tolerate it and neither should others, especially your employer. It can take the form of name-calling, discrimination, threatening behaviour, verbal or physical abuse but can also include unreasonable demands upon you, such as asking you to do work that's not within your job description. Whether bullying is physical or not, it is still a form a violence – psychological violence can be just as damaging as physical violence. Usually bullies do what they do in order to cover up their own inadequacies and to deflect attention from their own failings. By putting someone else down, bullies may also make themselves feel more worthy. Do not be fooled by fellow employees that a bully is just using a tough form of management. If you feel that you are being bullied, try and get something done about it. Most companies have a discrimination procedure, which may include a bullying procedure also. This should outline how staff are expected to behave and will also detail how complaints are dealt with. The normal procedure is to resolve bullying issues by talking about them. If that fails, companies may have a disciplinary procedure that can be implemented if necessary.

Bully Online
www.bullyonline.org

Basic rights at work
www.adviceguide.org.uk/em/wales/life/employment/basic_rights_at_work/wales/life/employment/basic_rights_at_work.htm

TUC guide to workplace bullying
0207 636 4030
www.tuc.org.uk/tuc/rights_bullyatwork.cfm

Equal Opportunities Commission
0845 601 5901
www.eoc.org.uk

Also check out:

> Discrimination Essentials
> Equal Opportunities
> Racism
> Contracts
> Employment Rights
> Working UK

When you are in employment you have a right to be treated fairly. You should not be expected to work in unhealthy or dangerous conditions, for more hours than the law states as legal and you should not be discriminated against for any reason. You can also expect to receive certain entitlements such as regularly paid wages, breaks, a holiday allowance and other benefits to make the workplace healthy. There are laws that govern how employers should treat their employees. Employees can find out what is expected of them and what they can expect from their employer by checking their contract and/or company handbook. If an employee has a grievance with their employer or feels they have been treated unfairly, there are several avenues that can be taken to resolve issues. Firstly, an employee should speak to their immediate superior and try to settle the problem through them. The next stop should be the company's human resources department (if your company has one). If the issue still cannot be resolved, seek external help. A union, the Citizens Advice Bureau or other more specific organisations such as the Equal Opportunities Commission can provide support.

Citizens Advice Bureau
www.adviceguide.org.uk

TUC guide to rights at work
www.worksmart.org.uk/rights/

Equal Opportunities Commission
0845 601 5901
www.eoc.org.uk

Also check out:

- Discrimination Essentials
- Legal Advice
- Careers Essentials
- Contracts
- Working UK

All employees are entitled to a minimum of four weeks paid leave a year. You'll be allowed four times the amount of days you work in a typical working week as paid leave. Your contract will say how much notice you must give before taking holiday. An employer may refuse holiday, providing that they give you the right notice. If you are sick when you are on leave or are unfairly refused leave, speak to your employer about it or seek professional advice if necessary. When you leave a company, you are entitled to be paid for any outstanding leave that you have. Similarly, if you owe leave, it may be deducted from your wages. Working parents are also entitled to paid leave, which can be granted for antenatal care and for looking after a newborn. Men are entitled to one or two week's paternity leave from the date that the child is born. Women are entitled to a minimum of 26 week's maternity leave and most women qualify for statutory maternity pay. Maternity leave will vary depending on your employer; speak to them or seek professional help for clarification.

Department of Trade and Industry
0207 215 5000
www.dti.gov.uk

Citizen's Advice Bureau page on holiday entitlement
http://www.adviceguide.org.uk/em/index/life/employment/holidays_and_holiday_pay.htm

Citizen's Advice Bureau page on Parental rights at work
www.adviceguide.org.uk/em/index/life/employment/parental_rights_at_work.htm

Also check out:

- Contracts
- Employment Rights
- Working UK
- Careers Essentials
- Discrimination Essentials
- Babies

When candidates apply for a new job, they are expected to provide referees. Referees are the names and contact details of someone who will be able to provide a reference (which says what type of employee and character the person is). Most employers ask for two referees, one of which should be your current or most recent employer, the other can be a colleague or previous employer but not a family member. If you've not worked before, your referee can be a previous teacher, lecturer or tutor. Only use a friend as a reference if none of these are available. You should ask permission before you put someone as your referee and tell them who might be contacting them and about what. Usually, employers will only use a reference to find out if there is any particular reason why the prospective employee should not be employed, such as continual absence or poor timekeeping. There are many legal issues that surround employment references. A previous employer may not make negligent or careless comments about a previous employee. The reference that they provide must be true, accurate and fair. An employer is under no legal obligation to provide a reference or to mention any particular incident so long as the reference is not misleading.

BBC page on Working Life
www.bbc.co.uk/radio1/onelife/work/index.shtml

Careers Wales
0800 100 900
www.careerswales.com

Also check out:

> Careers Essentials
> Applying for a Job
> CVs and Application Forms
> Interviews and Assessments
> Contracts

Sexual harassment at work can take many forms. In general, it is unwanted behaviour of a sexual nature. It can be anything from unwanted lewd comments about sex or appearance, physical behaviour such as brushing up closely against someone, the displaying of sexual material such as posters, inappropriate forwarded messages or any other sexual behaviour that makes the working environment uncomfortable. Sexual harassment should not be tolerated on any level and there are laws to protect employees against it. If you do experience sexual harassment at work it can be very damaging both physically and emotionally. The first thing to do is to make it clear in a calm and sensible manner that you do not like that kind of behaviour and wish for it to stop. It is a good idea to make a note of what occurs, when it does and who else was there to witness it. If the behaviour continues, approach your line manager or your human resources department and, hopefully, the issue can be resolved in-house. If you do not feel that your employer has dealt with the problem sufficiently, you can take legal action against them – see your union or contact the Equal Opportunities Commission for advice.

BBC guide to sexual harrassment
www.bbc.co.uk/crime/law/sexualharassment.s
html

Connexions Direct
0808 001 3219
www.connexions-direct.com

Citizens Advice Bureau page on sex discrimination
www.adviceguide.org.uk/em/index/your_rights
/civil_rights/taking_action_about_sex_discrimi-
nation.htm

Also check out:
> Bullying In The Workplace
> Employment Rights
> Working UK
> Harassment
> Discrimination Essentials
> Equal Opportunities

Unfair Dismissal

Unfair dismissal is when an employer ends a contract with an employee for a reason that is not deemed legal. It can be a complicated issue with various possible factors involved. Firstly, you need to be sure that your contract of employment does identify that you are an employee and not a contractor etc. There are various types of dismissal also. Your contract may not be renewed, you may be sacked instantly or you may be forced into resignation. If you have been discriminated against, which led to a dismissal then you will automatically have been unfairly dismissed. There are various other reasons (such as not being allowed to return to work after pregnancy) that are automatically considered as unfair dismissal. If the reason for dismissal is not one of those, there are various factors that will decide if you have been fairly dismissed or not such as how long you have worked for the company and the reason for dismissal. All companies are bound by laws that state the procedure that they must follow in order to dismiss an employee. In all cases, you should seek advice from the Citizen's Advice Bureau or your union.

Department of Trade and Industry
0207 215 5000
www.dti.gov.uk

BBC's page on unfair dismissal
www.bbc.co.uk/crime/law/unfairdismissal.shtml

Advisory Conciliation and Arbitration
Service (ACAS)
08457 47 47 47
www.acas.org.uk/rights/discipline.html

Citizens Advice Bureau page on unfair Dismissal
www.adviceguide.org.uk/em/index/life/employment/dismissal.htm

Also check out:

- Bullying In The Workplace
- Careers Essentials
- Contracts
- Employment Rights
- Discrimination Essentials
- Equal Opportunities

Before you start a new job, you need to sign a contract. You will sign two copies of your contract, one of which will be kept by your employer, the other being for your records. Your contract outlines the important details of your employment. These include your salary, your working hours, company policy rules concerning health and safety, annual and sick leave and the period of notice that you must give your employers before leaving (or the period of notice they must give you before dismissal!). Some companies may also have a company handbook, which goes into further details about the rules and regulations that the company have. Once a contract has been signed, both the employer and the employee are bound by law to it and must stick to what it says. So, before you sign it, have a good read through it and make sure that you are happy with it. If there are any parts of it that are not clear to you, mention it to your prospective employer and they'll be happy to explain all for you. Remember, the contract is there to protect the employer, the company and the employee.

The Advisory Conciliation and Arbitration Service
08457 47 47 47
www.acas.org.uk

Department of Trade and Industry page on Employment Relations
0207 215 5000
www.dti.gov.uk/er/regs.htm

Citizens Advice Bureau guide to Contract of Employment
www.adviceguide.org.uk/em/index/life/employment/contracts_of_employment/index/life/employment/contracts_of_employment.htm

Trade Union Congress
0207 636 4030
www.tuc.org.uk

Also check out:
- Employment Rights
- Time off Work
- Wages
- Working Hours
- Careers Essentials
- Rights Essentials

As well as standard annual leave, employees are entitled to receive other kinds of time off work, the details of which should be written in your contract or company handbook. Employees are entitled to sick pay (which may be less than full pay) for the first 28 weeks of sickness. Each company will have different rules as to what evidence is needed for proof of sickness. After 28 weeks off work, you may be entitled to unpaid sick leave. Most employees are also entitled to receive paid compassionate leave for such things as family funerals etc. Some companies may also offer their employees the chance to take unpaid leave. This will only occur once all paid leave has been used and the employee wishes to take extra holiday. It is also possible that an employer may offer their employees the chance to take sabbaticals. If, for example, you wanted to take a year out from your career to go travelling or volunteering, your company may allow you to return afterwards. If you want to take time off work, speak to your employers and find out what their rules and regulations are.

Advisory Conciliatory and Arbitration Service (ACAS) page on time off work
08457 47 47 47
www.acas.org.uk/rights/timeoff.html

Department of Trade and Industry (DTI) page on rights at work
0207 215 5000
www.dti.gov.uk/er/individual/rights-pl716.htm

Also check out:

> Careers Essentials
> Contracts
> Employment Rights
> Working UK
> Volunteering Abroad
> Travel Essentials

All workers are entitled to be paid for work done, for being at work and not being given work and for not being able to work due to sickness, holiday, maternity or paternity leave. If you are aged 16 or over, you are entitled to earn, at least, the National Minimum Wage (NMW), which is £3 an hour. For workers aged between 18 and 21 or workers aged 22 and above starting a new job with a new employer and doing accredited training, the NMW is £4.25 an hour and for those aged over 22, it is £5.05 an hour. From October 2006 the rates will increase. The adult rate will rise to £5.35, the "development rate" will be £4.45 and the rate for young people (older than school leaving age and younger than 18) will rise to £3.30.

There is no law on how wages should be paid to a worker. Instead, the method of payment is likely to be detailed in a written contract. If there is no written contract, this needs to be agreed with your employer beforehand. All employees are also entitled to receive a payslip at or before the time of payment. This details exactly how much has been earned, how much tax and national insurance has been deducted from payment and other information such as employee number, tax code and the total amount earned over the year. At the end of the financial year (April) your employer will give you a form, known as a P60, which should be kept as it shows details of earnings for the whole previous year.

Citizens Advice Bureau
www.adviceguide.org.uk

Advice Now
www.advicenow.org.uk

Also check out:

> Budgeting Essentials
> Income Tax
> Careers Essentials
> Contracts
> National Insurance (NI)
> Value Added Tax (VAT)

First of all, check that your normal working hours are clearly laid out in your contract of employment. The average working week is 37.5 hours long (your typical 9-to-5, Monday to Friday shift with half an hour each day for lunch). The maximum hours that you can be made to work in a week is 48. You can, occasionally, chose to work more hours than this (if you average less than 48 hours a week) and, sometimes, a longer working week is a requirement (but this should be made aware to you upfront and should be in your contract).

Working Hours for over 16s: You can work full-time when you are no longer of compulsory school age (from the last Friday in June for 16-year-olds).

14-16 Year Olds: You can work part-time between the ages of 14 and 16. However, you can't work during school hours, for more than two hours on a school day or before 7am or after 7pm. You also can't work more than 12 hours in a school week and not for more than five hours on a Saturday (or during the holidays) and not for more than 2 hours on a Sunday. There are also certain jobs you can't do for health & safety reasons. See the links below for more info.

13 Year Olds: You can only do work that is approved by local authority by-laws.

Under 13: As a rule, you are not allowed to work if you are under 13 (you can sometimes apply for a special license).

Citizens Advice Bureau
www.adviceguide.org.uk

Advice Now (site providing information on law and your rights)
www.advicenow.org.uk

Directgov page on working hours
www.direct.gov.uk/Employment/Employees/WorkingHoursAndTimeOff/fs/en

Worksmart
www.worksmart.org.uk/rights/viewsearchresults.php?q=children

Also check out:

- Careers Essentials
- Contracts
- Income Tax
- National Insurance (NI)

Volunteering abroad is a great way for you to give something back to the planet. You could help out on an environmental project, work with underprivileged children or with impoverished communities. Either way, you'll be using your skills, experience and character to help in an area where help is needed. As well as experiencing the pleasure of giving, you'll get the chance to experience a new language, meet lots of new people, learn new skills and you'll have great fun whilst doing it too. Volunteering is no easy ride though. Expect to be worked hard. It may be tough both physically and emotionally. There are many different types of voluntary work. Projects can be paid, unpaid, skilled, unskilled and some may provide other benefits such as accommodation etc. Some organisations may ask for you to raise money to take part, some may ask you to organise your own travel arrangements. When considering volunteering abroad, you need to know that you are committed to doing it, are willing to work hard and are doing it for the right reasons. You should also consider the culture, language and environment of the country where you volunteer.

I to I (provides volunteering experiences to people of all ages) 0800 011 1156
www.i-to-i.com

Job Centre's advice on volunteering
0113 307 8090
www.jobcentreplus.gov.uk/cms.asp?Page=/Home/Customers/WorkingOrTrainingInEurope/Wanttoworkorvolunteerabroad

Working Abroad (networking service for volunteers)
www.workingabroad.com

Careers Europe
01274 829600
www.careerseurope.co.uk

Also check out:

- Qualifications Essentials
- Volunteering UK
- Environmental Issues
- Poverty
- Travel Essentials
- Culture

Do you want to give something back to the community? If so, volunteering might just be the thing for you. There are countless opportunities for those with some spare time who want to help charities, gain new skills and experiences, improve their CVs, get involved in teamwork and meet new people. There are many ways that you can get involved. There are projects that aim to clean up and improve local areas so you may use your gardening skills to brighten up a piece of derelict land. If you like working with people, you could get involved with a team that distributes food to the homeless or you could volunteer at a day centre, looking after elderly people. If you like working in a shop, you could volunteer in a charity shop. It's unlikely that you'll be paid for your efforts but some organisations may pay your expenses. If you're thinking about volunteering, think about who it is that you wish to help, where your skills lie and how much time you can spare to do it. The range of volunteering opportunities is very wide, so carry out some research and find exactly what you're looking for. It is also possible to volunteer whilst claiming benefits.

Volunteering Wales
www.volunteering-wales.net

Youth Information
0116 242 7350
www.youthinformation.com

Wales Council For Voluntary Action
0870 607 1666
www.wcva.org.uk

Community Service Volunteers
0207 278 6601
www.csv.org.uk

CWVYS Council for Wales Voluntary Youth Services
www.cwvys.org.uk

Also check out:
> Personal Development
> Unemployed Essentials
> Volunteering Abroad
> Working UK
> Careers Essentials
> CVs and Application Forms

Just like humans, animals have rights too. There are many laws in the UK that protect animals. They state that animals have the right to food, shelter and water, as well as the right to live free from distress. They also have the right to perform their natural behaviour whether domesticated or held captive. If broken, those who are responsible for the cruelty can be fined, banned from keeping animals or even given a prison sentence. Currently, animal welfare laws are under review and, once complete, are expected to be toughened. Many people do not believe that the law protects animals enough and campaign to change the law. There are many ways to get involved with animal rights campaigning from collecting money to organising marches. The RSPCA exists in order to protect animals. They investigate cases where cruelty is suspected and can help in prosecuting those responsible. They are often involved in caring for sick and injured animals also. Additionally, the RSPCA run animal rights campaigns. You can get involved by donating or signing up as a member of the RSPCA.

Royal Society for the Prevention of Cruelty to Animals (RSPCA) Cruelty Line
0870 55 55 999
www.rspca.org.uk

BBC page on the ethics of animal rights
www.bbc.co.uk/religion/ethics/animals/index.shtml

Pro-Animal Rights
www.animal-rights.com

Animal Rights Coalition
0845 458 0146
arcnews.redblackandgreen.net

Also check out:
> Animal Testing
> Hunting
> Pets
> Wildlife, Zoos and Safari Parks
> Farming and Agriculture
> Ethical Trade

Testing on animals is an extremely complex and emotive issue. Worldwide, animals are tested on for research purposes (known as vivisection) and to improve cosmetic products such as make-up. In the UK, animal testing for cosmetics is banned. However, there are still some products available in the UK that have been developed using animal testing and labelling on products can often be misleading. The Humane Cosmetics Standard is like a kitemark that proves that the product and none of its ingredients have been developed using testing on animals. Currently, the EU is looking at new laws that will reduce the number of animals used for testing, reduce the amount of suffering caused and replace animals with alternatives. Scientists believe that using animals for medical research is necessary to improve knowledge into human diseases, medical cures and to gain medical knowledge such as research into genetics. Some animal rights campaigners believe that the research causes unnecessary harm to animals and doesn't provide accurate results. It's a difficult issue with no clear right or wrong. It's up to you to look at the issue and decide how you feel.

The British Union for the Abolition of Vivisection (BUAV)
0207 700 4888
www.buav.org

Home Office page on animal testing
0207 035 4848
www.homeoffice.gov.uk/science-research/animal-testing/

BBC guide to animal testing
www.bbc.co.uk/science/hottopics/animalexperiments/index.shtml

Ethical Consumer Magazine
www.ethicalconsumer.org

Also check out:
> Animal Rights
> Consumer Labelling
> Hunting
> Pets
> Wildlife, Zoos and Safari Parks
> Cloning and Genetics

Up until February 2005, some forms of hunting were legal in the UK. However, after much public debate the Government brought in a law (the Hunting Act 2004) that made hunting with dogs illegal. The issue caused a lot of controversy across the country. Pro-hunters believed that the hunting of animals such as foxes, deer and mink was necessary to keep their population under control. This was because farmers saw these animals as pests and a threat to their livestock. They also believed that such a ban would have a big impact on the rural economy. Anti-hunters believed that hunting was inhumane and unnecessary for pest control. Eventually, hunting with dogs was banned. However, the law does still permit some forms of hunting. For example, farmers are allowed to use dogs, in certain circumstances (to 'flush out' or chase into the open animals if they are causing a threat to livestock, for example). They can then only be shot by a competent person afterwards. Many people still feel very strongly about the issue and want the law to be changed.

Department for Environment, Food and Rural Affairs (DEFRA) page on Hunting with Dogs
08459 33 55 77
www.defra.gov.uk/rural/hunting/default.htm

BBC's Q&As on hunting
news.bbc.co.uk/1/hi/uk_politics/4021627.stm

Countryside Alliance (pro-hunting group)
0207 840 9200
www.countryside-alliance.org.uk

The League Against Cruel Sports (LACS)
www.league.uk.com

Also check out:
> Farming and Agriculture
> Countryside
> Animal Rights
> Animal Testing
> Wildlife, Zoos and Safari Parks
> Pets

Pets can be great fun but they are a big responsibility too. It can be easy to get carried away when you are getting a pet. Puppy dog eyes, cute cat paws and fluffy bunny rabbits can easily make you rush into something that you might not be ready for. Before you get a pet, make sure that you are aware of how much care they will need and if you are capable of providing that, not just for the first few months but for the rest it's life. You need to think about how much space your animal takes up, the mess it could make, if it needs any accessories, what food it requires and how often it will need to go to the vet. You'll need to think about if you have the time and energy to give it the exercise it needs, if you'll always be able to afford to pay for what it needs and if you are willing to do things like worm your pet and check your pet for fleas. Remember that cruel owners can be prosecuted. You also need to consider other laws that govern things like dog fouling and the keeping of exotic pets.

Royal Society for the Prevention of Cruelty to Animals (RSPCA)
0870 55 55 999
www.rspca.org.uk

BBC's pet page
www.bbc.co.uk/cbbc/wild/pets/

Page for pet lovers
www.petwebsite.com

Also check out:
> Animal Rights
> Animal Testing
> Hunting
> Wildlife, Zoos and Safari Parks
> Farming and Agriculture
> Ethical Trade

3.1 The Animal Kingdom

Wildlife: Most countries have agreed that we need to protect the world's animals and plants. It's time to take a walk on the wild side. Many wildlife habitats are either under threat or influenced by environmental pollution. Being sensitive to change, they can never be replaced. In Wales there are SSSIs (Sites of Special Scientific Interest) that you can visit and help maintain by volunteering. These areas make sure the wildlife and flora are protected. You can watch from afar, go on wildlife holidays, help out at a wildlife centre, watch wildlife on the TV, plant up your garden to encourage wildlife, volunteer or get involved in national or local projects.

Zoos & Safari Parks: Many zoos and safari parks are involved in protecting endangered animals and helping to boost populations in the wild. But do you think they're educational and interesting or outdated and cruel? You will have an opinion about the need for zoos and the reasons behind them. Much is being done to ensure that zoos are now becoming areas of environmental enhancement and natural places to help wildlife throughout the world. Safari Parks and Federation Zoos are good examples.

The Wildlife Trust
0870 036 7711
www.wildlifetrusts.org

The Captive Animals' Protection Society
0845 330 3911
www.captiveanimals.org

Guide to Britain's safari parks
www.safaripark.co.uk

World Wildlife Fund UK
www.wwf-uk.org/core/index.asp

Also check out:

> Animal Rights
> Conservation
> Animal Testing
> Pets
> Countryside
> Earth

Biodiversity relates to the range of species of animals and plants (fauna and flora) that exist in the natural environment. It has been shaped by millions of years of natural evolution and provides the basis for what life on earth depends upon. Biodiversity is in a state of constant change but is increasingly influenced by human behaviour, to a potentially dangerous level. Species are disappearing faster than ever before. Most reasons for this can be attributed to humans. The increasing human population, which is taking up more and more land, is leaving less room for wildlife. The illegal trade of wildlife (thought to be worth £5 billion a year) affects numbers of wild animals and plants. And, the introduction of non-native species is damaging to a natural environment. The decline in biodiversity could lead to a lack of food for poorer regions, fewer potential medicines and, at worst, could lead to the earth becoming unable to sustain life. The Convention on Biological Diversity (signed in 1992) ensured that most of the world's Governments agreed aims to preserve biodiversity. In 2002, it was agreed that these nations would do more to reduce the extinction rate of species. In the UK, The Wildlife and Countryside Act protects wild species from being killed or taken from their natural habitat and provides for the notification of Sites of Special Scientific Interest (SSSIs), where species are protected.

UK Biodiversity Action Plan
www.ukbap.org.uk

BBC page on Biodiversity
www.bbc.co.uk/nature/environment/conservationnow/global/biodiversity/index.shtml

Brief guide to The Wildlife and Countryside Act
www.naturenet.net/law/wca.html

Friends of the Earth (FoE) page on Biodiversity
0808 800 1111
www.foe.co.uk/campaigns/biodiversity/links.html

Also check out:
> Sustainable Development
> Conservation
> Environment
> Hunting
> Countryside
> Ethical Trade

The Earth's climate has always been and always will be in a state of change. In modern times, the term 'climate change' has come to mean the heating of the Earth caused by human intervention. Currently, there is much debate around the degree to which human behaviour is affecting the heat of the globe. It has become generally accepted by most people that climate change is occurring, due to the increased burning of fossil fuels, which creates greenhouse gases such as carbon dioxide, and that it needs to slow down dramatically to avoid a potentially disastrous situation. However, there are also some climate change sceptics. They believe that the changes that are occurring are natural and human behaviour is not to blame. Additionally, there are those who believe that current scientific thought is not able to accurately predict the changes that may occur to our climate. In 2005, the Kyoto Protocol became part of international law, requiring many nations to limit their carbon dioxide emissions. However, the US, the country that produces the largest amount of carbon emissions, did not sign up to the protocol. If you are concerned about climate change, why not get involved with a campaigning group such as Friends of the Earth?

Friends of the Earth
0808 800 1111
www.foe.co.uk

BBC pages on Climate Change
www.bbc.co.uk/climate/

United Nations Framework on Climate Change (agreement to tackle climate change)
unfccc.int/2860.php

The UK Climate Impacts Programme (UKCIP) 01865 285717
www.ukcip.org.uk/

Also check out:

> Logging
> Renewable Energy
> Going Green
> United Nations
> Pollution
> Flooding

A major modern scientific and ethical issue is cloning and genetics. Cloning is where an exact copy of a living organism is made using DNA from the original. Genetics is the study of heredity, where scientists look at exactly how qualities and traits are passed on from parents to offspring. Scientists have already cloned some animals including pigs, sheep and cats. The most debatable point, though, is whether there should be an attempt to clone a human being. Those in favour believe that this kind of scientific advancement could improve knowledge into ways of treating illness. Some also believe that it may become possible to produce children with a perfect genetic make-up who will therefore be free of disability and disease. Some less in favour believe that the research could do some harm so should be approached with a degree of caution. Those against cloning believe that science is not yet advanced enough and that cloned animals often die quickly or develop unknown illnesses. Many also have ethical reservations about cloning, believing that it is unnatural, humans should not be produced in this manufactured way and that scientists are 'playing God'. If you have a strong opinion on this, let us know.

Group in favour of human cloning
www.humancloning.org

Human Genetics Alert (anti-cloning group) 0207 704 6100
www.hgalert.org

Department of Health page on genetics
0207 210 4850
www.dh.gov.uk/PolicyAndGuidance/HealthAndSocialCareTopics/Genetics/GeneticsGeneralInformation/fs/en

I-bio (website about biotechnology)
plus.i-bio.gov.uk/biolinks/oip_ibio/cloning.html

Also check out:
> Animal Rights
> Animal Testing
> Wildlife, Zoos and Safari Parks
> Sustainable Development
> Earth
> Religion & Beliefs

Many products that you buy have consumer labels on them. In fact, manufacturers have a responsibility to tell consumers certain details about their products. It might be that the product is dangerous to certain people (i.e., food containing nuts to those with a nut allergy), it could just be to notify you what a product is made from, where it was made and if it was made to a certain standard or to an agreed set of principles. Some particularly important things to check for on labels are whether the product has been tested on animals, if it is suitable for Vegans, if the product has any safety warnings, whether it is organic, the best before dates and care instructions (especially if it's an item of clothing). If you are an ethical consumer, with a bit of research, you can use label information to be sure that you are buying the most ethically produced product. For example, chickens produce eggs in differing conditions ranging from cruel battery farms to more natural free range, organic farms. If you don't want to contribute to a company that sell products in a way that you feel is unethical or harms the environment, then check the labels first. If the consumer label claims something that is not true and is misleading, the trader or manufacturer could be prosecuted.

Ethical Consumer magazine
www.ethicalconsumer.org

Consumer Direct 08454 04 05 06
www.consumerdirect.gov.uk

Citizen's Advice Bureau
www.adviceguide.org.uk

Welsh Consumer Council 02920 255 454
www.wales-consumer.org.uk

Food Standards Agency 0207 276 8152
www.foodstandards.gov.uk

Also check out:
> Training Essentials
> Basic Skills Essentials
> Vocational Qualifications
> Personal Development

3.2 Environmental Issues

Welcome to planet Earth: the blue planet. It seems that drought, extinction and disaster are all we hear about our planet these days. Is this really all that's in store for Earth? Our planet is having a hard time, but our Earth keeps going and has done for millions of years, tangled up in a connected web of life.

The good news:
The hole in the ozone is repairing because 114 countries have reduced their use of harmful chemicals and air pollutants. Five times as much of the Earth is now protected than thirty years ago. Species that were under threat are coming back because of conservation groups and action groups.

And the bad:
Every year, the amount of concrete roads, cities and buildings peppering the Earth's surface increases. More and more forests, woodlands and countryside are being destroyed in the name of progress and industrial development.
Thousands of species of birds and mammals are threatened with extinction. The supply of fresh water to humans and animals will fall at an alarming rate.

There are ways you can help Earth overcome its problems and get involved in national campaigns and environmental pressure groups. Look forward to a better future.

Nations Online
www.nationsonline.org/oneworld/earth.htm

Earth Summit
www.earthsummit.info

The Environment Agency
08708 506 506
www.environment-agency.gov.uk

Friends of the Earth 0808 800 1111
www.foe.co.uk

Also check out:
> Biodiversity
> Climate Change
> Environmental Issues
> Flooding
> Pollution
> Sustainable Development

In the world today, millions of people are still affected by famine and drought. The vast majority of those affected are in Africa. The chief reason for famine in Africa is drought. The lack of rain means that it is difficult to grow crops and raise livestock, leading to food and water shortages. As well as drought, there are other factors that contribute to African famine. Political corruption, war and conflict, reliance on imported food, unfair trade policies and the spread of AIDS all place pressure on the food security of many African nations. Over the years, developed nations have attempted to help those in the grip of famine through fundraising events such as Live Aid in 1985. Money and supplies help in the short term, however, for the long term, African nations need tools to build themselves a better infrastructure and to have fewer restrictions placed upon them by richer nations (such as fairer trade laws and a decreased debt burden). Nowadays, campaigners are more concerned with changing laws and reducing debt levels in order to let Africa fend for itself. Live 8 in 2005 was an event organised to raise awareness of the issues. If you want to help, organisations like Save The Children and Make Poverty History campaign against poverty in Africa.

Make Poverty History
www.makepovertyhistory.org

United Nations World Food Programme
www.wfp.org

Save the Children
www.savethechildren.org.uk/scuk/jsp/index.jsp?flash=true

BBC page on famine in Africa
news.bbc.co.uk/1/hi/world/africa/2027079.stm

Also check out:
> Asylum Seekers
> Farming and Agriculture
> Poverty
> Sustainable Development
> United Nations
> World Politics – One World

3.2 Environmental Issues

Wales is a predominantly rural nation and has a longstanding, proud tradition of farming and agriculture. The actions and the fortune of the Welsh rural community has a wider effect on the nation as a whole. The issues that surround farming and agriculture are constantly changing and are affected by worldwide changes. Here are some of the current issues:

Genetically Modified (GM) foods: GM foods are foods that are grown using genes from another living organism in order to make the food better, i.e., bigger, better colour etc. Those against GM foods argue that they may not be safe for consumption, that their cultivation may harm the environment and damage biodiversity. Currently, GM foods are not grown in the UK but the Government is likely to allow production from 2008.

Organic foods: Organic food has been produced to a certain set of standards, which guarantee such things as animal welfare and chemical-free production. Currently, it is more expensive than non-organic food as it is more labour-intensive to produce. Those in favour of organic food argue that non-organic food contains chemicals (like pesticides) that may be harmful and do not agree with some of the conditions in which non-organic food is produced.

Farming Methods: As a result of increased competition, some farming methods have developed into ways that many feel are cruel to animals such as battery farms (where chickens are kept in dark, cramped conditions). Campaigners believe that animals should be able to lead more natural lives.

National Farmers Union 0870 845 8458
www.nfu-wales.org.uk

Department for Food and Rural Affairs page on GM crops 08459 33 55 77
www.defra.gov.uk/environment/gm/crops/faq.htm

The Soil Association 0117 314 5000
www.soilassociation.org

Compassion in World Farming (CIWF)
01730 264 208 www.ciwf.org.uk

Also check out:

- Animal Rights
- Hunting
- Biodiversity
- Environmental Issues
- Countryside
- Going Green

Recent events in South-East Asia and New Orleans prove the damage that water can do. Flooding usually occurs as a result of a natural disaster (although it can happen if a dam breaks). Heavy rainfall over a short period of time can cause an area to flood, particularly if it occurs immediately after a dry period when the ground is hard and less capable of absorbing the water. Extreme weather such as hurricanes and earthquakes can cause sea levels to swell, which in turn can lead to the sea overwhelming flood defences. Rivers can also be the cause of flooding. Heavy rainfall and water travelling down mountains can cause river levels to rise quickly and overflow. Wales has its share of flood problems. In the UK, around two million properties are at risk from flooding, which may make it difficult for them to be protected by home insurance (check first before buying), although across the world, the areas to which flooding causes the greatest risk are the poorer regions, which do not have the resources to cope in such events. The Environment Agency warns people about the risk of flooding from rivers and the sea. You can check if you are in a flood risk area by entering your postcode on this website: www.bbc.co.uk/weather/features/environment_search.shtml

Environment Agency
08708 506 506
www.environment-agency.gov.uk

UK Resilience (advice for when flooding occurs)
www.ukresilience.info/flooding.htm

The Met Office
0870 900 0100
www.met-office.gov.uk

The World Bank (source of funds for dam construction)
www.whirledbank.org/index.html

Also check out:
- Climate Change
- Earth
- Environmental Issues
- Poverty
- Famine and Drought
- Buying a Home

Every year, fires rage through forests all over the world, destroying wildlife, animals, buildings and sometimes people. Fires can start naturally and accidentally or can be set intentionally. Recently, forest fires have become more common across parts of Europe including Spain and France, as summers have become hotter and drier, causing death and destruction. Many think that this could be due to the effects of global warming.

In some forests, especially commercial ones grown specifically to sell trees to industry, firebreaks are used to try to prevent and control forest fires. These are wide gaps between rows of trees to try to stop the spread of the fire.

However, fire is essential to some ecosystems. Some species (including some types of woodpecker and squirrel) benefit from occasional fires, which help to maintain the diversity of plant life necessary for these species to feed themselves adequately. In some areas, authorities conduct carefully controlled fires for this purpose. Natural and controlled fires also help clear forests of dead wood. Without them, dead wood accumulates – making it more dangerous when an accidental fire breaks out, as the forests are more densely packed.

Forest fires can be caused accidentally by: discarding lit cigarettes, failing to properly extinguish campfires & discarding matches. If you are in a forest or an area of woodland, be very careful to extinguish any fires properly and don't drop lit cigarettes or matches.

Fire kills (fire safety)
www.firekills.gov.uk

Fire prevention 0207 215 5000
www.dti.gov.uk/homesafetynetwork/index.htm

Article on forest fires
www.peopleandplanet.net/doc.php?id=1876

World Wildlife Fund page on forest fires
01483 426 444
www.wwf.org.uk/researcher/issues/forests/0000000196.asp

Also check out:

> Climate Change
> Earth
> Environmental Issues
> Logging
> Countryside
> Conservation

Rainforests are the richest source of life on earth, home to over half the world's species of plants and animals containing unknown cures to thousands of illnesses and disease and we - as human beings - are chopping them down and clearing them (logging) largely for money (chopping the trees down for pulp and paper, or clearing areas of land where the rainforest grows for oil palm plantations etc). Commercial logging is the biggest threat to the ecological integrity of these forests.

Clearing large areas of rainforest can also have a harmful affect on the indigenous people (the people native to the area) – their homes, communities and natural habitat can be completely destroyed. It can also damage local and "downstream" environments, through flooding, soil erosion and fire.

Logging also intensifies global warming. Trees absorb some of the carbon dioxide that causes global warming and cutting them down reduces that effect.

Each year an area the size of Wales and England is destroyed. Want to help stop it? Great apes don't have a choice, but you do. If you want to say something about it, then do. Download a DIY campaign pack from Greenpeace and get active.

Friends of the Earth
0808 800 1111
www.foe.co.uk

Greenpeace
0207 865 8100
www.greenpeace.org.uk

World Wildlife Fund
01483 426 444
www.wwf-uk.org

Forestry Commission
0131 334 0303
www.forestry.gov.uk

Also check out:
- Volunteering Abroad
- Biodiversity
- Earth
- Environmental Issues
- Recycling
- Sustainable Development

Over Population
3.2 Environmental Issues

When there are more people in an area than the resources that are available to support them, overpopulation occurs. There are currently over six billion humans living on Earth and that number is increasing with rising speed. It is not known how many people the Earth can support and whether population levels can continue rising in the current manner. At some point, it is assumed that the Earth's resources will be stretched beyond breaking point. In China, the population problem was so large that the Government controversially introduced laws to limit the number of children that families were allowed to have.

Currently, one of the biggest problems with this issue is the way in which resources are used and distributed. People in wealthy areas have access to more and better resources than those in poor areas. Many people live in poverty because of this and are vulnerable to disease, natural disasters and famine. There are several organisations including Oxfam and Save The Children who are working in poverty-stricken areas to improve the situation of the poor.

Population Action International
www.populationaction.org/issues/index.htm

Oxfam
0870 333 2700
www.oxfam.org.uk

Save The Children
www.savethechildren.org.uk

Population information
www.population.com/

Also check out:
> Asylum Seekers
> Earth
> Sustainable Development
> Poverty
> Famine and Drought
> Contraception

Pollution
3.2 Environmental Issues

Our planet is not as clean as it could be and it's mainly down to us. Human behaviour is responsible for damaging our land, sea and air. This has an adverse affect, not just on our immediate surroundings, but also on all other species and the environment as a whole. We pollute the air in many ways. Fumes from cars and aeroplanes and chemicals, gases and smoke from industry darken the skies, leading to global warming and also causing health problems such as respiratory disease. Much human waste is dumped into the sea, causing dirty water and affecting sea life. Lots more of our waste is dumped into landfills (big holes in the ground), which are quickly filling. You can do your bit by using the right products such as environmentally sensitive washing powder, organic food (uses no harmful pesticides) and green energy (produced using renewable resources). You can travel in the right way (trains are better for the environment than cars, buses or planes). Also, you can recycle as much waste as you can to reduce the amount that goes into landfills.

The Environment Agency
08708 506 506
www.environment-agency.gov.uk

Department for Environment, Food and Rural Affairs page on pollution
08459 33 55 77
www.defra.gov.uk/environment/ppc/index.htm

National Society for Clean Air
www.nsca.org.uk

Friends of the Earth
0808 800 1111
www.foe.co.uk

Also check out:
> Climate Change
> Environmental Issues
> Renewable Energy
> Bin It!
> Going Green
> Recycling

At the moment, the majority of our energy comes from the burning of fossil fuels such as oil, natural gas and coal. As well as leading to global warming and pollution, these fuels (known as 'non-renewable') will eventually run out. If we continue to use energy at the same rate as we do now, we'll soon need an alternative. Unless a new source of energy is found, this alternative will have to be from 'renewable energy' (energy generated from a source that will last forever, such as the sun, wind or water). Currently, only 2.7% of the UK's electricity is being produced using renewable energy but the Government has set the industry a target of 20% by the year 2010.

There are different types of renewable energy that may replace existing non-renewable energy. These include solar power (energy panels heated by the sun), wind power (generators charged by the wind) and hydro-electric power (generators charged by the movement of water). Nuclear power also exists as an extremely efficient alternative energy source. However, the dangers associated with it (such as radioactive leaks like the Chernobyl disaster) mean that it is rarely used. If you care about the type of energy that you use, switch to a 'green' energy supplier. They may be a little more expensive but, as they use more renewable sources, are better for the environment.

Department of Trade and Industry page on renewable energy 0207 215 5000
www.dti.gov.uk/renewables/

Compare prices of green electricity
www.greenelectricity.org

Renewable Energy news
www.renewableenergy.com

Centre for Alternative Technology's guide to renewable energy in Wales 01654 705950
www.cat.org.uk/grew/index.tmpl

Also check out:
- Earth
- Environmental Issues
- Sustainable Development
- Going Green
- Countryside
- Recycling

Sustainable development is development by present generations that doesn't have a negative effect on future generations and their ability to meet their own requirements for good quality of life. Progress is a necessary and vital part of human evolution, but shouldn't be at the expense of the planet or future generations. In short – take care of the planet and the people now, so that they are still there in the future!

This means protecting the environment and not using up all of the planet's natural resources (so developing and pushing the use of renewable energies), encouraging stable economic growth and employment worldwide, delivering everyone equal rights to education, healthcare etc – all the vital ingredients for a decent standard of living.

Sustainable development should combat poverty, pollution, social exclusion and support global prosperity for present and future generations - everyone working together for a brighter future. There are simple things such as recycling and consuming ethically that you can do to help sustainable development.

UK Government sustainable development homepage 0207 238 5811
www.sustainable-development.gov.uk

Department for Environment, Food and Rural Affairs page on sustainable development 08459 33 55 77
www.defra.gov.uk/environment/sustainable/

Recycling information centre
www.recycle-more.co.uk

Wales Ecological Footprint
02920 454970
www.walesfootprint.org/about_us/index.htm

Also check out:
> Climate Change
> Over Population
> Renewable Energy
> Going Green
> Recycling
> Bin It!

Bin It!
3.3 Get Active

As a responsible citizen and member of your community, one of the simplest things that you can do to improve your local environment is to use bins properly. There's nothing that makes a place look more unattractive than if it's covered in litter. You'd be surprised how much difference it can make if an area is kept clean. Whilst individuals can only make a small difference, collectively the effect has a much greater impact, improving the look and feel of an area, as well as the mood of those living within it. As community members, we all use public spaces so the responsibility of keeping them as clean as possible lies with each and every one of us. As well as improving the look of your local environment, using bins correctly improves health and safety and cuts the cost of cleaning by the local authority. It's not difficult to do; there are bins everywhere. So, the next time you think about throwing your rubbish on the floor, think for a second what it'd be like if everyone else did the same and hang on to it until you find a bin.

Bins
0845 331 31 31
www.recyclenow.com/home_composting/bins_accessories/bins_.html

Keep Britain Tidy
01942 612 621
www.encams.org

Waste Awareness Wales
0845 330 5540
www.wasteawarenesswales.org.uk

Sign up to the Mail Preference Service to stop unwanted junk mail
0845 703 4599
www.mpsonline.org.uk

Also check out:
- Pollution
- Recycling
- Environmental Issues
- Earth
- Going Green

Over the world, there are many species of animals whose numbers are so low that they are faced with extinction. Conservationists spend their lives trying to halt the decline of these species and to preserve the natural habitat in which they live. There are numerous factors that affect the decline of species. It might be that their natural habitat has been lost to humans, they may be used for sporting purposes such as hunting, for food, clothing or for trade. There are many ways that you can get involved if you want to help conserve creatures and their natural habitats. There are plenty of organisations such as Born Free out there, each of which are looking for donations and volunteers. Research using the internet and find out the contact details of the type of organisation you're interested in and write them an email or a letter to get involved.

BBC page on conservation
www.bbc.co.uk/nature/animals/conservation/

Born Free
01403 240 170
www.bornfree.org.uk

World Wildlife Fund
www.worldwildlife.org

Care for the Wild International
01306 627 900
www.careforthewild.org

Also check out:
> Animal Rights
> Hunting
> Wildlife, Zoos and Safari Parks
> Biodiversity
> Logging
> Volunteering UK

You might love or you might hate the countryside but its importance cannot be denied. Across the countryside are countless species of plants and animals, each with their own part to play in our unique natural environment. Many species are protected and certain areas of the countryside are known as Sites of Special Scientific Interest. These areas are our most precious areas of countryside due to the species that live in them or simply because of their beauty or uniqueness. If you live in a rural area, you'll probably already appreciate the beauty, tranquillity and joy of the countryside. If you're a town or city-dweller, the countryside can be a great place to get away from it all, get some fresh air and take in some nature. However, there are a few rules to remember if you are in the countryside.

- Leave gates and property as you find them
- Take you litter home with you
- Be considerate to others in the countryside
- Keep pets under control
- Protect plants and animals
- Keep the noise down
- If you are walking along a road without a pavement, walk towards the direction of oncoming traffic so that they can see you

The Countryside Agency
01242 521 381
www.countryside.gov.uk

Countryside Council for Wales
08451 306 229
www.ccw.gov.uk

The Welsh Assembly Government
Department for Environment, Planning and Countryside 02920 825 111
www.countryside.wales.gov.uk/index.asp

Also check out:
> Animal Rights
> Pets
> Hunting
> Environmental Issues
> Conservation
> Bin It!

3.3 Get Active

You don't need to be some kind of eco-warrior to do your bit for the environment. Here are some everyday tips that'll make you go green:

• Find out what recycling facilities your local authority has and cut down your waste.
• Some products, such as washing-up liquid and washing powder, are major pollutants. There are some brands that are better for the environment than others – find them and use them!
• Dishwashers use a lot of water and energy so pull on your marigolds and get scrubbing!
• Wash your clothes in big loads and using cooler water to save energy.
• Use energy-saving light bulbs for more economic use of electricity.
• Turn off lights and electrical equipment when they are not in use.
• Buy locally produced goods where possible thereby saving on fuel emissions caused by the importing of goods. Buying organic also reduces carbon emissions.
• Don't get in the bath, take a shower instead – it saves water.
Turn the heating down by just 1 degrees C.
• Only fill a kettle with as much water as you need, the rest is just a waste of energy.
• Take public transport, walk, ride a bike or lift-share.
• Turn the tap off while you brush your teeth.

The Green Party
0207 272 4474
www.greenparty.org.uk

Friends of the Earth
0800 800 11 11
www.foe.co.uk

Ethical Consumer magazine
www.ethicalconsumer.org

Environmental resources page
www.envirolink.org

Also check out:
> Renewable Energy
> Ethical Trade
> Climate Change
> Bin It!
> Pollution
> Recycling

England and Wales currently produce around 122 million tonnes of waste each year, most of which gets dumped in landfill sites (big holes filled with rubbish). These sites are quickly running out, meaning that we need to find somewhere else to dump our waste or find an alternative to simply discarding rubbish. One way of reducing waste is recycling. By taking products that are no longer needed and turning them into something new, we can reduce the environmental and economic impact of landfill waste. All sorts of things can be recycled. Plastic can be made into clothing, glass can be crushed to make sand, paper can be made into newspaper and old food can be made into compost for the garden. Whilst not every local authority in Britain has adequate recycling facilities, the number of schemes is increasing. Check with your local authority to find out what schemes they offer. They may provide a green bin for things like paper and bottles, they may do a regular collection of old newspapers or they may provide an area that you can take recyclable waste to. So, if you want to do your bit for the environment, find out what facilities are available to you and spend a little extra time sorting out your waste.

Recycle More
www.recycle-more.co.uk

Waste Awareness Wales
0845 330 5540
www.wasteawarenesswales.org.uk

Centre for Alternative Technology
01654 705 950
www.cat.org.uk

Department for the Environment, Food and Rural Affairs page on waste and recycling
08459 33 55 77
www.defra.gov.uk/environment/waste/topics/

Also check out:

> Climate Change
> Pollution
> Citizenship
> Bin It!
> Renewable Energy
> Going Green

Disability Travel
4.1 Travel Essentials

A disability should not be a barrier to travelling. In recent years, facilities for disabled people have improved immeasurably. There are now many schemes and provisions that allow those with disabilities to get around with as much ease as everyone else. The Disability Discrimination Act means that travel and transport operators cannot treat you less favourably than anyone else. If you're travelling locally, most transport operators have facilities such as ramps for wheelchair access and concessionary fees for a disabled person and a helper. If you need extra assistance, phone the operator in advance and make them aware of your journey details and your needs. Taxi companies are also required to provide access for disabled people. When travelling further afield, those with disabilities should be equally well catered for. Airlines have provisions for disabled people but you'll need to phone them with your needs ahead of your flight. When travelling abroad, remember that provisions for the disabled may not be as advanced as they are in the UK. Find out about what kinds of facilities are available before you go. There are also many organisations out there who organise holidays specifically for the disabled, providing extra care and helpers where needed.

Citizens Advice Bureau page on transport options for disabled people
www.adviceguide.org.uk/em/index/your_world/travel/transport_options_for_disabled_people.htm

RADAR (disability network) 0207 250 3222
www.radar.org.uk

Holidays for disabled people 01942 888844
www.access-travel.co.uk

Global Access (information page for disabled travellers)
www.geocities.com/Paris/1502/

Also check out:

> Disability Education and Courses
> Travel Essentials
> Discrimination Essentials
> Health and Safety
> Money Abroad
> Passports and Visas

4. WORLD, EUROPE, UK & WALES

Holidays should be great fun, but if you don't take the right precautions yours could be ruined by a number of things. Here are some of the most common holiday horrors to beware of:

The sun: too much sun can cause severe sunburn, heatstroke and skin cancer. Keep out of the sun at the hottest times of the day, use high factor sun cream and wear a hat. If you're worried that you have heatstroke, seek medical advice instantly.

Alcohol: it can be easy to get carried away on holiday. Drink sensibly, make sure you know what you're drinking and if you drink too much, find a trusted friend to look after you.

Personal Safety: holiday resorts and travellers are often a target for criminals. Take extra care to keep hold of your valuables and don't go off with any strangers.

Illness: wherever you are, find out if it is OK to drink the water first. If not, use bottled water and watch out for ice in drinks.

Before you go away, think about whether you need any injections, if you have adequate insurance to cover you for all eventualities whilst abroad and that the area you are travelling to is a safe area to visit.

You can find this information and more on the Foreign and Commonwealth Office travel advice website or by calling their Travel Line.

Foreign and Commonwealth Office (for travel advice)
0207 008 1500
www.fco.gov.uk

Department of Health (health advice for travellers) 0207 210 4850
www.dh.gov.uk

Travel Health
www.travelhealth.co.uk

Travel Safety Q and As
www.timesonline.co.uk

Also check out:
> Disability Travel
> Money Abroad
> Passports and Visas
> Travel Essentials
> Sunbathing
> Alcohol

When travelling, most tourists take a certain amount of money with them that lasts for the whole trip. So, would-be thieves know that you may have all of your money either on your person or kept in one place. Reduce the risk of having your money stolen by keeping it locked away (most hotels have a safe facility), only carrying as much as you need and never leaving your money unattended (for example when you go for a swim). It's a good idea to carry money using a money-belt or a bag with a zip. It's not such a good idea to leave your money openly visible in your hotel room and to flash wads of cash around when you're out. Having a variety of money types reduces the risk of theft. Keep small amounts of currency for things like drinks and taxis, a credit card for emergencies and travellers cheques for larger amounts of money (changing as much as you need every day or so). You can protect your credit and debit cards and your travellers cheques by taking out insurance policies on them too. Currency can be exchanged at banks, bureau de changes, post offices and travel agents with most charging commission. These days, debit and credit cards are accepted in more and more worldwide locations but check with your bank what charges there are first.

Foreign and Commonwealth Office advice for money abroad
www.fco.gov.uk

Information on travelling
www.thetravellerslounge.co.uk

The Post Office
08457 22 33 44
www.postoffice.co.uk

Currency Converter
www.moneyextra.com/rates/currency/converter

Also check out:
> Health and Safety
> Passports and Visas
> Travel Essentials
> Backpacking
> Holidays for Young People
> Tourism

4. WORLD, EUROPE, UK & WALES

Passport – If you travel outside the UK, you'll need a valid passport. The only passport office in Wales is in Newport, but application forms can be obtained online or from Post Offices. The cost of a passport varies (depending on whether it's your first one, a replacement etc.) but it can reach as high as £90. It's also worth sorting out your passport well in advance of travel as it often takes time for the UK Passport Service to process applications and some countries will only let you in if you have six or more months to go on your passport. Note down your passport number and keep it separate from your passport in case it's lost or stolen. If it's stolen, report it to the local police and UK Passport Service (if abroad, you can also use the British Foreign and Commonwealth Office (FCO) Consulate, Embassy or High Commission). Apply for a passport online here - www.passport-application.gov.uk

Visas - Some countries require that you have a visa to enter. Visas are generally not required to travel to an EU country providing you are a resident of a country belonging to the EU. For more details on visas, contact the Consulate or Embassy of the country you intend on visiting. You will most likely have to pay a fee for a visa.

Advice on applying for a visa
0207 008 8438
www.ukvisas.gov.uk

The United Kingdom Passport Service
0870 521 0410
www.ukpa.gov.uk

The Visa Service 0870 8900 185
www.visaservice.co.uk

Citizen's Advice Bureau page on travelling abroad
www.adviceguide.org.uk/em/index/your_world/travel/travel_abroad.htm

Also check out:
- Disability Travel
- Health and Safety
- Money Abroad
- Travel Essentials
- Backpacking
- Tourism

4. WORLD, EUROPE, UK & WALES

Travelling can be a great life experience but there are plenty of dangers that you may face along the way. Take care of the following essentials and make yours the trip of a lifetime:

Documents: Tickets? Check. Passport? Check. Visas? Check. EHIC card (for free or reduced emergency medical treatment)? Check.

Insurance: if anything bad should happen whilst you're away, from lost luggage to personal injury, having insurance will be a lifeline. If you're planning on any extreme sports, check that you have the right cover first.

Injections: to enter some countries, you need certain injections. Check with your GP or MASTA (see links below) to find out which ones you'll need.

Alcohol: have fun but be careful. Remember, when you're away from the comfort and familiarity of home, you're more vulnerable, so indulge with caution.

Drugs: the law in some countries may legalise some drugs – even if it is legal it may not be healthy for you and you may not know what substances are being used.

Culture: different cultures have different rules and laws. If you're going somewhere exotic, check what the main differences are first to avoid unnecessary trouble.

Personal safety: tourists are often seen as targets by criminals so, remain vigilant at all times and you'll have no worries.

The sun: if you're going somewhere hot, take care. Keep out of the sun at the hottest times and stay covered in high factor sun cream.

Sex: don't get carried away just because you are away. Use protection and don't do anything you wouldn't do at home.

Medical Advisory Services for Travellers Abroad (MASTA) - www.masta.org

British Insurance Brokers Association
www.biba.org.uk

Department of Health advice for travellers
0845 606 2030 - www.dh.gov.uk

Playing Safely (safe sex advice)
0800 567 123 - www.playingsafely.co.uk

Also check out:

> Passports and Visas
> Culture
> Contraception
> Alcohol
> Drugs Essentials
> Sunbathing
> Travel Insurance

4. WORLD, EUROPE, UK & WALES

It might just be for peace of mind or it might save your bacon, but one thing's for sure - travel insurance is a must for every traveller. It can help you if your luggage is lost, if you fall ill, have an accident, experience delays or cancellations or if you're the victim of a crime. Some travel operators offer travel insurance as part of a deal but you don't have to buy from them; there are a whole host of companies looking for your travel insurance business. You can buy a single-trip policy, which covers you purely for the duration of your trip or if you plan on travelling regularly, you can buy an annual scheme that covers you for all of your travelling during the whole year. When travelling to a country within the EEA (all EU countries plus Iceland, Liechtenstein, Norway and Switzerland), get a European Health Insurance Card (EHIC) for free or reduced emergency medical treatment. You can apply for an EHIC card by phone, post or online. If you're considering doing any sports (especially extreme sports) whilst away, check with your insurance provider that you are adequately covered.

British Insurance Brokers Association (BIBA) page on travel insurance
870 950 1790
www.biba.org.uk/consumer/support/products/travel.html

BBC Watchdog guide to holiday insurance
www.bbc.co.uk/watchdog/guides_to/holidayinsurance/

Citizen's Advice Guide to insurance in general
www.adviceguide.org.uk/em/index/your_world/consumer_affairs/insurance.htm

Department of Health information on the European Health Insurance Card (EHIC)
0207 210 4850
www.dh.gov.uk

Also check out:
- Health and Safety
- Travel Essentials
- Money Abroad
- Passports and Visas
- Backpacking

If the thought of spending a week or two doing nothing but lounging by the pool leaves you cold, then an activity holiday may be the thing to warm you up. You can try anything from deep sea diving to white water rafting or if you prefer something gentler, a walking holiday or riding a donkey through the Grand Canyon could be for you. You can organise an inclusive trip through a specialist activity holiday company, where you pay for everything including a list of activities, or you can find a resort or hotel that specialises in activities that you can pick and choose from once you arrive. Be careful and check out the credentials of the company and the experience of the tutors and guides before you go. Make sure that you have travel insurance that covers you for the activities that you're planning. Some policies may exclude certain activities (particularly extreme sports) so check first. It's also a good idea to be certain that you know what you're getting before you go. Some packages may not include 'extras' like equipment hire and other hidden costs. Think about all of the possible extra charges that there may be and find out beforehand if they are included in the price or not.

British Activity Holiday Association
0208 842 1292
www.baha.org.uk

Outdoor Holidays (information on activity holidays)
www.outdoorholidays.com

World Outdoor Web (outdoor sports, travel and adventure)
www.w-o-w.com

Youth Information page on adventure holidays
0116 242 7350
www.youthinformation.com/Templates/Internal.asp?NodeID=91007

Also check out:
> Disability Travel
> Health and Safety
> Travel Essentials
> Sport & Leisure

Backpacking
4.2 Holidays

What better way to have freedom whilst travelling than to go backpacking? With all of the belongings that you need on your back, you can go anywhere at any time. Take care to find a backpack that suits you. Remember, you'll spend a lot of time in uncomfortable positions with that bag on your back, so make sure it fits you comfortably first. Spend some time packing your bag properly so that everything fits snugly too. Before you go, try and draw up a plan of where you intend to travel and leave a copy with friends and relatives. Most countries have email access so try and keep in regular contact with loved ones. Find as much as you can about places before you visit them (either through travel guides or fellow backpackers) to avoid any nasty surprises. Check that your accommodation is fire safe before you stay anywhere. If it's not, move on to one that is. Before you go, make sure you have all of the necessary documents, including passports, visas and insurance and check out how much living costs are where you intend to travel so that you'll have enough to get by.

BBC page on crime prevention whilst backpacking
www.bbc.co.uk/crime/prevention/backpacking.shtml

The Backpacking Site
www.the-backpacking-site.com

Outdoor Holidays
www.outdoorholidays.com

Backpacking Europe
www.backpackingeurope.com

Also check out:

- Tourism
- Health and Safety
- Money Abroad
- Passports and Visas
- Travel Essentials
- Culture

Holidays can often seem out of reach because of the expense. However, if you're young and have to watch the pennies, you can still find a way to have a great holiday without breaking the bank. The Youth Hostel Association provides budget accommodation all over the UK and can give you discounts on youth hostels all over the world. Stay in a youth hostel and you may find yourself in a country mansion or in a prime city centre location for a budget price. Youth hostel accommodation is usually in bunk-bedded rooms, sharing with the same sex (with bathroom facilities also shared). If there are enough of you, it is sometimes possible to book a whole room. Most hostels provide cheap meals and each hostel has a star rating (from one to five) in the same way that hotels do. Some youth hostels also provide activities such as climbing and kayaking. If you're not ready for a holiday on your own, why not try a staffed residential camp, where you stay in a hostel supervised by adults who will help organise your holiday and provide activities for you? Young people can also benefit from cheaper travel around the world. There are also a host of discount cards available to young people (usually for those aged under 25).

Youth Hostel Association
0870 770 8868
www.yha.org.uk/Home/Home_Page/index.html

Camp Beaumont
www.campbeaumont.co.uk

Youth Travel
0870 887 0135
www.youthtravel.com

International Student Travel Confederation
www.istc.org

Also check out:
> Activity Holidays
> Backpacking
> Buses and Coaches
> Trains
> Exchanges for Young People
> Travel Essentials

For the inexperienced traveller, package holidays are ideal. The tour operator takes care of everything; you just pay one lump sum. They may arrange your flights, transfers (travel from the airport to your accommodation and back again), accommodation, car hire and travel insurance, depending on which options you choose. You'll also benefit from having an English-speaking holiday rep so any problems that you have should be simply resolved. You can choose how much independence you have with a package holiday. If you go all-inclusive, you get everything paid for up front. They'll cover all of your food and drink and may include activities and trips too. If you go full board, you'll get breakfast, lunch and dinner included. Half board means that you'll just get breakfast and dinner. Bed and breakfast does what it says and self-catering means that you'll have a small kitchen to cook your own meals. When booking your holiday, check exactly what you will and won't get for your money. Package holidays are a great, cheap way to see the world, have fun and meet loads of new people. If you want to get a real bargain, look for some last minute deals. It's a risk, but it might be worth it.

The Association of British Travel Agents
0207 637 2444
www.abta.com

Department of Trade and Industry factsheet and FAQs on package holidays
0207 215 5000
www.dti.gov.uk/ccp/topics1/facts/package.htm

The Independent's complete guide to package holidays
travel.independent.co.uk/europe/mediterranean/article58481.ece

BBC Watchdog guide to package holidays
www.bbc.co.uk/watchdog/guides_to/package-holidays/

Also check out:
> Disability Travel
> Money Abroad
> Passports and Visas
> Travel Essentials
> Flying Essentials
> Holidays for Young People

From rolling hills to golden beaches, castles and monuments - have you really explored your own country, Wales, yet? Wales has many tourist attractions – for a full list, contact Wales Tourist Board and get exploring your homeland!

For any other city or location around the UK and Ireland, ring directory enquiries asking for their tourist board numbers or local tourist information shop. You can also check out the Yellow Pages for more details www.yell.com.

Wherever you visit, you'll have an impact. The host country you're visiting may have local customs and, as a guest, it's up to you to stick to them. You are the visitor and should know how to behave while you're there. There are many guidelines now available for long-distance travel, so make sure you get all the facts about the country you're visiting to maximise your pleasure and minimise your environmental impact whilst you're there.

Are you an eco-tourist? Natural habitats are being threatened by human activity and tourist development. You can get involved helping to conserve areas around you or throughout the world.

Visit Wales (official site of the Welsh Tourist Board)
www.visitwales.com

Visit Britain (official site of the British Tourist Authority)
www.visitbritain.com

BBC's holiday guide
www.bbc.co.uk/holiday/

Tourism Concern (campaigning for ethical and fairly traded tourism)
0207 133 3331
www.tourismconcern.org.uk

Also check out:
- Environmental Issues
- Conservation
- Backpacking
- Tourism
- Culture
- Language

What more convenient way is there to travel than by bus or coach? Buses and coaches go absolutely everywhere. If you fancy a quick nip into town, the bus will get you there, cheap as chips, in no time at all. Visiting a mate at Uni? Hop on the coach for a hassle-free journey. Maybe you're up for a trip around Europe? Well, there are coach trips that can take you to all the best sites for a reasonable price. With more and more bus lanes, journey times are quicker and the environmental impact is less by bus or coach than by car.

Tickets for buses and coaches can be bought either at the station or as you get on the bus (be careful, as some companies only accept the correct change). For coach journeys, you can also buy or reserve tickets in advance that can be sent to you or picked up at the station. Most bus routes go to and from major towns or cities, so if you are travelling to a rural location, you may need to change. If you're not sure where to get off or change, just ask the driver. Each bus and coach company normally operates discount card schemes for young people, so check with your local operator to get some good deals.

National Express coaches
08705 808080
www.gobycoach.com

Traveline Cymru
0870 608 2608
www.traveline-cymru.org.uk

UK Bus Timetable Directory
timetables.showbus.co.uk/wales.htm

Busweb (public transport information)
www.busweb.co.uk

Also check out:
> Trains
> Ferries
> Tourism
> Travel Essentials
> Flying Essentials
> Motorbikes, Mopeds and Scooters

It's usually one of the biggest purchases of your life and can be a bit of a minefield, but armed with the right knowledge, buying a car needn't be a nightmare. As well as the price of the car, you need to consider the cost of road tax, insurance, petrol, money for MOTs and regular services, as well as factoring in the cost of repairs, which every car needs at some point. There are all sorts of car traders out there from big name garages to private sellers and independent car dealers. When you're looking for a car, take a list of questions with you and don't be afraid to ask them. If you're no expert on cars or don't feel confident speaking to professionals, take a family member or friend who knows a thing or two along with you. When thinking about which car you want to buy it's worth thinking about what their safety record is, how economic the car's fuel consumption is and how much damage the car does to the environment. The key thing to buying a car is to not let the excitement get to you. Instead, take your time, do lots of research, speak to those in the know and make a sensible decision. You won't regret it in the end!

Parker's (independent website for car prices and reviews)
www.parkers.co.uk

Office of Fair Trading guide to buying a car
08457 22 44 99
www.oft.gov.uk/Consumer/Your+Rights+When+Shopping/Cars/default.htm

Citizen's Advice Bureau guide to buying a second hand car
www.adviceguide.org.uk/em/index/your_world/consumer_affairs/buying_second_hand_vehicles.htm

BBC guide to buying a car
www.bbc.co.uk/motoring/buying_advice/index.shtml

Also check out:

> Environmental Issues
> Pollution
> Going Green
> Driving Essentials
> Motorbikes, Mopeds and Scooters
> Trains

Before you start:
You can ride a moped at 16, but can't drive a car until you're 17. Before you get behind the wheel of a car and drive on a public road or highway, you must apply for and receive your provisional driving licence. D1 forms are available from main Post Offices. Complete the form and send it to the DVLA. Provisional licenses cost £38 and cover cars, motorcycles, medium/large vehicles, minibuses and buses.
To get your full licence and drive unaccompanied you need to pass a theory and practical driving test (changing your license from provisional to full is free). You can start learning the theory at any age – just buy a copy of The Highway Code. The DVLA website offers lots of info on driving essentials.
If you're really keen to drive, look for a driving school that offers starter lessons on private sites where you can actually drive off-road before you're 17. You can also get involved in Motor Sports at an early age.

Well done – you've passed:
You've passed your test – you're officially a driver! Being a driver and a car-owner is great but comes with certain responsibilities:

Continued on next page...

DVLA Swansea
0870 240 0009
www.dvla.gov.uk

Learning to drive info
www.learners.co.uk/starting

Driving Standards Agency
Driving tests & theory info
www.driving-tests.co.uk

Also check out:
> Motor Sports

Speed Limits - if you're caught breaking the speed limit, you could face a fine, points on your license and even a criminal record if you are involved in an accident.

MOT (Ministry of Transport) Certificate – every car over 3 years old needs to be put in for a new MOT every year. This is to ensure that the car is roadworthy & safe to travel on public roads (working breaks, lights, steering etc). The maximum anyone can charge for a car MOT is £44.15 – so shop around for a good deal.

Road Tax – every car owner has to pay road tax each year. If you're caught without it, you could face a fine of up to £1,000. To tax your car you must have valid insurance.

Irresponsible Driving - driving while under the influence of alcohol if over the limit is illegal and very irresponsible and if you're caught, you face a year ban and a large fine. The limit at present is 35 micrograms of alcohol per 100 millilitres of breath (or 80 milligrams of alcohol per 100 millilitres of blood). Driving when very tired is also irresponsible and could cause serious accidents. If you are drowsy or sleepy and struggling to stay awake, pull over in a safe place as soon as possible and get some rest. Driving whilst using a hand-held mobile phone is also now illegal (since 1st December 2003).

DETR
For more info on staying safe and the Highway Code
www.roads.detr.gov.uk/roadsafety

The Homes of British Motorsport
01474 872331
Driving experiences in closed off areas near the tracks for young people aged 13-16
www.octagonmotorsports.com

Also check out:
> Motorbikes, Mopeds &Scooters

You never quite know what you're going to get when you step onto a ferry. If the sea is calm, expect a relaxing, smooth journey. If not, you might find yourself in the middle of a rollercoaster ride, lurching from side to side, up and down, objects sliding off of tables, passengers turning a strange shade of green and, of course, the odd visit to the toilet! If you suffer from sea sickness, there are plenty of treatments that may help. Most are available from your local pharmacy. To keep you entertained, most ferries have onboard shops, restaurants, bars, cinemas and amusement arcades.

In Wales, there are ports at Swansea, Holyhead, Fishguard, Pembroke and Mostyn that go to various ports in Ireland. Ports in the UK go to France, Belgium, Holland, Spain, Germany, Norway, Denmark and Sweden. Prices tend to vary depending on the distance of your journey and if you're travelling by foot or car. There are special offers available if you book in advance so keep an eye out for them. Booking ferry tickets can be done online or by phone. The tickets will be sent to you and you'll have to present them before you can board the boat.

Ferry information
0871 222 3312
www.ferries.co.uk

Wales Index Water and Sea Travel In Wales links
www.walesindex.co.uk/pages/381_627.html

Also check out:
> Travel Essentials
> Sport & Leisure
> Holidays for Young People
> Buses and Coaches
> Driving Essentials

The world is getting smaller: you can fly to Paris in just over an hour, New York in 7 hours and the other side of the world in 24 hours.

Before you book

Check flight times, how long the flight is and whether there are any stopovers. It is also a good idea to find out exactly which airport the flight lands at, you may find that, especially with low-cost carriers, that they fly into an airport that is miles away from the city you thought you were flying to. When you come to book your flights, always specify if you need any special help, special meals such as vegetarian, vegan or kosher. Some airlines charge extra for meals, decide if you're willing to pay it. You can sometimes specify if you want a specific seat as well for example if you're tall or are travelsick.

Before you travel

Find out how much baggage allowance you are allowed. You may be charged extra if your bags are too heavy, use bathroom scales to check. There are certain things that you are not allowed to pack in your hand luggage such as knives, nail scissors or any sharp object. You will receive this information with your ticket, read it and listen: if you have anything you shouldn't they will take it away from you. Mark your bags, with your name and details, it's best to just put your first initial and a surname, especially if you're a female traveller. Don't carry anything for anyone else either. Wear loose comfortable clothing and shoes you can take off easily on the flight. It's often a good idea to pack a jumper in your hand luggage as flights can be quite cold. For long haul flights, make up a little overnight bag including a toothbrush and toothpaste, wet wipes, deodorant, spare underwear and some warm socks.

Continued on next page...

Plan how you are going to get to the airport and leave enough time to get there, especially if you are traveling through rush hour. If you're going to be parking at the airport, pre-book a parking space, it's much cheaper.
Check which terminal you are flying from, Heathrow for example has 4 terminals and it takes a long time to get from one to the other if you've gone to the wrong one. Your ticket will also say how long before the flight you need to check in.
Check that you have your passport, insurance document, tickets and visa if you need one.

At the airport

Depending on how big the airport is, you will usually find a screen giving your flight number, destination and which desk you need to check in at on your arrival in the airport. Have your passport and ticket ready to make check-in as quick as possible. The check-in staff will ask you a few security questions and then give you a boarding pass. Keep this safe - you will not be able to board the aircraft without it. You can then go through to departures. Relax, have a walk around but keep an eye on the screens that will tell you when to go to the gate, you should also hear an announcement. You can pick up some great bargains at the airport, but many items may be cheaper when you get there or even on the High Street, so don't spend all your money at once. You will need your boarding card if you do make any purchases. It may be tempting to start your holiday at the bar, but the airline have the right to refuse you to fly if you're drunk and you will have to pick up the tab for another flight. Once they announce your flight is boarding go straight to the gate, the TV screens will say which one, as soon as possible to avoid holding up or missing your flight. Some airports are very big and it might take a while to get to your gate, there are usually signs saying how long it will take.

Continued on next page...

On the Flight

Listen to the safety announcements and make sure your mobile phone is switched off. Drink plenty of water during the flight and avoid too much alcohol, tea, coffee and heavy meals. If you're going a long way, make sure you move around a bit to avoid the risk of DVT. You will often find tips on exercises to do in the in-flight magazine. Try and get some sleep if you can.

Getting there

Make sure you have your passport (and visa) and any other documentation you may need such as immigration cards (they will issue these on the flight if you need them) ready to go through customs. When collecting your bags, make sure you have picked up the right bag. If your bag doesn't arrive take your ticket, on which the check-in staff should have stuck your baggage tickets, to the information desk immediately. They will be able to help you find it. Most airports will have public transport links to the city centre or there is sometimes a bus that will take you to a central location or even to the hotel. Taxis can be very expensive, so go only in registered taxis and ask how much it will cost before you get in.

World Airport Guide
www.worldairportguide.net

Safety Regulation Group
Complaints or queries about air safety or standards
01293 567171
www.srg.caa.co.uk

STA Travel
0870 160 6070
www.statravel.co.uk

BAA – British Airport Authority
www.baa.com

Also check out:
> Backpacking
> Health & Safety
> Holidays

Motorbikes, Mopeds & Scooters

To drive a motorbike, moped or scooter on the road you need a provisional licence and to have taken part in a Compulsory Basic Training course (CBT). To obtain a licence, you need to fill in form D1, which is available from the Post Office. To find your nearest provider of the CBT course, look under 'Motorcycle Training' in the Yellow Pages. When you have a provisional licence to drive a motorbike, you need to display 'L' plates ('D' plates in Welsh) at all times, you cannot carry any passengers and you must not ride on the motorway. There are two types of motorcycle licence – the light motorcycle licence (A1) and the standard motorcycle licence (A). The two licences differ slightly, with the A licence allowing you to ride a greater range of motorcycles. After two years of riding with the A licence, you are able to ride a motorcycle of any size. From the age of 16 you are allowed to ride a moped up to a 50cc engine and from 17 you are allowed to ride a motorbike of up to 125cc. From the age of 21, it is legal to ride motorbikes with larger engines.

Driver and Vehicle Licensing Agency
0870 240 0009
www.dvla.gov.uk

Driving Standards Agency
0115 901 2500
www.dsa.gov.uk

The Highway Code for motorcyclists
www.highwaycode.gov.uk/motorcyclists.htm

Citizens Advice Bureau page on driving licences
www.adviceguide.org.uk/wales/your_world/travel/driving_licences.htm

Also check out:
- Travel Essentials
- Buses and Coaches
- Driving Essentials
- Trains
- Ferries
- Pollution

4. WORLD, EUROPE, UK & WALES

The train is a great way to get around not just your local area but also the rest of the country and maybe even the world too! Planning your journey is the key to successful train travel. You can buy tickets in advance (on-line at www.thetrainline.com or by phone on 08457 484950) that can be posted to you, you can reserve and pick up tickets at the station or you can buy them at the station, either from a ticket booth or a ticket machine. For the best deals, reserve your ticket more than seven days in advance of your journey. If you're aged between 16-25, the Young Persons Rail Card is invaluable – £20 a year saves you 1/3 on most rail fares. When you get to the station, take a look at the departure board to find out which platform your train leaves from. And remember, don't just look at the destination as this is where the train terminates – your station may be along the way. Make sure you're aware of any changes that you need to make and be sure that you don't fall asleep and miss your stop! Rail networks work by using main stations as hubs, which most journeys go to and from. The main stations in Wales are Cardiff, Newport, Wrexham and Swansea.

British Rail
08457 484950
www.thetrainline.com

Rail Europe
08708 30 20 08
www.raileurope.co.uk

Also check out:
> Backpacking
> Buses & Coaches
> Travel Essentials
> Holidays for Young People

Every time you buy a product or a service, your actions have an effect on the wider world. The cheap plane flight that you just bought may get you a nice holiday but what effect will the engine fumes have on the environment? Those trainers might make you the talk of the town but how much is the worker who stitched them together paid and how are they treated? The scrambled eggs you scoffed for your breakfast? They were tasty, yes, but in what condition were the chickens kept? Consuming ethically is something that we can all do to reduce the impact we have on the environment and workers around the world. It doesn't take much effort to find out which companies operate ethical trade policies. If you're concerned about it, contact the company and ask if they have such a policy and if you can see it. There are websites, books and magazines that can provide information on how companies around the world operate, so check them out first. If you don't think about consuming ethically, your actions could contribute towards global warming, the exploitation of workers and animals and the persistence of poverty around the world. Think before you buy.

Ethical Trade Initiative (improving labour standards)
0207 404 1463
www.ethicaltrade.org

Ethical Consumer magazine
www.ethicalconsumer.org

British Association for Fair Trade Shops (BAFTS) (promoting fair trade retailing in Britain)
07796 050045
www.bafts.org.uk/about_ethical.asp

Wales Fair Trade Forum
02920 614 435
www.walesfairtradeforum.org.uk

Also check out:
> Animal Rights
> Climate Change
> Consumer Labelling
> Farming & Agriculture
> Pollution
> Poverty

The European Union (EU), established in 1992 when 12 European countries signed a document known as The Maastricht Treaty, is a union of nations that can have influence on laws and policy throughout its member states. There are now 25 members: Belgium, France, Germany, Italy, Luxembourg, The Netherlands, Denmark, Ireland, UK, Greece, Portugal, Spain, Austria, Finland, Sweden, Cyprus, Czech Republic, Estonia, Hungary, Latvia, Lithuania, Malta, Poland, Slovakia and Slovenia. The influence that the EU can have differs from region to region. Currently, 12 of the member states use the same currency, the Euro, with the aim being that eventually all of the member states will use it. They also aim to set up a single market, which means developing certain common policies across all member states. At the moment, the future of the EU is unclear, as they have been unable to agree on one of the main aims of the EU - a Constitution For Europe. The EU is of importance to you because the laws and policies made by it and the role of the Union affects every member state.

Europa, Gateway to the European Union
00 800 67891011
www.europa.eu.int

Euro <26 card
www.euro26.org

The European Commission Representation in the United Kingdom
www.cec.org.uk

Encyclopaedia page on the EU
en.wikipedia.org/wiki/European_union

Also check out:

> Citizenship
> United Nations
> European Government
> National Assembly for Wales
> World Politics – One World
> UK Parliament

It works in tiers. At the top are the Council of Ministers, then European Parliament, the European Commission and the Council of Ministers. European Parliament represents all the people that live in the EU and, with The Council of Ministers, they pass the majority of laws that affect people throughout Europe.

The Council of Ministers makes big decisions. A person from each European member state meets to discuss big issues like Education. Parliament is elected every five years and has powers based on a series of treaties. There are 732 members (MEPs) that are elected every five years. The Parliament gets proposals from the European Commission. It looks at them, makes any changes and then moves them to the Council of Ministers for them to make the final decisions. There are 87 members of Parliament in Brussels representing different groups e.g. Socialists. The European Commission has a head (President) and 20 members (EU Commissioners) who are chosen by the governments of the member states. They manage community issues, budgets and carry out decisions made by the Council of Ministers. You can get a booklet from the West Wales European Centre called 'Serving the people of Europe – how the European Commission works' for more detailed info.

Council of the European Union
http://ue.eu.int/cms3_fo/index.htm

UK Office of the European Parliament
www.europarl.org.uk/index.htm

The European Commission
http://ec.europa.eu/index_en.htm

The EU in the United Kingdom
http://ec.europa.eu/unitedkingdom/

Also check out:
> EU
> National Assembly for Wales
> United Nations
> World Politics – One World

Local Government in Wales is split into 22 Unitary Local Authorities (UAs, local councils or authorities). The Welsh Assembly's Local Government Group makes sure that each UA delivers efficient services and helps local people. Local Government is there to develop communities and provide decent housing, good local facilities and a high quality environment, which is non-threatening and free from crime. Local Government Members have to be elected and are responsible for providing the services in your area, like Housing, Transport, Refuse Collection, Libraries and Social Services.

Each Unitary Authority has Council Departments which deal with these services that you can contact for more information or any queries in your area.

>>> For details of your local government go to the **Local Info** pages

The Welsh Local Government Association
02920 468600
www.wlga.gov.uk

Website of the UK Government
www.direct.gov.uk

National Assembly for Wales
02920 825111
www.wales.gov.uk

Also check out:
> European Government
> National Assembly for Wales
> UK Parliament
> World Politics – One World
> Voting and Elections
> Youth Councils

National Assembly for Wales

4.4 Politics

In 1999, the UK Government gave away some of its powers to the Welsh Government. This process, known as devolution, resulted in the creation of the National Assembly for Wales, which enabled Welsh politicians to develop policy and approve legislation that would take effect in Wales. Wales is still subject to the laws passed by the UK Government but is now responsible for governing itself in certain areas such as the Welsh language, housing, agriculture and transport. There are 40 constituencies in Wales and each one has its own Assembly Member (AM) voted for by the public (there are 20 additional members voted for on a regional basis) in elections that take place every four years. The Assembly is chaired by the Presiding Officer (voted for by the whole Assembly) who is the equivalent of the Speaker of the House of Commons. The Assembly's powers are delegated to the First Minister (currently Rhodri Morgan) who, in turn, delegates responsibility to Assembly Ministers, each taking their own area of expertise, who form the Cabinet. Together, the First Minister and his Cabinet are known as the Welsh Assembly Government. There are regional committees to discuss local issues and subject committees, responsible for certain political areas such as education etc. The main meetings, known as Plenary Meetings, take place on Tuesday and Wednesday afternoons and are broadcast live on the digital TV channel, S4C2 and on the internet at www.webcasting.wales.gov.uk

National Assembly for Wales 02920 825111
www.wales.gov.uk

Welsh Labour Party 02920 877 700
www.welshlabour.org.uk

Welsh Conservative Party 02920 616 031
www.conservatives.com

Welsh Liberal Democrats Party
02920 313 400 www.welshlibdems.org.uk

Plaid Cymru 02920 646 000
www.plaidcymru.org

Also check out:
> UK Parliament
> Local Government
> Voting and Elections
> European Government
> EU
> World Politics – One World

The British Royal Family is steeped in hundreds of years of tradition. Currently headed by Queen Elizabeth II, who is the UK's Head of State, the Royal Family represents Britain around the world. Members of the Royal Family usually have more than one role. They may patronise charities or other organisations (sporting, health etc.) as well as perform their official duties. Others may take on their own careers, in the Armed Forces for example. Who plays what role in the Royal Family is decided by birth. So, for example, Prince Charles is heir apparent to the throne because he is the queen's first-born child (heir apparent is the term used to describe the first in line to the throne).

There are many arguments for and against the monarchy. Anti-monarchists believe that the Royal Family is an out of date, out of touch institution that is a waste of tax-payers money (much of the Royal Family's income is taken from public taxes) and they usually favour a Republic State. Those in favour of the Monarchy believe that the Royal Family is an important part of British tradition and to lose it would mean losing some of our identity. They also believe that the role they play is important and that the money recouped by tourism generated by the Royal Family means that the country also benefits financially from them.

The Official Website of the British Monarchy
0207 930 4832
www.royal.gov.uk

Children's BBC guide to the UK Monarchy
news.bbc.co.uk/cbbcnews/hi/find_out/guides/uk/princess_margaret/the_uk_monarchy/newsid_2149000/2149012.stm

Throne Out (anti-monarchy website)
www.throneout.com

British Royal Family History website
www.britroyals.com

Also check out:
- Culture
- UK Parliament
- Income Tax

The Houses of Parliament in Westminster, London are made up of two chambers - The House of Commons and House of Lords. The Prime Minister and his or her chosen group of Members of Parliament (MPs) are called the Cabinet. The Cabinet has responsibility for major things like economy and law and order, and contains the Home Office Minister and Chancellor of the Exchequer. It's an incredibly powerful body. The House of Commons is the main meeting place and 'battle arena' for MPs. Issues are debated here between all party members and British laws decided and made. It's the activity centre for how the country is run. There is also a shadow cabinet, which is made up of members of the second largest party (currently the Conservatives). They analyse the work of the cabinet and are ready to take over should they win the next General Election. The House of Lords is the second legislative chamber in Parliament. It keeps a beady eye on the activities in the Commons. Some powers have been taken away from the UK Parliament and given to Wales, Scotland and Northern Ireland. This is called Devolution.

The House of Commons still discusses Welsh, Scottish and Northern Irish business, and many matters still remain in the power of the UK Government. Scotland has a Parliament that can pass laws and, since the approval of the Government of Wales Bill in July 2006, the Welsh Assembly Government has Increased powers and can make laws without going through Parliament.

The United Kingdom Parliament
www.parliament.uk

Parliament broadcast live on the Internet
www.parliamentlive.tv

10 Downing Street website
www.pm.gov.uk

National Assembly for Wales
02920 825111
www.wales.gov.uk

Also check out:

> National Assembly for Wales
> Local Government
> European Government
> Voting and Elections
> World Politics – One World
> Laws

The United Nations (UN) is an organisation to which 191 of the world's countries are members. Established in 1945, the UN has four purposes: to maintain international peace and security; to develop friendly relations among nations; to cooperate in solving international problems and in promoting respect for human rights; and to be a centre for harmonizing the actions of nations. It has six main organs, each with their own specific role within the organisation. These are: the General Assembly; the Security Council; the Economic and Social Council; the Trusteeship Council; the Secretariat; and the International Court of Justice. When nations become members, they have to agree to a document called the UN Charter, which spells out the UN's principles. The UN is not a government and it does not pass any laws. Instead, it acts as a central organisation that exists primarily to help preserve world peace and resolve disputes using peaceful and non-forceful means. Their work is wide-ranging and varied. They may offer solutions to potentially hostile situations, help countries provide better, more peaceful governance, help to establish and preserve ceasefires and buffer zones and they may impose sanctions on nations who do not abide by their decisions. The current UN Secretary General is Kofi Annan.

United Nations homepage
www.un.org

United Nations Development Programme
www.undp.org

Amnesty International UK (working on behalf of human rights victims)
02920 375 610
www.amnesty.org.uk

Campaign for Nuclear Disarmament
01495 773 180
www.cnduk.org

Also check out:
> Peace
> Terrorism
> EU
> UK Parliament
> National Assembly for Wales
> Youth Councils

A political party is a group of people who hold similar views. Each party has different views but some views between the parties may be similar. You have a right to your views and at 18, you can vote at elections for the MP or party that holds views most similar to your own. Many parties have youth sections that you can join before you're 18. In order to vote, you must have your name on the electoral register, which catalogues all the people who can vote at an election. Every year, in autumn, this registration form will come to your house. Even if you're only 16/17 make sure your name is on the register. As soon as you're 18 you'll then be able to vote on paper or via mobile phone or internet. Everyone over 18 has a right to vote.

There are five types of election:
General - To choose the Government at least every five years
By - To choose an MP for an area if someone dies or resigns
European - To choose MEPs to represent Parliament in Europe
Local - To choose local councillors
Assembly - To choose local Assembly Members in Wales every four years

Elections are vital for the public to have a say in what happens. They're free, fair and essential to maintaining democracy.

The Electoral Commission
0207 271 0500
www.electoralcommission.org.uk

BBC site on the General Election 2005
news.bbc.co.uk/1/hi/uk_politics/vote_2005/default.stm

Welsh Labour Party 02920 877 700
www.welshlabour.org.uk

Welsh Conservative Party 02920 616 031
www.conservatives.com/tile.do?def=wales.index.page

Welsh Liberal Democrats Party
02920 313 400
www.welshlibdems.org.uk

Plaid Cymru 02920 646 000
www.plaidcymru.org

Also check out:
> UK Parliament
> National Assembly for Wales
> Local Government
> European Government
> EU
> World Politics – One World

4. WORLD, EUROPE, UK & WALES

The World is a big place. Isn't it? Getting from Wales to Australia by plane takes around 24 hours. You can get to New York in around 7 hours. Still think it's such a big place? It's easy to get caught up in what's happening on your doorstep and to forget about what's going on all over the world. Here's a quick roundup of some global issues:

TRADE

People and economies worldwide depend on international trade – buying, selling or bartering commodities. Trade allows countries to strengthen their economy by exploiting their strengths. Tea, for example, doesn't grow in the UK, so we have to buy it in from countries like India. Likewise, the UK exports produce and products to other countries around the world. The UK is the world's fifth largest exporter of goods, and our economy depends heavily on the ability to trade and invest without constraints.

However, countries can set tariffs on imports from certain countries to protect their own market, which can make it impossible for third-world or developing countries to export their goods, which has a negative effect on their economy and growth.

Also, countries can introduce trade sanctions against other nations for political reasons – the US introduced sanctions against the EU in 1998 because of the way the EU regulated the import of bananas into the European Market – favouring mostly former European colonies.

The US complained to the World Trade Organisation and later introduced sanctions. For further info on trade policies and campaigns to make trade fairer check our contacts out.

Oxfam (UK) 01865 312610
www.oxfam.org.uk

One World 0270 914 503
www.oneworld.net

The World Trade Organisation
www.wto.org/

Traidcraft Exchange & Traidcraft plc
www.traidcraft.co.uk

Save the Children 029 2039 6838

Continued on next page...

THE DEVELOPING WORLD

The World used to be split into three categories:
First World (the most affluent areas of the World - mostly Western countries) Second World (mostly Eastern countries) Third World (poverty-stricken areas – mostly in Africa, Asia and Latin America)

Third World Countries are now referred to as "Less Developed Countries" or LDCs and have little or no home industry. Characteristics of an LDC are high rates of population growth (little or no birth control systems), high infant mortality rates, low life expectancy, general poverty and unbalanced distribution of wealth and poor literacy skills. Who actually owns land in a country? In LDCs, it's relatively simple - the richest do. In many cases the poor are forced to work on rented land where they give part of their crops or produce to the landowner. Oxfam fight for this to stop and always need volunteers. Many organisations are trying to help Less Developed Countries to eliminate poverty and implement sustainable development projects to try and help the local economies and social development.

WORLD DEBT

Many countries in the developing world owe money to western countries including the UK. Many countries are finding it impossible to pay it back, leaving them high and dry with no proper Education and Health Services. Do you think the debts should be dropped? Young people are joining together in a campaign to drop them. If you want more info contact the Jubilee + Campaign through their website: www.jubileecampaign.co.uk.

World Development Movement
0800 328 2153 www.wdm.org.uk

People & Planet
www.peopleandplanet.org

CEWC – Cymru (Council for Education in World Citizenship – Cymru)
029 2022 8549
www.cewc-cymru.org.uk

Also check out:
- Ethical Trade
- Poverty

4. WORLD, EUROPE, UK & WALES

Besides voting or joining a political party, there are other ways to make your views heard and try to change things. If there's a cause you feel strongly about, make your voice heard. It can let people in power stop and think and make other people view things differently. You have an active part to play in your own life.

Youth Councils get their voices heard through forums, meetings, exchanges and online votes and chats. They may even collect names from the public to show that they have support for a cause and send it to an Assembly Member/Member of Parliament/Member of European Parliament. This is a petition. They get publicity to draw attention to what they're doing. They may be involved in demonstrations, marches or pressure groups. There should be a youth forum in your local authority; contact them for more information. There are many debating forums on UK and European policies and politics, and ways to express your views on issues such as environmental issues, youth crime, the future of transport and cloning to name a few. You are a citizen of Wales, the UK and Europe. Play your part. Have your say on our website, don't be shy! Tell us what you really think.

British Youth Council 0845 458 1489
www.byc.org.uk

Funky Dragon (the Children and Young People's Assembly for Wales)
www.funkydragon.org

The Youth Forum (representing the interests of young people from all over Europe)
www.youthforum.org

School Councils (elected groups of students making a positive contribution towards schools) 0845 456 9428
www.schoolcouncils.org

Also check out:
> UK Parliament
> Voting and Elections
> Local Government
> National Assembly for Wales
> World Politics – One World
> European Government

An asylum seeker is someone who is seeking sanctuary, protection and help in a country that is not their homeland. Asylum seekers worldwide and in the UK often have nowhere else to go; they may be running from war, hunger, religious or political persecution and seeking safety. Asylum seekers leave their own countries very often not out of choice, but out of necessity. Certain countries in the world accept more asylum seekers than others. The matter remains that asylum seekers have human rights and need somewhere to live.

Currently, the issue of asylum seekers is high on the news agenda as there is a debate about how many the UK accepts. Some believe that we take too many and others believe that it is our duty as a civilized country to provide sanctuary for those that need it. When a refugee seeks asylum in this country, he or she is subject to a process to determine whether they truly require sanctuary in this country. If not, they may be ordered to return to their country of origin.

Many people in the UK have concern at the number of illegal immigrants in the UK and sometimes confuse genuine asylum seekers with these people.

Committee to Defend Asylum Seekers (CDAS) 07941 566 183
www.defend-asylum.org

BBC page on asylum seekers with loads of facts, information and news
news.bbc.co.uk/1/hi/in_depth/uk/2001/destination_uk/default.stm

The Home Office
www.homeoffice.gov.uk

Refugee Council
0207 346 6700
www.refugeecouncil.org.uk

Also check out:
- Basic Skills Essentials
- Famine and Drought
- Poverty
- Terrorism
- Human Rights
- Benefits Essentials

4. WORLD, EUROPE, UK & WALES

In today's world it's important to understand global issues affecting you and other young people. To become a good citizen of Wales, UK, Europe and the world, you need to understand the issues that affect you and how you can be involved in making decisions about your life and the lives of others. Do you know your rights as a young person? How can you get involved in your local community? Do you understand environmental issues and that there are different communities at local, regional, national and international levels?

With a little more understanding and co-operation, young people around the world are starting to take on global issues and challenges. Citizenship helps you to understand these issues so everyone can live together in this multicultural world and have their say.

Institute for Citizenship
0207 844 5444
www.citizen.org.uk

Department for Education and Skills Citizenship website
www.dfes.gov.uk/citizenship/

The Citizenship Foundation
www.citizenshipfoundation.org.uk

Community Service Volunteers Wales
0800 284 533
www.csv.org.uk/Wales/

Also check out:
> Human Rights
> World Politics – One World
> Youth Councils
> Voting and Elections
> Volunteering UK
> Bin It!

War and conflict is a common thing in our world and while many people are fighting each other, many organizations are fighting for world peace. When a conflict arises, most Governments try to resolve them peacefully first and will only resort to violence as a last resort. You may believe that violence is never the answer or you might think that it's necessary to sort out certain situations. People fight for many reasons and only you can decide if you believe in the cause – the reason for the conflict. Organizations such as the United Nations (UN) and the North Atlantic Treaty Organisation (NATO) work to peacefully resolve conflicts before they become violent. On a smaller scale, you may be simply wishing for peace in your house - a bit of quiet from tense moments or the conflict and arguments around you. There are projects and events you can get involved in to help the cause. A little understanding and compassion can go a long way to understanding the causes of conflict and making sure that people have their human rights without taking them away from others.

United Nations (UN) (worldwide peace-keeping organization)
www.un.org

North Atlantic Treaty Organisation (NATO) (safeguarding the freedom of 26 countries in North America and Europe)
www.nato.int

Stop The War Coalition
0207 278 6694
www.stopwar.org.uk

BBC Relationships page on how to avoid arguments
www.bbc.co.uk/relationships/couples/comm_avoid.shtml

Also check out:
> Asylum Seekers
> Terrorism
> United Nations
> World Politics – One World
> Arguments
> Living Together

Generally, poverty refers to hardship which is unacceptable. This may mean those who don't have enough material or financial wealth or are socially excluded. The word poverty is most commonly associated with those living in undeveloped or developing nations. This is because these countries are less wealthy so a greater percentage of their population tend to live in difficult conditions. However, developed countries also have many people who live in poverty (often referred to as 'living below the poverty line'). Almost one in four people in the UK currently live in poverty. The Prime Minister has outlined his plans to end child poverty in the UK within a generation. There are also many organizations that are fighting to end worldwide poverty. Currently, some nations have more money than others meaning that some people have too much whilst others go without (known as the 'uneven distribution of wealth'). Campaigns like Make Poverty History aim to get Governments to redistribute wealth more evenly so that each and every human on the planet can live in comfort, above the poverty line.

Make Poverty History
www.makepovertyhistory.org

Child Poverty Action Group
0207 837 7979
www.cpag.org.uk

Welsh Assembly page on Child Poverty
www.wales.gov.uk/subichildren/content/child-poverty-e.htm

OXFAM (facts about poverty)
0870 333 2700
www.oxfamgb.org/ukpp/poverty/thefacts.htm

Also check out:
> Asylum Seekers
> Peace
> Famine and Drought
> Over Population
> Homelessness Essentials
> Budgeting Essentials

Terrorists use violence and the threat of violence in an attempt to achieve something political (they want to change opinion and have an effect on Governments). Each terrorist group has its own motive. It may be that they are unhappy with their own Government, the actions of another Government or want to spread or enforce their own religious or ideological values. Terrorism has featured heavily in the news lately as Western countries such as the UK, Spain and the US have recently been subject to terrorist attacks. Many of the attacks have been carried out by suicide bombers (those willing to kill themselves in order to harm or kill others) and the rise in these cases is causing grave concern.

People turn to terrorism for different reasons and people that commit acts of terrorism are not all the same. For example, some people may act out of desperation, while other people may believe that they are carrying out "God's" work.

Terrorism is a very emotive issue, with opinions on terrorists and what constitutes as "terrorism" varying widely (for example, some people are of the opinion that going into Iraq without UN backing was an act of terrorism). In the UK, there is currently much discussion and change taking place around how we reduce and deal with the threat of terrorism.

Home Office Security page
0207 035 4848
www.homeoffice.gov.uk/security/?version=1

Government page improving UK security
www.ukresilience.info/terrorism.htm

Foreign and Commonwealth Office (gives advice on travelling abroad)
0207 008 1500
www.fco.gov.uk

United Nations Action against Terrorism
www.un.org/terrorism/

Also check out:
- Peace
- Citizenship
- United Nations
- Cultures & Religion
- UK Parliament
- Backpacking

Culture is a word that describes a group of people who have a similar identity. In general, cultural identity is formed by customs and habits that change and develop over time. Youth culture changes around the world but some aspects remain the same. Certain features of a culture make it stand out. Food, dress, music, language and so on. What's your culture all about?

Having lots of different cultures makes Britain a wonderfully diverse country. Where else in the world can you eat Welsh cakes, porridge, curry, stir fry, sushi and fish and chips all in one day? It's not just about the food either; look and listen out and you'll see sights and hear sounds from a wide range of cultures. Many people are proud of their culture and rightly so. However, some believe that certain cultures are superior to others. All cultures have their own place in the world and should be given the respect they deserve, free from discrimination. When in a different culture, be sure to understand and stick to the rules.

Department for Culture, Media and Sport
0207 211 6200
www.culture.gov.uk

National Assembly for Wales Culture, Sport and Welsh Language
02920 825111
www.wales.gov.uk/subiculture/

Urdd Gobaith Cymru
01970 613100
www.urdd.org

BBC Society and Culture pages
www.bbc.co.uk/society/

Also check out:
> Citizenship
> Tourism
> Travel Essentials
> Language
> Discrimination Essentials
> Heritage

Visiting another country, experiencing their life, language and culture can be an exciting, informative and valuable life experience. Through youth exchanges, you can get involved. You can visit another country by yourself or as part of a group, through various organizations around the country such as youth centres, schools or community groups. As well as finding out the differences between people and cultures, you'll experience their similarities. Your exchange may have a theme. It might be citizenship, Europe or the arts and you may attend talks and workshops or you may carry out activities and discussions on these subjects. Some exchanges may also involve working or studying abroad and most will include some kind of planning beforehand and assessment afterwards. Most exchange participants stay with the family of another young person, which is a great way to experience what life is really like for a young person abroad. Usually lasting between one and three weeks, exchanges are often funded by youth organizations, many of which look to involve those young people with less opportunities than others.

The Commonwealth Youth Exchange Council
0207 498 6151
www.cyec.org.uk

British Council European Youth Exchange Programmes
0207 389 4030
www.britishcouncil.org/connectyouth-programmes-european-youth-exchange-programmes.htm

Inter Cultural Youth Exchange
www.icye.co.uk

Also check out:

- Gap Years
- Personal Development
- Careers Essentials
- Volunteering Abroad
- Travel Essentials
- Culture

Wales has hundreds and thousands of years of history behind it, all of which has gone towards making it the great nation that it is today! But how much do you know about Wales' past? There's so much that you can discover about the history of the nation from relics of the past that were left behind. Historic monuments, buildings, parks and artefacts that have remained tell us something about the people who used to live here and what their lives were like. Additionally, they tell us something about who we are and where we come from. All over Wales, you'll find organizations that look after and present this history to us in a fascinating, informative way. Many of the organizations that do this often provide work experience for young people or offer voluntary work. So, whether you just want to find out about the past or get involved in helping to preserve it, now's your chance to do so!

Cadw
01443 33 6000
www.cadw.wales.gov.uk

The National Trust
0870 458 4000
www.nationaltrust.org.uk

The Welsh Heritage Schools Initiative
www.whsi.org.uk

Visit Wales
08708 300 306
www.visitwales.com

Also check out:
> Volunteering UK
> Citizenship
> Conservation
> Countryside
> Museums and Galleries

Language in Wales will always be one of the big issues. The Welsh language has officially been spoken since as long ago as the 9th century, although in a very different form to what it is now. Suppressed for hundreds of years (including a practice in some schools whereby anyone caught speaking Welsh would be made to wear a 'Welsh Knot', a symbol that meant the child in question could be bullied and ridiculed, weakening the language), the Welsh language has only recently made a significant return. In 1993, the Welsh Language Act meant that Welsh was given equal footing with English in public life. There are still those who work to preserve and give greater prominence to the Welsh language today. Being bi-lingual in Wales today is useful as many companies and organizations work using both languages. Many employers offer Welsh courses. If not, there are many other options, such as evening courses, that can teach you Welsh. Learning more than one language can be beneficial for many reasons. You may just want to survive on holiday but equally you might want to live or work abroad, or work for a company that do business in a certain part of the world. As well as improving your career prospects, learning a language is a great way to meet new people, improve communication skills and have fun whilst you're doing it.

Welsh Language Board
02920 878000
www.bwrdd-yr-iaith.org.uk

BBC Learn Welsh
www.bbc.co.uk/wales/learnwelsh/

Online dictionary of the Welsh language
www.aber.ac.uk/~gpcwww/

The National Centre for Languages
0207 379 5101
www.cilt.org.uk

Also check out:

> Courses and Subjects
> Careers Essentials
> Citizenship
> Travel Essentials
> Working Abroad
> Culture

The word 'paranormal' refers to events or forces that cannot be explained by nature or science. Also known as the 'supernatural', it can mean anything from ghosts to telepathy and speaking to the dead. Generally, you either believe in this kind of thing or you don't. It's up to you to decide. There are many books, magazines and website that cover this sort of thing and can help you make up your mind. Here's a guide to some paranormal activities:

Astral Projection – the projection of a person's astral or ethereal body outside of their physical one.
Extra Sensory Perception (ESP) – communicating using a sense outside of the standard five (touch, taste, sight, sound, smell). This includes telepathy (mind reading or communicating with another person through thought alone), precognition (seeing the future) and clairvoyance (seeing details of objects and events in the present). Many people also argue that intuition is a paranormal phenomenon.
Mediumship - communicating with the dead or the spirit world.
Poltergeist – when a spirit manifestation makes rapping noises and moves objects such as furniture – often linked with haunting.
Spontaneous Combustion – when something ignites completely independently of being introduced to an external source of heat.
Telekinesis – Moving objects using only the power of the mind.

Vampires, werewolves and demons are all classed as supernatural creatures (if you're a believer - if not, they are classed as fiction or myth).

The Paranormal Science homepage
www.parascience.org.uk

Paranormal Investigations Cymru
hometown.aol.co.uk/picymru/AboutUs.html

A quick guide to the supernatural
www.thesupernaturalworld.co.uk

A quick guide to the paranormal
www.paranormality.com

Also check out:
> Religion & Beliefs
> Culture
> Witchcraft and Wizardry
> Astronomy

Loosely speaking, religion can be thought of as any kind of code of values or belief system that people live their lives by. Latest figures show that, in England and Wales, more than 40 million people follow some form of religion. The most popular faith in England and Wales is Christianity but many also follow Islam, Hinduism, Sikhism, Judaism and Buddhism. Many people do not have a religious faith. These people are called atheists. Those who are not sure as to the existence of a God are known as 'agnostic'. In today's multicultural society, it is important to be respectful of the beliefs of others, regardless of their faith or lack of it. Some groups or individuals may believe that their religion is superior to others. Often known as fundamentalists, they tend to believe in the original teachings of their religion and are often the cause for tension between religions. Despite the mix of religions that we have in Wales and the rest of the UK, there is still much ignorance to the beliefs and values of different faiths. Learn about the principles of each faith, what it means, where it comes from and what the beliefs are and become a more tolerant, understanding person able to contribute to a better society.

BBC Religion and Ethics homepage
www.bbc.co.uk/religion/

Comparative Religion (religious resources)
www.comparative-religion.com

British History Online (digital library of British history resources, including religious information)
www.british-history.ac.uk

Current statistics for religion in Wales
www.statistics.gov.uk/CCI/nugget.asp?ID=451&Pos=1&ColRank=1&Rank=160

Also check out:
- Citizenship
- Peace
- Terrorism
- Culture
- Paranormal
- Personal Development

Abortion

Abortion is a big step to take and must only be taken once you are 100% sure that it will be the right thing for you. If you do decide that an abortion is the best thing for you, here are some facts about it:

- Abortions should only be carried out in a hospital or a licensed clinic.
- During the first nine weeks of pregnancy, an abortion pill can be taken which terminates the pregnancy. The pill causes the lining of the womb to break down and results in bleeding through the vagina, which can sometimes be painful.
- Abortion between week nine and fourteen is carried out using a procedure known as vacuum aspiration, where the foetus is gently sucked from the womb.
- Between fourteen and nineteen weeks of pregnancy, an abortion is carried out using a process known as surgical dilation and evacuation (D&E). Under general anaesthetic, the foetus is removed with forceps.
- There are two ways of carrying out an abortion between twenty and twenty four weeks of pregnancy. The first is similar to D&E and the second involves the injection of a drug into the womb followed by the D&E procedure. Both of these involve an overnight stay.
- After twenty-four weeks of pregnancy, abortion is illegal.

Deciding on an abortion may be one of the most difficult decisions of your life. Don't be rushed into doing anything you're not sure about. Talk it through with someone you trust and get some advice from a counsellor (or you can contact one of the helplines below).

NHS abortion information
www.nhsdirect.nhs.uk/en.asp?topicid=1&areaid=2214&linkid=1817

BBC page about the ethics of abortion
www.bbc.co.uk/religion/ethics/abortion/

Family Planning Association 0845 310 1334
www.fpa.org.uk

Childline 0800 1111
www.childline.org.uk

Also check out:

> Doctors
> Contraception
> Problems and Emotions
> Babies
> Children
> Parenthood

Abuse

Abuse can exist in relationships in many ways. Families, friends, partners and professional relationships can all become abusive. Anyone can be the victim – a child, adult, male or female and anyone can be the perpetrator. Abuse can occur in relationships between those of the opposite sex and those of the same sex. It can be not only physical, but emotional as well. Physical abuse can range from restraining someone to hitting them or sexually abusing them. Emotional abuse can be anything from verbal abuse to threats. If you are neglected, that also counts as abuse. If you are under the care of another (parent, carer etc.) and they do not provide for you adequately or if a partner restricts another financially, that could be neglect. Young people are particularly vulnerable to abuse as they are dependant on adults for food, shelter, clothes etc. and some adults know how to take advantage and manipulate young people. Abuse must never be tolerated in any relationship. If you are unhappy or uncomfortable at the way you are being treated in a relationship, tell someone. Sharing your worries can help you understand the behaviour and whether it's acceptable or not. If not, tell a professional (see links below) and get the abuse stopped. In an emergency situation, dial 999.

Childline 0800 1111
www.childline.org.uk

National Society for the Prevention of Cruelty to Children (NSPCC)
0808 800 5000
www.nspcc.org.uk

Women's Aid 0808 2000 247
www.womensaid.org.uk

Hidden Hurt
www.hiddenhurt.co.uk

Also check out:

- Arguments
- Care
- Family
- Friends
- Problems and Emotions
- Counselling

5. FAMILY & RELATIONSHIPS

Giving a child up - The decision to put a child up for adoption is always a very difficult one. It needs a lot of thought and discussion with those you are close to, as well as professionals including council adoption social workers and adoption agencies. Professionals can give you both legal and emotional advice. Once your child has been adopted, you are not allowed to contact them unless the adoptive family agree to it. When your child turns 18, he or she will have the choice of finding out about you. It is up to you how much you know about your child's adoptive family.

Being adopted - If you have been adopted, you may, at 18, wish to find out more about your birthparents; there are organisations that may be able to help.

Adopting a child

As long as you are over 21, you can be considered for adoption regardless of your background. The only hindrances may be criminal records or health issues. To apply for adoption, you will need to contact an adoption agency. The process normally takes about six months to complete. It involves interviews with the agency, application forms, checks such as police and medical checks, interviews between the agency and two or three of your friends and attendance at adoption workshops. Finally, you'll work with the agency to produce a report, which is then considered by an adoption panel.

The British Association for Adoption and Fostering 0207 593 2000
www.baaf.org.uk

Department for Education and Skills page on adoption
www.dfes.gov.uk/adoption/

Adoption and Fostering Information Line
0800 783 4086 - www.adoption.org.uk

BBC Radio One Life page on adoption
www.bbc.co.uk/radio1/onelife/personal/parenthood/adopt_practical.shtml

After Adoption - 029 2066 6597
www.afteradoption.org.uk/youngpeople

Also check out:
- Babies
- Parenthood
- Fostering
- Children
- Care
- Family
- Friends

Arguments

Arguments happen for all sorts of reasons. You may have fallen out with your best mate or your parents may argue all the time and it may get you down. Everyone has off days, but if it seems as though you're always shouting and arguing, there may be an underlying problem in your relationship. Speak to the other person or someone else that you feel comfortable with and tell them how arguing upsets you and try not to bottle up the hurt. By speaking out, you'll let people know and help them to understand your feelings.

You may be the one that feels angry all the time, especially with your parents or brothers and sisters. If you feel yourself getting angry, try and get yourself out of the situation by going for a walk or breathing in and counting to ten. It may be difficult in a busy household but try and get some time alone to read or listen to music or do something you really enjoy and relax. Check out the Sport & Leisure section for information on lots of different activities for you to try.

Relate (providing relationship counselling) 0845 456 1310
www.relate.org.uk

Institute of Family Therapy
0207 391 9150
www.instituteoffamilytherapy.org.uk

British Association for Counselling and Psychotherapy 0870 443 5252
www.bacp.co.uk

United Kingdom Council for Psychotherapy
www.psychotherapy.org.uk

Also check out:
> Abuse
> Attitudes & Stereotypes
> Family
> Friends
> Problems and Emotions
> Living Together
> Love and Relationships

Attitudes and Stereotypes
5.1 Family & Relationship Issues

Do you always see the glass as being half empty or half full? Being positive and looking forward to the future is an attitude that keeps you on track. Don't be afraid to have dreams and ambitions. No matter what point you are at in life, it's always inspiring to have future goals to aim for. Set yourself targets, no matter how small, and feel the satisfaction when you reach them. But don't expect life to fall into your lap. It takes hard work to achieve. If you sit and wait for a stroke of good luck, you may find that life passes you by and you look back with regret.

If you want to get on in life, think about your attitudes to other people. Getting on with people is the key. Don't judge others before you get to know them. Never think that you know someone just because of their appearance or their interests. Stereotyping people can be a very negative way of approaching people and you might just find that you get it totally wrong. Be open to new people with different interests than your own. That way you'll get a variety of opinions, subjects and lifestyles to talk about. You might not get on with everyone but give people a chance and then make your decision.

Handling people at work
www.troubleatwork.org.uk/ViewADocument.asp?ID=134

Relate (relationship advice)
0845 456 1310
www.relate.org.uk

How to make friends
www.youngminds.org.uk/education/y2.php

Also check out:
> Family
> Friends
> Problems and Emotions
> Holidays
> Discrimination Essentials
> You
> Racism
> Culture

Those of you who've been around babies will know how much hard work they can be. They need love, care and attention and they'll sure let you know when they're not getting enough of it (usually by screaming their little heads off!). The arrival of a new baby will mean that you'll have to change your life around completely. Your main responsibility in life now should now be your child. And sometimes, it can be a hard, stressful time to get through. You must be prepared to respond to your baby's demands at all hours, no matter what you are doing. If they are crying it's probably because they are hungry, wet, tired or they just want to play. Most of the time, you don't need to worry about the tears and tantrums. If you are worried that your baby is ill though, see a GP immediately. Many parents, especially those without support, can find it difficult to cope with raising a child so don't be afraid to use all the help that you can get your hands on. That help might be professional or simply from family or friends but if it's there and you need it, use it.

Government information on bringing up children -
www.direct.gov.uk/Bfsl1/BenefitsAndFinancialSupport/Expecting_or_bringing_up_children/fs/en

BBC's parenting homepage
www.bbc.co.uk/parenting/

Parentline Plus Helpline 0808 800 2222
www.parentlineplus.org.uk/templates/home/index.cfm

National Society for the Prevention of Cruelty to Children 0808 800 5000 www.nspcc.org.uk

www.midwivesonline.com - for you and baby

Also check out:
- Parenthood
- Doctors
- Adoption
- Fostering
- Children
- Fertility

5. FAMILY & RELATIONSHIPS

When children are put at risk from the way they are being looked after by their parents, the Social Services department of the nearest local authority may step in and take a child into care. The process that decides exactly what will happen in the end is known as 'care proceedings', which usually takes between nine and twelve months to complete. Through discussion between the Social Services, the child and anyone who has 'parental responsibility', it will be decided exactly what is best for the child (detailed in a 'care order') so that they will be safe and properly looked after. Each child going through care proceedings has a Children's Guardian, who represents their welfare. For parents whose children are going through care proceedings, solicitors are free of charge.

A care order can last up until a child is 18. A child in care may live in a children's home or with foster parents. Whilst in care, they are encouraged to keep up regular contact with their parents, friends and relatives. Any child in care aged 16 or above is given a 'Pathway Plan', which prepares them for independent life, giving support and guidance on housing, education and training.

Children and Family Court Advisory and Support Service 0207 510 7000
www.cafcass.gov.uk

Citizens Advice Bureau page on Children and Local Authority Care in Wales
www.adviceguide.org.uk/wales/family_parent/family/children_and_local_authority_care.htm

Carelaw (information for young people in care)
http://nchacti01.uuhost.uk.uu.net/carelaw

Childline 0800 1111
www.childline.org.uk

Also check out:
- Adoption
- Family
- Friends
- Children
- Parenthood
- Qualifications Essentials
- Housing Options

Many parents say that having children is the greatest joy that you can have in life. But with that pleasure comes responsibility and lots of hard work. Put the effort in and you'll be rewarded with children bought up exactly the way you want them to be. Once you're a parent you have a legal responsibility too for the safety and welfare of your child. Your priorities should change so that the more important person in the world now is your child. They need you, not just for love but for guidance, food, warmth, health and education.

Managing behaviour can be tricky with children who always seem to have a few tricks up their sleeves with which to manipulate their parents. Remember though that children have needs and wants just like adults and are only trying to get their needs satisfied, no matter how they try and achieve this. If bad behaviour is stressing you out, try your hardest to remain calm and deal with the situation sensibly. If you need help, there are lots of people who'll be willing to provide it. From local authorities to helplines, charities and support groups and not forgetting friends and family, there's plenty of support for you so use it when you need it.

Practical Parenting
www.practicalparent.org.uk

Parents Information Network
www.pin.org.uk

Raising Kids
0208 883 8621
www.raisingkids.co.uk

BBC page on Parenting
www.bbc.co.uk/parenting/

Also check out:
> Family
> Friends
> Babies
> Parenthood
> Arguments
> Benefits Essentials
> Care

Divorce

When a marriage is terminated, it is known as a 'divorce'. To get divorced, you need to have a marriage recognised by UK law that has existed for at least one year. If both people agree to the divorce, it is an 'undefended divorce', which is a relatively simple procedure that doesn't necessarily require a solicitor. If one partner doesn't agree, it's a 'defended divorce' and requires a solicitor. For a divorce to be granted, it must be proven that the marriage no longer exists. Any one of the following reasons need to be proven – adultery, unreasonable behaviour, desertion, two years separation without consent or five years separation. Divorce can be a complex, traumatic process and should only be approached with much forethought and advice. There are many issues that arise from divorce including the welfare of children, dividing possessions and property and arranging finances. Be sure to seek personal and professional advice from the organisations below before jumping in. Divorce often has a large impact on children so re-assure them that it's not their fault and that you both still love them. If your parents are going through a divorce, it can be a hard time. Talk to them, tell them how you are feeling and if you need further help, call an organisation like Childline.

Childline 0800 1111
www.childline.org.uk

NCH's It's Not Your Fault
0845 7626579
www.itsnotyourfault.org

Citizens Advice Bureau
www.adviceguide.org.uk

Liberty's page on rights for those involved in divorce 0845 123 2307
www.yourrights.org.uk/your-rights/chapters/the-rights-of-children-and-young-people

Also check out:

> Arguments
> Care
> Problems and Emotions
> Legal Advice

5. FAMILY & RELATIONSHIPS

5.1 Family & Relationship Issues

The bonds that exist between family members are extremely important. As well as biological bonds, you're also likely to spend a lot of time with your family members over the years. Because of these ties, time spent with your family can be great. You probably know each other better than anyone else so it's easy to relax and enjoy time together. Your elder family can be great for advice. Remember, they've been through it all before. Take the time to talk to your family, tell them how you feel and if you have any problems. Be open, honest and positive and keep in mind that your family have your best interests at heart. Family life isn't always harmonious though. Life can sometimes be hard in a family, when you may know each other so well that sometimes you can drive each other mad! Remember though that it's precisely because you are so close that you may irritate each other from time to time. There's no such thing as a normal family who get on well all of the time so keep things in perspective.

Care for the family (help for those hurting due to family breakdown)
02920 810 800
www.careforthefamily.org.uk

Relate (relationship advice)
www.relate.org.uk

Home Start (family support charity)
0800 068 63 68
www.home-start.org.uk

Childline
0800 1111
www.childline.org.uk

Also check out:
> Abuse
> Arguments
> Divorce
> Problems and Emotions
> Parenthood
> Living Together

Fostering

Children are fostered because their family, for whatever reason, are not able to look after them at that time. Fostering is a measure that is taken for the good of the child but it can be a confusing time for them. Each child has a social worker who is there to make sure that they are being looked after correctly and that they understand what is happening to them and why. Fostering is usually a temporary measure and Social Services will work to get the fostered child back to their birth family. If this is not possible, they will try to find long term care for the child, either with a permanent foster family or adoptive family.

Becoming a foster carer is a big decision to make. People decide to become foster parents for many reasons. They may feel that they can provide children with a good home when they need it or they may just like children. Anyone can become a foster carer regardless of age, gender, marital status and sexuality, although the minimum age is normally 21. Those who wish to become foster parents can either contact their local Social Services or a fostering agency. They will then have to go through training and an application process to decide if they are suitable.

Fostering Information Line
0800 783 4086
www.fostering.org.uk

BBC Radio One Life information on fostering
www.bbc.co.uk/radio1/onelife/personal/families/fostered.shtml

Government Information on fostering
www.direct.gov.uk/Audiences/Parents/AdoptionAndFostering/AdoptionAndFosteringArticle/

Also check out:
- Care
- Adoption
- Family
- Friends
- Babies
- Children
- Parenthood

Friends come and friends go. Some will stick around for a few months, some for a lifetime. With your friends you'll share experiences, ideas, memories, good times and bad. Having friends makes your path through life much easier and much more fun. In many ways, friends are just as important as family. The close ties that a family have often make it difficult to discuss or do certain things with them. Friends can take a step back and enjoy you for who you are and vice versa. A true friend should be there in times of trouble as well as joy. Be positive, communicate openly and try to let friends make their own choices and decisions in life. Being a friend doesn't mean that someone can take liberties though. If you feel you're being treated unfairly or used in a friendship, try to sort it out, and if it can't be resolved, there are plenty more deserving people worthy of your friendship. Within groups of friends, peer pressure often exists. This is when the behaviour, opinions and/or ideas of friends influence others to follow suit and do the same. Try and go your own way. Have your own thoughts and ideas and don't just go along with the crowd for the sake of it.

Kidscape guide to making friends
08451 205 204
www.kidscape.org.uk/childrenteens/makingfriends/1makingfriends.shtml

Childline page on friends
0800 1111
www.childline.org.uk/Friends.asp

How to make friends
www.uncommon-knowledge.co.uk/emotional_wellbeing/friends/making-friends.html

Friends Reunited
www.friendsreunited.co.uk

Also check out:
> Arguments
> Attitudes
> Problems and Emotions
> You
> Attitudes & Stereotypes
> Youth Clubs

Getting married is a huge commitment and should be one of the biggest decisions of your life, so make sure it's for the right reasons! Getting married to escape a problem or family, because everyone else is doing it or because you want the ring, the wedding day and a nice outfit, is a recipe for disaster. Your husband or wife should be someone that you love and want to spend the rest of your life living with. You can get married from the age of 16 but if you're under 18 you'll need written consent from your parents/guardian. The ceremony doesn't have to be religious and you can get married in any approved building. You can also get married abroad (contact the Embassy of the country for information). Same-sex relationships can now also be officially recognised through a civil partnership, which is similar to a wedding.

Many cultures living in Wales still practice arranged marriages. The bond between these two families is usually very strong and secures many marriage agreements. Are your parents responsible for finding you your future husband or wife? Do you want to be matched? If you have any concerns or need to be reassured contact Relate.

General Register Office
www.gro.gov.uk/gro/content/marriages/

Government information on marriage
www.direct.gov.uk/RightsAndResponsibilities/RightsAndResponsibilitiesArticles/fs/en?CONTENT_ID=10026937&chk=/et8pN

Relate (relationship advice)
0845 456 1310 www.relate.org.uk

Foreign and Commonwealth Office Forced Marriage Unit
0207 008 0230
www.fco.gov.uk/servlet/Front?pagename=OpenMarket/Xcelerate/ShowPage&c=Page&cid=1094234857863

Also check out:
- Boyfriends & Girlfriends
- Living Together
- Love & Sex
- Culture & Religions
- Sexuality

Miscarriage

Miscarriage is when a pregnancy is lost before 24 weeks. It normally occurs because of the fragile nature of conception. When a baby is created, half the genes come from the sperm and half from the egg. Occasionally when they meet, some information may be lost. It is when that information is needed that the baby dies and the mother miscarries. It also sometimes occurs because the baby doesn't implant itself in the womb properly. The very large majority of miscarriages occur purely because of bad luck. It is very rarely because of something the mother did or didn't do during pregnancy. However, there are some other factors such as smoking and exposure to solvents that can cause miscarriage and are avoidable. When a miscarriage occurs, a woman may experience a loss of blood that lasts for around seven to ten days and is quite similar to a normal period. The next period should return approximately six weeks later. If you are concerned at all, see your GP for information and help. A miscarriage can be traumatic for those involved; the Miscarriage Association (see link below) provides free support and information.

The Miscarriage Association Helpline
01924 200 799
www.miscarriageassociation.org.uk

NHS Direct page on miscarriage
0845 46 47
www.nhsdirect.nhs.uk/he.asp?articleID=249&LinkID=1567

Women's Health page on miscarriage
www.womens-health.co.uk/miscarr.asp

Web Health page on miscarriage
www.webhealth.co.uk/a_to_z_of_health/miscarriage.asp

Also check out:
- Doctors
- Fertility
- Substance Misuse
- Smoking
- Contraception
- Pregnancy

Becoming a parent is the biggest responsibility most people face throughout their lives. It can bring love, joy and pride but can also be daunting, hard and tiring work and, at times, can be boring. The needs of a child will call on all of your skills, as you'll constantly make decisions about what's best for your child. There is no right or wrong way to bring up children, no manual can tell you how to do it. But, there is help for parents. Don't be afraid to look to your family, friends, support lines and local community services for support.

Make no mistake, there will be hard times but there'll be good times too. It's worth hanging onto the good memories and recalling them during the bad times – they may just get you through them. Ultimately, the responsibility comes as your child looks to you for help, guidance and understanding. They will look up to you to see how you behave. So, show your child that you love them no matter what, listen to and encourage them, use positive parenting and they should respond by behaving in the same sensible way. And don't forget, you are more than just a parent so take time out for yourself too.

BBC page on parenting
www.bbc.co.uk/parenting

Raising Kids (parenting advice)
0208 883 8621
www.raisingkids.co.uk

For Parents By Parents (parenting advice)
www.forparentsbyparents.com

UK Government's parenting advice
www.direct.gov.uk/Parents/fs/en

Also check out:
> Children
> Relaxing
> Adoption
> Family
> Friends
> Fostering
> Babies

Friends are wonderful things – they pick you up when you're down, they laugh and cry with you, they share your experiences and they want the best for you. At least, they should.

Sometimes, though, "friends" may try and get you to do things that you don't want to do. For example, they may try to get you to shoplift by teasing you about being too chicken to do it, or they may say that you're too much of a mammy's boy to smoke to try and goad you into having a drag on a fag. If you're the only one in a group not drinking alcohol, for example, your "friends" may start excluding you on purpose, just to get you to join in and have a drink. These are all examples of peer pressure.

It's hard to stand your ground if you're worried about loosing friends, but you should never bow to pressure and allow yourself to be swayed into doing something that you don't want to do – especially if it's an illegal act or could endanger your health. Keep your self-respect and stick to your guns – you've got a mind of your own and don't be afraid to let others know it.

A true friend will never try and coerce you or force you into doing something that you are uncomfortable with - a true friend will always respect your decision. Remember - you can choose who you are friends with and if someone is pushing you and pressuring you into doing things that you don't want to, you don't have to be friends with them any more.

Childline page on friends
0800 1111
www.childline.org.uk/Friends.asp

Likeitis.org on peer pressure
www.likeitis.org/peer_pressure.html

Also check out:
> Arguments
> Attitudes
> Friends
> Problems & Emotions
> You
> Stereotypes
> Stress

Young Carers
5.1 Family & Relationship Issues

A young carer is someone who is under the age of 18 who carries out caring tasks and is at least partially responsible for another person. That person may be unable to care for themselves adequately because of their age, illness, a disability or an addiction. A carer's work may involve washing and cleaning the person they are caring for, helping them use the toilet, dressing them, feeding them and helping them with their medication. Being a carer can be hard for a young person. Young people need time to develop and have a life of their own, so looking after the needs of another can be stressful. As well as your education or employment, you need time to socialise and to relax on your own. However, there is help available for young carers. The Government may be able to provide financial assistance. Local authorities can often provide transport and mobility assistance to those in need. It's also possible to receive respite care. This is when another professional carer takes over your care duties for anything from a couple of hours upwards. Young Carers Projects are available. They offer young carers the chance to get away from the house, relax and socialise. If you think you need help, contact one of the organisations below.

Young Carers Initiative
www.youngcarer.com

NCH information for young carers
0845 762 6579
www.nch.org.uk/information/index.php?i=244

The Princess Royal Trust for Carers
0207 480 7788
www.carers.org

Young Carers
0207 480 7788
www.youngcarers.net

Also check out:
> Care
> Family
> Friends
> Problems and Emotions
> You
> Health
> Benefits Essentials

Boyfriends & Girlfriends

Boyfriends and girlfriends should make each other happy, be there for each other and be able to laugh and have fun together. Don't just choose any old person for the privilege of getting to be your partner because everyone else has one or because he or she is the only option available. It should be someone special that you hold dear. Every relationship between partners is different, none is normal. Some may argue like cat and dog, others never. Some may see each other from time to time, others once a week. What works for you, works for you, so don't judge yours or anyone else's relationship by others.

Be open and honest in your relationship. If you can talk freely about anything then you'll both know where you stand. Listen and respect your partner, don't keep secrets and do different things together. Don't cut yourselves off from your friends. It's all very well being with someone that you love but everyone needs a little independence some time. Having a boyfriend or girlfriend isn't the be-all and end-all in life. There's someone for everyone so if a relationship isn't working, don't be afraid to end it. Most of all though, enjoy your partner. That's what they're there for!

Dear Cupid (agony aunt)
www.dearcupid.org

BBC page on relationships
www.bbc.co.uk/relationships/

Relate (relationship advice)
0845 456 1310
www.relate.org.uk

Like It Is (Sex education for young people)
www.likeitis.org

Also check out:

> Arguments
> Family
> Friends
> Problems and Emotions
> Dating
> Love & Sex
> Splitting Up

Many people often ask what the most effective method of contraception is and there's only one answer to that question - celibacy. Celibacy simply means not having sexual intercourse. It doesn't mean that you can't get involved in a relationship or kiss and hug your partner but it does mean that you won't go the whole way. Celibacy doesn't mean that you are a virgin as some sexually active people decide to become celibate.

People are celibate for many reasons. They may be waiting for the right person to come along. Many people believe sexual intercourse to be of such importance that it is necessary only to do it with someone that you truly love. Others may be celibate because the rules of their religion say that they must not have sex before marriage. Some may not enjoy sex so decide not to take part in it with anyone. Whatever the reasons, celibacy is a perfectly reasonable life choice and provides a guarantee that you will remain free of STIs and unaffected by pregnancy.

Family Planning Association
0845 310 1334
www.fpa.org.uk

Avert (international AIDS charity)
www.avert.org

Playing Safely (Sex questions answered)
0800 567 123
www.playingsafely.co.uk

BBC Wales' Come Clean
0800 567 123
www.bbc.co.uk/wales/comeclean/

Also check out:
> Babies
> Contraception
> HIV and AIDS
> STIs
> Sex Essentials
> Love & Sex

If you want to avoid pregnancy, you need to use contraception. The most effective form of contraception is to not have sexual intercourse at all. However, if you are having or planning on having sex, you need to use another form of contraception. There are many types (see links below for more information) so you should be able to find a method that suits you. Here's some information on the two most common forms of contraception:

Condom – A sheath (for men or women) that traps sperm. If used properly, it's 98% effective. Put a condom on with care, as any splits or tears could greatly reduce its effectiveness. Free condoms are available for free from family planning centres, sexual health and GUM clinics (condoms can protect you from STIs (Sexually Transmitted Infections), while other methods of contraception won't). They can also be bought from many shops including newsagents, supermarkets and pharmacies.

The Pill – A pill taken by women to stop them ovulating and therefore becoming pregnant. If used properly, it is likely to be almost 100% effective (not having sex is the only 100% effective contraception). To get a pill prescription, visit your GP or family planning clinic. The pill occasionally has side effects. Usually they are minor but in some rare cases, there have been serious side effects. Make sure you discuss it in full with your GP before you go on tho pill.

Family Planning Association
0845 310 1334
www.fpa.org.uk

Playing Safely (STI and contraception information)
www.playingsafely.co.uk

NHS
0845 46 47
www.nhsdirect.nhs.uk

Net Doctor (in-depth guide to contraception)
www.netdoctor.co.uk/sex_relationships/facts/contraception_which.htm

Also check out:

- Babies
- Celibacy
- Fertility
- Love & Sex
- Sex Essentials
- STI

Butterflies and excitement all rolled into one. Going on a date can be fab. 'What are they going to be like? Are we going to get on? What am I going to wear? Where are we going to go?' Be clear in your own head about what you want out of your date and be honest with your partner about it, otherwise you could end up in a world of confusion! Be yourself at all times, it's really easy to spot when someone isn't and even if you do convince well, you'll be found out eventually and that moment won't be fun. Relax and enjoy yourself and if it doesn't work out, it's not your fault, it just wasn't meant to be.

There are dangers however if you're meeting up with someone you may not know very well. Here are some tips on how to be date-safe:

- Get the facts about the person you're meeting.
- Don't meet up with people alone if you've never met in person before - they may not be who they say they are.
- Always go to open, sociable places on your dates, busy cafes and restaurants etc. are a good choice.
- Tell someone else where you're going on the date.
- Don't let them talk you into anything you don't want to do.

Dating Advice
www.dating-advice.uk.com

BBC page on relationships and dating
www.bbc.co.uk/relationships/singles_and_dating/

The Suzy Lamplugh Trust (personal safety) 0208 876 0305
www.suzylamplugh.org

Also check out:
> Boyfriends & Girlfriends
> Kissing
> Love & Sex
> You
> Email and Internet

Love can be a pretty powerful emotion and once it's got hold of you, you'll certainly know about it! It is easy to get it wrong though. Don't mistake a crush or lust for love. Sure, he or she might look great and be the coolest person in town but if you have nothing to say to them, forget about it. However, if it's the real deal then go for it. The old cliché that it's better to have tried and failed than to never have tried at all is true when it comes to love. Perhaps the trickiest thing when falling in love is knowing whether the object of your desire feels the same as you do. Check their body language, do they make an effort to speak to you and compliment you? Do they hang around with you even when their mates are gone? Do they touch you quite a lot? If you're getting good signs, then you should be onto a winner. If you find that they stick with their friends and avoid making eye-contact and conversation with you then it's probably best to leave it. If your love is unrequited (you love them but they don't you) then it's not the end of the world. It just wasn't meant to be and to use another old cliché – there are plenty more fish in the sea!

Relate (relationship counselling)
0845 456 1310
www.relate.org.uk

Relationship advice
www.uncommon-knowledge.co.uk/relation-ship_advice.html

BBC relationships page
www.bbc.co.uk/relationships_advice.html

Also check out:

> Basic Skills Essentials
> You
> Boyfriends & Girlfriends
> Kissing
> Love & Sex
> Relaxing
> Contraception

If you are able to produce a baby, you are fertile and if not, you are infertile. Roughly one in seven couples is affected by infertility, although most can still conceive with medical help. There are lots of different reasons why couples cannot conceive. Women may have problems due to being underweight or overweight, because of an STI like Chlamydia, which often has no obvious symptoms, or because of various other medical conditions. Men can become infertile because of hormone problems, side effects of medicines etc. Often, doctors are unable to find a reason why a couple may be infertile. If you have reason to think you may be infertile, see your GP with your partner. A GP or a specialist may then carry out a series of tests to determine the problem (usually couples need to have been trying unsuccessfully for a baby for at least 18 months first). If there is a problem, there are a variety of methods that may help conception including egg donation, In Vitro Fertilisation (IVF) or drug treatment. Finding out you're infertile can be a stressful experience. It may help to join a counselling or support group to help you deal with it.

NHS
0845 46 47
www.nhsdirect.nhs.uk

British Infertility Counselling Association (BICA) 01744 450 660
www.bica.net

British Fertility Society
01454 642217
www.britishfertilitysociety.org.uk

Infertility Network UK
08701 188 088
www.infertilitynetworkuk.com

Also check out:
- Adoption
- Fostering
- Problems and Emotions
- Babies
- Parenthood
- Counselling

Kissing is a sure sign that you like someone and is the easiest way to show someone you care. Even a peck on the cheek makes someone feel special and loved. A kiss is great, but snogging, well you either love it or think it's gross! If you're all tongues and not sure whether you're doing it right...welcome to your own snog masterclass.

Snog Masterclass

Brush your teeth twice a day – not only will it give you shiny teeth but also fresh breath. Keep a mint handy if you've been eating strong food
Don't smoke –fag breath is not pleasant
Get close - not miles away.
Turn your head - not your body.
Grip their waist - to stop them going anywhere.
Eyes closed - unless you want to see if people are watching.
Get those lips together - don't suck, blow or chew!
Avoid the goldfish pose - mouth open and mouth closed.
Don't clean their tonsils with your tongue - be sensitive.

Surveys have shown that most couples that kiss in public turn their heads to the right. Even the couple in Rodin's 'The Kiss' turn to the right. It's thought that it could be that whilst in the womb a baby naturally turns its head to the right, and it may simply be more natural and comfortable to turn it that way.

How to kiss
www.howtokiss.info

NHS
0845 46 47
www.nhsdirect.nhs.uk

Teen Advice
teenadvice.about.com

The Art of kissing
www.kissing.com

Also check out:

> Boyfriends & Girlfriends
> Dating
> Love & Sex
> Sex Essentials
> Orgasms
> Oral Sex
> Contraception

Living with your partner can improve and develop your relationship. You'll get closer, find out more and more things about each other and you'll get to spend all that time having fun together, away from mates and parents. It's a big commitment though. It's always very difficult to know what it will be like to live with someone before you do so. There might be things that you don't notice beforehand that drive you crazy when you're in the same house as that person all day, every day. You might have to get used to your partner's unpleasant habits too! Also, once you've moved in together, your relationship will be put under new and different pressures. You'll have cooking, cleaning and bills to pay. Before you move in together, talk about it honestly and make sure that it's something that you both want and can afford to do. Once you've moved in, you need to find your own way of getting by and getting along. Be honest with each other, share the responsibilities equally and give each other time and space alone.

Relate (relationship counselling)
0845 456 1310
www.relate.org.uk

Citizens Advice Bureau page on your rights when you move in with someone
www.advicenow.org.uk/livingtogether/

Article on moving in together
www.confetti.co.uk/weddings/advice_ideas/families_relationships/moving_in.asp

Laws for those living together and rights if you separate 0845 345 4345
www.clsdirect.org.uk/legalhelp/leaflet27.jsp?section=1&lang=en

Also check out:

> Arguments
> Attitudes
> Problems and Emotions
> Love & Sex
> Housing

Making love is another term for sexual intercourse. By having sex, you are getting as close to your partner as is physically possible, so most people think of sex emotionally as well as physically. As well as being great fun and physically pleasurable, when you're in a relationship sex is also about feeling close to and loved by your partner. Casual sex is when you have sex with someone who you do not have an emotional relationship with. It might be a one-night stand or someone whom you have a relationship with that is based purely on sex. Either way, you and no-one else should be the one who decides who, how often and when you have sex. When you're having sex, be confident and don't let anyone make you do anything that you don't feel comfortable with. If you're in a sexually active relationship, be honest about your sex lives. If you're not happy in any way, don't be embarrassed about it - tell your partner and talk things through. If things really aren't working out, there are ways and means to improve your sex life. If you're not trying for a baby, use protection and, if you have had unprotected sex (especially with someone you're not in a relationship with), make sure you have an STI test.

Like It Is (sex advice for young people)
www.likeitis.org

Brook
0800 0185 023
www.brook.org.uk

Channel 4 page on sex
www.channel4.com/health/microsites/0-9/4health/sex/

Lover's Guide (advice for sex and relationships)
www.loversguide.co.uk

Also check out:
- Celibacy
- Contraception
- Love & Sex
- Sex Essentials
- Sexuality
- STIs
- Safe Sex

Oral sex is using the tongue or the mouth to excite your partner's sexual parts (genitals). It can be done independently or as a part of sexual intercourse, often during foreplay. Getting oral sex right can be a delicate business. The trick with oral sex is to try different things to find out what you like and what you don't. If you and your partner can talk openly and honestly about it, you'll both know where you're going right – and where you going wrong! As a general tip, if you're unsure of how to begin, it's best to be gentle at first rather than diving in headlong, so to speak, and scaring the wits out of your partner. Oral sex can sometimes be a bit of a messy business and, whilst some people enjoying giving it, some people don't. Again, if you can let your partner know exactly how you feel, you can always find compromises and other ways of pleasuring each other. There are few health concerns with oral sex, although there is a small chance of an HIV infection. Use a condom or avoid getting semen or pre-ejaculatory (precum) fluid in the mouth to reduce the risk. And no, you can't get pregnant through oral sex!
Remember: don't do it if you don't want to.

Other words for oral sex are 'blowjob' (received by a man) or 'head' (received by either sex).

Playing Safely (sex Q and As)
www.playingsafely.co.uk

Relate (relationship counselling)
0845 456 1310
www.relate.org.uk

Brook (free sex advice for young people)
0800 0185 023
www.brook.org.uk

All Sex Guide (sex guidance)
www.allsexguide.com

Also check out:
> Boyfriends & Girlfriends
> HIV and AIDS
> Love & Sex
> Sexuality
> STIs
> Safe Sex
> Contraception

You may hear the term 'come'. To come means to have an orgasm – the peak of sexual excitement. These are pleasurable waves of rhythmic contractions in your genital area and happen to both sexes. Orgasms can be caused by penetrative sex, masturbation and/or oral stimulation. Men have a very obvious sign of orgasm – ejaculation – whereas women do not. Whilst orgasms are nice, they should not be seen as the objective of sex. They are merely part of it and as long as you enjoy the sexual experience as a whole, you needn't worry. Orgasms are different for everyone, there is no normal. Some may feel a little 'tingle' whereas others may feel as though the Earth is moving beneath them! Different people have different things that can make them orgasm and some may 'come' more easily than others. There are many factors, more than just physical, that can affect your orgasm. The most important things are to be relaxed, awake and happy in your relationship and sex-life. Try different things out, don't be afraid to experiment and be honest with your partner about what you do and don't like. If you're having problems reaching orgasms, it's not unusual at all. See your GP if you think the problem may be medical or seek counselling or self-help otherwise.

BBC page on orgasms
www.bbc.co.uk/relationships/sex_and_sexual_health/enjsex_orgasms.shtm

British Association for Sexual and Relationship Therapy
0208 543 2707
www.basrt.org.uk

Sex education for young people
www.likeitis.org.uk

Brook (Confidential sex advice)
0800 0185 023
www.brook.org.uk

Also check out:
> Celibacy
> Kissing
> Love & Sex
> Sexuality
> Relaxing
> Safe Sex
> Contraception

The Sexual Offences Act in the UK covers what sexual activity is and isn't allowed in this country. Here are the most important points of the Act:

The age at which you are allowed to have sex (known as the 'age of consent') is 16 for both heterosexual and homosexual sex.

To have sex, you need to have the full consent of your partner, no matter what their age.

Sex in public places or where others may be offended is illegal.

Flashing (exposure of the genitals in public) is an offence but only if it is done for sexual gratification or to scare people. If someone is a naturist or is stripping off for fun, it might be considered exhibitionism, which is much less likely to result in a conviction.

Voyeurism (secretly watching people in intimate surroundings such as changing rooms) is an offence.

Incest (sex with close family members including grandsons/daughters, brothers and sisters, sons and daughters or mothers and fathers) is illegal. This includes half-blood relatives.

Remember, sex isn't just about the law; it's about when you're ready to do it. For more information, see Making Love.

Avert (AIDS charity) page on teens, sex and the law
www.avert.org/teensex.htm

The Sexual Offences Act
www.opsi.gov.uk/acts/acts2003/20030042.htm

Citizens Advice Bureau page on young people, sex and sexuality
www.adviceguide.org

Channel 4 page on sex and the law
www.channel4.com/health/microsites/0-9/4health/sex/sar_law.html

Also check out:
> Boyfriends & Girlfriends
> Orgasms
> Oral Sex
> Rape
> Personal Safety

Are you sure which sex you're attracted to? Are you attracted to both? Are you confused? Discovering your sexuality may take time, it could be blatantly obvious to you, but not to others. Follow your feelings inside and find out where your true feelings lie. If you want a private chat with people who understand, or want to 'come out' but don't know how to tell people, there are many organisations that can help. These organisations can also help if you find it difficult to meet people especially if you live in a small town or in a rural area where everyone knows you.

QUICK GUIDE – to sexuality

- Gay – A man who's attracted to other men.
- Lesbian – A woman who's attracted to other women.
- Bisexual – Someone who's attracted to both sexes.
- Transsexual – Someone who is one sex and feels as if they should be the other. Often, transsexuals complete sex reassignment surgery, an operation to realign their genitals with their gender.
- Transgender – Another term used to describe transsexuals.
- Transvestites – People who dress in clothes of the opposite sex.
- Heterosexual – A man or woman attracted to the opposite sex.
- Homosexual – Attracted to the same sex (gay or lesbian).

The Gender Trust (Gender identity charity)
07000 790 347
www.gendertrust.org.uk

Avert (AIDS charity)
www.avert.org

Like It Is (sex education for young people)
www.likeitis.org.uk

Stonewall Cymru
02920 237 744
www.stonewall.org.uk

Also check out:

> Problems and Emotions
> Attitudes & Stereotypes
> HIV and AIDS
> Love & Sex
> Cosmetic Surgery
> Discrimination Essentials

Ending a relationship, whether you're the one doing the dumping, the dumpee or if you've mutually agreed to part, is no fun. For a relationship to end, there is usually a good reason for it, but it can still be hard to take. Finding yourself on your own can be a shock to the system and there will undoubtedly be times when you miss things about your relationship. If you're unhappy in your relationship, talking openly, honestly and calmly about it means that you'll both know where you stand and how you feel. It always helps to talk things through with close family and friends too.

If you've been dumped, don't take it too personally. All relationships are about two people and, despite the fact that you might feel bad for being the one to be dumped, the fact is that you need to find the right balance in a relationship. And if your relationship didn't provide that, it's nobody's fault.

If you're the one ending the relationship, find a good way to do it and that should be in person, not by phone, text or email. Everyone deals with the end of relationships differently so find your own way of coping and remember, it may seem like the end of the world but it might just be a new beginning.

Relate 0845 456 1310
www.relate.org.uk

Connexions relationship advice
0808 001 3219 www.connexions-direct.com/index.cfm?go=relationships

BBC One Life page on splitting up
www.bbc.co.uk/radio1/onelife/personal/relationships/splitting.shtml

Department for Constitutional Affairs guide for young people whose family's are splitting up www.dca.gov.uk/family/leaflets/splitting-english/default.htm

Also check out:
- Arguments
- Attitudes & Stereotypes
- Boyfriends & Girlfriends
- Problems and Emotions
- Living Together

If someone dies there's no magic wand or formula to take away the pain of grief. People deal with grief in very different ways, some may carry on as if nothing has happened, others feel numb, some get very angry, others go over and over it in their head. There is no typical or correct way of dealing with it but it's best not to bottle things up for too long. Give yourself time to think it over and deal with it in your own way. There are plenty of people out there that you can talk to and there are lots of places where you can just chat to someone like a qualified counsellor, who can help you deal with your feelings. They will also be able to help you if you're worried about someone else. For more information, contact Cruse Bereavement Care on 0808 808 1677

If a friend has been bereaved you may feel as though you don't know what to say or what to do, just let them know you are there for them if they need you. Phone them, send a card or even just a text message to say that you care and are there if they need someone to talk to or any other kind of help.

Cruse Bereavement Care 0808 808 1677
www.crusebereavementcare.org.uk

RD4U (advice for young people affected by bereavement)
www.rd4u.org.uk

The Child Bereavement Trust
0845 357 1000
www.childbereavement.org.uk

Childline
0800 1111
www.childline.org.uk

Also check out:

> Family
> Friends
> Problems & Emotions
> Depression
> Counselling
> Death and Wills

We all have problems and emotions and deal with a variety of them every day. Most of the time, they aren't too much bother but sometimes, problems and emotions can become too much. When they get on top of you, it can seem difficult to find a way out. In fact, you could find yourself stressed and your health could suffer as a result of it. The trick is to understand when a problem has become too much and you can't deal with it by yourself any longer. The saying 'a problem shared is a problem halved' is true. Coping with problems by yourself can only get you so far. Talk to someone whose opinion you trust and you'll find that the problem can seem much easier to approach; you might also find new ways of looking at it and thinking about it. If there's no-one you know that you can talk to, there are plenty of advice phone-lines, support groups and Internet forums that may be able to help you put a problem into perspective.

Problem solving tips:

Think about who, what and where the problem is... be honest with yourself. How and why is this problem affecting you? List the problems so you can deal with them one-by-one. Look into ways of dealing with the problem and be realistic. Set up an action plan you can stick to.

Childline 0800 1111
www.childline.org.uk

Relate 0845 456 1310
www.relate.org.uk

Samaritans 08457 90 90 90
www.samaritans.org

Worried? Need to talk? 0808 800 5000
www.worriedneed2talk.org.uk

Also check out:

- Stress
- Arguments
- Attitudes & Stereotypes
- You
- Depression
- Counselling

Your self esteem is how you feel about yourself. If you have low self esteem, you have a low opinion of yourself and vice versa. Your self esteem changes all the time, depending on exactly what is happening in your life. Whilst some people may have self esteem that regularly changes dramatically, most people's self esteem is fairly stable. Your self esteem level is affected by a whole host of factors such as your mood at the time, your current situation, your upbringing, family and friends. Your upbringing as a child can have a great effect on your self esteem. It may be higher or lower depending on the level of encouragement and approval shown throughout childhood. Those with low self esteem may think that they aren't good people, are ugly, don't deserve love and aren't much good at anything. In short, they don't like themselves. If you have low self esteem, it's not always easy to change it. Keep in mind that you are an individual and because of that, you're special. Don't judge yourself too harshly, nobody's perfect. Instead, try to think and accentuate positive things that you do or have done. If you can't seem to shake low self esteem, there are counsellors and support groups that may be able to help. Use them because you're worth it!

Support Line page on self esteem
0208 554 9004
www.supportline.org.uk/problems/selfesteem.php

Free self confidence course
www.self-confidence.co.uk

Net Doctor article about self esteem
www.netdoctor.co.uk/sex_relationship/facts/selfesteem.htm

BBC page on self esteem
www.bbc.co.uk/health/conditions/mental_health/emotion_esteem.shtml

Also check out:

> Attitudes and Stereotypes
> Family
> Friends
> You
> Depression
> Counselling

As you go through life, you'll be confronted with all manner of problems and dilemmas. If you know yourself, you'll be more capable of tackling them. Try out new and different things, expose yourself to a variety of opinions and keep an open mind; that way, you can make your own, informed decision on what you like and what your true opinions are. Don't give in to peer pressure. If you don't want to do something or disagree with someone, stick to your guns and go your own way. That doesn't mean you shouldn't listen to anyone else – other people can be full of great advice – just take in all the options and make up your own mind. Be confident in yourself and the way you look. You are the way you are and, so long as you believe you're doing the right thing as best you can, others should accept that. Everybody makes mistakes and you will too. Learn from them and don't dwell on them. Instead, put them down to practice and move on - lesson learned! Dealing with family can be tough sometimes. Try to remember that they have your best interests at heart and only want you to take the right direction in life so listen to them but follow your own path.

Heads Up (online political debating space for young people)
www.headsup.org.uk

Debating Matters (debating competition for 6th formers)
www.debatingmatters.com

Free self Confidence course
www.self-confidence.co.uk

Also check out:

> Arguments
> Attitudes and Stereotypes
> Family
> Friends
> Problems and Emotions
> Self Esteem

First Aid Essentials
6.1 First Aid

Knowing a few basic first aid skills can be handy and, in an emergency, could save lives. You don't have to be an expert or a qualified surgeon, but a little knowledge in a first aid situation can go a long way. It's useful to know how to treat wounds, bites and burns, the recovery position, resuscitation and how to cope when someone is choking. There are plenty of resources including manuals, Internet sites and local-run courses that are available to teach you these skills and more. All employers must have a first aid policy, which usually includes having at least one designated first aider in the workplace. Employers will usually pay for employees to receive first aid training for this. In your home, make sure that you have a first aid kit. This should include plasters, dressings, non-alcoholic wound cleansers, disposable gloves and bandages. There are many other items that can be included too like scissors and blankets. It's also worth knowing or having easy access to contact details for your local GP. Remember, if the situation is an emergency, dial 999 and ask for an ambulance. If you want to get involved in first aid, organisations like The British Red Cross and the St John Ambulance service are always looking for volunteers to help them out.

BBC Health First Aid Action
www.bbc.co.uk/health/first_aid_action/

St John Ambulance
08700 10 49 50
www.sja.org.uk

British Red Cross
0870 170 7000
www.redcross.org.uk

Family First Aid
www.familyfirstaid.co.uk

Also check out:
- Emergencies
- Volunteering UK
- Doctors
- Donor Services
- Health Services

Take a quick stroll down your local high street on a Saturday night and you'd be forgiven for thinking that drinking was our favourite national pastime. But why is it so popular?

Alcohol is a mood-altering drug that can make you feel happy, relaxed and less inhibited. One drink a day is considered, by some, to be good for your health! However, beware; alcohol can affect your balance, speech and vision and the more you drink, the greater the effects. Overdo it and you may find walking, talking and keeping down the contents of your stomach difficult. Alcohol can also affect your mood negatively. If you're feeling low and drink, your mood may become worse (some become violent). Alcohol also affects a man's ability to get an erection.

One of the most dangerous effects of alcohol is that it impairs judgement and, because of this, people under the influence often put themselves at risk – by walking into traffic or going off with a stranger (for example). Stick with your mates and always tell them where you're going. The list of illnesses (some cancers, high blood pressure, liver disease and many more) linked to excessive alcohol consumption is pretty off-putting too. Drinking too much alcohol regularly can also lead to a physical addiction - 1 in 15 people in Britain have an alcohol problem. All of that and we've not even mentioned how horrific a hangover can be! The trick is, if you do drink, do it sensibly.

Alcohol Concern
0207 928 7377
www.alcoholconcern.org.uk

UK Government information
www.direct.gov.uk

NHS page on safe drinking
0845 46 47
www.nhsdirect.nhs.uk/interactivetools/alcohol

BBC Health page on alcohol
www.bbc.co.uk/health/healthy_living/nutrition/drinks_alcohol.shtml

Also check out:
> Headaches
> Impotence
> Smoking
> Doctors
> Health Essentials
> Diet & Exercise
> Crime prevention & Personal Safety

There are hundreds of different types of drugs, each with their own name, form, price, legal classification and effect. People break the law by taking illegal drugs for a number of reasons including curiosity, relaxation, to have a good time on a night out, to escape from an unfulfilling life and for medicinal purposes. However, the negative effect of drugs often far outweighs any other concerns. Many drugs are either physically or psychologically addictive. This can lead to long-term health problems and, at worst, death. In order to pay for their addiction, some find themselves drawn into a world of crime.

It can be hard to tell exactly what you are getting with some drugs, meaning that knowing the effects of the drug can be difficult. This can lead to illness, physical and mental health problems and, in some cases, death. Regular drug use frequently leads to a change in character and behaviour and of course, there is the law to contend with. Illegal drugs are classified (Class A, B and C) in order of addictiveness and danger to health levels and possession of any illegal drug can result in a criminal record or, at worst, a custodial sentence. Before you consider taking drugs, think about what might happen to you and make sure that you're clued up about what it is that you are taking. Inappropriate use of any drug, even Paracetamol, can be dangerous. Also, just because a drug hasn't been classified (currently there are various legal stimulants, such as EX-1, on the market) doesn't mean it's safe - approach with caution.

Talk to Frank (drugs advice)
0800 77 66 00
www.talktofrank.com

Drugscope 0207 928 1211
www.drugscope.org.uk

NHS Wales drugs facts 0845 46 47
www.nhsdirect.wales.nhs.uk/nhsdirect.aspx?id=301

Home Office page on drugs
www.drugs.gov.uk

Also check out:
> Legal Rights
> Drinking
> Smoking
> Stop & Search
> Criminal Records

Smoking
6.2 Substance Misuse

Fags, ciggies, tabs, rollies, smokes, call them what you will, cigarettes are smoked by millions of people across Britain and the arguments that surround them are here to stay. Tobacco was introduced to Europe in the fifteenth century and in the last century has become a national habit. The leaves of a tobacco plant are dried and rolled into pre-prepared or hand-made cigarettes which, when lit, produces smoke which is inhaled into the mouth and/or lungs. The nicotine that is present in tobacco increases heart rate and affects both the brain and the body. It is the nicotine in cigarettes that is addictive. Some people smoke because they think it makes them more social, others think it makes them look cool or confident and some argue that it helps them relax or calm down in a stressful situation. In fact, cigarettes do none of these things. Nicotine is actually a stimulant so it doesn't relax at all. In fact, most people smoke because they are addicted and think that it makes them feel better when actually they are suffering from withdrawal. Smoking also carries many health risks. The most common disease that is caused by smoking is cancer. Half of all smokers will have their lives ended prematurely as a result of smoking.

Action on Smoking and Health UK
0207 739 5902
www.ash.org.uk

Giving Up Smoking
www.givingupsmoking.co.uk

NHS Smoking Helpline 0800 169 0 169

Welsh Assembly Health Challenge page on smoking
www.healthchallenge.wales.gov.uk/smoking-e.htm

NHS page on how much money you'll save by quitting smoking
www.nhsdirect.nhs.uk/interactivetools/smoking/default.asp

UK Charity helping people to give up smoking 0800 00 22 00
www.quit.org.uk

Also check out:
> Cancer
> Alcohol
> Acne
> Relaxing
> Drugs

Anxiety

Anxiety is caused when your brain sends messages to the rest of the body that prepares it for trouble. We all experience some form of anxiety every day. Any stressful situation will be met with a certain amount of it. In fact, sometimes anxiety can actually help you deal with some difficulties. However, if anxiety becomes prolonged, severe or is unexplainable, it can become a major problem. As your body prepares for stress (what's known as the 'fight or flight' response), you may experience shortness of breath, stomach pain, dizziness and/or a rapid heartbeat. As well as physical symptoms, you may find it hard to sleep, difficult to concentrate and you become easily irritable. Some people are thought to be more prone to anxiety but anyone can be affected by it. Anxiety can be triggered by different things: it may be that someone has a problem that they cannot stop worrying about, the use of drugs such as LSD and Esctasy or it may be that someone has been through a life-threatening event such as a car crash from which, emotionally, they cannot recover. There are a variety of treatments for those suffering from anxiety. Therapy, counselling and drug treatment can all benefit sufferers. If anxiety is a problem for you, see your GP for advice, treatment or support.

NHS page on anxiety
0845 46 47
www.nhsdirect.nhs.uk/en.aspx?articleid=28

Royal College of Psychiatrists
0207 235 2351
www.rcpsych.ac.uk

Mental Health Foundation page on anxiety
0207 803 1100
www.mentalhealth.org.uk/page.cfm?pageurl=anxiety.cfm

National Phobics Society (the anxiety disorders charity) 0870 122 2325
www.phobics-society.org.uk

Also check out:
> Problems and Emotions
> Drugs
> Depression
> Panic Attacks
> Counselling
> Relaxing

Compulsions (perhaps more commonly known as 'habits') are extremely common and, on the whole, are fairly harmless. Habits can seemingly come from nowhere or can have an obvious cause. For example, if you were once burgled, you might check all the locks before leaving the house, or if you're feeling anxious or stressed, you might bite your nails. We've all got habits and some of them can even be good (for example, getting into the habit of saving your work onto disk regularly can only help you!). If you're irritated by one of your habits though, it's up to you to try and rid yourself of it. Just be disciplined with yourself and try to be aware of when you are doing your habit and tell yourself to stop each time.

Obsessive Compulsive Disorder (OCD) is when you have an obsession that creates a compulsion (for example, a person obsessed with germs might be constantly compelled to wash their hands), which comes to dominate your life. Sufferers can be severely debilitated, their lives turning into a repetitive, never-ending ritual. Help is available, the best of which is currently thought to be therapy. If you have a habit that you are worried about, see your GP for advice.

National Health Service (NHS)
0845 4647
www.nhsdirect.nhs.uk

Net Doctor
www.netdoctor.co.uk

OCD Action (OCD charity)
0845 390 6232
www.ocdaction.org.uk/ocdaction/index.asp

The National Phobics Society (anxiety disorders charity)
0870 122 2325
www.phobics-society.org.uk

Also check out:
> Anxiety
> Phobias
> Stress
> Counselling
> Relaxation
> Doctors

Depression is a very normal reaction to life sometimes. You're out of control, everyone hates you, you hate everyone, moods swing up and down and everything in life is a drag. It happens and then life carries on and it's all forgotten. Sometimes though, it doesn't go away. The feelings don't get better and your moods don't swing back up. It's despairing. You might lose sleep, lose weight, feel guilty, think you are a failure, get anxious and contemplate suicide. You should seek help. Talk to your doctor, a friend – anyone – but tell them how you feel. There are relaxation techniques and medication that can help you get through this. Physical exercise is also thought to help ease depression, hence the slogan 'healthy body, healthy mind'.

Autumn and winter get you down sometimes, make you sad? SAD is Seasonal Affective Disorder, a condition that's slightly more than the winter morning blues. Some people suffer with extreme fatigue and lack of energy, needing more sleep, cravings for carbohydrates and pile on the pounds. The lack of sunlight doesn't help, but spending more time outdoors and exercise do. In extreme cases, SAD patients are exposed to bright, artificial light, anti-depressants and counselling.

Depression Alliance (charity for people affected by depression) 0845 123 23 20
www.depressionalliance.org

MDF, the Bipolar Organisation (charity helping those affected by manic depression) 08456 340 540
www.mdf.org.uk

MIND (National Association for Mental Health) 0845 766 0163
www.mind.org.uk

The Seasonal Affective Disorder Association
www.sada.org.uk

Also check out:

> Problems and Emotions
> Self Esteem
> You
> Suicide
> Exercise & Keep Fit
> Counselling

A panic attack is a sudden feeling of fear that can seemingly come from out of nowhere and have no apparent cause. Some of the symptoms of a panic attack are feelings of dizziness, shortness of breath, fear of death, feelings of unreality, sweating and an increased heart rate. Because they seem to occur at random, it can often be hard to pinpoint the cause of panic. Most panic disorders are associated with a change in life, such as going to university. However, they could be caused by a stressful event, anticipation or substance abuse. There is also a possibility that panic may be genetic and could be passed down from parents or that it occurs as a result of an incorrect brain response to anxiety. Some sufferers develop agoraphobia (a fear of open spaces and other specific places) as they may associate physical places with attacks, causing them to avoid those places after an attack. Most panic disorders arise in people between 15 and 25, a period of great change for most. It is important for sufferers to recognise that they have a problem and get help straight away, as quick diagnosis could quicken recovery. Therapeutic and drug treatment (or a combination of both) is the most common form of treatment; see your GP for advice.

NHS Direct page on panic disorders
www.nhsdirect.nhs.uk/en.aspx?articleid=1499

National Phobics Society (anxiety disorders charity) 0870 122 2325
www.phobics-society.org.uk

No Panic (support for sufferers of panic attacks) 0808 808 0545
www.nopanic.org.uk

Online course to help sufferers of panic attacks
www.panic-attacks.co.uk

Also check out:
- Anxiety
- Phobias
- Stress
- Counselling
- Doctors
- Drugs

A phobia is a fear (often an extreme one) of something that cannot be adequately explained. They are very common. In fact, most of us have at least one and most are not too much of a problem. However, when a phobia comes to change the entire structure of your life, it can be a big problem. It might be spiders, the dentist, flying or the colour green but phobias, no matter how small, can be frightening and embarrassing. You might know full well that there is no reason to be afraid and no reason to panic but you just can't help it. You might feel fear, your heart rate may speed up and you might feel sick but these are all normal responses to a fear, even if the fear does seem illogical. Don't be ashamed of a phobia. It's better to come out and admit that you have an irrational fear of something than to panic, seemingly, for no reason. Most phobias can be overcome or the fear lessened. Depending on the severity and specific phobia, there are techniques, courses and guides to help overcome them. See Links below for support and guidance.

National Phobic Society (anxiety disorders charity)
0870 122 2325
www.phobics-society.org.uk

Triumph Over Phobia (charity helping sufferers of phobia)
0845 600 9601
www.triumphoverphobia.com

NHS Direct page on phobias
0845 4647
www.nhsdirect.nhs.uk/en.aspx?articleid=284

BBC One Life page on phobias and fears
www.bbc.co.uk/radio1/onelife/health/healthy_mind/phobia1.shtml

Also check out:
> Anxiety
> Compulsions
> Panic Attacks
> Stress
> Counselling
> Relaxation

Schizophrenia is when somebody cannot distinguish between their own thoughts and imaginings and real life. They may experience hallucinations (both visual and auditory), jumbled up thinking, delusions, paranoia and may be subject to mood swings and irrational behaviour. There is no consensus on what exactly causes schizophrenia but it is thought that it may be a brain condition that certain people are born with, it could be caused by other abnormal brain activity, bought on by recreational drugs such as cannabis, a stressful experience, or it could run in families. Anyone from any background of any age can be affected, but young people are particularly at risk, as most sufferers first develop symptoms in their late teens or early twenties. There is a disproportionate amount of fear of schizophrenics. The vast majority of schizophrenics are not dangerous. In fact, they're more likely to be a danger to themselves than anyone else. There are a lot of organisations and many different types of treatment available to sufferers of schizophrenia. Depending on the exact type and the severity of the problem, help can include drug treatment, therapy and community care. There are also organisations such as MIND and Rethink, who can provide advice and support.

Rethink (help for those affected by severe mental illness) 0208 974 6814
www.rethink.org

MIND (National Association for Mental Health) 0845 766 0163
www.mind.org

NHS Direct page on Schizophrenia
0845 4647
www.nhsdirect.nhs.uk/en.aspx?articleid=329

The Royal College of Psychiatrists leaflet for those worried about themselves, friends or relatives
www.rcpsych.ac.uk/info/help/schiz/index.asp
x

Also check out:

> Drugs
> Anxiety
> Self Harm
> Stress
> Counselling
> Doctors

Self harm is when somebody purposefully causes themselves injury. It might be cutting, scratching, taking a drug overdose, picking, tearing or burning skin, punching walls or tearing out hair or eyelashes. Self-harmers do this in order to help them cope with their lives, as usually they have an underlying problem, which cannot immediately be overcome. This problem can be anything from depression, physical or sexual abuse to parents divorcing to the loss of a loved one. No matter how big or small the reason is, some people seem to find that injuring themselves can help reduce the anger, aggression or emotion that they feel. Some people use self harm as a release for their emotions and others use it as a way to get back some element of control over their lives. However, self harm can have terrible consequences and most self-harmers want to stop themselves from doing it. To end the cycle of self harm, the underlying problem usually needs to be resolved first. Many people are unsure of why they self-harm so it's useful to think about when you started it and what was happening in your life or if any memories recur during self harming. There is plenty of help available to self-harmers including self-help groups, specialist counselling, therapy and drug treatment. Talk to a close friend or relative first, but if you need further help, see Links below.

National Self Harm Network
www.nshn.co.uk

Young People and Self Harm
www.selfharm.org.uk

NHS Direct
0845 46 47
www.nhsdirect.nhs.uk

Childline
0800 1111
www.childline.org.uk

Also check out:
> Problems and Emotions
> Self Esteem
> Drugs
> Depression
> Suicide
> Counselling

We all experience some form of stress on a daily basis. Late for the train? Having trouble with the DIY? Struggling to hand in coursework on time? All these situations will result in a degree of stress which may in fact spur you on to achieve your goal. However, when a person is under too much stress, it can become dangerous for their physical and mental health. Too much stress can lead to sleeplessness, irritability, increased use of cigarettes and/or alcohol and tension. There are many different factors that may cause stress and some people may be more prone to it than others. You may have suffered a loss such as the death of a loved one, your life may have changed (for example, going to university) and you're struggling to cope with the changes or you may have too much work on. Things like moving house can also increase stress (albeit in the short term). Once you've recognised that you are under too much stress, you need to find a way to reduce your stress levels. This can be done by accepting help from others, taking time off, relaxing and doing things that you enjoy. Physical exercise, like going for a walk in the countryside, can also ease stress. Remember, cigarettes, alcohol and drugs won't help cure stress, they'll do the exact opposite.

The Stress Management Society
0870 199 3260
www.stress.org.uk

NHS Direct page on stress
0845 46 47
www.nhsdirect.nhs.uk/en.aspx?articleid=350

Uncommon Knowledge's page on Relaxation techniques
www.uncommon-knowledge.co.uk/relaxation/techniques.html

Yoga In Wales
www.yogawales.co.uk

Also check out:
- Anxiety
- Depression
- Counselling
- Meditation
- Relaxation
- Arguments

When someone takes their own life, it is usually because they feel that their problems in life outweigh their ability to cope with them. It is the most extreme expression of desperation that there is and most who commit suicide put a certain amount of planning and preparation into it. Suicide can affect anyone but those with mental health problems such as Schizophrenia, depression and those who misuse substances are at a greater risk. If you're considering suicide, try and take a step back from your problems and understand that there is another way. Try talking to a friend or relative. If there's no-one that you feel you can talk to who'll listen properly and not judge you, try phoning the Samaritans or getting in touch with your local mental health team (through your GP). There are also local support groups where you may be able to get non-judgemental, professional help. Those who consider suicide or actually go ahead with it will feel they have a solid reason for doing it; if someone comes to you to discuss suicidal feelings, it might not make sense to you. Hold judgement, listen carefully and don't try to offer advice or solutions. Get your friend or relative to talk as much as they can and, if possible, suggest that they seek professional help ASAP. If you are worried about someone you know try speaking in confidence to a teacher, youth worker or other adult who may be able to help

The Samaritans
08457 60 90 90
www.samaritans.org.uk

Papyrus
01706 214449
www.papyrus-uk.org

Befrienders (support website for those considering suicide)
www.befrienders.org

Mental Health Foundation 0207 803 1100
www.mentalhealth.co.uk

Also check out:
> Problems and Emotions
> You
> Anxiety
> Depression
> Self Harm
> Counselling

Counselling gives you the chance to chat with professionals about problems you may be having emotionally. It can be done on a one-to-one basis or as part of a group. Talking about things helps. It helps you look at what's bothering you and why and tries to find ways of making it better in the future. It can help you get your life back together and get over a major event in your life like divorce, rape, bullying etc. or it may help with a condition such as Schizophrenia. You might think that your friends or family will give you the best advice but sometimes, it's difficult for them to be impartial and non-judgemental. As counsellors have been trained so that they will know the best way for you to approach and overcome your problems, they will be able to listen to you and they won't judge you. Your doctor will be able to advise you about NHS counselling services in your area (some of which may be free). Or look up your Health Authority in the Yellow Pages and contact them directly for more info.

If you have a more severe behavioural or emotional problem, you may be referred to a psychotherapist. Psychotherapy is a form of counselling specifically for people with more severe conditions or problems that have built up over many years.

British Association of Counselling and Psychotherapy 0870 443 5252
www.bacp.co.uk

Relate (relationship advice) 0845 456 1310
www.relate.co.uk

Counselling Wales
www.counsellingwales.org

The Brandon Centre (help and advice for young people)
0207 267 4792
www.brandon-centre.org.uk

Also check out:

- Losing a Loved One
- Self Esteem
- Drugs
- Depression
- Phobias
- Suicide

There are many different forms of meditation. Some are intended purely as a relaxation technique, some as a religious practice. However, all forms of meditation hope to achieve roughly the same effect – that of a calmed state of mind and body. Most meditation involves sitting in a certain position, breathing in a particular way and controlling your thoughts. The effect is intended to free you of concerns about the past or the future, focussing your mind on the present. The idea is that by doing so you will be able to approach life and deal with problems more calmly. In recent years, meditation (especially yoga, a practice that incorporates meditation) has increased in popularity in Wales, with many local centres and teachers providing yoga classes. Meditation has also begun to be used in healthcare, helping to reduce stress. Whilst most meditation can be quite tricky to master, you can do your own exercises similar to meditation that, hopefully, will achieve a similar effect. Try sitting alone in your room once a day with no distractions, concentrating on your breathing and trying to free your mind from worries. This should, at least, provide some respite from the trials and tribulations of everyday life.

Insight Meditation
www.insightmeditation.org

Channel 4 page on meditation
www.channel4.com/health/microsites/c/comp_medicine/meditation.html

Yoga In Wales
www.yogainwales.co.uk

Uncommon Knowledge's page on relaxation techniques
www.uncommon-knowledge.co.uk/relaxation/techniques.html

Also check out:
> Counselling
> Relaxation
> Exercise and Keep Fit
> Healthy Eating
> Alternative Medicine
> Yoga

In today's hectic world, the time for relaxing is often the first to be sacrificed if things get a bit too much. You should never undervalue the benefits of relaxation though. Taking some time out from everyday stresses and strains can improve your life in countless ways. For one, your relaxation time should be spent doing something that you enjoy. Secondly, a little bit of relaxation goes a long way. You'll find it easier to cope with stress when you've had a chance to relax properly. If you miss out on relaxation, you may actually find that the work you do suffers as a result. Remember, it's far better to work for half a day and achieve something than to work for a whole day and achieve nothing. You can relax anywhere at any time without the use of any equipment. It's probably best to find a place away from distractions such as other people, phones and emails. Find somewhere comfortable, where the light and furnishings are soft. Do something you enjoy. You might want to chill in front of the telly, listen to a CD, read or book or practice some simple breathing exercises. Whatever you do, it should be of little physical and mental effort. That way, you'll be much better prepared to tackle the next day ahead.

MIND (National Association for Mental Health) guide to relaxation
0845 766 0163
www.mind.org.uk/information/booklets/mind+guide+to/the+mind+guide+to+relaxation.htm

Uncommon Knowledge's page on relaxation
www.uncommon-knowledge.co.uk/relaxation/techniques.html

BBC page on relaxation
www.bbc.co.uk/health/conditions/mental_health/coping_relaxation.shtml

Yoga information
www.yogaclass.com/central.html

Also check out:
> Stress
> Meditation
> Yoga
> Sleeping and Dreaming
> Exercise and Keep Fit
> Healthy Eating

The majority of people need to spend roughly eight hours each day asleep. Sleep is an extremely important part of our lives, helping to keep us more active and alert throughout the day. No-one really knows for sure exactly why we sleep but it is agreed that without it, our brain's ability to function would suffer.

Dreaming occurs during a period of our sleep cycle known as Rapid Eye Movement (REM) sleep. Some think dreams may help commit the events of the day to memory, others think they have a deeper psychological meaning and others think them completely meaningless. We all need different amounts of sleep (Maggie Thatcher famously said that she got by on just four hours a night) but so long as you don't feel too sleepy during the day, you should be OK. If you're having trouble sleeping (insomnia), here are a few tips that may help you snooze:

- Avoid alcohol, caffeine (tea, coffee, cola etc.) and exercise the hour before bedtime
- Get yourself a bed that you feel comfortable in
- Take a warm bath before bed

If you think you have a serious sleeping problem (including snoring, which can be very disruptive to sleep), see your GP for advice.

Science Museum pages on sleep
www.sciencemuseum.org.uk/exhibitions/brain/130.asp

The Sleep Research Centre
www.lboro.ac.uk/info/help/sleep/index.asp

Royal College of Psychiatrists leaflet on sleep including tips on how to sleep better
www.rcpsych.ac.uk/info/help/sleep/index.asp

NHS pages on Insomnia 0845 46 47
www.nhsdirect.nhs.uk/en.aspx?articleid=216

Also check out:

> Problems and Emotions
> Depression
> Stress
> Meditation
> Relaxation
> Doctors

People with eating disorders use food to try and cope with their lives and to get back an element of control when they feel that areas of their lives are in turmoil. The most common types of eating disorder are:

Anorexia - A person suffering from Anorexia Nervosa will limit the amount of food and drink that they consume on purpose in order to gain control over their bodies, lives and emotions. Most people don't intend to harm themselves or indeed to become Anorexic - some people take weight-loss too far because they hate their bodies (these people will only see fat when they look in the mirror, even when there is none there to see (this is called Body Dysmorphic Disorder (BDD)) and some people control their intake of food because other areas of their lives are out of control and they are very unhappy.

Bulimia - Sufferers 'binge' eat (consume a large amount of food in one go) and then rid themselves of the it, either by making themselves sick or by taking laxatives.

Over-eating – When a sufferer eats too much and obsesses over food.

Most eating disorders are very harmful for your health. In some cases, eating disorders can lead to death. There is lots of help available to those with eating disorders though. As well as there being treatment available on the NHS, there are many professional organisations, charities and support groups specifically designed to help those affected by eating disorders. If you know someone who you think may have an eating disorder, try and persuade them to seek professional help (see Links for advice).

The National Centre for Eating Disorders
0845 838 2040 www.eating-disorders.org.uk

NHS Direct 0845 46 47
www.nhsdirect.nhs.uk

Eating Disorders Association 0845 634 7650
www.edauk.com

Young Minds pages on eating disorders
www.youngminds.org.uk/eatingproblems/y0.php

Also check out:
- Problems and Emotions
- Self Esteem
- You
- Counselling
- Exercise and Keep Fit
- Healthy Eating

It doesn't matter if you're tall, short, fat, skinny, young or old, exercise is essential to lead a healthy life. Exercise not only helps you lose weight and tone your body but it also increases the amount of Serotonin (a hormone that is thought to give feelings of well being) that your brain produces. Additionally, exercise can reduce stress and help keep many life-threatening diseases such as heart disease at bay, but the fact is that most of us don't do nearly enough exercise. In fact, many see exercise as something that might be painful and humiliating. Around about 30 minutes of moderate exercise (anything that means you breathe more heavily than normal) a day is thought to be the absolute minimum that we need to keep healthy. You don't have to go crazy and buy a multi-gym, a headband and a leotard; a brisk walk, some gardening or over-enthusiastic hoovering will do the job. If you want to put more effort in and dedicate some time to sport or fitness, don't be put off by your memories of P.E. Find a sport or activity that you enjoy. It might mean a bit of suck-it-and-see but you'll find something to your taste in the end.

NHS Direct page on exercise 0845 46 47
www.nhsdirect.nhs.uk/en.aspx?articleid=456

Fitness Wales (The Welsh governing body for exercise and fitness) 02920 575 155
www.fitnesswales.co.uk

BBC page on exercise for young people
www.bbc.co.uk/health/healthy_living/fitness/motivation_young.shtml

Netfit (loads of information on keeping fit)
www.netfit.co.uk

Also check out:
> Self Esteem
> You
> Relaxation
> Healthy Eating
> Sport & Lesiure

When it comes to food, you really are what you eat. It's important for all of us to eat well but healthy eating doesn't have to be a chore or take over your life. The trick is to maintain a balanced diet. And that means balancing out all the bad things that you eat – the take-aways, fast food and sweet things – with good things – fruit, vegetables, breads, potatoes and cereals. The only way to get all the vitamins, minerals and fibre that your body needs to remain in peak condition is to eat a wide variety of food. So, try new things and don't get stuck in a rut. A balanced diet will mean that not only will you look good, but you'll feel good too. Cut out fatty foods and watch the weight disappear. Eat fresh food, lots of fruit and veg, and you'll have more energy. The word 'diet' means what you eat generally not what you eat in order to lose weight. Going on a diet to lose weight is fine so long as the plan is a sensible one and you stick with it after you've lost weight. There's no point in putting in all of that effort to go back to your old ways and put the pounds back on once you've finished.

British Nutrition Foundation
0207 404 6504
www.nutrition.org.uk

Food Standards Agency guide to healthy eating
www.eatwell.gov.uk

BBC page on Do Detox Diets Work?
www.bbc.co.uk/health/healthy_living/your_weight/eatingwell_detox.shtml

Connexions advice for young people on healthy eating
0808 001 3219
www.connexions-direct.com

Also check out:
> Consumer Labelling
> Eating Disorders
> Exercise and Keep Fit
> Vegetarianism and Veganism
> Food

The choice to go vegetarian or vegan is usually a choice that's made on moral grounds. Many people believe that it is cruel for humans to keep and kill animals for food. Vegetarians don't eat any meat or fish whereas vegans also don't eat anything that has been made using an animal product. For example, vegetarians can eat eggs and butter but vegans can't. If you want to go vegetarian or vegan, it's your choice. It might mean that you have to cook a few meals for yourself but if you believe in the cause, it'll be worth it. Meat is a big source of protein, so once you make the change, you need to find a way to replace that protein in your diet. Nuts, seeds, grain, cereals and pulses like lentils are some of the many foods that can do just that for you. If you agree with the moral side of vegetarianism and veganism but can't face the idea of not eating meat or food made with animal products, there are plenty of foods that can adequately replace these foods like soya, tofu and Quorn.

Vegetarian Society
0161 925 2000
www.vegsoc.org

Vegan Society
01424 427393
www.vegansociety.com

Veggie Global
www.veggieglobal.com

Vegan Village
www.veganvillage.co.uk

Also check out:
> Animal Rights
> Farming and Agriculture
> Eating Disorders
> Exercise and Keep Fit
> Healthy Eating
> Food

Acne is a skin condition that causes spots to appear on the skin. The most common areas of the body where Acne occurs are on the face, arms, back and chest. Despite what you may have been told Acne is not caused by eating certain foods like chocolate or by a lack of hygiene. In fact, it is caused by glands producing too much sebum, a fluid which, along with dead skin cells, causes hair follicles to be blocked, giving rise to spots. It usually first appears in people around the time of puberty. This is due to changes in hormone levels that occur during puberty, leading to greater sebum production. The good thing is that Acne clears itself up over time. The best way to reduce the effects of Acne are to eat healthily (contributing to your general health) and to touch your face as little as possible. You should also wash your face and remove all make-up, as bacteria may multiply on your skin otherwise, causing Acne to worsen. Depending on how severe the Acne is, it is possible to get treatment for it on the NHS. There may be gels, creams or lotions that help and they can also offer support for the psychological effects of having Acne. Your GP may be able to prescribe something to help, so go and have a chat with them.

NHS page on Acne
0845 46 47
www.nhsdirect.nhs.uk/en.aspx?articleID=4

The Acne Support Group
0870 870 2263
www.m2w3.com/acne/home.html

BUPA factsheet on Acne
0800 600 500
http://hcd2.bupa.co.uk/fact_sheets/Mosby_fact sheets/acne.html

Support for sufferers of Acne
www.acnehelp.org.uk

Also check out:
- Self Esteem
- Exercise and Keep Fit
- Healthy Eating
- Eczema
- Looking Your Best
- Sunbathing

Allergies

Sometimes, the body may react to a particular substance, causing an allergic reaction. Any substance that does this is known as an allergen. When the body encounters the offending substance, it thinks that it must be harmful so reacts in order to repel it. This causes the body to release chemicals including histamines, which are responsible for producing the most common symptoms of allergic reactions. Allergies are very common, with the most common allergens being pollen, dust and nuts. Typical symptoms of an allergic reaction are sneezing, coughing, shortness of breath and itchy eyes. In some severe cases, an allergic reaction can cause anaphylactic shock, which affects the whole body and can lead to death. If you think you may have an allergy but aren't sure of what you may be allergic to, you can visit your GP who can carry out various tests to determine what the problem is. Usually, the best way to cope with an allergy is to avoid the allergen as much as possible. In fact, repeated exposure to allergens tends to make allergies worse. There are certain treatments that are available to treat the symptoms of allergies. These include tablets, sprays and eye drops, some of which may be available over the counter at a pharmacy (see your GP for advice).

Action Against Allergy
0208 892 2711
www.actionagainstallergy.co.uk

NHS Direct page on allergies 0845 46 47
www.nhsdirect.nhs.uk/en.aspx?articleID=11

Food Standards Agency page on allergens in food
www.eatwell.gov.uk/healthissues/foodintolerance/allergicreactions/

Allergy UK (medical charity for allergy sufferers)
www.allergyuk.org

Also check out:
> First Aid Essentials
> Food
> Hay Fever
> Stings and Bites
> Alternative Medicine
> Doctors

Anaemia is a condition by which people have a shortage of red blood cells leading to a lack of oxygen. There are various different types of Anaemia with causes, symptoms and treatment varying between them. The most common type is called Iron-Deficiency Anaemia (caused by a lack of iron) which can be down to an insufficient diet and/or unusually heavy periods for women. Other types of Anaemia can be caused by a lack of vitamin B12 or folic acid, as a result of an inherited condition or as an after-effect of certain viruses such as measles or because of pregnancy. The symptoms of Anaemia can be hard to spot, often for some time. In its early, less severe stage, sufferers can expect to feel tired and may experience occasional dizziness. However, if Anaemia gets worse it can lead to pale skin, weight loss, headaches and palpitations. Because Anaemia is usually caused by a deficiency in certain nutrients in the blood, to treat it means replacing these nutrients. To avoid Anaemia, eat a diet rich in nutrients, which includes foods such as red meat, green vegetables, fish and nuts. Those with Anaemia may be treated by being given iron, B12 or folic acid tablets.

NHS Direct page on Anaemia
0845 46 47
www.nhsdirect.nhs.uk/en.aspx?articleID=19

BBC page on Anaemia
www.bbc.co.uk/health/conditions/anaemia1.shtml

Homehealth page on Anaemia
www.homehealth-uk.com/medical/anaemia.htm

BUPA factsheet on iron-deficiency Anaemia
http://hcd2.bupa.co.uk/fact_sheets/mosby_factsheets/anaemia_iron.html

Also check out:
> Healthy Eating
> Vegetarianism and Veganism
> Headaches
> Pregnancy
> Doctors
> Food

Arthritis is a painful condition that affects the joints of your body (the parts of your body where two limbs meet, enabling them to move freely). It occurs when bone rubs on bone in the joint or when swollen joints lead to the breakdown of bone and cartilage. There are many different types of Arthritis, with most affecting older people. However, Juvenile Idiopathic Arthritis can affect young people. Sufferers of Arthritis experience pain and swelling in the affected joints (most commonly the knuckles and knees), tiredness and, as a result of the condition may become depressed. As yet, the exact causes of Arthritis aren't fully known. It is thought possible that people may be born with it or that obesity and/or jobs that require repetitive movement may increase the chances of Arthritis. There are a variety of treatments for Arthritis depending on the type and severity of the condition. Medical treatment can include certain types of drugs, specific exercises and surgery to replace or realign joints. To help prevent Arthritis, keep your weight down and exercise regularly, as this will decrease the pressure on the joints. As well as medical help for sufferers, there is also a network of psychological help that can benefit those affected by, what can be, a debilitating condition.

NHS Direct page on Arthritis 0845 46 47
www.nhsdirect.nhs.uk/en.aspx?articleID=32

BBC page on Arthritis
www.bbc.co.uk/health/conditions/arthritis

Arthritis Research Campaign
0870 850 500 www.arc.org.uk

Net Doctor page on Arthritis
www.netdoctor.co.uk/diseases/facts/Arthritis.htm

Homehealth page on juvenile Arthritis
http://www.homehealth-uk.com/index.html?f=body|fr=http://www.homehealth-uk.com/medical/juvenileArthritis.htm|r

Also check out:
> Depression
> Counselling
> Relaxation
> Exercise & Keep Fit
> Doctors

Asthma is a breathing condition that affects the airways. The airways are the tubes that carry air in and out of your lungs. Asthma causes the airways to swell and narrow, making breathing more difficult. The causes for this can vary. It may be brought on by allergens (substances to which the sufferer is allergic) such as dust, pollution or cigarette smoke or it could be brought on by exercise or low temperatures. It isn't known for sure how people get the condition of Asthma. However, it is thought that it could be hereditary (passed onto you by your parents), that sufferers may be born with it or that the environment may bring it on. Those with Asthma will experience coughing, wheezing, a tightening of the chest and breathlessness. There are various ways to treat and prevent Asthma. If it is caused by an allergen, it's best to try and avoid the allergen. Asthma can be treated by using an inhaler, a device which means that sufferers can inhale drugs that open the airways, improving breathing. Severe Asthma attacks can be very dangerous. Symptoms may develop quickly and, as well as normal symptoms an attack may result in lips or fingernails turning blue and tightening of the skin around the neck. If you have these symptoms, seek immediate medical help.

NHS Direct page on Asthma
0845 46 47
www.nhsdirect.nhs.uk/en.aspx?articleID=36

Asthma UK (Asthma charity)
08457 01 02 03
www.Asthma.org.uk

Medinfo's page on Asthma
www.medinfo.co.uk/conditions/Asthma.html

BBC page on Asthma
www.bbc.co.uk/health/conditions/asthma/

Also check out:
> Pollution
> Smoking
> Exercise and Keep Fit
> Allergies
> Hay Fever
> Doctors

Autism is a disorder that affects the way people communicate with others. It is believed to occur because a certain part of the brain is underdeveloped. There are several other disorders which are similar to Autism. These are known as Autism Spectrum Disorders (ASD). The most common ASD is Asperger's syndrome, which is not as severe as Autism itself. Autism is a lifelong disorder and is usually diagnosed during a child's first three years, although some aren't diagnosed until they are as old as 12. It affects sufferers' social skills, their imagination and their behaviour. They may not be able to get on well with other people, they may show an interest in repetitive behaviour such as lining up their toys and they may have obsessive behaviour. Additionally, more severe Autism can result in sufferers rocking back and forth, clapping their hands and having difficulty with speech (more extreme cases may have no speech at all). Treatment varies between individuals but may include medicine, behavioural training and special education. There are also provisions available for parents of children with Autism such as respite breaks, where a carer may take care of the child for some time to give the parent a break from what is often a demanding disorder.

NHS Direct page on Autism
0845 46 47
www.nhsdirect.nhs.uk/en.aspx?articleID=41

The National Autistic Society
0845 070 4004
www.nas.org.uk

Autism Independent UK
01536 523 274
www.Autismuk.com

BUPA factsheet on Autism
http://hcd2.bupa.co.uk/fact_sheets/html/Autism.html

Also check out:
> SEN Special Education Needs
> Care
> Young Carers
> Stress
> Counselling
> Doctors

Burns occur frequently and knowing how to deal with one can be a handy first aid tool. Burns occur when skin tissue is damaged, usually by excessive heat from such things as flames, hot objects (such as irons) and chemicals. A scald is slightly different in that the injury is caused by hot liquid or steam. However, treatment is the same. Most burns can be treated in the home but more serious ones may require hospital treatment. In extreme cases burns can lead to death. Many young children experience burns so it's important to take preventative measures to avoid this. If there are children in your home, be careful not to leave hot objects and liquids within reaching distance of them. If you need to treat a burn or scald, follow these tips:

- Remove the person from the source of heat
- Run the burn under cool water, preferably for around 20 minutes. Avoid using very cold water or ice, as it may cause further damage
- If the burns are extensive or stuck to clothing, don't attempt to remove the victim's clothes
- If the burn needs hospital treatment, wrap it in either a plastic bag or layers of cling film to reduce pain and keep the wound clean
- Discomfort from minor burns may be eased with painkillers

NHS Direct page on accidents and first aid 0845 46 47
www.nhsdirect.nhs.uk/en.aspx?articleId=450§ionId=2665

BUPA factsheet on burns
http://hcd2.bupa.co.uk/fact_sheets/html/burns.html

Patient UK page on burns
www.patient.co.uk/showdoc/23068955/

European Federation of Associations of Burned Persons
www.euroburnfederation.org

Also check out:
> Babies
> Children
> First Aid Essentials
> Stings and Bites
> Doctors
> Health Service

Cancer is a medical condition that occurs when a person's cell dividing process goes wrong. They normally divide in a controlled manner, but sometimes get out of control and keep on dividing, causing a lump. The lump is called a tumour and can be benign (harmless and may not need treatment) or malignant (harmful and could spread the Cancer around the body). There are many different types of Cancer and anyone can be affected by it, although the risk of getting the disease increases as you get older. What causes Cancer isn't always clear but some, such as Lung Cancer, are known to be caused by smoking. When diagnosed with Cancer, a patient can be treated in various ways. An operation may remove the tumour, radiotherapy uses powerful rays to destroy Cancer cells and chemotherapy uses strong drugs to try and fight the disease. Most patients receive a mix of treatments. There are ways to help prevent some types of Cancer, such as eating and drinking healthily, not smoking and wearing high factor sun cream in hot weather. Cancer is also best treated if caught in its early stages. You can help do this by checking for unusual lumps, changes in skin moles, changes in bowel habits, any abnormal bleeding, unexplained weight loss and coughing or hoarseness that won't go away. Cancer can be overcome and many go on to lead fulfilled lives for many years after diagnosis.

Macmillan Cancer Relief (helping people living with Cancer)
0808 808 2020
www.macmillan.org.uk

BBCs page on Cancer
www.bbc.co.uk/health/conditions/cancer/

Cancer Bacup
0808 800 1234
www.Cancerbacup.org.uk/Home

Cancer Research
0207 121 6699
www.Cancerresearchuk.org

Also check out:
> Sunbathing
> Smoking
> Exercise
> Keep Fit
> Doctors
> Nutrition

Diabetes is an incurable condition in which there is too much glucose in the blood. Normally, glucose is turned into energy but Diabetes means that this isn't done. There are two types of Diabetes – type I/Insulin-Dependent Diabetes and type II/Non-Insulin-Dependent Diabetes. Type I Diabetes is when the body produces no Insulin and type II is when either insufficient amounts of Insulin are produced or the Insulin that is produced doesn't work. The cause of Diabetes is unclear. It is thought that type I Diabetes may run in families and it's known that a virus infection can often trigger it. Type II Diabetes is more common in people with obesity, those who are physically inactive, those of Asian, Afro-Caribbean or Middle Eastern backgrounds and it may also run in families. Those with type I Diabetes need to replenish the Insulin in their blood. This is done by injecting Insulin (there are various methods of injection - using a syringe is the most common). Type II Diabetes may need to be treated in the same way but losing weight and exercise may improve the condition. The symptoms of Diabetes are increased thirst, blurred vision, needing to urinate frequently, tiredness, recurrent thrush and loss of weight. If you think you may have Diabetes, see your GP immediately as early detection may help.

Diabetes UK (charity for people with Diabetes)
www.diabetes.org.uk

Net Doctor page on Diabetes
www.netdoctor.co.uk/diseases/facts/Diabetes.htm

NHS Direct page on Diabetes
0845 46 47
www.nhsdirect.nhs.uk/en.aspx?articleID=128

Diabetes information
www.diabetes.co.uk

Also check out:
> Exercise & Keep Fit
> Healthy Eating
> Thrush
> Doctors
> Eyes
> Injections & Immunisations

Eczema (pronounced 'exma') is a non-contagious condition that affects the skin. Sufferers may find that certain parts of their skin (typically, the elbows and behind the knees, but it can appear anywhere on the body) become dry, itchy, red and painful. Eczema can be extremely uncomfortable and may affect sufferers' confidence due to its appearance. It can run in families and those who suffer from other allergies such as hay fever tend to have the condition also. Some types of Eczema can be triggered by the skin coming into contact with allergens. These can include detergents, dust, nuts and animal fur. It may also be triggered by stress. The best form of prevention is for sufferers to avoid their allergens. If Eczema occurs, there are a range of creams that can be rubbed into the affected areas, which may help. Skin affected by Eczema can be very itchy and, unfortunately, scratching the skin can actually cause further damage. Some creams are available that can help reduce itching. There are also a range of other types of complimentary medicines, which may help those with Eczema. Different things work for different people but some have found acupuncture, homeopathy and relaxation techniques to be of benefit.

The National Eczema Society
0870 241 3604
www.eczema.org

Eczema Voice
www.eczemavoice.com

BUP factsheet for those affected by Eczema
http://hcd2.bupa.co.uk/fact_sheets/Mosby_factsheets/Eczema.html

NHS Direct page on Eczema
0845 46 47
http://www.nhsdirect.nhs.uk/en.aspx?articleID=145

Also check out:
> Acne
> Allergies
> Dermatology
> Hair and Scalp
> Looking Your Best
> Alternative Medicine

Epilepsy & Fits

Epilepsy is a brain condition that causes sufferers to experience fits (or seizures). The human brain consists of millions of nerve cells, each sending and receiving messages to and from one another. This works in a balanced way but, occasionally the sending and receiving of messages can become unstable. This results in a fit. Epilepsy is when a person has repeated fits of this nature. There are different types of fits. Some may be mild and result in just the twitching of a limb. Others may be more severe, producing muscle contractions (twitching limbs), shaking, stiffening of the body and even unconsciousness. They can last for any time up to a few minutes. The cause of epilepsy is often unclear although head injuries, other medical conditions and alcohol abuse are known to increase the chances of it. There are certain things that may trigger an epileptic fit including strobe lighting, alcohol and certain illegal drugs. Most sufferers of epilepsy are successfully treated using drugs. If you're with someone who has a fit, you can help. Move away anything that may cause injury (sharp objects etc.) and cushion their head (if they're on the ground). Move them as little as possible and, once it's over, turn them on their side and stay with them, talking to them and keeping them calm.

Epilepsy Action
0808 800 5050
www.epilepsy.org.uk

The National Society for Epilepsy
01494 601300
www.epilepsynse.org.uk

The Fund for Epilepsy
01422 823508
www.epilepsyfund.org.uk

Net Doctor page on epilepsy
www.netdoctor.co.uk/diseases/facts/epilepsy.htm

Also check out:
> First Aid Essentials
> Alcohol
> Drugs
> Panic Attacks
> Stress
> Doctors

If you've had food poisoning (and most of us have done at some point), you'll know how unpleasant it can be. Diarrhoea, vomiting and stomach pain will make you want to avoid food poisoning forever! Most of the time, it isn't too severe and goes away after a couple of days. If it doesn't, you'll need to see your GP and find out why. It's caused by bacteria, parasites and viruses that have contaminated food or drink that you've consumed. Depending on the type of food poisoning, it usually takes between 12 and 48 hours to develop after you've consumed the offending food or drink. The nasties that cause food poisoning usually get there due to low standards of hygiene when preparing food. Not washing hands, not cooking meat thoroughly, mixing raw meat juices and other food and the incorrect storage of food can all encourage the growth of bacteria and result in food poisoning. Those who have food poisoning should take extra care with their personal hygiene (especially when preparing food) so that they do not pass it on to others. Most food poisoning doesn't require medical treatment but dehydration may occur if there is a lot of diarrhoea and vomiting. Drink rehydration solutions or fruit juice to rehydrate yourself.

Food Standards Agency page on food poisoning
www.eatwell.gov.uk/keepingfoodsafe/

Foodlink page on food poisoning
www.foodlink.org.uk/factfile.asp?file=1

BBC page on food poisoning
www.bbc.co.uk/health/conditions/foodpoisoning1.shtml

NHS Direct page on food poisoning
www.nhsdirect.nhs.uk/en.aspx?articleID=411

Also check out:
> First Aid Essentials
> Healthy Eating
> Vegetarianism and Veganism
> Doctors
> Food

When summer comes around, most of us just want to step outside, enjoy the sun and revel in the outdoors. Unfortunately, many people are inhibited from doing this because of hay fever. Caused by pollen getting into the nose, throat and eyes, symptoms of hay fever are sneezing and a runny nose, itchy eyes, coughing and wheezing and itching at the top of the mouth. It is very common in Wales and is at its worst during spring and summer. Sufferers can use the pollen count (now included in most weather reports) to gauge how bad their hay fever may be on any given day. The pollen count can be affected by the season and the weather. It also tends to rise during the day and can often be at its highest in the early evening. As hay fever is an allergy, the best way to prevent it is to avoid the allergen. As pollen is in the air, this can be very difficult (unless you want to stay in all summer!). So, you can help yourself by not going out in the early evening, avoiding mowing grass (and walking through long grass), keeping windows shut and keeping furry pets out of the house. There are also many types of medication that can help. These can be nasal sprays, eye-drops or tablets.

NHS Direct page on hay fever
0845 46 47
www.nhsdirect.nhs.uk/en.aspx?articleID=453

Net Doctor page on hay fever
www.netdoctor.co.uk/diseases/facts/hayfever.htm

Asthma UK page on hay fever
www.asthma.org.uk/all_about_asthma/hay_fever_rhinitis/index.html

More information on hay fever
www.patient.co.uk/showdoc/342/

Also check out:
> Pets
> First Aid Essentials
> Allergies
> Asthma
> Headaches
> Doctors
> Alternative Medicine

Most of us experience the odd headache from time to time and most of them are nothing more than a slight inconvenience. Ordinary headaches can be caused by things like bad posture, stress and straining your eyes. There are actually two types of headache, one of which, the cluster headache, is quite rare. It usually comes and goes very quickly and can be very painful. Most, however, are ordinary headaches known as tension-type headaches. These can be treated using commonplace over-the-counter painkillers such as Paracetamol and Ibuprofen. Any symptoms additional to a headache such as blurred vision, drowsiness and vomiting could mean something more serious so see your GP if this is the case.

Migraines are recurring severe headaches. The pain occurs on one side of the head and is often accompanied by increased sensitivity to light, dizziness, nausea and vomiting. Vision can also be impaired with many migraine sufferers seeing flashing or moving patterns in front of their eyes. It is not completely understood why they occur but they could be triggered by a number of things, from food to stress. Ordinary painkillers are sometimes effective to treat migraines and there are a range of other drugs that may help. Some also find alternative medicine such as relaxation techniques helps their migraines.

Migraine Action Association
0870 050 5898
www.migraine.org.uk

The Migraine Trust
0207 436 1336
www.migrainetrust.org

NHS Direct page on headaches
0845 46 47
www.nhsdirect.nhs.uk/en.aspx?articleID=496

NHS Direct page on migraine
0845 46 47
www.nhsdirect.nhs.uk/en.aspx?articleID=248

Also check out:

> First Aid Essentials
> Alcohol
> Stress
> Relaxation
> Sleeping and Dreaming
> Doctors

Many young children wet themselves and then grow out of it. But, sometimes it continues into teenage life and adulthood. Incontinence is a loss of control over the bladder, releasing urine. It's common, but because it can be an embarrassing problem, most people never admit it. It most commonly occurs during physical activity, meaning that it may happen when you sneeze, laugh or during sex. It may also mean that you need to go to the toilet a lot during the night. Its causes can be stress, pelvic floor damage caused by childbirth, an infection of the bladder, as an after-effect of various diseases such as Cancer or because of Senile Dementia or Alzheimer's disease. Do not be embarrassed if you are suffering from incontinence. It's not your fault and by seeing your GP about it, you should be able to get something done about it. Treatment can be exercises that improve bladder control, using electric stimulation to improve pelvic muscles, drug treatments and in some cases, surgery.

In Contact (support for those with bladder and bowel problems)
0870 770 3246
www.incontact.org

The Continence Foundation
0845 345 0165
www.continence-foundation.org.uk

NHS Direct page on incontinence
0845 46 47
www.nhsdirect.nhs.uk/en.aspx?ArticleID=211

Net Doctor page on incontinence
www.netdoctor.co.uk/diseases/facts/urinaryincontinence.htm

Also check out:
> Making Love
> Anxiety
> Stress
> Exercise & Keep Fit
> Diabetes
> Doctors

M.E.

M.E. stands for Myalgic Encephalomyelitis and is often also referred to as chronic fatigue syndrome. It is a medical condition that can affect anyone of any age, although women are twice as likely to contract the illness. It affects the nervous and immune systems and can be a debilitating condition. Its symptoms are extreme tiredness that won't go away, feeling generally unwell (often including flu-like symptoms), muscle pain and difficulty sleeping and concentrating. What causes M.E. isn't really known or agreed upon. It is possible that it runs in families and that other illnesses or events such as physical injury could trigger the illness. Because so little is known about M.E., there is no single proven way to treat it. What works for some, may not for others. Drug treatment and physical exercises are the most common types of treatment and some may also benefit from cognitive behavioural therapy (CBT). M.E. is a serious condition that shows few outward symptoms. If you think you may have it, speak to your GP. There are also various support groups for sufferers of M.E. (see links below).

Action for M.E.
0845 123 2380
www.afme.org.uk

The M.E. Association
0870 444 1836
www.meassociation.org.uk

The National M.E. Centre
01708 378050
www.nmec.org.uk

NHS Direct page on M.E.
0845 46 47
www.nhsdirect.nhs.uk/en.aspx?articleID=102

Also check out:
> Stress
> Counselling
> Relaxation
> Exercise & Keep Fit
> Headaches
> Doctors

Meningitis is an infection that can be, at best, mildly disturbing and, at worst, can lead to death. In all suspected cases, immediate advice must be sought in order to control the infection. Meningitis is an infection of the meninges, which are membranes that act as a barrier between the central nervous system and the rest of the body. There are two types of Meningitis:

Bacterial Meningitis
This is the less common of the two, but is always serious. It's caused by bacteria that live at the back of throat and in some people overcome the body's defences. Treatment for Bacterial Meningitis involves hospital care and antibiotics (full recovery is possible although long-term damage, such as brain damage, is a risk). Early treatment can help prevent long-term damage, so if you think you or a friend or family member has Meningitis, seek medical help as soon as possible.

Viral Meningitis
This is caused by a range of viruses. It is less severe than Bacterial Meningitis, but untreated can lead to coma. Viral Meningitis is treated with nursing care (recovery is normally complete).

Meningitis can be passed on by coughing, sneezing, kissing and prolonged contact with others. Symptoms of Meningitis are flu-like symptoms, drowsiness, vomiting, aversion to light, a stiff neck, stomach pains and a rash of red or purple spots that does not fade when a glass is pressed against it. There are vaccines available to prevent some types of Bacterial Meningitis. Other Meningitis vaccines are also now part of the routine national immunisation schedule.

Meningitis Cymru 0800 652 9996
www.meningitiscymru.co.uk

Meningitis Research Foundation
0808 800 3344
www.meningitis.org

Meningitis Trust 0845 6000 800
www.meningitis-trust.org

NHS Direct page on meningitis 0845 46 47
www.nhsdirect.nhs.uk/en.aspx?articleID=245

Also check out:
> Kissing
> First Aid Essentials
> Doctors
> Emergencies
> Health Service
> Injections and Immunisations

Stammering (also known as 'stuttering') is when your words don't come out smoothly. They may get stuck on their way out or sounds may be repeated (e.g., "s-s-s-s") or prolonged (e.g., "ssss"). It's not known why so many people stammer but it is known that more boys than girls do it and that the chances of having a stammer are increased if someone else in your family has one. It usually develops during childhood and can often be triggered by physical or emotional things happening during childhood, when speech skills are developing. It can be an embarrassing problem and can lead to those with stammers being afraid to speak out or becoming very shy. Not all those with stammers are stuck with them for life, full and partial recovery is possible. Speech and language therapists have methods to help those with stammers overcome them. There are also various exercises that can be done on your own to improve the problem. A stammer does not have to ruin your life (famous stammers have included Charles Darwin and Gareth Gates). Others, including employers, should see you for what you say not how you say it.

The British Stammering Association
0845 603 2001
www.stammering.org

BBC page on stammering
www.bbc.co.uk/radio1/onelife/health/atoz/stammer.shtml

Embarrassing Problems page on stammering
01235 523533
www.embarrassingproblems.co.uk/stammering.htm

The Stammer Trust
www.stammertrust.co.uk

Also check out:

- Bullying in the Workplace
- Bullying at School
- Self Esteem
- Anxiety
- Stress
- Discrimination Essentials

Imagine all biting and stinging creatures as venomous or non-venomous. Venomous creatures attack as a defence mechanism, injecting painful, toxic venom through their stingers to punish you so you'll stay away next time, like wasps and bees. Non-venomous creatures bite and usually inject their spit into you in order to feed on your blood, like bed bugs and fleas. Most bugs in the UK are harmless but seek advice and take extra care when travelling abroad.

If you've been stung, you should remove the sting with your fingers as soon as you can. Be careful not to push the sting further in and take care of the area which has been stung. Wash the area and try not to scratch it, as this could cause an infection. To prevent flea bites, make sure any pets are regularly checked and to help prevent bites from bed bugs, regularly wash and change your bed sheets.

Symptoms can be itching, pain, redness and/or swelling and sometimes a severe allergic reaction (anaphylactic shock) can happen from venom stings. If you start to experience swelling or itching on the body, wheezing or feeling faint immediately after a sting or bite, call 999 immediately. Also, if you notice a strange rash appear on you in the first 1-2 days after a bite, see your GP.

Insect Stings
www.insectstings.co.uk

Travel advice on insects and stings
www.traveldoctor.co.uk/stings.htm

BUPA factsheet on stings and bites
http://hcd2.bupa.co.uk/fact_sheets/html/bites_and_stings.html

NHS Direct
0845 46 47
www.nhsdirect.nhs.uk

Also check out:
> Travel Essentials
> First Aid Essentials
> Allergies
> Emergencies
> Doctors
> Injections and Immunisations

Mainly made up of fatty tissue, breasts are a pair of glandular organs that produce milk in response to the hormonal changes caused by pregnancy. They normally begin to develop in girls aged nine to eleven but it can be earlier or later. They come in all manner of shapes and sizes. It's not unusual for one breast to be larger than the other, for nipples to be inverted or for the nipples to have a few hairs around their areola (dark area around the nipple). It's important for women to be fitted with the right size bra. The main thing that a bra should do is provide comfort so don't be afraid to be properly measured so that you can find the right fit for you.

Every woman should take care to get to know her breasts well. Breast cancer is the most common cause of cancer amongst women. So, check your breasts regularly. Get to know what they feel like and remember that the shape and size of breasts change all the time so get used to your normal changes. If you spot any unusual lumps, pock-marked skin or the pulling in of nipples, consult your GP. Most lumps found in breasts are nothing to worry about, but it's better to check and be safe than sorry.

CancerBACUP's page on breasts
0808 800 1234
www.cancerbacup.org.uk/Cancertype/Breast/General/Thebreasts

NHS page on breast lumps
0845 46 47
www.nhsdirect.nhs.uk/he.asp?ArticleID=64

Guide to breast health products, services and information
www.thebreastsite.com

BBC page on breast awareness
www.bbc.co.uk/health/womens_health/body_breast1.shtml

Also check out:
> Cancer
> Doctors
> Body Hair
> Plastic & Cosmetic Surgery
> Periods and PMS
> Pregnancy

Cystitis

Cystitis is an infection of the bladder. It can affect anyone but is much more common in women, especially sexually active, pregnant or menopausal women. It is caused by bacteria from nearby skin travelling up the urethra (the tube used to empty urine from the bladder) and into the bladder. You'll know you've got cystitis when it becomes painful to pass urine, if you need to go to the toilet a lot (usually only producing a small amount of urine) or if you need to go to the toilet, but pass no urine at all. Other symptoms may be traces of blood in the urine, cloudy, dark or strong smelling urine and pain in the lower back or abdomen. It can be prevented by drinking a lot of water (around eight glasses a day), drinking a glass of cranberry juice daily, by wiping yourself from front to back after going to the toilet, by wearing loose clothing and cotton underwear and by washing before and after sex. Most cases of cystitis can be treated at home by following the prevention tips above, taking painkillers such as Paracetamol or by drinking a glass of water with a teaspoon of bicarbonate of soda in. If your symptoms do not go away, if you have blood in your urine or are pregnant, you should see your GP who may prescribe antibiotics.

The Cystitis and Overactive Bladder Foundation 01908 569 169
www.interstitialcystitis.co.uk

NHS Direct page on cystitis 0845 46 47
www.nhsdirect.nhs.uk/en.aspx?articleID=119

BBC page on cystitis
www.bbc.co.uk/health/conditions/cystitis1.shtml

BUPA factsheet on cystitis
http://hcd2.bupa.co.uk/fact_sheets/html/cystitis.html

Also check out:
> Genitals
> Pregnancy
> Safe Sex
> Making Love
> Doctors

Genitals
6.7 Women's Health

Your genitals are made up of the clitoris, outer and inner lips (labia), the urethra and vagina. Everyone's 'bits' are different. The clitoris gives you sexual pleasure and is where the inner lips join at the top in a small fleshy bump. The outer lips cover the clitoris and go back to just in front of the anus. They are hairy on the outside and darker on the inside. One outer lip may be bigger than another. It's perfectly normal. The inner lips are thinner and vary in colour from light pink to dark brown. They may even hang below the outer lips.

It's very important for you to have regular cervical smears. From the age of 25, the NHS invites all women registered with a GP for a test, which is usually repeated every 3-5 years. The test looks for abnormalities that could lead to cervical cancer. Cervical cancer can be detected, treated and cured with regular smear tests. They are available at your doctor's or health clinic and should be part of your health routine. This simple process can save your life.

It's also important to keep yourself healthy and safe. Keeping your genitals clean can help prevent infections such as cystitis. If you're having sex, use a condom to stop yourself getting an STI.

NHS Cervical Screening Programme
www.cancerscreening.nhs.uk/cervical/

NHS Direct page on cancer of the vagina 0845 46 47
www.nhsdirect.nhs.uk/en.aspx?articleID=471

Also check out:
> Cystitis
> Periods and PMS
> Pregnancy
> Thrush
> Safe Sex
> STIs

During puberty, the female body produces hormones that cause the eggs that all women are born with to mature. This is the first menstrual cycle, which usually begins between the ages of 9 and 16 and continues, monthly, until the menopause, which is usually between 45 and 55. It causes bleeding from the vagina that normally lasts for 5 days but can last for as long as 10 days. Sometimes periods can be painful: stomach cramps, backache and headaches are all quite common. Each person experiences it differently. The pain is nothing to worry about; it's just to do with the levels of certain hormones that are present in the womb at the time. Certain painkillers may help with painful periods – see your GP if you're concerned.

Premenstrual Syndrome (PMS) is a collection of physical and emotional symptoms caused by the menstrual cycle. Most women experience some symptoms to varying degrees. It can make you feel depressed, bloated, irritable and can cause tender breasts and backache. Most experience mild PMS but, for some, it can disrupt their lives. Your GP can prescribe different types of medication to help (including diuretics to help with fluid levels in the body) and you can also help yourself by taking regular exercise and dietary supplements such as vitamins.

NHS Direct page on Periods
0845 46 47
www.nhsdirect.nhs.uk/en.aspx?articleID=636

BBC page on the menstrual cycle
www.bbc.co.uk/science/humanbody/body/articles/lifecycle/teenagers/periods.shtml

National Association for Premenstrual Syndrome 01622 872 578
www.pms.org.uk

NHS Direct page on Premenstrual Sydrome 0845 46 47
www.nhsdirect.nhs.uk/en.aspx?articleID=295

Also check out:

- Relaxation
- Exercise & Keep Fit
- Genitals
- Pregnancy
- Doctors
- Health Services

Depending on your situation, a pregnancy can be a thing of great joy or heartache. Either way, the most important thing is to find out if you are pregnant as early as possible. Then you can make a firm decision on whether to keep the baby or not. The main sign that you are pregnant is a missed period. If this happens, see your GP or use a home pregnancy test immediately. Other symptoms (but not necessarily signs) of pregnancy are morning sickness, tender breasts, headaches, bloating and a slight increase in vaginal discharge. If you decide that you want to keep your baby, the next vital thing is that you keep yourself healthy and get clued up about pregnancy and giving birth. Keep your diet varied and healthy so that you and your baby get all of the necessary vitamins and nutrients. Take folic acid tablets (to reduce the possibility of birth defects). Avoid smoking and drinking and cut down your caffeine intake. If you decide that you do not want to keep your baby, you need to seek professional help as soon as possible to ensure that you do the right thing for yourself and your baby.

British Pregnancy Advisory Service
01564 793 225
www.bpas.org

NHS page on pregnancy
0845 46 47
www.nhsdirect.nhs.uk/articles/article.aspx?articleid=294

Women's Health Information
www.womens-health.co.uk

Baby Centre (pregnancy A-Z)
www.babycentre.co.uk/refcap/546144.htm

Also check out:
> Contraception
> Babies
> Family & Friends
> Abortion
> Children
> Miscarriage

Thrush is an infection that can affect the vagina and the mouth (although men are occasionally infected, affecting the head of the penis). It is caused by naturally-occurring bacteria that usually pose no problem. Changes in the body can result in a rapid growth in bacteria, which causes an infection. It can be triggered when you are feeling 'run down', by pregnancy, by the oral contraceptive pill and in those with diabetes or on steroids. The result of vaginal thrush is itching, irritation, soreness and a thick, white vaginal discharge. Oral thrush may cause a sore mouth and throat and may result in white discharge around the mouth. It can be passed on through sexual intercourse so refrain from sex whilst you have thrush. However, it can't be passed on through kissing or toilet seats. Thrush can be treated quite easily. It actually goes away by itself with time, but to reduce the amount of time in discomfort, there are a variety of creams and tablets that are available over the counter or from your GP that will help.

NHS Direct page on thrush
0845 46 47
www.nhsdirect.nhs.uk/en.aspx?articleID=87

BBC page on thrush
www.bbc.co.uk/relationships/sex_and_sexual_health/stis_thrush.shtml

Net Doctor page on oral thrush
www.netdoctor.co.uk/diseases/facts/oralthrush.htm

MedInfo page on thrush
www.medinfo.co.uk/conditions/thrush.html

Also check out:
> Cystitis
> Genitals
> STIs
> Doctors
> Health Service

Athlete's Foot and Jock Itch are both very similar fungal infections. In fact, Jock Itch is often caused by the spread of Athlete's Foot. We all have the fungi that causes Athlete's Foot on our body but sometimes certain conditions mean that the fungi gets out of control and causes an infection, meaning you'll have a red, itchy rash between your toes and scaly, flaky skin. In some cases, it'll also cover some of the skin near the toes. The type of fungi that causes Athlete's Foot loves warm, moist conditions, which is how the infection gets its name – because athletes tend to get sweaty feet, encouraging the nasty fungi. The best way to avoid it is to make sure that you dry well between your toes after you wash. If you are prone to Athlete's Foot, try changing your socks regularly and going barefoot as often as you can. It's easily treated with a variety of over-the-counter creams and you shouldn't need to visit the doctor (unless the infection won't go away). Jock Itch is basically the same thing, but the rash appears in the groin and sometimes on the skin beneath the scrotum. Jock Itch can be prevented by drying thoroughly after washing and wearing loose underwear.

Net Doctor page on Athlete's Foot
www.netdoctor.co.uk/diseases/facts/athletesfoot.htm

NHS page on treatments for Athlete's Foot
www.besttreatments.co.uk/btuk/conditions/10527.html

NHS Direct page on Athlete's Foot
www.nhsdirect.nhs.uk/en.aspx?articleID=38

Embarrassing Problems page on Jock Itch
www.embarrassingproblems.co.uk/jockitch.htm

Also check out:
> Exercise & Keep Fit
> Testicles
> Dermatology
> Doctors
> Health Service

When a man repeatedly can't get or maintain an adequate erection to perform sexual intercourse or in a way that interferes significantly with his sex life, this is known as impotence or erectile dysfunction. It happens to around 1 in 10 men and can be very distressing for those affected and can affect relationships badly. The reasons for it can be physical or psychological but are usually a combination of both. Physical reasons that could cause a lack of erection are things like having diabetes or other similar conditions, taking certain forms of medication or being under the influence of alcohol, smoking or other illegal drugs. Psychologically, erectile dysfunction can be caused by stress, relationship worries and depression. Impotence can be an embarrassing problem for men and one that can be hard to admit. Because of this, it can harm relationships, making partners feel isolated and as if it's their fault. It happens to most men at some point during their lives but occasional dysfunction is nothing to worry about. If it keeps happening though, it's sensible (for you and your partner) to talk about it and try to get something done. Your GP can offer advice and, if necessary, can recommend counselling or therapy that may help the problem. There are also treatments that may help.

Sexual Dysfunction Association
0870 7743571
www.sda.uk.net

NHS Direct page on erectile dysfunction
0845 46 47
www.nhsdirect.nhs.uk/en.aspx?articleID=210

Male Health article about erectile dysfunction
www.malehealth.co.uk/userpage1.cfm?item_id=129

BUPA factsheet about impotence
http://hcd2.bupa.co.uk/fact_sheets/html/Impotence.html

Also check out:
> Stress
> Exercise & Keep Fit
> Penis
> Doctors

Penis

Big, small, thin, wide, long, dark or light – each penis is as distinctive as a face. It's a vital piece of equipment and it needs to be well looked after. Consisting of two main parts, the head (the bit at the end) and the shaft (the main bit) it has two main functions – weeing and sex. The urethra is a tube that comes from the bladder and allows urine and semen to be emptied through the penis. When sexually aroused, the penis fills with blood allowing it to go hard (erection). Some men are circumcised, either for medical or religious purposes. This is when the foreskin (the skin at the end of the penis) is removed. It makes no difference to the actual operation of the penis. Keeping your penis clean is of prime importance. Make sure it's washed thoroughly and regularly (those with uncircumcised penises should take care to wash under the foreskin) otherwise it might smell and look unpleasant. Things do go wrong with penises. It's possible to get infections in it and you'll know you've got one if it's sore, itchy or if there's a discharge or any rashes or spots. Don't be embarrassed about seeing your GP to look at the problem – they've seen it all before!

Men's Health page on the penis
www.menshealth.co.uk/health/penis/

Humorous but informative owner's guide to the penis
www.vasectomy-information.com/humour/manual.htm

Male Health page on penis problems
www.malehealth.co.uk/userpage1.cfm?item_id=1020

Net Doctor page on penis size
www.netdoctor.co.uk/menshealth/facts/penissize.htm

Also check out:
> Making Love
> Impotence
> Prostate Cancer
> Testicles
> Safe Sex
> Doctors

The prostate is a gland that only men have. It is around the size of a walnut and is situated just beneath the bladder. Its job is to produce semen, which mixes with sperm produced by the testes. Prostate cancer is currently the most common form of cancer among men in the UK.

It is not really known what causes prostate cancer, but if other close relatives have had the disease, the risk increases. Also, black men are more at risk from it. Prostate cancer is rarely found in men aged under 50 and is most common in men over 70. The initial symptoms of it are urinating more frequently (especially at night), pain or difficulty whilst urinating, difficulty starting to urinate, back pain or blood in the urine. Often, cancer can be present before any symptoms show so it is recommended that all men aged over 50 be screened for it. Treatment for prostate cancer can by done by removing the prostate gland, which requires surgery and radiotherapy. If the cancer is not diagnosed in its early stages, the cancer can spread to other parts of the body.

The Prostate Cancer Charity
0845 300 83 83
www.prostate-cancer.org.uk

CancerBACUP page on prostate cancer
0808 800 1234
www.cancerbacup.org.uk/Cancertype/Prostate

Cancer Research Wales
02920 316 976
www.crw.org.uk

BBC health page on prostate cancer
www.bbc.co.uk/health/awareness_campaigns/mar_prostatecancer.shtml

Also check out:
> Cancer
> Penis
> Testicles
> Doctors

The testicles (or ëballsí) are the part of the male reproductive system that produces sperm and the male hormone, testosterone. They are two small oval-shaped balls that sit below the penis suspended in a pouch called the scrotum. At the top and back of each testicle is the epididymis, which feels like a soft swelling and can be quite tender (this is where sperm is stored). At the back and top of the testicles are vas deferens, which are the tubes that carry the sperm to the penis. Testicles should be smooth and soft. It is normal for one to be larger than the other and for one to hang slightly lower than the other.

It's important for men to keep a regular (once a month) check on their testicles. The most vital check that men can do is for testicular cancer, which is the most common form of cancer among young men. Make sure that you are familiar with your testicles so that you easily spot any changes in them. It's best to check them after you've had a warm bath or shower so that the skin around them is properly relaxed. If you notice any swelling, lumps, an ache in the testicles or stomach and back pain, go and see your GP or sexual health clinic.

CancerBACUP page on testicular cancer
0808 800 1234
www.cancerbacup.org.uk/Cancertype/Testes/

Cancer Research page on testicles
www.cancerhelp.org.uk/help/default.asp?page=2674

NHS page on testicular cancer 0845 46 47
www.nhsdirect.nhs.uk/articles/article.aspx?articleid=85

BBC page on testicular cancer
www.bbc.co.uk/wales/bllcks/

Also check out:
> Penis
> Cancer
> Doctors
> Impotence
> Athlete's Foot and Jock Itch

Ever noticed that the plughole seems to need unblocking more these days? Is your hairbrush full of hair and your pillow covered in it in the morning? If so, you may be suffering from hair loss (also known as alopecia). It happens to a lot of people – mostly men, but occasionally women too – and can be a traumatic experience. The most common kind of baldness happens naturally and is usually genetic, meaning that it can be passed down to you from your parents. There's nothing much you can do about it so the best thing is to try and deal with it and learn to love it. Baldness doesn't mean anything; it's just a fact of life. There's no reason to think that you won't look so good without hair. In fact, many people prefer men with little or no hair. Although there are some treatments that are available to help hair re-growth, there is no definite cure or remedy and what may have an effect on one person might be useless on another. Hair loss can also be caused by certain medical treatments such as chemotherapy and as a result of shock or stress.

Alopecia UK
0208 333 1661
www.alopeciaonline.org.uk

Net Doctor's guide to baldness remedies
www.netdoctor.co.uk/menshealth/feature/baldness_remedies.htm

Patient UK article on male pattern baldness
www.patient.co.uk/showdoc/23069043/

BUPA
www.bupa.co.uk

Also check out:
> Relaxation
> Cancer
> Body Hair
> Hair and Scalp
> Looking Your Best
> Doctors

We're all covered in hair. You should be thankful that it's there because it exists for a good reason – to help protect us from the cold. Some have more hair than others. It can be dark, light, fine or thick and some might have it in places you didn't realise could be so hairy! Chests, bums, backs, legs, arms, faces, noses, ears, pubic areas and, of course, your head all have their fair share of it. You'll find that most of your body hair starts growing when you're going through puberty – aged between 12 and 18 - and it carries on growing and changing as you get older too, especially in places like your ears and nose. Just as we all look different, we all like different looks too and some will love your body hair whereas some will prefer smooth skin. Keeping your body hair in check is a routine that you'll have to get into. You can shave or use cream, gel or wax to keep it trim. There's also electrolysis or laser treatment that can permanently remove hair but it may take time, be uncomfortable and damage your wallet too. Eyebrow, nasal and ear hair is probably best removed by plucking (using tweezers for minimal pain). If you're really hung up about your body hair, speak to a beauty therapist for advice.

BBC Health page on excess body hair
www.bbc.co.uk/health/ask_the_doctor/excess bodyhair.shtml

Embarrassing Problems page on hairiness in women
www.embarrassingproblems.co.uk/hair-women.htm

British Association of Dermatologists page on body hair
www.bad.org.uk/public/skin/hair/

Net Doctor's Q&As on hair
www.netdoctor.co.uk/ate/health/skin_hair/600 243.shtml

Also check out:
> Balding
> Hair and Scalp
> Looking Your Best
> Alternative Medicine

We all sweat. And it's when we sweat that a body odour (B.O.) is released. It's not the sweat itself that smells; it's the process of bacteria breaking down the sweat that causes it. Most people don't start to produce a body odour until they hit puberty as the hormone changes that occur in your body around this time lead to the production of more sweat. The best way to avoid B.O. is to wash regularly and with particular care to areas like the armpit and the groin, which have more sweat producing glands than the rest of the body. Your feet need special attention too. Because we cover them in socks and shoes, they can get warm and moist, allowing smelly fungi, as well as bacteria, to thrive. If you sweat a lot, you might need to wash more often than most. Change your clothes every day (especially your underwear) and don't wear clothes that you've sweated in again before washing them. Wear an anti-perspirant, which reduces the amount of sweat your body produces. You should also avoid eating spicy and strongly flavoured foods, as their smell can come out in your sweat and might make your breath smell bad too. For bad breath, brush your teeth regularly, use an anti-bacterial mouth-wash and avoid alcohol and smoking.

NHS Direct (features pages on body odours and bad breath)
0845 46 47
www.nhsdirect.nhs.uk

BBC page on body odours
www.bbc.co.uk/health/conditions/bodyodour2.shtml

Net Doctor page on halitosis (bad breath)
www.netdoctor.co.uk/diseases/facts/badbreath.htm

Connexions page on body odour
www.connexions-direct.com/index.cfm?pid=105&catalogueContentID=171&render=detailedArticle

Also check out:

- Alcohol
- Smoking
- Relaxation
- Exercise & Keep Fit
- Healthy Eating
- Looking Your Best

Cellulite & Stretch Marks
6.9 Looking Good?

Lumpy, bumpy, dimply skin around the thighs, breasts, arms or bottom is perfectly normal and is nothing to worry about. Sometimes this type of skin is known as cellulite, although not everyone agrees that cellulite actually exists and isn't just an effect of fat getting pulled around, changing the appearance of skin. We all have fat beneath our skin (even the skinniest supermodels) so anyone can be affected by cellulite, although men very rarely suffer from it. It's not in any way unhealthy to have cellulite but most who have it don't like it as they believe it looks unpleasant.

Stretch marks are caused by the skin stretching during periods of rapid growth such as pregnancy, adolescence or during dieting. They appear as streaks on the skin that are usually a lighter shade than your normal skin colour. There are hundreds of products out there that claim to cure or improve cellulite and stretch marks. However, there is very little evidence to say that any of them work, although some may help for some people or using them may just make you feel better about yourself. Medical evidence suggests that cellulite and stretch marks are irreversible processes (although stretch marks do fade over time) so the best thing is to try and learn to love it!

British Association of Dermatologists
0207 383 0266
www.bad.or.uk/about/

NHS Direct page on stretch marks
0845 46 47
www.nhsdirect.nhs.uk/en,aspx?articleID=633

Net Doctor article on cellulite
www.netdoctor.co.uk/features/cellulite_003809.htm

Also check out:
> Exercise & Keep Fit
> Healthy Eating
> Dermatology
> Doctors
> Alternative Medicine

6.9 Looking Good?

Everyone sees your skin so most people want it to look as good as it can. Spots on the skin are caused by grease-producing glands, which go into overdrive around the time of puberty. You might not be able to completely rid yourself of spots (everyone suffers from the odd pimple from time to time) but there are some simple ways that you can help improve the condition of your skin. You just need to wash regularly (but no more than twice a day), be sure to remove your make-up, drink a lot of water and exercise regularly. Eating healthy food like lots of fruit and vegetables also helps your skin. Try not to touch your face too often as it could lead to an increase in bacteria on your skin, which will make spots worse. If you suffer from dry skin, be sure to moisturise regularly or, instead of using soap to wash your face, use a moisturising face-wash. There are shelves full of products out there that all claim to improve the condition of your skin, keep it looking young etc. Be aware that the most expensive product won't necessarily be the most effective one; the important thing is to find what works for you.

Dermatology homepage
www.dermatology.co.uk

British Association of Dermatologists
0207 383 0266
www.bad.org.uk/about

Skin Care Campaign
www.skincarecampaign.org

BUPA factsheet on acne
http://hcd2.bupa.co.uk/fact_sheets/Mosby_fact sheets/acne.html

Also check out:
> Exercise & Keep Fit
> Healthy Eating
> Acne
> Body Hair
> Looking Your Best
> Tattoos

Flushing & Blushing
6.9 Looking Good?

From time to time, we all get embarrassed. It might be when you talk to a group of people, when you say or do something stupid, when you're talking to the girl or boy you fancy or when you're having a word with the boss. If you feel anxiety in a situation, your brain sends a signal that tells your body you need more oxygen, which is when a large quantity of blood flows to your face, causing it to go red. It can vary from a mild flush to blotchy, dark red patches and you'll probably get a bit hot under the collar too, depending on your level of fear and skin type. It's difficult to control blushing when it happens – in fact; thinking about it tends to make the situation worse! However, there are ways that you can reduce the fear factor. You probably aren't as red as you think you are and others know the fear associated with your embarrassment so they'll understand why you're blushing and won't think less of you for it. Get out there and confront your fear. The more you do so, the more you'll get used to it and the less blushing you'll do. Wearing loose clothes made from natural fibres and in colours that won't show sweat should help too.

Embarrassing Problems
www.embarrassingproblems.com

BBC page on building self confidence
www.bbc.co.uk/dna/h2g2/A841358

Sympathectomy (resources for the treatment for over-sweating and facial blushing)
www.sympathectomy.co.uk

NHS Direct page on blushing
0845 46 47
www.nhsdirect.nhs.uk/en.aspx?articleID=55

Also check out:
- Self Esteem
- Anxiety
- Panic Attacks
- Stress
- Relaxation
- Meditation

Everyone has the occasional bad hair day and getting it right all the time is virtually impossible. Try to accept and love your hair the way it is. The more you mess with your hair (straightening, dying etc.) the more damaged it will become. Get yourself a shampoo that suits your hair and make sure that you wash regularly. The minimum number of weekly washes is three but make sure you don't wash it too much (no more than once a day) as it can be bad for your hair. Regular brushing encourages hair renewal (your hair falls out, it's normal, but don't worry, it replaces itself naturally) but never brush wet hair (comb through gently instead). Eating well is essential for healthy hair. Lots of protein and B vitamins are best for your barnet. Dandruff is a condition that's caused by increased renewal of skin cells on the scalp, leading to white flakes in your hair. Regular washing, brushing and a change in diet (cutting down on sugar and refined carbohydrates and loading up on vitamin B and essential fatty acids) helps prevent dandruff. If the problem persists, there are specialist shampoos that should help.

BBC page on how to have healthy hair
www.bbc.co.uk/dna/h2g2/A467921

NHS Direct page on dandruff
0845 46 47
www.nhsdirect.nhs.uk/en.aspx?articleID=121

Embarrassing Problems page on hair loss
www.embarrassingproblems.co.uk/hairloss.htm

The Fit Map page on hair care tips
www.thefitmap.co.uk/beauty/hair/tips/

Also check out:

- Healthy Eating
- Balding
- Body Hair
- Dermatology
- Looking Your Best
- Sunbathing

6.9 Looking Good?

If you want to look your best, get healthy. With a balanced diet and regular exercise, you'll keep trim and toned, have a great complexion and shiny hair. On top of that, you need to keep up your personal hygiene. Get a routine that looks after your skin, teeth, hair and nails and you'll stay beautiful. There is a huge market out there for products that claim to make you look better. Don't believe the hype and be fooled by manipulative advertising. Instead, try out different things and be honest with yourself about what works and what doesn't. Your clothes matter too. It's all about individuality. You should work out what looks good on you (not what everyone else is wearing) and what you feel comfortable in. If you're not sure about fashion, ask a trusted friend to help you out. Not everyone likes the way they look. Most aren't born with supermodel looks and buff bodies so you've got to make do with what you've got. Learn to love the looks you were given and so long as you feel happy with the way you look, you'll be brimming with all-important confidence.

BBC's What Not To Wear (fashion advice)
www.bbc.co.uk/lifestyle/tv_and_radio/what_not_to_wear/

How to Look Good by Caryn Franklin
www.howtolookgood.com

Today's Woman (beauty tips for women)
www.todays-woman.co.uk

Channel 4's page on male grooming
www.channel4.com/health/microsites/L/lust4life/look_young/treat_groom.html

Also check out:

> Self Esteem
> You
> Exercise & Keep Fit
> Healthy Eating
> Dermatology
> Plastic & Cosmetic Surgery

These days, you can get pretty much any part of your body pierced. Studs, bars, diamonds, rings, you can have what you want. But watch out, body piercing can be painful and, if it's not carried out properly can be very dangerous. You also need to look after your piercing otherwise it could be unhealthy. Anyone can get a body piercing at any age but if you're under 16, it's illegal to have your genitals (and female breasts) pierced as this would be considered to be indecent assault. Many body piercers have their own informal guidelines about whom they pierce; some will ask for parental permission to pierce those aged under 16. Before you decide to have your body pierced, think about it and discuss it with someone whose opinion you trust. Despite what people may tell you, having your body pierced will hurt (piercers aren't legally allowed to use anaesthetic injections and other numbing creams, gels etc, could be unhygienic). You should make sure that your chosen piercer is reputable, that they operate using a packaged and sterilised needle and that they have clean hands and wear surgical gloves. Be sure also that they will provide you with aftercare advice. On top of all that, piercing can be expensive so make sure you're 100% certain before you dive in.

NHS Direct page on piercings
0845 46 47
www.nhsdirect.nhs.uk/en.aspx?articleID=422

The British Body Piercing Association
01458 831 666
www.profound-piercing.co.uk/association.html

Dan Aid (raising awareness about the dangers of body piercing)
www.danaid.com

BBC One Life page on body piercing
www.bbc.co.uk/radio1/onelife/personal/body_image/bodyart_piercing.shtml

Also check out:
> Body Hair
> Dermatology
> Looking Your Best
> Plastic & Cosmetic Surgery
> Tattoos

Plastic & Cosmetic Surgery
6.9 Looking Good?

We all have parts of our body that we don't particularly like. Cosmetic surgery is when someone has surgery because they don't like the way they look whereas plastic surgery is when it is required due to illness or injury. The immediate after effects of plastic surgery can be painful – not just for your body but your wallet as well. You should find a reputable surgeon who's a member of the British Association of Aesthetic Plastic Surgeons (BAAPS). If you're under 16, you'll need parental permission to get plastic surgery. The NHS only provides cosmetic surgery to those with serious psychological problems and will undertake extensive consultation with you before agreeing to do it.

COSMETIC SURGERY (INTENTIONAL) - Breast enlargement, breast reduction, nose jobs, face lifts, ear pinning, chin tucks and liposuction are all popular cosmetic surgery procedures. Surgery can be an option for you if you are very unhappy, but you should never feel pressured into changing your appearance because of someone else's opinion of how you look, especially not through a surgical procedure. Cosmetic surgery can be expensive and risky, and isn't guaranteed to give you what you're looking for, so think carefully before committing yourself to any procedure. Make sure you talk it over with friends, family and possibly a counsellor, research the facts and ask your doctor lots of questions in the first instance and don't ever rush into it.

RECONSTRUCTIVE (PLASTIC) SURGERY - People also have reconstructive surgery for a number of reasons – to correct birth defects, following accidents or violent attacks or following an illness such as breast cancer for example. The aim of reconstructive surgery is to restore normal function or appearance and can significantly boost self-confidence. Reconstructive surgery can sometimes involve one operation or require multiple procedures and a positive outlook is important to the person undergoing surgery – it can help the recovery process. If you or someone you know is undergoing reconstructive surgery, there are support networks that can offer help and advice. Check out the BAAPS website.

British Association of Aesthetic Plastic Surgery (BAAPS) 020 7405 2234
www.baaps.org.uk/

BBC One Life • Health • A-Z
Loads of further info on cosmetic surgery
www.bbc.co.uk/radio1/onelife

NHS Direct (has pages on plastic and cosmetic surgery) 0845 46 47
http://www.nhsdirect.nhs.uk

Also check out:

- You
- Healthy Eating
- Burns
- Cellulite and Stretch Marks
- Looking Your Best
- Doctors

6.9 Looking Good?

In Britain, the moment the sun peeks out from behind a cloud, we tend to whip off most of our clothes and worship! But whilst a bit of sun is undoubtedly good for us, it pays to sunbathe sensibly. UV rays from sunlight are the major cause of skin cancer, which causes over 1000 deaths in Britain each year. Exposure to sunlight also increases the risk of developing cataracts, a cloudy patch that appears over the lens of the eye leading, in worst cases, to blindness. Spending too much time in the sun without protecting your skin can also cause sunburn - which anyone who has had it will tell you is extremely unpleasant – and can lead to sunstroke (when the body cannot re-hydrate itself) which can, in some cases, lead to death. It's not difficult to protect yourself and sunbathe sensibly. Limit the amount of time spent in the sun, building a tan gradually rather than in one go. Use at least factor 15+ sun lotion and be sure to cover every part of your body that's exposed. Re-apply sun lotion regularly, especially after swimming. Keep out of the sun during the peak hours of 11am – 3pm. It's also a good idea to know your skin type. Fairer skin is more at risk from the sun than dark skin so be aware of what measures you should take to protect yourself.

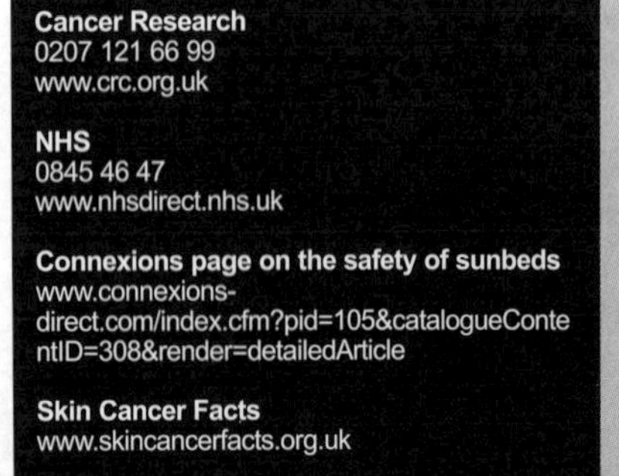

Cancer Research
0207 121 66 99
www.crc.org.uk

NHS
0845 46 47
www.nhsdirect.nhs.uk

Connexions page on the safety of sunbeds
www.connexions-direct.com/index.cfm?pid=105&catalogueContentID=308&render=detailedArticle

Skin Cancer Facts
www.skincancerfacts.org.uk

Also check out:

> Cancer
> Acne
> Travel Essentials
> Looking Your Best
> Doctors
> Health Essentials

Tattoos
6.9 Looking Good?

People have been tattooing themselves for centuries and, currently, body art is in fashion with many prominent celebrities sporting tattoos. Before you rush in and get one, have a think about it. You need to be 18 to get a tattoo and although some claim they can give you one that will disappear after five years, tattoos actually stay with you for life. Your opinion changes and what you like now, you might not like in a couple of years, let alone in 20 years time. Remember too that bodies change shape, which means your tattoo will too, so make sure you get tattooed in the right place. If you do decide that body art is for you, go to a registered tattooist and speak to them first. Make sure you trust them, check that they provide after-care advice and work in clean conditions. Tattoos are made by injecting ink into a layer of your skin using a vibrating needle, which may be painful or uncomfortable. They must use a clean, sterilized needle for every tattoo, otherwise there is a great risk of infection of diseases such as HIV and Hepatitis. Tattoos can be removed by laser surgery but it's a very expensive procedure that's not always successful. If you want to decorate your body but aren't sure you want a permanent tattoo, try henna or transfer tattoos for temporary body art.

Tattoo Info
www.tattooinfo.net/Scripts/default.asp

BBC One Life page on body art
www.bbc.co.uk/radio1/onelife/personal/body_image/bodyart_tattoo.shtml

Embarrassing Problems page on tattoos
www.embarrassingproblems.co.uk/tatoos.htm

Tattoo Club of Great Britain
01865 716877
www.tattoo.co.uk

Also check out:
> Dermatology
> Looking Your Best
> Piercings
> Plastic & Cosmetic Surgery
> HIV and AIDS
> Injections and Immunisations

HIV is a virus that affects the body's immune system, which fights off illness and disease. Those affected are often known as being HIV positive. Over time, the immune system weakens, leaving the body open to infections and cancers. Once infections become serious, a sufferer is referred to as having AIDS (Acquired Immune Deficiency Syndrome).

HIV - HIV is short for Human Immunodeficiency Virus and is the virus that causes AIDS. HIV can be only be passed on through the transfer of blood, semen, vaginal fluids and breast milk. The most common ways that HIV is passed on are unprotected sex, a mother passing it on during pregnancy or breastfeeding and through contact with needles used by someone with HIV. There is currently no cure for HIV. However, there is treatment available to those infected with the virus that can help prevent illness and increase life expectancy. The way to find out if you have the HIV virus is through a simple blood test that can be done by your GP or at your local GUM clinic but the virus needs three months from infection before it can be detected. To help avoid contracting HIV, use a condom during sex and don't share needles with anyone if injecting drugs. Finally, you can't catch HIV from shaking hands or using the same toilet as someone with the virus.

Continued on next page...

Avert
www.avert.org/young.htm

Aids Trust Cymru
01792 461848
www.aidstrustcymru.co.uk

International HIV/AIDS Alliance (organisation trying to reduce the spread of HIV internationally)
www.aidsalliance.org/sw1280.asp

Also check out:
- Contraception
- Sex Essentials
- Drugs

AIDS - AIDS is short for Acquired Immune Deficiency Syndrome - the disease that invades your immune system and strips it of its infection-fighting powers. It's a mixture of illnesses and conditions that happen to the body because the immune system has been damaged by HIV.

There's no cure or vaccine for either disease, but treatment can relieve some symptoms. Tests at GUM (Genito-Urinary Medicine) Clinics are confidential and won't appear on your medical records. An HIV test is a simple blood test and you can usually get a result within 10-days. It's best to get things checked out as soon as you can and save a lot of worry. You may be clear anyway, and be worrying for nothing.

Terence Higgins Trust (HIV/AIDS charity)
0845 12 21 200
www.tht.org.uk

The UK Coalition of People Living with AIDS and HIV
0207 564 2180
www.ukcoalition.org

Also check out:
> Safe Sex
> Doctors

Practicing safe sex is absolutely essential for two reasons. Unplanned pregnancies and sexually transmitted infections (STIs) can both occur as a result of unprotected sex, which can lead to dire consequences for those involved. Whether you have a long-term sexual partner, indulge in a one-off fling or are having regular sex, practicing safe sex could save your life. The number of people who have been diagnosed with an STI has increased in recent years, with young people (especially females aged under 20) most at risk. There are different types of STI, some of which are less dangerous than others. At worst, an STI can be life threatening. An unplanned pregnancy can also be traumatic for all concerned. Babies are a huge responsibility and need a lot of care and attention. There are many different forms of contraception but all are easily available to those who need them. Before having sex, be honest with yourself and your partner. Even if raising the subject of contraception may interrupt proceedings, cause embarrassment or perhaps mean that full sex doesn't take place, when you consider what the consequences of an STI or an unwanted pregnancy could be, is it really worth ignoring it?

Avert (International AIDS charity)
www.avert.org/young.htm

Playing Safely (NHS Safe Sex information)
0800 567 123
www.playingsafely.co.uk

BBC Wales Come Clean (sexual health advice)
www.bbc.co.uk/wales/comeclean/content/safersex.shtml

Net Doctor article on safe sex
www.netdoctor.co.uk/sex_relationships/facts/safesex.htm

Also check out:
- Contraception
- Sex Essentials
- Babies
- HIV & AIDs
- Love & Sex

The latest government figures have shown a huge rise in the number of STIs being diagnosed in the UK. If you're having unprotected sex, at any age, you can get an infection and pass one on. From viral infections to bacteria and mites, most STIs can be quickly and easily treated if discovered early with antibiotics or lotions. Be safe, always use a condom.

Common symptoms:
- Unusual discharges and smells
- Needing to pee more than usual
- Itching
- Rashes
- Lumps
- Blisters or pain in the genitals during sex
- Bleeding after sex or between periods

Symptoms can take anything from two days to four weeks to develop, but STIs like HIV and Chlamydia often have no symptoms at all. If you suspect you may have an STI, get it checked out immediately at your doctors, GUM (Genitourinary Medicine) clinic, local hospital or family planning clinic. An STI test is nowhere near as scary as you may have been told. It can be a little uncomfortable but it's worth it to know one way or the other. If you do have an STI, you need to tell current and former partners straight away so that they can get themselves checked out too.

The Family Planning Association
0845 310 1334 www.fpa.org.uk

R U Thinking?
0800 28 29 30 www.ruthinking.co.uk

BBC Wales Come Clean campaign
0800 567123
www.bbc.co.uk/wales/comeclean/

Brook (sexual health advice for young people) 0800 0185 023
www.brook.org.uk/content/

Also check out:
> Celibacy
> Contraception
> Making Love
> Sex Essentials
> HIV & AIDS
> Safe Sex

Alternative medicine (also known as complementary medicine is a term used to describe a wide range of therapies that differ from typical medical practices. These are the most common types of therapy:

Acupuncture – fine needles are inserted into the skin to balance the body's energy

Herbal Medicine – the use of plants to treat illness

Homeopathy – small doses of drugs specially prepared to treat illnesses and conditions

Osteopathy/Chiropractic – (also known as manipulation) – use of the hands to help muscle and joint problems

Reflexology – Massage of reflex points on the feet to help various ailments

Alternative medicine attempts to concentrate on the individual as a whole, rather than on a specific problem. This means that practitioners look at your lifestyle, diet, environment and your emotional health. At the moment, little scientific research into alternative medicine has taken place so it's not known how well it works. However, more and more people seem to be benefiting from alternative medicine. A small amount of alternative medicine is carried out by the NHS and some GPs may recommend it. However, the majority of alternative medicine is carried out by private practices. Most private practices have codes of conduct that regulate how they work and ensure safe practice. If you are considering using alternative medicine, check out your practitioner first. Make sure they are registered, that they provide good advice and support and that you trust them.

The Institute for Complementary Medicine
0207 237 5165 www.i-c-m.org.uk

The British Complementary Medicine Association 0845 345 5977
www.bcma.co.uk

BBC Health page on complementary medicine
www.bbc.co.uk/health/healthy_living/complementary_medicine/

Also check out:

- Allergies
- Asthma
- Eczema
- Hay Fever
- Doctors
- Health Service

Your doctor should always be the first port of call for any matters that you have relating to your health. They'll be able to provide treatment, advice, support, information and will have the knowledge to refer you to the right person or organisation if necessary. You need to book an appointment before you go, unless it's an emergency, in which case you should dial 999. Different practices have different rules on booking appointments. Some may ask you to phone them on the same day as your appointment whereas others may accept advance bookings. Some practices may run at the weekend and some won't but all practices offer 24 hour service, in some form. You can also call NHS Direct on 0845 46 47 for medical advice. Until you're 16, you'll be registered with a GP by your parents. However, if you wish, you can ask for confidential appointments with GPs. If they consider you mature enough, your GP will let you make your own decisions on medical treatment. If not, they'll consult with your parents or guardian. Once you're 16 you can choose your own GP and make your own medical choices, including changing your GP for any reason. In Wales, under-25s are entitled to free prescriptions.

Citizens Advice Bureau (has information on doctors and medical treatment)
www.adviceguide.org.uk

NHS Direct
0845 46 47
www.nhsdirect.nhs.uk

The Department of Health
0207 210 4850
www.dh.gov.uk/Home/fs/en

Also check out:
> First Aid Essentials
> Counselling
> Alternative Medicine
> Emergencies
> Health Service
> Patients' Rights

Currently there is an urgent need for organ donors in the UK. Every year hundreds of people die whilst waiting for a suitable donor. Donating organs and tissue can help seriously ill people live longer, healthier lives. To become an organ donor, you need to register with the NHS Organ Donor Register. You'll get an organ donor card and can choose which organs and tissues you wish to donate (from your heart, lungs, kidneys, pancreas, liver, small bowels, corneas, skin, bone and heart valves). If you're under 16, you'll need to have parental consent and to understand exactly what's involved to become an organ donor. You should also tell your close relatives of your wishes as medical professionals will usually consult relatives to find out your most current wishes before removing organs. You can also donate whilst you're alive – the most commonly donated organ being the kidney. You can also donate blood. You can do it up to three times a year, it's safe, doesn't hurt (you might feel a bit woozy for a bit but there's nothing to worry about) and your body naturally replaces your blood within days. The National Blood Service has units that travel around the country - look out for posters advertising local sessions (see www.blood.co.uk for more details). If you wish to leave your body for medical research, you can make arrangements by contacting the HM Inspector of Anatomy.

How to become an organ donor
0845 6060 400
www.uktransplant.org.uk/ukt/how_to_become_a_donor/how_to_become_a_donor.jsp

British Organ Donor Society
01223 893636
http://body.orpheusweb.co.uk

The National Blood Service
08457 711 711
www.blood.co.uk

Her Majesty's Inspector of Anatomy
www.dh.gov.uk/PolicyAndGuidance/HealthAndSocialCareTopics/HMAnatomy/fs/en

Also check out:
> Losing A Loved One
> Doctors
> Emergencies
> Health Service
> Patients' Rights
> Death & Wills

Would you know what to do in an emergency situation? Would your mates or family?

In an emergency call 999 or 112. They'll ask 'which service?' you then tell them if you want the police, fire brigade or ambulance service. Dial 999 or 112 only in the event of a real emergency. Hoax calls cost lives and money and can get you fined.

Many hospitals have a 24-hour A & E (Accident and Emergency) department. Check out the Yellow Pages (www.yell.com) for the number of your local hospital A & E unit just in case.

Drug-use by young people throughout Wales is a problem. Would you know what to do if your mate collapsed? Make sure they have plenty of cool, fresh air. Don't frighten them in any way. Don't throw water over them. Turn them on their side and put them in the recovery position. Ring 999 for an ambulance crew.

Do you know how to put someone in the recovery position? Contact the British Red Cross or St John's Ambulance for info on First Aid courses.

999 Where are you? (how to be sure that the emergency services can find you)
www.999whereareyou.org

The UK Police Service
www.police.uk

The Welsh Ambulance Service
www.was-tr.wales.nhs.uk

List of UK fire services
www.fireservice.co.uk/information/offcontacts.php

Also check out:

- First Aid Essentials
- Drugs
- Donor Services
- Health Service
- Patients Rights

If you experience a problem with your eyes, the important thing is to get it checked out as soon as possible. You may not like the idea of wearing glasses or contact lenses but, if you're having vision problems, they'll only get worse if you don't get tested. Under-16s, under-19s in full-time education, those with certain eye conditions, those who claim certain Government benefits and those who are prescribed complex lenses can get free eye tests and vouchers for glasses on the NHS. You can use your voucher at any opticians. After the age of 16, you'll have to pay for eye tests and glasses from your opticians. As well as glasses, contact lenses can correct vision. There are many types of contact lens. Some are permanent and some get replaced every day. Some need special cleaning treatments and others don't. Some are hard and some are soft. Speak to your opticians for advice and further information. Laser surgery is also becoming more popular but there are concerns over the safety of it. It's a procedure that uses a laser to correct your vision so you'll no longer need to wear glasses or contact lenses. It can also be very expensive and is not generally available through the NHS. If you are thinking of having laser eye correction, thoroughly check the credentials and history of the centre or person carrying out the treatment.

NHS page on how to find your nearest optician
www.nhs.uk/England/Opticians/Default.aspx

NHS Direct 0845 46 47
www.nhsdirect.nhs.uk

The Eyecare Trust (charity raising awareness of eye care issues) 0845 129 5001
www.eye-care.org.uk

Royal National Institute for the Blind (RNIB) 0845 766 9999
www.rnib.org.uk/xpedio/groups/public/documents/code/InternetHome.hcsp

Also check out:

- Diabetes
- Headaches
- Looking Your Best
- Health Service
- Doctors
- Teeth

Funded by the Government through taxes, the National Health Service (NHS) is a free service to all people in Wales. They provide health care through general practitioners (GPs), opticians, dentists, pharmacists, hospitals with a wide range of specialist healthcare professionals, the ambulance service and mobile units, providing health care in the community. As well as the traditional services offered by the NHS, they also provide help, information and support in other areas such as counselling and alternative medicine. Basically, if you have any issues with your physical or emotional health, you should approach your GP first. If they can't help you, they'll be able to point you in the right direction, at the very least. There are some things that the NHS charges a fee for such as prescriptions, dental treatment and sight tests. However, in Wales, many people (including under-25s, those on benefits) are entitled to financial help with NHS charges. If you think you may be entitled to help, just ask your GP. The NHS also provides an online and telephone service called NHS Direct, which can provide information on a wide variety of health issues. If you have a problem or question that you think doesn't require an appointment with your GP, phone them on 0845 46 47 or go online at http://www.nhsdirect.nhs.uk/.

NHS Wales
www.wales.nhs.uk

NHS Direct
0845 46 47
www.nhsdirect.nhs.uk

Government website on your local doctor
www.direct.gov.uk/HealthAndWellBeing/HealthServices/fs/en

Citizens Advice Bureau (includes information on health and the NHS)
www.adviceguide.org.uk

Also check out:

> First Aid Essentials
> Counselling
> Alternative Medicine
> Doctors
> Emergencies
> Injections and Immunisations
> Patients' Rights

The human body has the ability to defend itself from infections, viruses and diseases but sometimes it needs a helping hand. Immunisation (or vaccination) is a process by which the body is helped to fight illness. The most common type of immunisation is done by injecting drugs into the body, although some immunisations are given through oral medication. It's important to be immunised against some diseases for a number of reasons. Some diseases have been wiped out completely and immunisation helps to stop their return. It also helps outbreaks of diseases within the community and helps to stop diseases coming into the country from other parts of the world where they are more common. Most immunisation is given during childhood. Amongst others, you'll be protected from diphtheria, tetanus, measles, mumps and rubella. When travelling abroad to certain countries, you'll need to get immunisation. You may be protected for a certain period of time or for life. As well as administering the vaccination, your GP will give you advice and information on what you'll need. Immunisation is also given to certain people in specific circumstances. For example, those aged over 60 are offered a flu 'jab' and those at risk of other infections (such as health workers) can be immunised against many diseases.

NHS Direct page on immunisation
0845 46 47
www.nhsdirect.nhs.uk/en.aspx?articleID=208

More detailed NHS immunisation information
www.immunisation.nhs.uk

Foreign and Commonwealth Office travel advice
www.fco.gov.uk/travel

Citizens Advice Bureau
www.adviceguide.org.uk

Also check out:
> Travel Essentials
> Babies
> Children
> Meningitis
> Doctors
> Health Service

As a patient, under the Health and Social Care Guide for Wales, you are entitled to certain rights from the NHS. Here are some of the most important ones:

- You have a right to be registered with a GP and to receive treatment from them
- Your GP must ensure that some kind of 24 hour service is available for patients
- You can change your GP at any time, without reason
- Hospitals are only obliged to treat you if you've been referred to them by your GP, if it's an emergency or if you're visiting a special clinic such as a GUM clinic
- Certain people (such as under 25s and those on benefits) are entitled to discounts from prescriptions and other medical services
- Pregnant women are entitled to a range of services and care programmes
- The NHS have maximum waiting times for treatment
- Medical examination, treatment and research all need your consent except under certain rare circumstances
- You have the right to refuse treatment
- You are entitled to see most of your health records
- When in hospital, you are allowed to receive visitors during certain periods

The Health and Social Care Guide for Wales
www.wales.nhs.uk/documents/4decH&ScareGuide.pdf

Citizens Advice Bureau page on NHS patients rights
www.adviceguide.org.uk/wales.htm

NHS Direct 0845 46 47
www.nhsdirect.nhs.uk

BBC page on patients rights
www.bbc.co.uk/dna/actionnetwork/C2108

Also check out:
> Counselling
> Doctors
> Donor Services
> Emergencies
> Health Service
> Injections and Immunisations

Looking after your teeth should be an important part of your regular health routine. If not, you could end up with bad breath, yellow teeth, you might lose your teeth and you could get a painful dose of toothache or worse, you might need treatment for a more serious problem. You need to make sure you brush your teeth twice a day, using a toothpaste containing fluoride. Cutting down on sugary food and drink and not smoking helps too, as these can make dental problems worse. You should also make sure that you visit your dentist regularly. Many people have an irrational fear of dentists. Yes, their procedures may sometimes be a little unpleasant and uncomfortable but, they could spot something that, left untreated, could lead to something much worse than a simple check-up at the dentist. You should visit your dentist at least once a year and consider having your teeth cleaned by a hygienist. You can get a list of NHS dentists from your local health authority or NHS Direct (see Links). You do have to pay for dental treatment but some are entitled to free or discounted treatment. In Wales, you're entitled to free check-ups up until the age of 25 and free treatment to the age of 18. Others, such as those claiming benefits, may be entitled to reductions on the cost of dental treatment.

British Dental Health Foundation
0845 063 1188
www.dentalhealth.org.uk

NHS Wales' list of dentists in Wales
www.wales.nhs.uk/localservices.cfm?type=dentist&allwales=1

Ask the Dentist (free dental advice)
www.askthedentist.info

Channel 4 page on dental hygiene
www.channel4.com/life/microsites/0-9/10yy/teeth.html

Also check out:

- Kissing
- Smoking
- Alcohol
- Healthy Eating
- Looking Your Best
- Health Service

7. HOUSING

7.1 Leaving Home

Leaving home is a big step. Most leave home through choice – either to go to university, to live independently or with friends or partners. Some are forced to leave home (usually because of bad family relations or abuse in the home) and may end up homeless. Either way, it's a big decision that shouldn't be taken without a great deal of thought and much discussion with a close friend or family member. When you do leave the family home to go to a new home, don't expect things to be easy. Give it time and get used to a new way of living. With independence comes responsibility. You'll be expected to keep up payment of your rent or mortgage, bills and insurance. You might have to look after maintenance and you'll certainly have to contribute to keeping the house clean and tidy, shopping for food, cooking, and washing your clothes. It's a lot to take on, so take all the support you want but if you feel it's not needed, just say so politely. Running away from home is an even bigger decision to take as you'll probably have even less support than those leaving through choice. See section 7.6 Homelessness for further information.

Shelter Cymru
0808 800 4444
www.sheltercymru.org.uk

Connexions Direct advice on moving out of home
080 800 132 19
www.connexions-direct.com/index.cfm?pid=116&catalogueContentID=464

Citizens Advice Bureau page on young people and housing
www.adviceguide.org.uk/wales/family_parent/housing/young_people_and_housing.htm

NSPCC page on running away from home
0808 800 5000
www.nspcc.org.uk/html/Home/Needadvice/runningaway.htm

Also check out:

- Who with?
- Rent or Buy?
- Renting
- Home Essentials
- Homelessness Essentials
- Sleeping Rough
- Hostels & Supported Housing

7. HOUSING

When you're leaving home, one of the biggest decisions to take is whether you should rent or buy. Some people prefer to own their own property and see it as security or an investment. Others prefer the freedom of renting. If you don't have the money to buy (you'll probably need to pay an amount of money up front as a deposit) renting is an option.

If you think you can afford to buy a property, as well as your deposit, you need to be certain that you can afford to keep up your mortgage repayments. If you can't, you could find yourself in big trouble with mortgage companies able to take personal possessions or repossess your property as payment. You also need to consider if your property needs any work doing to it, if you'll need to buy furniture and equipment, like a fridge or a microwave, and other costs such as agency fees, taxes etc.

Fortunately, renting is a much more simple process. Remember, if you rent, the property does not belong to you. This means that you can't make changes to the property itself (such as painting, building work etc.) but it also means that any problems with the property are to be dealt with and paid for by the landlord or property agent. Renters still have a lot to think about, including agency fees, taxes, contract lengths and contents insurance.

BBC Watchdog guide to buying and renting
www.bbc.co.uk/watchdog/guides_to/buyingandrenting/

Citizens Advice Bureau page on housing in Wales
www.adviceguide.org.uk/wales/family_parent/housing.htm

Connexions Direct
www.connexions-direct.com

National Association of Estate Agents
01926 496800
www.naea.co.uk

Also check out:
- Renting
- Mortgage Options
- DIY
- Insurance
- Neighbours

7. HOUSING

7.1 Leaving Home

Where are you going to live and what kind of property are you going to live in?

Finding the right area to live in is not as simple as you might think. You need to do a bit of research before you go rushing into anything. Is the area a nice place to live? Is there much crime? How much do properties cost to buy or rent? What are the insurance prices like? How about the local amenities? Are there nearby shops and public transport routes? Is there a place for you car or bike? Can you get to your college, university or workplace? What will your neighbours be like? The more of these questions that you can answer before you move in, the better your choice will be.

You also need to consider what type of property you want to live in. Houses are great for a homely feel, getting to know your neighbours and often have gardens too (which you may or may not want!). Flats are good for city living, but it's unlikely you'll have a garden, you might have to climb flights and flights of stairs and you might find that it's harder to get to know your neighbours. Studio apartments (also called bedsits) are properties where everything (apart from your bathroom, which is separate and often shared with others) is in one room. Great for independent living but could get cramped and claustrophobic.

Britain.tv (guide to how to choose the right area to live in)
www.britain.tv/property_choosing_area.shtml

BBC property
www.bbc.co.uk/homes/property/

Also check out:

- Who with?
- Rent or Buy?
- Where to Look
- Insurance
- Neighbours
- Anti-Social Behaviour

7. HOUSING

Who are you going to live with and how long are you going to live there for?

So you're thinking about moving into a new home and there's a lot to think about. Like how long you'll be there and who you'll live with. If you're renting, most agencies offer one-year or six-month contracts, although some may be more flexible if you approach them. You'll be expected to stay in the property for the duration of the contract, although some agencies may let you break the contract midway through if you can find new tenants to replace you. You also need to be sure that you can afford to pay your rent for the length of the contract or else you could find yourself in hot water. If you're buying a property, you need to have a rough idea of how long you'll stay there. It could affect how much furniture and equipment (fridges, ovens etc.) you buy and you may not be able to sell it for the same or a better price later, depending on the market.

Deciding who to live with is a huge decision. You can never really know what someone will be like to live with until you've done it. Make sure it's someone you trust, know well and can talk openly and honestly with. Being able to discuss problems and issues with your housemates frankly will help your house remain harmonious.

Citizens Advice Bureau page on tenancy agreements
www.adviceguide.org.uk/wales/family_parent/housing/tenancy_agreements.htm

Channel 4's guide to renting
www.channel4.com/4homes/renting-2.html

Housepals (find a flatmate)
www.housepals.co.uk

Also check out:
> Friends
> Living Together
> Problems and Emotions
> Moving Essentials
> Renting
> Mortgage Options

Moving Essentials
7.2 Where to start?

People often say that moving house is one of the most stressful experiences that you can go through. There's an awful lot to think about when you move house so the key is to plan ahead. Have you got everything you need for your new home? You need to think about everything from cutlery to couches. Does it make more sense to buy the items you need once you've moved in, so that you don't have to transport them with the rest of your gear? Can you fit all of your belongings in a car or will you need to hire a van? Maybe you have so much stuff that you'll need to hire a removal company to do the hard work for you? If so, check with the company that you use if they provide insurance whilst your belongings are on the move. If you already have contents insurance, you'll need to check with your current company if they are covered whilst they are being moved. The actual move is something that you need to budget for before you commit to buying or renting a property. Make a plan, make lists, talk to friends or family who've moved before and do it all a long time in advance of your move. That way, you'll be prepared and you may avoid stressing out!

Help, I Am Moving (independent website offering advice for those moving house)
www.helpiammoving.com

Houseweb's guide to moving house
www.houseweb.co.uk/house/pros/moving/

Really Moving (a free UK service providing help to those moving house)
www.reallymoving.com

BBC Property
www.bbc.co.uk/homes/property/

Also check out:
- Who with?
- Where to?
- Rent or Buy?
- Where to look
- Insurance
- Budgeting Essentials

7.2 Where to start?

Whether you're looking to buy or rent a property, there are a whole host of places where you can find them on offer. Your first port of call should be your local estate agents. If you're buying, they'll have loads of property details on show in their windows and will probably have lists of further properties inside. Prospective renters should go into the estate agents and ask for the list of properties to rent. Usually, these lists will have descriptions of properties but no pictures. It's a great idea to look for properties over the Internet. Most estate agents have their own website, where they'll put property details and can usually feature a few photos too. You'll also find websites that compile properties from different estate agents. The Internet can save you time traipsing around agencies and you might find more information. However, it's worth remembering that Internet sites may not be continually updated so give the agency a call before you get excited. Most local newspapers have a property section too, with the majority dedicating a pull-out section once a week to it. Expect to find a small amount of information and usually a photograph as well. Try asking around friends, work colleagues and in shop windows or local notice boards for private property advertisements too.

BBC Watchdog guide to renting and buying
www.bbc.co.uk/watchdog/guides_to/

National Association of Estate Agents
01926 496800
www.naea.co.uk

Lease (The Leasehold Advisory Service)
0207 374 5380
www.lease-advice.org

Also check out:

- Where to?
- Rent or Buy?
- Moving Essentials
- Lodging
- Renting
- Mortgage Options

A lodger is a person who lives in a room in a house belonging to someone else, who also lives there at the same time. Lodging has benefits for both parties. Home owners get added income and lodgers get a room of their own, plus the use of facilities in the rest of the home. It might be that you lodge with family or friends or with someone you don't know. If it's with someone you do know, the details of your stay such as rent, house rules etc. can usually be agreed between you without need for a contract. If you're staying with someone you've never met, it's usually a good idea to get some kind of formal agreement, although it's not legally necessary. Only those who own their homes can take in a lodger. If you rent, you need to check with your landlord or estate agent first and they may not agree to it. The main advantage of lodging is its informal nature. As notice periods are shorter or rarely required, lodgers are usually free to leave when they wish (or they could be asked to leave). The major disadvantage of lodging is that you may not feel as though you are a fully fledged member of the household. Those taking in lodgers should let their insurers know beforehand, as it could affect the terms of their contract, leaving them uninsured.

The Rent-a-room scheme (tax-free scheme for those taking in lodgers)
www.direct.gov.uk/moneytaxandbenefits/taxes/taxonpropertyandrentalincome/

Government page on letting
www.direct.gov.uk/homeandcommunity/rentingandletting/

Shelter page on lodging
www.sheltercymru.org.uk

Also check out:
- Who with?
- Where to?
- Moving Essentials
- Bills
- Home Essentials
- Insurance

Renting a property is cheaper, easier and more flexible than buying one. You pay rent to an agency or landlord and, as the owners of the property, they look after it. As you have no financial investment in the property, you can (more or less) move on at will, as your situation changes. The disadvantage is that the money you pay is, essentially, lost, unlike when you buy a property and your money is invested.

Before you rent, find out:
What changes, if any, can you make to the property, i.e., decoration, maintenance etc?
How long is your contract and what period of notice do you (or your landlord) have to give before moving out?
Is it furnished, unfurnished or part-furnished?
How much is the deposit (bond) and on what conditions is it refundable (most will require that the property is left in the same condition as when you moved in)?
Who maintains the property, the landlord or the agency?
How much are agency fees and when will you have to pay them?
What references do your agency require?

Tips for tenants:
Before you move in, make sure your landlord or agency carries out a witnessed inventory.
If you have a maintenance issue or complaint, don't be afraid to make a nuisance of yourself to get something done.
Put major complaints in writing as proof, should you need it.
Read the contract before signing it.

Channel 4's guide to renting
www.channel4.com/4money/mortgages/features/guide_to_renting.html

Rentamatic
rentamatic.co.uk

Up My Street
www.upmystreet.com

Also check out:
> Where to?
> Rent or Buy?
> Where to Look
> Bills
> Neighbours

7.4 Buying a Home

When buying a house, you need to enlist the help of a solicitor in order to carry out what is known as conveyancing. This refers to all of the administration and legal work associated with the transfer of buildings and/or land between owners. It is not essential to hire a solicitor but conveyancing is complex work that requires legal training so most people cannot do it themselves. During the sale of a house, solicitors will contact the seller's solicitor and draw up, negotiate and check contracts and other forms. All solicitors can do conveyancing work but it might be best to go to a specialist firm. Your mortgage provider may be able to provide you with a list of recommended firms. The cost of a solicitor varies depending on the circumstances of your sale, the area you live in and the company itself. However, expect to pay at least £600 and at most £2,000 for solicitor's fees.

Government information on conveyancing and solicitors
www.direct.gov.uk/HomeAndCommunity/BuyingAndSellingYourHome/BuyingYourHome/BuyingArticles/fs/en?CONTENT_ID=4001326&chk=Mk9Zew

Law Society of England and Wales
0870 606 6575
www.lawsociety.org.uk/choosingandusing/findasolicitor.law

Citizen's Advice Bureau guide to buying a home
www.adviceguide.org.uk/index/family_parent/housing/buying_a_home.htm

BBC Homes property guide
www.bbc.co.uk/homes/property/

Also check out:

- Who with?
- Where to?
- Moving Essentials
- Mortgage Options
- Survey
- Legal Advice

A mortgage is a loan provided by a bank, building society or independent financial company to those needing money to buy a house. The amount must be paid back on a monthly basis with interest (either a fixed rate of interest or a variable one that depends on interest rates). The property acts as security on the loan so that, if the loan cannot be repaid, the lender can use the property to get back (recoup) their loss. Lenders usually offer a loan of three times the buyer's salary. Most mortgages can be split into one of two main types – repayment and interest-only mortgages. With a repayment mortgage, you will pay off both the capital and the interest on the mortgage. By the end of the term (usually 20 to 30 years), you will have paid off the whole amount. With interest-only mortgages, you only pay off the interest on the capital on a monthly basis. The remaining capital is then paid off in full at the end of the term. The idea is that you'll invest elsewhere to save the money to pay the capital off. There are several types of interest-only mortgage including flexible, 100%, endowment and pension-linked mortgages. Each one differs in the way that the money is paid back to the lender.

Explanation of the different types of mortgage
www.mortgages-options.co.uk/About/types.shtml

Council of Mortgage Lenders
0207 437 0075
www.cml.org.uk/cml/home

Financial Services Authority (FSA) (consumer information on mortgages)
0845 606 1234
www.fsa.gov.uk/consumer/07_MORTGAGES/

BBC guide to mortgages
www.bbc.co.uk/homes/property/moneyandlegal_mortgages.shtml

Also check out:
> Who with?
> Legal Advice
> Survey
> Budgeting Essentials
> Interest Rates & Inflation
> Investing

Getting a survey done on a house that you are considering buying is not compulsory but most people would agree that it is worth spending the money on one. Initially, your mortgage provider will survey the house to check that it is worth what you are paying (this is mandatory in order to get a mortgage). This survey doesn't go into great detail, which is why it is worth getting a further one. There are two other types of survey. The first (often called a Home Buyers Survey) is a reasonably thorough check, which should outline the possible threat of such things as subsidence and rising damp. The most thorough check available (often known as a Building Survey) is only really worth taking if there are obvious signs of problems, if the house is old or made of unusual materials. The Home Buyers Survey usually costs around £300 and the Building survey can cost up to £1,000. If the survey does throw up a new problem, you can then decide either to lower your offer or to withdraw from the sale completely. Either way, it's best to know what potential problems there are before committing yourself to what is likely to be the largest financial commitment of your life.

Royal Institution of Chartered Surveyors
0870 333 1600
www.rics.org/default

Citizens Advice Bureau (info. on buying a house)
www.adviceguide.org.uk/wales/family-parent/housing.htm

The Move Channel guide to buying a home
www.themovechannel.com/howto/buy/buying-overview.asp

Also check out:

> Who with?
> Where to?
> Moving Essentials
> Legal Advice
> Mortgage Options
> DIY
> Budgeting Essentials

Whether you're renting, buying or lodging, you'll still have bills to pay! Council tax, TV licence, electricity, gas, water, telephone, Internet and subscription TV – they all add up. Before you decide to move into a property, you need to do yourself a budget. And this should include bills. It's impossible to know for sure exactly how much you'll have to pay. Speak to friends, family, even the companies who'll be charging you to find out the average costs, add on a few pounds for safety and there you have it. Can you still afford to move in? If so, you need to be organised. When you move in, take any meter readings that you can and let the utility companies (water, electricity and gas) know that you've moved in. They'll set the ball rolling by sending you piles of forms and bills. Keep these filed in an organised, safe place then remain calm when you receive that incorrect, overcharged bill! If you're sharing, try and divide the burden between you so that each person is responsible for one set of bills. Then try and arrange regular meetings to sort out who owes what to whom. Finally, make sure you have the money in your account to pay and if you have problems, let the company know ASAP – they may be able to help.

Government website offering advice to those having trouble paying utility bills
www.direct.gov.uk/moneytaxandbenefits/managingdebt/

Channel 4's guide to organising bill-paying for students
www.channel4.com/4money/smartmoney/features/student_accommodation_010805_page6.html

Credit Action (money education charity)
0800 138 1111 www.creditaction.org.uk

Consumer Credit Counselling Service
0800 138 1111 www.cccs.co.uk

Citizens Advice Bureau page on energy efficiency and saving money
www.adviceguide.org.uk/wales/family_parent/housing/energy_efficiency.htm

Also check out:

> Who with?
> Lodging
> Home Essentials
> Insurance
> Budgeting Essentials
> Debt Essentials

DIY - Do it yourself! Some of you will, some of you won't. Doing up a new pad can be great fun or a pain. It can be a hands-on experience with amazing results or a living disaster. There are some excellent Internet sites and also loads of books and mags on the subject. You'll find basic DIY tips, as well as advice on larger projects, like customising furniture, room makeovers and paint effects. DIY also includes things like tiling, laying floors and wiring plugs.

Please get advice before doing anything you know nothing about, or you could end up having an accident or damaging your property beyond repair! Unless you know what you're doing, things such as electrics and plumbing are best left to the professionals.

You can certainly be creative with DIY. The best idea is to get a picture or a clear idea of what you want to achieve before you get started. Think about the space you have, colours, accessories and furniture. Dark colours make rooms look smaller, while white has the opposite effect and opens up a room. Planning with a scrapbook and scribbles is a good idea.

If you're renting, you MUST ask the landlord's permission before doing anything major! Remember that if you're a home owner and planning to sell your property then bright colour schemes may turn buyers off!

DIY Fix It (DIY tips)
www.diyfixit.co.uk

DIY Doctor (DIY help from qualified tradesmen)
www.diydoctor.org.uk/home.htm

BBC Home's DIY guide
www.bbc.co.uk/homes/diy/diy_guide/

Also check out:

> Modern Apprenticeships
> NVQs and GNVQs
> Who with?
> Where to?
> Rent or Buy?
> Survey

Having your own place gives you freedom but it also gives you responsibility. You (and anyone that you live with) are responsible for the payment of rent or your mortgage and bills (including council tax) and if you don't plan well enough to be able to meet these payments, you could be in big trouble. You could be kicked out, taken to court or have your house repossessed. If you own a TV, you'll need a TV licence. Annually, they cost £126.50 for colour TVs and £42 for black and white ones. Non-payment could result in a fine of up to £1,000. If you own your house, you have to have building insurance by law and whether you own or rent, having contents insurance is a sensible decision. If you own a property, you need to make sure it's kept in good condition. This requires regular maintenance and DIY. Tenants must make sure that all maintenance problems are reported and dealt with. Getting on with whomever you live with can be surprisingly difficult at times. Try to give your housemates space, respect their differences and if you have a problem, speak out rather than bottle it up. Finally, you need to find a way to cope with household chores. We all have our own way of doing this, but so long as the responsibility is shared equally, there should be no room for complaint.

TV Licensing
0870 241 6468
www.tvlicensing.co.uk/index.jsp

Citizens Advice Bureau page on insurance
www.adviceguide.org.uk/wales/your_world/consumer_affairs/insurance.htm

Government page on council tax
www.direct.gov.uk/moneytaxandbenefits/counciltax/fs/en

Also check out:
> Friends
> Living Together
> Who with?
> Bills
> DIY
> Insurance

If you're buying a house, your mortgage provider will insist that you have buildings insurance and an estate agent will not let you complete purchase on a property until you have valid documents. Your buildings insurance protects the actual physical structure of your house – basically, as long as it's attached to the ground, it's covered. You will be protected from things like weather damage, fire, vandalism and falling trees. Whether you own, rent, lodge or are in student accommodation it's a wise move to get your contents insured. Contents insurance covers everything in your property that isn't tied down such as your TV, furniture, washing machine etc. You will be covered against such things as theft, loss, fire and flood damage. You may also be covered against accidental damage but this is usually an optional extra on most insurance policies. Some policies can also cover your contents when they are away from the home. Most buildings and contents insurance policies are essentially the same but check with your insurance provider for the finer details. Paying out for insurance can seem like a drag. That is, until something goes wrong - then you'll be glad you paid up!

Your Mortgage
www.yourmortgage.co.uk

UK Insurance Directory
www.ukinsurancedirectory.com

Houseweb on Building Insurance
www.houseweb.co.uk/house/buy/insure/build.html

British Insurance Brokers' Association
0870 950 1790
www.biba.org.uk

BBC Watchdog guide to insurance
www.bbc.co.uk/watchdog/guides_to/insurance/

Also check out:
- Rent or Buy?
- Moving Essentials
- Renting
- Mortgage Options
- Home Essentials
- Budgeting Essentials

When you move into a new home, you immediately become a part of that community. You'r local community consists of all of the people that live in your local area. Each person has a role to play in their local community and it's down to you to decide exactly what that role is and how much difference you'll make to the community. There are a few basic things that everyone should do as part of their local community, no matter what. Respecting your fellow community members is the most important thing. This means letting others live in the way that they wish and if you have any complaints, making them through the official channels. You should not disturb others with unnecessary noise and you should respect your local environment by keeping it clean and free of vandalism and graffiti. You should also look out for your neighbours. If they're in trouble, help them out. If you spot a crime, report it to the police. If you want to, there are further ways to get involved such as local volunteering projects and if you really want to make a difference, you could try and become a local councillor.

Change Makers (encouraging young people to get active in their community)
01458 834767
www.changemakers.org.uk

BBC Action Network (help to make a difference in your neighbourhood)
www.bbc.co.uk/dna/actionnetwork/

Youth Justice Board (get involved as a volunteer) 0207 271 3033
www.youth-justice-board.gov.uk/youthjustice-board/gettingInvolved/

WRVS (volunteering charity)
www.wrvs.org.uk

Also check out:
- Volunteering UK
- Bin It!
- Local Government
- Citizenship
- Neighbours
- Vandalism & Graffiti

Everybody needs good neighbours. You might live half a mile from the nearest house or be surrounded by people above, below and side by side but we all need to get on with our neighbours. When you move in, try to meet as many of your neighbours as you can. You don't have to pop round and ask for a bowl of sugar or anything. In fact, all you really have to do is say "hi" and introduce yourself when you see them around. It's good to be able to recognise people in your neighbourhood as it helps everyone feel safer and gives a greater feeling of community. Being on good terms with your neighbours is also really handy for when you need favours. You might want to borrow tools or they might need your help fixing a fence. Either way, neighbours should be there to help out one another – in fact, you might find that your neighbours have skills or knowledge that could come in pretty handy. One of the main problems that neighbours can have with each other is noise. Respect your neighbours and keep noise at a reasonable level during acceptable hours of the day. If you have a problem with your neighbours, first of all, try approaching them voicing your concerns in a polite manner. If this doesn't work, contact the Citizens Advice Bureau to find out the right method of complaint.

Neighbours From Hell in Britain (positively managing negative neighbours)
www.nfh.org.uk

Citizens Advice Bureau
www.adviceguide.org.uk

Community Legal Service Direct page on Neighbourhood and community disputes
0845 3454 345
www.clsdirect.org.uk/legalhelp/leaflet30.jsp?lang=en

BBC page on dealing with nuisance neighbours
www.bbc.co.uk/dna/actionnetwork/A1174727

Also check out:

- Who with?
- Where to?
- Renting
- Home Essentials
- Local Communities
- Anti Social Behaviour

Some people choose not to live in a permanent home but instead live a nomadic lifestyle, moving from place to place. There are different types of travelling people. Gypsies are a recognised ethnic group, coming from a Romany background originating in Asia. Irish travellers are also a separate ethnic group and New Age travellers are a group of travelling people that came from the Free Festival Movement in the 1970's. People live nomadic lifestyles for a number of reasons. It may be part of family tradition or it might be a political or ideological decision (to 'opt out' of modern-day living). There is often opposition to the lifestyle of travelling people from the public and the Government. New laws have made it hard for travelling people to live the way they want to. Most live in caravans on authorised sites, provided by the local authority. However, many live on sites not belonging to them or sites established without planning permission. Most travellers make a living, usually from practical work such as tree-felling and gardening. The travelling lifestyle isn't for everyone. Some may thrive but others may find constantly moving on and having to deal with opposition difficult. There are many myths about travelling people. See links below for more information to find out what's true and what's not.

Liberty page on rights of gypsies and travellers
www.yourrights.org.uk/your-rights/chapters/rights-of-gypsies-and-travellers/

Commission for Racial Equality page on gypsies and travellers
02920 729 200
www.cre.gov.uk/gdpract/

Department for Communities and Local Governnment
0207 944 4400
www.odpm.gov.uk

New Age travellers in the UK
http://tash.gn.apc.org/trav1.htm

Also check out:

> Countryside
> Citizenship
> Culture
> Home
> Local Communities
> Discrimination Essentials

Homelessness can affect anyone, from any background and of any age. It doesn't only apply to those living on the street but to those with no fixed address. Homelessness can happen for a variety of reasons. It might be that someone cannot pay their rent or mortgage, it's dangerous to stay at home or someone may be evicted by their landlord. Becoming homeless can be a frightening experience but there is a lot of help available. The first thing to do is to register yourself as homeless and to get as much advice as you can. Organisations like Shelter and the Citizens Advice Bureau all provide professional advice and support on homelessness. To register as homeless, you need to speak to your local council. They will then try and find accommodation for you, depending on your individual circumstances and the reason for your homelessness. Young people (especially under-18s) are usually given some form of priority. Sleeping rough should be a last resort and should only be done if all other possibilities have been exhausted (see Sleeping Rough for details).

The Big Issue is an organisation that helps homeless people help themselves. The magazine is available to buy by the registered homeless and is then sold by them for a profit.

Shelter Cymru
0808 800 4444
www.sheltercymru.org.uk

Citizens Advice Bureau
www.adviceguide.org.uk

The Big Issue Cymru
0207 526 3252
www.bigissuecymru.co.uk

BBC One Life guide to homelessness
www.bbc.co.uk/radio1/onelife/housing/crisis/homeless.shtml

Also check out:
> Hostels & Supported Housing
> Sleeping Rough
> Benefits Essentials

For many homeless people, hostels or supported housing may be the only option. Supported housing tends to be for those staying for longer periods whereas hostels are usually more short-term. In many cases you may have to pay rent, but you may be able to claim benefit to help you. There are many types of hostel from shared houses and flats, to shared rooms and dormitories or emergency night shelters that simply provide a bed for the night. Whilst some hostels ask that you be referred to them from a homelessness agency to fill up their vacancies, many hostels now offer support and advice on homelessness and accommodate anyone. There are also short-stay and cold weather hostels that are free at certain times of the year. Contact Shelter Cymru for more advice. As facilities tend to differ between regions, speak to your local council to find out what is available in your area.

Supported housing and hostels are available in most areas for young people aged 16-25 and usually have facilities to help you find work. Projects differ, but usually provide affordable and safe accommodation, advice and/or training.

Shelter Cymru
0808 800 4444
www.sheltercymru.org.uk

Citizens Advice Bureau
www.adviceguide.org.uk

Centrepoint (charity for young homeless people) 0845 466 3400
www.centrepoint.org.uk

Nightstop UK (charity providing safe emergency accommodation for young people) 01274 533004
www.nightstop-uk.org

Also check out:

> Homelessness Essentials
> Leaving Home
> Sleeping Rough
> Benefits Essentials
> Who with?
> Where to?

Sleeping rough should only be done if all other possibilities of sleeping with a roof over your head have been exhausted. It should be an absolute last resort. If there really is no option, you need to be prepared for what could be a tough, dangerous experience. Not only are you at risk from the elements but also from criminals. Here's some guidance for those who sleep rough:

- Try and find a sleeping place sheltered from wind and rain where there are other people
- Never sleep directly on the floor – always try and lie on something to protect you, like cardboard boxes or newspapers
- Dress up warm, preferably wearing many layers
- Keep your head, feet and hands covered for maximum warmth
- Keep your valuables hidden
- Eat a hot meal every day and try to drink as many hot drinks as you can
- Avoid people who could be a threat or danger to you
- Never resort to alcohol or drugs for comfort. In the long run, they'll only make your problems worse

Crisis (national charity fighting homelessness) 0870 011 3335
www.crisis.org.uk

Shelter Cymru
www.sheltercymru.org.uk

Citizens Advice Bureau
www.adviceguide.org.uk/wales.htm

Centrepoint (charity for young homeless people) 0845 466 3400
www.centrepoint.org.uk

Nightstop UK (charity providing safe emergency accommodation for young people) 01274 533004
www.nightstop-uk.org

Also check out:
> Alcohol
> Drugs
> Homelessness Essentials
> Hostels and Supported
> Leaving Home
> Laws

8. LAW & RIGHTS

8.1 Law & Police

There are two types of law, criminal and civil. Break them and there are penalties and consequences. Criminal law lists what a 'crime' is and what the punishments are. If you're accused of a criminal offence and go to court, this is called a prosecution. If you're guilty you're convicted and become an offender. If you're not, you're free to go. From the age of 10 you're responsible enough to be charged with and convicted of a criminal offence and get a criminal record. Civil law deals with non-criminal areas of the law: your rights as a consumer, issues on marriage and divorce, housing rights etc. When a civil law is broken, you can take the person who broke it to court or sue them.Laws aren't set out to catch you out or restrict you, but to give you limits that maintain your human rights and keep you safe. You need to know and understand the law. You live in a society that puts a lot of emphasis on rights. Laws can be complicated and confusing, so check out the rest of this section for more information. Whether you feel the laws of our land are fair and just doesn't really count for much if you get caught breaking them!

contributed to and supported by Legal Services Commission

Citizens Advice Bureau page on Young People and the Law
www.adviceguide.org.uk/wales/your_rights/legal_system/young_people_and_the_law.htm

The Law Commission
0207 453 1220 www.lawcom.gov.uk

The Law Society
0207 242 1222 www.lawsociety.org.uk

Citizenship Foundation guide to legal rights and responsibilities in England and Wales
www.citizenshipfoundation.org.uk

Legal Services Commission leaflet on dealing with the police.
Leaflet line 0845 3000 345
www.clsdirect.org.uk/legalhelp/leaflet11.jsp?lang=en

Also check out:
> Employment Rights
> UK Parliament
> Police
> Arrested?
> Rights Essentials
> Youth Crime

The Police are a vital workforce that keep law and order in this country. Police officers can work in a variety of settings: they may work in an office, in a Police station or on the street (using cars, bikes or on foot). Being a Police officer is about more than just arresting people. They may help to control crowds, deal with traffic incidents, act as a reassuring presence on the street and provide advice to those in need also. Remember, the Police are there to help, not hinder, the public. Treat them with respect and they will do the same for you. If you need to contact the Police in an emergency, dial 999. If it is not an emergency, the number of your local Police force will be in your Yellow Pages or phone-book. Police staff also have to operate within many rules and regulations. The Police and Criminal Evidence Act 1984 is the main law on Police powers. There is also a document, known as 'the Codes of Practice', which details what the Police can and can't do when searching, arresting and detaining. If the Police do not follow the codes of practice, they may be taken to court.

contributed to and supported by Legal Services Commission

The UK Police Service homepage
www.police.uk

Police Recruitment page
www.policecouldyou.co.uk/default.asp?action=article&ID=1

Independent Police Complaints Commission
08543 002 002
www.ipcc.gov.uk

Citizens Advice Bureau page on young people and the law in Wales
www.adviceguide.org.uk/wales/your_rights/legal_system/young_people_and_the_law.htm

Legal Services Commission leaflet on dealing with the police.
www.clsdirect.org.uk/legalhelp/leaflet11.jsp?lang=en **Leaflet line** 0845 3000 345

Also check out:
- Laws
- Arrested?
- Rights Essentials
- Stop and Search
- Street Crime & Violence
- Legal Advice

Arrested?
8.2 Your Legal Rights

If you have been arrested, you need to know your rights. Here's a list of the most important ones:

- You have the right to let one person know that you have been arrested.
- You have the right to speak with a solicitor in private (if you can't afford it, one will be provided).
- You have a right to look at Police codes of practice.
- You cannot normally be held for more than 24 hours without charge, unless special permission is given by a magistrate.
- The Police must caution you, if possible, as soon as you have been arrested.
- You should be taken to a Police station as soon as possible.
- You should be given a written notice of your rights once you are in the Police station.
- You do have the right to silence but, if your case goes to court, it could count against you.
- If you are aged under-17, you cannot be interviewed by the Police without the presence of an appropriate adult (usually a parent or guardian).
- There are also rules that govern the questioning process such as regular breaks, food etc. If you wish to see them, just ask at the Police station.

contributed to and supported by Legal Services Commission

Citizens Advice Bureau page on police powers
www.adviceguide.org.uk/wales/your-rights/legal-system.htm

Urban 75 (guide to your rights on arrest)
www.urban75.org/legal/rights.html

The Liberty Guide to Human Rights
www.yourrights.org.uk

The Site's guide to rights on arrest
www.thesite.org.uk/homelawandmoney/law/introuble/rightsonarrest

Children's Legal Centre 0845 456 6811
www.childrenslegalcentre.com

Also check out:
> Employment Rights
> UK Parliament
> Police
> Rights Essentials
> Youth Crime

Bail

Once you have been charged with an offence, the Police may release you on bail. There are two types of bail – conditional and unconditional. If you're released on conditional bail, you'll have to commit to certain conditions like reporting into the Police station regularly, a curfew, remaining within a certain area or you may even be electronically tagged. Unconditional bail means that you have to appear at court on a set date but don't have to do anything else until then. You won't be released on bail if the Police believe that you may be a danger to yourself or others, that you may interfere with witnesses, if they doubt your given name and address or if they think you won't turn up in court. The conditions of your bail can be changed if you apply to the Magistrates' Court. They may change them or add conditions such as a financial bond to guarantee that you appear in court. If you do not conform to the conditions of your bail or appear in court on the specified date, you have breached your bail. This is a prosecutable offence in itself and can lead to arrest, you could be remanded in custody and you are likely to be refused bail in future.

contributed to and supported by Legal Services Commission

Youth Justice Board for England and Wales 0207 271 3033
www.youth-justice-board.gov.uk/YouthJusticeBoard/

Criminal Justice System for England and Wales www.cjsonline.gov.uk

The Liberty Guide to Human Rights
www.yourrights.org.uk

Police information on bail
www.police-information.co.uk/legislation/legislationindexeng.html#B

Legal Services Commission
www.legalservices.gov.uk

The Community Legal Service
www.clsdirect.org.uk

Also check out:
- Arrested?
- Rights Essentials
- Human Rights
- Police
- Remand
- Youth Court

Whenever you buy goods you enter into a contract with the seller, you become a consumer and have rights. The law that details your consumer rights is the Sale of Goods Act 1979. The three main points are that when you buy goods, they are of 'satisfactory quality', they are 'as described' and they are fit for their purpose. If your purchase fails on any of these counts, you have the right to demand your money back from the seller. You are not entitled to anything if you simply change your mind about buying the product, were told about a fault beforehand, if a fault was obvious and should have been noticed or if you caused damage yourself. Traders also have to ensure that products are safe to use. If not and they cause damage, you could claim compensation. Those who shop from home have the right to see clear product information before purchase, can cancel an order within five days of making it and can claim a refund if the product hasn't arrived within 30 days or another agreed period. You should be extra careful when buying goods through an auction as the seller doesn't have to accept responsibility for their goods, so make sure you get clear, detailed information before you part with your cash.

contributed to and supported by Legal Services Commission

Trading Standards Central
www.tradingstandards.gov.uk

Consumer Direct
08454 04 05 06
www.tradingstandards.gov.uk

Citizens Advice Bureau page on Consumer Affairs in Wales
www.adviceguide.org.uk/wales/your_world/consumer_affairs.htm

Government page on consumer rights
www.direct.gov.uk/rightsandresponsibilities/rightsandresponsibilitiesarticles/fs/en?content_id=10015892&chk=l8hfa1

Legal Services Commission leaflet – problems with goods and services.
www.clsdirect.gov.uk/legalhelp/leaflet13.jsp?lang=en **Leaflet line 0845 3000 345**

Also check out:
> Consumer Labelling
> Rights Essentials
> Legal Advice
> Online Shopping
> Shopping
> Fraud

We all deserve to be treated like humans. This means that we each have certain rights that we can demand and that others can expect from us. These are our human rights. In Britain, the law that details our human rights is the Human Rights Act 1998, which incorporates the European Convention on Human Rights. In general, the term 'human rights' refers to things like the right to life, freedom and dignity. It also covers torture, slavery and forced labour, fair trials, respect for private and family life, freedom of thought, conscience and religion, freedom of expression, freedom of assembly and association, the right to marry, discrimination, property, education and free elections. As well as the law, which protects our human rights, there are also many organisations that look out for abuses of human rights and campaign for more rights around the world. The most well known human rights campaigners are Amnesty International and Liberty. If you think that your human rights have been breached, you need to seek legal advice. You can take a person or an authority to court to get your case heard. If the courts in this country do not help satisfactorily, you may need to take your case to the European Court in Strasbourg.

contributed to and supported by Legal Services Commission

Human Rights Watch
0207 713 1995 www.hrw.org

Amnesty International
0207 033 1500 www.amnesty.org

Department for Constitutional Affairs, Human Rights Unit pages 0207 210 8614
www.humanrights.gov.uk

Liberty page on human rights
0207 403 3888 www.liberty-human-rights.org.uk

Legal Services Commission
www.legalservices.gov.uk

Legal Services Commission. Leaflet on Human Rights. www.clsdirect.gov.uk/legal-help/leaflet07.jsp?lang=en
Leaflet line 0845 3000 343

Also check out:
> Poverty
> Terrorism
> United Nations
> Laws
> Rights Essentials
> Legal Advice

8.2 Your Legal Rights

In almost every aspect of your life, you are entitled to certain rights. This doesn't mean that you have the right to do anything you like but that you can expect to be treated in a certain way that is governed by UK, European and International law. Our rights are looked after in this country by the Government and the Police force, as they are able to get involved in possible rights disputes. From walking down the street to buying a car to being arrested, you have rights. Be aware of what your rights are and then you won't get taken for a ride. If you think your rights may have been violated, contact the Citizens Advice Bureau, find out if they have and if so, what you can do about it. As well as having your own rights, remember that we all have the same rights so be respectful of others and don't deny them the rights that you expect. Human rights do change over Europe and the rest of the world but there are basic rights that must countries grant their citizens and visitors to their countries. Where human rights violations may occur, there are many organisations such as Amnesty International and Liberty who fight for the preservation of human rights.

contributed to and supported by Legal Services Commission

Citizens Advice Bureau
www.citizenadvice.org.uk

Amnesty International
0207 033 1500
www.amnesty.org

Liberty
0207 403 3888
www.liberty-human-rights.org.uk

National Assembly for Wales page on Human Rights
02920 825 111
www.wales.gov.uk/subihumanrights/

Also check out:
> Laws
> Police
> Arrested?
> Human Rights
> Discrimination
Essentials
> Legal Advice

If a Police officer has reasonable grounds for suspicion, they are able to stop and search you or your vehicle. The most likely reason to do this would be if they suspected you of carrying stolen goods, drugs or weapons. The suspicion of a Police officer must not be based on race, age, gender, clothing etc. This would be classed as discrimination. Before you are searched you should be informed of the Police officer's name and station, the grounds for the search and you should be shown proof of identity by the Police officer (uniformed Police officers are not legally obliged to show ID but, if asked, they probably will). Police are only allowed to search outer clothing. They are not able to force you to remove any items of clothing but they may ask you to do so. It is possible for a more thorough search (though not an intimate one) to take place in private, i.e. in a Police van. Searches must be carried out by members of the same sex and not in front of anyone of the opposite sex. To search your house, the Police will usually need a warrant but they can search without one under certain circumstances. If property is taken from you it must be listed while you're there. You then have to sign to say that the Police have taken the items listed.

contributed to and supported by Legal Services Commission

Liberty Guide to Human Rights
0845 123 2307 www.yourrights.org.uk

Police Authorities Association guidelines on stop and search 0207 664 3096
www.apa.police.uk/apa/features/stop+and+search/stop+and+search.htm

Home Office information on stop and search 0207 035 4848
www.homeoffice.gov.uk/police/powers/stop-and-search/

Citizens Advice Bureau
www.adviceguide.co.uk

Legal Services Commission. Leaflet on dealing with the police 0845 3000 345
www.clsdirect.org.uk/legalhelp/leaflet11.jsp?lang=en

Also check out:
- Police
- Laws
- Arrested?
- Bail
- Rights Essentials
- Remand

Child abduction is something that is currently on the increase in Britain. It most commonly occurs when a parent who is no longer legally in care of their child takes the law into their own hands and takes the child to live with them without permission. Abduction also known as kidnapping - is both a criminal and a civil offence and can result in a prison sentence. The effects of abduction can be varying. For the person who is abducted it depends on the experience that they have. It is possible that the experience may be traumatic but it is also possible that no harm may occur as a result of it. The abduction of a child will also have an effect on the parent left without the child. They may focus their efforts into legally regaining care of their child or they may find that they become depressed or angry because of it. If you have been the victim of abduction or have been taken without consent, it is important to know that the courts will work to do whatever is best for you. There are also plenty of organisations providing help and advice to the victims of abduction.

contributed to and supported by Legal Services Commission

Reunite (advice and information on child abduction) 0116 2556 234
www.reunite.org/page.php?alias=newabout00

National Missing Persons Helpline
0500 700 700
www.missingpersons.org

Foreign and Commonwealth Office (advice on child abduction whilst travelling abroad)
www.fco.gov.uk/servlet/Front?pagename=OpenMarket/Xcelerate/ShowPage&c=Page&cid=1094234677305

Channel 4 article on parental child abduction
www.channel4.com/health/microsites/F/family/rights/abduction.html

Also check out:
> Care
> Divorce
> Culture
> Laws
> Police
> Personal Safety

Within your community, each person behaves differently and, usually, your behaviour has an effect on those around you. Anti-social behaviour is behaviour in a manner that causes harassment, alarm or distress to one or more persons not of the same household. Types of anti-social behaviour are begging, intimidation and harassment, vandalism, noise, hoax calls, street prostitution and rowdy behaviour. If you are the victim of anti-social behaviour, you can do something about it. Make a note of each incident that occurs and inform your local Anti-Social Behaviour (ASB) co-ordinator (find your local ASB co-ordinator on the Together website, below). ASB co-ordinators can then intervene and try to resolve the problem. They may use warning letters, interviews, contracts and agreements, penalty notices or other orders or Anti-Social Behaviour Orders (ASBOs), which can ban people from certain activities or areas. If an ASBO is breached, it could lead to a prison sentence. It's important to tackle anti-social behaviour seriously to let the perpetrators know that their actions are unacceptable. Behaving anti-socially can cause much distress and alarm to those around you and, in some cases, can cause much disruption within a community. Respect your fellow citizens and treat them in the way that you would wish to be treated yourself.

contributed to and supported by Legal Services Commission

Together, tackling anti-social behaviour (find your local ASB co-ordinator here) www.together.gov.uk

Crime Reduction 0870 000 4848 www.crimereduction.gov.uk/toolkits/as00.htm

Home Office page on anti-social behaviour 0207 035 4848 www.homeoffice.gov.uk/anti-social-behaviour/

Youth Justice Board page on anti-social behaviour www.youth-justice-board.gov.uk/PractitionersPortal/PreventionAndInterventions/AntiSocialBehaviour/

Also check out:
> Arguments
> Harassment
> Crime Prevention
> Joy Riding
> Street Crime & Violence
> Vandalism & Graffiti

Crime Prevention & Personal Safety
8.3 Crime

Crime is an everyday part of our society. It happens and it probably always will, but you can do your bit to help reduce crime. If you witness a crime, report it. Know the phone number of your local Police station or dial 999 in an emergency. If you witness a crime, it's not always sensible to intervene. Judge the situation for yourself and if you think it's too dangerous to get involved then walk away and contact the police. If you think it's safe to try stop a crime being committed, get involved and do your bit for your community. Personal safety is an important part of crime prevention. By sticking to certain rules you can reduce the chances of being the victim of crime. When you're out, remain aware, keep your hands by your side and your bags, mobile phones, i-pods etc. hidden or close to your body. Stick to well-lit roads and paths, avoiding dark alleys, short-cuts etc. if possible. Always tell someone where you'll be and when. If necessary, carry a personal attack alarm, wear sensible footwear (better for running in!) and take a self-defence course, in case of attack.

contributed to and supported by Legal Services Commission

Crime Reduction page on personal safety
www.crimereduction.gov.uk/personalsafety.htm

The Suzy Lamplugh Trust (personal safety charity)
0208 876 0891
www.suzylamplugh.org

BBC page on crime prevention
www.bbc.co.uk/crime/prevention/

Government pages on crime prevention
www.direct.gov.uk/crimejusticeandthelaw/crimeprevention/fs/en

Also check out:

> Police
> Street Crime & Violence
> Theft
> Vandalism and Graffiti
> Victims
> Witnesses

Domestic violence is when one partner in a relationship is violent towards the other. Violence can be both physical and verbal. Physical violence can take the form of punching, slapping, kicking, sexual abuse and restraining. In some cases, domestic abuse has led to rape or even murder. Emotional abuse can be just as damaging. Threats, harassment, restrictions on who a person can see, where they can go, what they can wear and what they can do, blackmail and verbal abuse are all forms of domestic violence. Usually, those who carry out domestic violence use a combination of both physical and verbal abuse. Most domestic abuse is carried out by men against women. However, domestic abuse by women against men and abuse in same sex relationships also happens. Victims of domestic violence should never feel ashamed of their plight and should always try to find a way out of their situation. There are many groups and organisations that can help those in abusive relationships. They can take steps to stop the abuse or can help a victim leave their abusive partner. No person in a relationship should ever feel scared of their partner or tolerate any kind of abuse.

contributed to and supported by Legal Services Commission

Women's Aid
0808 2000 247 www.womensaid.org.uk

Campaign Against Domestic Abuse
0208 520 5881 www.cadv.org.uk

Refuge
0808 2000 247 www.refuge.org.uk

Mankind (helping male victims of domestic violence) 0870 794 4124
www.mankind.org.uk

Legal Services Commission. Leaflet on Domestic Violence, Abuse and Harassment. 0800 3000 345
www.clsdirect.org.uk/legalhelp/leaflet26.jsp?lang=en

Also check out:
- Arguments
- Harassment
- Problems & Emotions
- Family & Relationships
- Splitting Up
- Police

There are many types of driving offences, each with their own punishment. Many offences are punished by having points placed on your licence. The number of points given increases with the seriousness of the offence. Your licence will show how many points you have, what offence you committed and when you did so. Reach more than 12 points during a three year period and you'll be automatically disqualified from driving. Most offences also are punished with a fixed penalty notice, which is a fine of £30 (minimum) but can be much higher, depending on the offence. Some offences can mean disqualification or worse, a prison sentence, so stick to the rules! Here are some of the most common offences and the possible number of points that may be handed out as punishment. Remember though that there are many more offences than listed below and that, as well as points, you may be given a much harsher penalty.

Speeding: 3-6 points
Driving without a licence/tax/insurance/MOT: 3-8 points
Dangerous driving: 3-11 points
Hit and run: 5-10 points
Drink/drug driving: 3-11 points
No seatbelt/broken headlight etc: 3 points

contributed to and supported by Legal Services Commission

The Crown Prosecution Service page on driving offences
www.cps.gov.uk/legal/section9/chapter_b.html

Department for Transport page on Road Safety 0207 944 8300
www.dft.gov.uk/stellent/groups/dft_rdsafety/documents/sectionhomepage/dft_rdsafety_page.hcsp

Driving and Vehicle Licensing Agency
0870 240 0009 www.dvla.gov.uk

Law on the Web page on motoring offences
www.lawontheweb.co.uk/motoringoffences.htm

Also check out:

> Driving Essentials
> Motorbikes, Mopeds and Scooters
> Laws
> Police
> Rights Essentials
> Crime Prevention

Drug Crime

UK law divides drugs up into three categories – A, B and C - with Class A drugs deemed to be the most harmful and Class C, the least. Class A drugs include Heroin, LSD, Ecstasy and prepared Magic Mushrooms, Class B drugs include amphetamines and barbiturates and Class C drugs include Cannabis and tranquilisers. The most common drug offences are for possession of a drug (you have the drug on you or knowingly possess it) and supply (you've an amount of drugs in your control that suggest you are supplying others or if you're caught passing drugs to others). You can also be prosecuted for driving whilst under the influence of drugs, allowing your home to be used for drug-taking and production of a drug. The punishments for drug offences vary, ranging from a fine to life imprisonment, depending on the class of drug, the amount involved, the offence committed and the number of times that you've been caught by the Police. Although Cannabis has been downgraded to a Class C drug, it is still illegal to smoke, possess or deal Cannabis and you can still be arrested, especially if you're under 17, near a school, smoking in public or are caught repeatedly. Police can stop and search you if they have reasonable grounds to suggest that you have committed a drug offence.

contributed to and supported by Legal Services Commission

Drugscope
0207 928 1211
www.drugscope.org.uk

The Home Office page on UK drug laws
0207 035 4848
www.drugs.gov.uk/drugs-laws/

Talk To Frank
0800 77 66 00
www.talktofrank.com

Release (drugs, the law and human rights)
0845 4500 215
www.release.org.uk

Community Legal Service Directory
www.clsdirect.org.uk

Also check out:

- Drugs Essentials
- Police
- Arrested?
- Legal Advice
- Stop and Search
- Rights Essentials

Fraud is a term used to describe a process in which personal gain is made using deception. In British law, the word 'fraud' is a catch-all term for many different types of fraudulent practice. These can include identity theft (where someone steals your personal details and uses them for their own, usually financial, gain), false advertising (where companies or individuals lie about what they are selling in order to generate interest), forgery (copying of documents such as passports etc.) and false insurance claims (pretending that you've made an insurable loss in order to falsely claim an insurance payout). You should be aware of what constitutes fraud as the law will punish those found guilty of it. For example, it's easy to fall foul of benefit fraud and copyright laws (including unauthorised copying such as downloading and CD duplication). It's also essential to be vigilant of others who may be practising fraud. For example, you need to keep your important items, such as passports and cash cards, safe to stop them from being stolen and used fraudulently. Internet fraud has also become common recently so make sure never to enter any financial or secret information unless you are on a secure website.

contributed to and supported by Legal Services Commission

Serious Fraud Office
0207 239 7272
www.sfo.gov.uk

Targeting Benefit Fraud
0800 854 440
www.targetingbenefitfraud.gov.uk

CIFAS (Fraud Prevention Service)
www.cifas.org.uk

Home Office Identity Fraud page
www.identity-theft.org.uk

Community Legal Service Directory
www.clsdirect.org.uk

Also check out:

> Passports & Visas
> Benefits Essentials
> Crime Prevention & Personal Safety
> Consumer Rights
> Online Shopping
> Legal Advice

Murder & Manslaughter
8.3 Crime

Murder and manslaughter are considered to be the most serious of crimes in the UK. The definition of murder is the intentional killing of another human being. Manslaughter differs in that intent does not have to be present, so if a death was caused by accident or if the killer could not be held responsible for his or her actions, it would be considered manslaughter. For both young people and adults, murder cases are tried in the Crown Courts, where more serious crime trials take place. The minimum sentence for those convicted of murder aged 21 or over is 15 years, for those aged 17 or under is 12 years and for those aged 18,19 or 20 is either 12 or 15 years. The maximum sentence for murder for both young people and adults is a life prison sentence. The murder or manslaughter of someone can lead to a traumatic time for those close to the victim. Victim support can provide those affected by murder and manslaughter with advice on how to deal with the emotional impact of such an event. If you witness a murder, phone 999 immediately.

contributed to and supported by Legal Services Commission

Victim Support
0845 30 30 900
www.victimsupport.org.uk

Rizer (advice for young people about crime and the law)
www.rizer.co.uk

Home Office information on manslaughter
www.homeoffice.gov.uk/documents/2005-corporate-manslaughter/

Also check out:
> Prison
> Crime Prevention & Personal Safety
> Laws
> Police

Rape is when someone is unwillingly forced to have sex. A victim may know their attacker, they may have never met them or they may have been drugged in order to comply. It is not just men that rape women either; male rape is currently increasing and is taken just as seriously as female rape. Rape victims react differently after the event: they may not want to talk to or be around other people and may find physical contact difficult to cope with. If you have been raped, whatever you decide to do, it is important to talk to someone when you feel ready. It may be a friend or relative, a rape support line or the Police. If you report it to the Police, you will be assigned a trained Police officer to deal with your case. You'll be asked to speak about what happened and they may take evidence, such as the clothes you were wearing at the time of the attack, skin from underneath your fingernails etc. For this reason, if possible, go to the Police immediately as it may help the case and help prevention of unwanted pregnancy and STIs. Rape victims are allowed anonymity for life and may be entitled to compensation. If you know someone who is a victim of rape, be sympathetic, listen to what they have to say and point them in the direction of professional help. There is a lot of help available to rape victims, so if you have experienced rape you are not alone.

contributed to and supported by Legal Services Commission

Victim Support
0845 30 30 900
www.victimsupport.org.uk

Rape and Sexual Abuse Support Centre
08451 221 331
www.rasasc.org.uk

Survivors (help for who men who have been sexually abused or raped)
0845 122 1201
www.survivorsuk.org

Rape Crisis (help for survivors of rape)
www.rapecrisis.org.uk

Also check out:
> Crime Prevention & Personal Safety
> Abuse
> Abduction
> Sex Essentials
> Victims
> Witnesses

Often known as 'the oldest profession', the sex trade is still evident all over the world in today's society. In the UK, most sex workers are women providing sexual services to men, but there are also male sex workers. There are many laws that relate to prostitution in the UK. The issues that surround the sex trade are very controversial and it's a subject commonly in debate, meaning that the law often changes. Currently in the UK, prostitution is legal but only if the sex worker is over 18 and working alone. It is illegal for anyone aged under 18 to offer sexual services. It is also an offence to offer sexual services from the street, to ask another person for an act of prostitution from a car (often known as 'kerb-crawling') and to manage or assist in managing a brothel. It is legal for over 18s to appear in a pornographic film/photo shoot and to work as a stripper or a lap dancer. The issues that surround the sex trade (the law, health, sexual equality, morals, drugs and poverty) are many and few agree on what the answer to the problem is.

contributed to and supported by Legal Services Commission

End Child Prostitution, Child Pornography and the Trafficking of Children for Sexual Purposes (ECPAT) 0207 501 8927
www.ecpat.org.uk

Child and Woman Abuse Studies Unit
0207 133 5014
www.cwasu.org

Crown Prosecution Service Offences Against Public Morals and Decency laws
www.cps.gov.uk/legal/section12/chapter_d.html

Also check out:
> Sex Essentials
> STIs
> Police
> Arrested?
> Human Rights
> Crime Prevention & Personal Safety

Sexual harassment is classed as unwelcome behaviour of a sexual nature. This can mean lewd comments or sexual innuendo, unwanted physical behaviour such as someone purposefully brushing against you or could be an intimidating work atmosphere (for example, the display of sexual material in the workplace). It can be very damaging for victims who may find their work, health and confidence affected. Your employer has a duty to protect you from sexual harassment. If you experience sexual harassment, there are steps that you can take to stop it. Firstly, approach the person concerned and let them know that you're unhappy with their behaviour (it may be sensible to do this in front of a trusted friend for evidence's sake). If the behaviour continues, let your employer know. They then have to investigate your claim. If possible, keep a diary of all instances of unwelcome behaviour so that, if necessary, you can provide evidence of the harassment. If you are harassed by your employer or if your employer does not take adequate steps to stop the harassment, they can be punished by law. When reporting sexual harassment, it is always best to do so as soon as possible. If you wait, it may be argued that it wasn't made clear that the behaviour was unacceptable at the time.

contributed to and supported by Legal Services Commission

Equal Opportunities Commission
0845 601 5901 www.eoc.org.uk

Citizens Advice Bureau page on Basic Rights At Work
www.adviceguide.org.uk/wales/life/employment/basic_rights_at_work.htm

Trouble At Work page on sexual harassment
www.troubleatwork.org.uk/ViewAQuestion_theme.asp?ID=290&Trail=SearchTheme:6

Employment Tribunals
0845 795 9775
www.employmenttribunals.gov.uk

Legal Services Commission leaflet on Equal Opportunities 0845 3000 345
www.clsdirect.org.uk/legalhelp/leaflet15.jsp?lang=en

Also check out:
> Employment Rights
> Rights Essentials
> Crime Prevention & Personal Safety
> Discrimination Essentials
> Equal Opportunities
> Legal Advice

Taking something from a shop without paying for it is shoplifting. It is a crime that is punishable by, at worst, a prison sentence. Other punishments are likely to be a fine or community service. Either way, if you are convicted of shoplifting, you'll have a criminal record, which may harm your chances of getting a job and hold you back in other areas of life. The punishment handed out will depend upon the value of the goods you shoplift and how many times you've been caught for it previously. If you're caught or suspected of shoplifting, the shopkeeper or their security can hold you until the Police arrive but they are not allowed to search you without permission. Theft costs shopkeepers and deprives them of what they deserve so think twice before committing the crime. As shoplifting costs so much to businesses, there are now many security measures that can catch you out like cameras, security guards and electronic tags. Some people cannot stop themselves from shoplifting. These people may have an Impulse Control Disorder, a brain condition which means that sufferers are unable to control certain urges. If you think you may have an Impulse Control Disorder, see your GP for advice and support.

contributed to and supported by Legal Services Commission

Crimestoppers Wales
0800 555 111
www.crimestoppers-uk.org/wales/

Crime Reduction
0207 035 4747
www.crimereduction.gov.uk

Victim Support
0845 30 30 900
www.victimsupport.org/vs_england_wales/index.php

NHS Direct
0845 46 47
www.nhsdirect.nhs.uk

Also check out:
> Counselling
> Arrested?
> Stop and Search
> Crime Prevention & Personal Safety
> Criminal Records
> Victims

Smuggling is when you import goods from another country that are either illegal in the destination country (pirate DVDs in the UK), are illegal themselves (weapons or child pornography) or have not had tax paid on them when they should have (more than your legal allowance of tobacco). By handling illegal goods, you are contributing to and committing a criminal offence. By avoiding paying tax on imported goods, you are costing the Government, and therefore the country, money. Smuggling is a crime that can carry harsh penalties under UK law and could carry even harsher penalties if you're convicted of smuggling under the law of another country, which, in certain places could mean execution. When travelling across borders, be particularly vigilant about your luggage. Smugglers may use innocent parties to help them commit their crimes. Don't offer to carry anything for a stranger, don't let someone else pack your bags and don't leave your bags unattended. That way, you'll avoid becoming an unwitting smuggler. In the UK, HM Revenue and Customs help stop illegal goods entering the UK. Check the law before you bring anything back to the UK to make sure, firstly, that it is legal and secondly, that it doesn't need to be declared.

contributed to and supported by Legal Services Commission

HM Revenue and Customs
0845 010 9000
www.hmrc.gov.uk

Department of Trade and Industry's page on customs tariffs
0207 215 5000
www.dti.gov.uk/europeantrade/importing-into-uk/import-tariffs/page11291.html

Foreign and Commonwealth Office (travel advice) 0207 008 1500
www.fco.gov.uk

Citizens Advice Bureau advice for people in trouble abroad
www.adviceguide.org.uk/wales/your_world/travel/travel_abroad.htm#People_in_trouble_abroad

Also check out:

- Travel Essentials
- Ethical Trade
- Human Rights
- Rights Essentials
- Prison
- Legal Advice

If you are being followed, watched or pursued illegally by someone, you are being stalked. This can mean being physically trailed, harassed, watched and/or being contacted by letter, email or post. It also includes being pursued over the Internet. Through chat rooms or forums, stalkers can find people to stalk with greater anonymity and simplicity. Stalking can cause huge emotional damage and often leads to physical violence, even murder. Stalking is usually reported only when celebrities are involved but the majority of cases concern ordinary people. It is much more common for women to be the victims of stalking than men but it can happen the other way around. Most stalking is carried out by people known to their victims. Often, victims are stalked by their former partners who cannot cope with rejection. In the UK, the Protection from Harassment Act protects the victims of stalking. The penalty for conviction can be a fine, a prison sentence of up to five years, a combination of both or a restraining order (where you are not legally allowed to go near your victim). If you think you are being stalked, make a note of every suspicious occurrence and contact the Police to seek advice on how to proceed. Various organisations and support groups can also provide counselling for those affected by stalking.

contributed to and supported by Legal Services Commission

Bully Online (include page on stalking)
www.bullyonline.org

The Network for Surviving Stalking
www.nss.org.uk

BBC page on stalking
www.bbc.co.uk/crime/support/stalking.shtml

Victim Support
0845 30 30 900
www.victimsupport.org/vs_england_wales/index.php

Also check out:

> Splitting Up
> Family & Relationships
> Counselling
> Rape
> Crime Prevention & Personal Safety
> Victims

When you're out and about you need to be safe and streetwise. Street crime and violence is a threat that it's sensible to be aware of. There's no need to panic or stay in the house but naivety can increase your chances of becoming a victim. Criminals may target people to steal their mobile phones, bags, wallets, personal audio systems or trainers. Others may be attacked because of their race, religion or sexuality. Some may be attacked sexually and some may be caught up in gang violence, which usually revolves around drugs, weapons, territory etc. Those who commit these kinds of crimes are simply cowards, seeking to profit from the vulnerability of others. However, there are increasingly more and more methods being employed to stop them. CCTV, more Police working on the street, Street Crime Action Groups and Neighbourhood Watch schemes are all out there, keeping an eye on the criminals and helping to keep the streets safe. Help keep crime away by learning a few simple personal safety rules such as keeping mobile phones hidden and bags close to your body etc. (see http://www.suzylamplugh.org/tips/safetyonfoot.shtml for more tips). If you witness a street crime, contact the Police immediately.

contributed to and supported by Legal Services Commission

Good 2 B Secure (the student crime reduction website)
www.good2bsecure.gov.uk

Street Crime Action Team
0207 035 4747
www.crimereduction.gov.uk/streetcrime01.htm

The Suzy Lamplugh Trust
0208 876 0305
www.suzylamplugh.org/home/index.shtml

NACRO (crime reduction charity)
0207 582 6500
www.nacro.org.uk

Also check out:
> Citizenship
> Police
> Crime Prevention & Personal Safety
> Victims
> Witnesses

The crime of theft is a very serious one. Theft is taking something that you know doesn't belong to you. It is slightly different from burglary, which is stealing from a dwelling and robbery, which is using force to steal from someone. Either way, get caught and you could end up in big trouble with punishment for theft or related offences reaching up to 14 years imprisonment. It's not just stealing that can be a crime. Handling stolen goods, carrying equipment with the intention to steal, threatening violence to steal and entering a dwelling with the intention to steal are all punishable crimes. Claiming ignorance in most cases is not an adequate excuse; the courts will rule that most people know what is allowed and what is not. If you are the victim of a theft, report the crime to the Police straight away. If your house has been burgled, don't touch anything as you might contaminate or disturb any evidence left by the thieves. Make sure that your contents are covered by home insurance (some policies can also cover items whilst they are away from the home like mobile phones).

contributed to and supported by Legal Services Commission

BBC page on crime prevention in the home
www.bbc.co.uk/crime/prevention/yourhome.shtml

Rizer (information on crime for young people)
http://rizer.co.uk

Victim Support
0845 30 30 900
www.victimsupport.org/vs_england_wales/index.php

Criminal Justice System
www.cjsonline.gov.uk

Also check out:
> Police
> Crime Prevention & Personal Safety
> Fraud
> Shoplifting
> Victims
> Laws

Vandalism is when somebody damages or destroys property that doesn't belong to them. It can include smashing your neighbour's window, breaking a public telephone, setting fire to a public bin and smashing up a bus shelter. Most vandalism is caused by young people who may be bored, frustrated or want to impress others. Anyone can vandalise, so don't think it's clever or fun and if you get caught, you'll only be more bored and frustrated. The result of vandalism is that places look ugly, run-down and poor. The area will become less attractive and pleasant for you and everyone else to live in. Graffiti is a style of art that is defined by a certain look, usually created using spray-paints. When it's done in a controlled, legal environment it can be a great form of painting and expression. It becomes a problem, however, when graffiti is painted in public, illegal places. It can make an area look unwelcoming and ugly (especially tagging, where people merely write a name or a word) and can cost local councils thousands of pounds trying to clear it. Just because some people like the look of it doesn't mean that everyone else wants to see it too! The maximum sentence for those caught vandalising and doing graffiti is a six-month prison sentence and a £5,000 fine.

contributed to and supported by Legal Services Commission

Together (tackling anti-social behaviour)
www.together.gov.uk

Crime Reduction
www.crimereduction.gov.uk

Keep Britain Tidy
01942 612621
www.encams.org

Create your own graffiti
www.graffiticreator.net

Connect to your Council
Get the graffiti in your neighbourhood cleaned up
http://local.direct.gov.uk/mycouncil/

Also check out:
> Citizenship
> Relaxing
> Police
> Arrested?
> Crime Prevention & Personal Safety
> Criminal Records

Being a victim of crime is always an unpleasant experience. No matter how small the crime, the effects of it can be damaging. Try to keep events in perspective. If you've been the victim of crime, you may blame yourself for not being careful enough. However, criminals always find a way to commit crime and it is not possible for everyone to remain vigilant all day, every day. Of course, there are measures that you can take to prevent crime occurring but you can only do what is reasonable to protect yourself. Make sure that you know what to do if you are the victim of crime. In an emergency, always call 999. If it is not an emergency, you'll need to contact your local Police force. It is also worth keeping hold of other important phone numbers such as bank and mobile phone companies in case of phone or wallet theft. If you have been a victim of crime, there is support to help you deal with the situation. Each person deals with the experience differently so talk to friends, family or professionals about your feelings. If you are required to be a witness in court, find out the procedures and what rights you have. It's a fact that crime happens and there are victims but you shouldn't have to suffer so get help if you need it.

contributed to and supported by Legal Services Commission

UK Police Service Portal
www.police.uk

Victim Support
0845 30 30 900
www.victimsupport.org.uk

Government information on victims of crime
www.direct.gov.uk/crimejusticeandthelaw/victimsofcrime/fs/en

Liberty guide to compensation for victims of crime 0845 123 2307
www.youthrights.org.uk/your-rights/chapters/how-to-get-redress/compensation-for-the-victims-of-crime/

Also check out:
> Crime Prevention & Personal Safety
> Witnesses
> Family
> Problems & Emotions
> Laws
> Police
> Friends

Weapons & Firearms

Get caught with an offensive weapon and you could be in big trouble, with maximum sentences being six months in prison and/or a fine of up to £5,000. An offensive weapon is something designed to cause injury such as a flick-knife or a knuckle-duster, an ordinary item adapted to cause injury such as a broken bottle or an ordinary item carried for no other reason than to cause injury such as a baseball bat. You might think that it's ok to go out with a weapon considered to be offensive but if you get caught and can't prove why you are carrying it, you could be prosecuted for it. It is ok, for example, to carry a knife if you use one for work but it will be down to you to prove you have a lawful reason for carrying it. Most guns are illegal in the UK. However, some types of guns such as airguns and shotguns are legal in certain circumstances. If you want to use a gun, join a shooting club and do it legally. Take extra care when travelling by plane as the authorities may not let you board a flight if you have something that could be considered an offensive weapon in your luggage.

contributed to and supported by Legal Services Commission

Rizer (Information on crime for young people)
http://rizer.co.uk

Liberty guide to the law on knives and other offensive weapons
0845 123 2307
www.yourrights.org.uk/your-rights/chapters/the-right-of-peaceful-protest/public-order-offences/knives_and_other_offensive_wea.shtml

Victim Support
0845 30 30 900
www.victimsupport.org/vs_england_wales/

National Rifle Association of the UK list of shooting clubs 01483 797 777
www.nra.org.uk/common/asp/links/links.asp?site=NRA&cat=4

Also check out:

> Police
> Arrested?
> Stop & Search
> Street Crime & Violence
> Fencing
> Target Sports

If you have heard about or seen a crime being committed first-hand, you may be required to act as a witness. If you do find out about a crime, contact the Police immediately either by contacting your local station or by dialling 999 in an emergency. The Police may want to speak to you if they think you may have information valuable to them. They may ask you about what you saw or heard, descriptions of people's physical appearance and/or vehicle descriptions. They will probably need to take down some of your personal details too, in case they need to get back in touch with you. If a criminal investigation goes to court, you may be called as a witness. People of any age can appear as a witness, as long as they can understand and answers the questions appropriately. Appearing in court can seem scary to some people. A witness may have to relive something that was painful for them or come face-to-face with someone they don't want to see. However, in some cases it is possible to give evidence from behind a screen, from another room (they are shown on TV in the court) or in private. There are also organisations such as Victim Support who can provide assistance for witnesses.

contributed to and supported by Legal Services Commission

Victim Support
0845 30 30 900
www.victimsupport.org/vs_england_wales/

Crime Reduction
0207 035 47 47
www.crimereduction.gov.uk

Criminal Justice System
www.cjsonline.gov.uk

Various Crown Office leaflets about being a witness in court
www.crownoffice.gov.uk/Witnesses/witnesses

Also check out:

> Victims
> Youth Court
> Rights Essentials
> Crime Prevention & Personal Safety
> Police
> Laws

From 14, you are responsible for your actions in criminal law just like an adult. You're considered a juvenile (under 17) and dealt with in a youth court. Crimes such as burglary, domestic violence, murder and manslaughter, racist incidents, sex offences, stabbing, joy-riding, traffic offences, petty thieving, shoplifting and hundreds more are offences and each offence is punishable by law. The Crime & Disorder Act 1998 and Youth Justice System now provide new measures to tackle youth crime. There are orders to deal with child safety and anti-social behaviour for those 10 and over, and power for the Police to remove truants from educational establishments. If you're charged with an offence, your case will be heard in a Youth Court (part of the Magistrates Court). If you're charged with a serious crime, your case can be handled by the Crown Court. Detention and Training Orders (DTOs) are given out to 12 to 17 year-olds who have committed an offence that is punishable with imprisonment (in the case of an adult). The first half of a DTO is spent in detention and the second, under supervision in the community. At 18 your crime is dealt with by an adult court. If you're convicted of an offence under 18, the court may ask for pre-sentence reports to be made. These reports will be made by a member of the Youth Offending Team, who help the court decide on the sentence and/or punishment most appropriate for you. The best advice you're going to get about what's going to happen in court is from your solicitor. Ask them to tell you everything, good and bad. It's better to be prepared and know what you're doing.

contributed to and supported by Legal Services Commission

Youth Justice Board
0207 271 3033 www.youth-justice-board.gov.uk/YouthJusticeBoard/

The Liberty Guide to Human Rights
www.yourrights.org.uk/your-rights/chapters/the-rights-of-children-and-young-people/young-offenders/index.shtml

Bar Pro Bono (free legal advice)
0207 611 9500 www.barprobono.org.uk

National Youth Advocacy Service
0800 61 61 01 www.nyas.net

The Court Service 020 7210 2266
Welsh Speakers 088 212 368
Textphone 020 7210 2231
www.courtservice.gov.uk

Also check out:

> Police
> Arrested?
> Crime Prevention & Personal Safety
> Criminal Records
> Prison
> Legal Advice

Criminal Records

Getting a criminal record is something that might hold you back in many important areas of life, so think first before breaking the law. A criminal record lists all of the convictions that you have. It does not include cautions, reprimands or final warnings given by the Police. However, these are kept on a Police database and may be used in Court if you are tried for another offence. Convictions don't necessarily remain on your criminal record forever. More serious sentences (such as more than 10 years in prison) do, but others remain on your record for a certain amount of time, after which they are removed (the conviction is then 'spent'). A criminal record can damage your life in some serious ways. You have to mention it when applying for a job, college, university, for credit cards and when you travel to some foreign countries. If you don't mention it and are found out, you could be dismissed. Convictions for certain crimes can mean that an employer can choose not to employ you because of it. Before you commit a crime, no matter how small, give a thought to the damage that you could be causing, not just to others, but to yourself too.

contributed to and supported by Legal Services Commission

Criminal Records Bureau
0870 90 90 811
www.crb.gov.uk

The Liberty Guide to Human Rights
www.yourrights.org.uk

Criminal Justice System
www.cjsonline.gov.uk

The Home Office – 'How Justice Works'
0207 035 4848
www.homeoffice.gov.uk/justice/how-justice-works/

Also check out:
> Applying for a Job
> Arrested?
> Crime Prevention & Personal Safety
> Youth Crime
> Prison
> Remand

Prison is the most severe punishment for a crime that you can get in the UK. It takes away the freedom of the criminal and removes someone who may be potentially harmful from public life. In England and Wales, there are 138 prisons, each with their own rules and regulations. There are four different levels of security, ranging from category A, the highest level of security housing prisoners thought to be dangerous to the public to Category D, where prisoners are trusted to roam freely. Prison cells are usually shared, with some having facilities such as TV and radio. Most prisons also have gym, education, religious, social and health facilities. Prisoners are also allowed visitors. Disobey the rules in prison and you may find yourself in a segregation unit (also known as 'the seg' or 'the block'), separated from the other prisoners and denied privileges such as TV. Prisons can be notoriously difficult places to live in. As well as being denied your basic freedom, life can be boring, repetitive, you're subject to a mountain of rules and regulations and frustration and tension often boils over, leading to violence.

contributed to and supported by Legal Services Commission

HM Prison Service
www.hmprisonservice.gov.uk

Action for Prisoners' Families
0208 812 3600
www.prisonersfamilies.org.uk

Home Office page on Justice and Prisons
0207 035 48 48
www.homeoffice.gov.uk/justice

The No-Way Trust
01482 224382
www.pmnw.co.uk

NACRO (crime reduction charity)
0207 582 6500
www.nacro.org.uk

Also check out:
> Laws
> Arrested?
> Crime Prevention & Personal Safety
> Criminal Records
> Remand
> Legal Advice

In Britain, prison is there not just as a deterrent to would-be criminals and punishment but also as rehabilitation for convicted criminals. They may provide education and/or counselling and courses for prisoners, all intended to help the prisoner avoid re-offending once they've been released. They may be encouraged to learn new, employable skills or to find out about housing and employment, easing their path from prison back to public life. They may be given psychological treatment to help them deal with certain situations differently, once released, and prisoners with drug problems may be given treatment to cure addiction. Organisations such as NACRO help ex-offenders cope with resettling into everyday life. They provide advice, support and guidance to ex-offenders, helping with housing, employment and drug treatment issues. If you're an ex-offender or member of their family, call their helpline on 0800 0181 259.

contributed to and supported by Legal Services Commission

NACRO (crime reduction charity)
0207 582 6500
www.nacro.org.uk

Crime Reduction
0207 035 4747
www.crimereduction.gov.uk

The Home Office
0207 035 4848
www.homeoffice.gov.uk

Crime Info
www.crimeinfo.org.uk

Also check out:
> Laws
> Rights Essentials
> Crime Prevention & Personal Safety
> Criminal Records
> Prison
> Legal Advice

When you're accused of committing a crime, you'll usually be put on remand before your case is heard in court. Remand can mean conditional or unconditional bail (where you are allowed to go free until the start of the hearing, often with conditions) or it can mean being held somewhere until your case begins. From the age of 15, young people can be held on remand in prison but, usually, if you're under 17, you'll go to a children's home or will stay with foster parents. If you've committed a serious crime or have repeated many times before, you may be held in secure remand. Remand should last up until your hearing begins, which can be anything from a few days to, in rare circumstances, nine months. Being held on remand can be a frustrating time, as you may not have committed any crime and your freedom is restricted whilst you wait to put your side of the story forward. Prisoners on remand have more rights than convicted prisoners. For example, you're still allowed to vote, can wear ordinary clothes and have greater visiting rights.

contributed to and supported by Legal Services Commission

Youth Justice Board for England and Wales
0207 271 3033
www.youth-justice-board.gov.uk

Prisoners' Families Helpline
0808 808 2003
www.prisonersfamilieshelpline.org.uk/php/bin/readarticle.php?articlecode=9241

HM Prison Service
www.hmprisonservice.gov.uk

Liberty's guide to the rights of prisoners
www.yourrights.org.uk/your-rights/chapters/the-rights-of-prisoners/index.shtml

Also check out:
> Police
> Arrested?
> Bail
> Rights Essentials
> Prison
> Legal Advice

Those who commit crime aged below 18 are treated differently to those aged 18 or over. People aged under 10 cannot be charged with a criminal offence. When a young person (under 18) is arrested, their parents or guardian must be informed and they must be accompanied by an 'appropriate adult' (usually parents, a guardian or a social worker) when interviewed by the Police. All but the most serious of crimes are dealt with in Youth Courts. These are like normal courts but are set up in order to suit the needs of young people. First time offenders are often dealt with outside of the courts. A young person can be warned, reprimanded, placed under a curfew or a special contract or issued with an Anti-Social Behaviour Order (ASBO). Reprimands and warnings, which are not placed on criminal records, can only be given under certain circumstances. The maximum prison sentence for young people is 24 months for cases heard in a Crown Court and 6 months if heard in a Youth Court. If the offence is murder, a young person can be detained indefinitely and if it is a 'grave' crime (rape etc.), a prison sentence of up to 24 months can be given. Those aged under 21 will be held in a Young Offender's Institution. Aged over 21, they'll be transferred to prison.

contributed to and supported by Legal Services Commission

Youth Justice Board 0207 271 3033
www.youth-justice-board.gov.uk/YouthJusticeBoard/

The Liberty Guide to Human Rights
www.yourrights.org.uk/your-rights/chapters/the-rights-of-children-and-young-people/young-offenders/index.shtml

Bar Pro Bono (free legal advice)
0207 611 9500
www.barprobono.org.uk/navigate/home.html

National Youth Advocacy Service
0800 61 61 01
www.nyas.net

Also check out:
> Police
> Arrested?
> Crime Prevention & Personal Safety
> Criminal Records
> Prison
> Legal Advice

8.5 Court Procedures

Whether you're on the right or the wrong side of the law, here's a brief guide to everything you need to know about the British court system.

Types of courts:
Magistrates' Courts – Deal with trials for less serious crimes, such as driving offences. **County Courts** – Look at family or property law cases, so may become involved in settling divorces or land disputes. **Crown Courts** – Crown courts take only more serious crimes such as armed robbery and murder. **Youth Court** – Take any cases where the offender is aged between 10 and 18. **Court Of Appeal** – If a convicted person feels that they have not had a fair trial, it is sometimes possible to take the case to the Court Of Appeal, who may reduce the sentence.

Types of Jobs:
Magistrates – Sit in a magistrates' court and may determine the guilt of a defendant, pass sentence, grant bail, adjourn a case or send it to a higher court. **Judge** – Presides over a crown court and, if the jury has found the defendant guilty, decides on punishment. **Lawyer** – The term lawyer refers to anyone who works as a barrister, solicitor or legal executive. **Barrister** – Barristers are similar to solicitors but deal mainly with a type of law called advocacy and tend to work in the higher courts. **Solicitor/Legal Executive** - Solicitors take instruction from the general public. They give advice on legal matters and may represent people in lower courts. **Crown Prosecutor** - Decide whether there is enough evidence and enough public interest for a case to warrant a prosecution.

contributed to and supported by Legal Services Commission

Department for Constitutional Affairs
0207 210 8614
www.dca.gov.uk/legalsys/structure.htm

Her Majesty's Court Services
www.hmcourts-service.gov.uk

Criminal Justice System
www.cjsonline.gov.uk

Guide to civil courts
www.justclaim.co.uk

Also check out:

> Legal Advice
> Witnesses
> Laws
> Police
> Jury Service
> Youth Crime
> Youth Offenders

Any case that goes to a crown court is tried by a jury, consisting of twelve randomly chosen members of the public. They are present for the full length of the trial and hear all of the evidence presented. Whilst in court, jurors are allowed to take notes and ask questions by passing notes if anything is unclear, but they aren't allowed to speak out. Once all the evidence has been given and the judge has summed the case up, the jury retire to a room where they discuss the case and decide whether the defendant is guilty or innocent.

Anyone on the electoral register aged between 18 and 70 can be called for jury service. It's compulsory to complete the service although there are exceptions, including those with criminal records, those who work in the justice system and those with mental health problems. Jury service can also be deferred (for example, if you're on holiday) but it is up to a jury summoning officer whether your reason will be accepted. Jury service normally lasts for two weeks, so it may take in more than one trial. However, if the trial goes on for more than two weeks, the jury must remain present throughout. Those called for jury service are not paid but may be reimbursed for expenses such as travel, accommodation, food and childcare costs.

contributed to and supported by Legal Services Commission

Criminal Justice System section on jurors
www.cjsonline.gov.uk/juror/

BBC page on jury service
www.bbc.co.uk/crime/support/juryservice.shtml

Home Office information on jury service
www.homeoffice.gov.uk/justice/what-happens-at-court/jury-service/

Her Majesty's Court Service
www.hmcourts-service.gov.uk/

Also check out:
- Laws
- Police
- Youth Crime
- Young Offenders
- Witnesses
- Victims

The initial event in a trial is that a person or persons (known as the defendant/s) will be accused of committing a crime. The Crown Prosecution Service (CPS) then decides whether there is enough evidence and public interest for the case to warrant a trial. If there is, all cases will firstly go to the Magistrates' Court. A Magistrate can only give a maximum sentence of six months imprisonment so will only try more minor cases, known as summary offences. These are seen and tried by a bench of magistrates, usually consisting of three non-professional judges. If the offence requires a greater punishment it is known as an indictable-only offence and the case will be passed on to the Crown Court; in these cases, the Magistrate will decide only on matters such as bail.

The trial itself begins with the prosecution presenting their case to the court. They will then call their witnesses who they will question first, followed by the defence. This is called cross-examination. The defence then presents their case to the court. They then call their witnesses, who are cross-examined. Once this process is complete, both sides sum their arguments up and the jury retires to decide on whether to give a guilty or not-guilty verdict. If guilty, the judge then decides on the defendants' punishment.

contributed to and supported by Legal Services Commission

Liberty guide to trials
www.yourrights.org.uk/your-rights/chapters/the-rights-of-defendants/venue/venue.shtml

Criminal Justice System
www.cjsonline.gov.uk

The Crown Prosecution Service
www.cps.gov.uk

Also check out:
> Arrested?
> Victims
> Laws
> Police
> Jury Service
> Youth Crime
> Youth Offenders

8.6 Discrimination

In today's society and by UK law, we all have the right to be treated equally. It doesn't matter about your race, gender, age, religion, marital status, sexuality or if you have a disability, you should be treated in the same way as anyone else. Discrimination can be very damaging. It can cause an individual or a group to feel ashamed, unwelcome, angry, physically scared and emotionally scarred. Discrimination can be direct. For example, you may not be considered for a promotion at work because of your gender or your looks. But, discrimination can also be indirect. This is a more subtle form of discrimination. An example may be that a job advert might limit the applicants to come from a certain group of people. If an employer, authority, company, organisation or an individual discriminates against someone, they can be punished by UK law. Under no circumstances should you be discriminated or prejudiced against. If you suffer any form of discrimination, however small it may seem, contact the relevant organisations.

contributed to and supported by Legal Services Commission

Citizens Advice Bureau page on discrimination because of sexuality, religion or age
www.adviceguide.org.uk/wales/your_rights/civil_rights/discrimination_sexuality_religion_age.htm

Advisory, Conciliation and Arbitration Service (ACAS) 08457 47 47 47
www.acas.org.uk

Equal Opportunities Commission
0845 601 5901
www.eoc.org.uk

Bully Online
www.bullyonline.org

Legal Services Commission leaflet on Equal Opportunities 0845 3000 345
www.clsdirect.org.uk/legalhelp/leaflet15.jsp?lang=en

Also check out:

> Laws
> Rights Essentials
> Equal Opportunities
> Racism
> Legal Advice
> Human Rights

You have a right, male or female, to equal pay, equal rights, equal facilities, equal uniforms in school and dress codes in the workplace, equal opportunities and equal chances in education and training. By working together to make sure that everyone, including you, is treated this way, we can help make our country a better place to live.

Be open-minded about yourself and others. Don't feel that if you're a girl, you can't be a car mechanic or, if you're a boy, you can't be a beautician. This is gender discrimination and simply doesn't cut it anymore. Some people try to use "tradition" as an excuse for discrimination, but don't let this dissuade you either. "Traditionally", women weren't allowed to vote or go to university, but just because it was "tradition", it didn't make it right.

The Government will be introducing a new Gender Equality Duty (GED) in April 2007, which will mean that sex equality will have to be promoted and services will have to be designed considering the different needs of men and women. The GED will apply to all public bodies and private and voluntary organisations providing services and will have a legal requirement for action on equal pay (did you know that currently, on average, men with full-time jobs earn around 17% more than their female equivalent?).

If your school does not allow girls to wear trousers, or boys to have earrings or long hair, you can contact Equal Opportunities Commission (Wales) for advice and they will tell you about your rights under the Sex Discrimination Act.

contributed to and supported by Legal Services Commission

Equal Opportunities Commission
www.eoc.org.uk

Also check out:

> Discrimination Essentials
> Racism
> Rights Essentials

Racism

Racism is when one person abuses another person, purely because of their race. If a white person is attacked by a black person, for example, it doesn't mean it's a racist attack but if they are attacked purely because they are white, then it is. Racism can occur between people of any race, colour or creed. Racist attacks can be verbal and/or physical. It is a crime to verbally abuse someone because of their race or to spread hatred about a race of people in written form. It is also a separate crime to physically attack someone because of their race and punishments tend to be harsher if racism is found to be a reason for an attack. All forms of racism can be extremely damaging. They can leave an individual or a group of people feeling scared, outcast, humiliated and angry. It is important to remember that we now live in a multi-cultural society and that racism only helps divide people and communities. If you are suffering or have suffered from racism, get a copy of 'Racial Discrimination – Your Legal Rights', which is available from the CLS Leafletline on 0845 3000 343.

contributed to and supported by Legal Services Commission

Community Legal Services Direct
0845 345 4345
www.clsdirect.org.uk

Campaign Against Racism and Facism
0207 837 1450
www.carf.demon.co.uk

The National Assembly against Racism
0207 247 9907
www.naar.org.uk

Bullying Online
www.bullying.co.uk

Legal Services Commission leaflet on racial discrimination
0845 3000 345
www.clsdirect.org.uk/legalhelp/leaflet16.jsp?lang=en

Also check out:

> Laws
> Human Rights
> Rights Essentials
> Crime Prevention & Personal Safety
> Discrimination Essentials

No-one particularly wants to spend time thinking about when they die but it's coming to all of us (eventually!) so it's best for everyone concerned if you do. A will sets out who benefits from your property and your possessions (known as your 'estate') after your death and who will ensure that your wishes are carried out (known as your 'executor(s)'). Although it isn't completely necessary to use a solicitor when drawing up a will, it is advisable (especially if your will is complicated) as any mistakes could cause big problems after your death. For a will to be valid it must be made by someone aged 18 or over who is not under pressure from anyone else and who is of sound mind. It must also be signed in the presence of two witnesses and by the witnesses themselves. A will can be kept anywhere but many choose to deposit theirs with a bank or solicitor for safe-keeping. It's important to know the laws that govern wills as they could affect what happens to your estate. For example, if you live with an unmarried partner, they may not inherit from you and if you don't prepare a will correctly, your estate may be subject to Inheritance Tax, so your benefactors won't receive as much as you intended to leave them.

contributed to and supported by Legal Services Commission

Citizens Advice Bureau page on Wills
www.adviceguide.org.uk/wales/family-parent/family/wills.htm

BBC page - 'How to Have Fun While Writing Your Will'
www.bbc.co.uk/dna/h2g2/A738821

Law On The Web information about wills
www.lawontheweb.co.uk/basics/wills.htm

Tesco Finance information about wills
www.tescofinance.com/personal/finance/smarter_money/protecting/will.html

Legal Services Commision
www.clsdirect.org.uk

Also check out:

- Counselling
- Rights Essentials
- Legal Advice
- Budgeting Essentials
- Tax & NI
- Banks & Building Societies

8.7 Solicitors & Legal Services

Solicitors are the people that will help you out the most if you're in trouble and can help you with legal advice in many other situations also. Whether you've been arrested, are writing a will or buying a house, you'll need a solicitor. They have different specialist areas of the law, like crime, family law, housing, business etc. so will have detailed knowledge of the laws that you're concerned with. Details of local solicitors can be found in the Yellow Pages (www.yell.com).

If you've been arrested, you can't be made to wait longer than 36-hours before seeing a solicitor at a Police station (48- hours in terrorism cases). Everyone is entitled to legal representation. If you don't have the means to pay for a solicitor, free legal representation may be available. If you have to go to court, you'll need a solicitor; they'll be your representatives in court, defending you or putting your case forward to the judge.

In other areas of life such as property and finance, solicitors can provide advice on complicated legal issues to avoid you accidentally breaking any rules, regulations or laws.

contributed to and supported by Legal Services Commission

Yellow Pages (find a local solicitor)
www.yell.com/ucs/HomePageAction.do

Community Legal Services Direct
0845 345 4345
www.clsdirect.org.uk

Advice Now (information on rights and legal issues)
www.advicenow.org.uk

Citizens Advice Bureau
www.adviceguide.org.uk

Also check out:
> Divorce
> Death and Wills
> Buying A Home
> Arrested?
> Youth Crime
> Young Offenders

9. MONEY

Everyone has to budget – even the seriously rich. It's true! A budget tells you how much money you've got coming in (income) and how much you've got going out (expenditure: i.e. how much you regularly spend on bills, petrol, rent etc) and how much you've got left over to spend (disposable income).

If you stick to your budget, you won't get into money difficulties – simple as that. In the real world, however, where beautiful, cool people constantly call to us to part with our cash so that we can be as uber-cool as them, this isn't always easy to do. The key thing is, as always, moderation! Treating yourself won't break the bank, as long as you do it now and again and not every day!

It can seem easy to run away from money problems, but ignoring them can lead you into a spiral of debt, so face up to your finances. Don't be scared to look at your bank balance: confront it. The quicker you try to deal with it, the easier it'll be. If you find yourself with money problems, tell your bank or building society. They'll be much more willing to help you if they know that you want to do something about it.

Register for a VIP account at www.credu.co.uk and you can get your very own online budgeting tool, called My Money.

Government website on taking the pain out of budgeting
www.direct.gov.uk/YoungPeople/Money/ManagingYourMoney/ManagingYourMoneyArticles/fs/en?CONTENT_ID=10027616&chk=NT%2B4Sy

Consumer Credit Counselling Service budget advice pages 0800 138 1111
www.cccs.co.uk/budget/budget.htm

Hot Courses guide to student money
www.studentmoney.org

BBC advice on budgeting
www.bbc.co.uk/dna/h2g2/brunel/A848676

Also check out:
> Bills
> Credit Cards
> Debt Essentials
> Loans
> Overdrafts
> Benefits Essentials

There are many cards around that get you money off your favourite things in life like travel, fashion, food, shopping, sport, cinema and loads more.

EURO<26 card – card that entitles young people, aged 26 and under, to thousands of discounts around Europe and here in Wales. You can grab yourself a card from Canllaw Online (www.canllaw-online.com) for only £7 each. If you're 16 you are entitled to a free card. See page 59 for more details.

NUS Card – card given to all students belonging to the National Union of Students (NUS) that offers access to discounts on everything from haircuts, entertainment and clothes to travel.

International Student Identity Card (ISIC) – card available to full-time students, secondary pupils aged 12 or over and gap year students with a firm higher education offer the following year. It offers discounts in over 100 countries on travel, accommodation, museums, cultural events entertainment and much more worldwide. Costs £7.

International Youth Travel Card (IYTC) – card for those who are not full-time students but are aged between 12 and 25, saving money on flights, rail passes, accommodation, phones, currency exchange, shopping and entrance to museums and other cultural events in more than 50 countries.

Euro 26
www.euro26.org

National Union of Students (NUS)
0871 221 8221
www.nusonline.co.uk

International Student Travel Confederation
www.isic.org/sisp/index.htm

Also check out:
- University Essentials
- Travel Essentials
- Budgeting Essentials
- Shopping
- Arts
- Concerts & Events

Taking out insurance is a way that you can cover yourself against various kinds of losses. For example, many people insure their possessions and the contents of their home. An insurance company would assess the value of all of your contents as well as considering the chances of the items being damaged, lost or stolen. They'd then set a monthly premium that you pay them (this usually ranges from around £10 to £30 a month depending on the value of the contents and the type of coverage taken out). If you suffered a loss (i.e. having your expensive watch stolen) your insurance company would either pay you the value of the watch or replace it as new. You can insure contents, buildings, cars, health, holidays, individual items (i.e. your mobile phone), items outside of the home and you can insure yourself if you lose your job. You can also get life assurance, which pays out money to beneficiaries such as family members, mortgage company etc. upon your death. When you get insurance you need to make sure that you get exactly what you want. Write a list of questions down before you start phoning around and make sure that you get a clear answer to them. Check all the small print before signing up to a policy and seek professional help if anything is unclear.

National Insurance

National Insurance (NI) is money that you have to pay to the Government when you're earning a certain amount. It contributes towards your pension or benefits, should you need it.

The Association of British Insurers
0207 600 3333
www.abi.org.uk

Financial Services Authority (FSA) page on insurance
www.fsa.gov.uk/consumer/05_INSURANCE/

BBC Watchdog guide to insurance
www.bbc.co.uk/watchdog/guides_to/insurance/

Also check out:

> Travel Insurance
> Driving Essentials
> Consumer Rights
> Budgeting Essentials
> National Insurance

Interest

Did you know that when you have money in a bank account, although you have instant access to it, the bank is effectively borrowing the money from you? Your bank then rewards you for letting them borrow this money by paying back a percentage of the money into your account (interest). The amount they pay depends on the interest rate of your bank account, which is usually expressed in percentage terms for the year. It works the other way around too. If you have an overdraft or a loan, the bank, building society or Loan Company who are lending you the money charge you to borrow the money from them. This is done in exactly the same way as when you are paid interest by the bank. If you are getting a bank account or are thinking about borrowing money, be sure to check the interest rates so that you get the best deal and don't get swizzled!

Inflation

In economic terms, the word 'inflation' refers to the rate at which prices go up. For example, a tin of beans may cost £1, then a year later may cost £1.10, meaning that the annual inflation rate is 10%. You may hear the term "cost of living" associated with inflation. This means that if inflation is high, the amount of money people need to live also goes up (for food, clothes, rent etc). Knowing the inflation rate is important so that economists can determine the strength or weakness of a national economy.

Bank of England page on inflation
0207 601 4444
www.bankofengland.co.uk/education/targettwopointzero/inflation/index.htm

BBC Economy
news.bbc.co.uk/1/hi/business/economy/default.stm

Financial Services Authority (FSA) page on Saving (including information on interest rates) 0845 606 1234
www.fsa.gov.uk/consumer/11_LEARN/financial_products/Saving/intro1.html

Also check out:

> Banks and Building Societies
> Credit Cards
> Debt Essentials
> Loans
> Overdrafts
> Student Loan

Ever heard the saying “save it for a rainy day”? Tempting though it is, you don’t have to go out and spend your money as soon as you get your hands on it, you know. Think of the future: if you spend it all at once, what will you have left for that special occasion or the dreaded day of boredom doom? You won’t even have enough for a pizza and a DVD – imagine the horror! Spending now might mean scrimping later, so save now and you can spend more down the road.

There are various ways that you can invest your money. The simplest way is to save. There are loads of bank accounts designed specifically for saving. Shop around and find the best account to give you interest on the money you put by. Putting your money in a bank account is a low risk way to invest. You’ll be sure that you get your money back but you won’t make a very big profit. Most other ways of investing are a higher risk. You might buy a property, a collectable antique, a piece of art or shares in a company. The risk comes because you can’t be sure of how the value of your investment will change. If it goes up then your luck is in. When you sell, you’ll make big bucks. But if the time to sell comes and the value has decreased, you’ll lose out. If you have money that you want to invest, get as much advice as you can and don’t be talked into anything you’re not sure of.

Government page on ways to save and invest money
www.direct.gov.uk/MoneyTaxAndBenefits/ManagingMoney/SavingsAndInvestments/

Financial Services Authority consumer information page 0845 606 1234
www.fsa.gov.uk/consumer

Radio One Life finance pages
www.bbc.co.uk/radio1/onelife/finance/index.shtml

The Gaeia Partnership (promoting ethical investment) 0161 434 4681
www.gaeia.co.uk

Also check out:
- Mortgage Options
- Fraud
- Budgeting Essentials
- Interest Rates & Inflation
- Savings (ISAs etc.)
- Stocks & Shares

A pension is like a long-term savings account that you pay a percentage of your wages into and get back when you retire from work. It might seem like a long way off when you're young and just starting work, but you need to make sure that you have something to live on when you retire and have no other regular income. The earlier you start to pay into a pension, the better, as you'll have more money when you retire.

There are different types of pension available to you. There is the state pension, which you contribute to by paying National Insurance (NI) when you work. It's paid out at a flat rate and is only given to those who've contributed enough by the time they've retired. Most employers offer occupational pensions, where you pay a percentage of your wages into the pension each month and sometimes, depending on the scheme and your employer's policy, your employer will also pay a monthly contribution into your pension. With occupational pensions, your contribution is usually taken directly from your pay before tax has been taken. There are also personal pensions, which are similar to occupational pensions but have nothing to do with your employment, and stakeholder pension, which are similar but tend to be more flexible. Pensions can be complicated so it's best to get as much information and advice as you can. Speak to your employer, parents or see Links below for more information.

The Pension Service
0845 60 60 265
www.pensionguide.gov.uk

The Pensions Advisory Service
0845 601 2923
www.opas.org.uk

Citizens Advice Bureau page on pensions
www.adviceguide.org.uk/wales/your_world/consumer_affairs/pensions.htm

BBC page on pensions
news.bbc.co.uk/1/hi/in_depth/business/2002/pensions_crisis/default.stm

Also check out:
> Careers Essentials
> Contracts
> Budgeting Essentials
> Investing
> Banks & Building Societies
> National Insurance

Whether you're saving for your retirement, a holiday, a hi-fi or a house, you need to think about where you save your money. There are numerous types of bank and building society accounts that suit different kinds of saving. You need to work out what you want to do and find out which type of account is best suited to your needs. Look out for differences in interest rates, bank charges, overdraft limits and how long it takes for you to withdraw the money from the account. Many banks and building societies have accounts specifically designed for young people and students, offering advantages including introductory offers.

Individual Savings Accounts (ISAs) are tax-free accounts set up by the Government in order to encourage people to save money. You can invest up to £7,000 (in cash or shares, depending on the type of ISA) in any tax year, which runs from April to April. They are good for gaining interest and avoiding having to pay tax on savings. However, shares ISAs should be considered a long-term investment, as they depend on movements in the stock market. Before agreeing to any kind of savings account, make sure you've shopped around, got advice and have read all the small print of the account.

Government website on young people and money
www.direct.gov.uk/YoungPeople/Money/fs/en

HM Revenue and Customs leaflet on ISAs
www.hmrc.gov.uk/leaflets/isa.htm

BBC News pages on savings and investments
news.bbc.co.uk/1/hi/in_depth/business/savings_investments/default.stm

Citizens Advice Bureau page on young people – money and consumer rights
www.adviceguide.org.uk/wales/your_world/consumer_affairs/young_people_money_and_consumer_rights.htm

Also check out:
- Budgeting Essentials
- Interest Rates & Inflation
- Investing
- Pensions
- Stocks & Shares
- Banks & Building Societies

When you buy shares, you invest money in a company (or loan money to a company) and in return own part of the business – you have a "share" in the company. As a shareholder, you are entitled to "dividends", which are part of the company's profits set aside to divide among shareholders.

Shares are bought in units. You can buy shares on the Stock Exchange. The idea is, if the value of each share goes up (i.e. the company is doing well) on the stockmarket, the value of your shares go up too and you make money. The problem is that if they go down, you lose money. Buying and selling shares can be a risky business, but do it wisely and you can save, invest and if you've got a long time to wait you can make money!

Talk to people who have bought and sold shares to learn about the ins and outs. Your bank should also be able to give you advice on buying shares, and may offer a share-buying service.

UK Net Guide
www.uknetguide.co.uk/Finance/

Directgov
www.direct.gov.uk/MoneyTaxAndBenefits/ManagingMoney/SavingsAndInvestments/fs/en

Also check out:
> Investing
> Savings
> Banks & Building Societies

9.3 Bank Accounts

Banks and Building Societies offer a range of different "accounts", targeted at different groups of people and offering different services. You can have a personal account or a business account, a savings account or a day-to-day living account and you can have a normal level account or a special colour coded one (like silver, gold or platinum) depending on how good a customer you are! There are many to choose from, so do your homework and a fair bit of "compare and contrast" to help you decide which is the best account to suit your needs. Though it's tempting to be wooed by offers of money in your account or free mobile top-up cards, CDs, travel vouchers etc., try to see past the gimmick. When the money's been spent or the voucher's expired, you'll still have your account.

Here's a quick checklist to help you find the right account:

Where's your nearest branch? How many cash points do they have and do they charge? How quickly can you get access to your money? Can you have an overdraft on your account? What is the overdraft interest percentage? What are the charges for going overdrawn without authorisation? Can you bank online? Is there a telephone helpline? Does your account provide free card insurance? Does your account provide free travel insurance etc? Are there any ongoing perks?

To open an account, you will usually need at least 2 forms of ID and some money! You may need only £1 or it might be as much as £1,000, depending on the bank or building society and the type of account. If you do your homework properly, you'll know this in advance!

Money Facts
www.moneyfacts.co.uk

BBC Finance
http://www.bbc.co.uk/radio1/onelife/finance/

Direct Debit
www.directdebit.co.uk

CardWatch
020 7711 6356 www.cardwatch.org.uk

Also check out:
- Investing
- Savings
- Online Banking

If you're on Tinterweb (aherm, Internet), then you could manage your bank account remotely. Imagine sorting out your overdraft from the comfort of your own home: welcome the miracle of online banking! Not all banks and building societies offer this service, so check out whether or not it's an option for you by phoning your branch or checking their website. If you're a customer, however, and your bank or building society is launching online banking, you'll soon know about it!

If you want to bank online, you'll get a username and a password (which will either be sent to you in the post, or will be created when you log on to the online banking website), which you will have to enter every time you login to your account on the website. This ensures your privacy and means that you and you alone have access to your account – so it's vital that you keep these details secret.

So, what can you do through online banking? You can...
Check your balance
Pay bills
Transfer money from one account to another
Increase or decrease overdraft levels
View statements
Cancel direct debits
Order chequebooks, statements etc.

If you're worried about the safety of banking online, check out the link below.

Bank Safe Online
www.banksafeonline.org.uk

Also check out:
> Overdrafts
> Banks & Building Societies

Think carefully before you get one. Credit cards allow you to borrow a lump sum of money to pay for something that you can't afford to buy in one go and pay it back in monthly installments. However, if you use your card too much, you might not be able to afford the monthly payments and get into debt that you can't handle. Remember, you have to be 18 to get a credit card.

When you get your credit card, you're given a spending limit, but this can be much higher than you can actually afford, it doesn't mean that you should be spending up to your limit. You receive monthly statements telling you how much you owe and how much you need to pay back for that month. You can pay the full balance each month, which means you don't have to pay any interest and is a useful way to pay for big purchases if you don't like carrying cash with you. You can also just pay the minimum amount stated on the statement, though this will mean that you will end up paying interest on the rest of the balance. This interest can be very high, so shop around for a credit card. The APR is the key.

The APR is how much interest (extra money) you pay back on top of the money you'll borrow. The lower the APR on the card, the better. Some credit card companies offer you six months interest free – but after the six months is up, you will start paying interest on what you've borrowed, so make sure you check out the small print and find out what interest rate you'll end up paying if you haven't cleared your balance within the six months.

Trading Standards
Advice leaflets on credit under the 'For consumers' section
www.tradingstandards.gov.uk

BBC Online
Advice on credit & credit cards
www.bbc.co.uk/radio1/onelife/finance/credit

Also check out:

- Debt Essentials
- Store Cards
- Fraud

Spending more than you earn means getting into debt and although, at times, we all owe money, sometimes it gets out of hand. When debt builds up, it can get really stressful, especially if you can't make the repayments and are worrying about legal action.
There is help at hand, though, so don't be tempted to borrow money to get yourself out of debt: you may end up in more trouble than when you started.

Speak to your bank and tell them of your troubles – a trained advisor should be able to give you good advice on the best course of action. Also, why not approach the companies you owe money to and try to set up a repayment scheme that is manageable for you? You could try and get them to suspend interest while you pay back your debt, for example. If you don't ask, you don't get and the results surely can't be as bad as suffering in silence while letting the debt mount up.

There are also debt management agencies about, however some are there to make money from you while they sort out your debt, so bear this in mind if you enter an agreement with them.

If you're a student and are worried about debt look at our section on Budgeting. For info on how to avoid getting into debt, contact one of the organisations below or the NUS in your college or uni, they will be able to help you. Get help before the situation gets too bad.

The UK Insolvency Helpline
Free National Debt Advisory Service
0800 074 6918 www.insolvencyhelpline.co.uk

National Debtline Helpline
0808 808 4000 www.nationaldebtline.co.uk

BBC Online/Radio 1/ Onelife
www.bbc.co.uk/radio1/onelife/finance

Community Legal Service (CLS)
0845 3000 343

Also check out:
> Loans
> Overdrafts
> Credit Cards
> Budgeting Essentials

9. MONEY

Sitting round with your mates, scoffing finger-food and playing cards for matchsticks can be a great laugh and there's no harm in it. Right?

Well - yeah, to a degree. Having a gamble can be harmless. Thousands of people enjoy a flutter on the gee-gees on Grand National day hoping to win a bob or two and millions buy the odd lottery ticket hoping to win enough money to change their lives forever. Some win but most lose and the people that put a few quid on a losing horse or bought a dud lottery ticket shrug their shoulders and get on with their lives – no harm done. However, when gambling becomes an addiction it can ruin lives.

So what do people bet on? Sports, slot machines, the lottery, bingo, in casinos: you can pretty much place a bet on anything these days. People gamble for all sorts of reasons. They might need money - some people see gambling as a genuine way to make a quick buck. If someone has a big win just after they start to gamble, it might make gambling look fun, easy and lucrative – the problem is that they might go their whole lives without another win, big or small, and could waste a lot of money trying to re-capture that first taste of winning. Some people do it for the adrenalin rush and can become addicted to the rush.

Continued on next page...

Gamcare
0845 6000 133
www.gamcare.org.uk

Gamblers' Anonymous
020 7384 3040
www.gamblersanonymous.org.uk

Home Office - General Enquiries
0870 000 1585
www.homeoffice.gov.uk

Also check out:

- Debts Essentials
- Budgetting Essentials
- Legal Advice
- Anxiety
- Compulsions
- Depression
- Counselling
- Panic Attacks
- Stress

Some gamble because of social pressure and others may be wooed by the glamorous world of gambling: gambling is often portrayed on the TV and in movies as being glamorous, cool and stylish.

Gambling addicts can be driven to extreme measures to keep up their habit: lying and stealing money from friends and family, spending money set aside for other things (like holidays, or even paying the bills) on gambling and even going as far as re-mortgaging their houses to feed their gambling addiction. Addicts can find it increasingly difficult to concentrate on work, family life etc, (anything other than gambling) and can be driven to feeling suicidal because of their addiction, especially if they have got into massive debt. If you think that you might be addicted to gambling or you are worried about a friend or family member, there are organisations that can offer you help and advice. Check out the contacts below.

The Law:
The fact is that though it's illegal for anyone under 18 to enter a betting shop or a club to bet or gamble, young people still find ways to gamble and more and more young people are becoming addicted to gambling. You can't play bingo for cash until you are 18, but you can play for non-cash prizes (also in fairs & amusement arcades). You have to be 16 or over to play the football pools or buy a National Lottery ticket or a scratchcard.

Hire Purchase is often referred to as HP (like the sauce!). When you have something on HP, it means that you have the product on hire, or on loan, for the length of the agreement (or contract). The difference between Hire Purchase and a loan is that the finance is taken out against a specific object and you don't own that object until you make the final payment.

The important thing to remember with HP is that you mustn't sell the goods while they are under the "hire" part of the agreement, as they don't belong to you! You should carefully check the terms of any HP agreement so that you don't make any mistakes like this. You haven't got the same freedom as you would if you had bought the goods, however if the goods develop a problem while under HP, you have the same rights as if you had bought them outright.

This works both ways though – if you fall behind with payments, the goods might be reclaimed (you will still have the debt of the unpaid instalments to clear). It's important to face up to money problems like this instead of hiding from them, so it could be a good idea to be frank with the money lender and ask them if you could sell the goods yourself to pay them back.

As with all contracts and agreements, read all the terms and conditions and the small print and make sure you understand it all before signing on the dotted line.

Watchdog
www.bbc.co.uk/watchdog/

Citizens' Advice Bureau
www.adviceguide.org.uk

Also check out:
> Debt Essentials
> Loans

A loan is a way of borrowing money now, then paying it back later. You have to be 18 to get a loan.

There are 2 types of loan - personal and secured.

With a personal loan, you're responsible to pay it back every month until the full amount (and however much interest you are being charged) is paid back. You can pay back a loan over different periods of time – usually anything between 12 months (1 year) and 96 months (8 years).

A secured loan means that if you fail to pay the loan back to the company, they can take and sell whatever you 'secured' it on, like your house, to get the money that's owed.

Always, when taking out a loan, look at the APR (Annual Percentage Rate). The higher the APR, the more money you will have to pay back on your purchase. Obviously, the longer you take the loan out over, the more interest you'll end up paying, so take this into consideration. It may be tempting to pay back your loan over a long period of time because the monthly payments will be less, but you'll pay more in the long run.

To get a loan you usually need to have a good credit record (how long you take to pay bills, where you live and how long you've been at your bank can all affect your credit rating), be a resident in the UK, have a regular income and in some cases pay a set up fee or a deposit.

The UK Insolvency Helpline
0800 074 6918
www.insolvencyhelpline.co.uk

Student Loans Company -
0800 405010 www.slc.co.uk

Career Development Loans
www.lifelonglearning.co.uk/cd

Channel 4 Money
http://www.channel4.com/4money/

Also check out:

- Overdrafts
- Debt Essentials
- Credit Cards
- Hire Purchase

If you get stuck for money, your bank or building society may give you an overdraft. It's a semi-loan because they know you'll be paying money back into your account. It can be handy at the end of the month when cash is running dry and if you need to pay bills long overdue. You agree a limit and you won't be allowed to go beyond that. Ask about how much you can have, but be warned - you may be charged. If you go over the overdraft limit it's very expensive and the charges shoot through the roof (you will get charged a flat fee for going over your overdraft without authorisation and, in some cases, you will get charged a further penalty for each day that you remain overdrawn over the limit) so keep an eye on your balance.

Check out the nitty-gritty details before getting an overdraft or extending an existing one.

BBC Online
Advice on overdrafts
www.bbc.co.uk/radio1/onelife/finance

The Site
Info on money, cards, credit & debt
www.thesite.org.uk/homelawandmoney/money

Support 4 Learning
A money advisory service to help you deal with & debt
www.support4learning.org.uk

Also check out:
> Banks & Building Societies
> Debt Essentials
> Loans
> Credit Cards
> Store Cards

When you take out a store card, you open an account with a finance company. When you use your card to buy goods in the store, the finance company pays the store and you pay back the finance company. You will get a monthly statement with a balance that you have to pay off before a certain date.

Some store card accounts will charge you interest unless you pay the entire balance off in one go, so make sure you check out the small print to see what kind of deal you're getting before you sign up. If you miss a payment deadline, you may get charged a penalty (usually around £20), so make sure you check your statements regularly and keep up to date with payments. It can be tempting to agree to a store card when you're standing at the checkout being offered a 25% discount, but try not to be pulled in by the hype, free gifts, fee mags, preview evenings and discounts - be careful, think first: it's easy to get into debt if you keep charging stuff to cards.

To avoid the stress of debt, keep an eye on your account, try to pay off the balance when the statement arrives so you don't accrue interest, learn how to budget and use your card responsibly (i.e. to treat yourself, not to buy things you don't really need). To really make store cards work for you, be sensible, be money aware and don't go overboard – remember, you still have to pay for it all in the end.

BBC Online / Radio 1 / Onelife
Advice on credit & credit cards
www.bbc.co.uk/radio1/onelife/finance/credit

The Site
Info on money, cards, credit & debt
www.thesite.org.uk/homelawandmoney/money

Money Facts
www.moneyfacts.co.uk/guides/guide_cards.asp

Also check out:
> Debt Essentials
> Credit Cards
> Loans

If you are going on to higher education, you can apply for a student loan to help you with living costs (not tuition fees – there is a separate loan of £3,000 available for coping with tuition fees). Whether or not you are accepted for a loan and how much you will qualify for will depend on your earnings, household income and whether or not you have an Assembly Learning Grant (if your household income is less than £17,500, you may be entitled to the full Assembly Learning Grant of £2,700). The maximum amount you can apply for under the student loan scheme is £4, 405 for students living outside of London and £3,415 for those living outside of London but with their parents. You still have to pay interest on student loans, although the rate is lower than with most other loans. The interest rate as of January 2006 is 3.2%. You will not have to pay back your student loan until you are earning £15,000 a year or more. Once you earn this much, your loan repayments will start from 6th April. The repayments will be deducted directly from your salary, which is why it's important that you provide your National Insurance number when applying. You can apply for a student loan by going to the Student Finance Wales website (see links) or you should be able to pick up a paper form from the administration office of your college or University.

There are other forms of financial assistance that you may qualify for, such as a childcare grant, a parent's learning allowance, an adult dependant's grant, a disabled students' allowance, a non-repayable bursary or an Assembly Learning Grant, for example. Ask at your college or University for a list of what you may be entitled to.

The Student Loans Company
www.slc.co.uk

Student Finance Wales
www.studentfinancewales.co.uk

Also check out:
> Debt Essentials
> University Essentials
> Loans
> Overdrafts

Benefits are there to support people that are on a low income (or out of work completely) or those with difficult personal circumstances. Here is a quick guide to some of the main benefits:

Income Support – is paid to those who are out of work or work less than 16 hours a week and don't have enough money to live on. You could qualify for Income Support if you're a single parent, disabled, or a carer, for example, and you don't have £8,000 or more in savings. Contact your local Jobcentre Plus to see if you qualify.

If you get Income Support, you can also get free prescriptions, free dental care, free school dinners, Housing Benefit and Council Tax Benefit.

Jobseeker's Allowance – or JSA – is paid to those who are unemployed but looking for a job (full-time students aren't usually eligible, unless they are also looking after children). You usually have to be over 18 to claim JSA, but there are exceptions, so check with your local Jobcentre Plus. The weekly rate for 18-24-year-olds is £44.50.

Continued on next page...

Department of Work & Pensions
www.dwp.gov.uk

Disability Benefits
www.disabilitybenefits.co.uk

Directgov
www.direct.gov.uk/MoneyTaxAndBenefits/

Citizens Advice Bureau
www.adviceguide.org.uk/wales.htm

Also check out:
- Budgeting Essentials
- Unemployed Essentials

Housing Benefit – is paid to those who are out of work or on low income and need help paying some or all of their rent. There are restrictions as to who is eligible, and Housing Benefits doesn't cover the cost of electricity, water etc, so make sure you read the application form carefully. Application forms can be collected from the council.

Child Benefit – is paid to anyone bringing up a child, or children, under the age of 16 (or under 19 and still in school or full-time education). Child Benefit is £17 a week for the first child and £11.40 a week for subsequent children (however it is usually paid on a monthly basis). Call the Child Benefit Office for more information on 0845 302 1444. You can e-mail them at child.benefit@hmrc.gsi.gov.uk

Carer's Allowance – is paid to those, aged 16 or over, that spend 35 hours a week or more caring for a relative, friend or neighbour. Contact The Carer's Allowance for more information on 01253 856 123 or E-mail cau.customer-services@dwp.gsi.gov.uk.

Department of Work & Pensions
www.dwp.gov.uk

Disability Benefits
www.disabilitybenefits.co.uk

Directgov
www.direct.gov.uk/MoneyTaxAndBenefits/

Citizens Advice Bureau
www.adviceguide.org.uk/wales.htm

Also check out:
> Budgeting Essentials
> Unemployed Essentials

9. MONEY

Benjamin Franklin once said "in this world, nothing is certain but death and taxes". Yes, no matter where you go and what you do, you'll always have to pay taxes.

The amount of income tax you pay depends on how much you earn. As a young person, you're given a personal allowance of £4,895. If you earn more than this you'll be taxed. The more you earn the more income tax you pay. Every time you get paid, some of the money is taken by the Government as income tax to pay for Social Security Benefits, Defence and the National Health Service.

If you earn up to £32,400 a year, you will pay 22% income tax. If you earn more than this, you will pay 40% income tax.

You can get more info from the Tax Office (in the phone book under Inland Revenue).

The financial tax year runs from the 6th April one year to 5th April the next. All your tax will be worked out between these two dates.

Citizen's Advice Bureau
www.adviceguide.org.uk

UK Government Guide To Taxes
www.direct.gov.uk/MoneyTaxAndBenefits

National Youth Agency guide to income tax
www.youthinformation.com/Templates/Internal.asp?NodeID=90970

Taxworld (tax information)
www.taxworld.org

HM Revenue and Customs (tax information leaflets)
www.hmrc.gov.uk/leaflets/index.htm

Tax Aid (help and advice with tax queries)
www.taxaid.org.uk

Also check out:
> VAT
> Wages
> National Insurance

Most working people have to pay National Insurance Contributions (NICs). If your parents have been claiming child benefit for you, you will be given a National Insurance (NI) number. When you are 16, you will be sent a national insurance card with your number on it. If you don't have a NI number, you are required by law to apply for one when you start work in the UK. Your NI number records all of the NICs that you make over the course of your life. The contributions that you make go towards benefits such as unemployment, child benefit and the state pension.

If you are employed or self-employed in the UK, you are required to pay NICs. There are also cases in which you may choose to pay NICs if you're working abroad (visit the Citizen's Advice Bureau for more information). There are various classes of NICs depending on your situation, some of which are charged at a set amount, some of which are linked to earnings. If you're employed, NICs are paid to the Government by your employer before you get paid. If you are self-employed, you are required to organise your own payment of NICs. Late payment of NICs may result in prosecution.

Business Link
www.businesslink.gov.uk

Citizens Advice Bureau
www.adviceguide.org.uk

Department for Work and Pensions
Benefit Enquiry Line 0800 88 22 00
www.dwp.gov.uk/lifeevent/benefits/ni_number.asp

Taxation Web (page on National Insurance)
www.taxationweb.co.uk/ni/

Also check out:
- Insurance
- Wages
- Income Tax
- Value added Tax (VAT)

VAT is Value Added Tax: tax that is paid by consumers each time they purchase a product or service in the European Union. In the UK, VAT is charged at 17.5%. This means that when you buy a product or service, you actually pay for the net price plus 17.5% of it. Some products and services have different rates of VAT, which may be 5% or zero. Sometimes you may see a receipt that shows exactly how much VAT you've paid. This is purely for information purposes and doesn't mean that you've paid any more than you should.

VAT is more of a concern for those with their own businesses. Most businesses must be registered for VAT, meaning that they must charge VAT on all taxable supplies. When a business buys taxable supplies, they must pay VAT and the difference between the amount of VAT they have charged for and the amount they have paid must be paid to or refunded by HM Customs & Excise. Businesses must be careful to keep full and accurate records of all business sales and purchases so that they can be charged or refunded the correct amount. When you start a business HM Revenue & Customs organise to send you a VAT return, through which the correct amount of VAT to be paid or refunded can be calculated.

Business Link
www.businesslink.gov.uk

Directgov
www.direct.gov.uk

Taxation Web
www.taxationweb.co.uk

Just Tax guide to VAT
www.just-tax.co.uk/guide_vat.htm

Also check out:
- Self Employment
- National Insurance
- Consumer Rights
- Income Tax

Anyone can play basketball – no matter how tall or short – so don't let height put you off. If you're interested in basketball, you could either find out where your nearest team is based and try to get on the squad or you could round up a couple of your mates and shoot a few hoops in the park (basketball is growing in popularity and many parks now have courts and hoops). Of course there's nothing stopping you from practising on your own – honing your shooting or dribbling skills. Fitness is important - the court may be small compared to a football pitch, but you still have to be fit to last out a match. Don't underestimate how physically demanding basketball can be.

You can pick up a basketball for around £8. A hoop will set you back a bit more, especially if it's free-standing (they range from around £60 to £200).

If you are interested in joining a team, contact the National Association for your nearest club or ask at your local Sports or Leisure Club.

Wheelchair Basketball is also growing in popularity, with clubs springing up all around the country and many tournaments and competitions being held (such as the Visa Paralympic Wheelchair Basketball World Cup). Check out the Great Britain Wheelchair Basketball Association website for more info (see below).

Basketball Association of Wales
029 2049 6696
www.basketballwales.com

Great Britain Wheelchair Basketball Association www.gbwba.org.uk

Hoops
www.hoops.co.uk

FIBA - European federation site
www.fiba.com

Sports Council for Wales
029 2030 0500
www.sports-council-wales.co.uk

Also check out:

> Exercise & Keep Fit
> Healthy Eating
> Team Sports

There are 11 players on a cricket team – all with different skills. Some might be good at bowling, some at batting and others at fielding. Some players are great at them all! In a cricket match, one team will bat while the other team will field (try to either bowl out or catch out the batters from the opposition) and then they will swap. The bowler's job is to get the cricket ball past the batsman and his bat. If he or she's successful and knocks the little pieces of wood (called bails) off the top of the stumps, the batter from the opposition will be out. The idea is to get the batter out before he/she can score lots of runs. The fielders & wicket keeper also have important roles to play as they try to catch out the batter (catch the ball in mid-air). There are also groups for cricketers with disabilities – check out the websites below for more info. To get started you don't have to be that fit, but it's a team game and as you get better, it'll get faster. You can learn the basics, bowling, batting stance and hand-eye co-ordination at your local school or club. Expect to pay a club membership fee and/or practice session and match fees. Once you start to play regularly you will need 'whites'. They will cost around £70 new and a good bat, pads and gloves around £100. However, schools and clubs normally provide some items of equipment to get you started. See how you like it first before shelling out a load of cash.

South Wales Cricket Association
www.swca.co.uk

Glamorgan Cricket
0871 282 3401
www.glamorgancricket.com

Sports Council for Wales
029 2030 0500
www.sports-council-wales.co.uk

British Association for Cricketers with Disabilities (BACD)
www.bacd.co.uk

Cricket Federation for People with Disabilities (CFPD)
www.cfpd.org.uk

British Blind Sport (BBS)
www.britishlindsport.org.uk

Also check out:
> Disability Sport
> Team Sports
> Exercise & Keep Fit

10. SPORT & LEISURE

The beautiful game – or so some say! 22 players, 2 teams, 45 minutes each way, a pitch, 2 goals, a ref and the baffling offside rule. Football – you either love it or hate it.

Footballers have to be incredibly fit – it's not all glamorous lifestyles and fast cars; footballers are basically running (and concentrating) for the full match time of 90 minutes. Premier league footballers train, train, train and then train some more. You don't have to be David Beckham to play in a football team – there are local clubs and amateur leagues that you can become involved in, whether you are able-bodied or have a disability. Check out the contacts below for more info and contact the Football Association of Wales for details of your local club or initiative. Expect to pay an annual club membership fee and/or practice session and match fees. The essential shin pads you can grab at all good sport shops from around £5.

The Football Association of Wales
029 2037 2325
www.faw.org.uk

Five-a-side
www.fiveaside.net

Sports Council for Wales
029 2030 0500
www.sports-council-wales.co.uk

Dragon Sport
www.dragon-sport.co.uk

Fit In
www.fit-in.co.uk

Disability Football Club Directory
www.disabilityfootball.co.uk

Also check out:
> Exercise & Keep Fit
> Healthy Eating
> Team Sports

Hockey: it's fast, furious, for both sexes and for able-bodied and disabled people. You can play in school or you can join a club. If you're lucky, the school or club will provide the necessary equipment (hockey stick, shin pads etc) otherwise you will have to buy your own. Hockey sticks can cost anywhere from £6.00 to around £200. Shop around for the best deals (online sites can offer good discounts, but make sure the payment part of the site is secure).

Hockey players have to be fit - there is a lot of strain on your back and knees when playing Hockey at a high level. Bear this in mind if you are thinking of taking up the sport professionally. Hockey Basics: Two teams of 11 compete in matches. They use sticks to control a ball (dribble it, pass it, hit it, shoot to score etc). Scoring is done by defeating the goalie and getting the ball into the other team's net (but the ball has to be hit from within the shooting circle, otherwise the goal is disallowed).

World Hockey
www.fihockey.org

Welsh Hockey Union
029 2023 3257
www.welsh-hockey.co.uk

Sports Council for Wales
029 2030 0500
www.sports-council-wales.co.uk

Ability Sports Association
www.abilitysports.org.uk

Fit In
www.fit-in.co.uk

Dragon Sport
www.dragon-sport.co.uk

Also check out:

> Ice Sports
> Exercise & Keep Fit
> Healthy Eating
> Team Sports

10. SPORT & LEISURE

Netball has traditionally been seen as a game for girls, but in these modern times, more and more boys are playing and enjoying the game. Two teams of seven players battle it out on court to see who can score the most goals. Each player has a specific role and responsibility (goal attack or goal defense, for example). Players score by "shooting" and getting the ball through an elevated hoop (similar to basketball). There are many rules to remember – check out the contacts below – and skills to learn (like the bounce pass, the chest pass, the high running pass, shooting, landing, pivoting etc). You don't really need any special equipment to start playing netball – a pair of comfy trainers and a tracksuit will do (unless you play in school or for a team where they might ask you to wear a uniform). Many people opt for a short pleated skirt or shorts with a loose polo T-Shirt. Netball is a great team sport whether you like playing or as a coach. There are also lots of opportunities for disabled people to play and get involved with netball. Check out Sportability and Ability Sports Association (contacts below). You can train to be a coach or help younger players learn with Dragon Sport Netball teams around Wales. Your best contact is the Welsh Netball Association, who can put you in touch with a local team. There are also summer schools and training sessions that you can go on to brush up on those shooting skills. But be prepared for lots of drills!

Welsh Netball Association
029 2023 7048
www.welshnetball.co.uk

International Netball Federation
www.netball.org

Sports Council for Wales
029 2030 0500
www.sports-council-wales.co.uk

Dragon Sport
www.dragon-sport.co.uk

Ability Sports Association
www.abilitysports.org.uk

Sportability
www.sportability.org

Also check out:
- Basketball
- Team Sports
- Exercise & Keep Fit
- Healthy Eating

10. SPORT & LEISURE

Have you ever noticed the hush that descends over Wales when an important rugby match is on? The streets are empty and the valleys silent as the majority of Welsh people crowd around TV sets to watch the glorious game. There are two styles of rugby: Union and League. Though both are similar, having come from the same original game, there are key differences: Rugby Union teams have 15 players, while League have just 13 (and 2 substitutions). Rugby Union is considered the faster of the two games as play doesn't stop after every tackle (like in Rugby League) and, until 1995, Rugby Union was an "amateur" sport, which meant that the players could not be paid for playing, whereas League became "professional" in 1895. Each player, regardless of League or Union, has a specific role within the team (hooker, winger, fly half etc) and defence is as important as attack. Both men and women, able-bodied and disabled people can play rugby – check out the contacts below for info about your nearest club if you want to get playing, or just want to go along and support your local team.

IRB
www.irb.com

Planet Rugby
www.planet-rugby.com

Welsh Rugby Union
www.wru.co.uk

Scrum.com
www.scrum.com

Sports Council for Wales
029 2030 0500
www.sports-council-wales.co.uk

Ability Sports Association
www.abilitysports.org.uk

Sportability
www.sportability.org

Welsh Wheelchair Rugby Association
www.wwra.co.uk

Also check out:

- Disabled Sport
- Exercise & Keep Fit
- Healthy Eating

BASEBALL & ROUNDERS: Baseball is traditionally an American game (along with its sister game softball). In Wales, "rounders" is pretty much the same game but a lot less competitive. All involve a combination of teamwork and individual skills like hitting, catching and throwing. All of them are very sociable and found being played in parks across Wales from April to October. It keeps you fit and you can play and join in at any level. It's more of a sociable game, so find a club, pay a small joining fee and away you go on a sunny evening or weekend. Use the contacts to find your nearest club.

LACROSSE: Lacrosse (or Lax) is a very fast paced team game originating from North America. The ladies game is non-contact but they wear a gum-shield as the game is played around the head. There is fast tackling, stick control and skills, plus ball throwing with a net at the end of a stick. Pop Lacrosse is a great fun game, played in lots of schools across Wales, and is a modified version of the full game. Contact the Wales Lacrosse Association or the Sports Council for Wales for details of under 18 teams and clubs around Wales.

VOLLEYBALL: Volleyball is a great team game that can be played pretty much anywhere, from the beach to grass and in sports centres. The idea is to score by hitting the ball, over a very high net with your hand, and involves a lot of skill and eye-ball co-ordination. You can play in single sex teams or mixed and in teams of 2 or 4. There are competitions and tournaments you can get involved in. Your local volleyball club will be able to keep you up-to-date about them.

Baseball Softball UK
020 7453 7055

Wales Lacrosse
www.waleslacrosse.org.uk

Welsh Volleyball Association
029 2031 3561

Sports Council for Wales
029 2030 0500
www.sports-council-wales.co.uk

Ability Sports Association
www.abilitysports.org.uk

Sportability
www.sportability.org

Also check out:

- Disabled Sport
- Exercise & Keep Fit
- Healthy Eating

Boxing is not a sport you should just take up lightly because you like hitting people. It's not about that at all. Boxing is about mental strength as well as physical. It takes a lot of practice, discipline and commitment. Boxing can be hard work and can sometimes hurt, but it's fantastic for all-round fitness and body conditioning, and is a very competitive sport. Expect to train hard and be pushed to your limits. If you still fancy it contact the Welsh Amateur Boxing Association to arrange a time and date for you to pop along to your local club. Ask about joining fees etc. Just popping in won't get you any brownie points.

Fencing is swordplay and one of the oldest of sports. You need to be fast, skilfull and dexterous to play and be prepared to train hard. There are 3 types of fencing. Foil, Epee or Sabre and in each there are different ways of attacking and defending. Fencing for wheelchair users is also a major sport in the Paralympic Games. A large number of clubs now exist throughout the UK. Some are run as evening classes and others are organised in sports centres, youth clubs, schools and colleges. Fencing is one of the safest of sports and, provided the correct equipment is used, even minor injuries are uncommon. Check out the BFA for details of local clubs etc.

Welsh Amateur Boxing Association
029 2062 3566

The Amateur Boxing Association
020 8778 0251

British Boxing
News, chat forums, and online merchandise
www.britishboxing.com

Welsh Fencing
029 2037 1844
www.welshfencing.org

British Fencing Association (BFA)
0208 742 3032
www.britishfencing.com

Also check out:
> Athletics
> Martial Arts

GYMNASTICS

Take to the beam, the parallel bars or even the floor. There are many aspects to gymnastics not just bouncing onto a box. Gymnastics is an amazing way to get fit and is extremely athletic, but it gets harder as you get older and less supple. The key is to start young. Gymnastics takes great skills in balance and concentration as well as a lot of practice to get good. There are gymnastic clubs that you can join. You can specialise in one area of gymnastics if you wish to. Gymnastics is one of the most popular Olympic Sports.

TRAMPOLINING

Are you the bouncy type? Trampolining is a great sport that keeps you very fit and lets you be creative while flying through the air. Many clubs meet up at local leisure centres and there are courses and sessions you can go on to get a taster and then work your way up the grades. There are lads and girls teams and you get judged on acrobatic skills, moves and height. Trampolining is very much like gymnastics in the air. Contact the Sports Council for further details about local clubs, training sessions and competitions.

Welsh Amateur Gymnastics Association
029 2062 4321

Sports Council for Wales
029 2030 0500
www.sports-council-wales.co.uk
www.fit-in.co.uk

Trampolining
www.welcome.to/trampolining

Also check out:
> Dance
> Athletics

10. SPORT & LEISURE

It's great to be able to get outside and run about but in winter when it's cold, wet and dark it's not really practical. So why not head off to your local leisure centre, there are activities to suit everybody.Usually you have to be over 16 to join in classes and use the gym, but many leisure centres are now introducing special classes and programmes for those under 16. So if you're under 16 contact your local leisure centre to find out what activities they have.

Aerobics & Step-Aerobics - There are Aerobics and Step-Aerobics classes for every level, if you're new to it go for a low or multi-level class, that way you'll be able to progress at your own pace. Classes usually combine a routine done to music (using a small step in the case of step-aerobics) with toning excercises like sit-ups and press-ups. Some classes also target specific areas like legs, bums and tums. The important thing at these classes, is not to overdo it, it is not a competition.

Badminton and Squash - You will need to book places on Squash and Badminton courts in advance, most leisure centres also provide equipment to hire. You need a partner for these so it's good for motivation as there'll be someone else to encourage you, so get you mate to come with you.

Boxercise - This involves doing many of the moves and techniques that are associated with boxing but without the physical contact. The classes usually incorporate some kind of circuit involving skipping, punch bags and pads and possibly kick-boxing to work the lower body. Boxercise mainly works the upper body, strengthening arms, abs, the chest and shoulders.

Circuit Training - Circuit training involves doing lots of different types of excercises, one after the other. The type of excercises vary but will often include sprinting, sit-ups, press-ups, skipping, squats and step-ups.

Continued on next page...

Gym - If you're going to use a gym it's a good idea to get the staff there to give you a fitness test and a programme to follow, many gyms don't allow you to use the equipment without an induction but if they don't offer, ask! The staff there will then be able to teach you how to use the equipment properly and determine the right length of time and weights.

Spinning - In this class, they use a special exercise bike, the instructor has one and each class member sits on another facing the front and follow the instructions. A lever on these special bikes to make it feel as though you're going up or down hill. These classes improve general fitness.

Swimming - If you're not a strong swimmer, most leisure centres do classes. Don't be embarrassed that you can't swim, everyone will be in the same boat and you'll soon be master the strokes. You can also try aqua-aerobics, again this is great exercise. It's good fun and great if the thought of getting all sweaty isn't appealing.

General Tips: Always drink enough water ? Take a drink whenever you need it, don't wait for the instructor to tell you ? Take a towel. You'll need it for putting under you during ab work and is essential in the gym for wiping the equipment after you use it, other people don't want to be covered in your sweat! All you need is comfortable clothing. A T-shirt and shorts is fine. Have a go at a few activites and find the one to suit you. You don't have to stick to one either, mix and match to keep yourself motivated. Have fun!
Contact your local authority for a list of Health & Leisure Centres and Private Health Clubs

Sports Council for Wales
029 2030 0500
www.sports-council-wales.co.uk

Also check out:
> Diet & Exercise
> Exercise & Keep Fit

Ice Skating (Figure Skating)

Ice-skating is a fab way to get fit and wet at the same time (if you're no good!).

Your local ice-rink will have lessons for beginners that are worth taking, and also for more advanced skaters. Ice skates start at around £60, but you can pay hundreds for professional skates.

Ice Hockey

Ice-hockey is fast, physical and skilful. It can sometimes be expensive kit-wise. You need to be very fit and powerful to play at a high level. Master skating first and then take on the game itself. If you can't skate learn first! Ice Hockey skates can cost between £45 and £400, so shop around!

Equipment list: Helmet, gloves, neck guard, body amour (all compulsory) and elbow pads, shorts and leg pads (all optional).

Sledge Hockey (Ice Hockey for people with a disability)

Sledge Hockey is a version of Ice Hockey for people with a disability. Players sit on specially designed sledges that have two skate blades and have two sticks instead of one (one end of the stick is pointy, so players can dig it into the ice and propel themselves along). Apart from the sledge and sticks, the rest of the equipment is the same as required for ice hockey.

Other Ice sports include curling, ice climbing and even ice carving.

Ice Hockey UK 0115 915 924
www.icehockeyuk.co.uk

National Ice-Skating Association
0115 9888 060
www.iceskating.org.uk

Sports Council for Wales
029 2030 0500
www.sports-council-wales.co.uk

British Sledge Hockey Association
www.bsha.co.uk

Wheel Power
www.wheelpower.org.uk/sports/dyncat.cfm?catid=16975

Also check out:
> Hockey
> Skiing & Snowboarding

From grappling to kicking, striking to aerobic fitness, self-defence and discipline, martial arts cover it all. Fitness levels, concentration and skill-building are the main elements in all martial arts. It takes time to become very good at any one of them. Don't expect it overnight. But, you can take part whatever you're age, size or ability. Expect to pay to join a club and for the right equipment. You can also get more info from your local leisure centre, where they may have lessons. Here's a quick list of martial arts:

Karate is a form of a fighting technique (attack and defence) developed in Japanese using only the human body (no weapons).

Judo is another weaponless fighting/defence method developed in Japan. Adapted from Jujitsu, Judo uses the opponent's strength to overcome him or her.

Kung Fu is an old form of martial arts consisting of many styles (including Shaolin, which has 170 moves divided into five styles named after animals the movements were supposed to resemble or represent; Tiger, Leopard, Snake, Dragon and Crane.

Tae Kwon Do is a Korean martial art, which grew from the basis of karate, which emphasises the use of kicking techniques.

Kick Boxing is a Japanese martial art where opponents are allowed to hit each other with fists and feet, hitting above the hip.

Aikido uses the opponents' energy against them. Based on aikijutsu, this is viewed as a non-aggressive martial art. Aikido is Japanese for "the way of harmony."

Welsh Judo Association
01792 869 460
www.britishjudo.org.uk

Welsh Karate federation
01834 813 776

World Kickboxing Association
www.kickboxing-wka.co.uk/Clubs/club_wales_40.htm

Taichi Finder
Clubs around Wales
www.taichifinder.co.uk/local

Also check out:
> Crime Prevention & Personal Safety
> Exercise & Keep Fit

SNOOKER & POOL - There's serious money in them if you're good. Snooker and Pool can be great fun for a laugh, for beginners to the more serious players. If you fancy getting good there are clubs and organisations that you can join to get you trained properly. There are lads and girls teams in all events, and tournaments that you can get involved in. Contact the organisation that you're most interested in for more details of local clubs around you.

TABLE TENNIS - Table Tennis is a very fast sport for 2-4 people and great if you don't like running but have good hand-eye coordination. If you fancy having a go, contact the Table Tennis Association of Wales who can put you in touch with your local Table Tennis community club or local league. You can then get more info on coaching and take part in competitions. The community clubs regularly meet up in leisure centres across Wales and the leagues give you the opportunity to compete against other local clubs.

TIDDLYWINKS - Tiddlywinks is a game for four people (who play in two pairs). Each match lasts 25 minutes. Tiddlywinks is a popular sport in universities. In 1961, HRH Prince Phillip established a British Universities Championship, and universities across Britain still compete in the competition. There are many rules to Tiddlywinks, so if you are interested in taking up the sport, it's probably best to join an association or club.

Great Snooker Sites
www.110sport.com/snooker
www.worldsnooker.com
www.worldofsnooker.co.uk

Welsh Pool Association
01639 830 990
www.welshpoolassociation.co.uk

Table Tennis Association of Wales
North Wales: 01286 881195
South Wales: 01446 740750
www.btinternet.com/~ttaw

Sports Council for Wales
029 2030 0500
www.sports-council-wales.co.uk

Also check out:
- Tennis
- Pubs & Clubs

Tennis, like Squash and Badminton, is a racquet sport. Health & Leisure Centres are the main places you'll find Tennis courts set up (although some cities, towns and villages have outdoor courts for general public use). For a small fee you can play for an hour and hire their equipment. If you want to buy your own, you will need a racquet, a set of tennis balls and the appropriate sportswear and trainers (note that some Leisure Centres won't allow people to wear trainers with black rubber soles on their courts). You can pick up a new racquet quite cheaply (from around £10). Professional racquets can cost hundreds.

Tennis is a fast-paced game between two players. Depending on the tournament, players have to win the best of three sets or of five sets. Players who win the most games win the set and the players with the most sets win the match (hence the saying "game, set, match"). Matches can go on for several hours, so professional tennis players have to be exceptionally fit.

If you are interested in Tennis, whether able-bodied or disabled, there are clubs, classes, tournaments and courses that you can get involved in. Ask at your local leisure centre for further details. Check out your yellow pages to find your nearest leisure centre. www.yell.com

Tennis Wales
029 2046 3335
www.tennis.wales.org

Sports Council for Wales
029 2030 0500
www.sports-council-wales.co.uk

Fit In
www.fit-in.co.uk

WheelPower – British Wheelchair Sport
www.wheelpower.org.uk

Also check out:
> Health & Leisure Centres
> Exercise & Keep Fit
> Healthy Eating

The practice of Yoga is intended to provide a better balance between mind, body and soul. With its origins in ancient India, it has only become popular in the UK fairly recently and has flourished in the last twenty years. Nowadays most areas will have a local Yoga course or teacher; some may even have a Yoga school. There are many different forms of Yoga, some of which will be quite light, others will be surprisingly hard work. Discovering which type of Yoga is right for you can be a tough task. Here's a quick guide:

Hatha – A series of stable poses that should be comfortable to hold, stretches, massage and relaxation.

Kundalini – The emphasis of Kundalini, thought to be one of the most powerful forms of Yoga, is on breathing and chanting, rather than Yoga poses.

Ashtanga – An eight-step sequence of postures synchronised with breathing exercises and meditation.

Bikram – A physically demanding series of 26 postures practiced in a heated room – sometimes to temperatures as much as 105 degrees Fahrenheit. Expect to sweat!

Pilates - Develops awareness of the body, aims to improve and change posture and increase flexibility and ease of movement.

Classes tend to cost between £3 and £8 per session. It is recommended that yoga should be practiced regularly for short periods. As Yoga can be quite disciplined, it is also advisable to stick at it – sometimes it can take time to feel its benefits. And be careful! Don't rush in and try to do everything at once or you could risk an injury. Yoga should be about getting your body into positions comfortably. It isn't a competition so don't tie yourself in knots trying to do it!

The British Wheel of Yoga
01529 306851
www.bwy.org.uk

YogaUK
www.yogauk.com

Pilates Foundation
www.pilatesfoundation.com

Also check out:
- Mental Health
- Diet & Exercise

FLYING - Training for each type of air sport may be slightly different, but ultimately the goal is the same - to obtain your Club Pilot (CP) rating. Air Law says that you must be at least 16 before you can attempt a solo flight. Once you have a Club Pilot rating, you can then enjoy the freedom of air flight in a club. **HANG GLIDING & PARAGLIDING** - Hang gliders strap themselves to a lightweight glider, run down an incline and launch themselves into an updraft to take off and soar the skies. They steer the craft by shifting their bodyweight. A hang glider has a rigid frame with fabric stretched over it (imagine a kite) and a rigid support bar for shifting bodyweight. Paragliders were developed from parachutes and don't have a framework. Paragliders jump off high points where there are strong updrafts and gently descend, using their paraglider in much the same way as a hang glider. To get started sign up for a hang gliding or paragliding course at a British Hang Gliding & Paragliding Association (BHPA) qualified training school. **PARCHUTING** - Throwing yourself off a platform, or a cliff, or out of a perfectly good plane might not be everyone's cup of tea, but as far as excitement goes, this is one activity that must be hard to top. If you want to get the blood rushing in your ears and your heart pounding, then maybe parachuting or skydiving is your cup of tea. It might be wise to contact your GP before you jump, especially if you have weak knees, a back injury, or high blood pressure etc. **SAFETY** – Take it seriously! Make sure that you check out the credentials of any centres or training schools you use, take out the proper insurance and make sure you use all the right equipment and follow all advised safety checks.

Sports Council for Wales
029 2030 0500
www.sports-council-wales.co.uk

South East Wales Hang Gliding & Paragliding Club
www.sewhgpgc.co.uk

British Parachute Association
www.bpa.org.uk

BHPA (British Hang Gliding & Paragliding Association) 0116 2611322 www.bhpa.co.uk

Also check out:
>Climbing & Mountaineering
>Exercise & Keep Fit
>Healthy Eating

You probably had an introduction to athletics at school, but in case you were off sick that day, here's a quick list of what classifies as "athletics":

Sprinting (100m & 200m), Running (400m, 800m, 1,500m, 5,000m, 10,000m & Marathon), Hurdles (110m & 400m), 3,000m Steeplechase, Walking (20km, 50km), Jumping (High Jump, Long Jump, Triple Jump & Pole Vault), Throwing (Discus, Javelin, Shot Put & Hammer). A Decathlon is a men's competition involving 10 athletic events and a Heptathlon is a women's competition involving 7 athletic events.

There are many tracks and clubs that you can join to get involved further and get better at something you may have only tried out at school – whether you are able-bodied or have a disability. Contact the Athletics Association of Wales for more details. If you're a pretty good sprinter for example and want to train, get professional help, start competing against others and, who knows, you could be in the next Olympics!

Athletics Association of Wales
01633 416633
www.welshathletics.org

British Olympic Association
020 8811 2677
www.boa.org.uk

The Olympic Games
www.olympic.org

Commonwealth Games
www.commonwealthgames.com

Sports Council for Wales
029 2030 0500
www.sports-council-wales.co.uk

Disability Sport Cymru
029 2030 0525
www.disability-sport-cymru.co.uk

Also check out:

> Disability Sport
> Exercise & Keep Fit
> Healthy Eating

Canoeing is a brilliant way to keep active and see some great sights. There are three kinds of canoe and various styles of canoeing. There is the kayak, a one-man canoe in which you sit and row with a double-ended paddle. A canoe is the same as a kayak but the paddler kneels and uses a single-ended paddle. An open canoe is an open boat in which more than one paddler kneels, using a single-ended paddle. In these canoes you can either just amble along up-river, which is known as recreational canoeing or you can compete in slalom, sprint, marathon, white water racing, rodeo events and there's even a ball sport called canoe polo.

Most people can canoe, regardless of age, gender or ability. To compete, the most beneficial attribute is upper body strength and the fitter you are, the better you'll be. To begin canoeing, it's probably best to approach your local canoeing club. Otherwise, there are plenty of places where you can try canoeing out to see if you like it. It's also a relatively cheap sport to take part in and, if you join a club, you can use their equipment whilst slowly acquiring your own equipment.

SAFETY – Take it seriously! Make sure that you check out the credentials of any centres or training schools you use, take out the proper insurance and make sure you use all the right equipment and follow all advised safety checks.

Plas Menai National Watersports Centre
01248 670 964 www.plasmenai.co.uk

Welsh Canoeing Association
01792 869 460 www.welsh-canoeing.org.uk

National White Water Centre
01678 521 083

Sports Council for Wales
029 2030 0500
www.sports-council-wales.co.uk

Disability Sport Cymru 029 2030 0525
www.disability-sport-cymru.co.uk

Also check out:
> Rowing & Sailing
> Surfing & Windsurfing
> Health & Leisure Centres

Climbing

If you want to try your hand at climbing, but you don't fancy braving the elements, then an indoor climbing wall could be just the ticket. There are loads of walls in Wales – check out the British Mountaineering Council website for a full list. Indoor climbing walls have developed over the years and some are now difficult/technical enough to keep even advanced climbers happy. For you novices out there, don't worry, there are still plenty of beginner walls.

Make sure you wear all the advised safety gear and pay attention to the instructor. As the walls get harder, the strain on the body increases. Climbers need good upper body strength (think Tom Cruise at the start of Mission Impossible 2!) and a head for heights.

Mountaineering

Did you know that there's a Regional Access Database, full of advice on crags and mountain areas in England and Wales? Well, there is! The database, accessed through the British Mountaineering Council website, has info on seasonal access restrictions, special advice for groups, delicate or banned access or specific parking and approach advice. If you're intending to do some outdoor climbing, it's vital that you know what you're doing and don't push yourself beyond your limits. For further safety info and a guide on what to take, check out Hiking & Walking.

British Mountaineering Council
www.thbmc.co.uk

Welsh Orienteering Association
01792 204 643
www.woa.org.uk

Activity Wales
www.activitywales.co.uk

YHA
020 7025 1900
www.yha.org.uk

Sports Council for Wales
029 2030 0500
www.sports-council-wales.o.uk

Also check out:
> Hiking & Walking

There are so many different types of cycling from mountain-biking to road-racing, trail-biking and stunt-biking. You get very fit and the options are endless, right from your front door to cycling across continents for charity or racing.

Wales is the ideal venue for mountain biking, so much so that the International Mountain Biking Association lists it as having some of the best trails in the world. So get out there and explore what Wales has to offer.

If you fancy yourself more as the next Lance Armstrong, there are cycle clubs in pretty much every big town. You can find out from a local bike shop or the contacts below. Get in touch with a club before splashing out on expensive gear. They'll advise you on what you need for the type of cycling you're interested in. A well fitting helmet is essential for all types of bike riding. There is also a national cycle network where you can get cycle maps for around the UK.

The Tour de France is one of cycling's most famous events and one of the hardest, most gruelling sporting events in the world - three practically non-stop weeks of cycling around France and up some of the highest (and steepest!) mountains in Europe. Find out more about Le Tour on their website.

Welsh Cycling Union
01633 671 814
www.cyclewales.co.uk

Mountain Biking Wales
www.mbwales.com

National Cycle Network
029 2065 0601
www.sustrans.org.uk

Sports Council for Wales
029 2030 0500
www.sports-council-wales.co.uk

Also check out:

> Exercise & Keep Fit
> Healthy Eating
> Health & Leisure Centres

There are many types of fishing and angling from fly to deep sea and there are loads of opportunities for you to enjoy fishing around the waters of Wales. Fishing is peaceful and a great way to while away those hours, or you could get involved in angling competitions.

Be careful, though – you can't simply fish anywhere that takes your fancy. Anybody aged 12 years or over fishing for salmon, trout, freshwater fish or eels in Wales must have an Environment Agency rod license. If you are caught fishing without one, you could be fined up to £2,500. Licenses cost between £3.25 for a 1-day license to £65 for a full season license.

Go to www.environment-agency.gov.uk/subjects/fish/399730/ to buy your license online.

Fishing & angling can also give you a real sense of the environment and a respect for the wildlife around you. There is a conservation code that you can stick to. Get your copy from The Countryside Council for Wales 01248 385500 www.ccw.gov.uk

Fishing in Wales
www.fishing-in-wales.com

Go-Fishing
www.go-fishing.co.uk

Activity Wales
Course-fishing, sea-angling, fly-fishing
01437 766888
www.activitywales.com

Sports Council for Wales
029 2030 0500
www.sports-council-wales.co.uk

Also check out:

> Pollution
> Conservation
> Countryside

Light exercise in beautiful surroundings; golf is sociable and you can expect to walk around 4-miles over 18 holes without even realising it. Expect to pay for a round of golf, even if it's pitch and putt. You can also hire golf clubs, so don't go buying until you know you like it.

The objective in golf is to get the ball in the hole! Players hit the ball from the tee (the starting place) and try to get it into the hole in the ground in as few strokes as possible. You have to count how many times you hit the ball before it goes in. There are 18 holes on a full size golf course and each hole has a "par" (an average amount of strokes that it should take a player to get the ball in the hole). As you get better, you may do it in fewer strokes than the "par". This is how you develop your handicap. For example, if the total "par" for the course is 76 and you go round in 100, your handicap is +26, which means you get 26 shots start before your opponent begins, if their handicap is 0. You can also play for points using the Stableford scoring system (points awarded at each hole). The winner is the one with the most points:
1 point = Bogey (one over par)
2 points = Par
3 points = Birdie (one under par)
4 points = Eagle (two under par)
5 points = Albatross (three under par)

World Golf
www.worldgolf.com

Anyone for Tee?
www.anyonefortee.com

Get into Golf
www.getintogolf.org]

Online Golf
www.onlinegolf.co.uk

Sports Council for Wales
029 2030 0500
www.sports-council-wales.co.uk

Also check out:
> Exercise & Keep Fit

From your front door to the mountains of Snowdonia and beyond, walking is something you may take for granted. Those little legs of yours can take you places nothing else can and let you escape for a few minutes, hours or even days. You don't have to be fit for a little ramble; as you get fitter you'll naturally take on more demanding walks and treks.

It's vital to check the weather forecast before you set off on a hike or a long walk, especially if it involves mountains. Don't ignore weather warnings and don't go out without the right gear, or you could find yourself caught out and in need of rescue. Take your mobile phone with you if you have one, but be mindful that you might not get a signal in remote areas. Last but not least, tell someone where you're going, show them the route and let them know when you think you'll be back so that they can raise the alarm if you don't return on time.

Here is a guide to some basic kit you'll need to take on longer treks:
Walking boots.
Sleeping bag and tent if you're sleeping over.
A small (or big) rucksack to carry your stuff in.
Water, sunscreen and waterproof jacket.
Torch, compass and maps on longer treks.

Welsh Orienteering Association
01792 204 643
www.woa.org.uk

Activity Wales
www.activitywales.co.uk

The Ramblers Association (Wales)
01978 855 148
www.ramblers.org.uk

YHA
020 7025 1900
www.yha.org.uk

Sports Council for Wales
029 2030 0500
www.sports-council-wales.co.uk

Also check out:
> Climbing & Mountaineering
> Exercise & Keep Fit

Horse-riding or equestrian activities are fantastic for fitness and can be immensely enjoyable. You'll soon find muscles you thought you never had! You don't have to own your own horse to go horse riding – you can join a stables or sign up for local riding classes at a riding school (to find a local riding school, contact the British Horse Society). Lessons cost upwards of £12 per hour for a group lesson and from around £15 for half hour private lessons, which are sometimes a good idea for first timers! Many schools offer good quality and well looked after horses and ponies (don't even think about booking if the horses aren't exceptionally cared for), along with excellent facilities such as floodlit outdoor riding areas, an indoor school for when it's raining, and maybe even a cross country course.

Once you've mastered the basics your options are endless. Some people prefer the freedom of a gentle hack in the country rather than the confines of a riding school, whereas other riders get the bug for the skill that experienced horsemanship requires, and are hooked to the discipline for life. Whatever you fancy, a good riding school should be able to offer you advice on riding and safety, horsemanship, buying a horse, and a wealth of other information to help you get the most out of your riding. You may even be able to take out a horse on loan, which means you look after and finance the care of the horse, without actually owning it – a great taster if you're thinking of buying your own one day. If you are seriously committed to horses, or maybe thinking about working in the industry, you may also be able to achieve some BHS qualifications or more basic certificates like stable management for example.

The British Horse Society (BHS)
08701 202244
www.bhs.org.uk

Directory of Riding Schools & Livery Stables in Wales
www.horseweb-uk.com

New Rider
www.newrider.com

Equine World
www.equine-world.co.uk

Also check out:

> Exercise & Keep Fit
> The Animal Kingdom

Motor Sports range from quad biking to Formula 1 (including karting, motorcross, scrambling, superbike and rallying, to name a few). If you've got petrol running through your veins and want to see if Motor Sports are for you, why not have a go at karting? There are lots of activity centres around Wales - check out the Activity Wales website below.

If you are taking part in Motor Sports, you should always follow the safety rules and wear the helmet, goggles, gloves, leathers, boots etc that the centre or staff advise you to. Always listen to the tutor and don't be tempted to break the rules and show off in front of your friends.

Wales is also a great place to go and watch rallies, but beware; road rallies in Wales rarely start before 11pm at night (dressing up really warm, taking a flask of hot tea and sitting watching cars thundering past is a top Saturday night out for some). The Wales Rally GB is a big sporting event attracting the big names in rallying. Get info on this year's rally from Wales Rally GB.

Wales Rally GB
www.walesrallygb.com

Quad-Racing Association
01264 354 259
www.quadriding.com

Activity Wales • Karting
www.activitywales.com

Newport Speedway Official Website:
freespace.virgin.net/ian.rodger/Newport.htm

Sports Council for Wales
029 2030 0500
www.sports-council-wales.co.uk

Also check out:
> Driving Essentials

Rowing: Steve Redgrave and Matthew Pinsent have raised the profile of rowing in recent years, with their first class performance at the Olympics. Then there's the Boat Race between Oxford and Cambridge every year. Rowing is becoming a popular sport. You can row on your own (single skull), in pairs (skull pairs or cox pairs), in fours (un-cox fours and cox fours) and in eights (cox eights). The "cox" is the person in the boat who steers the boat and motivates and calms the crew. **Sailing:** Messing about in boats (safely of course!) not only builds up your strength and muscle tone but it can help you improve at other sports and activities. Plus, it's great fun. Loads of people take to the waves and lakes to enjoy sailing and boating. You can do it at any age and in any size boat. You can do it on your own or as a team, the list is endless. The Royal Yachting Association (RYA) has set up a National Sailing Scheme for people who want to try out their sea legs for the first time and learn basic skills to skippering your own boat. Contact them for details. The Cirdan Sailing Trust also gives young people the chance to experience living and working on board a large sailing vessel. **Tall Ships:** The Tall Ships Youth Fund is a registered charity dedicated to the personal development of young people through the crewing of Tall Ships – check out their website for more info. **Disabled Sailing:** There are many opportunities to sail if you have a disability – check out the International Foundation for Disabled Sailing.

Welsh Amateur Rowing Association
www.wara.org.uk

Welsh Yachting Association
01248 670 738
www.welshsquad.in4mation.org.uk

Cirdan Sailing Trust
07000 784751 www.cirdan-faramir.co.uk

Royal Yachting Association (RYA)
0845 345 0400 www.rya.org.uk

Tall Ships Adventures
www.tallships.org

International Foundation for Disabled Sailing www.sailing.org

Also check out:
- Canoeing
- Surfing & Windsurfing

Jogging and running are both ideal for losing those pounds and sightseeing at the same time. Jogging is great aerobic exercise, making it great for working your heart and burning fat, but it can be quite hard on your joints, especially on your knees, so take it easy if you have weak ones. Don't try and run a marathon on your first day. Start off by warming up at a fast walk then slowly build up to a pace where you can still have a conversation (if you are going at a pace where you can't hold a conversation you're pushing yourself too hard and slow down). Try and run for 10 minutes to begin with, then build up gradually as you get fitter.

Jogging and running don't have to just be plodding the streets either. You can do it as road-running, cross-country running and distance running. You can also do it in a team event in races, or on your own for fun, or in marathons and half marathons. A good way to get started is to do a small run for charity and work your way up. There are also many clubs you can join where there are other people like you to run with. It can be fun to run with others, not to mention safer, especially in the darker winter evenings. If the weather means you can't get out and about, you could always try the running machine at the gym instead.

British Athletics Wales Page
www.british-athletics.co.uk/clubs/county50.htm

BBC Fitness
www.bbc.co.uk/health/fitness/active.shmtl

Sports Council for Wales
029 2030 0500
www.sports-council-wales.co.uk

Also check out:
> Exercise & Keep Fit
> Athletics
> Crime Prevention & Personal Safety
> Health & Leisure Centres

Roller sports take a lot of balance and as a result, great bum and fab legs is what you can expect. Roller sports include Roller Skating & Blading, Skateboarding and Inline Puck Hockey. There are many leagues that you can now join around Wales. Contact the Sports Development Officer of your local Council. You can speed around parks, skate parks or in your drive. You may be the pavement type or the local at the roller disco. However you choose to skate, blade or board, you'll need the right equipment.

ROLLER BLADING & ROLLER SKATING - Whether it's Blading or Skating you're into - if you're zipping along on wheels you should wear a helmet and protective pads. You can get pads to protect your wrists (which suffer a lot if you're not the most steady person on wheels), knees and elbows.

SKATEBOARDING - If you want to try skateboarding, why not get yourself a board, some pads (to protect your wrists, knees and elbows) and a helmet and get down to the nearest skate park or ramp park and give it a go? You might be a born natural. There are skateparks in Cardiff, Cwmbran, Swansea, Pontypool, Rhyl, Tywyn, Blaenau Gwent, Tregaron, Llandudno, Newport, Aberavon and other places.

INLINE PUCK HOCKEY - Inline Puck Hockey is like Ice-Hockey, without the ice! If you fancy a go, check out the websites below for club details. Make sure you wear all the safety gear.

British Inline Puck Hockey Association
www.bipha.co.uk

Street Skater
www.streetskater.co.uk

SK8M8 – list of skateparks in Wales.
www.sk8m8.com

Sports Council for Wales
029 2030 0500
www.sports-council-wales.co.uk

Also check out:
> Ice Skating & Ice Hockey

It's no life without snow life. Snow sports are for everyone, including those with disabilities. Skiing and Snowboarding are the two most popular, but there's also Blading, Telemarking, Touring, Cross Country Sking, Sledging and Rubber Inner-tubing. There are hundreds of holidays you can go on and plenty of places throughout Wales for you to learn the basics before hitting the real snow elsewhere. That way you can really enjoy the snow and take it to the next level.

It's important to have the right equipment if you're going to try snow sports. However, Ski and Snowboard equipment can be expensive, so it may be a good idea to hire kit at first, incase you decide it's not for you after all. Dry Slopes - no excuse

Llangrannog Ski Centre - 01239 654656
Pembrey Ski Slope - 01554 834443
Pontypool Ski Centre - 01495 756955
Llandudno Ski & Snowboard Centre - 01492 874707
Plas-y-Brenin National Centre - 01690 720214 www.pyb.co.uk
Rhiw Goch Ski Centre 01766 540578
Ski & Snowboard Centre 029 20 561793 www.skicardiff.com
Swansea Ski Centre 01792 645639

Snowsport Cymru Wales
029 2056 19094

Snowlife
www.snowlife.org.uk

Sports Council for Wales
029 2030 0500
www.sports-council-wales.co.uk

Ski Club of Great Britain
www.skiclub.co.uk

Snowlife page on skiing with disabilities
www.snowlife.org.uk/ski/skiing-with-disabilities.asp

Disability Snowsport UK
www.disabilitysnowsport.org.uk

Also check out:
> Ice Skating & Ice Hockey
> Surfing & Windsurfing

SURFING - So what if the weather is bad? If you're wet, you may as well be in the water! Surf is definitely up in Wales. There are surf schools everywhere offering surfing lessons to absolute beginners and upwards. There are also surf courses and surf shops where you can hire surfboards and wetsuits. Sessions are available for lads and girls, plus there are lots of tournaments around the UK that you can go to and simply watch from the shore. If you are going to give surfing a go, make sure you've got the right kit and follow the safety rules of the beach. You need to be a strong swimmer, so practice (in the sea if you can), but please be careful of tides. Check first and stay safe.

WINDSURFING - Windsurfing is similar to surfing – you still stand upright on a board and ride the waves, but this time there's a big sail attached to the board which catches the wind and propels you along (sometimes very quickly, so be careful). You don't have to be mega strong to take part – it's more about technique than muscles! If you've never tried windsurfing before, it may be a good idea to get lessons – there's a lot to learn (how to get upright, how to use the wind to move, how to control the direction of the board, how to "ditch" safely if you're going to fast or in the wrong direction etc). Beginners courses cost around £50. You can pick up a second-hand board and rig for upwards of £150.

Welsh Surfing Federation Surf School
01792 386 426
www.wsfsurfschool.co.uk

Gower Surfing Development
01792 360 370
www.gowersurfing.com

UK Windsurfing Association
http://ukwindsurfing.com/

Plas Menai National Watersports Centre
01248 670 964
www.plasmenai.co.uk

Also check out:
> Rowing & Sailing

ARCHERY is highly skilled but not hugely physically demanding. The sport is split into Target Archery (the Olympic, fixed target discipline) and Field Archery (shooting mock animals on the move). Strength in your legs and back are more important than bulging biceps, and you don't have to have training beforehand. It's easy to fire an arrow, but it takes years to get good. Clubs have open days to give you a taster and lend you the equipment.

DARTS - There's serious money in them if you're good. Darts can be great fun for a laugh, for beginners to the more serious players. If you fancy getting good there are clubs and organisations that you can join to get you trained properly. There are lads and girls teams in all events and tournaments that you can get involved in.

PAINTBALLING - slightly different from the other target sports in that you are the target! - is a great laugh. Usually, two teams compete and try to capture each other's barracks or a flag first. Once you've been shot, you're out of the game. Don't try to paintball on your own – go to an organised event, where they will provide you with all the equipment you need to paintball safely (boots, camouflage gear and most importantly – eye goggles). NEVER take your goggles off during a session and NEVER shoot at someone who isn't wearing goggles. **SHOOTING** - Clay Pigeon Shooting involves firing a gun (usually a shotgun) at clay discs that are fired up into the air by a machine (so requires good hand-to-eye coordination). It can be taken up by people aged 9 up. You should contact a local gun club or shooting school for proper training and tuition. Make sure that they are properly insured and licensed.

BASC Wales - The British Association for Shooting & Conservation
www.basc.org.uk

Grand National Archery Society
01952 677888 www.gnas.org

Welsh Darts Organisation
01495 247 732 www.welshdarts.org

Just Paintball
www.justpaintball.co.uk

Also check out:
> Outdoor Pursuits
> Disability Sports

10.4 Disability Sport

A disability doesn't have to stop you from taking part in sport. Wales has many opportunities for disabled people to take part in sport and has world champions as a result. On a smaller scale there are teams you can get involved in and there are the Paralympics that you can get involved in as well. Contact Disability Sport Cymru at the Sports Council for Wales for details.

You could also contact your local Health & Leisure Centre to find out if they offer any programmes, sessions or classes.

Every 4 years there is also a Special Olympics held for people with learning disabilities. Check it out at http://www.specialolympicsgb.org/

Disability Sport
www.disabilitysport.org.uk

Disability Sport Cymru
029 2030 0525
www.disability-sport-cymru.co.uk

Wales Council for the Blind
029 2047 3954
www.wcb-ccd.org.uk

Wales Council for the Deaf
01443 485687
www.wcdeaf.org.uk/

British Paralympics Association
020 7662 8882
www.paralympics.org.uk/

Sports Council for Wales
029 2030 0500
www.sports-council-wales.co.uk

Also check out:
> Athletics

Astrologers study the planets and their motions to determine their influences on people's lives. A person's date of birth dictates which sign of the Zodiac they are (the Zodiac is a region in space, on the sun's path, made up out of 12 constellations (configurations of stars). If someone asks you what your birth sign is, they are asking what sign of the Zodiac you are.
Some astrologers use the Zodiac and the positions of the stars to produce horoscopes (forecasts or predictions for people or individuals of a specific sign). This is also sometimes referred to as divination.

Signs of the Zodiac and their symbols and elements:

Sign	Symbol	Element	Dates
Aries	Ram	Fire	Mar 21- Apr 19
Taurus	Bull	Earth	Apr 20 - May 20
Gemini	Twins	Air	May 21 - Jun 20
Cancer	Crab	Water	Jun 21 - July 22
Leo	Lion	Fire	Jul 23 - Aug 22
Virgo	Virgin	Earth	Aug 23 -Sep 22
Libra	Scales	Air	Sep 23 - Oct 22
Scorpio	Scorpion	Water	Oct 23 - Nov 21
Sagittarius	Archer	Fire	Nov 22 - Dec 21
Capricorn	Goat	Earth	Dec 22 - Jan 19
Aquarius	Water	Air	Jan 20 - Feb 18
Pisces	Fish	Water	Feb 19 - Mar 20

The Astrological Association of Great Britain
www.astrologer.com/aanet/

Faculty of Astrological Studies
www.astrology.org.uk

Paranormality.com
www.paranormality.com

Also check out:
> Astronomy
> Witchcraft & Wizardry

Astronomy

Astronomy is the study of the sky and beyond - from stars to meteors, comets to planets and even black holes – and should not be confused with astrology, which is the study of the alleged affects of the stars and planets on people's lives!

Astronomers scientifically study the Universe and all that's in it. There are books, magazines and thousands of websites covering astronomy, and local clubs that you can join to share your passion in the cosmos and outer space. There are many careers in astronomy, from working as an astro-physicist to working for NASA.

The University of Glamorgan runs a 3 year BSc Honours Degree in Astronomy & Space. Check out their online prospectus on www.glam.ac.uk/. Cardiff University also has a course in Physics & Astronomy – check it out at http://www.cardiff.ac.uk

British Astronomical Association
www.britastro.org

NASA
www.nasa.gov

Also check out:
> Astrology

Have you ever watched a tightrope walker and thought "I'd like to try that"? Wales has a thriving network of circuses, where you can watch trained professionals performing their special skills. Everyone seems to be getting in on the Circus buzz - even the Scouts, who have a Circus Skills Badge! Why don't you have a go? There are tons of Circus skills that you can try your hand at: **Glass walking** - when someone walks a length of distance over broken glass, with nothing on their feet! Don't try this at home – not without some prior tuition first. Make sure you get expert help with this one. **Wire walking** (or tightrope walking - technical term: Funambulism) - when a person walks a length of distance on an elevated wire that's approximately 1/2 inch thick. Sometimes the person holds a long pole up to 12 meters in length to help balance. **Plate spinning** - Plates used for spinning should have a large rim on the underside, and should slope towards the centre point. To get started, put your stick on the rim of the plate, so that the plate is hanging from the stick (almost vertical). Slowly move your wrist in a circular motion, so that the plate starts to spin around the stick. By increasing the circular wrist motion, the plate speeds up and becomes horizontal. The stick will move the middle of the plate because of the sloped underside. **Juggling** - you can juggle all sorts of thing – balls, rings, clubs etc. - but if you're a beginner, it's probably best to use 3 lightweight squishy beanbags (there's less of a chance of winding up in casualty!).

SAFETY – Take it seriously! Make sure that you check out the credentials of any centres or training schools you use, take out the proper insurance and make sure you use all the right equipment and follow all advised safety checks.

Circus Malarkey
www.circus-malarkey.org.uk

Cirque du Soleil
www.cirquedusoleil.com

Dr Bliss Circus Skills workshops
www.drbliss.org

Circus Arts
www.circusarts.org.uk

Also check out:
> Animal rights

Don't let the rain stop you. Even without the great weather there are great days out throughout Wales and the UK, from theme parks to skate parks.
Keep an eye on your local newspaper for good days out that are coming up, as well as checking out the front pages of your yellow pages for a list of attractions in your area. Remember to check out entry fees before hand (many museums are free of charge, or ask for a contribution).

THEME PARKS
Wey hey! You know what we're talking about – the feeling that your guts are about to spill out at any moment while you cling desperately to the arms of your seat. We're talking roller coasters, of course! There are 3 types of coaster: Steel, Shuttle and Wooden, and hundreds of theme parks just waiting for you to try out. The buzz, the thrill, the high - what a feeling! There are loads to check out in the UK and abroad if you dare.

For pure coaster heaven and loads of great facts, world records and where to go for the ultimate ride, check out this site www.ultimaterollercoaster.com

Make sure that the park you visit meets the proper health and safety regulations.

Oakwood Theme Park
01834 861889
www.oakwood-leisure.com

Wales Tourist Board
Things to do, events & attractions for great days out
www.visitwales.com

Also check out:
> Concerts & Events
> Museums & Galleries

The Award (as the Duke of Edinburgh's Award is known) is a programme of activity and personal development for young people aged between 14 and 25. There are three levels to the Award: Bronze (for those aged 14 and over), Silver (for those aged 15 and over) and Gold (for those aged 16 and over). Bronze Awards take between 6 and 12 months to complete, Silver takes between 12 and 18 months and Gold Awards take between 18 and 24 months to complete.

There are also four sections to the Award, involving Service (helping people in the community), Skills (covering almost any hobby, skill or interest), Physical Recreation (sport, dance and fitness), Expeditions (training for, planning and completing a journey on foot or horseback, by boat or cycle) and Residential Project (Gold Award only) (a purposeful enterprise with people not previously known to the participant)
10 Key Principles of the Award: Non-competitive, available to all, voluntary, flexible, balanced, progressive, achievement focused, marathon not a sprint, personal development, enjoyable.
Benefits of the Award for the participants include increased confidence, self-reliance and leadership skills, better practical and inter-personal skills, the discovery of new interests and talents, meeting new people and making new friends and having fun. Taking part in the Award would certainly count as "extra curricular activity" and could look good on your CV.

Check out your local youth clubs, voluntary organisations, Open Award Centres, schools, colleges, etc to see if they are running the Award.

The Duke of Edinburgh's Award
www.theaward.org

The Duke of Edinburgh's Award (Wales)
www.theaward.org/wales/

Also check out:
- Education
- Employment & Training
- Outdoor Pursuits

Fashion & Clothing

It's hard to keep ahead of all the fashion trends, but you don't necessarily need a complete new wardrobe every time fashions change. If you choose a few key basics such as jeans, black trousers and great shoes, you can add the fashion element either with accessories or with just one cheap 'disposable chic' item.

If you like buying clothes abroad, check out our size guide to help you get the right size.

The Size Sorter (ladies)

UK	8	10	12	14	16	18
US	4	6	8	10	12	14
ES/IT/FR	36	38	40	42	44	46
D	34	36	38	40	42	44

The Size Sorter (lads shirts)

UK & US	14	14.5	15	15.5	16	16.5	17	17.5
EUROPE	35	36/37	38	39/40	41	42/43	44	45

(lads suits)

UK & US	36	38	40	42	44	46	48	50
EUROPE	46	48	50/52	54	56	58/60	62	64

Shoes (men and women)

UK	2	3	4	5	6	7	8	9	10	11	12
EUROPE	34	35.5	37	38	39	41	42	43	44.5	46	47

Fashion
www.fuk.co.uk

London Fashion Week
www.londonfashionweek.co.uk

Also check out:
> Looking Good?
> Online Shopping
> Shopping

Food

10.5 Hobbies & Leisure Activities

Nifty with the pots and pans, or a whizz with the pastry and blender? Cooking has become incredibly trendy. With so many programmes on TV, mags, books, tips and catering courses, you can specialise in any type of cooking you like from all over the world. If you don't feel confident enough to go it alone, you could take evening classes or go to a catering college. Keep an eye out in your local paper for courses, or ask your careers advisor about catering colleges where you can study. For more info on how to train to become a chef/cook go to www.wise1520.info then Employment & Training then I Wannabe.

Here are some top tips on handling food:
* Wash hands before touching food * Wash utensils and plates in between use (not a good idea to dice raw chicken then slice veg with the same knife!) * Keep raw food away from cooked food (especially raw meats, which should be kept away from all other food) * Use separate chopping boards for raw and cooked food (especially meat, fish etc) * Wash "garden" ingredients like veg, salad ingredients and fruits * Keep your kitchen clean and tidy – wipe down surfaces and wash utensils immediately after use to avoid food poisoning * Remember to wash T-Towels and dishcloths regularly.

Food Standards Agency
www.food.gov.uk

Foodlink
www.foodlink.org.uk

BBC Food
www.bbc.co.uk/food

Careers Wales
www.careerswales.com

Also check out:
> Careers Essentials
> Healthy Eating
> Vegetarianism & Veganism

You don't need a huge garden to enjoy gardening; a small pot or window box is fine. There is lots of help at hand to create the garden of your dreams: shows on TV, books, specialist mags and supplements in Sunday papers, plus of course the Internet. You could also sign up for a course if you're really interested. You can pick up fact sheets from large DIY stores and hundreds of books on gardening. Have a think of what you want to achieve first – moss garden, rock garden, decked area, water feature, patio, flower beds, natural garden, herb garden etc – then get some advice on how to make it happen.
Remember that some plants need a lot of attention, while others thrive on their own. It may be worth baring this in mind if you have a hectic life with little time to spare to tend to your garden.

The National Botanic Garden of Wales runs school programmes, courses and workshops. Contact their educational department for details on 01558 667 150.

The UK's biggest annual show is the Chelsea Flower Show – check out the RHS website for more details.

BBC Gardening
www.bbc.co.uk/gardening

The National Botanic Garden of Wales
01558 668 768
www.gardenofwales.org.uk

Royal Horticultural Society (RHS)
www.rhs.org.uk

Also check out:
> DIY
> Environment

Buying online is great - you don't even have to leave the building - BUT it's also full of dangers if you don't know what you're doing. Make sure the site is secure before giving your credit card details. Orders must be confirmed in writing, usually via e-mail. Shop around for the best deals and prices. You are now entitled to a 7-day cooling off period if you change your mind.

Tips

- Type the web address in carefully, there have been cases where duplicate sites have been set up that look exactly the same as the real site, so that you put in your credit or debit card details.
- Watch out for hidden costs, high postage rates, VAT etc.
- Get sites from your mates, at least that way they are tried and tested!
- Check that there is always a yellow padlock in the corner when you pay – this means it's a secure site.
- Goods from abroad may take time to arrive: set a date, but if you can't, delivery must be within 30-days.
- Check the returns policy, just in case.
- If you buy from abroad, your contract is there! If you face problems you may have difficulties getting money back etc.
- Print out the order and terms and conditions that appear on the web site, just in case of probs.

Trading Standards
Contact them for your nearest office
www.tradingstandards.gov.uk

Office of Fair Trading
Your rights as a consumer
08457 22 44 99
www.oft.gov.uk

Consumer Gateway Site
www.consumer.gov.uk

Also check out:
> Shopping
> Consumer Rights

Some people read to relax, some write poetry to unwind. Some like to go for a run to shake off tension and some like a swim to wash away the daily grime…and others like to pamper. Pampering is for both sexes, not just for girls – more and more fellas openly admit to taking pride in their appearance these days (just think David Beckham) – so there's nothing stopping you blokes from indulging. Having a good old pamper can make you feel like a million dollars and is a great confidence booster. It needn't cost the earth, either –you don't need to go to an expensive salon or spa, you can pamper yourself at home. Canllaw Online recommends that you put aside one day every month to pamper yourself rotten and return your outer glow* Canllaw Online's guide to your once-monthly-pamper: **Hair:** Wash your hair twice with shampoo, apply conditioner twice and make sure you rinse very thoroughly for super clean, super shiny, super condition hair. If you've got straight hair, why not curl it for a change? Or straighten naturally curly hair for a breath of fresh hair (groan!). **Nails:** Give yourself a manicure. Start by filing your nails into the shape you want (curved tips are better for those with weak nails –square tips require strong nails), remembering to file in one direction, not back-and-forth in a sawing motion. Next, remove or push back your cuticles using a proper cuticle remover and taking care not to damage your nails (it might help to soak your finger tips in warm water for a minute or two to soften the cuticle) and then buff your nails until they shine (you can buy a buffing block from any high-street chemist – they don't cost a lot). Apply nail varnish (if you want to polish your nails) in long, continuous strokes. The last step is to apply cuticle oil and hand cream (which you should then try and apply daily to keep your hands looking gorgeous!). **Skin:** Why not get yourself a face mask? You can buy a sample pack for around 99p. Wash your face carefully to remove grease and dirt (making sure you are thorough but gentle – skin on the face is delicate) and apply the face mask (you might need to do an allergy test first – see on-pack instructions). Make sure you rinse off the mask properly. You could also apply some fake tan to give yourself a golden glow (follow the on-pack instructions carefully to avoid streaking and allergic reactions).

* see Healthy Eating and Exercise & Keep Fit for your inner glow!

Hints and Things
www.hintsandthings.co.uk/bathroom/beauty.htm

BBC Health
www.bbc.co.uk/health/

Also check out:
> Healthy Eating
> Fashion & Clothing

PUBS

From 14-16 you can, by law, go into a pub/bar but not drink alcohol (this includes beer gardens and family rooms). You must have permission from the landlord, who will have a suitable license to allow this. At 16 and 17 you can buy, or be bought, beer or cider shandy to go with a meal, but not otherwise. Buying drinks for people under 18 is against the law and hanging around in pubs when you know you're underage gets you and the pub into trouble. Pubs are pretty wise to the under-age-drink culture in Wales and should ask to see proper I.D. Be sociable but be responsible. Pubs offer a range of tasty non-alcoholic drinks too you know!

CLUBBING

Nightclubs are a major part of the social scene at a young age, but at 15/16/17 you shouldn't be doing it, unless they're under 18 clubs. Clubs can be great places, but at the same time they have their own dangers that you must be aware of like alcohol abuse, drink spiking, drugs etc. and you need to make sure that you and your mates are as safe as you can be. Do yourself and others a favour; if you suspect anything 'dodgy' going on tell the owner, bouncer or bar staff. Without your help, the club owners can't keep clubs safe for you. Enjoy your dance scene, be sensible and stay safe.

24-Hour Drink Law

In November 2005, the law changed to allow 24-hour-drinking in certain circumstances. Places that want to open later or round-the-clock have to apply for a license and if there is trouble in pubs because of the longer opening, they may be closed or billed for police costs.

Drug Prevention Advisory Service
For a copy of the 'Safer Clubbing' document
www.drugs.gov.uk

Also check out:
> Dance
> Personal Safety
> Substance Misuse

Reading

Do you want to be an astronaut, a private detective, a gangster's moll or a mermaid? Well, you can – all through the magic of books. Reading can take you into worlds and places you never dreamt of. It can tell you things, help you learn skills and find out loads of info. Reading also increases vocabulary and challenges ways of thinking, broadening minds and inspiring imaginations.

Reading need not be a solitary activity, believe it or not. Reading groups (also known as reading circles and book clubs) are becoming very popular. If you're passionate about reading, why not pop along to your nearest group? You'll meet new people and get to chat about your favourite authors (and maybe find some new authors to enjoy).

Reading is a key skill and the only way to get better at it is to read more, so pop to your local library and get yourself a library card – you can borrow the books for free (so long as you return them)! If English is not your first language, you can buy dual language books. Ask in a large bookshop for details.

National Library of Wales
01970 632 800
www.llgc.org.uk

Welsh Books Council
01970 624 151
www.cllc.org.uk

Academi
National organization which promotes writers & literature of Wales
www.academi.org

Literacy Trust
020 7828 2435
www.literacytrust.org.uk

Also check out:

- Basic Skills
- Home Learning
- Writing & Poetry

Canllaw Online's guide to shopping:

• Planning a shopping trip can be almost as fun and exciting as the actual shopping itself, so why not map out where you're going to go, where you're going to start, when you're going to break for coffee and what you're going to buy. Write yourself a list so that you don't forget anything when you get there.

• Set yourself a spending limit before you hit the shops. Work out how much you can afford and stick to it so that there's no guilt attached to your shiny new purchases and you can enjoy them to the max.

• Wear comfy shoes – you'll be on your feet for hours if the shopping spree's going well!

• Don't wear lots of layers, especially if you're planning on trying on clothes. Shopping can be hot and exhausting business!

• Check out the charity shops for bargains (you can find just about anything in charity shops – albums, vintage clothes, bric-a-brac, designer labels – and you'll be helping a good cause).

• Very often when you get to the checkout, especially in clothes shops, you get asked whether or not you would like to open an account with the store and get a discount. Don't be talked into taking out a store card if you don't want to. Smile and politely, but firmly, refuse. "No thank you, I'm not interested" usually does the trick.

• Check out the return & refund policies before you part with your money and keep the receipt until you're sure that you're satisfied with the item.

Guardian Unlimited – Shopping
shopping.guardian.co.uk

BBC Consumer Guide to Shopping
www.bbc.co.uk/consumer/guides_to/shopping_index.shtml

Consumer Direct
www.consumerdirect.gov.uk

Trading Standards
www.tradingstandards.gov.uk

Also check out:

- Debt
- Fashion & Clothing
- Online Shopping
- Store Cards

What do you get up to in your spare time? Have you considered checking out your local youth club / centre or making a difference to how it's run and looks to fill your time? They're a great way to meet people your own age, broaden your horizons, try out new activities and fulfil your potential depending on how active you feel! Youth clubs are set up to create somewhere for you, as a young person, to hang out, develop and try out new experiences and spend your spare time. They are a place to meet, have a laugh, get out of the house and get involved in activities, or simply chill out away from home. The size and the number of facilities that youth clubs and centres have across Wales vary hugely. Youth clubs and centres grow and develop over time with everyone in them, and using them, working hard together to make it a better and more enjoyable place to be for young people. You can make a difference to your local youth club or centre by telling the right people what you would like, what would make a difference, what would make a good youth club even better for the young people in your area. A youth club or centre is a way that you can be involved in your community and make a difference. You could start a project, you could raise money for a snooker table, you could paint a place to make it look good, it is after all meant to be for young people, so tell your local youth club and centre what you want and think of ways to get it. If you have ideas, don't be afraid to go to the person in charge and ask them if you can have a chat, put your ideas forward and think of a plan. These places want feedback from young people, if you don't say anything, nothing will change.
Many youth clubs have CREDU Digilabs, so why not pop along and see what's on offer?

For further information check out the local pages and the page on National Voluntary Organisations situated at the back of the book. Also check out Info Outlets and Digilabs on pages 15 - 47 for your nearest centres.

Have you ever fancied being an extra on TV or the leading star on the stage? Do you have ideas of bright lights or being a Bollywood or Hollywood star? There are loads of opportunities to get acting through youth drama groups and theatres across Wales. You can also get involved in stage schools that hold courses and productions for young people. Contact your local theatre who may be able to help you find a local theatre group or stage school.

A theatre is a performing space where you can be entertained, or take part in the entertaining. Productions, plays, ballet and dance, comedy, music, opera and musicals are all performed in theatres and there are many youth theatre groups that you can get involved in. You may not want to act but like the buzz of a theatre. A theatre is run by a team of people, from lighting and set designers to publicists and stage crews. You can get involved in workshops, courses, or even get a part time job working behind the scenes at a theatre.

The Wales Millennium Centre, in addition to showing musicals, operas, plays and other performances, also holds creative classes during the holidays. Contact them on 08700 402000 or http://www.wmc.org.uk/

National Youth Arts Wales
www.nyaw.co.uk

Theatre in Wales
www.theatre-wales.co.uk

Amdram.co.uk
www.amdram.co.uk

Welsh National Opera 029 2046 4666
www.wno.org.uk

Arts and Young People
www.youtharts.org.uk

BBC New Talent Drama
www.bbc.co.uk/newtalent/drama/

Stagecoach Theatre Arts Plc
www.stagecoach.co.uk

Also check out:

- Cinema
- Concerts & Events
- Film Making

The animation industry is thriving in Wales and there are plenty of opportunities for you to get involved. There are annual Welsh Animation Festivals held in both Swansea and Cardiff where you can talk face to face with animators, script writers, editors and producers working within the industry and pick up some handy hints on how to get started. Becoming a runner for an animation company is an excellent way to get a real insight into the industry, and you get a wage packet at the end of each month! However, the money's minimal to start with, the hours can be long, and it's usually very, very hard work!

Remember, animation doesn't just mean making clay models, or illustrating characters – it covers a broad range of specialist subjects:
Storyboard Artist
Animator (from Flash animation used on the BBC Wales series 'The Bobinogs' to Computer Generated Imagery (CGI) animation used in 'Toy Story')
Claymation Animator / Claymation Modelmaker (as seen in 'Fireman Sam')
After Effects/Sound
Editing & Directing

Study the different styles of animation all around you – on the TV, at the Cinema, in Comic Books. Find out what your style is.

Cyfle national training provider for Television, Film and Interactive Media in Wales.
Caernarfon office: 01286 671000
Cardiff office: 029 20 465533
www.cyfle.co.uk

British Animation Awards
www.britishanimationawards.com

Also check out:
- Acting, Drama & Theatre
- Arts
- Cinema
- Film Making

The arts cover such a wide range of things to do and see. The 'arts' are literature, performing arts, visual arts, craft & design, media and multimedia. It covers a huge range of topics from dance to acting & drama, opera to mime (theatre), sculpture to drawing, photography to digital arts, poetry to scriptwriting, acting to storytelling and in Wales you can be involved in the arts as a participant, a creator of art or as a person who just loves looking at it through projects, workshops and classes.

Arts Wales
029 2026 5197
www.artswales.org.uk/

Youth Arts
www.artswales.org

BBC Blast
0800 011 011
www.bbc.co.uk/blast

Art Cymru
www.artcymru.co.uk

Interactive space for artists
www.voluntaryarts.org

Also check out:
> Dance
> Acting, Drama & Theatre
> Music
> Writing & Poetry
> Photography & Digital Imagery
> Museums & Galleries

Going to the movies is a great way to spend a couple of hours – you can lose yourself in the ups and downs and thrills & spills of someone else's world. Whatever your viewing tastes are, with around five new films released each week ranging in genres such as action, comedy, horror, drama, thriller, animation etc, there's bound to be something to your fancy!

The price per viewing ranges from approximately £3 in the smaller more local cinemas to £5.60 (ish) in the larger complexes. Check out your local cinema for their "offer" nights, where the prices are usually reduced by a couple of pounds. These nights are usually busy – so get there well in advance!

Until you're 18 (and can watch any release without supervision), your age can govern which films you are allowed to see. The British Board of Film Classification give movie releases ratings to ensure that children and young people don't watch unsuitable material.

Film ratings

* U - Universal (suitable for all).
* Uc - Universal (suitable for young children).
* PG - Parental Guidance (watched with parents).
* 12a - Suitable if 12 & over, and for under 12s with an adult present.
* 15 - Suitable if 15 & over.
* 18 - Suitable if 18 or over.

British Board of Film Classification
www.bbfc.co.uk

Wales Screen Commission
www.walesscreencommission.co.uk

Also check out:
> Film-Making
> Animation
> Acting, Drama & Theatre

The best way to catch up with local events and concerts is through your local paper. Going to gigs can be a great laugh, whether it's a local band in the back room of a pokey pub or Madonna at the Millennium Stadium. Here's a quick guide to getting the most out of a gig: * Get there early if you want to get to the front (especially if it's a big gig in a large venue) * Expect you and your bag to be searched on the way in. If you've got anything dangerous or pointy (or illegal, like drugs), expect it to be confiscated. Some venues don't allow you to take in alcohol, so you might have to leave your booze at the door * Shoes – wear sensible ones! You could be on your feet for hours and will probably get trodden on at some stage, so high heel strappy sandals (for example) might not be the best idea, no matter how good they look * Some venues might not allow you to take photographs during the gig, so check in advance * Even at the smallest of gigs, there's usually a market stall selling the artist's merchandise. You can usually pick up items like CDs, T-Shirts, mugs, posters and signed photos. These can be expensive, so make sure you take enough money if you want to pick up a memento.

Finally, be safe. Don't be tempted to drink more than you want or take anything at the urging of friends, keep an eye on your drink to avoid spiking, stay in a group and don't go off with anyone you don't know. Enjoy the gig responsibly and you'll have fond memories forever, not nightmares.

Ticketmaster
0870 333 6207

Millennium Stadium
www.millenniumstadium.com

Wales Millennium Centre
www.wmc.org.uk/

Cardiff International Arena
www.ticketmaster.co.uk/venue/188514

Gig-Guide.co.uk
www.gig-guide.co.uk/

Also check out:

> Pubs & Clubs
> Dance
> Days Out
> Festivals

There are so many opportunities for you to be involved in dance for fun or professionally. You can line dance or ballet dance, tap or ballroom, disco or salsa. Dancing is also a great form of exercise.

There are hundreds of classes you can join, college courses you can take, leading to (with a bit of luck) opportunities to dance in musicals, films and theatre productions. You can also be involved in other ways with dance. Dance is a huge industry giving artists the chance to work in dance circles, like teachers, choreographers, technicians and managers or as a promoter, producer, designer or physiotherapist. Contact Community Dance Wales, Welsh independent Dance or Dance UK for more info.

For more info on how to train to become a dancer go to www.wise1520.info then Employment & Training then I Wannabe

Community Dance Wales
029 2057 5075
www.communitydancewales.com

Welsh Independent Dance
029 2038 7314
www.welshindance.co.uk

Dance UK
020 7228 4990
www.danceuk.org

BBC Blast
Advice & contacts for youth in dance
0800 011 011
www.bbc.co.uk/blast

Arts and Young People in Wales
www.youtharts.org.uk

Also check out:
> Arts

Noisy, lazy, hazy days filed with music, arts, dance, literature, theatre, street entertainment, concerts, exhibits and much more. The UK comes alive in summer but there's always some kind of festival or outdoor event happening throughout the year. Not all festivals are free. Some may charge a one-off entry fee or a day-by-day ticket charge. Always ask if there are any hidden costs to work out how much it will really cost you!

Eisteddfods are the largest festivals of music, culture, dance, poetry, song & literature, arts, competitions & even science for young people, held at different times of the year throughout Wales. There's plenty going on in the Pavilion and there are lots of stalls on site, for those die-hard shoppers. You don't have to be a Welsh speaker to enjoy the Eisteddfod.

Wales has a number of successful festivals, such as the Green Man Festival in Brecon, described by some as "the hippest UK festival", the HSBC Brecon Jazz Festival and Bryn Terfel's Faenol festival.

Green Man Festival
www.thegreenmanfestival.co.uk

HSBC Brecon Jazz
www.breconjazz.co.uk/

Bryn Terfel's Faenol festival
www.brynfest.com/

Get your tickets for all the big festivals here
www.ticketmaster.co.uk

Best festival sites around
www.urdd.org
www.virtualfestivals.co.uk
www.efestivals.co.uk
www.artsfestivals.co.uk

Also check out:
> Concerts & Events
> Days Out

There are many opportunities within the film making industry: actor, director, producer, editor, casting agent, sound manager, make up artist, lighting technician, stunt person etc. The list is endless. There are many training courses available if you are interested in any aspect of the film making industry. Or, have you got a great idea for a film? Do you have something inventive, unique and very appealing? If you have a good idea up your sleeve, then have a go at doing something with it.

Wales is an exciting place to be for budding film makers, especially with the development of Dragon International Studios, a multi-million pound development in South Wales scheduled to open in 2007. Dragon International Studios (dubbed Valleywood!) will be a purpose-built film, TV, and multimedia complex and has the backing of Lord Richard Attenborough. Dragon International Studios will offer state-of-the-art production facilities and advanced digital technology and will also house The Film Academy. The Film Academy, currently based at the University of Glamorgan, offers post-experience and postgraduate professional courses in the creative and business dimensions of film.

There are also many other film companies in Wales – check out this link for a full list: http://journalism.cf.ac.uk/2004/baoj/filmwales/contacts.html

Sgrin
029 2033 3314 www.sgrin.co.uk

BBC Talent
www.bbc.co.uk/talent

BBC Blast (for 13-19 year olds)
0800 011 011 www.bbc.co.uk/blast

Cyfle – provides training in TV & Film, Interactive Media and Production Development
029 2046 5533 www.cyfle.co.uk/

Film Academy
www.glam.ac.uk/filmacademy/news

Also check out:
> Acting, Drama & Theatre
> Animation
> Cinema

Wales is packed full of museums and galleries that offer everyone access to a range of exhibitions, interactive workshops, behind-the-scene activities and lots more.

The 7 National Museums and Galleries of Wales are all FREE to get into, so why not go along to your nearest and have a look at what they've got on offer. The 7 are: The National Museum Cardiff, St Fagans: Natural History Museum, Big Pit: National Coal Museum, National Wool Museum, Nation Roman Legion Museum, National Slate Museum and National Waterfront Museum.

Museums aren't fossils anymore, they're real-life, interactive and interesting, covering everything from dinosaurs to art. You'll never know until you give it a try, so don't stay away.

If more traditional museums aren't your thing, you could always try one of these, erm, alternative, museums:

Baked Bean Museum of Excellence
www.bakedbeanmuseumofexcellence.org.uk

The Alice in Wonderland Centre
www.wonderland.co.uk

The Museum of Childhood Memories
1, Castle Street, Beaumaris, Isle of Anglesey, Anglesey

National Museums & Galleries of Wales
www.nmgw.ac.uk

Also check out:
- Arts
- Days Out
- Concerts & Events

Music is everywhere in Wales (we are, after all, the Land of Song!). Check out Concerts and Events for more info on what's on.

You may want to be directly involved in making music, be it musical theatre, R'n'B, hip-hop, gospel, jazz, garage, soul, classical music or pop. Whatever your taste or interest, the opportunities are plentiful. Use our contacts, they can get you started and give you advice and put you in touch with the right people who deal in the music you love.

Some schools provide free or subsidized music lessons. If yours doesn't (or didn't, if you're out of school), try and find out if there are any local organizations offering lessons – you might not have to pay a lot. Learning a musical instrument takes a lot of practice (and can take a lot of time), so the sooner you start, the better!

Immtech -Courses & recording facilities and loads more
029 2064 0500
www.immtech.co.uk

ProMo-Cymru - 029 2046 2222
www.promo-cymru.org
info@promo-cymru.org

Welsh Music Foundation
www.welshmusicfoundation.com

Community Music Wales
DJ schools, courses, projects & training
029 2083 8060
www.communitymusicwales.org.uk

Ty Cerdd
One-stop music info service
www.tycerdd.org

Arts Council Wales
www.artswales.org.uk

Also check out:
> Festivals

You can get involved in photography at any age – disposable cameras are cheap and durable enough these days (and are excellent to take on nights out or to the beach, or on an adventure holiday or to anywhere that you don't want to take an expensive bit of camera kit!). If you are interested in photography, why not buy a couple of disposable cameras and see what kind of eye for pictures you have before splashing out on kit? If you find you want to take it further, there are many specialist shops that sell second hand professional cameras and the shop assistant will probably be able to give you some handy tips on how to use the equipment. If the idea of taking photographs on reels of film seems archaic and you want to be able to take your piccies and send them to all your friends and family straight away without going to the expense of getting them developed, then digital photography is for you. Why not pick up a magazine on digital photography or get a book from the library and read up on the subject so that you've got a handle on the latest developments before buying? The best way to learn photography is to join a local photography club, where you can share ideas with others and even use their equipment. There are many camera clubs, libraries and galleries that run courses, as well as colleges and universities that have design & photography departments.

"Credu" is a partnership project between Canllaw Online & Fujitsu Services that offers young people opportunity to access and be trained in the use of digital cameras. Find your nearest CREDU Digilab here: http://www.credu.co.uk/izone/digilabs/

The Welsh Photographic Federation
www.thewpf.co.uk

Film Academy – University of Glamorgan
International centre for advanced training, education and research in film, animation, digital video and the moving image
01443 484111
www.glam.ac.uk
cmyer@glam.ac.uk

Also check out:
- Film Making
- Animation
- Arts
- Cinema
- Technology & Communication

Talent Competitions

Talent shows are everywhere, Pop Idol, X Factor, Strictly Dance Fever etc (well, if you have a talent why not flaunt it?). Talent competitions aren't just for budding singing stars, there are talent competitions in science, dance and lots more weird and wacky fields. There are also competitions for young writers, film-makers and artists. Make sure that the talent competition is genuine (be wary of any competitions asking big entry fees) – it may be a good idea to take a friend or family member along for moral support.

The biggest talent competition, where you can really show what you're made of is held every year by the BBC. They hold talent competitions in radio, presenting, singing, Djing and loads more. In Wales, the Eisteddfods are the places where you can show what you're made of.

List of talent competitions:
www.vocalist.org.uk/singing_competitions.html

X-Factor
www.xfactor.tv

BBC Talent
www.bbc.co.uk/talent

Urdd Gobaith Cymru
www.urdd.org

Also check out:

> Careers Essentials
> Festivals
> Acting, Drama & Theatre
> Art
> Writing and Poetry

Witchcraft and wizardry is very much in vogue at the moment, thanks to a certain orphan boy with a lightening bolt scar on his forehead. Of course, many people believe that there is no such thing as magic and that's that! Fans of Buffy the Vampire Slayer and Charmed may contest that opinion, but which one are you – a believer or a sceptic?

During the 1500s to the 1700s, people thought to be witches were hunted down and either imprisoned or executed, as witches were alleged to be evil (the majority of witches at this time were female - male witches were rare back then).
Witchcraft & wizardry today is closer to paganism or druidism than to satanism or the black arts. Witchcraft today includes learning herbalism, practising spiritualism & meditation etc. Witchcraft is considered to be a practise, like a trade or a craft that is learned, not a religion. There are many websites dedicated to witchcraft & wizardry, so if you are interested in the subject, get online and have a look. There are also many books on the history of witches & wizards, so don't forget to check out your local library. There is even a Witchcraft and Wicca magazine and an annual festival called Witchfest Wales (check out details below).

We'd like your opinion on this. Do you believe in witchcraft and wizardry? Do you practise it? Do you think it's all a load of nonsense? Let us know by e-mailing ed@canllaw-online.com or writing to Ed, Canllaw Online, Unit 5, The Octagon, Caerphilly Business Park, Van Road, Caerphilly, CF83 3ED.

Witchfest Wales
www.witchfest.net/wf_wales.htm

Also check out:
> Astrology
> Religions & Beliefs

Writing & Poetry

Be it writing novels, short stories or poetry, writing is a very personal way of expressing your innermost thoughts and feelings and the most important thing is to find a style of your own. There are no right or wrongs (though there are a couple of rules you may want to remember which could make you a better writer) and the best thing that you can do is practise! Stephen King states in his book 'On Writing' – "All I can suggest is that you read, read, and read some more, and write, write and then write some more".

There are a number of creative writing classes, writer's workshops and text books which could all help you along the path to becoming a writer – see below for details. Why not check out your local youth organisations and find out if there are any book clubs or writers associations in your area.

Why not start by writing something for the Canllaw Online's websites? We are looking for young writers to contribute news articles, special reports etc on loads of topics.

If you are interested in becoming a young writer for Canllaw Online, send an e-mail to ed@canllaw-online.com

Books: A must for any budding writer is 'The Writers Handbook' & 'The Writers' and Artists' Yearbook'. They list UK & Irish publishers and Literary Agents (with a small write-up about them), News Agencies etc., and tips on how to approach them.

Stephen King – 'On Writing – A Memoir of the Craft'. This book is filled with useful tips and inspirational advice on the dos and don'ts, editing processes etc.

Ty Newydd National Writers' Centre for Wales
www.tynewydd.org

Writing Magazine
www.writersnews.co.uk

Arts Council of Wales
029 20 376500 www.artswales.org.uk

Also check out:
> Arts
> Reading
> Talent Competitions

Computers

Mac or PC, laptop or palm pilot... computers are very much part of your life. Whatever system you use, computers are getting better and better and you'll need to keep up to speed with the latest software if you want to stay in touch with technology. Computers can do so many things: you can surf the web, make a movie, store digital photos, have live web cam chats over the internet, store masses of info, graphics and images, listen to music, chat, play games, burn CDs, tune in to internet radio, shop, bank and watch TV on them.

Think about what you want out of your computer before buying one. You may spend more on software trying to get it to do what you want it to if you don't think about it first. Hacking (breaking into other computer systems in business and national security systems etc) is against the law. Do it and you can get heavily fined and a long prison sentence.

If you don't have your own computer, check if your local library or youth organization has kit. "Credu" is a partnership project between Canllaw Online & Fujitsu Services that offers young people opportunity to access and be trained in computers and new technologies. Find your nearest CREDU Digilab here: http://www.credu.co.uk/izone/digilabs/

Technology Buzzwords for Students
www.tekmom.com/buzzwords

Apple Mac
www.apple.com/uk

PC World
0870 2420 444
www.pcworld.co.uk

Also check out:
> Computer Games
> E-mail & Internet
> Inventions

It's easy to loose yourself in the virtual world of computer games – they can be absorbing, challenging and addictive – but you should be careful not to risk your physical health or mental wellbeing. It's easy to loose track of time when you're absorbed in a game, so it's easy to forget to eat, to rest your eyes, to move about, to get fresh air etc. There are also whole communities of online gamers who compete against each other through the Internet. Beating a person rather than a computer can make online gaming particularly addictive. It's been reported that some online gamers have played for around 18 hours straight, seriously risking their health. If you think that you might be addicted to gaming, contact Addictions.co.uk (details below). If you play a lot of computer games, you should be careful of the following: Epilepsy – flashing imagery on screen could trigger epilepsy, so read the warnings on the packaging. DVT – sitting in a cramped position for hours on end could cause DVT (Deep Vein Thrombosis), so take regular breaks and move around. Isolation & Anti Social Behavior – locking yourself away for hours playing games could make for a very lonely existence. Try to balance the amount of time you spend gaming with going out and hooking up with friends to keep in the social loop. Don't let computer games ruin your relationships. Staring at the screen for too long could lead to eye strain and headaches and RSI (Repetitive Strain Injury) could be a problem for those gamers fused to their joypads for hours - take regular breaks to avoid.

Don't forget to check out the GameZroom on the CREDU Portal. Try to get on the leader board of the Blockboggler (it's harder than you think!), test your memory on The Sizzler or try to fathom out the Brainteaser. Check it out at www.credu.co.uk.

CVG – Computer and Video Games
www.computerandvideogames.com/home-page.php

Addtictions.co.uk
www.addictions.co.uk

Also check out:
> Computers
> E-mail & Internet
> Inventions

E-MAIL - E-mail is a wonderful thing - it allows you to communicate with people all around the world in seconds. You can share experiences with friends & family that can't be with you, keep people up-to-date with your progress if you're travelling or just e-mail your pal to ask them if they want to get together after work/school. As a communication tool, E-mail is fab – if it's used properly, by responsible people. If you give out your e-mail address to strangers then you could be putting yourself at risk. Would you give out your phone number to anyone that asked you for it? Probably not. E-mail addresses are no different – they allow people access to you. Only share your address with people that you know and trust.

INTERNET - Like e-mail, the Internet is an amazingly useful information tool. Unfortunately, as with e-mail, there is a darker side to the Internet when it's used by irresponsible people and for illegal purposes. The Internet is used to view child pornography, buy illegal weapons from abroad and is used by paedophiles to target young people through chat rooms (they can disguise themselves and pretend to be a young person). Chat rooms can be great fun and it's great to talk to other people. But, it's very easy to lie about who you are online because others can't see your face. Someone might say that they are a gorgeous looking 15 year old, but in reality they might be a very dodgy 50-year-old. Never give out any personal information such as your full name, address, phone or mobile number, e-mail address, the name of your school etc. If you are meeting someone you met online, take a friend with you and tell someone responsible where you're going. Always meet in a public place and NEVER go to someone's house or get in their car.

Childnet International
www.childnet-int.org

The Suzy Lamplugh Trust
www.suzylamplugh.org

WiseKids - Promoting Positive and Safe Internet Use
www.wisekids.org.uk

Also check out:
- Computer Games
- Personal Safety

Inventions

Inventors are crucial to progress and evolution. Without inventors, we wouldn't have phones, cars, TVs, clockwork radios, computers, airplanes or even safety razors! Nearly everything you use on a day-to-day basis has been "invented" by someone and some inventions have made their inventors a stack load of cash to boot!

I've got an invention - how do I make sure no one steals my idea? Patent your invention. A patent taken out on an invention in this country will give the inventor sole right to make, use or sell their invention in the UK. Patents can be taken out for specific periods of time, so if you are patenting an invention, make sure you know when the patent runs out so that you can renew if you want to. Your invention will have to meet a certain criteria to be patented. It will have to be new (not been made or sold, or in production, anywhere in the world at the time of the patent application), be inventive (not just a copy of someone else's invention with small changes) and must be able to be used in industry (must be some kind of device or piece of equipment). Things like scientific discoveries and computer programmes are not eligible. Patents cost money, so check out the full costs before you proceed. For more info on Patents, go to the Patent Office website (see below).
Have you got a great idea for a new invention? Check out Inventions Help for UK Inventors (details below).

Inventions Help for UK Inventors
020 7354 5640
www.inventions-help-for-uk-inventors.com

Government website on Inventions
www.dti.gov.uk/innovation/

Design Technology Department
Info on Inventions and Inventors
www.design-technology.org

Patent Office
www.patent.gov.uk

Also check out:
> Computers
> Technology

There are hundreds of magazine and newspaper titles available in Wales. They range from publications covering very obscure subjects to the most general ones. Newspapers are produced more regularly than magazines so are a better way at keeping up with all the latest news and current affairs. These days, newspapers contain much more than just that though. They cover an array of topics, may feature quizzes, opinions, longer interview pieces and a host of different types of writing. In short, newspapers are likely to give you a wide range of information and expose you to a variety of writing styles. Each newspaper is distinctive in some way though. Whether they tend to focus on serious news or gossip, if they contain left or right wing views or if they cover a wide or specific range of topics, there will be a newspaper for you. Magazines tend to come out less regularly so don't contain as much up-to-date news, instead tending to feature longer, more in-depth articles. Again, the variety of available magazines is staggering. From knitting to politics to fashion, mags are likely to give you more specific information about your preferred subjects. Here are some of Wales' papers and magazines:

Cambria, Wales' National Magazine - www.cambriamagazine.com
V – teenage magazine in Welsh language - www.v-cylchgrawn.com
Golwg – Welsh language magazine - www.golwg.com
Woctorn Mail & Echo newspapers - icwales.icnetwork.co.uk

If you're in Further Education, check to see whether your college or Uni has a newspaper or magazine. It should be full of local news and events and you may be able to get involved.

The Newspaper Society
www.newspapersoc.org.uk

Periodical Publishers Association
0207 404 4166 www.ppa.co.uk

National Council for the Training of Journalists
www.nctj.com/journalist.htm

The Writer's Bureau
www.writersbureau.com

Also check out:
> Reading
> Writing & Poetry

Mobile Phones

With so much choice these days, buying a mobile phone can be trickier than you think. There are lots of things to consider and you need to do your homework before going into the shop or you might find yourself being lured by promises of great deals and free gifts only to find out that they're not so great after all. Here are the things to think about:- Do some networks have better signals than others in your area? Who do you phone? If all your mates are on one network you might find it expensive to call them from a different one. When do you call? It's no good having free minutes in the day if you're in school anyway. Do you want Internet access from your mobile? Do you travel a lot and need to use your phone abroad? Do you want a camera phone? Do you want radio on your phone? Do you want to play music on your phone? How do you want to pay for calls, by monthly contract, or pay-as-you-go?

Mobile phone dos & don'ts:
• Don't use your mobile in a hospital, on an airplane or in a restricted area – the signal could interfere with electrical equipment – or in a petrol station. • Don't use your mobile without a hands-free-kit while driving. Using mobile phones while driving (without hands-free kit) is illegal and you could be fined a minimum of £30. • Don't give out your mobile number to people that you don't know, even if it's to the sexiest boy or girl in the club. Mobile phones can be used to stalk, bully and harass people, so keep your number safe. • Don't flash around your mobile or you may make yourself a target for thieves. • Do take your mobile with you when you go out – mobiles can save lives in emergencies and you never know when you'll need it.

There has been a lot of concern over possible health risks associated with using mobiles, so check out the Department of Health website for safety guidelines on using mobile phones.

Oftel
Mobile phone information
www.oftel.gov.uk

Department of Health
www.dh.gov.uk

Also check out:
> Technology
> Crime Prevention & Personal Safety
> E-mail & Internet

Radio

Most people still listen to the radio at least once every single day. It's an enormously popular medium for transmitting information, entertainment, education and music. With new technologies such as digital and Internet radio, it is becoming easier to hear what you want, when you want. Turn the dial on your radio set and, at any given moment, you'll hear a wide range of programming. There are stations devoted to music (including many who play only a specific kind of music), discussion and news. There are local, national and international stations; some are funded by advertising and some by the Government. As a medium, radio is obviously restricted to just using sound so there is a big challenge to make sound interesting, fresh and inventive. To make good radio, you need to be very creative. The scope of radio programming means that there are lots of ways to get involved. From just playing records to chatting, interviewing, writing, reporting, discussing and producing, radio can be a surprisingly diverse form of media. So whether it's Chris Moyles being nasty to people or some lively political debate, radio has it all.

If you're in Further Education, check to see whether your college or Uni has a radio station. Shows should be full of local news and events and you may be able to get involved. Immtech, based in Cardiff, also offer training in "Radio production" – check it out at http://www.immtech.co.uk/

British Broadcasting Corporation (BBC)
www.bbc.co.uk/radio/

Radio Now (List of UK radio stations)
www.radio-now.co.uk

Directory of worldwide internet radio stations
www.radio-locator.com

Skillset (guide to working in radio)
www.skillset.org/radio/

Also check out:

> E-mail & Internet
> Mags & Newspapers
> TV

The history of man can also be seen as the history of the development of technology. From man's earliest inventions to the latest gadgets being developed today, technology has shown how the human race has developed. For example, the development of the first tool, which was quite simply a stone fashioned into a blade, meant that humans could hunt with improved efficiency. This led to a more comfortable and less dangerous life for early humans and allowed the human race to prosper as more people ate well and were better able to defend themselves from attackers. Similarly, a more modern invention such as the Internet has led to wholesale changes to the way that we shop, communicate and find information. Just think what technology lets us do: talk to people on the other side of the world (phones), store music on tiny portable machines (MP3 players), take hundreds of photos (digital cameras), increase security (biometric scanners, CCTV)…the list goes on and on.

If you want to learn a bit more about technology, why not visit Techniquest in Cardiff Bay? There are also New Technology courses available at colleges and universities in Wales – most have websites and online prospectuses.

"Credu" is a partnership project between Canllaw Online & Fujitsu Services that offers young people opportunity to access and be trained in new technologies. Find your nearest CREDU Digilab here: http://www.credu.co.uk/izone/digilabs/

Technology Buzzwords for Students
www.tekmom.com/buzzwords

The latest news on technology from the BBC
news.bbc.co.uk/1/hi/technology//default.stm

Centre for Alternative Technology
www.cat.org.uk

Techniquest
www.techniquest.org

Also check out:
> Computer Games
> E-mail & Internet
> Inventions

TV

In around one hundred years, television has gone from being an unproven theory to an enormous, multi-million pound industry that has changed the lives of virtually every human on the planet. The range of programmes that have developed is immense. And today, you can take whatever you want from TV. If it's lying back, switching your mind off and gawping at reality TV, watching a fascinating nature documentary or taking in a political debate, your needs will be catered for. Sometimes TV gets a bad press with critics saying that it makes your mind and body inactive. If you watch too much TV, they're probably right but that doesn't mean that TV can't be good for you. It can be a great way to unwind, can encourage conversation, it can open your eyes and ears to new ideas and experiences, it can be used to keep up to date with the world we live in today and it can be used to improve your education and knowledge.

The Digital Switchover - The UK's TV broadcast system is switching from analogue to digital (starting in 2009 in Wales). If your TV doesn't receive digital signals or hasn't been converted by the time the switchover happens in your area, you won't be able to get any channels! All you need to convert your TV is a digital box – available from around £40+. If you're thinking of buying a new TV, look out for the digitala logo – this shows that the TV can receive the digital signal (you can get your digital TV signal through an aerial (Freeview), by satellite or through cable). Don't forget your video and DVD player – they may need adapting too.

Digital UK
0845 6 50 50 50 www.digitaluk.co.uk

BBC TV
www.bbc.co.uk/tv/

ITV
www.itv.com

Channel 4
www.channel4.com

Channel 5
www.five.tv

Learn Direct
www.learndirect-advice.co.uk

Also check out:
- Cinema
- Film Making
- Radio
- Mags & Newspapers

Index: A-Z

Index: A-Z

Index: A-Z

Index: A-Z

Notes

Notes

Notes

Notes

LOCAL INFORMATION: EVERYBODY NEEDS TO KNOW SOMETHING - SOMETIME!

If you are looking for information and advice locally, the following pages are for you! They contain contacts in your local areas where people will help you find what you are looking for whether it be the latest health advice or the latest movie release! See also pages 37 - 47 for a list of all of the local Canllaw Info-Outlets in your area which will be able to help you find the information that is available in your area. The following local pages cover all topics that interest young people using the 10 headings of the Canllaw-Online Info Index, and can include a spectrum of activities: informing, counselling, advising, guiding, supporting, training and referral to specialised services. These activities may be delivered by youth information centres, or through youth support services in other agencies,or using websites & telephone services. **All contacts have been researched by one of our young staff at Canllaw Online and we make sure that they offer a youth-friendly service and will be able to answer all of your enquiries under the topic that you are calling about.** All projects registered for the Canllaw Online Info-Outlets Scheme operate under the European Information Charter for Young People which was adopted by the 15th General Assembly of the European Youth Information and Counselling Agency (ERYICA) in Bratislava (Slovak Republic) on 19 November 2004.

The principles of this Charter are intended to apply to all forms of generalist youth information work. They constitute a basis for minimum standards and quality measures which should be established in each country as elements of a comprehensive, coherent and co-ordinated approach to youth information work, which is a part of youth policy. A copy of the charter can be obtained from Canllaw Online by calling 02920 887868 or e-mail mickconroy@canllaw-online.com

Education
Education Department
01248 752900

Employment & Training
Holyhead Careers Office
01407 762177
Ynys Mon Voluntary Services - 01248 752550
Employment and Training Schemes - 01248 752526/5

Environment
Environmental Health Department - 01248 752820
Recycling - 01248 752860

World, Europe, UK & Wales
To find out about your representatives @ all levels and local services, contact: The Isle of Anglesey County Council, Council Offices Llangefni, Anglesey, LL77 7TW
01248 750057

Family & Relationships
Amlwch Family Planning Clinic - 01407 830760
Holyhead Sexual Health Clinic - 01407 766026 or 370376
(Recorded message giving clinic times & locations)
Llanrwst Family Planning Clinic - 01492 640345

Health
Ynys Mon Community Health Council - 01248 723283

Housing
Homeless Section – 01248 752168
Housing Association
01248 752294
Housing Benefit – 01248 752299

Law & Rights
Anglesey Police - 999 in an emergency (or 112 from a mobile phone)
For all non-urgent calls to North Wales Police on 0845 607 1002.
Anglesey Police Division - 01407 722222
Crimestoppers: 0800 555111

Money
Citizens Advice Bureau Ynys Mon - 0845 120 3708
Trading Standards
01248 752840

Sport & Leisure
Anglesey Youth Service
01248 752938
Holyhead Leisure Centre
01407 764111
Llangefni, Plas Arthur Leisure Centre – 01248 722966
Amlwch Leisure Centre
01407 830060
Children's & Young People Library Services – 01248 752096
Mobile Library Service
01248 752095
Information Services and Local Studies Information
01248 752095

For details of your nearest INFO Outlet contact:
Sharon Jones or Gareth Jones – 01248 752940

Education
Education Department
01495 303544

Employment & Training
Abertillery Careers Office - Careers Wales (Gwent) – 01495 322000
Ebbw Vale Careers Office - Careers Wales (Gwent) – 01495 353110
Cross Keys Careers Office Careers Wales (Gwent) – 01495 270320
Tredegar Careers Office – Careers Wales (Gwent) – 01495 722355
Gwent Association of Voluntary Organisations Ebbw Vale
01495 306602

Environment
Environmental Health Department 01495 355054

World, Europe, UK & Wales
To find out about your representatives @ all levels and local services, contact: Municipal Offices, Civic Centre, Ebbw Vale, NP23 6XB
01495 350555

Family and Relationships
Abertillery Sexual Health Clinic
01495 322742/3
Ebbw Vale Young Peoples Clinic
01495 333007 ext 3083
Ebbw Vale Health Centre and Divisional Office - 01495 303013
Tredegar Family Planning Clinic
01495 725231

Health
Gwent Community Health Council
01495 740555

Housing
Housing Department
01495 354600
Homelessness Department
01495 355665

Law & Rights
Caerphilly & Blaenau Gwent Police
01495 223673
Crime Prevention – 01495 232305
Domestic Violence Unit
02920 857338 – ask for Domestic Violence Unit

Money
Citizens Advice Bureau –
Abertillery – 01495 212424
Tredegar - 01495 722110

Sport & Leisure
Blaenau Gwent Youth Service
01495 355804
Abertillery Leisure Centre
01495 212206
Ebbw Vale Leisure Centre
01495 303766
Nantyglo Leisure Centre
01495 310785
Tredegar Leisure Centre
01495 723554
Library Services – 01495 355318

For details of your nearest INFO Outlet contact:
Catapult Youth Information Shop: 01495 711499
or Damian Briggs on 01495 212244

Education
Education Department
01656 642696

Employment & Training
Bridgend Careers Centre
0800 1830283 / 01656 653600
Bridgend Job Centre
01656 682100
Bridgend Association of Voluntary Associations
01656 647255

Environment
Environmental Health Department - 01656 643643 / 643260

World, Europe, UK & Wales
To find out about your representatives @ all levels and local services, contact:
Bridgend County Borough Council, Civic Offices
Angel Street, Bridgend
CF31 4WB
01656 643643

Family & Relationships
Bridgend Sexual Health Clinic - 01656 752752 / 01443 443597 to arrange Appointment
Social Services
01656 642200

Health
Bridgend Community Health Council
01656 645700
Bridgend Local Health Group 01656 754400

Housing
Housing Department - 01656 643551 / 663247
Outside Working Hours
Homeless Department
01656 643551

Law & Rights
Bridgend Advocacy and Mediation Service
01656 659876
Bridgend Police Station
01656 655555

Money
Bridgend Citizens Advice Bureau - 01656 654951
Consumer Advice
01656 643260

Sport & Leisure
Bridgend Youth Service
01656 724057
Bridgend Recreation Centre
01656 657491
Maesteg Sports Centre
01656 737121
Ogmore Valley Life Centre
01656 840880
Garw Valley Life Centre
01656 870886
Bridgend Library & Information Service
01656 767451
Ynysawdre Swimming Pool
01656 720806

For details of your nearest INFO Outlet contact: 01656 724057

Education
Education Department
01443 864956

Employment & Training
Caerphilly Careers Centre
0800 1830283
Blackwood Careers Centre
01495 227650

Environment
Environmental Health Office
01495 235004 / 235213

World, Europe, UK & Wales
To find out about your representatives @ all levels and local services, contact:
Dyffryn Industrial Estate
Ystrad Mynach, Hengoed
CF82 7RJ
01443 863183

Family & Relationships
Blackwood Sexual Health Clinic
01495 226284
Church Village Sexual Health Clinic
01443 218218
Newbridge Sexual Health Clinic
01495 243280
Risca Sexual Health Clinic
01633 618012

Health
Abuse – alcohol/drugs/substance
02920 880090
Drugaid Caerphilly
02920 881008

Housing
Housing Advice Centre
01443 863039
Housing Benefits – 01443 815588

Law & Rights
Police Station – 02920 852999

Money
Caerphilly Benefits Agency
02920 428000
Caerphilly Citizens Advice Bureau
02920 882105
Bargoed Citizens Advice Bureau
01443 831112
Blackwood Citizens Advice Bureau
01495 224456

Sports & Leisure
Caerphilly Youth Service
01443 863268
Caerphilly Libraries
01495 235581 / 235587
Leisure Centres:-
Bedwas – 02920 852538
Caerphilly – 02920 851845
Cefn Forest – 01443 830567
Cwmcarn – 01495 272010
Heolddu – 01443 828950
Newbridge – 01495 248100
New Tredegar – 01443 875586
Pontllanfraith – 01495 224562
Risca – 01633 600940
St. Cenydd – 02920881448
Ystrad Mynach – 01443 813982

Education
Cardiff Education Department
02920 872700

Education & Training
Cardiff Careers Centre
02920 906700
Voluntary Action Cardiff
02920 485722

Environment
Environmental Health Office
02920 871134/5

World, Europe, UK Wales
To find out about your representatives @ all levels and local services, contact:
Cardiff Council
County Hall
Atlantic Wharf
Cardiff
CF10 4UW
029 2087 2000

Family & Relationships
Sexual Health Clinics:
Cardiff Royal Infirmary
02920 492233
Llanderyn - 02920 731671
Riverside - 02920 371221
St Mellons - 02920 778667
Trowbridge - 02920 791011

Health
Community Alcohol Team
02920 372244
Drugaid - 02920 881000

Housing
Housing Help Centre
02920 871448

Law & Rights
Eastern Area:
029 2022 2111
Central Area:
01656 655 555
Western Area:
01792 456 999

Money
Cardiff Citizens Advice Bureau
0870 1264028 /
02920 346490
Cardiff Benefits Agency
02920 428000 /
02920 586158

Sport & Leisure
Cardiff Youth Service
02920 892719
Library Services
02920 382116
Eastern - 02920 796616
Western - 02920 593592
Pentwyn - 02920 549211
Fairwater - 02920 552210
Health Sports Centre
02920 755607

For details of your nearest INFO Outlet contact:
Grangetown Information Shop: 02920 666385
Dusty Forge Information Zone: 02920 594914

Education
Education Department
01267 234567

Employment & Training
Ammanford Careers
01269 598100
Carmarthen Careers Centre
01267 244100
Llanelli Careers Centre
01554 740100
Carmarthen Youth Gateway
01267 234164
Llanelli Youth Gateway
01554 749213
Carmarthen New Deal Centre
01267 223345
Carmarthen Association of Voluntary Organisations
01267 236376

Environment
Environmental Health
01554 742303

World, Europe, UK & Wales
To find out about your representatives @ all levels and local services, contact: Carmarthenshire County Council, County Hall, Carmarthen Carmarthenshire, SA31 1JP
01267 234567

Family & Relationships
Sexual Health Clinics
Carmarthen – 01267 227833
Llanelli – 01554 744053

Health
Dyfed Powys Drug and Alcohol Action Team – 01267 225018

Housing
Housing Offices
Ammanford – 01558 825408
Carmarthen – 01267 228955
Llanelli – 01554 742300
Llandeilo – 01558 825408

Law & Rights
Camarthenshire Police Division – 01267 232000

Money
Citizens Advice Bureau:
Ammanford – 01269 591091
Carmarthen – 01267 234488
Llanelli – 01554 759626

Sport & Leisure
Carmarthenshire Youth Services – 01994 232015
Leisure Centres:
Amman valley – 01269 598150
Carmarthen – 01267 230874
Llanelli – 01554 774757
Newcastle Emlyn – 01239 711025
St Clears – 01994 231253
Libraries:
Ammanford – 01269 598150
Carmarthen – 01267 230873
Llanelli – 01554 773538

For details of your nearest INFO Outlet contact:
Carmarthenshire Youth info Service – 01267 228208

Education
Education & Community Services - 01970 633655

Employment & Training
Aberystwyth Careers Centre
01970 636150
Cardigan Careers Centre
01239 622100
Lampeter Careers Centre
01570 423232
Ceredigion Association of Voluntary Organisations
01570 423232

Environment
Recycling - 01545 572572

World, Europe, UK & Wales
To find out about your representatives @ all levels and local services, contact:
Town Hall
Aberystwyth
Ceredigion
SY23 2EB
01970 617911

Family & Relationships
Sexual Health:
North Road Clinic, Aberystwyth
01970 636216

Health
Bronglais Hospital
01970 523131

Housing
Housing Department
01545 572181
Housing Benefit
01970 633252

Law & Rights
Ceredigion Police Division
01970 612791

Money
Citizens Advice Bureau
Aberystwyth - 01970 612817
Cardigan - 01239 613707
Tregaron - 01570 423606

Sport & Leisure
Ceredigion Youth Service
01570 470697
Library Service
01970 617464
Leisure Centres
Aberystwyth Penglais
01970 615303
Aberystwyth Plascrug
01970 624579
Cardigan
01239 621287
Lampeter
01570 422552
Tregaron
01974 298960

For details of your nearest INFO Outlet:
Aberaeron Youth Info Zone - 01545 571572

Education
Education Department
01492 575031/032

Employment & Training
Llandudno Careers Centre
01492 871900
Colwyn Bay Careers Centre
01495 534079
Rhyl Careers Centre
01745 330012
Conwy Voluntary Services
01492 534091

Environment
Environmental Health Department
01492 574000

World, Europe, UK & Wales
To find out about your representatives @ all levels and local services, contact:
Conwy County Borough Council
Bodlondeb
Conwy
North Wales
LL32 8DU
01492 574000

Family & Relationships
Sexual Health Clinics:
Llandudno – 01492 860066
Llanrwst – 01492 640345

Health
Conwy Local Health Group
01492 536586

Housing
Housing Offices:
Colwyn – 01492 530341
Conwy – 01492 576272
Llandudno – 01492 574031

Law & Rights
North Wales Police Divisional Headquarters – 01492 511000

Money
Citizens Advice Bureau
Abergele – 01492 825627
Colwyn Bay – 01492 531310
Llandudno – 01492 878818
Llanrwst – 01492 531310

Sport & Leisure
Conwy Youth Service
01492 863040
Library Service - 01492 576140
Leisure Centres:
Abergale – 01745 833988
Colwyn – 01492 533223
Dyffryn Conwy – 01492 642028
Llandudno Junction
01492 583592
Y Morfa, Kinmel Bay
01745 360410

For details of your nearest INFO Outlet contact : Bus Stop Info Mobile – 07733012993 – www.the-busstop.co.uk or contact David Price or Brian Watson at Colwyn Bay Info Zone, Douglas Road, on 01492 535961

Education
Department of Education
01824 706777

Employment & Training
Rhyl Careers Centre - 01745 330012
Denbighshire Voluntary Services Council - 01824 703805

Environment
Environmental Health Offices:-
Rhyl - 01824 706444 / 706446
Ruthin - 01824 703805 / 706083 / 706086

World, Europe, UK & Wales
To find out about your representatives @ all levels and local services, contact:
Denbighshire County Council
County Hall
Wynnstay Road
Ruthin
LL15 1YN
01824 706000

Family & Relationships
Denbigh Sexual Health Clinic 01745 812624
Rhyl Sexual Health Clinic
01745 534455
Ruthin Sexual Health Clinic
01824 702361

Health
Clwyd Community Health Council 01978 356178

Housing
Housing Services - Rhyl
01824 708451
Housing Services - Ruthin
01824 706081

Law & Rights
Denbighshire Police
01745 852341

Money
Caledfryn Credit Union
01745 817444

Sport & Leisure
Denbighshire Youth Service
01824 708214
Corwen Library and One Stop Shop 01490 412378
Denbigh Library, Museum and Gallery 01745 816313
Llangollen Library and One Stop Shop 01978 869600
Rhyl Library, Museum and Arts Centre 01745 344153

For details of your nearest INFO Outlet contact:
Denbighshire Youth Service - 01724 708214 or
Kim Dovaston at Rhudland Info Shop on01745 591932

Education - Education and Children's Services 01352 704032 * Education Department 01352 704012 * Deeside College 01244 834511 * Welsh College of Horticulture - 01352 841000 **Employment and Training** - Careers Wales 0800 919 520 * Local Voluntary Council 01352 755008 * Jobcentre Plus 01352 896400 * Princes Trust 0800 842842 **Environment** - Environmental Health 01352 703440 * Environmental Services: * Pest control, etc. 01352 703366 * Waste Control 01352 703350 * Recycling 01352 703347 * Flintshire Friends of the Earth - 01352 710714 * North Wales Wildlife Trust 01352 810469 **World, Europe, UK & Wales** - To find out about your representatives @ all levels and local services, contact: Flintshire County Council County Hall, Mold, Flintshire CH7 6NB, 01352 752121 **Family & Relationships** - CHAT (Confidential Health Advice for Teenagers) Clinics * Connah's Quay Clinic (Connahs Quay Health Centre) - 01244 813486 * Holywell Clinic (Park Lane) - 01352 712002 * Buckley Clinic (Padeswood Road Health Contro) 01244 545277 * Deeside Clinic (Deeside College Campus, G22) - 01244 834511 * Family Planning Clinics * Flint, Borough Grove - 01352 732280 * Mold Health Clinic, Kings Street - 01352 753637 * Connah's Quay, Civic Centre, Wepre Drive - 01244 813486 * Children's Information Service - 01244 547017 * Family Group Meeting Project - 01352 701000 * North Wales Family Mediation Service - 01492 870876 * Home Start - 01352 753666 * Sure Start - 01244 823234 * Delyn

Local Info - Flintshire

Women's Aid - 01352 712 150 * Deeside Women's Aid - 01244 830436 * NSPCC Cymru - 0808 100 2524 * Social Services – Adult - 01352 701386 * Social Services – Children - 01352 701000 **Health** - NHS Wales Direct - 0845 46 47 * North Wales Smoking Cessation Service - 01352 755543 * Community Drugs and Alcohol Team - 01244 831 798 * Child & Adolescent Mental Health Service (CAMHS) - 01244 813486 / 822244 * Clwyd Community Health Council - 01978 356178 * Community Advice Listening Line - 0800 132737 * Youth Service - Drugs Education Team - 01352 752588 **Housing** - General Housing Enquiries - 01352 703532 * Wales & West Housing Association - 0870 0131930 * Clwyd Alyn Housing Association - 01352 763376 * Shelter Cymru – Buckley - 01244 545653 * Wrexham Foyer - 01978 262222 * Neighborhood Wardens - 01352 701826 **Law & Rights** - Flintshire Police - 01352 752321 * Trading Standards - 01352 703189 * Flintshire Victim Support - 01352 751538 * Flintshire Neighbourhood Watch - 01352 707545 * Save the Children 01352 750630 **Money** - Citizens Advice Bureaux: * Holywell - 01352 711262 * Mold 01352 753520 * Flint 01352 733187 * All Flintshire Credit Union - 01352 715555 * Flintshire Unified Benefit & Advisory Service 01352 702900

continued on the next page...

Sport & Leisure - Flintshire Youth Service (general enquiries) - 01352 704032 * Library & Information Service - 01352 704405 * Sports Development (for all leisure Centres) - 01352 702461 * Flintshire Arts, Culture and Events - 01352 704408 * Play Development - 01352 702456 * Theatre Clwyd Mold - 0845 330365 * Deeside Ice Rink & Leisure Centre - 01244 8124725 * Flintshire Cycling Officer - 01352 704633 * Disability Sport Cymru Development Officer - 01352 702480 * Sports Council for Wales - 01244 822600 * NW Indoor Athletic Centre - 01244 834 546 * Walkabout Flintshire - 01352 702477 * Hollowater-outdoor water based activity centre - 01352 770123 * Youth Service Duke of Edinburgh Award Team - 01352 758139

Local Info - Gwynedd

Education Department
Education – 01286 679162

Employment & Training
Bangor Careers Office 01286 662930 * Caernarfon 01286 662930 * Porthmadog Careers Office 01766 514501 * Mantell Gwynedd (Voluntary Opportunities) 01286 672626

Environment
Environmental Health Offices:
Arfon 01286 682731 *
Dwyfor 01758 704018 *
Meirionydd 01341 424385

World, Europe, UK & Wales
To find out about your representatives @ all levels and local services, contact:
Gwynedd Council
Council Offices
Caernarfon, Gwynedd
LL55 1SH
01286 672255

Family & Relationships
Bangor GUM Clinic 01248 370376 * Caernarfon Family Planning Clinic 01784 821624 * Dolgellau Family Planning Clinic – 01341 422479 * Bala Family Planning Clinic 01678 520542

Health
Ysbyty Gwynedd Bangor
01286 674961

Housing
Housing Enquiries:
Arfon 01286 682834 *
Dwyfor 01758 613131 *
Meirionnydd 01341 424318 *
Housing Benefit 01286 613131/682698

Law & Rights
North Wales Police – Gwynedd 01286 673333 * North Wales Police – Gwynedd South 01341 422222

Money
Citizens Advice Bureau
08707 502350

Sport & Leisure
Gwynedd Youth Service
Principal Youth Officer 01286 679190 * Arfon Area Officer 01286 679351 * Dwyfor and Meirionnydd Area Offier 01341 424304 * Leisure Centres: Arfon 01286 676451 * Plas Ffrancon 01286 882047 * Dwyfor 01758 613437 * Glaslyn 01766 512711 * Pavilion 01341 280111 * Blaenau Ffestiniog 01766 861953 * Bro Dysynni 01654 711763

Local Info - Merthyr Tydfil

Education
Education Department
01685 724600

Employment & Training
Merthyr Careers Centre
01685 353900
Merthyr Voluntary Action Centre - 01685 353900

Environment
Recycling - 01495 235336

World, Europe, UK & Wales
To find out about your representatives @ all levels and local services, contact:
Civic Centre, Castle Street
Merthyr Tydfil, CF47 8AN
01685 725000

Family & Relationships
Social Services * Community Care - 01685 724537 * Childcare - 01685 724506

Health
Prince Charles Hospital
01685 725000
Drugs & Alcohol
01685 721671

Housing
Housing Department
01685 725000

Law & Rights
Merthyr & Cynon Valley Police Division
011685 722541

Money
Trading Standards
01685 725021

Sports & Leisure
Merthyr Tydfil Youth Service
01443 724601
Rhydcar Sports & Leisure Centre
01685 371491

For details of your nearest INFO Outlet contact: Lesley Jones at the Merthyr Info Shop on 01685 727081

Education
Basic and Key Skills Project 01291 671274 * Coleg Gwent 01495 333333 * Lifelong Learning & Leisure Directorate 01633 644644

Employment & Training
Careers Offices Abergavenny 01873 853662 * Chepstow 01291 635647 * Monmouth 01600 713288 * Careers Wales Gwent 0800 0289212
Gwent Association of Voluntary Organisations 01291 672352

Environment
Abergavenny Watch and RSPB Wildlife Explorer (AWARE) 01873 832072 *
Environmental Directorate 01633 644644 * Friends of the Earth * Abergavenny & Crickhowell 01873 852245
Chepstow & District 01291 625977 * Gwent Wildlife Trust 01600 715501

World, Europe, UK & Wales
To find out about your representatives @ all levels and local services, contact:
Monmouthshire County Council, County Hall
Cwmbran, Gwent
NP44 2XH , 01633 644644

Family & Relationships
Abergavenny Bereavement Support Group 01873 857903
Young People's Clinic - Abergavenny, Caldicot, Chepstow, Monmouth 01633 623714

Health
Abergavenny & District Diabetes Group 01291 672288 * Community Against Drugs 01633 644039 *
Monmouthshire Local Health Board 01291 636400 *
Monmouthshire Young Persons Substance Misuse Service 01873 735567 *
Gwent Community Council 01495 740555

Housing
Monmouthshire Community Housing Advice Service 02920 556120 * Council Housing Services * Abergavenny 01873 735813 * Caldicot 01291 426415 * Chepstow 01291 635715 * Monmouth 01291 775210

Law & Rights
Citizens Advice Bureaux *
Abergavenny 01873 735865 *
Caldicot 01291 423840 *
Chepstow 01291 623437 *
Monmouth 01600 712590 *
Monmouthshire Consumer Advice 0845 1203727 *
Gwent Police 01633 838111

Money
Trading Standards – 01633 644644

Sport & Leisure
Leisure Centres *
Abergavenny 01873 735360 *
Caldicot 01291 426850 *
Chepstow 01291 635745 *
Monmouth 01600 775135

For details of your nearest INFO Outlet contact: Monmouthshire Youth Information Service – 01291 674605

Education
Education Department
01639 763599

Employment & Training
Neath Careers Centre
01639 636391
Port Talbot Careers Centre
01639 871933
Neath Youth Gateway
01639 635475
Neath Port Talbot Council for Voluntary Services
01639 631246

Environment
Recycling – 01792 512571

World, Europe, UK & Wales
To find out about your representatives @ all levels and local services, contact:
Port Talbot Civic Centre
Port Talbot
SA13 1PJ
01639 763333

Family & Relationships
Port Talbot GUM Clinic
01639 762672

Health
Neath & Port Talbot Hospitals
General Enquiries
01639 641161

Housing
Housing Department
01639 764777

Law & Rights
Neath & Port Talbot Police Division
016369 635321

Money
Trading Standards
01639 764325

Sports & Leisure
Neath & Port Talbot Youth Service
01639 765190
Afan Lido Lesiure Complex
01639 642827

For details for your nearest INFO Outlet contact: Neath Port Talbot Youth Info Service – 01639 765190

Education
Education Department
01633 656656

Employment & Training
Newport Careers Office
01633 844700
Gwent Association of Voluntary Organisations 01633 213229

Environment
Recycling – 01633 233398
Wastesavers – 01633 216855

World, Europe, UK & Wales
To find out about your representatives @ all levels and local services, contact:
Civic Centre
Newport
South Wales
NP20 4UR
01633 656656

Family & Relationships
Newport Sexual Health Clinic (GUMed) 01633 2345555

Health
Royal Gwent Hospital
01633234234
Young People's Sexual Health outreach Worker
07884 314368
Fusion Young Peoples Drug and Alcohol Service
01633 252053
Child and Adolescent Primary Mental Health Team
01633 283667

Housing
Housing Department
01633 656656

Law & Rights
Crime Prevention Unit
01633 245282
Domestic Violence
01633 245329
South East Wales Race Equality Council (SEWREC)
01633 250006

Money
Trading Standards
01633 271127

Sport & Leisure
Newport Youth Service 01633 784070 / 01633 875054
Leisure Centres
Bettws 01633 855420
Liswerry 01633 274919
Maindee Pools 01633 671820
Newport Centre 01633 662662
Underwood 01633 412090

For details of your nearest INFO outlet contact:
Newport's Information Shop,
133 Commercial Street, Newport NP20 1LY
Phone 01633 784054/255031
Minicom txt: 01633 784054
E-mail: infoshop@newport.gov.uk

Education
Education Department
01437 764551

Employment & Training
Haverfordwest Careers Centre
01437 764551
01437 772100
Milford Haven Careers Centre
01646 623510
Pembroke Dock Careers Centre
01646 623510
Pembrokeshire Association of Voluntary Organisation
01686 626220

Environment
Recycling 01437 764551

World, Europe, UK and Wales
To find out about your representatives @ all levels and local services, contact:
Pembrokeshire County Council
County Hall
Haverfordwest
Pembrokeshire
SA61 1TP
01437 764551

Family & Relationships
Pembroke Dock Sexual Health Clinic 01437 773315
Haverfordwest GUM Clinic
01437 773315

Health
Withybush General Hospital
01437 764545

Housing
Housing Department
01437 764551

Law & Rights
Pembrokeshire Police Division
01437 763355

Money
Pembrokeshire Trading Standards
0437 764551

Sports & Leisure
Pembrokeshire Youth Service
01437 775234
Preseli Leisure Centre
01646 684434
Pembroke Leisure Centre
01646 684434
Meads Sport & Leisure Centre
01646 694011

Education
Education Department
01597 826422

Employment & Training
Careers Wales Mid Galmorgan and Powys - Llandrindodd Wells
01597 825898
Careers Wales Powys Newtown
01686 626959
Careers Wales Powys Brecon
01874 624619
Careers Wales Powys Ystradgynlais
01639 842002
Powys Association of Voluntary Associations
01874 622631

Environment
Recycling – 0845 6076060

World, Europe, UK & Wales
To find out about your representatives @ all levels and local services, contact:
Powys County Council
County Hall
Llandrindod Wells
LD1 5LG
01597 826000

Family & Relationships
Powys Social Services
01597 827650
Young Persons Centres (Sexual Health)
Llandridnodd Wells
01597 828702
Brecon
01874 615622

Health
Powys Health Care Trust
01874 624206
PDAC – Powys Drug and Alcohol Council
01597 825102

Housing
Housing Department
01597 826659

Law & Rights
Dyfed Powys Police: Powys Division
01686 625704

Money
Citizens Advice Bereaux
Brecon 01874 624595
Llandridnodd Wells
01597 823508
Machynlleth 0870 126 4067
Newtown 01686 626557

Sport & Leisure
Powys Youth Service
01597 826483
Leisure Centres
Brecon 01874 623677
Bro Ddyfi 01654 703300
Caereinion 01938 810634
Maldwyn 01686 628771
Rhayader 01597 810355
The Flash 01938 555953

Education
Education Lifelong Learning 01443 744000

Employment & Training
Careers Centres: * Aberdare 01685 875795 * Tonypandy 01443 432555 * Pontypridd 01443 486741 * Careers Wales 01443 842207 * Interlink (Voluntary Opportunities) 01443 485337

Environment
Recycling – 01443 494700

World, Europe, UK & Wales
To find out about your representatives @ all levels and local services, contact:
Rhondda Cynon Taff County Borough Council
The Pavilions
Cambrian Park
Clydach Vale
Tonypandy
CF40 2XX
01443 424000

Family & Relationships
Aberdare GUM Clinic 01685 872411
Church Village Sexual Health Clinic 01443 218218 * Dewi Sant Sexual Health Clinic 01443 486222 * Royal Glamorgan Sexual Health Clinic 01443 443597

Health
Hospitals * Aberdare General 01685 872411 * Royal Glamorgan 01443 443597 * Dewi Sant 01443 486222

Housing
Housing Department 01443 407811 * Adref, Aberdare 01685 881202 * Housing Benefit 01443 681081

Law & Rights
Police Stations * Merthyr & Cynon Valley 01685 722541 * Pontypridd & Rhondda 01443 485351

Money
Rhondda Cynon Taff
01443 406441

Sport & Leisure
Caerphilly Youth Service 01443 863268 * Leisure Centres
Hawthorn 01443 843406
Llantrisant 01443 224616
Llantwit Fardre 01443 201721
Tonyrefail 01443 670578

For details of your nearest INFO Outlet contact the information workers for Rhondda Cynon Taf: Leanne Thomas – 07786523825 * Bethan Jones – 07786523826 * Centre Base – 01443 424400 ext: 4457 / 4454

Education
Education Department
01792 636000

Employment & Training
Gorseinon Careers Centres
01792 897333
Swansea Careers Centre
01792 644444
Swansea Youth Gateway
01792 461230
Swansea Council for Voluntary Services
01792 544000

Environment
Recycling – 01792 635600

World, Europe, UK & Wales
To find out about your representatives @ all levels and local services, contact:
County Hall
Oystermouth Road
Swansea
SA1 3SN
01792 636000

Family & Relationships
Swansea GUM Clinic
01792 285016

Health
Morriston Hospital
01792 702222
Singleton Hospital
01792 205666

Housing
Housing Department
01792 635013

Law & Rights
Swansea Police Division
01792 635600

Sport & Leisure
Swansea Youth Service
01792 648081
Swansea Leisure Centre
01792 649126
Penlan Community Leisure Centre 01792 588079
Penyrheol Leisure Centre
01792 897039

For Details of your nearest INFO Outlet contact:
Info Nation, 47 the Kingsway, Swansea SA1 5HG
Tel: 01792 484010
Fax: 01792 484012
Text 07956503902
Email: Info-Nation@swansea-edunet.gov.uk

Education
Education Department
01495 762200

Employment & Training
Cwmbran Careers Office
01633 482363
Pontypool Careers Office
01495 750015
Tredegar Careers Office
01495 750015
Torfaen Voluntary Alliance
01495 766204

Environment
Recycling 01495 762200

World, Europe, UK & Wales
To find out about your representatives @ all levels and local services, contact:
Torfaen County Borough Council
Civic Centre, Pontypool
Torfaen, NP4 6YB
01495 762200

Family & Relationships
Pontypool GUM Clinic
01495 768768
Pontypool Family Planning
01495 757788

Health
Torfaen Local Health Board
01495 745868

Housing
Housing Department
01495 762200

Law & Rights
Garnddiffaith Police Station
01495 772540
Blaenavon Police Station
01495 790452
Fairwater Police Station
01633 868616
Pontypool Police Station
01495 764711
New Inn Police Station
01495 764044
Cwmbran Police Station
01633 838999

Money
Trading Standards 01633 648464

Sport & Leisure
Torfaen Youth Service
01495 766326
Blaenavon Leisure Centre
01495 790646
Fairwater Leisure Centre
01633 872811
Llantarnam Leisure Centre
01633 482832
Pontypool Leisure Centre
01495 755764
Cwmbran Stadium
01633 628969

For details of your nearest INFO Outlet contact:
Steve Thomas, Youth Service – 01495 758868
The Doorway, Blaenavon – 01495 793109
Zone 2, New Inn Pontypool – 01495 762859
Tŷ Rosser Gwyn, Pontypool – 01495 775692
Coed Eva, Cwmbran – 01633 861190
Cwmbran Centre for Young People – 01633 875851

Education
Education Department
01446 709146

Employment & Training
Barry Careers Centre
01446 410600
Vale Council for Voluntary Services
01446 741706

Environment
Recycling
02920 673091

World, Europe, UK & Wales
To find out about your representatives @ all levels and local services, contact:
Vale of Glamorgan County Council
Civic Offices
Holton Road
Barry
CF63 4RU
01446 700111

Family & Relationships
Barry Sexual Health Clinics
01446 746722

Health
Vale of Glamorgan Local Health Board
02920 350600

Housing
Housing Department
01446 706500

Law & Rights
Barry & the Vale of Glamorgan
01446 734451

Money
Trading Standards
01446 709105

Sports & Leisure
Vale of Glamorgan Youth Services
01446 792141
Cowbridge Leisure Centre
01443 775533
Penarth Leisure Centre
02920 700717
Holm View Leisure Centre
01446 700258
Colcot Leisure Centre
01446 735182
Barry Leisure Centre
01446 744770
Llantwit Major Centre
01446 793947

Education
Education Department
01978 297401
Yale College FE 01978 311794
NEWI HE 01978 290666

Employment & Training
Job Centre 01978 203400
Wrexham Careers Shop
01978 266802
Association of Voluntary
Organisations in Wrexham
01978 297018

Environment
Groundwork 01978 363555

World, Europe, UK & Wales
To find out about your representatives @ all levels and local services, contact:
Wrexham County Borough Council
The Guildhall, Wrexham
LL11 1AY, 01978 292000

Family & Relationships
Children's Information Bureau
01978 292094
Sexual Health Clinics
Wrexham Maelor Hospital GUM Department 01978 326510
Health Clinic, Queens Park
01978 262191
Wrexham Hightown
01978 358900
Contact Young People's Clinic and Info, Chester St 01978 358900
RELEASE, Bereavement Counseling for YP 01978 316800
Stepping Stones, for over 18s who were abused as Children
01978 352717
Relate, Relationship Counseling
01978 265028

Health
Ysbyty Wrexham Maelor
01978 291100
Wrexham MIND 01978 366155

Housing
Homelessness 01978 292919
Housing Benefit 01978 292033
Shelter Cymru 01978 353649
Barnado's Compass Project
01978 315130

Law & Rights
North Wales Police Wrexham
01978 290222
NACRO 01978 314313

Money
Wrexham Citizens Advice Bureau
01978 364639
Benefits Agency 01978 316500

Sports & Leisure
Wrexham Youth Service 01978 358900
Leisure Centres 01978 297410
Library Service 01978 292090

Youth Hostels Association Wales, 4th Floor, 1 Cathedral Road, Cardiff, CF11 9HA

Wales Young Farmers' Clubs, YFC Centre, Royal Welsh Showground, Llanelwedd, Builth Wells, Powys, LD2 3NJ

Boys' and Girls' Clubs of Wales Western Business Centre, Riverside Terrace , Ely Bridge, Cardiff, CF5 5AS

St John Cymru Wales, Priory House, Beignon Way, Ocean Way, Cardiff, CF24 5PB

Weston Spirit, 1 Guilford Crescent, Cardiff, CF10 2HJ

Play Wales, Baltic House, Mount Stuart Square, Cardiff, CF10 5FH

Urdd Gobaith Cymru, Swyddfa'r Urdd, Ffordd Llanbadarn, Aberystwyth, SY23 1EY

Gwerin y Coed, Y Ganolfan, Llanfrothen, Gwynedd, LL48 6LJ

British Red Cross Wales, River House , Ynys Bridge Court, Gwaelod y Garth , Cardiff, CF15 9SS

Prince's Trust Cymru, 120 Broadway, Cardiff, CF24 1NJ

Welsh Scout Council, The Old School, Wine Street, Llantwit Major, CF61 1RZ

MENCAP Cymru, 31 Lambourne Crescent, Cardiff Business Park, Llanishen, Cardiff, CF14 5GF

The Boys' Brigade in Wales, 80 Woodville Road, Cathays, Cardiff, CF23 4ED

UNA Exchange, Temple of Peace, Cathays Park Cardiff, CF10 3AP

Duke of Edinburgh's Award, Oak House, 12 The Bulwark, Brecon, Powys, LD3 7AD

Girlguiding Cymru, The Lodge, Broneirion, Llandinam, Powys, SY17 5DD

Adran Ieuenctid Undeb yr Annibynwyr Cymraeg, 1 Lister Close, St Davids Manor, Pentre'r Eglwys, Pontypridd, Rhondda Cynon Taff, CF83 1GL

CSV Volunteering Partners, CSV House Williams Way, Cardiff, CF10 5DY

YMCA Wales, Unit 17, J Shed, Kings Road, Swansea, SA1 8PL

British Deaf Association, British Sign Language Culture Centre , 47 Newport Road, Cardiff, CF24 0AD

Youth Cymru, HQ/Training Centre, Sachville Avenue, Heath, Cardiff, CF14 3NY

Groundwork Wales, 20 Centre Court, Main Avenue, Treforest Industrial Estate, Pontypridd, CF37 5YR

Cyfarwyddwr Gwaith Plant/Ieuenctid Eglwys Bresbyteraidd Cymru, Canolfan Hyfforddi, Coleg y Bala, 23-25 Ffrydan Road, Y Bala, L23 7RY

Methodist Youth Committee, 15 Guys Road, Barry, CF63 3QA

The Army Cadet Force Association Wales, Centre Block, Maindy Barracks, Cardiff, CF14 3YE

Youth Work in Wales...

choose life...choose a job...choose a career...choose a family... choose a rollocking big television...choose washing machines, cars, and MP3 players...choose good health, low cholesterol, and dental insurance...choose fixed interest mortgage repayments...choose a starter home...choose your friends...choose leisurewear and matching luggage...choose a three-piece suite on hire purchase in a range of man-made fabrics...choose DIY and wondering who the hell you are on a Sunday morning...but most of all, **choose your future!**

choose to get in touch with your local youth service team...and make your mind up about all of the above.

Get in touch now..... check out the local pages on (pages 97 to 119) for your nearest youth service details!!......

What will you choose?

Youth Work in Wales...

Wherever you are in Wales, there is a local youth service team that wants to listen to you and offer you opportunities and activities which are designed to tap into your energy and potential as a young person. Your local youth service wants you to have the best possible preparation for adulthood and will work with you right up to your early twenties to help you make the best possible choices in learning and in life. The Standing Conference for Youth Work meets regularly to make sure that those in charge of delivering local services to young people understand the benefits of youth work, the best way in which to engage with young people, and the importance of offering EVERY young person the chance to learn, develop, and make the most of their potential regardless of their circumstances. So, check out the localised information for your area in this book and get in touch with your local youth service team. Then you can pop along to meet your local youth workers who will welcome you into a friendly and supportive environment where you will have a voice, be listened to and will be able to take up many opportunities to learn new skills and make a journey of your own choosing. Also, check out pages 528-529 for information on CWVYS (Council for Wales Voluntary Youth Service) and other National Voluntary Organisations who can help you find made-to-measure volunteering experiences that could enrich your life. You will learn a lot about yourself through the wide range of things on offer and most importantly you will get to have loads of fun at the same time! So come on get in touch with these people ... they are there waiting to help you on your way!!

Internet & Mobile Safety

The Internet and mobile phones are great tools, but a small number of people misuse them. Here are some things to remember:

>> Anyone can have a website, so not everything you read online is reliable.
>> On websites like Myspace and Bebo, remember that your pages can be seen by anyone on the Internet, unless you protect them.
>> With Messenger programmes, watch what's in your profile, who's on your contact list and remember to log off.

To learn more, see www.wisekids.org.uk/guides

WISE KIDS provides training programmes for young people and adults on positive and safe Internet use.

Useful links to the language!

Here you'll find handy links for more info on the internet about Welsh medium activities and music, including where to download Welsh language music on the internet....

Mentrau Iaith (Language Initiatives) www.mentrau-iaith.com - Help on anything linked to the Welsh language in your community * **Yr Urdd** - www.urdd.org - The Urdd is the main youth organisation in Wales with almost 50,000 members, and it provides opportunities for young people in clubs, camps, sports, leisure and music activities. * **Duke of Edinburgh Award Scheme** - www.theaward.org - Aged between 14 and 25? Fancy a challenge? Contact the Award! * **YFC** - www.yfc-wales.org.uk - The organisation for all young people in rural Wales * **Maes E** - www.maes-e.com - What's on, what's in and what's it all about? Find out at maes-e and share your views *****Music***** To download Welsh medium music on the internet go to: iTunes - http://www.apple.com/itunes/ or Last.fm - http://www.last.fm/ or Myspace Music - http://www.myspace.com/ * **Dan y Cownter** - www.danycownter.com - A brand-new free compilation CD of the best talent from the Welsh language scene, all compiled by Radio One DJ Huw Stephens, and available on the Dan y Cownter website * **Welsh Music Foundation** - www.welshmusicfoundation.com - The WMF is there to provide assistance, advice, information and contacts to the music industry in Wales * **Ciwdod** - www.myspace.com/ciwdod - Get yourself heard! Help, advice and support for fresh, young, Welsh language bands * **BBC Radio Cymru C2** - www.bbc.co.uk/c2 - Live accoustic sessions, news, sports, competitions, music and much more, on air from Monday to Friday, 8pm-1am. * **Bandit** - www.bandit247.com - Music Programme on S4C with all the latest on the music scene in Wales * **Maes B** - www.maesb.com - For gigs, gigs and more gigs check out the latest on Maes B.

BWRDD YR IAITH GYMRAEG · WELSH LANGUAGE BOARD

...nportant things to know!

Produced by...

This publication was written and produced by Canllaw Online Cyf (© 2006 Canllaw Online Cyf). If you would like more copies, please contact Canllaw Online on 029 2088 7868 or e-mail ed@canllaw-online.com

For more information about Canllaw Online, go to www.canllaw-online.com

Canllaw Online Cyf, Suite 5, The Octagon, Caerphilly Business Park, Van Road, Caerphilly, CF83 3ED

For...

This publication has been written specifically for young people between the age of 16 and 25

Printed by...

This publication was printed by The Westdale Press Limited - www.westdale.co.uk

A big thanks to...

Canllaw Online would like to thank everyone who contributed towards this publication. You know who you are - thank you!

Remember...

Every precaution has been taken to ensure that the info in this publication is trustworthy, accurate, reliable and written with a young person's perspective in mind. Whilst we always endeavour to be as accurate as possible, we can't be held responsible for any inaccuracies as information goes out of date very quickly. This publication gives general info only and should not be treated as a complete and authoritative statement.